Effective Consultation in School Psychology

Ester Cole & Jane A. Siegel (Editors)

Ester Cole & Jane A. Siegel
(Editors)

Effective Consultation in School Psychology

2nd revised and expanded edition

 Hogrefe & Huber

Library of Congress Cataloging-in-Publication Data

is available via the Library of Congress Marc Database under the
LC Control Number 2002111971

National Library of Canada Cataloguing-in-Publication Data

Effective consultation in school psychology / edited by Ester Cole and
Jane A. Siegel. — 2nd rev. and expanded ed.

Includes bibliographical references.
ISBN 0-88937-252-7

1. School psychology. 2. Psychological consultation. 3. Personnel service in education.
I. Cole, Ester, 1946- II. Siegel, Jane A., 1944-

LB1027.55.E44 2003   371.4'6   C2002-906005-2

PUBLISHING OFFICES
USA: Hogrefe & Huber Publishers, 44 Brattle Street, 4th Floor,
            Cambridge, MA 02138,
            Phone (866) 823-4726, Fax (617) 354-6875, E-mail info@hhpub.com
Europe: Hogrefe & Huber Publishers, Rohnsweg 25, D-37085 Göttingen, Germany,
            Phone +49 551 496090, Fax +49 551 49609-88, E-mail hh@hhpub.com

SALES & DISTRIBUTION
USA: Hogrefe & Huber Publishers, Customer Service Department,
            30 Amberwood Parkway, Ashland, OH 44805,
            Phone (800) 228-3749, Fax (419) 281-6883, E-mail custserv@hhpub.com
Europe: Hogrefe & Huber Publishers, Rohnsweg 25, D-37085 Göttingen, Germany,
            Phone +49 551 496090, Fax +49 551 49609-88, E-mail hh@hhpub.com

OTHER OFFICES
Canada: Hogrefe & Huber Publishers, 12 Bruce Park Avenue, Toronto, Ontario, M4P 2S3
Switzerland: Hogrefe & Huber Publishers, Länggass-Strasse 76, CH-3000 Bern 9

Hogrefe & Huber Publishers
Incorporated and Registered in the State of Washington, USA, and in Göttingen, Lower Saxony, Germany

Printed and bound in Germany
ISBN 0-88937-252-7

Table of Contents

Part 2: The Psychologist as a Change Agent

Part 3: Consultation in School-Based Programs

Preface

When we published the first edition of *Effective Consultation in School Psychology* in 1990, it was the result of collaborative synergy between practitioners and academics committed to the field of school psychology. Dr. Jane Siegel and I developed our model and conceptual framework with the belief that it would facilitate equitable and inclusive services in education. We also hoped that it would aid service providers to broaden their roles in school communities and highlight the central role psychologists have in promoting multi-disciplinary consultation. Since that time, our model has been taught at universities, discussed in many education systems, and lectured about on several continents. The book was reprinted in 1992, and continued to be sought after.

When Dr. Christine Hogrefe had the vision to approach us to write a second edition, Jane was gravely ill. Shortly before her untimely death in 1999, I broached the subject with her. Near the end of her life, she noted that our model was "ahead of its time." As I facilitated the development of the second edition, I kept her words in mind. This second edition of *Effective Consultation in School Psychology* contains seven updated chapters from the original publication, as well as twelve new chapters. Once again, the work reflects the evolution of research, advocacy, creativity, and the culture of school psychology and consultation.

Finally, this book is dedicated to the memory of the late Dr. Jane Siegel, whose contributions to this publication and to the field of psychology are sadly missed. The second edition is published with the original trust she and I hoped would promote partnerships and services for the benefit of students, educators, and parents.

Dr. Ester Cole
Toronto, 2002

Dedication

David, Mihael, and Anat
COLE

Bill, Hallie, and Kathryn
SIEGEL
And in memory of Jane Siegel

ALL THE RAINBOW COLORS

About the Editors

Dr. Ester Cole is currently a psychologist in private practice. Previously, she was a supervising psychologist at the Toronto Board of Education from 1984–2000. Her work has focussed extensively on the development of multicultural consultation, clinical and school psychology services. She has taught at the Ontario Institute for Studies in Education/University of Toronto for over two decades, and for the past two years at York University. Following a teaching career and undergraduate studies in Israel, she received her PhD from the University of Toronto in 1979. She is a registered psychologist with the Ontario College of Psychologists and the Canadian Register of Health Service Providers in Psychology.

Dr. Cole has written and co-authored numerous research and advocacy articles in recognized journals and professional publications, and has contributed to several manuals and books. She previously co-edited two books – *Effective Consultation in School Psychology* (1990) and *Dynamic Assessment for Instruction* (1996). In addition to the provision of direct services in a variety of educational and clinical settings, Dr. Cole has developed psychological service models for school settings and consultation modalities which focus on the adaptation of immigrant and refugee children and their families. Her lectures and workshops to mental health professionals and educators in Canada, the United States, Portugal, Sweden, and Israel include topics such as multiculturalism, special education, depression and suicide prevention, and system consultation services.

Over the years, Dr. Cole has been a member of various committees and task forces focussing on program development in school systems. She was the 1993 President of the Canadian Association of School Psychologists and the Chair of the Psychology Foundation of Canada from 1996–2000. She is the current President of the Ontario Psychological Association.

Dr. Jane Siegel (Oct 6, 1944–March 25, 1999). Prior to her untimely death, Dr. Siegel was a part of Longwoods International, a marketing research firm, for close to a decade. She became renowned for the research methodology she developed. Her "Return on Investments" model, which measures advertising effectiveness, has since impacted marketing budgets throughout Canada and the United States.

Dr. Siegel completed her undergraduate degree at Purdue University, and obtained her PhD from the University of Michigan in 1971. She taught psychology at the University of Michigan and the University of Western Ontario before joining the field of school psychology.

Dr. Siegel's background was in cognitive psychology, learning and memory, and her research in these areas was published in internationally recognized journals – including the *Psychological Review*. She was the co-editor of the first edition of *Effective Consultation in School Psychology*. She joined the Toronto Board of Education in 1977, and was promoted to Senior Psychologist in 1980. She was responsible for supervision of psychological staff and took a special interest in staff and program development. She gave numerous workshops to teachers, school administrators, and psychologists in the United States, Canada, and Europe.

The Contributors

C. Tane Akamatsu is a psychologist at the Toronto District School Board, Toronto, Ontario, Canada.

Aron Blidner is a graduate student at McGill University, Montreal, Quebec, Canada.

Rob Brown is a researcher at the Toronto District School Board, Toronto, Ontario, Canada.

Laurie Carlson Berg is an assistant professor at the University of Regina, Regina, Saskatchewan, Canada.

Glenn DiPasquale is the Chief Psychologist at the York Region District School Board, Aurora, Ontario, Canada.

Esther Geva is a professor at the Ontario Institute for Studies in Education/University of Toronto, Toronto, Ontario, Canada.

Lisa Hagermoser is a doctoral candidate at the University of Wisconsin-Madison, Madison, Wisconsin, U.S.A.

Nancy Lee Heath is an associate professor at McGill University, Montreal, Quebec, Canada.

Thomas R. Kratochwill is a professor at the University of Wisconsin-Madison, Madison, Wisconsin, U.S.A.

Patrick Kumke is a doctoral candidate at the University of Wisconsin-Madison, Madison, Wisconsin, U.S.A.

Lisa Marie Lanaro is a graduate student at McGill University, Montreal, Quebec, Canada.

Nancy Link is the Clinical Director of the Ontario Institute for Studies in Education/University of Toronto, Toronto, Ontario, Canada.

Sharone Maital is the Head of Psychological Services in Megido Area, Israel.

Ilze A. Matiss is a school psychologist, Toronto District School Board, Toronto, Ontario, Canada.

Solveiga Miezitis is a professor at the Ontario Institute for Studies in Education/University of Toronto, Toronto, Ontario, Canada.

Michele Peterson-Badali is an associate professor, Ontario Institute for Studies in Education/University of Toronto, Toronto, Ontario, Canada.

Anat Scher is a professor at the University of Haifa, Haifa, Israel.

Teeya Scholten is a chartered psychologist in Calgary, Alberta, Canada.

Ingrid E. Sladeczek is an associate professor at McGill University, Montreal, Quebec, Canada.

C. Lisa Steinbach is a doctoral candidate at McGill University, Montreal, Quebec, Canada.

Judith Wiener is a professor at the Ontario Institute for Studies in Education/ University of Toronto, Toronto, Ontario, Canada.

Janet Zarb is the director of psychological services at Providence Center Hospital, Toronto, Ontario, Canada.

Part 1

Perspectives on Consultation and Training

Chapter 1
Role Expansion for School Psychologists:
Challenges and Future Directions

Jane A. Siegel and Ester Cole

"School psychology was born in the prison of a test, and although the cell has been enlarged somewhat, it is still a prison." [Seymour Sarason, 1977]

School psychology in North America continues to be at a crossroads. While nearly every school board employs psychologists, there is little consensus regarding their role: traditionalists view them as technocrats whose purpose is to provide mental testing services to teachers, while a more encompassing perception views them as consultants who are able to draw on a wide body of knowledge for the benefit of students, parents, and educators. Although most psychologists seem to prefer this more innovative approach, to date it has not been widely or consistently implemented and remains underused in school systems.

Our aim in preparing both editions of this book has been to provide practical help to those school psychologists who wish to free themselves from the constraints of testing, as a sole rule; to assist them in identifying the skills and tools they need for fostering a consultative approach; and to provide them with useful information for implementation.

This first chapter is intended as an organizer in which we present an overall service delivery model that we ourselves found useful over the years in expanding the role of consultation in school psychology. The goal of this model is to provide a framework that encourages increased use of consultation, while at the same time recognizing educators' legitimate need for traditional psychological assessment services. As well, the model will help readers understand how information presented in the rest of the book can contribute to an expansion of their roles.

As background to the introduction of our service model, in Part I we briefly discuss the current state of school psychology from an historical and cultural perspective, and consider why, in spite of a stated wish to do so, school psychologists have been only partially successful in expanding upon the traditional testing role. The model itself is presented in Part II, along with a review of its chief benefits and operating principles. Part III discusses the implications of the model for school psychologists' training and continuing education, as well as for the use of this book. Finally, an overview of the book in terms of our service model is presented and the content of each chapter briefly discussed.

Section I: Historical and Cultural Perspectives

In considering options for change, school psychologists should be aware of the historical and cultural forces that have influenced the development of their current role. In North America, school psychology and mental testing have been closely linked in the thinking of both educators and the public at large. Yet in a historical review, French (1984) documents that the involvement of early mainstream psychologists in educational issues went far beyond the testing role. No fewer than eight of the first ten presidents of the American Psychological Association were school psychologists, in interest if not in title. That these early psychologists wished to provide educators with information about the implications of their new science for teaching and learning is illustrated by William James' *Talks to Teachers on Psychology* (James, cited by French, 1984).

In spite of these promising beginnings, however, the idea of the school psychologist as problem solver rather than merely "tester" has rarely caught on with educators. Although many practitioners with psychological training worked in the schools, their titles of "Binet-testers" or "examiners" reflected their narrowly defined roles. Gesell, the first practitioner with the title of "school psychologist," spent most of his time in a diagnosis-for-placement-in-special-education role (Fagan, 1987). The focus on assessment and testing continues to the present day, with recent surveys showing that many school psychologists spend extensive amounts of their time in these activities (Canter, 1997; Huberty & Huebner, 1988; Reschly & Wilson, 1995; Stewart, 1986; Wilson & Reschly, 1996).

Testing services do not seem to have played as important a role in school psychology outside North America. In their review, Oakland and Saigh (1987) note that both national priorities and cultural factors help to determine the nature and scope of school psychological services. In the former Soviet Union, for example, the use of tests was banned in 1936 as being ideologically incompatible with Marxist philosophy (Pambockian & Holowinsky, 1987). Psychological services in education in that country were not oriented toward individual student needs; instead, they focused on research into the nature of learning and its implications for curricular and teaching practices. In general, in school psychology outside of North America, testing is seen as but one part of a broad range of services, including both direct and indirect services, consultation and research.

In North America as well, cultural values appear to have had an impact on school psychologists' roles. Kaplan and Kaplan (1985) suggested that the rapid growth of both special education and the mental testing movement can be traced to the pervasive influence of the North American commitment to individualism. Concern for the individual learner, combined with a commitment to compulsory education for all children in increasingly diverse multicultural populations, led to graded classrooms that would allow teachers to plan instructional programs according to developmental needs. Such classrooms, however, also made more obvious the problems of children whose rates of learning departed from the norm, thus fostering the growth of special education programs.

In psychology, a focus on the individual led to an emphasis on individual differences and a tendency to ignore the role of social and environmental variables in development (Cole, 1996; Cole & Siegel, 1990; Sarason, 1988, 1997). These biases allowed school psychologists to adjust comfortably to an educational system that focused on factors within the child as responsible for learning problems. They also provided a rationale for removing underachieving children from classrooms rather than altering learning environments.

Today, in spite of the lack of sufficient documentation regarding its efficacy, special education continues to be a dominant force in North America (Cole & Siegel, 1990; Johnson, 1969; Shinn, 1986). Attitudes that are fundamental to the thinking of both school psychologists and educators perpetuate the importance of the assessment-for-placement model (Braden, 1997; Cole & Siegel, 1990; Kovaleski, 1988). In many jurisdictions, psychological assessment is a legislated requirement for placement decisions, and educators see this as the most needed psychological service (Abel & Burke, 1985; Cole, 1996; Hartshorne & Johnson, 1985; Kamphaus, 1996). They recognize that psychologists possess a wide range of knowledge and skills and seem to appreciate the benefits of such services; however, with few exceptions, they are not accepting of such modes of service as appropriate alternatives to assessment (Genshaft, 1984; Stewart, 1986). Very few school systems seem prepared to devote sufficient monetary resources to provide for a wide range of services in addition to psychological assessments. For that matter, many jurisdictions fail to provide the minimal funds necessary for adequate support of even that function (Kicklighter & Bailey Richardson, 1984).

Reacting to service needs identified by educators, many school psychologists themselves view assessment skills, especially the evaluation of cognitive functioning and information processing skills, as among the most important for their work and the area for which most feel they have been best prepared in graduate school (Braden, 1997; Mckee, Witt, Elliott, Pardue, & Judycki, 1987; Sarason, 1988). Testing is seen as the skill shared by all psychologists (Page, 1982) and as the most essential component of school psychologists' training, both now and in the future (Cole, 1996; Cole & Siegel, 1990; Copeland & Miller, 1985). Curriculum in university level training programs reflects this judgment (Brown, 1994; Brown & Minke,

1986). Even scholarly research within school psychology, which presumably reflects the thinking of those at the leading edge of the field, continues to emphasize problems associated with test development and assessment, according to published data (Canter, 1997; Fagan, 1986b, 1994; Hutton, Dubes, & Muir, 1992; Kamphaus, 1996; Reynolds & Clark, 1984; Sattler, 2001).

There is some evidence, however, that attitudes are changing. Forward-looking educators have questioned whether special education classes are the most effective way of dealing with academic underachievement (Reschly, 1988; Will, 1988) and there is an increasing skepticism of the diagnostic powers of traditional psychological assessment (Kamphaus, 1996; Luther, Cole, & Gamlin, 1996; Reschly, 1988; Shapiro, 1990). School psychologists themselves began to consider a wider range of skills as important to practice and would like ongoing information about and better training in a variety of areas (Brown, 1994; French, 1996; Graden et al., 1984; Mckee et al., 1987; Sandoval, 1996). Over the past two decades, journal articles and other publications, both scholarly and practical, have led practitioners in the direction of expanded services. Organizations such as the National Association of School Psychologists (NASP) are playing a crucial role in identifying and improving upon training standards (Fagan, 1986a) and in providing information to practitioners. The publications *Best Practices in School Psychology* (Thomas & Grimes, 1985, 1990), *Children's Needs: Psychological Perspectives* (Thomas & Grimes, 1987), *Children at Risk: Poverty, Minority Status and Other Issues in Educational Equity* (Barona & Garcia, 1990) and *NASP Blueprints* (Ysseldyke, Dawson et al., 1997; Ysseldyke, Reynolds, & Weinberg, 1984) are examples.

In spite of these promising developments, the fundamental pace of change has been and will likely continue to be slow (Cole, 1996; Fagan & Wise, 1994; Stewart, 1986). Assessment-for-placement work will continue to be a major part of the school psychologist's role as long as there are children whose learning needs sufficiently depart from the norm to require special services. We support the profession's involvement in this activity, since we believe that individuals with psychological training have expertise that can contribute to fairer, more balanced decision-making in the best interests of children. However, as discussed in Chapter 11, we advocate an approach to assessment that is less test-dependent than is typical of many practices (Cole, 1991, 1992, 1996, 1998; Kicklighter & Bailey-Richardson, 1984; Sandoval, 1996). This approach includes an evaluation of the impact of factors affecting learning that are external to the child, and is oriented toward suggesting a variety of recommendations, not just special education solutions.

What can school psychologists do to overcome longstanding ingrained biases to broader, more problem-solving oriented services? As both educators and psychologists themselves see legislated requirements as the dominant factor influencing the provision of service in schools (Benson & Hughes, 1985; Fagan, 1990; Fagan & Wise, 1994), it is important that our professional organizations have input into such legislation so that established structures and regulations will more adequately meet the needs of children (Cole, 1992, 1996; Stewart, 1986). Training is another obvious area of concern, since the current focus on assessment skills as the core competencies helps to perpetuate the diagnostically oriented model (Brown, 1994; French, 1996; Reschly, 1984; Thomas & Grimes, 1990; Sattler, 2001; Shapiro & Kratochwill, 2000).

However, focusing on changes in legislation and training only takes responsibility for effecting change out of the hands of individual practitioners and provides them with a convenient rationale for inaction. We feel that in adopting such an approach, school psychologists not only abrogate their responsibilities to children but fail to act in their own best interests: job-related stresses are reduced when one engages in innovative services and can benefit from the advantages of personal and professional growth (Huberty & Huebner, 1988; McMahon, 1993; Siegel & Cole, 1990). Our assumptions that practitioners themselves can do much to implement change - and that they desire to do so - have been the main motivations for preparing this book.

The following key avenues for change have been suggested by the literature, and are supported by our own experience. Specifically, we suggest to you, our readers, that as advocates of school psychology you should:

(1) Ask different questions about children. Focus on "What can be done to help the child?," not "What is wrong with the child?"

(2) Be realistic about setting goals. Determine what is both acceptable and possible for educators, parents, children, and yourself.

(3) Understand educators' needs and attitudes. Evaluate possible areas for change, and be assertive about what you can do to help.

(4) Encourage mechanisms such as School Teams and Assessment Consultation to cut down on assessment time (see Chapters 2 and 5).

(5) Consider responding to children's needs in a variety of ways, including preventative programs. That is, consider yourself a member of the system and ask how you can use your skills to help change it.

(6) Develop the habit of self-evaluation: "What skills do I have? What skills do I need? How can I learn?"

(7) Be patient. Set realistic, short-term goals and do your best to achieve them.

These steps are critical to successful implementation of our model for service delivery, which we will now discuss.

Section II: An Effective Service Model

Models of service tend to provide common directions for school psychologists. Yet, many psychologists employed by school systems tend to be reactive in their provision of supports, often citing lack of time for planning in view of service demands. However, unless the principles on which a service delivery model is based are made explicit, staff and schools are less likely to prioritize service needs and are more likely to underutilize valuable psychological knowledge and skills.

In general, psychological services are governed by three interrelated factors. First, school psychologists are often employed by school systems because of legislative requirements (such as assessment needs concerning special education identification and placement). Second, school systems may create internal mechanisms for services that identify specific roles for psychological staff. In many school systems, for example, psychologists are members of multidisciplinary school teams that provide consultation and monitor interventions. Also, psychologists are often members of centralized tragic-events response teams. These roles are not part of a legislative requirement, but are tied to school policies and organizational goals. Finally, local school needs in part dictate the third level of service. Schools facing a rapid transformation of the community may require an emphasis on specific services. In other instances, valued projects or early intervention programs have become part of a school's culture and provide an avenue for valued services to be made available to the community. It is thus common for psychologists to note that each of the schools they are assigned to may tend to utilize different types of services, allowing either for expanded roles or for unidimensional functions (Cole, 1996).

These three levels of service can all be coordinated within a coherent conceptual framework. The advantages of developing a service model are numerous as they foster a broader understanding of the role psychology has in education and guides service delivery practices. It is likely to help consciousness raising during periods of downsizing and to assist in explaining to educators and parents the importance of the role psychology has in enhancing children's learning and development. In addition, an integrated model is more likely to facilitate the coordination of prevention and intervention functions and to generate possibilities for alternative services.

Models are abstractions and are therefore inadequate descriptions of everyday life. For many busy school psychologists the idea of having a service delivery model may seem of relatively little value. Yet most of us do have an underlying set of beliefs that govern our behavior, and it is important to take the time to make these beliefs explicit. We therefore will here describe the service delivery model that has guided our practice for years and has served as the inspiration for this book. We have found that having such a model has helped us gain a better understanding of our role and assisted us in explaining that role to educators, parents, and other psychologists. The model has provided us with insight into the significance of our day-to-day activities and helped to establish priorities. Finally, it has provided us with a framework for generating and evaluating alternate methods of service delivery.

Our model assumes that the ultimate goal of school psychologists' services is to enhance children's learning and adjustment; that services are available to all students; and that multiple approaches to service delivery are desirable (see Thomas & Grimes, 1990; Ysseldyke, 1986; Ysseldyke et al., 1997). The model consists of the simple two-dimensional grid illustrated in Figure 1. The horizontal dimension of the grid elaborates the goals of service delivery as primary, secondary, and tertiary prevention. These concepts are borrowed from the work of Caplan (1970), a pioneer in the area of preventative mental health. Primary prevention services are provided for the benefit of all students; secondary prevention services for the benefit of students who are at risk; and tertiary prevention services for those who are experiencing significant difficulties with school adjustment.

The vertical dimension of the grid was suggested by the work of Parsons and Meyers (1984) and illustrates that, although the goal of a service is ultimately to benefit students, their needs may sometimes best be met indirectly through services to teachers, principals, or the entire school system. That is, rather than services always being provided directly to students or their parents by the school psychologist, they may also be carried out by someone else, such as a teacher, with consultation from the psychologist, or through their impact on school personnel or the school system at large.

	Goals of Service		
Recipients of Service	*Primary Prevention* Identify resources, provide and analyze information; Program for all students	*Secondary Prevention* Program for students "at risk"	*Tertiary Prevention* Program for students whose problems significantly interfere with their adaptation to school
The Organization – School system or school – Provide information, consult, advise			
School Staff – Teachers or administrators – Provide information, consult, advise			
Students/Parents (Mediated) – Provide information, consult, advise			
Students/Parents (Direct) – Group and individual counseling – Assessment – Consultation			

Figure 1 A Model for Psychological Service in Schools

The model shown in Figure 1 is a bare-bones skeleton into which most, if not all, activities of school psychologists may be incorporated. Traditional roles, such as student assessments and counseling, fall in the lower right-hand corner of the grid; such roles have the advantage of providing practitioners with firsthand knowledge of student needs, but are limiting in terms of the number of individuals served. Moving upwards and to the left, service becomes more indirect and systems-oriented. Innovative services are possible in all roles suggested by the model, and many illustrative examples that fit into each of the cells of the grid will be presented later throughout the book. For now we have left the cells blank and invite readers to fill them in on the basis of their own experiences.

As discussed thus far, the model describes alternative roles for school psychologists but does not show *how* one goes about expanding services. The acceptance of several key assumptions is necessary if one wishes to achieve this goal. These will now be discussed in turn.

(1) Consultation Is a Key Skill

With its emphasis on preventative services, the model is explicit in identifying the proper role of the school psychologist as change agent and problem solver. Central to the successful execution of this role, we believe, is the effective use of consultation. In school systems, the important decisions are usually made by educators and parents, sometimes by students, and almost never by psychologists. Therefore, psychologists can effect change only through influencing and/or facilitating the decisions of others.

In our view, the most effective method of accomplishing this goal is through collaborative consultation (Caplan, 1970; Parsons & Meyers, 1984). By this we mean a process through which psychologists and educators work coordinately to resolve educational problems from positions of mutual respect for one another as professionals. The key assumptions of collaborative consultation are summarized in Chapters 3 and 4, and suggestions for implementing it have been discussed by such writers as Parsons and Meyers (1984).

In our view, if psychologists are to function effectively as consultants they must avoid presenting themselves as "experts" or being cast into such a role by educators. Chapter 5 details an explicit model for avoiding this trap in the face of the many forces that propel psychologists toward it (see Anserello & Sweet, 1990; Cole, 1996; Davison, 1990; Stewart, 1986; Witt & Martens,1988). In our experience, when psychologists adopt an "expert" role their input is rejected by educators, who quite rightly resent the advice preferred by members of another professional group in areas about which they themselves should be most knowledgeable and for which they have ultimate responsibility. These impressions are supported by literature that documents the preference of educators for collaborative approaches (Cole & Brown, 1996; Fullan, 1991, 2000, 2001; Pryzwansky & White, 1983; Wenger, 1986).

In common with Curtis and Meyers (1985) and Reschly and Ysseldyke (1995), we see consultation not only as an alternative to direct services but as a key component of them, in such activities as student assessment or counseling (see Chapters 9 and 11). Minimally, consultation will lead to more systematic decisions as to which and how many students should receive direct services. However, once initiated, direct service contacts inevitably result in ideas about what actions could be taken. Collaborative consultation then facilitates the implementation of these interventions.

(2) Approach Traditional Services From a Perspective That Acknowledges Multiple Causes Of Children's Learning Difficulties, and Be Open To a Variety Of Interventions

If consultation is seen as an important component of direct services, then the traditional referral can become a vehicle for role expansion. For this to occur, the psychologist must go beyond asking "What is wrong with the child?" to consider "What can be done to help the child?" One should adopt a model that acknowledges multiple and interacting influences on children's learning, and be prepared to evaluate them using a variety of methods. Interactions between a student and his or her teacher, peers, family, school environment, and community, should all be examined as positive or negative interrelated influences. The developmental model proposed by Chris tenson and colleagues (Christenson, Abery, & Weinberg, 1986) has served as the basis for our own assessment model discussed in Chapter 11. Traditional testing may be undertaken, but only when it will contribute significant information (Carner, 1982; Cole, 1991, 1996).

Consideration of the multiple influences on children's learning leads automatically to an evaluation of avenues for change. The key to success is a consideration of all the options and the adoption of those strategies that have the greatest likelihood of success. Of particular importance is an evaluation of the ability of significant others in a child's life (parents, siblings, classmates, teachers) to make changes in their own attitudes and behaviors. As well, the possibility of altering the instructional program or the classroom or home environments should be considered, and the positive or negative contribution of special education services evaluated. In real-life consultation cases, a number of intervention strategies must often be tried (see Cole, 1992, 1996; Reschly & Ysseldyke, 1995; Wenger, 1986).

As the person who interacts most frequently with the student at school, the classroom teacher is often seen as a potential change agent. However, if change is to come about as a result of collaborative effort, it is important to gain an understanding of what and how many changes teachers feel are possible to make. Changes in classroom management tactics or curriculum that make a great deal of sense to the psychologist may be rejected by teachers as too time-consuming, intrusive, or incompatible with their educational approach (Borghese & Cole, 1994; Fullan, 2000, 2001; Fullan &

Miles, 1992; Witt, 1986; Witt, Martens, & Elliott, 1984). Sometimes teachers may be opposed to the idea of *any* change, feeling they have already done all they can and that putting a problem child in a special education program is a more sensible alternative. As well, they may lack confidence in their ability to implement the changes effectively, or may simply be too stressed due to factors beyond the particular child or classroom to even try.

The psychologist who is insensitive to a teacher's beliefs regarding change may be frustrated in any efforts to help students, as teachers who sense that it is unacceptable to express their opinions are likely to passively resist interventions, thus dooming them to failure. The psychologist should be prepared to listen to the teacher's concerns, to respect them, and to avoid judging their legitimacy. Often, such an approach will open the door to collaboration or problem-solving that will generate solutions acceptable to all concerned.

Teachers may be more open to change themselves if they feel that other avenues are being explored as well. When the focus is solely on them, they may feel inadequate and blamed for a child's problems. Such beliefs are likely to reduce trust and induce guilt and defensiveness. Thus, focusing solely on the teacher for the solution is no better an alternative than relying only on special education. All options need to be considered.

In evaluating possible solutions for a child's learning difficulties, it is important to provide those who have an influence on the child's life with a sense that they have both the competency and the strength to make things better. This philosophy of "empowerment" has been discussed by several writers in relation to helping teachers become better classroom managers (Fullan, 1991, 2001; Newberry, 1992; Royal Commission on Learning, 1994; Speck, 1996; Witt & Martens, 1988). However, the principles they articulate apply equally well to the solution of almost any problem. These are: i) Build on existing strengths; ii) Use existing resources, if possible; iii) Be aware of seemingly unrelated environmental variables that may be producing additional stress; iv) Help is more often accepted if it is provided proactively; v) The process of change should leave those directly involved with a feeling of empowerment, not dependency.

(3) Develop a Preventative Mindset. Allow Bottom-up As Well As Top-down Information To Identify Service Needs

The model presented in Figure 1 provides for many preventative activities. In most school systems, however, primary prevention is not an explicit part of the psychologist's role (Cole, 1992, 1996; Cole & Siegel, 1990; Genshaft, 1984). Faced with a high case load and too many referrals, psychologists often feel that they simply do not have the time for preventative work or the sanction of educators to become involved in it.

Occasionally, preventative programs are implemented because a high-level administrator, school trustee, or principal has identified a particular need. Unfortunately, if school psychologists are associated only with a testing role, they may not be thought of as resources that are available and willing to help. Whether such programs are mounted at the systems or at the school level, it is important for psychologists to be assertive about making educators aware of their interest and skills, and, if their involvement is requested, to make the time to facilitate the implementation of the program. Chapters 16 and 17 provide examples of a department-wide implementation of two preventative programs initiated at the system level.

Because school psychologists are in touch on a daily basis with students who have special learning needs, they are in a position to identify recurring patterns of difficulty and to suggest what preventative actions might be taken to deal with them. Providing educators with solid information about the scope of a particular problem is important, although time-consuming. As well, it will often be necessary to invest time in self-education and identification of resources. We would suggest that school psychologists allocate a small amount of their time each week to preventatively oriented work, even if it has not been explicitly sanctioned (see Brown, 1994; Carner, 1982; Cole, 1996; Thomas & Grimes, 1990; Sladeczek & Heath, 1997).

(4) Pick and Choose Among Service Options In Response To Educators' Needs

Lest the reader feel overwhelmed by the variety of activities suggested in Figure 1, we should make it clear that it is inconceivable that any one individual would be involved in all aspects of the model during the course of a particular week or even an entire school year. The multiple options are intended to provide a framework for innovation, rather than to delineate an ideal service role. We feel that school psychologists, both as individuals and as members of their departments, should try to achieve a balance of direct and indirect service delivery.

Parsons and Meyers (1984) have suggested that systems-level interventions should always be attempted as a first priority because they benefit more people and are therefore more cost-efficient. We recognize, however, that such a decision rule may be unrealistic in many cases. Many educators will reject psychologists' involvement at this level, as their competencies are seen as related to the evaluation of "problem students" and not to decision-making at the systems level.

In identifying service priorities, the psychologist must place the greatest emphasis on the needs identified by educators. Within a particular school, it is especially important to become familiar with and accept the priorities of the principal, who is the ultimate educational decision maker in that setting (Carner, 1982; Cole & Brown, 1996; Fullan, 1991; Sladeczek & Heath, 1997).

Section III: Implications for Training and for Using This Book

We have prepared this book because we believe that improved knowledge and skills must go hand in hand with role expansion. By describing the approaches of practicing psychologists in actual school settings, we acknowledge the realities of service delivery, which at times may differ from the "ivory tower" perspective of academic research. Our experience with the service model described in this chapter has a number of implications for the skills and knowledge that school psychologists need, both for the nature of their training programs and for their professional development.

(1) Knowledge and Skills

Knowledge and skills are not entirely separable concepts. However, we have found the distinction useful in thinking about the ideal training program in school psychology.

The NASP Blueprint-II (Ysseldyke et al., 1997) identified specific domains of knowledge that the school psychologist should be prepared to offer to educators, and suggested that training programs restructure their required course work and practicum experience accordingly. These domains, listed in Table 1, were intended to illustrate in concrete terms the wide-ranging knowledge base needed in practice. As prac-

---

Table 1 Recommended Domains of School Psychology*

(1) Data-based decision making and accountability
(2) Interpersonal communication, collaboration, and consultation
(3) Effective instruction and development of cognitive/academic skills
(4) Socialization and development of life compentencies
(5) School structure, organization and climate
(6) Home/school community collaboration
(7) Research and program evaluation
(8) Legal, ethical practice and professional development
(9) Student diversity in development and learning
(10) Prevention, wellness promotion and crisis intervention
(11) School-community relations
(12) Instruction
(13) Legal/ethical concerns
(14) Assessment
(15) Multicultural concerns
(16) Research

*From Ysseldyke, Dawson, Lehr, Reschley, Reynolds, and Telzrow, 1997

---

titioners, we find this list both exciting and overwhelming. It is exciting because of its graphic demonstration of the many possibilities for practice: successful delivery of service in each of the domains for the benefit of students and educators would be extremely rewarding for any psychologist. The extent of the list is overwhelming, however, and seems to deny the possibility of any one individual, no matter how well trained or experienced, ever becoming fully competent to practice.

In addition to these domains of knowledge, our experience suggests that school psychologists require skills in a number of specific areas: (a) consultation, (b) communication, including both public speaking and writing, (c) individual, group, and family counseling, (d) assessment, (e) research, and (f) team building. These skills overlap somewhat with the knowledge domains, but the two lists taken together suggest a lifetime of learning.

(2) Implications for Training

Lifetime self-education is a desirable goal. However, it is important to be realistic about the core skills and knowledge bases that should be required for entry level training. This book is not the place to debate the perennial PhD versus MA entry level issue (Fagan, 1989, 1990; Fagan & Wise, 1994; Reschly & Wilson, 1997) or to outline the specifics of course or supervision hours that should be required for credentialed training programs. Instead, we present, in Table 2, a list of suggestions for basic competencies regardless of professional degree.

Comparison of our core competencies in Table 2 with the NASP domains listed in Table 1 reveals that the two lists overlap with one another extensively, although we focus more on basic psychology while the NASP domains are more applied. We feel that a good grounding in the core knowledge and skills listed in Table 2 will provide school psychologists with an excellent foundation for acquiring the more extensive applied knowledge implied in the NASP Blueprint-II. The vehicles for this continuing education are ongoing supervision and professional development, ideally directed by service needs as they arise in schools. In our view, school psychologists should make these activities a priority throughout their professional lives.

Our list of core competencies contrasts with published information about both school psychology training programs (Brown & Minke, 1986; Cole, 1996) and training needs as perceived by practitioners (Copeland & Miller, 1985; Ross & Goh, 1993). For instance, neither source seems to identify a comprehensive look at individual differences or organizational theory as key knowledge areas, yet, in our view, such information is critical to the role of the psychologist as change agent within the complex organizational setting of the school. Of the core skills we have listed, few courses, such as assessment and interviewing, are offered as compulsory requisites in graduate programs. Practitioners identify consultation and therapeutic skills as important but do not mention either communications or multicultural service and research skills as re-

---

Table 2 Basic Competencies for Entry Level School Psychologists

Core Knowledge:[*]
(1)   Theories of learning – cognitive and behavioral perspectives
(2)   Theories of personality-behavioral, psychodynamic, humanistic
(3)   History and systems of psychology
(4)   Child development – biological, affective, social, cognitive, linguistic, academic
(5)   Individual differences – biological, developmental, environmental, social, cultural determinants, and transcultural adaptation
(6)   Psychopathology – emphasis on childhood, adolescence, and family
(7)   Ethics and standards of practice
(8)   Organizational theory – organizational change
(9)   Effective teaching – effective schools
(10) In-depth study of one or two practical problems including possible interventions

Core Skills:[**]
(1)   Consultation skills
(2)   Interpersonal communication skills
(3)   Assessment skills
(4)   Research skills
(5)   Interview skills
(6)   One therapeutic modality (e.g., cognitive behavioral therapy)

[*]   Core knowledge is covered in course work that links theory to application. Ideally, trainees will be able to approach applied problems from a number of theoretical perspectives.
[**] Core skills are practiced under supervision.

---

quiring formal training. They apparently do not see these skills as an explicit part of training, even though they report spending a substantial amount of time involved in activities that require them. If school psychologists undertake in-service of teachers as part of their role, communications will be increasingly involved in their work, while research skills are required for such areas of activity as program evaluation and other applied research.

While there is a clear need to reorient graduate programs, this brief discussion suggests that the degree of change required is not that extensive and is more a matter of adding to rather than replacing existing programs.

(3) How to Use This Book

This book is not intended as a comprehensive text, but to provide illustrative examples of innovative services with a hands-on, how-to-do-it orientation. The content and problem areas were dictated by our pragmatic wish to present the perspectives of those currently practicing in the field so as to reflect the reality of service in today's school settings. Most chapters provide case material, references, and suggestions of useful tools for implementing the strategy or programs being described.

It is not necessary that this book be read through from cover to cover by everyone: rather, we invite practitioners, students, and trainers to sample according to their needs and stages of professional development. To provide an overview, in Figure 2 we have reproduced the model outlined in Figure 1 in such a way as to relate it to the various chapters, indicating where each is relevant to the suggested roles in the model.

	Goals of Service		
Recipients of Service	*Primary Prevention* See Chapters 1, 2, 3, 4, 7, 11, 15, 16, 17, 19	*Secondary Prevention* See Chapters 1, 2, 5, 8, 9, 11, 12, 13	*Tertiary Prevention* See Chapters 1, 2, 9, 17, 18
The Organization – School system or school – Provide information, consult, advise	Setting up an early intervention program to facilitate later school adjustment (Chapter 15)	Establish in-school teams (Chapter 2)	Co-write a suicide prevention booklet (Chapter 17)
School Staff – Teachers or administrators – Provide information, consult, advise	Facilitate teacher discussion of effective management strategies (Chapter 7)	Provide in-service for teachers on multicultural students' needs (Chapters 11 and 13)	Facilitate teachers' problem solving (Chapters 5 and 7)
Students/Parents (Mediated) – Provide information, consult, advise	Consult with teachers as they assess students' cognitive abilities and learning styles (Chapter 16)	As a member of the school team, develop plans for students "at risk" (Chapters 2 and 8)	Pre-referral consultation (Chapters 2 and 5)
Students/Parents (Direct) – Group and individual counseling – Assessment – Consultation	Facilitate in-class communication (Chapters 16 and 19)	Facilitate a study skills group for multicultural students (Chapters 11 and 13)	Assessment and short-term intervention for depressed or underachieving students (Chapters 9 and 17)

Figure 2 A Model for Psychological Service in Schools: Examples from this Book

In each cell we have given one or more illustrative examples of a specific service drawn from a relevant chapter. These examples were selected arbitrarily and are only intended to provide the reader with a more concrete understanding of the model; many more examples are provided throughout.

We conclude by discussing each section of the book in turn and relating the various chapters to the model shown in Figures 1 and 2. The first section, *Perspectives on Consultation and Training,* reflects our conviction that consultation should join assessment as a core skill for school psychologists. The chapters here are, in a sense, relevant to all aspects of the model, as consultation skills are important in carrying out any of the roles described. Chapter 2 discusses how the establishment of school teams can influence the psychologist's role. Chapters 3, 4 and 5 deal with the practice of consultation and with school psychologists' understanding of the term "consultation." These chapters present models for the consultation process that facilitates collaborative problem-solving while de-emphasizing the psychologist's status as an expert. Chapter 6 discusses consultation skills for future trainees, illustrating the impact of graduate university models towards the realities of school psychology. Becoming a school consultant is clearly a step-by-step process for which on-site, practical experience is a necessary component.

Section II, *The Psychologist as a Change Agent,* discusses a variety of strategies including short-term cognitive and family therapy, consultation, and in-service training. Both direct and indirect services oriented toward primary, secondary, and tertiary prevention are included. Thus, Chapter 7 presents a model of consultation that incorporates in-service training for teachers as well as case-specific problem-solving. Chapters 8 and 9 discuss ways in which the school psychologist can intervene with two commonly encountered problems, depressed elementary students and underachieving adolescents. Both discuss strategies for assessing the problem as well as considering appropriate interventions. These chapters deal specifically with direct service to students; however, once school psychologists develop experience with these strategies, expansion to other parts of the model are possible. For example, service may be mediated by teachers and guidance counselors with the psychologist adopting a consultant role, and developing an understanding of the needs of students in serious difficulty may eventually lead to consultation at the systems level on appropriate early identification strategies and prevention programs.

Chapters 10, 12, 14, and 15 show how service models can facilitate the psychologist's role as consultant and change agent, discussing both how this approach facilitates in-class problem solving, and the implications for parent education. It is shown here how the same principles that facilitate interaction in the classroom can be extended to services of a more preventative nature.

Section II also includes Chapters 11 and 13 which describe services to the multicultural community and the special needs of immigrant students and their families. An assessment model that is specifically tailored to the needs of multicultural students is presented, and examples given of preventatively oriented interventions.

In Section III, *Consultation in School-Based Programs,* we consider the implementation of systems-wide initiatives. Organizational factors and intervention at the systems level are discussed within the context of three different initiatives: implementating a systems-wide consultation-oriented school psychology service; facilitating preventative curriculum change in classrooms (Chapter 16); and developing a suicide prevention program (Chapter 17). This section demonstrates that educational change is seldom sweeping, but occurs gradually and is contingent on the involvement of all who are affected by the process (see Fullan, 1982, 1991, 2000, 2001). As illustrated in all four chapters, role change on a systems basis requires professional development for school psychologists as well as educators. The process is facilitated when systems change is accompanied by relevant performance review procedures, as illustrated in all chapters (see Fullan, 1988; Fullan & Miles, 1992; Speck, 1996). Chapters 18 and 19 also suggest that involvement in primary prevention programs impacts positively on other aspects of the school psychologist's role.

References

Abel, P. R., & Burke, J. P. (1985). Perceptions of school psychology from a staff perspective. *Journal of School Psychology, 33*, 121-131.

Anserello, C., & Sweet, T. (1990). Integrating consultation into school psychological services. In E. Cole & J. A. Siegel (Eds.), *Effective consultation in school psychology* (pp. 173-199). Toronto: Hogrefe & Huber Publishers.

Barona, A., & Garcia, E. (Eds.). (1990). *Children at risk: Poverty, minority status and other issues in educational equity.* Washington, DC: National Association of School Psychologists.

Benson, A. J., & Hughes, J. (1985). Perceptions of role definition processes in school psychology: A national survey. *School Psychology Review, 14(1),* 64-73.

Borghese, N., & Cole, E. (1994). Psychoeducational recommendations: Perceptions of school psychologists and classroom teachers. *Canadian Journal of School Psychology, 10(1),* 70-87.

Braden, J. P. (1997). The practical impact of intellectual assessment issues. *School Psychology Review, 26(2),* 242-248.

Brown, D. T. (1994). Will the real school psychologists please stand up: Is the past a prologue for the future of school psychology? *School Psychology Review, 23,* 589-600.

Brown, D. T., & Minke, K. M. (1986). School psychology graduate training: A comprehensive analysis. *American Psychologist, 41(12),* 1328-1338.

Canter, A. S. (1997). The future of intelligence testing in the schools. *School Psychology Review, 26(2),* 255-261.

Caplan, G. (1970). *The theory and practice of mental health consultation.* New York: Basic Books.

Carner, L. A. (1982). Developing a consultation contract. In J. L. Alpert (Ed.), *Psychological consultation in educational settings* (pp. 8-32). San Francisco: Jossey-Bass.

Christenson, S., Abery, B., & Weinberg, R. A. (1986). An alternative model for the delivery of psychological services in the school community. In S. N. Elliott & J. C. Witt (Eds.), *The delivery of psychological services in schools.* New Jersey: Erlbaum.

Cole, E. (1991). Multicultural psychological assessment: New challenges, improved methods. *International Journal of Dynamic Assessment and Instruction, 2(1),* 1-10.

Cole, E. (1992). Characteristics of students referred to school teams: Implications for preventive psychological services. *Canadian Journal of School Psychology, 8,* 23-36.

Cole, E. (1996). An integrative perspective on school psychology. *Canadian Journal of School Psychology, 12(2),* 115-121.

Cole, E. (1998). Immigrant and refugee children: Challenges and opportunities for education and mental health services. *Canadian Journal of School Psychology, 14(1),* 36-50.

Cole, E., & Brown, R. (1996). Multidisciplinary school teams: A five-year follow-up study. *Canadian Journal of School Psychology, 12(2),* 155-168.

Cole, E., & Siegel, J. A. (Eds.). (1990). *Effective consultation in school psychology.* Toronto: Hogrefe & Huber Publishers.

Copeland, E. P., & Miller, L. F. (1985). Training needs of prospective school psychologists: The practitioners' viewpoint. *Journal of School Psychology, 23,* 247-254.

Curtis, M. J., & Meyers, J. (1985). Best practices in school-based consultation: Guidelines for effective practice. In A. Thomas & J. Grimes (Eds.), *Best practices in school psychology* (pp. 79-94). Kent, OH: National Association of School Psychologists.

Davison, J. (1990). The process of school consultation: Give and take. In E. Cole & J. A. Siegel (Eds.), *Effective consultation in school psychology* (pp. 53-69). Toronto: Hogrefe & Huber Publishers.

Fagan, T. K. (1986a). School psychology's dilemma. *American Psychologist, 41(8),* 851-861.

Fagan, T. K. (1986b). The evolving literature of school psychology. *School Psychology Review, 15(3),* 430-440.

Fagan, T. K. (1987). Gesell: The first school psychologist. Part H-Practice and significance. *School Psychology Review, 16(3),* 399-409.

Fagan, T. K. (1989). Guest editor's commentary on the entry-level debate. *School Psychology Review, 18(1),* 34-36.

Fagan, T. K. (1990). A brief history of school psychology in the United States. In A. Thomas & J. Grimes (Eds.), *Best practices in school psychology – II.* Washington, DC: National Association of School Psychologists.

Fagan, T. K. (1994). A critical appraisal of the NASP's first 25 years. *School Psychology Review, 23(4),* 604-618.

Fagan, T. K., & Wise, P. S. (1994). *School psychology: Past, present and future.* White Plains, NY: Longman.

French, J. L. (1984). On the conception, birth and early development of school psychology. *American Psychologist, 39(9),* 976-987.

French, J. L. (1996). Recycling the basics for evolving schools: Psychologists as fulcrums for leveraging improved schooling. In R. C. Talley, T. Kubiszyn, M. Brassard, & R. J. Short (Eds.), *Making psychologists in schools indispensable: Critical questions & emerging perspectives* (pp. 15-19). Washington, DC: American Psychological Association.

Fullan, M. (1982). *The meaning of educational change.* New York: Teachers College Press.

Fullan, M. (1988). Performance appraisal and curriculum implementation research. In E. S. Hickcox, S. B. Lawton, K. A. Leithwood, & D. F. Musella (Eds.), *Making a difference through performance appraisal* (pp. 71-83). Toronto: Ontario Institute for Studies in Education Press.

Fullan, M. (1991). *The new meaning of educational change* (2nd edition). Toronto: OISE Press.

Fullan, M. (2000). The three stories of educational reform. *Phi Delta Kappan, 81(8),* 581-584.

Fullan, M. (2001). *Leading in a culture of change.* San Francisco: Jossey - Bass, John A. Wiley Company.

Fullan, M., & Miles, M. B. (1992). Getting reform right: What works and what doesn't. *Phi Delta Kappan, 73*(10), 744-752.

Genshaft, J. (1984). A reaction to "A national survey of students' and practitioners' perceptions of training. " *School Psychology Review, 13*(3), 406-407.

Graden, J., Christenson, S., Ysseldyke, J., Meyers, J., Genshaft, J., & Reschley, D. J. (1984). A national survey of students' and practitioners' perceptions of training. *School Psychology Review, 13(3),* 397-407.

Hartshorne, T. S., & Johnson, M. C. (1985). The actual and preferred roles of the school psychologist according to secondary school administrators. *Journal of School Psychology, 23,* 241-246.

Huberty, T. J., & Huebner, E. S. (1988). A national survey of burnout among school psychologists. *Psychology in the Schools, 25,* 54-61.

Hutton, J. B., Dubes, R., & Muir, S. (1992). Assessment practices of school psychologists: Ten years later. *School Psychology Review, 21 (2),* 271-284.

Johnson, J. L. (1969). Special education and the inner city: A challenge for the future or another means for cooling the mark? *Journal of Special Education, 3,* 241-251.

Kamphaus, R. W. (1996). Measurement consultation. In R. C. Talley, T. Kubiszyn, M. Brassard, & R. J. Short (Eds.), *Making psychologists in schools indispensable: Critical questions & emerging perspectives* (pp. 153-158). Washington, DC: American Psychological Association.

Kaplan, M. S., & Kaplan, H. E. (1985). School psychology: Its educational and societal connections. *Journal of School Psychology, 23,* 319-325.

Kicklighter, R. H., & Bailey-Richardson, B. (1984). Psychological assessment: Tasks and time. *School Psychology Review, 13(4),* 499-502.

Kovaleski, J. F. (1988). Paradigmatic obstacles to reform in school psychology. *School Psychology Review, 17(3),* 479-484.

Luther, M., Cole, E., & Gamlin, P. (Eds.). (1996). *Dynamic assessment for instruction: From theory to application.* Toronto: Captus University Publications.

Mckee, W. T, Witt, J. C., Elliott, S. N., Pardue, M., & Judycki, A. (1987). Practice informing research: A survey of research dissemination and knowledge utilization. *School Psychology Review, 16(3),* 338-347.

McMahon, T. J. (1993). On the concept of child advocacy: A review of theory and methodology. *School Psychology Review, 22(4),* 744-755.

Newberry, A. J. H. (1992). *Strategic planning in education.* Vancouver, BC: Educational Services.

Oakland, T., & Saigh, P. (1987). Psychological services in schools: A summary of international perspectives. *Journal of School Psychology, 25,* 287-308.

Page, F. B. (1982). Foreword. In C. R. Reynolds & T. B. Gutkin (Eds.), *The handbook of school psychology* (pp. xi-xii). New York: John Wiley

Pambockian, H. S., & Holowinsky, I. Z. (1987). School psychology in the U. S. S. R. *Journal of School Psychology, 25,* 209-221.

Parsons, R. D., & Meyers, J. (1984). *Developing consultation skills: A guide to training, development and assessment for human services professionals.* San Francisco: Jossey-Bass.

Pryzwansky, W B., & White, G. W. (1983). The influence of consultee characteristics on preferences for consultation approaches. *Professional Psychology: Research and Practice, 14,* 457-461.

Reschly, D. J. (1984). A reaction to "A national survey of students' and practitioners' perceptions of training. *School Psychology Review, 13(3),* 405-406.

Reschly, D. J. (1988). Special education reform: School psychology revolution. *School Psychology Review, 17(3),* 459-475.

Reschly, D. J., & Wilson, M. S. (1995). School psychology faculty and practitioners: 1986-1991 trends in demographic characteristics, roles, satisfaction, and system reform. *School Psychology Review, 24(1),* 62-80

Reschly, D. J., & Wilson, M. S. (1997). Characteristics of school psychology graduate education: Implications for the entry-level discussion and doctoral-level specialty definition. *School Psychology Review, 21(1),* 74-92.

Reschly, D. J., & Ysseldyke, J. E. (1995). School psychology paradigm shift. In A. Thomas & J. Grimes (Eds.), *Best practices in school psychology – III* (pp. 17-31). Washington, DC: National Association of School Psychologists.

Reynolds, K. R., & Clark, J. H. (1984). Trends in school psychology research (1974-1980). *Journal of School Psychology, 22,* 43-52.

Ross, R. P., & Goh, D. S. (1993). Participation in supervision in school psychology: A national survey of practices and training. *School Psychology Review, 22(1),* 63-80.

Royal Commission on Learning (1994). *For the love of learning.* Queen's Printer of Ontario.

Sandoval, J. (1996). Becoming indispensable through mental health promotion. In R. C. Talley, T. Kubiszyn, M. Brassard, & R. J. Short (Eds.), *Making psychologists in schools indispensable: Critical questions & emerging perspectives* (pp. 3-7). Washington, DC: American Psychological Association.

Sarason, S. B. (1977). The unfortunate fate of Alfred Binet and school psychology. In S. Miezitis & M. Orme (Eds.), *Innovation in school psychology* (pp. 19-32). Toronto: Ontario Institute for Studies in Education Press.

Sarason, S. B. (1988). *The making of an American psychologist.* San Francisco: Jossey-Bass Publishers.

Sarason, S. B. (1997). NASP distinguished lecture series: What should we do about school reform? *School Psychology Review, 26(1),* 104-110.

Sattler, J. (2001). *Assessment of children (4th Edition).* San Diego: Jerome Sattler.

Shapiro, E. S. (1990). An integrated model for curriculum-based assessment. *School Psychology Review, 19,* 331-349.

Shapiro, E. S., & Kratochwill, T. (2000). *Conducting school-based assessments of child and adolescent behavior.* New York: Guilford Press.

Shinn, M. R. (1986). Does anyone care what happens after the refer-test-place sequence: The systematic evaluation of special education program effectiveness. *School Psychology Review, 15(1),* 49-58.

Sladeczek, I. E., & Heath, N. L. (1997). Consultation in Canada. *Canadian Journal of School Psychology, 13(2),* 1-14.

Speck, M. (1996). Best practices in professional development for sustained educational change. *Spectrum – Journal of School Research and Information, 14(2),* 33-41.

Stewart, K. J. (1986). Innovative practice of indirect service delivery: Realities and idealities. *School Psychology Review, 15(4),* 466-478.

Thomas, A., & Grimes, J. (Eds.). (1985). *Best practices in school psychology.* Kent, OH: National Association of School Psychologists.

Thomas, A., & Grimes, J. (1987). *Children's needs: Psychological perspectives.* Washington, DC: National Association of School Psychologists.

Thomas, A., & Grimes, J. (Eds.). (1990). *Best practices in school psychology - II.* Washington, DC: National Association of School Psychologists.

Wenger, R. D. (1986). A longitudinal study of an indirect service case. *School Psychology Review, 15(4),* 500-509.

Will, M. (1988). Educating students with learning problems and the changing role of the school psychologist. *School Psychology Review, 17(3),* 476-478.

Wilson, M. S., & Reschly, D. J. (1996). Assessment in school psychology training and practice. *School Psychology Review, 25(1),* 9-23.

Witt, J. C. (1986). Teachers' resistance to the use of school-based interventions. *Journal of School Psychology, 24,* 37-44.

Witt, J. C., & Martens, B. K. (1988). Problems with problem solving consultation: A re-analysis of assumptions, methods, and goals. *School Psychology Review, 17(2),* 221-226.

Witt, J. C., Martens, B. K., & Elliott, S. N. (1984). Factors affecting teachers' judgments of the acceptability of interventions: Time involvement, behavior problem severity, and type of intervention. *Behavior Therapy, 15,* 204-209.

Ysseldyke, J. E. (1986). Current practice in school psychology. In S. N. Elliott & J. C. Witt (Eds.), *The delivery of psychological services in schools.* Hillsdale, NJ: Laurence Erlbaum Associates.

Ysseldyke, J. E., Dawson, P., Lehr, C., Reschly, D., Reynolds, M., & Telzrow, C. (1997). *School psychology: A blueprint for training and practice II.* Bethesda, MD: National Association of School Psychologists.

Ysseldyke, J. E., Reynolds, M. C., & Weinberg, R. A. (1984). *School psychology: A blueprint for training and practice.* Minneapolis: National Psychology In-service Training Network.

Chapter 2
Multidisciplinary School Teams:
A Five-Year Follow-up Study

Ester Cole and Rob Brown

Introduction

Multidisciplinary School Teams continue to provide a vehicle for service delivery in many school boards in Canada and the United States. Overall, Teams are designed to support teachers, school administrators, and parents in providing appropriate interventions for students in need of assistance in regular and special education settings. Some Canadian and American school systems have expanded Team mandates to include consultative services to educators, parents and community agencies (Adelman & Taylor, 1998; Cole & Brown, 1996b; Cole, Siegel, & Yau, 1992; Davidson & Wiener, 1991).

Schools have become recognized as intervention sites for numerous learning, social, and emotional problems affecting children and adolescents (Cole, 1992). Because mental health problems tend to interfere with learning and socialization, schools have come to rely on multidisciplinary supports to plan effective interventions at school and at home. Although some studies document that, to date, this service vehicle has not been as facilitative as it could potentially become, others have provided support for this service delivery model. Advocates of Multidisciplinary Teams often emphasize that this mechanism provides an avenue for cost-effective sharing and coordination of school based services (Cole & Brown, 1996a; Cole & Siegel, 1990; Huebner & Gould, 1991; Kaiser & Woodman, 1985).

The composition of Multidisciplinary Teams is closely tied to school policies and organizational goals. The roles of members and the functions of Teams vary. In the United States, for example, legislation requires that Multidisciplinary Teams provide for the assessment and programming of special education students. In Ontario, Canada, on the other hand, Teams are not mandated by special education legislation and are free to adopt a wide variety of roles.

In schools facing a rapid transformation of communities, Teams have focused on consultation and coordination of education and early intervention programs (Cole, 1992; Cole & Brown, 1996b; Elliott & Sheridan, 1992; Rosenfield, 1987). The consultative problem-solving that Teams develop may be described as including several phases:

a) *Clarification of presenting problem* – a clear definition of the presenting problem is crucial for planning appropriate interventions. In order to avoid ambiguity, Team members must discuss and state the issues in concrete, explicit terms.

b) *Analysis of identified problem(s)* – presenting students' problems should be assessed by eliciting information from multiple sources, including background information, review of school records and observational data. During Team meeting(s), teachers and Team members can clarify the needs of individuals or groups of students. Questions asked during discussion often lead to a better understanding of needs in the context of the current learning environment.

c) *Brainstorming alternative solutions* – once the problem analysis has been completed, the Team should consider, together with invited members, as many solutions as possible. All alternatives should be discussed without making value judgements. By being open minded, all participants will feel that their ideas are listened to and respected.

d) *Developing plans for intervention* – during this phase, Team members choose among alternative strategies. Short and long term action plans for class, school and/or community based supports are selected by consensus.

e) *Assigning responsibilities and time lines* – once recommendations have been obtained by consensus, Team members have to assume responsibility for different aspects of the agreed upon solutions. In addition, time lines for program implementation have to be stated clearly. The questions Why? Who? What? When? Where? must be answered before the conclusion of the consultation meeting.

f) *Monitoring interventions and follow-up* – follow-up meeting dates have to be established in advance in order to evaluate the effectiveness of interventions. This phase provides the Team with opportunities to review programs and receive feedback about services. By evaluating the effectiveness of programs, the Team can make additional recommendations or adjustments on an as-needed basis.

Effective teams tend to have several common characteristics discussed in the literature. Those include clarity of goals and roles, leadership support, effective planning, composition of membership, and team performance (Adelman & Taylor, 1998; Cole, 1992; Cole & Brown, 1996b; Wagner, 2000).

(1) **Goals and Roles** – in effective consultation teams, goals and roles are clear to all team members and school staff. Professionals and invited members are ap-

praised about this type of consultation service model. Moreover, team members are committed to multidisciplinary services and develop a sense of ownership about collaborative consultation.

(2) **Leadership support** – democratic leadership results in an inclusive atmosphere and following of agreed-upon guidelines. Parents are invited to team meetings together with classroom teachers. Administrative support results in consulting relationships which evolve among staff and parents.

(3) **Regular and effective meetings** – scheduled meetings that allow for a broad range of services and agendas are set by team members. Frequent meetings address individual and group needs, and multiple recommendations are considered. Consultative discussions and focused and written summary forms are developed by team members.

(4) **Team Membership** – team membership is multidisciplinary and may vary according to the objectives of the consultation process. Teachers are viewed as key participants at all phases of the consultation. In addition, in multilingual community schools, translators are included in order to support family participation.

(5) **Team Performance** – group dynamics ensure democratic participation in the consultative process. As a result, members are more likely to review their own role in facilitating collaboration. Team members participate in professional development with a focus on skill development including: communication, intervention strategies, collaborative problem-solving, and cross-cultural consultation. Last, team members view one another as bringing different skills and knowledge to the team.

In 1990, a study on the goals, roles and functions of the Multidisciplinary Team surveyed 50% of elementary and secondary schools in a Metropolitan school board in Ontario (Cole, 1992; Cole et al.,1992). Teams had been formerly introduced to all elementary and secondary schools in 1986. Research findings documented that: a) most referred students were discussed on more than one occasion, b) three quarters of meeting time was devoted to discussing individual students, c) referred students were described as having academic problems, especially in language and study skills, d) secondary school students tended to have more social and emotional problems, and e) overall, members indicated that their Teams usually achieved their goals. Following this study, results were discussed by school board staff. This led to professional development activities aimed to expand team functions. The purpose of the 1995 study was to provide a follow-up on current Team goals and functions and referred student characteristics, and to provide new information on recommendations formulated during consultation. This chapter concludes with a discussion of the implications for on-going school-based services provided by school psychologists and other consultants.

Method

Subjects

In the 1995 study, 50% of the school board's elementary and secondary schools were randomly selected. Forty-four elementary schools (83% of the sample) and 11 secondary school (78%) responded. Each sampled school returned several sets of multidisciplinary questionnaires, including those of Multidisciplinary Team members and classroom teachers.

The 341 respondents included members from the following professional groups: 112 (33%) classroom teachers, 56 (16%) special education teachers, 51 (15%) principals/vice principals, 39 (11%) social workers, 29 (9%) school psychologists, 12 (4%) guidance counsellors, and 11% other professionals. Fifty-three of the 55 Team chairpersons replied to the survey. Nearly three quarters of the participants (74%) had at least five years of experience with Teams, including a quarter of the respondents who had 11 or more years of experience.

Instrument and Procedures

The questionnaire was a modified version of that used in the 1990 study. It was comprised of three main sections. The first asked Team members to evaluate the importance of school team goals (i.e., "to facilitate referrals to specialized services"). In the second section, respondents were asked how frequently students referred to Teams had characteristics related to academic performance, learning style/study skills, social skills, emotional problems, and psycho-social attributes (i.e., "is motivated to learn;" "is quiet, withdrawn"). The third section (which was an addition to the 1990 questionnaire) asked respondents to indicate the frequency with which class-based, school-based, family-based, and community-based recommendations were made during Team consultation (i.e., "referral to community services;" "individual counselling").

For each question, respondents were asked to rate each item on a five point Likert scale, with one corresponding to "seldom" or "not important," and five corresponding to "very often" or "very important."

Each principal of the selected schools was sent the questionnaires, which were distributed to team members (chairperson, school psychologist, social worker, guidance counsellor, special education teachers) and four randomly selected classroom teachers. Subjects were asked to return their anonymous questionnaires approximately three weeks after the date of mailing.

Data Analysis

The analysis duplicated the procedures used in examining results of the 1990 study. As in the first study results, overall responses were analyzed using three statistical procedures: simple frequencies, cross-tabulations, and chi-square analysis. The first procedure was employed for tabulating the overall responses while the last two procedures were used for comparing responses among different professional groups and between elementary and secondary school respondents. (Significant differences were defined here as at or below .05 probability). Questionnaire items were five scale points (e.g., from "seldom" to "very often") which for the analysis were collapsed into three scale points (e.g., "seldom," "sometimes," and "often"). The focus was on identifying general patterns or respondents' opinions and perceptions.

Results

Multidisciplinary Team Goals

Eight school team goals were listed in the questionnaire. These were consistent with the broad Team model established at the school board to reflect prevention and intervention services (Cole, 1992; Cole et al., 1992). All respondents were asked to rate the personal importance they attributed to each goal. Table 1 below indicates the percentages of respondents who rated each of the following goals as "very important" or "important." Present responses convey similar patterns and slightly higher percentages to those found in the 1990 study. The most important goal continued to address the needs of individual students and planning appropriate modifications and interventions for them (94% in 1995 compared to 89% in 1990). Other important goals were: providing multidisciplinary consultation to school personnel around the needs of individual students (85% in 1995 compared to 82% in 1990); facilitating referrals for specialized services, i.e., educational, psychological, and social work services (85% in 1995 compared to 77% in 1990); and co-ordinating specialized group work or other programs for "at risk" students (77% in 1995 compared to 73% in 1990).

In both the 1990 and 1995 studies, there was a high degree of consensus among professional groups regarding the role of the Team in addressing the needs of individual students. However, a closer examination of the more current data indicated some discrepancies as to the degree of importance given to other Team functions. Consistent with the 1990 study findings, over 70% of the principals rated all the stated goals as important, except for monitoring referrals for Special Education placement (57%) and monitoring integration from Special Education (49%). Also consistent with previous findings, classroom and special education teachers' most highly rated goals continued to be understanding of individual student needs (85% for classroom

Table 1 LST Goals by Professional Groups

LST Goals	1990 Study TOTAL	1995 Study TOTAL	Principal	Classroom Teacher	Sp. Ed Teacher	Guidance Counsellor	Psycho-ed Consultant	Social Worker	Dept Head
	n=331	n=341	n=51	n=112	n=56	n=12	n=29	n=39	n=16
					1995 Responses				
Understanding individual student needs and plan appropriate interventions	89%	94%	96%	85%	98%	100%	97%	100%	100%
Providing multidisciplinary consultation to school staff re: individual student needs	82%	85%	88%	71%	88%	92%	93%	100%	100%
Facilitating referrals for specialized services: (Educational, Psychological, Social Work)	77%	85%	71%	88%	96%	100%	62%	85%	100%
Co-ordinating specialized group work or other programs for students "at risk"	73%	77%	80%	72%	79%	92%	66%	82%	75%
Co-ordinating the work of team members	71%	74%	71%	65%	80%	75%	83%	72%	94%
Identifying common student needs and placing schoolwide preventative programs/procedures	66%	74%	80%	61%	71%	92%	83%	92%	75%
Monitoring referrals for Special Education placement	67%	71%	57%	80%	95%	67%	48%	56%	63%
To monitor integration from Special Education *	–	53%	49%	59%	61%	58%	35%	54%	50%

Note: Owing to the small sample size of guidance counsellors and department heads, one should be cautious about interpreting their group percentages.
* Added in the 1995 study.

teachers and 98% for special education teachers); facilitating referrals for specialized services (88% for classroom teachers and 96% for special education teachers); and monitoring referrals for Special Education placement (80% for classroom teachers and 95% for special education teachers).

Teachers placed a much higher priority on referrals for Special Education placement (80% of classroom teachers, and 95% of special education teachers), compared to all other sampled groups. However, a lower priority was placed on monitoring integration of students from Special Education into the classroom (59% and 61% respectively). Data concerning monitoring integration from Special Education are more consistent with other professional groups (between 35% and 54% of other groups consider monitoring integration from Special Education to be important). This may indicate that a higher priority for Team activity is placed on monitoring referrals for Special Education placement, as compared to consulting about the integration of special education students into regular classrooms.

The other two support groups, school psychologists and social workers, also bore many similarities in their perceptions of Team goals. In both groups, over 80% of their members rated planning schoolwide prevention programs as one of the important goals. The main differences between the groups were that social workers were more likely to agree that: referrals for specialized services were important (85% of social workers versus 62% of school psychologists); that coordinating specialized group work for students at risk was important (82% of social workers versus 66% of school psychologists); and that monitoring integration from Special Education was important (54% of social workers versus 35% of school psychologists).

Students Referred to Teams

The number of students referred and discussed each year continued to vary from team to team. For elementary students, the mean number of students discussed increased from 62 in 1990 to 78 in 1995, with a range of 8 to 300 students. For the secondary school Teams, the mean number of students discussed dropped from 79 to 48, with a range of 8 to 75 students; the secondary range in 1990, by comparison, was 30-200. (However, one should be cautious in interpreting differences in secondary school responses, due to the small sample size.) Total average referrals increased from 66 in 1990 to 72 in 1995.

According to chairpersons' information, on average, two thirds of meeting time was allotted for individual students' needs. Around a third of the time was devoted to issues concerning classrooms, groups of students, school and Team issues. The proportion of students discussed on more than one occasion dropped somewhat– from over half in 1990 to 46% in 1995 (an average of 45% for the elementary and 48% for the secondary).

Characteristics of Referred Students

Altogether, 52 student characteristic items were listed in the 1995 questionnaire, as compared to 50 in the 1990 questionnaire (Cole, 1992). Two additional characteristics were: "Acts violently," and "Refugee & Immigrant adjustment needs." The items related to a) academic performance; b) learning style and study skills; c) social skills; d) emotional problems; and e) psycho-social attributes. Respondents were asked to rate, on a scale of 1 to 5, how frequently students referred to Teams had the characteristics mentioned. About half of the items were positive statements, and the other half were problem oriented statements. The respondents tended to rate "seldom" for positive characteristics, but "often" for items that were problem related. Overall, both academic characteristics and social-emotional attributes are consistent with those documented in the earlier study.

1. **Academic Performance.** Respondents were asked to rate referred students on academic performance in eight areas: oral language, reading, spelling, written language, math, handwriting, general knowledge, and advanced/enriched programming. Consistent with ratings on school Team goals, respondents focused on referrals of students with deficit skills rather than those in need of enrichment. For example, 65% responded that discussions about enriched programming "seldom" occurred.

Overall, perceptions of the referred students' academic profiles were similar by elementary and secondary staff. However, significantly fewer secondary school respondents found their referred students functioning academically at or above grade level in: spelling (59% of secondary staff, 76% of elementary staff); written language (59% of secondary staff, 77% of elementary staff). More secondary respondents found their referred students functioning academically at or above grade level in math (55% of secondary staff, 40% of elementary staff).

2. **Active Learning and Study Skills.** Eight active learning and study skills statements were rated by participants. Results indicate that active learning attributes such as work completion, class participation, and enjoyment of academic challenges were seldom discussed (over 50% of participants indicated this). These findings are consistent with the academic performance characteristics which continue to document that School Teams tend to focus their consultation on students who exhibit academic weaknesses, as compared with students who are in need of enrichment and expanded opportunities due to their academic strengths.

3. **Specific Learning Characteristics.** Students brought for discussion to the Team were described as less likely to have academic strengths. They were often viewed as more passive learners, who required assistance when new work was presented in class (70%). They were said to "often" forget new routines and instructions (72%). Elementary and secondary students exhibited similar learning weaknesses, and were viewed as dependent learners who worked best when watched or compelled (63%).

4. Social Skills. Most respondents did not describe their referred students as especially strong or weak in the social skills area. There was a tendency to identify positive social attributes less often and negative attributes more often, as in the 1990 study. The students brought to the Team for consultation continued to be characterized as appreciating their teachers' attention. This is the only positive item in the entire list of characteristics which was frequently attributed to referred students, who tend to be passive learners. Withdrawn and quiet students were more often noted at the secondary school level. 87% of respondents in the secondary panel, as opposed to 75% in the elementary panel, described students as "often" or "sometimes" quiet and withdrawn. As well, 46% of secondary respondents and 59% of elementary respondents described students as "often" or "sometimes" exhibiting violent behaviors.

5. Emotional Problems. In describing students' emotional problems, significantly higher proportions of secondary school respondents characterized students as exhibiting depressive symptoms (59% versus 30% of elementary respondents), anxiety-related problems (58% versus 36% of elementary respondents), and phobias (18% versus 7% of elementary responses). A higher proportion of secondary school respondents than elementary school respondents also characterized students as having nervous habits (35% versus 24% of elementary respondents), although that difference was not statistically significant.

6. Psychosocial Stressors. For psychosocial stressors, the patterns observed in 1990 were nearly identical in 1995. Students tended to have problems related to family stressors and school non-attendance, yet seldom had problems related to substance abuse, child abuse, or medical needs. A significantly higher proportion of secondary school respondents characterized their students as having all psychological stressors. As can be expected, a higher proportion of school psychologists (82%) and social workers (79%) identified family stressors than did special education teachers (58%), principals/vice-principals (54%) and classroom teachers (52%).

7. ESL and Refugee Needs. Respondents were asked to rate English as a Second Language (ESL) needs and refugee needs as two characteristics. About a third of Team members saw ESL needs as an attribute that was often related to student referral, while about a quarter of Team members saw refugee needs as an attribute related to referral. One cannot tell from survey responses the extent to which ESL and refugee students may have student characteristics discussed earlier. However, other research has indicated that refugees and immigrants share common difficulties in coping with a new language and culture. Refugees, in particular, "carry with them extraordinary social and emotional needs that make their overall adjustment complicated." Refugees made up 7% of the school board's elementary students and 13% of secondary students (Yau, 1995, pp. iv-v). ESL students make up 23% of the Board's elementary students and 26% of secondary students (Toronto Board of Education, 1995b).

School Team Recommendations

Twenty-eight School Team recommendations concerning consultation outcomes were listed. For analysis purposes, these were organized in clusters of a) class-based; b) school-based; c) family-based; and d) community-based recommendations. Chi-square tests of significance were conducted on each recommendation to see if there were differences between elementary school Team respondents and secondary school Team respondents.

1. Class-Based Recommendations

Results documented in Table 2 indicate that the in-class recommendations most frequently discussed (over 50%) were specific teaching strategies, expanded opportunities (remedial and enrichment) and specific consequences for misbehavior. Findings suggest that curriculum consultants were least frequently recommended for class recommendation supports (only 11% of respondents often recommended involving curriculum consultants). Overall, result patterns indicate that elementary Teams as compared to secondary Teams tended to make in-class recommendations more often. Using chi-square tests of differences, elementary teams were significantly more likely to recommend teaching strategies (66% of elementary Team respondents, 47% of secondary), group activities (40% of elementary respondents, 24% of secondary), projects (21% of elementary respondents, 11% of secondary), class profiles (43% of elementary respondents, 25% of secondary), classroom observations (44% of elementary respondents, 23% of secondary), and involvement of curriculum consultants (13% of elementary respondents, 3% of secondary). However, secondary Teams were more likely to make recommendations about classroom environment than were elementary Teams (38% of secondary respondents, 34% of elementary respondents). See Table 2 for more details.

2. School-Based Recommendations

School recommendations listed in Table 3 tended to include most frequently (over 50%): referral for psychological and social work involvement, family interviews, and referral to local IPRC[1]. The least frequently recommended in-school activities included referral for psychiatric assessment (11%), referral for first language assessment (14%), mentoring programs (16%), and ESL consultation (19%).

---

1   Area IPRC is Identification, Placement, and Review Committee for full time Special Education placement. Local IPRC is Identification, Placement, and Review Committee for part-time Special Education support.

Table 2 Class-Based Recommendations

	Overall (n=341)			Elementary (n=270)			Secondary (n=71)		
	Often	Sometimes	Not or Infrequent	Often	Sometimes	Not or Infrequent	Often	Sometimes	Not or infrequent
Class-Based recommendations									
Teaching strategies	62%	21%	14%	66%	18%	14%	47%	31%	16%*
Group activities	37%	29%	30%	40%	27%	30%	24%	38%	28%*
Expanded opportunities	60%	22%	15%	62%	21%	14%	49%	24%	18%
Projects	19%	22%	53%	21%	24%	50%	11%	13%	65%*
Specific consequences for misbehavior	50%	23%	24%	49%	24%	26%	55%	21%	18%
Consultation about classroom environment	35%	27%	36%	34%	24%	41%	38%	39%	14%*
Consultation about resource materials	31%	32%	34%	33%	31%	34%	23%	35%	34%
Class profiles	39%	24%	32%	43%	25%	28%	25%	20%	47%*
Classroom observation(s)	40%	31%	26%	44%	30%	25%	23%	37%	32%*
Involvement of curriculum consultants	11%	25%	61%	13%	29%	57%	3%	11%	78%*

* Statistically significant difference between elementary and secondary responses at $p < .05$

Table 3 School-Based Recommendations

School-Based recommendations	Overall (n=341)			Elementary (n=270)			Secondary (n=71)		
	Often	Sometimes	Not or Infrequent	Often	Sometimes	Not or Infrequent	Often	Sometimes	Not or Infrequent
Involvement of Translators/Interpreters	30%	22%	46%	30%	20%	47%	27%	30%	41%
Monitor effectiveness of program modifications/interventions	49%	31%	17%	51%	30%	17%	42%	34%	16%
Psychological involvement	60%	25%	13%	56%	28%	15%	76%	16%	4%
Social Work involvement	60%	26%	13%	57%	28%	13%	70%	17%	10%
ESL consultation for programming	19%	25%	51%	14%	26%	56%	37%	23%	32%
Referral for assessment – psychological	56%	31%	11%	53%	33%	13%	65%	21%	7%
Referral for assessment – social work	55%	28%	15%	51%	30%	18%	70%	21%	3%
Referral for assessment – psychiatric	11%	15%	70%	10%	14%	73%	16%	17%	61%
Referral for assessment – language	28%	29%	39%	29%	30%	40%	28%	25%	35%
Referral for assessment – first language	14%	20%	60%	12%	22%	61%	20%	13%	55%

	Overall (n=341)			Elementary (n=270)			Secondary (n=71)		
	Often	Sometimes	Not or Infrequent	Often	Sometimes	Not or Infrequent	Often	Sometimes	Not or infrequent
Referral for assessment – reading	41%	31%	24%	43%	32%	23%	34%	28%	25%
Interviews with family	70%	18%	10%	69%	19%	10%	72%	13%	9%
Referral to Area IPRC	34%	39%	21%	37%	42%	17%	25%	30%	38%*
Referral to Local IPRC	54%	30%	11%	56%	31%	9%	45%	27%	21%*
Review diagnostic placement in Special Education	36%	30%	28%	36%	32%	28%	38%	24%	31%
Review integration from Special Education	30%	25%	39%	28%	26%	40%	37%	21%	34%
Mentoring program(s)/transition issues	16%	18%	60%	10%	16%	69%	39%	24%	25%*
Review of Team processes and activities	21%	28%	44%	16%	25%	52%	41%	37%	16%*

* Statistically significant difference between elementary and secondary responses at p < .05

Table 4 Family-Based Recommendations

	Overall (n=341)			Elementary (n=270)			Secondary (n=71)		
	Often	Sometimes	Not or Infrequent	Often	Sometimes	Not or Infrequent	Often	Sometimes	Not or infrequent
Family recommendations									
Consultation with parents	80%	14%	4%	79%	16%	4%	80%	9%	4%
Family counselling	37%	32%	29%	34%	32%	33%	49%	32%	14%*
Individual counselling	48%	28%	23%	38%	33%	28%	85%	9%	4%*

* Statistically significant difference between elementary and secondary responses at p < .05

As seen in Table 3, findings show statistically significant differences between secondary school and elementary school Team respondents in recommendations around psychological involvement (76% of secondary Team respondents, 56% of elementary), ESL programming (37% of secondary respondents, 14% of elementary respondents), social work assessment (70% of secondary respondents, 51% of elementary), referrals to area IPRC's (25% of secondary respondents, 37% of elementary), local IPRC's (45% of secondary respondents, 56% of elementary), mentoring programs (39% of secondary respondents, 10% of secondary) and reviewing of Team processes and activities (41% of secondary respondents, 16% of elementary respondents).

3. Family-Based Recommendations

Consultation with parents was viewed by both elementary and secondary team members as a highly important recommendation (80% of secondary and 79% of elementary). As documented in Table 4, this recommendation received the highest rating by all participants, reinforcing the need to strengthen school-home ties.

Recommendations for family counselling and individual counselling were significantly higher at the secondary panel. Specifically, 85% of secondary Team members indicated that the Team recommended individual counselling for referred students; 38% of elementary Team members indicated this. Nearly half (49%) of secondary Team members recommended family counselling, compared to a third (34%) of elementary Team members.

4. Community-Based Recommendations

Recommendations most frequently made (over 20% recommended "often" or "very often") concerned referral to community agencies for counselling (33%) and consultation with external agencies (23%). The least frequent recommendation was related to Tragic Event Support (this may reflect both identified needs and the fact that the school board has developed Tragic Event Support Teams, which provide follow-up services on an as-needed basis).

Again, there were statistically significant differences between elementary and secondary panels (see Table 5), in that at the secondary level, there were more referrals to community services for medical issues (27% of secondary Team members, 16% of elementary Team members) counselling issues (54% of secondary Team members, 28% of elementary Team members), welfare issues (38% of secondary Team members, 5% of elementary Team members), and legal issues (18% of secondary Team members, 4% of elementary Team members), as well as reporting abuse (16% of secondary Team members, 5% of elementary Team members) and Tragic Events Support (16% of secondary Team members, 2% of elementary Team members). These

Table 5 Community-Based Recommendations

Community-Based recommendations	Overall (n=341)		Elementary (n=270)			Secondary (n=71)		
	Often	Sometimes	Not or Infrequent	Often	Sometimes	Not or Infrequent	Often	Sometimes	Not or infrequent
Referral to community services – medical issues	18%	25%	54%	16%	24%	59%	27%	27%	35%*
Referral to community services – counselling issues	33%	28%	36%	28%	29%	41%	54%	23%	16%*
Referral to community services – welfare issues	12%	12%	72%	5%	12%	80%	38%	16%	38%*
Referral to community services – legal issues	7%	7%	81%	4%	5%	88%	18%	16%	56%*
Request for written information from external agencies	18%	24%	54%	18%	25%	55%	18%	23%	51%
Consultation with external agencies	23%	33%	41%	22%	32%	44%	27%	39%	28%
Reporting abuse	7%	13%	75%	5%	9%	82%	16%	27%	49%*
Tragic Events support	5%	11%	80%	2%	7%	87%	16%	24%	52%*

* Statistically significant difference between elementary and secondary responses at $p < .05$

recommendations are consistent with the patterns of identified higher socio-emotional needs amongst secondary students.

Conclusions and Recommendations

The 1995 study results documented that Team members tend to have a greater breadth of experience with team consultation (with most of the members having seven or more years of experience). Consequently, the patterns of findings are more likely to reflect reinforced Team processes and practices. In comparing the 1990 and 1995 results, one is struck more by the similarities than the differences. Many of the findings indicate that over the past five years, Teams continued to focus on the same needs and the same model of service. This may be due, in part, to the fact that the first study documented that most members were satisfied with their Teams as addressing the needs of referred students (Cole, 1992; Cole & Brown, 1996b; Cole et al., 1992).

Results continued to show a high degree of consensus regarding the role of Teams in understanding and planning interventions for individual students at school and at home, and of providing consultation to educators. There was less consensus regarding multi-dimensional prevention services. For example, in both the 1990 and 1995 studies, two thirds or more of meeting time was allotted for discussion of individual students; one third of the time was devoted to discussion of broader issues concerning groups of students or the school as a whole. However, when the school board formalized Multidisciplinary Teams in the mid 80's, it reflected a mission which advocated the importance of broad based prevention programs. As school board cultures evolve, teams may be wise to re-evaluate their mandate and goals for school teams.

Overall, the characteristics of students referred to School Teams continued to emphasize academic and social-emotional needs. Schools have become intervention sites for numerous learning and social problems affecting students. Those who are at risk for educational failure and social maladjustment continue to pose challenges to teachers and highlight the need for coordinated multidisciplinary consultation services (Reeder et al., 1997; Shaw & Swerdlik, 1995).

A growing and consistent body of research has shown that children who exhibit early signs of academic and social difficulties are at risk for problems later on in life if effective intervention is not provided (American Psychological Association, 1993; Brown, 1995; Hargreaves & Earl, 1990; Offord & Boyle, 1993; Offord, Boyle, & Racine, 1990; Reeder et al., 1997). For example, Rush and Vitale (1994) have described how "at risk" secondary school student characteristics can be identified at the elementary school level (the most important of these characteristics relate to academic achievement and social emotional difficulties). Without support, however, the older the students get, the more crystallized their problems become in both academic and social emotional areas. As well, students at risk for conduct problems often exhibit low tolerance for frustration in early childhood, tend to have attention deficit problems, and poor problem-solving skills (Cole, 1995). In the 1990 and 1995 studies, although elementary and secondary students exhibited similar learning weaknesses, secondary students were more likely to be viewed as having emotional problems and psychological stressors. These findings may be seen as supportive of the literature emphasizing the importance of cost-effective early identification and prevention programs (Cole, 1996; Cole & Siegel, 1990; Thomas & Grimes, 1995).

Early violence-prevention efforts, such as conflict resolution, are practiced in many schools. Those encompass a range of efforts through the curriculum and school-based activities (see for example, Gibbs, 1995; Girard & Koch, 1996). When discussing individual students whose maladjusted behavior interferes with their learning, Teams are advised to form recommendations in the context of broad school-based initiatives, rather then focus on individual modifications only. Multimodal intervention approaches tend to be more effective with groups of students who exhibit similar needs. These types of programs can be facilitated through Team consultation. It is only a minority of individuals who usually require intensive treatment and the coordinated efforts of school and community-based treatment settings. Nevertheless, of concern is the high overall percentage of respondents (56%) who described referred students as "often" or "sometimes" exhibiting violent behaviors.

Clearly, given the complex problems related to acting out behaviors and victimization, an ecological approach to programming is called for. There is encouraging evidence that multi-disciplinary programs employed on a school-wide basis can be effective in reducing levels of anti-social behavior and improving the school climate. Specifically, longitudinal studies based on Olweus' (1991) model have documented a significant reduction of bullying incidents when a comprehensive plan was developed and employed on the level of community, school, classroom, and individual students (Ziegler & Pepler, 1993).

A continuum of individual and group interventions is also needed in addressing the high proportion of referred students who were described by respondents as "often" or "sometimes" exhibiting depressive symptoms (71%). The causes for such characteristics are multiple and interrelated as quiet students rarely call attention to themselves. Withdrawn behaviors may be symptomatic of academic struggles, social rejection or complex family problems (Cole, 1995; Eber & Nelson, 1997). Again, comprehensive assessment of individual and small groups may provide avenues for short-term school based counselling and consultation by school psychologists and social workers.

Consultation with parents was viewed by both elementary and secondary respondents as a highly important recommendation (this recommendation in fact received the highest rating by respondents). This is consistent with educational policies and goals concerning parental involvement in the school. The importance of parental consultation as recommended by Team members may be tied to student achievement and motivation, as documented by Ziegler (1987) and others (Christenson, 1995;

Christenson, Hurley, Sheridan, & Fenstermacher, 1997; Comer & Haynes, 1992; Graham-Clay, 1999; Swap, 1993).

Immigrant and refugee students are often brought for Team consultation, reflecting the transformation of the North American student population, especially in large urban centres. These students comprise heterogeneous groups whose language development and learning profile are linked to psychological, socio-cultural, and educational factors. In any school, there is great variability as to how much help they may need in the process of adaptation (Cole, 1998). The Canadian 1995 study by Yau documented that refugees who attended the school board suffer from many post-migration obstacles including post-traumatic stress symptoms and an on-going sense of fear; frequent relocations; and disadvantages in academic performances.

Yau suggested that the Multidisciplinary Teams could play an important role in addressing these issues, through utilizing the Team to "address and monitor the needs of individual and groups of refugee students on a regular basis in order to ensure immediate intervention and long-term prevention programs, rather than waiting for teacher-initiated referrals." (Yau, 1995, p. 99).

It appears from the 1995 findings that the number of individual students referred to Multidisciplinary Teams has somewhat increased. Referred students continue to exhibit academic performance deficits, especially in language and study skills. It is thus important to explore learning outcomes detailed in curriculum documents, and link those to specific recommendations discussed at the Team (see, for example, Carnine, 1994). It is evident from the number of students who are recommended for special education programs, that School Teams continue to facilitate referrals to Identification, Placement and Review Committees for Special Education services. Recommendation #38 of the Ontario Royal Commission on Learning (1994), highlights the needs for program modifications and for accountability before decisions to alter students' programs are made: "School Boards look for ways to provide assistance to those who need it, without tying that assistance to a formal identification process." At the same time, following early consultation, interventions and parental consent, Special Education may best serve the needs of some students. School Teams will be required to document which early recommendations were implemented successfully before considering out-of-class program changes.

Overall, analysis of recommendations documented that secondary Teams were more likely to focus on school recommendations; elementary Teams were more likely to focus on class recommendations. This shows a connection between structural variables within schools and student recommendations that might be further examined. Class profiles, for example, are a valuable consultation service for many elementary and some secondary schools. Although research findings indicate that class profiles are recommended by School Teams (according to 43% of elementary, and 25% of secondary respondents), it is not clear from these findings how many schools actually use their team for this type of consultation.

Given the student characteristics that have been documented consistently, it is important to re-evaluate the functions of Multidisciplinary Teams as they relate to educational goals and programs. During an era of diminishing resources, Multidisciplinary Teams need to refine their operations and monitoring of recommendations for both individuals and groups of students.

One of the implications derived from this research study, concerns the provision of comprehensive psychological services including direct and indirect interventions. Given the high number of students who are newcomers to cities in the United States and in Canada, and students who are referred for special education support, it is incumbent upon psychologists to provide comprehensive services linked to school processes and learning outcomes. A consultative framework can provide an umbrella for understanding common patterns for identified needs at the classroom, school, and systems levels. As a result, by shifting the focus from being primarily directed to individual student needs, school teams have an opportunity to provide a range of services in a coordinated way (Cole & Brown, 1996b).

Consultation services are likely to expand when schools provide feedback about the value of indirect service delivery models which are advocated by psychologists. Moreover, by validating consultation services psychologists may expand their services to include school-wide initiatives such as professional development for teachers and parenting programs (Carnine, 1994; Haynes & Comer, 1996; Wagner, 2000).

Graham-Clay (1999) highlighted a central role school psychologists can play in the consultation process by stressing that:

"School psychologists understand both schools and families. By virtue of their expertise and role, they are in a strategic position to promote, facilitate and support the development of strong partnerships which will ultimately benefit schools, parents and children." (p. 43)

Professional development for psychologists as consultants is also likely to enhance their contributions to the development of ecological service models. For school teams, in-service is a vehicle for changing the culture of decision-making and effectiveness of multidisciplinary collaboration.

References

Adelman, H. S., & Taylor, L. (1998). Involving teachers in collaborative efforts to better address the barriers to student learning. *Preventing School Failure, 42(2)*, 55-60.

American Psychological Association. (1993). Commission on Violence and Youth, *Report, 1*.

Brown, R. S. (1995). *Mentoring of at risk students: Challenges and potential*. Research Services, Toronto Board of Education.

Carnine, D. (1994). Introduction to the mini-series. Diverse learners and prevailing, emerging, and research-based educational approaches and their tools. *School Psychology Review, 23(3)*, 341-350.

Christenson, S. L. (1995). Best practices in supporting home-school collaboration. In A. Thomas & J. Grimes (Eds.), *Best practices in school psychology-III* (pp. 253-267). Washington, DC: National Association of School Psychologists.

Christenson, S. L., Hurley, C. M., Sheridan, S. M., & Fenstermacher, K. (1997). Parents' and school psychologists' perspectives on parent involvement activities. *School Psychology Review, 26(1),* 111-130.

Cole, E. (1992). Characteristics of students referred to school teams: Implication for preventive psychological services. *Canadian Journal of School Psychology, 8(1),* 23-36.

Cole, E. (1995). Responding to school violence: Understanding today for tomorrow. *Canadian Journal of School Psychology, 11(2),* 10-20.

Cole, E. (1996). An integrative perspective on school psychology. *Canadian Journal of School Psychology, 12(2),* 115-121.

Cole, E. (1998). Immigrant and refugee children: Challenges and opportunities for education and mental health services. *Canadian Journal of School Psychology, 14(1),* 36-50.

Cole, E., & Brown, R. (1996a). Multidisciplinary school teams: Challenges and opportunities. In M. Luther, E. Cole, & P. Gamlin, (Eds.), *Dynamic assessment for instruction: From theory to application* (pp. 43-55). Toronto: Captus University Press.

Cole, E., & Brown, R. (1996b). Multidisciplinary school teams: A five-year follow-up study. *Canadian Journal of School Psychology, 12(2),* 155-168.

Cole, E., & Siegel, J. (Eds.). (1990). *Effective consultation in school psychology.* Toronto: Hogrefe and Huber.

Cole, E., Siegel, J., & Yau, M. (1992). Multidisciplinary school teams: Perceptions of goals, roles and functions. *Canadian Journal of School Psychology, 8(1),* 37-51.

Comer, J. P., & Haynes, N. M. (1992). Parent involvement in school: An ecological approach. *The Elementary School Journal, 91(3),* 271-278.

Davidson, I. F., & Wiener, J. (1991). Creating educational change: The in-school team. *Exceptionally Education Canada, 1(2),* 25-44.

Eber, L., & Nelson, C. M. (1997). School-based wraparound planning: Integrating services for students with emotional and behavioral needs. *American Journal of Orthopsychiatry, 67(3),* 385-395.

Elliott, S. N., & Sheridan, S. M. (1992). Consultation and teaming: Problem solving among educators, parents and support personnel. *The Elementary School Journal, 92(3),* 315-338.

Gibbs, J. (1995). *Tribes, a new way of learning and being together.* Sausalito, CA: Center Source Systems.

Girard, K., & Koch, S. J. (1996). *Conflict resolution in the schools: A manual for educators.* California: Jossey-Bass Inc.

Graham-Clay, S. (1999). Enhancing home-school partnerships: How school psychologists can help. *Canadian Journal of School Psychology, 14(2),* 31-44.

Hargreaves, A., & Earl, L. (1990). *Rights of passage.* Toronto: Ministry of Education/OISE.

Haynes, N. M., & Comer, J. P. (1996). Integrating schools, families, and communities through successful school reform: The school development program. *School Psychology Review, 25(4),* 501-506.

Huebner, E. S., & Gould, K. (1991). Multidisciplinary teams revisited: Current perceptions of school psychologists regarding team functioning. *School Psychology Review, 20(3),* 428-434.

Kaiser, S. M., & Woodman, R. W. (1985). Multidisciplinary teams and group decision-making techniques: Possible solutions to decision-making problems. *School Psychology Review, 14(4),* 457-470.

Offord, D., & Boyle, M. (1993). Helping children adjust: A tri-ministry project. *ORBIT, 24(1),* 25.

Offord, D., Boyle, M., & Racine, Y. (1990). *Ontario child health study: Children at risk.* Toronto: Queen's Printer of Ontario.

Olweus, D. (1991). Bully/victim problems among school children: Basic facts and effects of school-based intervention program. In D. Pepler & K. Rubin (Eds.), *The development and treatment of childhood aggression.* Hillsdale, NJ: Erlbaum.

Ontario Royal Commission on Learning. (1994). *For the love of learning.* Toronto: Queen's Printer.

Reeder, G. D., Maccow, G. C., Shaw, S. R., Swerdlik, M. E., Horton, C. B., & Foster, P. (1997). School psychologists and full-service schools: Partnerships with medical, mental health, and social services. *School Psychology Review, 26(4),* 603-621.

Rosenfield, S. A. (1987). *Instructional consultation.* Hillsdale, NJ; Erlbaum.

Rush, S., & Vitale, P. A. (1994). Analysis for determining factors that place elementary students at risk. *Journal of Educational Research, 87(6),* 325-333.

Shaw, S. R., & Swerdlik, M. E. (1995). Best practices in facilitating team functioning. In A. Thomas & J. Grimes (Eds.), *Best practices in school psychology* – III (pp. 153-160). Washington, DC: National Association of School Psychologists.

Swap, S. M. (1993). *Developing home-school partnerships: From concepts to practice.* New York: Teachers College Press.

Thomas, A., & Grimes, J. (Eds.) (1995). *Best practices in school psychology* – III. Washington, DC: National Association of School Psychologists.

Wagner, P. (2000). Consultation: Developing a comprehensive approach to service delivery. *Educational Psychology in Practice, 16(1),* 9-18.

Yau, M. (1995). *Refugee students in Toronto schools: An exploratory study.* Research Services, Toronto Board of Education.

Ziegler, S. (1987). *The effect of parent involvement on children's achievement.* Research Services, Toronto Board of Education.

Ziegler, S., & Pepler, D. (1993). Bullying at school: Pervasive and persistent. *ORBIT, 24(1),* 29-31.

Chapter 3
Canadian Consultation in an International Context: A Review of the Literature

Ingrid E. Sladeczek, Nancy Lee Heath, Aron Blidner, and Lisa Marie Lanaro

School psychologists, school counsellors, special education teachers, and other special needs service providers working in the schools are faced with increasing demands for diagnostic, assessment, and intervention services while simultaneously undergoing budgetary cutbacks (Bartell, 1996; Carney, 1996; Cole, 1996; McKay, 1995). Increasing budgetary constraints have resulted in the recognition of the need to move towards a more cost-effective model of service delivery in the field of school psychology (e.g., Cole, 1996; Janzen, Paterson, & Paterson, 1993; Kratochwill, Elliott, & Callan-Stoiber, 2002). Specifically, in the United States there has been an increasing focus on indirect service delivery as being more cost-effective, time-efficient, preventative, and available to more children and teachers than the direct service model (e.g., Parsons & Meyers, 1984; Zins, Kratochwill, & Elliott, 1993). Traditionally, direct delivery systems have been the venue for providing services for children with special needs. Direct delivery systems are distinguished from indirect delivery systems in that the former provides services on a one-to-one basis. A school psychologist who provides individual therapy for a child with conduct problems is one example of a direct service, other components within a direct delivery system include: (a) special classes; (b) resource rooms; (c) crisis intervention; (d) itinerant teachers; (e) academic tutoring; (f) homebound instruction; and (g) psychiatric consultation (Dworet & Rathgeber, 1996). In contrast, indirect services include in-service training, consultation with parents, teachers, or other educators, in-school teams, parent training, and curriculum advisement (e.g., Elliott & Witt, 1986; Wiener & Davidson, 1990).

Indirect service delivery systems for students with behavioral difficulties, including consultation and parent training, will be the foci of the current chapter, with the primary purpose being to describe the development and current status of consultation in the United States, in other countries, and in Canada. In this vein, we strive to convey the unique aspects of consultation in Canada within an international context, but also to highlight the similarities, and to conclude with a vision for the future practice of consultation in an international arena.

In the last 40 years, consultation, as an indirect method of service delivery, has received widespread attention in the United States. There is a large body of empirical evidence from the United States that documents and attests to the effectiveness of consultation in helping children with special needs (see for example, Alpert & Yammer, 1983; Bergan, 1993; Bergan & Kratochwill, 1990; Bergan, Sladeczek, & Schwarz, 1991; Gibson & Chard, 1994; Gutkin & Curtis, 1990; Mannino & Shore, 1975; Medway, 1979, 1982; Medway & Updyke, 1985; Reddy, Barboza-Whitehead, Files, & Rubel, 2000; Sladeczek, 1996). Since 1967, over 100 books have been written on consultation by individuals affiliated with school, counselling, community psychology, and special education (Zins et al., 1993) and three major journals exist which specifically focus on articles relevant to human service consultation (i.e., *Consultation: An International Journal*, *Journal of Educational and Psychological Consultation*, and *Consulting Psychology Journal*). With the launching in 1990 of the *Journal of Educational and Psychological Consultation*, consultation solidified its status as a field with its own theoretical base, research, and practice.

The behavioral consultation model has been one of the major models of consultation used in the United States. Briefly, behavioral consultation involves the collaboration between a consultant and at least one consultee (usually a parent and/or teacher) that together work towards bringing about behavior change with a client (usually a child). Typically, four stages are involved in the consultation process: Problem Identification, Problem Analysis, Treatment Implementation, and Treatment Evaluation. During the *Problem Identification Interview* the consultant and consultee(s) identify the initial problem and agree upon a data collection strategy to collect baseline information (e.g., number of aggressive acts per day). During the *Problem Analysis Interview* baseline data is reviewed, antecedents, consequences, and sequential conditions linked with the problem behaviors are identified and analyzed. A treatment plan based on effective behavioral management strategies is developed and plans for implementation are confirmed. Finally, after treatment implementation has occurred, the *Treatment Evaluation Interview* is held, where the data is reviewed, and the consultant, teacher, and parent discuss the effectiveness of treatment, and if treatment should be continued or terminated. In between the *Problem Analysis Interview* and the *Treatment Evaluation Interview* the consultant and consultee maintain contact and determine how the client is responding to treatment, and if revisions need to be made to the treatment plan. The most impressive feature of this type of consultation is that the relationship between the consultant and consultee is viewed as collaborative, and secondly, that the approach to problem identification and the monitoring of treatment is data driven. In summary, over the last 40 years a clearly delineated form of consultation, namely behavioral consultation, has emerged in the United States and within the last 25 years this approach has been recognized as the most prominent form of consultation throughout the United States.

In contrast to the substantive nature of the consultation field in the United States, the status of consultation in the international arena remains ill defined. An exhaustive search of the literature with the focus on accessing international journals and other resources (e.g., direct contact with international colleagues) yielded surprisingly few investigations that would be considered within the purview of "consultation." Nevertheless, some evidence of consultative research was found in Sri Lanka and Australia. Nastasi and colleagues (Nastasi, Varjas, Bernstein, & Jayasena, 2000; Nastasi, Varjas, Sakar, & Jayasena, 1998) are American researchers who imported consultation to Sri Lanka, since school-based intervention services are non-existent. They implemented a participatory approach to consultation, which builds upon a contemporary model of best practices in consultation and is designed to address the students' behavioral, social and emotional functioning with a culturally specific approach. They refer to this model as *Participatory Culture-Specific Consultation* (PCSC) which consists of a participatory interpersonal process and ethnographic and action research methods to guide the development of culture-specific interventions. Their conceptual framework includes: (a) the cultural definition of mental health or personal/social competence and adjustment; (b) identification of the main mechanisms that explain social development and personal/social competence; (c) the personal and familial stressors existing within the Sri Lankan society; and (d) the personal and social resources available to youth to cope with stressors. The authors indicate that although PCSC has been shown to be successful in Sri Lanka, the model needs to be tested in the United States as well.

In Australia, Sanders (2001) and his colleagues have developed the *Triple P – Positive Parenting Program* which can be conceptualized as a home-based consultation model designed to reduce the incidence of child abuse, mental illness, behavioral problems, delinquency, and homelessness. These aims are achieved by enhancing parents' knowledge, skills, and confidence in dealing with their preadolescent children; by providing a protective, nurturing, and non-violent environment; and by providing the resources necessary for parents to be more self-sufficient in meeting the needs of their children. As such, behavioral interventions form the cornerstone of the Triple P multi-level family intervention program, and the focus of consultation is on the prevention and remediation of disruptive and problematic behaviors (e.g., Connell, Sanders, & Markie-Dadds, 1997; Sanders, 1999; Sanders & Markie-Dadds, 1996; Sanders, Markie-Dadds, Tully, & Bor, 2000; Sanders & McFarland, 2000; Sanders, Montgomery, & Brechman-Toussaint, 2000). Empirical evidence from Australia and Germany (Hahlweg et al., 2001) attest to the efficacy and benefit to parents of this program.

In contrast to the difficulty in accessing international literature using key words such as "consultation," we found a substantial literature base on consultation in Canada. Although there are numerous sources regarding consultation in Canada, the Canadian literature is characterized by a less formalized conceptualization of consultation than in the United States. Indeed, it appeared that consultation in Canada varied extensively across time as well as disciplines. Certain time periods demonstrated an unusual dearth of literature on consultation whereas other periods were marked by a notable increase of literature in the field. Similarly, in contrast to the American consultation field which centred around school psychology, the Canadian consultation literature emerged in school counselling, special education, as well as school psychology. In light of this unexpected diversity, the authors undertook to conduct a systematic evaluation of the field of consultation in Canada.

An extensive literature search was conducted on consultation in Canada. The search included the following journals: *Canadian Journal of School Psychology, Canadian Psychology, Canadian Psychological Review, Canadian Psychologist, Canadian Journal of Counselling, Canadian Counsellor, Canadian Journal for Exceptional Children, Canadian Journal of Education, Canadian Journal of Behavioral Science, Canadian Education and Research Digest, The Alberta Journal of Educational Research*, and *School Guidance Worker*. The search spanned the period from 1960 to 1999. Only in the 1960s did the term "consultation" emerge (Caplan, 1963), therefore serving as a logical starting point for a review of the field. Furthermore, the chronological organization of the articles was based on the observation that change in the consultation literature appeared non-linear, and a chronological framework would facilitate a clearer depiction of the nature of that change. The number of articles on consultation in the 1960's, 1970's, 1980's, and 1990's were 1, 10, 2, and 11, respectively.

Consultation in Canada from 1960 to 1999

The 1960's

During the 1960's, "mental health consultation" as initially proposed by Caplan (1963) was discussed as an alternative method for delivering services in Canada's schools (e.g., Halpern, 1964). Mental health consultation, as described by Caplan, involved the interaction between a consultant (a specialist or recognized "expert") and a consultee (a professional) who was seeking assistance with a client. An essential aspect of Caplan's description of the consultative process, is that the consultee can accept or reject the advice given by the consultant and furthermore, that the consultee accepts the professional responsibility for the client. Interesting, as well, is the notion that the consultant not only engages in this process in order to assist the consultee, but also to gain a better understanding of diagnostic, assessment, and treatment issues that are relevant to the consultee, and to thus be able to offer assistance when similar problems are encountered in the future. Notable here is that the consultant-consultee relationship is seen as a mutually beneficial relationship although clearly hierarchical.

Caplan differentiated between four central types of mental health consultation:
(a) Client-Centered Case Consultation,
(b) Program-Centered Administrative Consultation,

(c) Consultee-Centered Case Consultation, and, finally,

(d) Consultee-Centered Administrative Consultation.

In *Client-Centered Case Consultation,* the primary goal is to help the consultee to bring about desired changes with the client of concern, a specific individual. In contrast, in *Program-Centered Administrative Consultation* the emphasis is at the group level with the consultant working with a group of consultees, to assist with the administration of prevention, treatment, or rehabilitation of individuals who evidence mental problems. *Consultee-Centered Case Consultation,* while similar to Client-Centered Case Consultation in its focus on a single individual, is unique as the change expected occurs in the consultee, not the client. With Consultee-Centered Case Consultation, the consultant is brought in to work with the consultee directly to address a lack of understanding with reference to the client's problems, to enhance the consultee's skills, to assist the consultee with themes that interfere with his/her ability to work with a particular client or situation, and to support the consultee and aid in building confidence and self esteem in the consultee. *Consultee-Centered Administrative Consultation,* as the title suggests, spotlights more administrative level change, with the consultant assisting the consultee(s) to manage program goals and to deal effectively with collegial interpersonal issues.

Halpern (1964) advocated the use of mental health consultation for school psychologists in Canada, and although, she describes mental health consultation in broad terms, it is clear from her discourse that her proposal focused on consultee-centred case consultation, with particular reference to consultation with teachers to bring about changes with a child. Halpern viewed a consultative model as a method to increase the effectiveness of school psychologists in communicating and integrating information in a way that was useful to educators; and as a means to enhance the implementation of recommendations by teachers. Further, Halpern highlights the usefulness of a consultative model in addressing the "manpower problem" (p.150) and views consultation as a method whereby more children may be provided with services in a more efficient manner. Thus, even in the 1960's, the notion that psychologists would be able to meet the demands of applied settings was deemed unrealistic by professionals (Bernhardt, 1961 as cited by Halpern, 1964). It could be argued that Halpern (1964) was a pioneer in highlighting the use of consultation in the Canadian context.

The 1970's

A surge of interest in the potential of consultation as an alternative delivery system was particularly evident in the school counsellor literature in the 1970's. Consultation was viewed as a viable method for the delivery of services to elementary, secondary, college, and university communities (e.g., Axford, 1977; Brosseau, 1973; Carr, 1976; Merchant, 1976; Simons & Davies, 1973; Waxer, 1972; Waxer & White, 1973; Young

& Borgen, 1979). Brosseau (1973) noted that the foci of consultation activities were diverse and marked by a lack of definitional clarity. However, certain commonalities existed in the consultation literature at this time. Consultation was viewed as developmental and preventive in nature, and as a preferred alternative to direct treatment. In addition, teachers were viewed as the major agents of change, and although the consultative relationship was viewed as mutually beneficial, the consultant was clearly seen in an "expert" role. Importantly, consultation was viewed as a mechanism to impart skills to teachers so that they would not only be able to effectively deal with a particular child's problem behavior, but to be able to address similar problems such as these in the future. As a consequence, counsellors would be free to attend to more severe problems (Simons & Davies, 1973).

As the decade progressed a new framework for consultation arose (Axford, 1977). During the mid-to-late 1970's "developmental consultation" emerged as an approach that involved the entire system or environment within which the child functioned. Merchant (1976) discusses developmental consultation as a more holistic approach within which to understand a child's functioning. This approach requires that the consultant engage the individuals who play a pivotal role in the child's life (e.g., sibling, parent, teacher) throughout the consultative endeavor. Thus, for the first time, with the advent of developmental consultation, the tremendous influence of the family on children's development was recognized as vital to the consultative process (Axford, 1977).

The 1980's

Theory, research, and practice in consultation appeared to come to a stand still in the 1980's. Up to this time, there had been a flurry of discussion on consultation in the schools, although a systematic analysis of the efficacy of consultation had not been undertaken. Carr (1981) provides compelling explanations for this state of affairs, namely, conceptual problems, little research activity in the field, limited numbers of consultants and lack of available training in consultation. Further, Carr (1981) argued that the grip of the medical model on education was another reason why consultation floundered in Canada. Typically, strict adherents to the "medical model" view abnormal behavior as emanating from "within" the child, therefore, the course of treatment is to "do" something to the child. The adherence to the medical model was puzzling in light of Jevne's (1981) finding that school consultants prefer a developmental, holistic orientation to problem solving and with reference to information suggesting that the medical model was "... the most costly, least efficient, and most likely ineffective system for implementing principles of developmental growth ..." (Carr, 1981, p. 85). In closing, the decade of the 1980s was singularly inactive in the field of consultation in Canada. Reasons for this stagnation have been tentatively suggested but no definitive explanation is revealed.

The 1990's

This decade marks a period of considerable growth for consultation theory, research, and practice in Canada. Notable is the publication of the comprehensive book *Effective Consultation in School Psychology* edited by Cole and Siegel (1990). Prominent Canadian scholars address the following critical issues: the expanding future role of school psychologists (Siegel & Cole, 1990); the process of school consultation (Davison, 1990); responding to teachers' needs (Miezitis & Scholten, 1990); parent-teacher mediated intervention (Cole, 1990); assessment and intervention with under-achieving adolescents (Zarb, 1990); dynamic assessment in the classroom (Bountrogianni & Pratt, 1990); and the integration of consultation in the delivery of school psychological services (Anserello & Sweet, 1990). The purpose of the book was to provide school psychologists with a blueprint for conducting consultation.

Siegel and Cole (1990) stressed the importance of "collaborative consultation." Collaborative consultation can be distinguished from mental health consultation in that the former model encourages the school psychologist to relinquish his/her role as an "expert" thereby paving the way for a mutually respectful relationship between school psychologists and educators. In addition, school psychologists are encouraged to maintain an open attitude toward diverse methods of delivering services to children and youth, to develop a preventive mind set, and importantly, to match the mode of service delivery to educators' needs. The service delivery model proposed by Siegel and Cole (1990) was innovative as it incorporated all activities of the school psychologist and thus included both indirect and more systems-oriented services. The three pronged model of primary prevention, secondary prevention, and tertiary prevention allowed for services to span the spectrum (services for *all* children as well as children with special needs) and the recipients of those services could include the organization, school staff, students/parents (mediated), and students/parents (direct). Several authors described the effective application of this model for providing services (e.g., Cole, 1990; Cole & Siegel, 1990; Miezitis & Scholten, 1990; Wiener & Davidson, 1990; Zarb, 1990).

Wiener and Davidson's (1990) study on the efficacy of collaborative consultation as a pre-referral intervention system represents one of the few empirical studies carried out in Canada. Heretofore, the research had been limited to reports of successful individual case studies or anecdotal information concerning the process of programmatic consultation. Wiener and Davidson (1990) found that collaborative consultation using resource teachers as in-house consultants coupled with an ecological approach to assessment decreased referrals to psychologists, other consultants, or special education placement by half.

Ross and Regan (1990) conducted a study investigating differences between experienced and inexperienced curriculum consultants and found that experienced consultants had more knowledge concerning the effort required to bring about desired change, and had a larger repertoire of strategies available to bring about that change.

In addition, the more experienced consultants arranged for individual and group sessions and provided practice sessions for teachers. Furthermore, their skill structures were more complex than the novice consultants, and they were more sensitive to task demands and the social system within which consultation occurred. They also involved other agents in the monitoring and implementation of objectives. Interestingly, however, Ross and Regan (1990) acknowledged that the nature of the system in which the consultant functioned did influence the consultant's performance. Consultants who worked within school systems that were highly supportive, demonstrated greater success than consultants in less supportive environments. Thus, Ross and Regan's (1990) work provided additional indication of the efficacy of consultation in Canadian schools.

In 1995, da Costa compared the effectiveness of four teacher collaboration strategies: collaborative consultation; collaborative consultation with team teaching; collaborative consultation with no classroom observation; and collegial consultation with no classroom observation. The four groups were found to differ and the identified essential element for this difference was deemed to be classroom observation. It was concluded that conducting classroom observations is crucial to collaborative consultation if the goal is to increase personal teaching efficacy and student achievement.

In addition, in the late 1990s the empirical investigation of conjoint behavioral consultation with children who have mild to moderate behavior problems was commenced in Canada with the work of Sladeczek and her colleagues at McGill University. Specifically, Sladeczek first sought to investigate the efficacy of conjoint behavioral consultation within a Canadian context and conducted a series of single-n studies with her colleagues that provided evidence for the effectiveness of this parent-teacher mediated approach for alleviating behavior problems in young children (e.g., Illsley & Sladeczek, in press; Wayland & Sladeczek, 1999). Second, due in part to the call by leading researchers in the field for comparative investigations, Sladeczek (1999a, 1999b) proposed a series of studies to compare the traditional conjoint behavioral consultation framework to consultant-led videotape therapy groups for parents and teachers, as well as self-administered videotape therapy. Outcome variables include the examination of change in children's target behaviors, social skills, overall social and emotional functioning, quality of friendships, and actual parent-child interactions. Moreover, changes in parental skills, attitudes, and knowledge about behavioral principles as a function of participating in the interventions have been examined (Illsley, 2002; Illsley & Sladeczek, 2001). Teachers' knowledge of behavior principles, intervention integrity, and intervention acceptability were also investigated. Furthermore, Sladeczek et al., (2001) published one of the few studies of the use of goal attainment scaling within a behavioral consultation framework. In brief, goal attainment scaling involves the selection of a target behavior(s); an objective description of a desired intervention outcome; and the development of three to five descriptions of the target behavior or behaviors that increasingly approximate the desired outcome (Elliott, Sladeczek, & Kratochwill, 1995). Through the use of a case study, Sladeczek, Elliott, Kratochwill, Robertson-Mjaanes, and Stoiber (2001) illustrated how goal attainment scaling can be used with consultees to identify the goals, progress, and outcomes of consultation interventions. Thus, Sladeczek and her colleagues have made inroads in the use of consultation in the Canadian context and she is now extending her work to children with developmental delays, their families, and teachers (Sladeczek & Heath, 2002; Sladeczek, Saros, Steinbach, Viola, & Blidner, 2002; Viola, 2000). To summarize, the 1990s, unlike the preceding decade, have been a productive period for the field of consultation in Canada. Indeed, so much so that the present review cannot claim to be exhaustive. The studies herein reviewed were chosen to illustrate this period's distinctive claim to the initiation of the systematic investigation of the efficacy of consultation in Canadian schools.

Examination of the evolution of consultation in Canada over the past four decades suggests an initial surge of interest with the advent of Caplan's (1963) seminal work on types of mental health consultation, followed by extensive discussion by academics and practitioners as to how school psychologists, school counsellors, and educators could incorporate consultation activities within a delivery system that can be described as primarily direct and hierarchical. In the 1980's, writing and research on consultation declined, the exact reason for this is unclear. Although published discourse declined, it is highly probable that practitioners included some type of consultation in their day-to-day functioning. Of course, the notion of consulting with teachers and parents was not an entirely novel idea, however, the conceptualization of the consultee and consultant roles with prescribed procedures for bringing about change was original. Momentum increased as consultation theory, research, and practice approached the 1990's. Professional organizations (e.g., National Association of School Psychologists) stressed the importance of formalized training in consultation for school psychologists and this tenet was mirrored by researchers active in Canadian schools. Established Canadian school psychologists and educators clearly state the necessity of consultation as a part of a comprehensive service delivery system (e.g., Carney, 1996; Cole, 1996; Janzen et al., 1993; Siegel & Cole, 1990). Significant here is the belief that consultation is an integral component of a delivery service system, and not viewed as a second best alternative. In this vein, Siegel and Cole (1990) developed an effective consultation model for the delivery of psychological services in schools and Sladeczek and her colleagues have launched comparative investigations of diverse consultative approaches and extended its use to a wider range of children with special needs.

Discussion

In summation, it appears that the field of consultation in the United States has been characterized by a continuous growth, although the basic tenets of behavioral consultation have been attacked (e.g., Noell & Witt, 1996; Witt, Gresham, & Noell, 1996) and rebutted (e.g., Kratochwill, Bergan, Sheridan, & Elliott, 1998). This lively debate has invigorated the field, especially as behavioral consultation relates or compares to other consultative modalities. More specifically, Noell and Witt (1996) critiqued the basic assumptions of behavioral consultation and concluded that there was a need for a more competitive and controversial stance toward models of consultation than presently exists in the United States. Noell and Witt's (1996) underlying premise appears to be that the consultation field has been dominated by the behavioral consultation model, which in turn, has led to minimal development of alternative models of consultation. In contrast, internationally it would appear that the systematic study of consultation is in its infancy, with the American model being imported and changed based on the consultative needs of the particular country. In Canada, however, consultation research, although somewhat different in its beginnings and more diverse in its models, has emerged as a viable alternative for the delivery of psychological services in schools. We conclude that the consultation field in the United States is the most clearly defined and substantive, whereas internationally there appears to be the least use of consultation and Canada's consultation field lies somewhere between these two extremes. In 1997, Sladeczek and Heath compared the status of consultation in Canada to the United States and concluded that Canada was still developing and remained far less clearly delineated as a field. However, in light of our present findings concerning the status of consultation internationally, we now contend that consultation in Canada is, in fact, far closer to consultation in the United States than previously thought.

If one contrasts the above observations concerning the evolution of consultation in Canada to the United States versus the international forum, several interesting findings emerge. First, in the United States the prominence and permanence behavioral consultation has enjoyed for 25 years in the United States is striking (Noell & Witt, 1996). However, despite the widespread support of the behavioral consultation model in the United States, it is not without its critics, and leading researchers have called for a re-examination of the empirical evidence regarding the basic tenets of consultation. However, in Canada or internationally, where the behavioral consultation model has not dominated consultation, it could equally be argued that the field has failed to establish itself to the same degree as in the United States. In summary, the prominence of the behavioral consultation model observed in the United States, while open to criticism, may have served an important role in the development of consultation as an established field, which has not occurred in Canada or elsewhere at this time.

A second interesting comparison between consultation in the United States versus Canada or internationally, revolves around the sheer magnitude of the published work in consultation. The amount of scientific inquiry generated by scholars and practitioners in consultation has been tremendous in the United States. In the most recent meta-analytic investigations of consultation outcomes, 1, 643 studies were reviewed by Gibson and Chard (1994) who concluded that the efficacy of consultation interventions was considerable. In a more recent meta-analysis by Reddy and her colleagues (2000) consultation was found to be particularly effective with children and adolescents with externalizing behavior problems and academic difficulties. A comparable meta-analysis of the Canadian literature on consultation outcomes has not been done. However, our own literature search from 1960 to 1999 uncovered only 24 articles on consultation. Interestingly in the international arena where consultation appears to be far less defined than in Canada, we only found 2 articles specifically on consultation. These startling findings may best illustrate the difference between the state of the consultation field in Canada versus the United States, while demonstrating Canada's relative strength in consultation within an international context.

Internationally, the virtual absence of consultation as understood in both the United States and Canada is of interest to the authors. In comparison with the establishment of a form of consultation in Canada, in the international forum we were unable to uncover a significant body of literature focusing on consultation, although there have been two examples of consultation practice (i.e., Sri Lanka, Australia, and the extension of the Australian parenting program to Germany). The question arises as to why there has not been a larger area of study on consultation internationally? One possibility is that the practice exists but is carried out using different terminology which leads to difficulty in accessing the literature. To address this possibility we continue to seek colleagues in other countries to further inform our existing knowledge base concerning the theory, research and practice of consultation. A second possibility is that this dearth of information accurately reflects an absence of consultation internationally. Is consultation a culturally North American phenomenon? Possibly consultation, or indirect service delivery models only begin to develop once direct services have been fully established. It may be that in many countries direct services for students with exceptionalities are still in the process of being developed due to resource limitations or cultural differences. However, this is purely supposition and requires an international discussion to either confirm or discredit.

In conclusion, it is the authors' contention that the formalized conceptualization of consultation that exists in the U.S. does not exist elsewhere, however, Canada, possibly due to the close American influence has the most similar use of the consultation construct. Despite the similarity between the Canadian and U.S. approaches when viewed through an international perspective certain essential differences remain. Consultation in Canada differs from consultation in the United States along two dimensions: qualitatively and quantitatively. The qualitative difference lies in the emphasis of the fields. In the United States there is a single leading model of consultation which has predominated in the literature and practice, whereas in Canada we see a more diverse, fluid understanding of consultation. This flexibility has had significant drawbacks in that little empirical investigation of the efficacy of consultation has been conducted in Canada and the field could be argued to be fragmented. Nevertheless, the future development of the field in Canada has enormous potential. The quantitative difference between the Canadian and the American consultation fields refers to the amount of literature in American sources versus their Canadian counterparts. Even allowing for proportional differences in number of existing journals, and population, there remains a greater emphasis on consultation in the American research literature relative to the Canadian.

Consultation in the United States, internationally, and in Canada is unique. Future investigators need to clearly define and operationalize what is meant by "consultation" or similar terminology (e.g., ecobehavioral consultation, problem-solving consultation). Only in this manner can we conduct empirical investigations of the efficacy of consultation in Canadian schools and extend our research into an international context, which is imperative for the continued growth of the field. It is only through international collaborative efforts that we can come to a better understanding of the true potential of consultation across cultural boundaries and surmise its universality as a viable approach for providing services to children, families, and systems.

References

Alpert, J. L., & Yammer, M. D. (1983). Research in school consultation: A content analysis of selected journals. *Professional Psychology: Research and Practice, 14,* 604-612.

Anserello, C., & Sweet, T. (1990). Integrating consultation into school psychological services. In E. Cole & J. A. Siegel (Eds.), *Effective consultation in school psychology* (pp. 173-199). Toronto: Hogrefe & Huber.

Axford, M. B. (1977). The elementary school counsellor-consultant and the family. *School Guidance Worker, 33,* 36-42.

Bartell, R. (1996). The argument for a paradigm shift or what's in a name? *Canadian Journal of School Psychology, 12(2),* 86-90.

Bergan, J. R. (1993). Foreword. In J. Zins, T. R. Kratochwill, & S. N. Elliott (Eds.), *Handbook of consultation services for children* (pp. xiii-xiv). San Francisco: Jossey-Bass Publishers.

Bergan, J. R., & Kratochwill, T. R. (1990). *Behavioral consultation and therapy.* New York: Plenum.

Bergan, J. R., Sladeczek, I. E., & Schwarz, R. D. (1991). Effects of a measurement and planning system on kindergartners' cognitive and educational programming. *American Educational Research Journal, 28(3),* 683-714.

Bountrogianni, M., & Pratt, M. (1990). Dynamic assessment: Implications for classroom consultation, peer tutoring and parent education. In E. Cole & J. A. Siegel (Eds.), *Effective consultation in school psychology* (pp. 129-140). Toronto: Hogrefe & Huber.

Brosseau, J. (1973). Consulting – A potpourri? *Canadian Counsellor, 7(4),* 259-267.

Caplan, G. (1963). Types of mental health consultations. *American Journal of Orthopsychiatry, 33,* 470-481.

Carney, P. J. (1996). A practitioner's view of challenges and issues for school psychologists in the 21st century. *Canadian Journal of School Psychology, 12(2),* 98-102.

Carr, R. A. (1976). The effects of preventive consultation with elementary school principals on changing teacher staff meeting behaviors. *Canadian Counselor, 10(4)*, 157-165.

Carr, R. A. (1981). A model for consultation training in Canadian counsellor education programs. *Canadian Counsellor, 15*, 83-92.

Cole, E. (1990). Parent-teacher mediated intervention: A growth-promoting process. In E. Cole & J. A. Siegel (Eds.), *Effective consultation in school psychology* (pp. 101-112). Toronto: Hogrefe & Huber.

Cole, E. (1996). An integrative perspective on school psychology. *Canadian Journal of School Psychology, 12(2)*, 115-121.

Cole, E., & Siegel, J. A. (Eds.). (1990). *Effective consultation in school psychology.* Toronto, Canada: Hogrefe & Huber.

Connell, S., Sanders, M. R., & Markie-Dadds, C. (1997). Self-directed behavioural family intervention for parents of oppositional children in rural and remote areas. *Behaviour Modification, 21*, 379-408.

da Costa, J. L. (1995). Teacher collaboration: A comparison of four strategies. *The Alberta Journal of Educational Research, 61(4)*, 407-420.

Davison, J. (1990). The process of school consultation: Give and take. In E. Cole & J. A. Siegel (Eds.), *Effective consultation in school psychology* (pp. 53-69). Toronto: Hogrefe & Huber.

Dworet, D. H., & Rathgeber, A. J. (1996, April). *Behaviour disorders in Canada.* Paper presented at the meeting of the Council for Exceptional Children, Orlando, Fl.

Elliott, S. N., Sladeczek, I. E., & Kratochwill, T. R. (1995, August). Goal attainment scaling: Its use as a progress monitoring and outcome effectiveness measure in behavioral consultation. Poster session presented at the annual meeting of the American Psychological Association, New York, NY.

Elliot, S. N., & Witt, J.C. (Eds.), (1986). *The delivery of psychological services in schools: Concepts, processes, and issues.* Hillsdale, NJ: Lawrence Erlbaum Associates.

Gibson, G., & Chard, K. M. (1994). Quantifying the effects of community mental health consultation interventions. *Consulting Psychology Journal: Practice and Research, 46(4)*, 13-25.

Gutkin, T. B., & Curtis, M. J. (1990). School-based consultation: Theory, techniques, and research. In T. B. Gutkin & C. R. Reynolds (Eds.), *The handbook of school psychology* (2nd ed., pp. 577-611). New York: Wiley.

Hahlweg, K., Kuschel, A., Miller, Y., Lubke, A., Koppe, E., & Sanders, M. R., (2001). Prävention kindlicher Verhaltensstörungen Triple P. Ein mehrstufiges Programm zu positiver Erziehung. In S. Walper & R. Pekreun (Eds.), *Familie und Entwicklung.* Göttingen, Germany: Hogrefe.

Halpern, E. (1964). Mental health consultations and the school psychologist. *Canadian Psychologist, 5(3)*, 149-153.

Illsley, S. D. (2002). Remediating conduct problems in children: Examining changes in children and parents following consultation. Unpublished doctoral dissertation, McGill University, Montreal, Quebec, Canada.

Illsley, S. D., & Sladeczek, I. E. (in press). Conjoint behavioral consultation for children with conduct problems: Examining changes in parental knowledge and skill. *Journal of Educational and Psychological Consultation.*

Janzen, H. L., Paterson, J. G., & Paterson, D. W. (1993). The future of school psychology in the schools. *Canadian Journal of School Psychology, 9(2)*, 174-180.

Jevne, R. (1981). Counsellor competencies and selected issues in Canadian counsellor education. *Canadian Counsellor, 15(2)*, 57-63.

Kratochwill, T. R., Bergan, J. R., Sheridan, S. M., & Elliot, S. N. (1998). Assumptions of behavioural consultation: After all is said and done more has been done than said. *School Psychology Quarterly, 13(1),* 63-80.

Kratochwill, T. R., Elliot, S. N., & Callan-Stoiber, K. (2002). Best practices in school-based problem-solving consultation. In A. Thomas & J. Grimes (Eds.), *Best practices in school psychology IV* (pp.583-608). Bethesda, MD: The National Association of School Psychologists.

Mannino, F. V., & Shore, M. F. (1975). The effects of consultation: A review of empirical studies of the literature. *American Journal of Community Psychology, 3,* 1-21.

McKay, R. (1995). Proposed cutbacks to psychological services provided in the schools. *Canadian Journal of School Psychology, 11,(2)* 101-102.

Medway, F. J. (1979). How effective is school consultation? A review of recent research. *Journal of School Psychology, 17,* 275-282.

Medway, F. J. (1982). School consultation research: Past trends and future directions. *Professional Psychology, 13,* 422-430.

Medway, F. J., & Updyke, J. F. (1985). Meta-analysis of consultation outcome studies. *American Journal of Community Psychology, 13,* 489-505.

Merchant, D. F. (1976). Creating stronger swimmers: The counsellor-consultant in the elementary school. *School Guidance Worker, 31,* 22-26.

Miezitis, S., & Scholten, P. T. (1990). Responding to teachers' needs: A case-study in consultation. In E. Cole & J. A. Siegel (Eds.), *Effective consultation in school psychology* (pp. 81-99). Toronto: Hogrefe & Huber.

Nastasi, B. K., Varijas, K., Bernstein, R., & Jayasena, A. (2000). Conducting participatory culture-specific consultation: A global perspective on multicultural consultation. *School Psychology Review, 29(3),* 401-413.

Nastasi, B. K., Varijas, K., Sakar, S., & Jayasena, A. (1998). Participatory model of mental health programming: Lessons learned from work in developing countries. *School Psychology Review, 27(2),* 260-276.

Noell, G., H., & Witt, J. C. (1996). A critical evaluation of five fundamental assumptions underlying behavioral consultation. *School Psychology Quarterly, 11(11),* 189-203.

Parsons, R. D., & Meyers, J. (1984). *Developing consultation skills: A guide to training, development and assessment for human services professionals.* San Francisco: Jossey-Bass.

Reddy, L. A., Barboza-Whitehead., S., Files, T., & Rubel, E. (2000). Clinical focus of consultation outcome research with children and adolescents. *Special Services in Schools, 16(1-2),* 1-22.

Ross, J. A., & Regan, E. M. (1990). Self-reported strategies of experienced and inexperienced consultants: Exploring differences. *The Alberta Journal of Educational Research, 36(2),* 157-180.

Sanders, M. R. (1999). The Triple P-Positive Parenting Program: Toward an empirically validated multilevel parenting and family support strategy for the prevention of behavior and emotional problems in children. *Clinical Child and Family Psychology Review, 2,* 71-90.

Sanders, M. R. (2001). Triple P – Positive Parenting Program. Retrieved November 11, 2001, from University of Queensland Web Site: http://www.pfsc.uq.edu.au

Sanders, M. R., & Markie-Dadds, C. (1996). Triple P: A multi-level family intervention program for children with disruptive behavior disorders. In P. Cotton & H. Jackson (Eds.), *Early intervention and prevention in mental health* (pp. 59-85). Melbourne, VIC, Australia: Australian Psychological Society.

Sanders, M. R., Markie-Dadds, C., Tully, L. A., & Bor, W. (2000). The Triple-P Positive Parenting Program: A comparison of enhanced, standard, and self-directed behavioral family intervention. *Journal of Consulting and Clinical Psychology, 68,* 624-640.

Sanders, M. R., & McFarland, M. L. (2000). The treatment of depressed mothers with disruptive children: A controlled evaluation of cognitive behavioral family intervention. *Behavior Therapy, 31*, 89-112.

Sanders, M. R., Montgomey, D., & Brechman-Toussaint, M. (2000). Mass media and the prevention of child behavior problems. *Journal of Child Psychology and Psychiatry, 41*, 939-948.

Siegel, J. A., & Cole, E. (1990). Appraisal for better curriculum. In E. Cole & J. A. Siegel (Eds.), *Effective consultation in school psychology* (pp. 201-245). Toronto: Hogrefe & Huber.

Simons, H., & Davies, D. (1973). The counsellor as consultant in the development of the teacher-advisor concept in guidance. *Canadian Counsellor, 7(1)*, 27-39.

Sladeczek, I. E. (1996). Aggressive and territorial behavior: The case of Ken. In S.N. Sheridan, T. R. Kratochwill, & J. R. Bergan (Eds.), *Conjoint behavioural consultation: A procedural guide.* New York: Plenum Publishing Corporation.

Sladeczek, I. E. (1999a). Parent-teacher mediated interventions for children with behavior problems.(Fonds pour la formation de chercheurs et l'aide a la recherche (FCAR)). Quebec, Canada: McGill University.

Sladeczek, I. E. (1999b). Indirect service models for children with behavior problems. (Social Sciences and Humanities Research Council of Canada). Quebec, Canada: McGill University.

Sladeczek, I. E., Elliott, S. N., Kratochwill, T. R., Robertson-Mjaanes, S., & Stoiber, K. C. (2001). Application of goal attainment scaling to a conjoint behavioral consultation case. *Journal of Educational & Psychological Consultation, 12(1)*, 45-58.

Sladeczek, I. E, & Heath, N. L. (1997). Consultation in Canada. *Canadian Journal of School Psychology, 13(2)*, 1-14.

Sladeczek, I. E, & Heath, N. L. (2002). Evaluation of an indirect intervention for children with developmental delays. (Council of the Canadian Institutes of Health Research Grant Application). Quebec, Canada: McGill University.

Sladeczek I. E, Saros, N., Steinbach, L., Viola, T., & Blidner, A. (2002). Evaluation of behavioral consultation with videotape therapies for children with developmental delays. Manuscript in preparation.

Viola, T. (2000). Remediating behavior problems in children with cognitive disabilities. Unpublished master's thesis. McGill University, Montreal, Quebec, Canada.

Wayland, L. A., & Sladeczek, I. E. (1999). Work in progress: Conjoint behavioral consultation with children who are socially withdrawn. *Canadian Journal of School Psychology, 14*, 45-50.

Waxer, P. (1972). Counsellors as consultants in a college community. *School Guidance Worker, 28*, 50-55.

Waxer, P., & White, R. (1973). Introducing psychological consultation to a university community. *The Canadian Psychologist, 14(3)*, 256-265.

Wiener, J., & Davidson, I. (1990). The in-school team experience. In E. Cole, & J. A. Siegel (Eds.), *Effective consultation in school psychology* (pp. 19-32). Toronto: Hogrefe & Huber.

Witt, J. C., Gresham, F. M., & Noell, G. H. (1996). What's behavioral about behavioral consultation? *Journal of Educational & Psychological Consultation, 7(4)*, 327-344.

Young, R.A., & Borgen, W.A. (1979). Developmental consultation in implementing career education programs. *Canadian Counsellor, 13(3)*, 179-183.

Zarb, J. (1990). Underachieving adolescents: Assessment and intervention. In E. Cole, & J. A. Siegel (Eds.), *Effective consultation in school psychology* (pp. 113-128). Toronto: Hogrefe & Huber.

Zins, J. E., Kratochwill, T. R., & Elliott, S. N. (Eds.). (1993). *Handbook for consultation services for children: Applications in educational and clinical settings.* San Francisco: Jossey-Bass.

Chapter 4
Problem-Solving Consultation in the New Millennium

Ingrid E. Sladeczek, Thomas R. Kratochwill, C. Lisa Steinbach, Patrick Kumke, and Lisa Hagermoser

The purpose of this chapter is to illustrate how two precursors of problem-solving consultation, behavioral consultation and conjoint behavioral consultation, fit into an effective school psychology service delivery system as initially described by Cole and Siegel in their book entitled *Effective Consultation in School Psychology* (1990) and refined in this new edition. Behavioral consultation (BC) and conjoint behavioral consultation (CBC) uniquely mesh into, and share several of the same assumptions of Cole and Siegel's proposed model that is summarized in Figure 1 (see Chapter 1). For example, the assumptions that (a) services need to help children learn, (b) services are available to the children, parents, and teachers who need them, and (c) multiple approaches be used for service delivery, underlie the basic premise of BC and CBC. Both BC and CBC represent intervention paradigms that can be described as primarily indirect, in that the client is usually a child with academic or social/emotional problem behaviors, and teachers or parents carry out the intervention plans through the assistance of a consultant. Traditionally, BC – pioneered by the work of Bergan (1977) and later refined by Bergan and Kratochwill (1990) – focused on the process of consultation via one consultee (the person implementing the intervention with the child, usually a parent or teacher). In contrast, CBC, as described by Sheridan, Kratochwill, and Bergan (1996) focused on the importance of including *both* teachers and parents in the consultation process.

Consultation can be a major catalyst in providing psychological and educational services within a traditional primary, secondary, and tertiary prevention paradigm (see Walker & Shinn, 2002 for a review of prevention approaches). For example, consultation can be viewed as secondary prevention for those students that are seen to be at-risk for more serious academic or behavior problems, but is also highly appropriate for students who are already exhibiting problems adapting to the school environment and the demands placed upon them. Thus, when examining Cole and Siegel's model (see Chapter 1), the recipients of consultation are school personnel (in particular, teachers acting as consultees) and students who receive services primarily through a mediator. Cole and Siegel (1990) stress that innovative services are possible in all parts or roles of the model, and we will demonstrate how BC and CBC in particular (henceforth both will be subsumed under the newer term *problem-solving consultation*), provide an innovative and effective paradigm for the provision of school psychological services, and underscore the role of the school psychologist as problem-solver. In this vein, the more recent use of the term *problem-solving consultation* (PSC) emphasizes the diverse and wide array of assessments, interventions, and theoretical orientations that can extend BC and CBC which have traditionally been associated with behavior modification and behavioral theory (Kratochwill, Elliott, & Callan-Stoiber, 2002).

Thus, the purpose of this chapter is to demonstrate how problem-solving consultation fits into Cole and Siegel's (1990) model of school psychology service delivery. In this endeavor, the following areas shall be emphasized: (a) a brief history of problem-solving consultation; (b) salient areas of inquiry that dominate the theory and practice of problem-solving consultation; and, finally (c) future challenges for researchers and practitioners in the new millennium.

Brief History of Problem-Solving Consultation

In the last 40 years, consultation, as an indirect method of service delivery, has received widespread attention in the United States and Canada (Sladeczek & Heath, 1997). This attention has been due, in large part, to the large body of empirical evidence that attests to the effectiveness of consultation in helping children with special needs (see for example, Alpert & Yammer, 1983; Bergan, 1995; Bergan & Kratochwill, 1990; Bergan, Sladeczek, Schwarz, & Smith, 1991; Gibson & Chard, 1994; Gutkin & Curtis, 1990; Mannino & Shore, 1975; Medway, 1979, 1982; Medway & Updyke, 1985; Sladeczek, 1996). Consultation has been found to be effective for a myriad of academic and behavior related problems such as social skill deficits (e.g., Sheridan, Kratochwill, & Elliott, 1990); school performance in underachieving students (e.g., Galloway & Sheridan, 1994); irrational fears and phobias (Sheridan & Colton, 1994); and behavioral excesses of children diagnosed with attention deficit disorder (e.g., Johnson & Tilly, 1993) to name but a few. To this end, several methods of consultation have evolved over the past 40 years including (a) mental health consultation, (b) developmental consultation, and (c) behavioral consultation.

Mental Health Consultation

Mental health consultation, the forerunner to other consultative models was developed by Caplan (1963) who described consultation as involving the interaction between a consultant, a specialist or recognized "expert," and a consultee, a professional who was seeking assistance with a client. Essential aspects of Caplan's description of the consultative process are that the consultee can accept or reject the advice given by the consultant and furthermore, that the consultee accepts the professional responsibility for the client. Interesting, as well, is the notion that the consultant not only engages in this process to assist the consultee, but also to gain a better understanding of diagnostic, assessment, and intervention issues that are relevant to the consultee, and to thus be able to offer assistance when similar problems are encountered in the future. Notable here is that the consultant-consultee relationship was seen as a mutually beneficial relationship although clearly hierarchical.

Caplan differentiated between four central types of mental health consultation: (a) Client-Centered Case Consultation; (b) Program-Centered Administrative Consultation; (c) Consultee-Centered Case Consultation; and, finally, (d) Consultee-Centered Administrative Consultation. In Client-Centered Case Consultation the primary goal is to help the consultee to bring about desired changes with the client of concern, a specific individual. In contrast, the emphasis in Program-Centered Administrative Consultation is at the group level with the consultant working with a group of consultees, to assist with the administration of prevention, treatment, or rehabilitation of individuals who have mental problems. Consultee-Centered Case Consultation, while similar to Client-Centered Case Consultation in its focus on a single individual, is unique as the change expected occurs in the consultee, not the client. Thus, the consultant is brought in to work with the consultee directly (a) to address a lack of understanding with reference to the client's problems, (b) to enhance the consultee's skills and to identify themes that interfere with his/her ability to work with a particular client or situation, and (c) to support the consultee and aid in building confidence and self esteem in the consultee. Consultee-Centered Administrative Consultation, as the title suggests, spotlights more administrative level change with the consultant assisting the consultee(s) to manage program goals and to deal effectively with collegial interpersonal issues.

Developmental Consultation

During the mid-to-late 1970's "developmental consultation" emerged as an approach that involved the entire system or environment within which the child functioned. Merchant (1976) discussed developmental consultation as a more holistic approach to understanding a child's functioning. This approach requires that the consultant engage the individuals who play a pivotal role in the child's life (e.g., sibling, parent, and teacher) throughout the consultative endeavour. Thus, for the first time in developmental consultation, the tremendous influence of the family on children's development was recognized as vital to the consultative process (Axford, 1977).

Behavioral Consultation

The "behavioral consultation" model has been one of the major models of consultation used in the United States, and more recently in Canada. Briefly, behavioral consultation involves the collaboration between a consultant and at least one consultee (usually a parent and/or teacher) that together work towards bringing about behavior change with a client (usually a child) (Bergan, 1977; Bergan & Kratochwill, 1990). Traditionally, four-to-five stages are involved in the consultation process: Problem Identification, Problem Analysis, Treatment Implementation, and Treatment Evaluation. During the *Problem Identification Interview* the consultant and consultee(s) identify the initial problem and agree upon a data collection strategy to collect baseline information (e.g., number of aggressive acts per day). During the *Problem Analysis Interview* baseline data are reviewed, and antecedents, consequences, and sequential conditions linked with the problem behaviors are identified and analyzed. A treatment plan based on effective behavioral management strategies is developed and plans for implementation are confirmed. Finally, after treatment implementation has occurred, the *Treatment Evaluation Interview* is held, where the data is reviewed, and the consultant, teacher, and parent discuss the effectiveness of treatment, and if treatment should be continued or terminated. In between the *Problem Analysis Interview* and the *Treatment Evaluation Interview* the consultant and consultee maintain contact and determine how the client is responding to treatment, and if revisions need to be made to the treatment plan. The most impressive features of this type of consultation are that the relationship between the consultant and consultee is viewed as collaborative, and that the approach to problem identification and the monitoring of treatment is data driven. Striking is the prominence and permanence behavioral consultation has enjoyed for the past 25 years. However, despite the widespread support of the behavioral consultation model it is not without its critics. Noell and Witt (1996) critiqued the basic assumptions of behavioral consultation and concluded that there was a need for a more competitive and controversial stance toward models of consultation than presently exists. Noell and Witt's underlying premise appears to be that the consultation field has been dominated by the behavioral consultation model, which in turn, has led to minimal development of alternative models of consultation. In summary, the prominence of the behavioral consultation model, while open to criticism, may have served an important role in the development of consultation as an established field (Sladeczek & Heath, 1997). Professional organizations (e.g., National Association of School Psychologists, American Psychological Association) continue to recognize the importance of formalized training in consultation for school psychologists and this tenet is mirrored by established school psychologists and educators (e.g., Carney, 1996; Cole & Siegel, 1990; Janzen, Paterson, & Paterson, 1993). Significant here is the belief that consultation is an integral component of a delivery service system, and not viewed as a second best alternative in schools.

Areas of Inquiry within Problem-Solving Consultation

We have identified four primary areas of inquiry within the problem-solving consultation field that are receiving wide spread attention by both researchers and practitioners alike. Each of these areas addresses significant issues that impinge upon the process and outcomes of consultation. The four areas we have chosen to highlight are: the collaborative nature of consultation, treatment acceptability, treatment integrity, and evidenced-based interventions.

Collaborative Consultation

Cole and Siegel (1990) identify consultation as a key skill for school psychologists as change often occurs indirectly through their influence on school personnel and/or parents. As such, Cole and Siegel (1990) emphasize *collaborative consultation* as the most effective method of providing consultation services, and define collaborative consultation as "… a process through which psychologists and educators work coordinately to resolve educational problems from positions of mutual respect for one another as professionals" (p. 9). The notion that consultation is collaborative in nature and that collaborative consultation leads to positive intervention outcomes has been accepted as a universal truth (Gutkin, 1999) within the consultation literature. However, Witt (1990) challenged this basic assumption, and suggested that the opposite may in fact be true. Three other seminal studies (i.e., Erchul, 1987; Erchul & Chewning, 1990; Witt, Erchul, McKee, Pardue, & Wickstrom, 1991) examined the verbalizations of consultation dyads and seriously questioned the collaborative aspect of the consultant-consultee relationship. Erchul (1987) in his study of eight behavioral consultation dyads concluded that because consultants were more domineering and dominant in their verbalizations than consultees were, the consultant-consultee relationship was viewed as non-equal and hierarchical in nature. Using these same set of dyads and adding two more, Erchul and Chewning (1990) reanalyzed their data and found that (a) consultants made requests six times more frequently than consultees; (b) consultees responded with more accepting or elusive responses than consultants; and (c) consultees' increased requests were negatively related to intervention outcomes in the problem identification interview. They concluded that this was evidence of perhaps a cooperative relationship, but not necessarily a collaborative one. Witt et al. (1991) used the work of Tracey, Heck, and Lichtenberg (1981) and Tracy and Ray (1984) to analyze the verbalizations of eight behavioral consultation dyads, and found that consultants determined topics significantly more frequently than consultees; and that consultants' perceptions of consultees' potential to carry out an intervention plan (i.e., treatment integrity) as intended was negatively related to both total initiation and topic determination by consultees during the problem identification interview. Further, they found that consultant topic determination was positively and significantly correlated with positive perceptions of the consultees' treatment integrity in the treatment evaluation interview. These findings led Witt et al. (1991) to conclude that consultants exerted more control than consultees in the consultative relationship, and that topic determination on the part of the consultant was positively related to intervention outcomes, whereas, the reverse was true for the consultee.

Gutkin (1999) in a thoughtful and influential paper reanalyzed all three of these studies and provided alternative explanations for their findings. First, he concluded that although consultants' attempts to control interactions were significantly more frequent than that of the consultees (referring to Erchul's 1987 study), this was not their primary mode of interaction, and the implicit assumption that dominance is indicative of a non-collaborative interaction style does not hold up under closer scrutiny. Second, there is nothing inherently non-collaborative about consultants making more requests for information than consultees (referring to Erchul & Chewning, 1990), and although there were a few isolated negative correlations between consultee requests for information and consultation outcomes, there was an equal number of statistically significant positive relationships between consultee requests and consultation outcomes. Thirdly, with respect to Witt et al. (1991), Gutkin seriously questioned the appropriateness of the presumption that higher levels of topic determination by consultants versus consultees are evidence of a non-collaborative interaction style. Gutkin suggests that collaboration "… reflects a process of joint/shared decision making between consultants and consultees, with both parties having the opportunity to exert leadership and provide input whenever they believe that would be appropriate" (p. 180). In addition, Gutkin developed a useful heuristic in describing a proposed model of collaborative consultation which views consultation along a directive-nondirective and a coercive-collaborative continuum. Along this continuum, consultation can be collaborative and directive, collaborative and nondirective, coercive and directive, or coercive and nondirective. At this point the research literature supports the use of collaborative-directive and collaborative-nondirective models of consultation (Gutkin, 1999). However, future empirical studies need to be conducted to determine whether there are situations where the other collaborative consultation models may indeed be useful. Erchul (1999) responded to Gutkin's proposed model of collaboration and while commending Gutkin for his significant contribution, indicated that he falls short in terms of finding a definition of this poorly defined construct, and that his model does not include an interpersonal perspective of the consultant/consultee relationship or the role of social influences on consultation outcomes.

While serious limitations are posed when constructs are ill defined, the definitions proposed by Cole and Siegel (1990) and Gutkin (1999) suggest a general conceptualization of what is meant by the term *collaborative* within a problem-solving model of consultation. Nevertheless, consultation researchers need to be precise in their definition and subsequent operationalization of this term and ascertain which specific characteristics of a particular type of collaborative consultant/consultee relationship are conducive to optimal intervention outcomes.

Treatment Acceptability

Assessing the acceptability of consultative interventions has been one way in which researchers have attempted to identify factors that may potentially influence compliance with behavioral or problem-solving strategies (Cross-Calvert & Johnson, 1990; Reimers, Wacker, & Koeppl, 1987; Witt & Elliott, 1985). Although initially interested in establishing the effectiveness of new intervention procedures, researchers have turned their attention toward a formal acknowledgement of the importance of the social validity of intervention or treatment approaches (e.g., Eckert & Hintze, 2000; Finn, 2000; Finn & Sladeczek, 2001; Freer & Watson, 1999; Graham, 1998; Reimers et al., 1987; Sheridan & Steck, 1995). It is no longer sufficient to demonstrate that treatment procedures are effective but they must also be acceptable to the individuals who will implement them (Eckert & Hintze, 2000; Kazdin, 1977; Wolf, 1978).

The term social validity, first coined by Wolf in 1978, has been used to collectively refer to judgments of the social significance of behaviors targeted for change, acceptability of intervention or treatment procedures, and the social importance of consequent behavior changes. Treatment acceptability is one aspect of social validity and is defined as "Judgments by laypersons, clients, and others of whether treatment procedures are appropriate, fair and reasonable for the problem or client" (Kazdin, 1980a, p. 483). The importance of assessing treatment acceptability is multifaceted. First, treatments deemed acceptable by a consultant may be more acceptable to a consumer/consultee than one that is not (Elliott, 1988). Second, assessing the acceptability of several effective interventions may help to identify which intervention is most acceptable for the consultee (Reimers et al., 1987). Third, assessing the acceptability of interventions may also help to discover variables, such as time, side effects, or the difficulty of implementing an intervention, that may affect a consultee's use of a particular intervention (Duggan, 2000; Elliott, 1988; Elliott, Turco, & Gresham, 1987; Elliott, Witt, Galvin, & Peterson, 1984; Frentz & Kelly, 1986; Reimers, Wacker, Cooper, & De Raad, 1992; Steinbach, 2000; Wickstrom, 1996; Witt, Elliott, & Martens, 1984; Witt, Martens, & Elliott, 1984; Witt, Moe, Gutkin, & Andrews, 1984). Fourth, interventions that are reported to be acceptable may be more likely to be implemented than those that are reported to be unacceptable (Elliott, 1988). Finally, providing the most acceptable intervention strategies may result in greater behavior change since the consultee's rating of the appropriateness of the recommended intervention may affect compliance with intervention procedures (Kazdin, 1980a). Consequently, determining the acceptability of several effective interventions could aid in identifying which intervention is most acceptable for a particular type of consultee (e.g., parents and teachers of children with special needs, conduct disorders, cognitive delays).

Several aspects of interventions have been found to influence the perceptions of treatment acceptability: (a) problem severity and type of problem, (b) time requirements, type of treatment, and reported effectiveness, (c) parent and teacher race, income, experience, and knowledge of behavioral or problem-solving principles; and (d) consultant use of psychological jargon and the amount of consultant involvement (Clark & Elliott, 1988; Ehrhard, Barnett, Lentz, & Stollar, 1996; Elliott et al., 1984; Elliott et al., 1987; Frentz & Kelly, 1986; Illsley & Sladeczek, 2001; Kazdin, 1980a, 1980b, 1981; Witt et al., 1984; Witt, Moe, et al., 1984).

Severity of the Problem and Difficulty of the Intervention Plan

Several researchers have suggested that the severity of a problem can influence the acceptability ratings of an intervention plan (Elliott et al., 1984; Elliott et al., 1987; Frentz & Kelly, 1986; Kazdin, 1980a; Martens, Witt, Elliott, & Darveaux, 1985; Von Brock & Elliott, 1987; Witt, Elliott, et al., 1984; Witt, Martens, et al., 1984). Generally, the results of these studies have indicated that the more severe a child's behavior problem, the more acceptable any given treatment will be.

In a two-part experiment, Elliott et al. (1984) examined teacher acceptability of behavioral interventions. In the first part of their study, teachers read one of three case descriptions of an elementary school student whose misbehaviors varied in terms of severity – low (daydreaming), moderate (obscene language), or high (destruction of other's property). Teachers were also asked to rate the acceptability of one of three positive intervention methods whose complexity was low (praise), moderate (home-based reinforcement), or high (token economy). The results suggested that the least complex positive intervention was the most acceptable treatment for the least severe problem behavior. Furthermore, the most complex intervention was rated as the most acceptable procedure for the most severe behavior problem. In the second part of their study, teachers were asked to rate the acceptability of one of three reductive intervention methods that were low (ignoring), moderate (response-cost lottery), or high (seclusion time-out) in complexity. Similarly, results suggested that the least complex reductive intervention was the most acceptable treatment for the least severe behavior problem.

Frentz and Kelly (1986) provide further support for the conclusion that treatment acceptability is affected by the difficulty of the intervention procedure. Eighty-two mothers were asked to rate five reductive treatment procedures (i.e., differential attention, response-cost, time-out, spanking alone, and time-out with spanking) applied to one of two case descriptions of children with behavioral difficulties. Results indicated that response cost was rated significantly more acceptable than the other four methods. Moreover, time-out was found to be significantly more acceptable to mothers than differential attention, spanking with time-out, and spanking alone. Interestingly, mothers also rated all treatments as being more acceptable when applied to severe behavior problems.

Type of Treatment

In general, researchers have found that acceptability ratings for teachers, parents, and children have been consistently higher for positive than for reductive interventions (Elliott et al., 1984; Kazdin, 1980a, 1980b; Kazdin, French & Sherick, 1981; Witt, Elliott, et al., 1984; Witt & Robbins, 1985). Kazdin and his colleagues (Kazdin, 1980a, 1980b; Kazdin et al., 1981) have carried out several studies exploring the influence of intervention type on treatment acceptability ratings. These studies used analogue methodology where evaluations by undergraduate students were used to rate one of several interventions in case descriptions. Overall, the results of these studies indicated that positive interventions were rated as more acceptable than reductive strategies.

Witt, Elliott et al. (1984) assessed 180 student teachers' acceptance of three positive (i.e., praise, home-based reinforcement, token economy) and three negative (i.e., ignoring, response cost, seclusion time-out) interventions. The problem behaviors varied in severity (mild to severe) and the interventions varied by type (positive vs. reductive) and teacher involvement time (low to high). Results revealed that amount of time involvement affected the judgments of intervention acceptability significantly and that positive interventions were evaluated consistently more acceptable than reductive interventions for the same behavioral problems. Specifically, if an intervention could be implemented with little preparation time or relatively quickly it would be perceived to be more acceptable than if it required considerable preparation time or took a long time to implement. Similarly, positive interventions like praise, rewards, token economies and sticker charts are perceived to be more acceptable than time-out and punishments.

Similarly, Miltenberger, Parrish, Rickert, and Kohr (1989) investigated the acceptability of alternative behavioral treatments of 100 parents and grandparents at an outpatient clinic for children with behavior disorders. Raters assessed the acceptability of behavioral interventions that were applied to one of four randomly selected behavior problems (i.e., non-compliance, aggression, tantrums, and hyperactivity). Results indicated that differential reinforcement, response cost, and time-out were rated as significantly more acceptable than spanking for all four behavior problems. For hyperactivity, spanking and medication were rated as significantly less acceptable than the other interventions. Interestingly, these findings differ from the results of previous studies. Previous research (Elliott et al., 1984; Kazdin, 1980a, 1980b; Kazdin, et al., 1981; Witt, Elliott, et al., 1984; Witt & Robbins, 1985) had generally indicated that aversive procedures were less acceptable than positive procedures, while this study showed that parents' ratings of positive and aversive behavior modification procedures were not significantly different.

Time Required to Implement a Treatment

Researchers have documented that the amount of time required to implement an intervention is an important factor influencing the acceptability of treatment procedures (Duggan, 2000; Elliott et al., 1984; Kazdin, 1981; Reimers et al., 1992; Wickstrom, 1996; Witt, Elliott et al., 1984; Witt, Martens et al., 1984). Time is a valuable commodity and this is particularly true for teachers who are frequently responsible for more than 25 children in the classroom. It is therefore not surprising that studies have shown that when evaluating a behavioral intervention teachers are concerned about time (Elliott, 1988; Kazdin, 1982; Witt, Elliott et al., 1984; Witt, Martens et al., 1984).

Witt, Elliott et al. (1984) examined the effects of intervention types, teacher time involvement, and behavior problem severity on ratings of acceptability. One hundred and eighty teachers were presented with written case studies describing a child with a behavior problem and an intervention that was applied to that behavior problem. Results suggested those teachers' ratings of acceptability of interventions varied as a function of the time needed to implement the procedures. In other words, as time involvement increased, acceptability decreased. Furthermore, it was found that time involvement interacted significantly with problem severity and treatment type. Thus, when teachers are confronted with a severe behavior problem they appear to adjust their expectations upward about the length of treatment and consequently the time involved to change the problem behavior.

In a similar study, Witt, Martens et al. (1984) examined the acceptability of several alternative interventions by asking 180 pre-service and student teachers to read a written case description of a child with behavior problems and then rate the interventions on a six-point Likert-type scale (IRP-20). The behavior problems ranged in severity (mild to severe) and the interventions varied by type (positive vs. reductive) and time involvement (low to high). Results indicated that the teachers rated interventions as more acceptable when they required less time to implement and when the treatment approach was positive.

Parents and teachers seek out and need interventions to improve children's behavioral problems and social skills. Over the past 20 years, as researchers and practitioners answer requests for evidence-based interventions, questions and issues have been raised regarding the responsiveness or treatment/intervention acceptability of those who are responsible for the implementation of strategies and techniques. Two decades of research and anecdotal evidence suggest that the degree of treatment acceptability for interventions most likely reflects the consultee's overall appraisal of the intervention in terms of the severity and type of the behavior problem, time requirements, type of treatment, and perceived effectiveness. Until now researchers have focused on investigating one piece of the acceptability puzzle at a time, however, perceptions of treatment acceptability appear to be multifaceted and cannot be reduced to a one-dimensional factor. Thus, future research on treatment acceptability needs to include an evaluation of the strength of association or effect size between diverse variables thought to influence treatment acceptability and to ascertain the possibility of interactions and possible trends of the variables discussed above.

Treatment Integrity

An important consideration in problem-solving consultation research and practice is treatment integrity or the extent to which a recommended intervention is being implemented as intended (Peterson, Homer, & Wonderlich, 1982; Yeaton & Sechrest, 1981). Prominent researchers (e.g., Gresham, 1989; Noell & Witt, 1999) continue to underscore the importance of assuring that the accurate implementation of interventions is one of the most fundamental challenges faced by school psychologists.

During consultation, consultees are often asked to alter their behavior in some fashion to implement an intervention. Assessment of treatment integrity allows researchers and practitioners to make valid conclusions about the functional relationship between the systematic implementation of an intervention by the consultee, and change in the dependent variable (i.e., targeted student behavior). Failure to ensure treatment integrity poses threats to the four main types of experimental validity that allow researchers to draw conclusions from experiments: (a) internal validity, (b) external validity, (c) construct validity, and (d) statistical conclusion validity (Cook & Campbell, 1979).

While most consultants assume that consultees implement interventions as planned as a result of successful consultation sessions, it is possible that consultees modify the intervention in ways unknown to the consultant, thus compromising internal validity. Such "therapist drift" (Peterson et al., 1982), may result in positive, neutral, or negative effects (Gresham, 1989). For instance, an effective, but poorly implemented intervention could be inferred to be ineffective based on changes in the dependent variables. Conversely, an ineffective intervention may be inferred to be effective as a result of modifications to the intervention unknown to the researcher.

In terms of external validity, interventions that are poorly defined, described or implemented make the replication, evaluation and generalization of treatments difficult, if not impossible. To this effect, treatment integrity measures are useful because they require an operational definition of the intervention components and thus can serve as roadmaps for others to follow in their attempts to replicate findings. Construct validity is also influenced by treatment integrity because without precise operational definitions of intervention components, it is difficult to rule out potential confounds that may compromise the interpretation of the causal relationship between the independent and dependent variables.

Currently, effect sizes are a common method of reporting the effectiveness of an intervention. The measurement of treatment integrity can influence the utility of effect size reporting as "…inconsistent application of or deviations in how treatments are implemented can increase the variability in an experiment that can produce lower effect sizes and thus create a threat to the statistical conclusion validity of an intervention study" (Gresham, MacMillan, Beebe-Frankenberger, & Bocian, 2000, p. 202).

Despite the inherent importance of treatment integrity, the specific variables that determine to what degree teachers and parents implement interventions with integrity and how this relates to the magnitude of intervention outcomes remains largely unexplored. A review of the literature spanning the last two decades by Gresham and Cohen (1993) suggested that many researchers have either failed to examine or to report treatment integrity data. Specifically, Gresham and Cohen reviewed 181 experimental school-based behavioral intervention studies published in seven journals from 1980 to 1990 and found that only 14% systematically measured treatment integrity in conjunction with treatment efficacy. A similar review of 65 experimental learning disabilities intervention studies published in three journals from 1995 to 1999 indicated that only 18.5% systematically measured and reported data on treatment integrity, while over 30% of the articles did not address or mention treatment integrity at all (Gresham et al., 2000). Thus, the reporting of treatment integrity has increased slightly, but is still well below what one would expect given the importance of the construct of treatment integrity in ensuring appropriate interpretation of the efficacy of intervention outcomes.

The findings of researchers who have examined treatment integrity in school-based consultation highlight the reality of "therapist drift" in consultation and thus the importance of assessing treatment integrity. In a study by Kratochwill, Elliott, and Busse (1995) only 25% of consultees fully achieved the goals stated during consultation. In addition, researchers have found that lack of treatment integrity has been related to the failure of numerous interventions and that over-reliance on teacher self report has possibly led to the inflation of estimates of the actual rate of intervention implementation (Gresham, 1989; Yeaton & Sechrest, 1981). As one would expect, high treatment integrity was linked with significantly more positive outcomes as compared to interventions with less treatment integrity (Gresham, 1989; Jones, Wickstrom, & Friman, 1997; Noell, Gresham, & Gansle, 2002; Noell, Witt, Gilbertson, Ranier, & Freeland, 1997; Wickstrom, Jones, LaFleur, & Witt, 1998; Witt, Noell, Lafleur, & Mortenson, 1997). Together these findings underscore the importance of measuring treatment integrity as it allows consultants to monitor the implementation of the planned intervention, thus improving the likelihood of positive intervention outcomes.

Factors Related to Treatment Integrity

Gresham (1989) identified several factors that appear to be related to the integrity of intervention implementation. Consultants may be able to influence the likelihood of high treatment integrity by taking the following factors into consideration when developing an intervention: (a) complexity of the intervention, (b) time required to implement the intervention, (c) materials/resources necessary to carry out the intervention, (d) number of consultees needed to implement the intervention, (e) perceived and actual effectiveness of the intervention, and (f) motivation of consultees.

Complexity of the intervention

The level of treatment integrity is directly related to the complexity of the intervention (Yeaton & Sechrest, 1981). For instance, an intervention plan that consists of numerous steps or the simultaneous use of multiple strategies may overwhelm consultees resulting in lower treatment integrity.

Time required to implement the intervention

Time is a highly valued commodity and the most frequent reason given by teachers for not implementing a consultation plan is lack of time. Happe (1982) for example, found that 82% of respondents in his survey reported lack of time as the most frequent reason given for not implementing an intervention.

It is important to note an interaction between the complexity of an intervention and the time required for its implementation–the more complex the intervention, the more time it will require to implement (Noell & Gresham, 1993). For example, the consultant who devises a plan consisting of " . . . token reinforcement, school home notes, frequent monitoring of behavior, and time-out is asking teachers to invest a great deal of time which they probably do not have or are not willing to invest" (Gresham, 1989, p. 39). Such a plan is likely to result in poor treatment integrity, which may compromise its effectiveness in changing behavior (Gresham, 1989).

Materials/resources necessary to carry out the intervention

Interventions that require materials and resources that are not readily available in a classroom or school may be implemented with lower levels of integrity. The reduction of integrity may not be evident until special resources, which are not readily available in schools are withdrawn (Gresham, 1989).

Number of consultees needed to implement the intervention

Interventions that require only one consultee are more likely to be implemented with better integrity than those requiring multiple consultees (Gresham, 1989). For example, if one parent's treatment integrity is high and the other's is low, the average integrity of the program will be different than if only one person had implemented the intervention. Generally, more complex interventions require more consultees or participants in the intervention, in addition to requiring more time, and therefore are more likely to have poor integrity. Conversely, interventions with multiple consultees may increase the strength and generalizability of interventions across multiple settings (Gresham, 1997).

Perceived and actual effectiveness of the intervention

If a teacher perceives the treatment to be effective, he or she is more likely to implement it with a high level of integrity. Similarly, the shorter the amount of time between the onset of intervention and behavior change, the more likely a teacher is to continue implementing the treatment with a high level of integrity. Witt and Elliott (1985) suggest that treatment integrity is a core element connecting the acceptability and the use of an intervention.

Motivation of consultees

The level of motivation of the consultee to invest their efforts in the intervention is another important factor impacting treatment integrity. For example, a teacher who has referred a student for services in the hope that the student will be removed from his or her classroom may be less likely to implement an intervention with a high level of integrity as compared to a teacher wanting the student to remain in his or her classroom. Even a teacher who wants the student to remain in his or her classroom may lack motivation to implement an intervention if he or she has not received adequate training in the theory, practice, and implementation of the intervention.

Treatment Integrity and Consultant Feedback

A recent line of research has indicated that when verbal instructions fail to improve parent or teacher implementation of an intervention, consultant feedback can be an effective strategy to increase treatment integrity (Jones et al.,1997; Mortenson & Witt, 1998; Noell et al., 1997; Noell et al., 2000; Witt et al., 1997). When using consultant feedback as a strategy to improve treatment integrity, consultants observe the consultee interacting with the client and provide constructive comments or feedback in a written or verbal format. This feedback is meant to shape the consultees' use of behavioral strategies with the ultimate goal of the consultee using the strategy with increased proficiency and effectiveness.

Jones et al. (1997) examined the effects of observational feedback on treatment integrity in school-based behavioral consultation. Three teachers participated in this study and treatment integrity was defined as the percentage of two-minute intervals during which a positive consequence was delivered by a teacher contingent on student on-task behavior. The consultant served as the primary observer for each case. Teacher and child behaviors were monitored across three phases – baseline, consultation alone, and consultation with performance feedback – in a multiple baseline design. During the consultation alone phase frequent disruptive behaviors necessitating reprimands were observed and mean levels of treatment integrity for the three teachers ranged from 9% to 37%. The addition of performance feedback increased treatment integrity to levels ranging from 60% to 83%.

In similar studies, Witt et al. (1997) and Noell et al. (1997) examined teacher integrity for a behavioral intervention for students with poor academic performance. Both studies supported the results of Jones et al. (1997), finding that teachers maintained treatment integrity for only a short period time during the consultation only phase, and that treatment integrity improved for all teachers during the daily performance feedback phase. A replication and extension of these studies by Mortenson and Witt (1998) provided further evidence that teacher's treatment integrity declined in the consultation only phase. In addition, the results indicated that teacher treatment integrity increased with weekly, as opposed to daily, performance feedback. The findings in the above studies suggest that treatment integrity in the absence of follow-up sessions is poor and that improvements can be maintained by follow up meetings which are more time efficient than restarting the consultation process.

The findings in a recent study by Noell et al. (2000) support the results of previous studies (Jones et al., 1997; Mortenson & Witt, 1998; Noell et al., 1997; Witt et al., 1997) in that teachers implemented interventions with lower levels of integrity prior to follow up meetings with the consultant. Additionally, the authors suggest that the type and intensity of the feedback necessary to maintain treatment integrity will vary across treatment providers and that holding brief structured meetings allows for individualized responses to specific concerns. Moreover, varying performance feedback procedures (for example, graphic presentation of results, praise for correct implementation, identification of implementation errors) is an effective means of ensuring higher levels of treatment integrity. Noell et al. (2000) suggest that making teachers accountable to administration and parents through feedback sessions may also result in higher treatment integrity.

Measuring Treatment Integrity

Indirect or direct methods can be used to measure treatment integrity. Indirect assessment methods include self-monitoring, self-report, rating scales, and behavioral interviews (Gresham, 1997). Self-monitoring has not received much attention from researchers as it forces the consultee to choose between self-monitoring and implementing the treatment (Gresham, 1997). Self-report, which is frequently used for assessing treatment integrity, requires (a) an operational definition of the intervention components, (b) a framework for rating each component, and (c) the completion of the self-report after implementation. Self-report measures, however, may produce reactive effects resulting in either an over- or under-estimation of the level of treatment integrity. Other options include the use of behavior rating scales or behavioral interviews, the length and complexity of which may make these methods less likely to be sustained during an intervention.

Direct observation is the most commonly used method of measuring treatment integrity. As noted by Gresham (1997), "Direct assessment of treatment integrity is identical to the systematic observation of behavior in applied settings" (p. 111). As such, it is essential to consider factors such as the amount of behavior being observed, the quality of the data, and the reactivity of observations when deciding to use direct observation (see Foster & Cone, 1986). Direct observation requires (a) an operational definition of the intervention, (b) a record of the occurrence or non-occurrence of each intervention component, and (c) calculation of the percentage of components correctly implemented (Gresham, 1997).

The results of a study by Wickstrom et al. (1998) highlight potential advantages and disadvantages of both observation and self-report as methods of assessing treatment integrity. Treatment integrity was examined for 27 teachers participating in behavioral consultation. Mean integrity was 54% based on teacher self-report, and 62% based on teacher use of stimulus products. In contrast, mean integrity was 4% based on direct observations. Nevertheless, multiple indices of child outcomes showed significant reductions in disruptive behavior. Thus, in this study, there was a significant discrepancy between reported and observed use of intervention tools and it was suggested by Wickstrom et al. that low treatment integrity was due, in part, to measurement error, missed observations of a consultee using a prescribed tool, and time of day/activity of the observations.

The first step in measuring treatment integrity, regardless of the method, is defining the intervention and all of its components in specific, behavioral terms. Peterson et al. (1982) coined the phrase "curious double standard" in describing the situation in behavioral research in which both measures of reliability and operational definitions are provided for behaviors when they serve as dependent variables, but are absent when the same behaviors serve as independent variables. Results from a review of school-based behavioral interventions by Gresham and Cohen (1993) support this notion, as only 35% of the studies provided an operational definition of intervention components. Operationally defining an intervention and its components and creating an assessment of treatment integrity does not need to be a daunting task when completed in a step-wise fashion. First, the intervention needs to be defined by specifying (a) who will implement the intervention, (b) where, when and how often the intervention components will take place, (c) the physical and verbal interactions that will occur during the intervention, (d) how long the intervention session will last, and (e) who will receive the intervention. Second, intervention components need to be divided into steps that retain the specific behavioral information included in the intervention definition. Third, each intervention component must be delineated in terms of (a) how implementation will be assessed (e.g., occurrence/nonoccurrence, degree of implementation), (b) how the frequency of implementation will be assessed,

(c) how the duration of implementation will be assessed (e.g., free response, multiple choice time ranges), and (d) how deviations from the original implementation plan will be assessed (e.g., have a check box for consultees to indicate that a deviation occurred and obtain a specific description). The information yielded from these steps can be used to create a treatment integrity assessment. Defining interventions in such a detailed manner will allow for the creation of a more thorough assessment of treatment integrity and allow practitioners and applied researchers to more easily replicate interventions.

Evidence-Based Interventions/Empirically Supported Interventions

Traditionally, behavioral consultation has been associated with a behavioral theoretical orientation or paradigm. Through the use of behavioral principles, inappropriate academic or social behavior is addressed. Most commonly, interventions are constructed by using positive and negative reinforcement, by modifying reinforcing contingencies for behaviors, or by using other operant learning principles. Nevertheless, the consultation framework has been expanding to include other assessment and intervention techniques from a variety of theoretical backgrounds (Kratochwill et al., 2002). This new framework has been renamed "problem-solving" consultation. The conventional five stages of the consultation structure are maintained (initiating a consulting relationship, problem identification, problem analysis, plan implementation, and plan evaluation), but are subsumed under the problem-solving approach.

Typically, within the problem solving process, specific and clearly operationalized problems are targeted for intervention. Once this has been completed, the selection of an intervention is the next logical step (the plan implementation stage of the consultation process). A myriad of possible treatment options or strategies that can be shared and used by a consultee are available. However, the challenge is to choose an intervention from all of the potentially effective strategies that can be implemented by a teacher or parent, the typical consultee. Taking into consideration available resources, the acceptability and the difficulty of the intervention plan, and consultee skills, an appropriate intervention should be chosen. Interventions with empirical support, regardless of theoretical orientation, are one option and can be a strategy that is helpful in plan design and implementation (Erlich & Kratochwill, in press).

History of Evidence-Based Interventions

There are several reasons for the increasing interest in the use of evidence-based interventions. One major influence in the field of psychology has been the evolution of the health care delivery system. Today, practitioners are being held accountable for their effectiveness and need to demonstrate in an empirical fashion the outcomes of their treatments (Hayes, Barlow, & Nelson-Gray, 1999). Furthermore, within the field of psychology, there also continues to be a research-practice gap. Although the field of psychology embraces a scientist-practitioner model, there still remains an apparent low use of research findings by clinicians in the field (Wilson, 1996). Evidence-based interventions are one potential source to facilitate the link between the practitioner and the scientist and bring about the true integration of research and practice.

To meet this need, Division 12 (Clinical Psychology) of the American Psychological Association (APA) formed the Task Force on Promotion and Dissemination of Psychological Procedures (1995). The aim of this Task Force was to review research to identify "empirically validated," what are now called "evidence-based," treatments. The initial 1995 Task Force report listed 25 treatments that met their criteria. Since that time, there has been a great deal of additional research and numerous publications identifying evidence-based treatments. For instance, Ollendick and King (1998) reviewed research on treatments for children with phobic and anxiety disorders, listing those treatments that were "experimental," "probably efficacious," or "well-established" following the Task Force guidelines (see Kaslow and Thompson's article on EST for child and adolescent depression, 1998; *A Guide to Treatments That Work* by Nathan & Gorman, 1998; *Empirically Supported Therapies: Best Practice in Professional Psychology* by Dobson & Craig, 1998; *Treatments That Work With Children: Empirically Supported Strategies for Managing Childhood Problems* by Christophersen & Mortweet, 2001). As of 2001, there were a total of 108 treatments for adults and 37 for children (Chambless & Ollendick, 2001).

For the field of school psychology, the educational reform movement (PL 94-142, The Education for all Handicapped Children Act; PL 101-476, Individuals with Disabilities Education Act, 1997; Goals 2000) and school accountability for students' poor performance have been the primary impetus for the introduction of evidence-based interventions. Kavale and Forness (1999) found through meta-analysis that many of the approaches used in special education do not have empirical support. However, school psychologists, teachers, and administrators are interested in finding interventions that work. Therefore, the APA Division 16 (School Psychology) and the Society for the Study of School Psychology (SSSP) formed a Task Force on Evidence-Based Interventions in School Psychology. Their goal is to identify evidence-based psychological and educational interventions for children with behavioral, emotional, and academic problems (Kratochwill & Stoiber, 2000b). To this end, the Task Force has recently put forth its own *Procedural and Coding Manual for Review of Evidence-Based Interventions* (Kratochwill & Stoiber, 2002a, 2002b). Of course, the ultimate and primary purpose of identifying evidence-based interventions is to give practitioners the procedures necessary to serve the needs of the children and families with whom they work.

Example Program: Parent/Teacher Mediated Intervention

Among all of the interventions that have thus far been identified as empirically supported, few are mediator-based. In fact, traditionally, within the child clinical literature, whether an intervention is mediated or not is usually not taken into account when it is studied. Nevertheless, one example of an intervention that is primarily mediator-based, and has also been shown to be effective, is Webster-Stratton's (2001) series of programs designed to prevent and treat conduct problems in young children. These programs, *The Incredible Years: Parents, Teachers, and Children Training Series*, focus on teaching parents and teachers the skills necessary to effectively deal with children who have, or are at risk for, conduct problems. Parents and/or teachers are taught new skills through the use of videotapes, manuals, and guided sessions by a "leader" who has been trained in the use of the programs.

Several studies have shown the effectiveness of these programs in improving parental attitudes and parent-child interactions, reducing parental use of violent forms of discipline, and in reducing child conduct problems. In one study, Webster-Stratton (1990) compared three groups: an individually administered videotape therapy group, an individually administered videotape therapy with therapist consultation group, and a waiting-list control group. She found that although both groups who used the videotape intervention had fewer child behavior problems, reduced stress levels, and used less spanking, the children in the videotape with consultation group were significantly less deviant than the children in the videotape alone group.

When the program was used with teachers, the results indicate that teachers in the intervention group were significantly less critical and more positive in their discipline approaches, reported making significantly more effort to involve parents in their classrooms, and had a significantly more positive overall classroom atmosphere (Webster-Stratton, Reid, & Hammond, 2001). In addition, their students exhibited significantly fewer behavior problems, non-compliance, and aggression towards peers. Naturally, the school psychologist is someone who can take on the group leadership role and, through the consultation process, help parents and teachers more effectively deal with conduct problems.

Example Program: Systemic Interventions

It should be remembered that the consultation process is also a useful framework for examining and tackling systemic problems found in schools. The collaborative structure offers a way to implement evidence-based interventions not only on the individual level, but also on much broader levels. Using a proactive and systemic approach, behavior support teams can be formed that can develop, implement, and monitor school-wide, specific-setting, classroom, and individual interventions (Carr et al., 2002; Sugai & Horner, 1999). In other words, the consultation process can be used to help address the needs of the consultee, whether the consultee is an individual or an entire school system. The focus and form of intervention may change, but the process remains the same.

Sugai and Horner (1999) propose that to effectively respond to the increase in behavior problems in schools today, there needs to be a shift from traditional discipline approaches to a more integrated, positive, and preventive strategy. Through the use of collaboration and teams, they suggest the development, implementation, evaluation, and maintenance of school-wide discipline efforts at the building level, at the classroom level, at the individual student level, and in specific settings (e.g., hallways). This approach, then, expands the consultation focus to include entire systems. In recognition of the fact that no single teacher or administrator can tackle all educational and behavioral problems alone, behavior support teams are established to carry out change in the above-mentioned systems. These teams can then implement effective interventions in a systematic and integrated manner. This team approach, then, is in line with the problem-solving consultation framework and allows the consultant to take full advantage of the evidence-based strategies available and effectively implement them in a school system.

Empirical Practice

Consultation, as the *sine qua non* of school psychology, has become extremely prominent in the practice of school psychology (Kratochwill & Stoiber, 2000b). The consultation framework, with its built in treatment monitoring and evaluation stages, allows psychologists to evaluate their services empirically. Even for those who have concerns that the evidence-based treatments will not fit their particular client or unique situation and needs, the consultation problem-solving framework provides a way for the evidence-based intervention to be evaluated. One such protocol, *Outcomes: Planning, Monitoring, Evaluating* (*Outcomes: PME*) facilitates this process by providing a means to select, design, implement, and evaluate intervention outcomes (Stoiber & Kratochwill, 2002). In the end, it will be necessary for practitioners to document the usefulness of the evidence-based treatments that are identified through the various task forces. At this time, evidence-based interventions are one source of treatment options available to the consultant and consultee who are endeavoring to help a child succeed academically and socially in school.

Future Challenges for Researchers and Practitioners

The school psychology delivery model developed by Cole and Siegel in 1990, and refined in 2002, presents a framework from which to view the issues that we have identified as being central to a problem-solving model of consultation. In this vein we underscored the importance and extreme complexity of defining and operationalizing key components of problem-solving consultation. These key components included: (a) the presumed collaborative nature of the consultant-consultee relationship; (b) the importance of assessing the acceptability of interventions and the factors that may influence acceptability in either a positive or negative fashion, and how acceptability relates to intervention outcomes; (c) the necessity of measuring treatment integrity as a vital component in assessing the validity of intervention outcomes; and (d) the increased interest in the use of evidence-based interventions. However, the model developed by Cole and Siegel (1990) encompasses other considerations that are seen as integral to the continuing practice of school psychology in the new millennium.

Kratochwill and Stoiber (2000b) present a thought-provoking analysis of critical research agendas that they believe will provide continued momentum for the field of school psychology, and, importantly, enhance intervention outcomes for children and adolescents, their families, and teachers. Although it is beyond the scope of this paper to discuss in detail the domains (diagnosis/classification and assessment, consultation, prevention and intervention, program evaluation and research) discussed in their article, several of their points are particularly relevant to our discussion. First, the standardization of consultation processes and practices is seen as a vital task within the consultation field. To this end, existing consultation interview and intervention manuals or other media used to convey the process and procedures to be used during the consultation process need to be standardized. This would allow practitioners and researchers to adhere to set procedures and intervention integrity could be assessed more readily. Furthermore, it would permit researchers to determine which components of the consultation process are absolutely critical for clinically significant intervention outcomes (Kratochwill & Stoiber, 2000b) and thereby foster a closer link between research and actual practice. Second, the importance of examining intervention outcomes using a versatile perspective enhances our ability to interpret intervention outcomes. For example, multiple means of examining client behavior should be used (e.g., direct observation by teachers and parents, observations by independent observers, behavior rating scales) as well as evaluation of client and consultee outcomes. Third, the authors suggest that researchers use a hybrid model of quantitative and qualitative research methodologies to better understand the process and outcomes of problem-solving consultation. Fourth, since problem-solving consultation is ideally suited for prevention *and* intervention, policy-makers in the U.S., Canada, and elsewhere are strongly urged to consider the reallocation of resources to support the amalgamation of research and practice. Thus, problem-solving consultation offers a promising and rich scaffold that can change how we conceptualize and conduct future research.

References

Alpert, J. L., & Yammer, M. D. (1983). Research in school consultation: A content analysis of selected journals. *Professional Psychology – Research & Practice, 14,* 604-612.

Axford, M. B. (1977). The elementary school counsellor – Consultant and the family. *School Guidance Worker, 33,* 36-42.

Bergan, J. R. (1977). *Behavioral consultation.* Columbus, OH: Charles Merrill.

Bergan, J. R. (1995). Evolution of a problem-solving model of consultation. *Journal of Educational & Psychological Consultation, 6,* 111-123.

Bergan, J. R., & Kratochwill, T. R. (1990). *Behavioral consultation and therapy.* New York: Plenum.

Bergan, J. R., Sladeczek, I. E., Schwarz, R. D., & Smith, A. N. (1991). Effects of a measurement and planning system on kindergartners' cognitive development and educational programming. *American Educational Research Journal, 28,* 683-714.

Caplan, G. (1963). Types of mental health consultations. *American Journal of Orthopsychiatry, 33,* 470-481.

Carney, P. J. (1996). A practitioner's view of challenges and issues for school psychologists in the 21st century. *Canadian Journal of School Psychology, 12,* 98-102.

Carr, E. G., Dunlap, G., Horner, R. H., Koegel, R. L., Turnbull, A. P., Sailor, W., Anderson, J. L., Albin, R. W., Koegel, L. K., & Fox, L. (2002). Positive behavior support: Evolution of an applied science. *Journal of Positive Behavior Interventions, 4,* 4-16, 20.

Chambless, D. L., & Ollendick, T. H. (2001). Empirically supported psychological interventions: Controversies and evidence. *Annual Review of Psychology, 52,* 685-716.

Christophersen, E. R., & Mortweet, S. L. (2001). *Treatments that work with children : Empirically supported strategies for managing child problems.* Washington, DC : American Psychological Association.

Clark, L., & Elliott, S. N. (1988). The influence of treatment strength information on knowledgeable teachers' pretreatment evaluation of social skills training methods. *Professional School Psychology, 3,* 253-269.

Cole, E., & Siegel, J. A. (1990). *Effective consultation in school psychology.* Toronto: ON: Hogrefe & Huber Publishers.

Cook, T., & Campbell, D. (Eds.). (1979). *Quasi-experimentation: Design analysis issues for field settings.* Chicago: Rand McNally.

Cross-Calvert, S., & Johnston, C. (1990). Acceptability of treatments for child behavior problems: Issues and implications for future research. *Journal of Clinical Child Psychology, 19,* 61-74.

Dobson, K. S., & Craig, K. D. (Eds.). (1998). *Empirically supported therapies: Best practice in professional psychology.* Thousand Oaks, CA: SAGE Publications.

Duggan, V. (2000). *Parent's and teacher's acceptability of conjoint behavioral consultation.* Unpublished Masters Thesis.

Eckert, T. L., & Hintze, J. M. (2000). Behavioral conceptions and applications of acceptability: Issues related to service delivery and research methodology. *School Psychology Quarterly, 15,* 123-148.

Ehrhard, K. E., Barnett, D. W., Lentz, F. E. Jr., & Stollar, S. A. (1996). Innovative methodology in ecological consultation: Use of scripts to promote treatment acceptability and integrity. *School Psychology Quarterly, 11,* 149-168.

Elliott, S. N. (1988). Acceptability of behavioral treatments: Review of variables that influence treatment selection. *Professional Psychology: Research and Practice, 19,* 68-80.

Elliott, S. N., Turco, T., & Gresham, F. (1987). Consumers' and clients' pretreatment acceptability ratings of classroom group contingencies. *Journal of School Psychology, 25,* 145-153.

Elliott, S. N., Witt, J. C., Galvin, G., & Peterson, R. (1984). Acceptability of positive and reductive interventions: Factors that influence teachers' decisions. *Journal of School Psychology, 22,* 353-360.

Erchul, W. P. (1987). A relational communication analysis of control in school consultation. *Professional School Psychology, 2,* 113-124.

Erchul, W. P. (1999). Two steps forward, one step back: Collaboration in school-based consultation. *Journal of School Psychology, 37,* 191-203.

Erchul, W. P., & Chewning, T. G. (1990). Behavioral consultation from a request-centered relational communication perspective. *School Psychology Quarterly, 5,* 1-20.

Erlich, M. E., & Kratochwill, T. R. (in press). Behavioral consultation and therapy. In M. Hersen & W. Sledge (Eds.), *Encyclopedia of psychotherapy.* New York, NY: Academic Press.

Finn, C. A. (2000). *Remediating behavior problems of young children: The impact of parent, treatment acceptability, and the efficacy of conjoint behavioral therapy and videotape therapy.* Unpublished doctoral dissertation.

Finn, C. A., & Sladeczek, I. E. (2001). Assessing the social validity of behavioral interventions: A review of treatment acceptability measures. *School Psychology Quarterly, 16,* 176-206.

Foster, S., & Cone, J. (1986). Design and use of direct observation. In A. Ciminero, K. Calhoun, & H. Adams (Eds.), *Handbook of behavioral assessment* (2nd ed., pp. 253-324). New York: Wiley Interscience.

Freer, P., & Watson, T. S. (1999). A comparison of parent and teacher acceptability ratings of behavioral and conjoint behavioral consultation. *School Psychology Review, 28,* 672-684.

Frentz, C., & Kelley, M. L. (1986). Parents' acceptance of productive treatment methods: The influence of problem severity and perceptions of child behavior. *Behavior Therapy, 17,* 75-81.

Galloway, J., & Sheridan, S. M. (1994). Implementing scientific practices through case studies: Examples using home-school interventions and consultation. *Journal of School Psychology, 32,* 385-413.

Gibson, G., & Chard, K. M. (1994). Quantifying the effects of community mental health consultation interventions. *Consulting Psychology Journal: Practice & Research, 46,* 13-25.

Goals 2000: Educate America Act of 1993, Pub. L. No. 103-227.

Graham, D. S. (1998). Consultant effectiveness and treatment acceptability: An examination of consultee requests and consultant responses. *School Psychology Quarterly, 13,* 155-168.

Gresham, F. M. (1989). Assessment of treatment integrity in school consultation and prereferral intervention. *School Psychology Review, 18,* 37-50.

Gresham, F. M. (1997). Treatment integrity in single-subject research. In R. D. Franklin, D. B. Allison & B. S. Gorman (Eds.), *Design and analysis of single-case research.* Mahwah, NJ: Lawrence Erlbaum Associates.

Gresham, F. M., & Cohen, S. (1993). Treatment integrity of school-based behavioral intervention studies: 1980-1990. *School Psychology Review, 22(2),* 254-272.

Gresham, F. M., MacMillan, D. L., Beebe-Frankenberger, M. E., & Bocian, K. M. (2000). Treatment integrity in learning disabilities intervention research: Do we really know how treatments are implemented? *Learning Disabilities Research & Practice, 15,* 198-205.

Gutkin, T. B. (1999). Collaborative versus directive/prescriptive/expert school-based consultation: Reviewing and resolving a false dichotomy. *Journal of School Psychology, 37,* 161-190.

Gutkin, T. B., & Curtis, M. J. (1990). School-based consultation: Theory, techniques, and research. In T. B. Gutkin & C. R. Reynolds (Eds.), *The handbook of school psychology (2nd ed.)*, pp. 577-611. New York: Wiley.

Happe, D. (1982). Behavioral intervention: It doesn't do any good in your briefcase. In J. Grimes (Ed.), *Psychological approaches to problems of children and adolescents* (pp. 15-41). Des Moines: Iowa Department of Public Instruction.

Hayes, S. C., Barlow, D. H., & Nelson-Gray, R. O. (1999). *The scientist-practitioner: Research and accountability in the age of managed care* (2nd ed.). Boston: Allyn and Bacon.

Illsley, S. D., & Sladeczek, I. (2001). Conjoint behavioral consultation: Outcome measures beyond the client level. *Journal of Educational and Psychological Consultation, 12*, 397-404.

Individuals with Disabilities Education Act of 1997, Pub. L. No. 94-142, 20 U.S.C. Ch.33, Sec. 1400.

Janzen, H. L., Paterson, J. G., & Paterson, D. W. (1993). The future of psychology in the schools. *Canadian Journal of School Psychology, 9*, 174-180.

Johnson, T. L., & Tilly, W. D. (1993, March). *Using conjoint consultation to enhance the effects of parent training for children with ADHD*. Poster session presented for the 25th Annual Meeting of the National Association of School Psychologists, Washington, DC.

Jones, K. M., Wickstrom, K. F., & Friman, P. C. (1997). The effects of observational feedback on treatment integrity in school-based behavioral consultation. *School Psychology Quarterly, 12*, 316-326.

Kaslow, N. J., & Thompson, M. P. (1998). Applying the criteria for empirically supported treatments to studies of psychosocial interventions for child and adolescent depression. *Journal of Clinical Child Psychology, 27*, 146-155.

Kavale, K., & Forness, S. (1999). Effectiveness of special education. In C. Reynolds & T. Gutkin (Eds.), *The handbook of school psychology* (3rd ed.). New York: Wiley.

Kazdin, A. E. (1977). Assessing the clinical or applied importance of behavior change through social validation. *Behavior Modification, 1*, 427-452.

Kazdin, A. E. (1980a). Acceptability of alternative treatments for deviant child behavior. *Journal of Applied Behavior Analysis, 13*, 259-273.

Kazdin, A. E. (1980b). Acceptability of time-out from reinforcement procedures for disruptive child behavior. *Behavior Therapy, 11*, 329-344.

Kazdin, A. E. (1981). Acceptability of child treatment techniques: The influence of treatment efficacy and adverse side effects. *Behavior Therapy, 12*, 493-506

Kazdin, A. E., French, N. H., & Sherick, R. B. (1981). Acceptability of alternative treatments for children: Evaluations by inpatient children, parent, and staff. *Journal of Consulting and Clinical Psychology, 49*, 900-907.

Kratochwill, T. R., Elliott, S. N., & Busse. R. T. (1995). Behavior consultation: A five-year evaluation of consultant and client outcomes. *School Psychology Quarterly, 10*, 87-117.

Kratochwill, T. R., Elliott, S. N., & Callan-Stoiber, K. C. (2002). Best practices in school-based problem-solving consultation. In A. Thomas & J. Grimes (Eds.), *Best practices in school psychology IV* (pp. 583- 608). Bethesda, MD: NASP.

Kratochwill, T. R., & Stoiber, K. C. (2000a). Empirically supported interventions and school psychology: Conceptual and practical issues: Part II. *School Psychology Quarterly, 15*, 233-253.

Kratochwill, T. R., & Stoiber, K. C. (2000b). Uncovering critical research agendas for school psychology: Conceptual dimensions and future directions. *School Psychology Review, 29*, 591-603.

Kratochwill, T. R., & Stoiber, K. C. (2002a). *Evidence-based interventions in school psychology: Conceptual foundations of the procedural and coding manual of division 16 and the society for the study of school psychology task force.*

Kratochwill, T. R., & Stoiber, K. C. (2002b). *Procedural and coding manual for review of evidence-based interventions.*

Mannino, F. V., & Shore, M. F. (1975). Accountability in a family oriented rehabilitation program. *Family Coordinator, 24,* 315-319.

Martens, B. K., Witt, J. C., Elliott, S. N., & Darveaux, D. (1985). Teacher judgments concerning the acceptability of school-based interventions. *Professional Psychology: Research and Practice, 16,* 191-198.

Medway, F. J. (1979). How effective is school consultation?: A review of recent research. *Journal of School Psychology, 17,* 275-282.

Medway, F. J. (1982). School consultation research: Past trends and future directions. *Professional Psychology – Research & Practice, 13,* 422-430.

Medway, F. J., & Updyke, J. F. (1985). Meta-analysis of consultation outcome studies. *American Journal of Community Psychology, 13,* 489-505.

Merchant, D. F. (1976). Creating stronger swimmers: The counsellor-consultant in the elementary school. *School Guidance Worker, 31,* 22-26.

Miltenberger, R. G., Parrish, J., Rickert, V., & Kohr, M. (1989). Assessing treatment acceptability with consumers of outpatient child behavior management services. *Child and Family Behavior Therapy, 11,* 35-44.

Mortenson, B. P., & Witt, J. C. (1998). The use of weekly performance feedback to increase teacher implementation of a prereferral academic intervention. *School Psychology Review, 27,* 613-627.

Nathan, P. E., & Gorman, J. M. (1998). *A guide to treatments that work.* New York, NY: Oxford University Press.

Noell, G. H., & Gresham, F. M. (1993). Functional outcome analysis: Do the benefits of consultation and prereferral intervention justify the costs? *School Psychology Quarterly, 8,* 200-226.

Noell, G. H., Gresham, F. M., & Gansle, K. A. (2002). Does treatment integrity matter? A preliminary investigation of instructional implementation and mathematics performance. *Journal of Behavioral Education, 11,* 51-67.

Noell, G. H., & Witt, J. E. (1996). A critical evaluation of five fundamental assumptions underlying behavioral consultation. *School Psychology Quarterly, 11,* 189-203.

Noell, G. H., & Witt, J. E. (1999). When does consultation lead to intervention implementation? Critical issues for research and practice. *Journal of Special Education, 33,* 29-35.

Noell, G. H., Witt, J. E., Gilbertson, D. N., Ranier, D. D., & Freeland, J. T. (1997). Increasing teacher intervention implementation in general education settings through consultation and performance feedback. *School Psychology Quarterly, 12,* 77-88.

Noell, G. H., Witt, J. E., LaFleur, L. H., Mortenson, B. P., Ranier, D.D., & LaVelle, J. (2000). A comparison of two follow-up strategies to increase teacher intervention implementation in general education following consultation. *Journal of Applied Behavior Analysis, 33,* 271-284.

Ollendick, T. H., & King, N. J. (1998). Empirically supported treatments for children with phobic and anxiety disorders: Current status. *Journal of Clinical Child Psychology, 27,* 190-205.

Peterson, L., Homer, A., & Wonderlich, S. (1982). The integrity of independent variables in behavior analysis. *Journal of Applied Behavior Analysis, 15,* 477-492.

Reimers, T. M., Wacker, D. P., Cooper, L. J., & DeRaad, A. O. (1992). Acceptability of behavioral treatments for children: Analog and naturalistic evaluations by parents. *School Psychology Review, 21,* 628-643.

Reimers, T. M., Wacker, D. P., & Koeppl, G. (1987). Acceptability of behavioral interventions: A review of the literature. *School Psychology Review, 16,* 215-227.

Sheridan, S. M., & Colton, D. L. (1994). Conjoint behavioral consultation: A review case study. *Journal of Educational and Psychological Consultation, 5,* 211-228.

Sheridan, S. M., Kratochwill, T. R., & Bergan, J. R. (1996). *Conjoint behavioral consultation: A procedural manual.* New York, NY: Plenum Press.

Sheridan, S. M., Kratochwill, T. R., & Elliott, S. N. (1990). Behavioral consultation with parents and teachers: Delivery treatment for socially withdrawn children at home and school. *School Psychology Review, 19,* 33-52.

Sheridan, S. M., & Steck, M. C. (1995). Acceptability of conjoint behavioral consultation: A national survey of school psychologists. *School Psychology Review, 24,* 633-647.

Sladeczek, I. E. (1996). Aggressive and territorial behaviors: The case of Ken. In S. M. Sheridan, T. R. Kratochwill, & J. R. Bergen (Eds.), *Conjoint behavioral consultation: A procedural manual* (pp. 138-147). New York: Plenum.

Sladeczek, I. E., & Heath, N. L. (1997). Consultation in Canada. *Canadian Journal of School Psychology, 13,* 1-14.

Steinbach, L. (2000) *Parent and teacher treatment integrity and conjoint behavioral consultation.* Unpublished Masters Thesis.

Stoiber, K. C., & Kratochwill, T. R. (2002). *Outcomes: Planning, monitoring, evaluating.* San Antonio, TX: The Psychological Corporation.

Sugai, G., & Horner, R. (1999). Discipline and behavioral support: Practices, pitfalls, and promises. *Effective School Practices, 17(4),* 10-22.

Task Force on Promotion and Dissemination of Psychological Procedures. (1995). Training in and dissemination of empirically-validated psychological treatments: Report and recommendations. *The Clinical Psychologist, 48,* 3-23.

Tracey, T. J., & Ray, P. B. (1984). Stages of successful time-limited counseling: An interactional examination. *Journal of Counseling Psychology, 31,* 13-27.

Tracey, T. J., Heck, E. J., & Lichtenberg, J. W. (1981). Role expectations and symmetrical/complementary therapeutic relationships. *Psychotherapy: Theory, Research & Practice, 18,* 338-344.

Von Brock, M. B., & Elliott, S. N. (1987). The influence of treatment effectiveness information on the acceptability of classroom interventions. *Journal of School Psychology, 25,* 131-144.

Walker, H. M., & Shinn, M. R. (2002). Structuring school-based interventions to achieve integrated primary, secondary, and tertiary prevention goals for safe and effective schools. In M. R. Shinn, H. M. Walker, & G. Stoner (Eds.), *Interventions for academic and behavior problems II: Preventive and remedial approaches.* Bethesda, MD: National Association of School Psychologists.

Webster-Stratton, C. (1990). Enhancing the effectiveness of self-administered videotape parent training for families with conduct-problem children. *Journal of Abnormal Child Psychology, 18,* 479-492.

Webster-Stratton, C. (2001). The incredible years: Parents, teachers, and children training series. In S. I. Pfeiffer & L. A. Reddy (Eds.), *Innovative mental health interventions for children: Programs that work* (pp. 31-45). Haworth Press.

Webster-Stratton, C., Reid, M.J., & Hammond, M. (2001). Preventing conduct problems, promoting social competence: A parent and teacher training partnership in Head Start. *Journal of Clinical Child Psychology, 30,* 283-302.

Wickstrom, K. F. (1996). *A study of the relationship among teacher, process, and outcome variables within school-based consultation.* Unpublished doctoral dissertation.

Wickstrom, K. F., Jones, K. M., LaFleur, L. H., & Witt, J. C. (1998). An analysis of treatment integrity in school-based behavioral consultation. *School Psychology Quarterly, 13,* 141-154.

Wilson, G.T. (1996). Empirically validated treatments: Reality and resistance. *Clinical Psychology: Science and Practice, 3,* 241-244.

Witt, J. C. (1990). Face-to-face verbal interaction in school-based consultation: A review of the literature. *School Psychology Quarterly, 5,* 199-210.

Witt, J. C., & Elliott, S. N. (1985). Acceptability of classroom management strategies. In T. R. Kratochwill (Ed.), *Advances in school psychology* (pp. 251-288). Hillsdale, NJ: Erlbaum.

Witt, J. C., Elliott, S. N., & Martens, B. K. (1984). Acceptability of behavioral interventions used in classrooms: The influence of amount of teacher time, severity of behavior problem, and type of intervention. *Behavioral Disorders, 9,* 95-104.

Witt, J. C, Erchul, W. P, McKee, W. T, Pardue, M. M., & Wickstrom, K. F. (1991). Conversational control in school-based consultation: The relationship between consultant and consultee topic determination and consultation outcome. *Journal of Educational & Psychological Consultation, 2,* 101-116.

Witt, J. C., Martens, B. K., & Elliott, S. N. (1984). Factors affecting teachers' judgments of the acceptability of behavioral interventions: Time involvement, behavior problem severity, and type of intervention. *Behavior Therapy, 15,* 204-209.

Witt, J. C., Moe, G., Gutkin, T. B., & Andrews, L. (1984). The effect of saying the same thing in different ways: The problem of language and jargon in school-based consultation. *Journal of School Psychology, 22,* 361-367.

Witt, J. C., Noell, G. H, LaFleur, L.H., & Mortenson, B. P. (1997). Teacher usage of interventions in general education: Measurement and analysis of the independent variable. *Journal of Applied Behavior Analysis, 30,* 693-696.

Witt, J. C., & Robbins, J. R. (1985). Acceptability of reductive interventions for the control of inappropriate child behavior. *Journal of Abnormal Child Psychology, 13* 59-67.

Wolf, M. M. (1978). Social validity: The case for subjective measurement or how applied behavior analysis is finding its heart. *Journal of Applied Behavior Analysis, 11,* 203-214.

Yeaton, W. H., & Sechrest, I. (1981). Critical dimensions in the choice and maintenance of successful treatment: Strength, integrity and effectiveness. *Journal of Consulting and Clinical Psychology, 49,* 156-167.

Chapter 5
What Does it Mean to Consult?

Teeya Scholten

School psychological services have begun to shift from a traditional, reactive mode to primary prevention programs. When proactive support services are developed to deal with issues and problems facing students and their teachers, the word "consultation" is often used. What does this term mean to practitioners in school psychology? What skills do they use in consultation? What skills are needed for fostering a consultation problem-solving approach?

This chapter describes a recent research study that explores ways in which the term is understood and applied by experienced practitioners. It will be shown that despite an agreement on a global definition of consultation, there is a lack of consensus on which aspects of psychological services one would consider consultative. Some differences in opinion seem, however, to cluster into four specific orientations identified with by individual practitioners. These role orientations seem to influence not only individuals' practices, but how they defined the term "consultation" and perceived its function within the referral process. A number of factors were identified by practitioners as facilitating or impeding the practice of consultation within the school system. These will be reviewed along with some ideas on ways to assess one's effectiveness as a consultant. Finally, implications of this research for enhancing the role of consultation in psychological service delivery will be discussed.

Background

It was Gerald Caplan (1970) who first introduced the concept of psychological consultation as a cost-effective form of psychological service delivery. His focus was on the primary prevention of emotional and learning problems, through early identification and intervention through consultative services to front-line staff who were directly involved with clients. He felt that a mental health professional could impact in an indirect way on a much broader basis than would be possible using direct service delivery models (e.g., individual or group psychotherapy).

Over the last thirty years, consultation has become an increasingly popular form of service delivery (Caplan & Caplan, 1993) and much headway has been made in our understanding of how it can be applied within the school setting (Conoley & Conoley, 1992; Dettmer, Dyck, & Thurston, 1996). Stages of the consultative process have been defined, specific skills identified that are needed in a consultant (Idol & West, 1987; Parsons, 1996; West & Cannon, 1988) and suggested methods proposed for assessing one's effectiveness (Noell & Witt, 1999; Sheridan, Welch, & Orme, 1996). The major models that have been developed can generally be divided into those that differ in terms of the type of problem *focus* (mental health, behavioral or organizational development), *the level of intervention* (individual child, classroom, or system) and the *approach* taken by the consultant (expert or collaborative).

However, much of this research on consultation has been model-specific, primarily behavioral in focus and carried out in highly controlled settings (Fuchs & Fuchs, 1989; Kratochwill, Elliott, & Rotto, 1995). What, specifically, is meant by "consultation" is not always clearly delineated. All of these factors lead to questions about the generalizability of the findings to day-to-day practice. In fact, it has long been known that a consultant may use a number of different models of consultation, depending on the referral problem, preference of the teacher, and the state of service delivery (Babcock & Pryzwansky, 1983). Despite all the research in this area, there still remains a need, as expressed by Medway (1982), for field research with experienced consultants. We need to find out how consultation is actually being practiced, what practitioners mean when they say they are "consulting" and ultimately, how to facilitate this process as an effective means of service delivery.

This chapter describes qualitative field research with experienced school psychological practitioners that explored ways in which the term "consultation" was understood and applied (Scholten, 1987). It will be shown that despite an agreement on a global definition of consultation, there was a lack of consensus on which aspects of psychological services one would consider consultative. These differences in opinion seemed, however, to cluster into four specific orientations to the role of school psychologist. There were distinct differences in how individuals with these role orientations viewed consultative activities within the framework of the referral process. A number of factors were also identified by practitioners as facilitative or not to the process of consultation within the school system. These will be reviewed along with some ideas on several ways to assess one's effectiveness as a consultant. Finally, the implications of this research for enhancing the role of consultation in psychological service delivery will be discussed.

The Study

Methodology

The study described here was designed to address some of the concerns discussed above. Twenty practitioners from a large metropolitan school board were interviewed following a semi-structured interview format. These were experienced psychologists who had been with their present board for approximately 15 years. See Appendix A for a summary of their demographic characteristics.

The interview questions were designed to elicit information on individual practices of consultation. Participants were asked specifically about their definition of consultation, how they practiced it, and factors that their experience had led them to believe influenced the process either favorably or adversely. While following the principles of qualitative research, particular use was made of ethnographic techniques. This involved the asking of descriptive, structural, and contrast questions (as outlined by Spradley, 1979), and comparing the responses given by successive participants. This method is predicated upon the belief that ten semantic relationships (see Appendix B) form the basis for the organization of much of our knowledge and are therefore very useful in the study of cultures or practices of groups of people (in this case, school psychological consultants). These semantic relationships formed the lens through which consultation was explored in this study. Thus, particular note was made if participants used words such as "kinds of," "places in," "causes of," "results of," "reasons for," "places for," "used as," "a way to," "a step in," or "a characteristic of."

In this way, by the time the first few participants had been interviewed, a large amount of descriptive data had been obtained in terms of areas of knowledge about school psychological consultation. Once this information had been collected it was possible to see which categories were saturated with information and which needed to be explored further. A number of analyses – domain, taxonomic, and componential (Spradley, 1979) – were performed.

Selection of Participants

The school board chosen for the study was selected on the basis of a pilot project, which had identified it as one of several school boards within southwestern Ontario in which the Chief Psychologist stated that his/her staff practiced consultation at least 10% of their time. Selection of the actual subjects was done by asking successive participants to nominate one or more of their colleagues who held a very different view from their own. Thus, subject selection was done in a purposeful way, designed to maximize variability in practice within a single school board setting.

Findings: The Meaning of Consultation

The composite definition of consultation that was generated by participants was that it involved "an exchange of information which is used for problem-solving purposes, in which the consultant may be asked to give an opinion, answer questions, solve problems or sometimes just listen" (Scholten, 1987, p. 45). However, during the process of reflecting not only upon what consultation meant to them, but which of their activities as psychological service providers (testing, report writing, crisis intervention, counseling, liaison work, committee work, in-service provision, research, supervision, and attending meetings) they would consider consultative, there was a wide discrepancy of opinion. Some practitioners felt that all these activities could be considered consultative, while others were more selective. Initially, no pattern of choice could be identified. In addition, the way in which consultation was practiced seemed to differ considerably from practitioner to practitioner.

As the participants were interviewed further and their reflections on consultation were compared, four different orientations to the role of psychological service provider were identified. These were labeled by the author as the Psychometrician, the Diagnostician, the Assessor, and the Problem-solver. Figures 1 to 4 represent a schematization of the referral process according to each of these four "role-orientations," while Table 1 summarizes their respective opinions of the various functions of consultation.

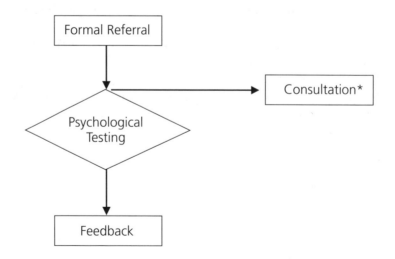

*only if child too young to test

Figure 1 The Function of Consultation Within the Referral Process: The Psychometrician's View

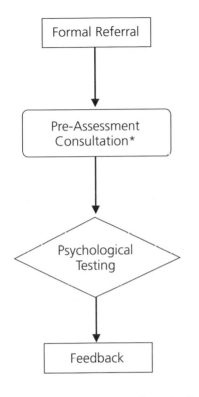

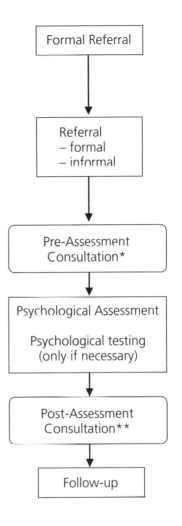

Figure 2 The Function of Consultation
Within the Referral Process:
The Diagnostician's View

*To brainstorm ways to solve problems without
having to do a psychological assessment.

** To give feedback on results of assessment
and to generate intervention strategies.

Figure 3 The Function of Consultation
Within the Referral Process:
The Assessor's View

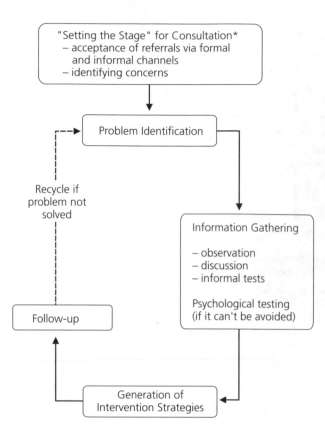

* All stages of the referral processes are viewed as CONSULTATIONS carried out for a variety of purposes within the problem solving process (i.e., problem identification, information gathering, generation of intervention strategies, follow-up).

Figure 4 The Function of Consultation Within the Referral Process: The Problem-Solver's View

An examination of the figures suggests that the Psychometricians and Diagnosticians viewed consultation as a part of the assessment process, whereas for Assessors and Problem-solvers it was the opposite: consultation was the main process in which assessment played a part. One can view these four role orientations as points along a continuum of time spent in consultation, with the Psychometrician spending the least and the Problem-solver the most.

Most of the practitioners interviewed seemed to fall within or around the Assessor category on this continuum: some seemed to be strongly identified as Assessors, while others had practices most similar to the Diagnostician, but were beginning to practice as more of an Assessor. There were also those who were most similar to the Assessor

Table 1 Functions of Consultation Within the Referral Process As Seen by Practitioners with Different Role-Orientations

Role-Orientation	Function of Consultation
Psychometrician	discussion with teacher only if child too young to test
Diagnostician	meeting held as a screening device to determine if psychological testing is appropriate
Assessor	meeting to brainstorm ways to solve problems without having to do a psychological assessment
	meeting to give feedback on results of assessment and to generate intervention strategies
Problem-solver	all activities with the problem solving process are viewed as consultation carried out for a variety of purposes (i.e., problem identification, info-gathering, generation of intervention strategies, and follow-up)

but who had a few practice preferences similar to those espoused by the Problem-solvers. Each of these four approaches will now be discussed in greater detail.

The Psychometrician

At one end of the continuum of consultation, there seemed to be some school psychologists whose practices consisted primarily of psychological assessments. These professionals tended to be trained in the area of psychometrics, and saw their role and seemed to judge their effectiveness in terms of their ability to provide information through the generation of psychological data (see Figure 1). Typically, this information was used by school personnel in making decisions regarding the educational needs of exceptional students within the school system, often decisions relating to whether or not a student should be placed into a particular special education class.

These practitioners reported that consultation played little or no part in their work, except where testing was felt to be inappropriate. In this case, the Psychometrician might observe a child in the classroom and then meet with parents or a teacher to discuss concerns. The following quotation describes one Psychometrician's view of the consultation process:

"Well, for example, we will have a kindergarten teacher who'd say, 'I have a kid who's aggressive. Would you come in and spend some time with him?,' which I would do. Then we usually have some suggestions to them, you know, 'Praise the child when he's not acting up.' I think this is one of our main functions in the consultation process because we don't then step in and give a whole lot of tests."

The Diagnostician

At the second point along the consultation continuum is the Diagnostician, whose perceptions of the process of psychological service delivery are illustrated in Figure 2. As with the Psychometrician, the orientation of these individuals still appears primarily to be toward the carrying out of psychological assessments. However, consultation, as they conceptualized it, did have its place before the assessment. The purpose of the pre-assessment consultation, which usually took place during school team meetings, was a type of screening device to ensure that psychological staff were involved only with cases in which an assessment was judged to be absolutely necessary. In the words of a Diagnostician:

"We'll have, say a pre-assessment conference. And we're all saying, 'Now the kid doesn't need to be tested,' or 'Let's try to modify the program first,' or 'That kid should get an assessment from the multicultural people.' So we have those (consultation) meetings that happen before testing or that prevent testing or something."

Both Psychometricians and Diagnosticians tended to prefer formal referrals for their services, in contrast to Assessors and Problem-solvers who preferred to operate with less formality. This Diagnostician explained what would happen if an informal request were made to him by a teacher:

"You're sitting in a staff-room over lunch or a break and somebody says, 'Oh, you should come in and see so-and-so. She's misbehaving or this or that.' If you have a school that has a real heavy caseload, you try to redirect the person and say 'O.K., let's bring it through proper channels.' Unless some teacher is just unloading and that's fine. You see, if a teacher wants an assessment done, she's got to go through the vice-principal or the guidance person. And that's the way those consultations are usually set up."

The Assessor

The Assessors' interpretation of their role is represented in Figure 3. These practitioners seemed to define their role primarily as problem-solvers rather than as generators of psychological data. Although they still reported spending a fair amount of their time doing testing, their perceived role was primarily to assist school personnel in the assessment of students' educational, emotional, and social needs in order to serve them more effectively. Their preference was to be involved in the problem-solving process right from the beginning of a teacher's concern about a particular student.

Consequently, they seemed open to referrals through both informal and formal channels. In fact, they welcomed stated concerns and liked to deal with problems at an early stage. Time spent in this type of discussion was considered well spent. Such dialogues with teachers were referred to as a "pre-assessment consultations," and could take place on an individual basis or during school team meetings. A school team consisted of as few as three participants (usually the principal, teacher, and consultant) to as many members as were felt to be needed. The following example was provided by an Assessor:

"The school team meeting is often what we would refer to as a pre assessment consultation. And in some instances we are talking about a number of kids that I don't ever see. Or I might be asked to observe the child and then we would go back and discuss the child the following week."

Psychological testing was viewed by these practitioners as an optional step in a multi-phased process, and was judged to be only one of a number of possible options for obtaining information about a child. It was also viewed as an option that they preferred to exercise only when necessary-that is, if the information couldn't be obtained in other ways (i.e., by talking to the teacher, reviewing school records, classroom observation). If testing were needed, a post-assessment consultation would follow.

"I think consultation is more when you're giving feedback and exchanging the information and deciding what to do as a result of it. That would fit into what I would describe as being a post-assessment consultation."

The Problem-solver

At the far end of the consultation continuum were the Problem-solvers (see Figure 4). Although their perceptions of the process appear to be similar to those of the Assessor, in this case a specific step for "consultation" was not mentioned, because the Problem-solver tended to define *all* activities carried out within the context of the problem-solving process as consultation. In addition, psychological testing was not mentioned as a stage or step in the referral process: in fact, these practitioners seemed to go out of their way to avoid it, using it only as a last resort. One Problem-solver stated clearly:

"I tell all the schools and all the staff in those schools that I'm working with that once I start there, that I don't want to be seen simply as a tester."

Like the Assessors, the Problem-solvers were receptive to both formal and informal referrals and tended to value the early identification and/or prevention of problems, if possible. However, in talking about their role, they described themselves as quite forceful in their attempts to "get the message out" about their preferred way of practice. This strategy consisted of resisting psychological testing and letting others know that they were interested in facilitating the problem-solving process wherever and whenever possible.

How to "Set the Stage" for the Consultation Process

Both Assessors and Problem-solvers identified a number of techniques that they referred to as "setting the stage" for effective consultation, which are briefly summarized in Figure 5. These practitioners were also able to describe specific activities or practices that they could undertake to facilitate this process, such as eating lunch at a school or having a chat with a teacher in the yard. In the mind of a Problem-solver, at least, these could serve a multitude of functions, including rapport-building, problem-identification and follow-up. On the other hand, to a Psychometrician or Diagnostician the same activity might just be considered a courtesy, but certainly not part of the consultation process. Thus, it seemed that the same activity or event tended to be differently perceived and valued by practitioners with alternate role-orientations.

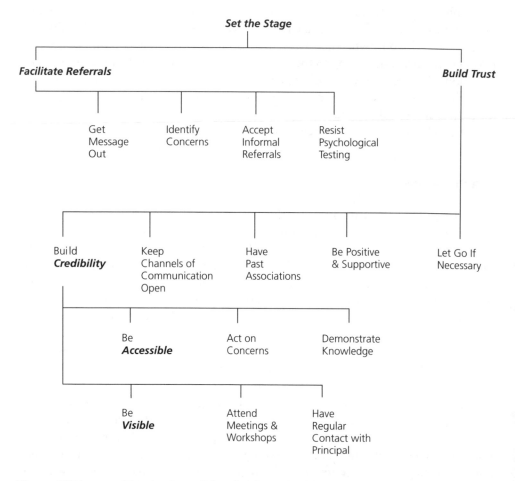

Figure 5 Ways to "Set the Stage" for the Consultation Process

Facilitating Referrals for Consultation

As mentioned, there were marked differences among the four role-orientations in terms of receptivity to referrals. It seemed that those who practiced more consultation or wished to do so (i.e., the Assessors and the Problem-solvers) often sought out referrals actively. They tried to stay aware of patterns of needs in teachers' classes and to identify concerns wherever possible.

There also seemed to be a real need to inform the system that one was interested in operating in an alternative fashion that differed from the "traditional" tester role. As we have seen, the Problem-solvers seemed to be more forceful than the Assessors in getting this message out. This might be done during a presentation to the school staff at the beginning of the school year, or in repeated contacts with the principal, teachers, and in school team meetings.

Trust-Building

By far the most widely acknowledged and crucial first step in the consultation process, as found both in the literature and in the opinion of the psychologists surveyed here, was what has been referred to as trust or rapport-building. There seem to be a multitude of practical ways to build trust: Figure 6 illustrates some of the more general methods reported in this study. These included building credibility through being accessible (such as being visible at school), demonstrating knowledge, and acting on the concerns expressed by potential consultees. It was also felt to be important to keep the channels of communication open, to have past associations with the school staff, and generally to be positive and supportive. Even occasionally "letting go" of an apparent problem or issue was mentioned as being important in a situation of conflict or disagreement with a teacher or principal in order to preserve a relationship.

Thus, it appeared that practicing school psychologists had very specific ideas concerning the referral process and the role of consultation within it. Those who wished to maximize their practices of consultation had, in addition, developed a number of ways to "set the stage" for it. These activities consisted not only of the commonly accepted trust-building actions, but also of "getting the message out" concerning one's preferred way to practice.

Factors Influencing the Process of Consultation

Practitioners were also asked their opinions on factors that seemed to either facilitate or impede the process of consultation. Facilitating factors are summarized in Figure 6. The ones identified as "key factors" were those considered to be essential, and referred primarily to the characteristics of the participants in the consultation process: ideally, a democratic principal, a teacher open to the consultation process, an organized school team leader, and a school psychologist with a pro-consultation role-orientation (i.e., an assessor or problem-solver).

KEY FACTORS

- *Consultant* with a Pro-Consultation Orientation
- Democratic *Principal*
- Open *Teacher*
- Organized *Team Leader*

ADDITIONAL FACTORS

- Positive *Reason* for requesting Consultation
- Congruent *Problem Definition*
- Consultation *Time* held during School Hours

Figure 6 Factors that Facilitate the Process of Consultation

Additional factors described as desirable conditions related to the reasons for which the consultation was being requested, how the problem was defined, and the time the meeting was held. Consultees were considered to have a positive reason for consultation when they truly wanted help in solving a problem and were not just doing it to cooperate with a principal or trying to get the student placed elsewhere. When there were several people involved in the problem-solving process, a congruent or mutually agreed upon definition of the problem was important. Finally, it was felt that if possible, consultation meetings should take place during the day rather than after school when the participants might not have the energy needed to engage in effective problem-solving. These factors are now discussed in turn in further detail.

Key Factors

Consultants distinguished among principals as having autocratic, democratic, or laissez-faire leadership styles. While there were some exceptions to the rule, they gave many examples that illustrated that consultation is facilitated when the leadership style of the principal is democratic. Such a style, they felt, fosters the environment of open communication and shared problem-solving which is most congruent with the goals of consultation. One notable exception involved the experience of one psychologist with an autocratic principal who also happened to be very committed to meeting the needs of the students in his school: in this case, the psychologist found that one-to-one consultation with the principal rather than with the school team was not only possible but more effective.

Although some of the participants described certain teachers as "rigid," this characteristic was seen within the somewhat broader context of teachers being either open or closed to the communication process. The type felt to be least receptive to consultation was described by several participants as being a "private kind of person" who preferred to do his or her own problem-solving.

"I see them as having a great deal of pride in their professionalism and in their ability. They have an enormous investment in their class and their interaction with kids in their class. And that is a privileged private kind of relationship and they operate almost on a little island within the school setting."

Other teachers might be closed to consultation because they felt that their privacy would be threatened by practices such as classroom observation. In these cases, one can see how trust-building would be an important ingredient in "setting the stage" for consultation to occur. Some consultants reported spending their time only with teachers who were open to shared problem-solving, while others would attempt to establish a relationship with those who didn't seem open to it:

"What I would normally do with the teacher whose door is closed, and who I think might be a little edgy about it, is that I would chat them up several times at recess time or lunchtime and say, 'You know, I've been visiting in (Grade) Two and you've got a Three, would you mind me popping in your room sometime and seeing what's going on? I'd like to see so-and-so whom I remember from last year.'"

This was just one of a number of techniques reported in order to "get through" the closed door and begin the long, slow process of trust and relationship building.

The role of the school team leader was to chair the school team meetings. This included being responsible for their scheduling, inviting appropriate participants, setting the agenda, keeping records of intervention ideas, and bringing forward cases at some future date in order to ensure proper follow-up. The team leader was often, but not always, the principal: it might have also been the vice-principal, another teacher, or even the psychologist. The quality of the team leaders felt to influence the consultation process most strongly was how well organized they were. If they were organized, cases would be discussed, decisions made as to intervention strategies, and definite follow-up dates set. Conversely, the involvement of a disorganized team leader usually resulted in a pattern of poor follow-up. The practitioners reported that in such situations, people didn't ask how suggested interventions worked, and consequently teachers had the feeling that "nothing was actually done" about their concerns.

"One of my schools which has an official school team worked very effectively under the direction of the vice-principal. The vice-principal left and the principal is not an effective individual. And although we still have team meetings, they do not occur as frequently. There is not the same follow-up. He gets things mixed up...or forgets and so the model is still there, but it is not operating as well. And I think that that is really unfortunate, because it was effective. But the teachers are not bringing forward problems much this year. People don't see the follow-up either. And I think because of that they are not as likely to bring forward another situation."

Additional Factors

One of the "additional factors" listed in Figure 6 that was felt to facilitate the process of consultation was that there be a positive reason for requesting consultation. In general, reasons were operational when a teacher or other consultee really wanted help in solving a problem. Positive reasons included a need to make a decision regarding placement, to obtain advice about how to manage a particular student or situation, or to receive some reassurance about an approach already being taken by the teacher. This list is congruent which areas identified by Gerald Caplan (1970) as valid reasons for consultation (i.e., lack of objectivity, skill, knowledge, or confidence), although they are phrased in a more positive way.

Negative reasons for requesting consultation generally involved hidden agendas of various types. The practitioners identified several situations in which these might occur, including the teacher wanting the student out of his/her classroom, or the teacher only agreeing to cooperate with a principal who had asked the psychologist to come in.

"Now consultation may be forced on them, but never occur. The principal may tell them to have me come in to consult and you can tell within five minutes whether it's going to happen."

There were also those situations in which there were political pressures of various sorts, and the intent of the consultation was really just to show that the "proper procedure" had been followed.

In situations in which there were a number of people involved in the consultation process, it became very important to come to a consensus regarding a definition of the problem. If this did not take place, members of a team could be working at cross-purposes, and it would be very hard to evaluate the success of any intervention strategy that was decided upon.

In terms of the question of when consultation sessions should be held, it was generally felt that although having meetings after school seemed to be a convenient time, it was probably not the most appropriate. By the end of the school day teachers are often tired and may not have the energy to put into participating fully in the process. The study participants gave numerous examples of ways in which teachers could be "freed up" during the day in order to attend these meetings. Some principals would hire a substitute teacher on the morning the school team met each week, in order to allow the homeroom teacher to come to the meeting at the point at which his/her student was being discussed. This arrangement allowed the teacher to concentrate fully on the problem-solving process and not to have to worry about the class being left unattended. In another school much the same arrangement was made, but instead of a substitute teacher the laissez-faire principal (who, it was felt, would not have contributed much to the discussion) volunteered to supervise classes when necessary. In schools where it is not possible to free teachers during class time, weekly team meetings may be held for half an hour before school or during lunch hour, with a limit placed upon the number of students to be discussed. The after-school time slot was considered the least desirable, with most consultants feeling that time should be made for consultation during school hours if possible.

In general, it appeared that there were a number of factors whose presence facilitated the problem-solving process, and in whose absence the process could become frustrating. It seemed that with experience practitioners had become adept at distinguishing between these situations, and were attempting to involve themselves in those that maximized the occurrence of successful consultation.

Ways of Assessing One's Effectiveness in School Psychological Consultation

A by-product of any activity undertaken on a personal or professional level are feelings and thoughts about the value of that activity. In terms of one's professional life, it seems that a major source of satisfaction results from the feeling of succeeding in "doing a good job," whatever that is taken to mean. Conversely, frustrations may arise out of a feeling of being prevented from being effective.

It appeared from the interviews that the role of the school psychologist is one in which it is very difficult to assess individual effectiveness. Nevertheless, practitioners were able to identify several methods that combined more traditional objective measures with some internal subjective considerations. In general, these methods addressed their feelings of satisfaction with their own *performance*, with the consultation *process*, and with its *outcome*. Specific ways of evaluating these are summarized in Figure 7.

In discussing ways of assessing their own performance, consultants felt that they had done well when they had either felt useful or had been successful in mobilizing the skills learned and used in counseling, such as empathy, respect, and genuineness.

"I have my internal measure, and that is if I have the feeling that I've been the best I can be in a consultation position. I get some satisfaction from that even if there hasn't been a change."

Feeling good about the process tended to occur in the presence of factors that facilitated consultation. When factors such as a democratic principal, open teacher, and organized team leader were present, chances were maximized that there would also be an openness of all parties to the process, respect for each others' perspectives and the involvement of all. When these conditions were present, one could hope for a congruent problem definition that would lead to consensus regarding an effective intervention strategy.

Feeling good re: performance	Feeling useful to others	Seen as a resource	Explicit commendation Request for service Others say felt supported
		Used as a resource	Information used Advice taken Recommendation followed
	Successfully using skills	Using interpersonal skills Using problem solving skills Using skills in area of expertise	
Feeling good re: process	Coordinated team action	Involvement of all parties in problem-solving process	Presence of all parties Review history Review past attempts at problem resolution Openness of parties to process Mutual respect for all participants
		Congruent problem definition	Opportunity to share ideas and perspectives of all parties Shared responsibility Absence of hidden agendas Definition of problem in terms acceptable to all parties
		Consensus re: solution to problem	
Feeling good re: outcome	Problem understood better		
	Some changes made	Short-term change observed Long-term change observed Client's needs met Some progress made towards goal	
	Review of records to suggest effectiveness		

Figure 7 Ways of Assessing One's Effectiveness in School Psychological Consultation

In terms of outcome, consultants reported feeling good when any amount of progress was made in the direction of problem resolution. It was sometimes good enough that a problem was simply understood better or that some short-term changes were observed in the student, consultee, or system. Despite the fact that the ultimate goal of any intervention was the long-term benefit of the student, it could take years to find out whether or not an intervention idea or placement decision had been in the child's best interests. Students' needs can change so much over time and there are such a variety of factors impinging on their lives, that no one consultant could ever seriously hope to take either the credit or the blame for a given outcome. Even if one could wait a great length of time for feedback, the mobile nature of the student population would greatly reduce the chances of finding a particular student in order to track outcomes. In this setting, then, finding out whether a student's needs had been met or even how he or she eventually "turned out" are highly unlikely:

"We never know the end result, so we never know if our intervention has been successful or not."

It was perhaps as a consequence of this lack or impracticality of long-term evidence that the word "outcome" took on a more immediate connotation from the viewpoint of practitioners. Those individuals who tended to judge their effectiveness in terms of outcome measures rather than performance or process considerations, bemoaned the fact that they often spent time engaged in problem-solving activities with "nothing to show for it" in terms of concrete results. One consultant handled this concern by devising a process he called "logging":

"I keep track over the year of the kinds of things and the proportions and the number of kids and that kind of thing. And I offer the principals an end-of-year report on the kinds of kids I have been working with at their school and the kind of work I have been doing for them."

This was an idea that seemed to hold promise for practitioners who wish to increase their consultation time and at the same time satisfy their need for some form of accountability within their complex and variable practices.

Implications of These Findings for the Practice of Consultation

The research that has been reported in this chapter is supportive of the view that "consultation" has become an overly generalized term (Gresham & Kendall, 1987). Not only does it tend to be used in a global way, but exploration of the term in further depth has revealed that it can have qualitatively different meanings to different practitioners. It would seem important, then, to clarify the meaning of the terms being used for both practice and professional development activities.

In this study, four role-orientations were identified within the field of school psychology. Consultation seemed to take on very specific meanings, particularly as to how its function was differentially perceived. In subsequent sessions at which these findings have been presented to psychological service staff at a variety of school boards, practitioners have been able to identify their own particular role-orientations and have reported that this understanding has helped them to see how they can begin to change their present practices. In some cases, they have noted how the ideas included in "setting the stage" could be used to expand the use of consultation.

Although school psychologists continue to provide traditional services, consultation skills are identified as a key factor in successful school-based programs. The model presented in Chapter 1 offers readers a comprehensive schema for evaluating their own roles as consultants. As practitioners aim to broaden the delivery of psychological services, it would seem that reflection upon one's style in relation to that of others is likely to facilitate further insight into one's practices and eventually contribute to professional growth.

It may be an appropriate strategy for practitioners to evaluate the conditions for consultation in the situations to which they are assigned. If some of these conditions are not favorable, the consultant could then see what he or she could do to change them. Setting such goals might eventually prove to be yet another method by which school psychologists can evaluate themselves. Finally, an awareness of the difficulty in assessing one's effectiveness along with some of the ideas presented here may facilitate further exploration in this challenging area.

For those readers interested in consultation research, the results of this study should assist in the development of clearer conceptualizations. The literature has provided an awareness that consultation models can be described in terms of focus, level of intervention, and approach; that it can be practiced with individuals and groups on either a one-shot or ongoing basis; and that the use of a "consultation" model may or may not include testing. Although the practitioners who were interviewed for this study did not seem to think of their roles in terms of distinct models, these descriptors were in fact incorporated into the different role-orientations that were identified. It would seem advisable that as more research is carried out in the field, a serious attempt be made to describe the actions being taken by individuals within these parameters. This type of rigor will, it is hoped, facilitate the development of future research that can be done with greater precision, bring with it heightened comparability, and ultimately contribute to a better understanding of this increasingly popular form of service delivery.

References

Babcock, N., & Pryzwansky, W. (1983). Models of consultation: Preferences of educational professionals at five stages of service. *Journal of School Psychology, 21(4)*, 359-366.

Caplan, G. (1970). *The theory and practice of mental health consultation.* New York: Basic Books.

Caplan, G., & Caplan, R. B. (1993). *Mental health consultation and collaboration.* San Francisco: Jossey-Bass.

Conoley, J. C., & Conoley, C. W. (1992). *School consultation: A guide to practice and training.* Elmsford, New York: Pergamon.

Dettmer, P. A., Dyck, N. T., & Thurston, L. P. (1996). *Consultation, collaboration, and teamwork: For students with special needs* (2nd edition). Boston: Allyn and Bacon.

Fuchs, D., & Fuchs, L. S. (1989). Exploring effective and efficient pre-referral interventions: A component analysis of behavioral consultation. *School Psychology Review, 18,* 260-279.

Gresham, F. M., & Kendall, G. K. (1987). School consultation research: Methodological critique and future research directions. *School Psychology Review, 16(3),* 306-316.

Idol, L., & West, J. F. (1987). Consultation in special education: Part 2. Training and practice. *Journal of Learning Disabilities, 20,* 474-497.

Kratochwill, T. R., Elliott, S. N., & Rotto, P. C. (1995). Best practices in school-based behavioral consultation. In A. Thomas & J. Grimes (Eds.), *Best practices in school psychology III* (pp. 519-535). Washington, DC: The National Association of School Psychologists.

Medway, F. J. *(1982).* School consultation research: Past trends and future directions. *Professional Psychology: Research and Practice, 13(3),* 422-430.

Noell, G. H., & Witt, J. C. (1999). When does consultation lead to intervention implementation? *Journal of Special Education, 33(1),* 29.

Parsons, R. D. (1996). *The skilled consultant.* Needham Heights, MA: Allyn and Bacon.

Scholten, P. T. (1987). *School psychological consultation in practice: A descriptive study of the consultant's perspective.* Unpublished doctoral dissertation. Ontario Institute for Studies in Education, University of Toronto, Toronto, Ontario.

Sheridan, S., Welch, M., & Orme, S. (1996). Is consultation effective? A review of some outcome research. *Remedial and Special Education, 17,* 341-354.

Spradley, J. (1979). *The ethnographic interview.* New York: Holt, Rinehart and Winston.

West, J. F., & Cannon, G. S. (1988). Essential collaborative consultation competencies for regular and special educators. *Journal of Learning Disabilities, 21,* 56-63.

Appendix A: A Summary of the Descriptive Characteristics of Participants

Total # of participants	20

Sex

males	10
females	10

Age

25-40 yrs.	5
over 40 yrs.	15

Education Level

BA	1
MA, MEd (non-registered)	11
PhD (non-registered)	5
Registered Psychologists (PhD, MA)	3

Appendix B: Semantic Relationships

Type of Semantic Relationship	Form and Example
(1) Strict Inclusion	X (is a kind of) Y e.g., case-centred (is a kind of) consultation
(2) Spatial	X (is a place in) Y e.g., the staffroom (is a place in) the school
(3) Cause-Effect (cause)	X (is a cause of) Y e.g., feeling useful(is a cause of) satisfaction with consultation
(4) Cause-Effect (result)	X (is a result/outcome of) Y e.g., effective follow-up (is a result of) an organized team leader
(5) Rationale	X (is a reason for doing) Y e.g., needing advice (is a reason for doing) consultation
(6) Location	X (is a place for doing) Y e.g., in the hallway (is a place for doing) consultation
(7) Function	X (is used for) Y e.g., classroom observation (is used for) information gathering
(8) Means-End	X (is a way to) Y e.g., being accessible (is a way to) build trust
(9) Sequence	X (is a step in) Y e.g., gaining trust (is a step in) the consultation process
(10) Attribution	X (is a characteristic of) Y e.g., satisfying (is a characteristic of) consultation

Spradley (1979) has suggested that much of our knowledge, particularly in the study of cultures of certain groups of people, can be organized into one of the ten semantic relationships here.

Chapter 6
Integrating School and Clinical Child Psychology: An Innovative Model for Training School Psychologists

Esther Geva, Judith Wiener, Michele Peterson-Badali, and Nancy Link[1]

Introduction

School psychologists play a variety of roles in the educational and health systems to meet the multiplicity of needs of children in our complex society (Nastasi, 2000). Therefore, the training of school psychologists must also be multidimensional, flexible, and dynamic. In this chapter we present a conceptual framework for training in professional child psychology that involves the integration of school psychology and clinical child psychology. We then describe a training program that strives to implement this model, discuss how the process of self-study guides the continuous renewal of the program, and outline some future directions for implementation of the conceptual framework.

Conceptual Framework

The traditional role of school psychologists is typically fairly circumscribed. The foundation of that role is based on a medical model in which students are referred for assessment due to hypothesized deficits or problems that reside within the child. Within this traditional model, the role of the psychologist is to do psychoeducational

---

[1] The authors wish to thank the colleagues and SCCP students who contributed to preparation of the accreditation document submitted to the American Psychological Association.

assessments in which they administer psychological tests in order to detect those deficits, and to prescribe, but not to implement, possible directions for intervention (Christenson, Abery, & Weinberg, 1986). Education of psychologists within this framework mainly entails providing intensive training in tests and measurement, in administration of standardized tests, and in categorical classifications of disorders (e.g., DSM-IV: American Psychological Association, 1994). The training in intervention, if provided at all, tends to be fairly prescriptive and de-contextualized, and mainly involves approaches to working with individual children (Swerdlik & French, 2000).

In response to the increasing demands that are now placed on the education system, this traditional role of the school psychologist is in the process of change. Models describing the role of the school psychologist within the context of the school are changing as well. Christenson et al. (1986), for example, propose an alternative model that they term the *developmental model*, in which ecology plays a prominent role. In this chapter, we use the term *developmental-ecological* to describe our adaptation of this model. By the use of the term *developmental*, we formally acknowledge an issue that is implicit in all work with children; namely that the child's developmental stage (i.e., preschooler, school age child, adolescent) is itself a factor that must be incorporated into our understanding of the child. By the use of the term *ecological* we emphasize the importance of understanding each child in dynamic relationship with his or her own specific context (e.g., cultural background, socioeconomic status, family stresses and resources, school setting).

In the developmental-ecological model, healthy functioning is conceived of flexibly and defined in terms of the perspective of the individuals involved as well as the community. This new model of child functioning necessitates a new role for the school psychologist, and relatedly, changes to training models. This conceptualization is based on the recognition of a multivariate definition of diversity that includes culture, race, language, disability, gender, socioeconomic status, and sexual orientation. Furthermore, diversity is not seen in static, or stereotyped ways (e.g., all persons who are Afro-Canadian share the same cultural viewpoint). Instead, the way individuals define themselves is related to context and is dynamic in nature (Geva, Barsky, & Westernoff, 2000; Meyers & Nastasi, 1999). In this model, child psychopathology or dysfunction is also viewed from a developmental and ecological perspective (Lewis, 1999; Prout, 1999).

The premise of the model is that when children are referred due to possible problems, the focus is on the mismatch between child's needs and behaviors and the demands of the classroom, the community, and home environment. An important consideration is that when children are referred, even for the same learning or behavioral problem, the underlying causes of the maladaptive learning or behavior patterns may not be the same. Thus, each child must be considered individually. Underlining this focus is the premise that behavior, no matter how superficially dysfunctional, occurs for a reason. A key task of the psychologist is to determine the factors (constitutional and environmental) that are supporting the behavior. Assessment is multi-faceted involving observation, interviewing, formal and informal testing and occurs across a range of contexts (e.g., home/school, structured/unstructured settings).

Although the role of the school psychologist in the developmental-ecological model clearly includes assessment, it is not limited to assessment. Within this model, diagnosis (labelling, identification) is a central but not the only consideration. More emphasis is placed on describing the mutual interaction between the child, school and family factors, and the larger context of culture and community. There is a direct link between assessment and intervention and home-school collaboration. Indeed, psychologists trained within this model are consultants who collaborate with school personnel, parents, other health professionals, and community members to implement structures that prevent the emergence of problems in children, and to intervene with children who are at-risk for a negative developmental trajectory due to learning problems, family problems, substance abuse, socioeconomic disadvantage, trauma related to war and immigration, disability, and so on. Primary prevention activities are generally directed at the entire school or community, and secondary prevention activities are directed at groups of at-risk children or families (Cole & Siegel, 1990; Meyers & Nastasi, 1999). Psychologists within this framework are change agents who work with professionals from other disciplines to achieve an environment that promotes health for children.

A key aspect of the consultation process is interprofessional practice, which is defined as:

"a highly integrated approach to assessment and intervention, one in which practitioners from different professional backgrounds come together with clients/students/patients. The professionals develop common objectives for work while still providing differential professional contributions. Throughout assessment and intervention, they maintain an open system of communication, coordination, and cooperation." (Geva et al., 2000, p. 3).

According to Geva et al. (2000), a key component of interprofessional practice is teamwork wherein professionals learn from each other the skills of their various professions in order to provide optimal service to the client.

The school psychologist "might best be described as a practicing scientist who uses systematic inquiry (social science methods) to address the real-life needs of individuals and systems" (Nastasi, 2000, p. 550). Consistent with this definition, within the developmental ecological model, school psychologists are expected to function simultaneously as scientists, practitioners, and scholars.

As scientists, school psychologists are attuned to the need to employ empirically supported approaches, and are capable of carrying out both action-based and formal program evaluation research. Furthermore, they are in an ideal position, due to the breadth of the populations with whom they work, to develop hypotheses for research and innovative preventive programs and interventions that could then be empirically validated either by themselves, or in collaboration with others whose role is to conduct research. School psychologists who are educated to work in accordance with the developmental-ecological model are also able to extrapolate policy implications from research.

As practitioners, school psychologists must be generalists who are able to access relevant information across a wide range of sub-specialties within the field (e.g., psychopathology, learning disabilities, psychometrics, differential diagnosis, developmental theory, parent-child relationships, intervention approaches). They must then weigh the relative importance of each factor in their application of this knowledge to specific problems and children. The implications for training practitioners within this developmental-ecological framework are far-reaching. It is still necessary but not sufficient to train students in psychometrics and categorical diagnosis. In order to gain an appreciation of the multiple contexts affecting children, however, students need to work in a variety of settings and be exposed to the range of diverse needs and modes of adaptation and dysfunction. Therefore, the training cannot be confined to the university classroom and the school system. Furthermore, students need a solid grounding in developmental psychopathology, systemic and dynamic assessment techniques, linking assessment and intervention, and methods of placing assessment within a counselling process. They need an in-depth understanding of the consultation process and the role of consultation in producing change. In order to do this, they need to have a broad understanding of social policy and ethical decision-making. Field placements in settings where supervising psychologists are actively engaged in intervention, consultation and prevention activities, and where students can be part of inter-professional teams are invaluable.

In discussing the role of school psychologists as *scientists* and *practitioners* we have described the essence of the scientist-practitioner model articulated at the Boulder conference in 1949 in relation to clinical psychology (Barlow, Hayes, & Nelson, 1984). However, the Boulder scientist-practitioner model does not explicitly discuss the role of reflective practice, scholarly inquiry, and life-long learning. The role of *scholar* implies that psychologists ought to be broadly informed about significant scientific and theoretical developments throughout the discipline. We believe that the concept of *scholarship* represents an important conceptual bridge between the *scientist,* who generates new knowledge by conducting research, and the *practitioner,* who applies that knowledge when working with children, youth, families, and organizations. Furthermore, the traffic on the bridge is bi-directional. One of the problems that has been inherent in the scientist-practitioner model is that the emphasis has been on science informing practice, without the component of theory informing research and practice, and practice informing theory and research. As will be discussed further below, having faculty who model this integration of practice, theory, reflection and research may be a key aspect of training school psychologists for the 21st century.

It follows that integrated training in both school and clinical child psychology is most likely to produce graduates who are able to undertake the diverse roles that are implied by this model. This is essential because the traditional approach to training school psychologists typically does not teach graduates the skills they require to promote the process of change. The way we approach training in the combined fields of school and clinical child psychology promotes examination of the whole child, and the child in context. There are no artificial divisions between academic and learning problems, on the one hand, and psychosocial problems, on the other hand. Psycho-educational assessment is part of a comprehensive clinical assessment that assumes that the person and environment are interconnected (Meyers & Nastasi, 1999), and that the psychologist must examine the compatibilities and mismatch between the needs and functioning of the child and those of primary stakeholders (Greene, 1995). Academic remediation, intervention, and psychotherapy are seen as complementary, mutually facilitative, and sometimes one fulfills the function of the other. In order to gain a comprehensive understanding of these issues, field placements in a variety of educational and clinical settings are essential.

The School and Clinical Child Psychology (SCCP) program at the Ontario Institute for Studies in Education of the University of Toronto embodies the conceptual framework outlined above. In the next section we describe the key components of our training model.

Training Model

Four components form the basis of the training model of the SCCP program: (1) we are training students to be skilled in both school psychology and clinical psychology with an emphasis on children, youth, and families; (2) we work to inculcate attitudes consistent with the scientist-scholar-practitioner model; (3) we have a curriculum which is both developmental and hierarchical; (4) the themes of development, diversity and ecology are predominant in most of the courses.

School *and* Clinical Child Psychology

The integration of school and clinical child psychology is a central feature of our program. We are convinced that integrated training in school and clinical psychology facilitates the development of highly competent psychologists who work very effectively in both educational and mental health settings. This is especially so when the developmental-ecological model, that incorporates both Christenson et al.'s (1986) developmental model in school psychology and the developmental psychopathology model in clinical child psychology (Garmezy & Rutter, 1983), is employed. Psychologists with this type of training are able to work with children, youth and families considering all aspects of their context.

Furthermore, professional psychologists who work in schools need much of the knowledge and skills traditionally viewed as the domain of clinical psychologists, who in turn need much of the knowledge and skills traditionally viewed as the domain of school psychologists. Although we recognize that there are some knowledge and skills which are more likely to be needed by school psychologists (e.g., understanding the social ecology of schools, instructional interventions) and clinical psychologists (e.g., individual and group psychotherapy), we are able to train students in both fields because the basic knowledge and skills of both fields overlap extensively.

A careful examination of the competencies that professional psychologists practicing in both school and clinical child psychology need indicates that they share many commonalities. As discussed above, psychologists working in both fields need to have a solid foundation in developmental psychology and developmental psychopathology. They require an in-depth understanding of ethical issues and their application to professional practice as well as knowledge of jurisprudence pertaining to psychological practice. Psychological assessment and the formulation of and communication of a diagnosis are obviously essential skills regardless of field. All professional psychologists need to have well-developed communication and counselling skills and need to be familiar with a broad range of psychosocial interventions. Ideally, both school and clinical child psychologists should be skilled in consultation and working in interprofessional teams, and should be sensitive to cultural and individual diversity. Finally, program evaluation, research design, and statistics are basic knowledge components for psychologists regardless of their area of specialty.

Often students who enter our program express the desire to study either school or clinical child psychology, and are reluctant to study and gain experience in the combined field. At the outset of our program, students are informed that they are all being trained to work in school and clinical settings, that there are no specific tracks, courses address issues that arise in both settings, and they must do practica in both settings. More experienced students have indicated that they find the integrated training to be extremely relevant and are pleased that these requirements are in place.

Scientist-Scholar-Practitioner Model

Our training model reflects the belief that empirically based knowledge in psychology should inform professional training and, at the same time, applied research should be informed by professional experience. The training model adopted by the program is the scientist-scholar-practitioner model, an extension of the Boulder scientist-practitioner model. It emphasizes the interaction of practice and theory. The goal is to develop professionals who are clinically competent and intellectually curious, and who are able to conduct applied and theoretical research relevant to the practice of psychology, use research to critically inform practice, and to provide services that enhance the well being of children, youth and families. We also view it as important that our graduates obtain a high level of competence in oral and written communication skills. These components are complementary, and training occurs in each of the components in an interwoven fashion throughout a student's program. We interpret the components of the scientist-scholar-practitioner model as follows:

Scientist

Research is a crucial element of the SCCP program. Students are expected to gain broad and general knowledge in the areas encompassed by school and clinical psychology, and to develop a firm foundation in the philosophy of science and scientific methodology. They are expected to become educated consumers of research as well as competent researchers themselves. Students are taught to critically evaluate and apply research through their substantive courses. The skills needed to conduct research are developed in research methods courses, colloquia, graduate assistantships, research groups, attendance at conferences, and masters and doctoral theses.

Scholar

The program emphasizes the importance of developing a breadth of basic and applied knowledge across several areas of psychology, including human development, developmental psychopathology, individual differences, social, cognitive-affective, and biological bases of behavior, and research and quantitative methods. The scholar generates questions from issues of practice and places these concerns in an appropriate theoretical perspective so as to guide the search for answers. Graduates are expected to be able to integrate knowledge from different domains and to interpret problems they encounter in a meaningful way.

Practitioner

Students develop competence in the practice of school and clinical psychology through practicum and other courses, practicum field experiences, and internships. They are expected to apply their scholarly and scientific knowledge to practice by engaging in critical reflection about their own practice, and by using empirically supported assessment and intervention techniques (Hunsley, Dobson, Johnson, & Mikhail, 1999).

A mentorship model, which emphasizes the development of knowledge and skills through professional relationships, is utilized in the SCCP program. Students are initially sponsored into the program by a faculty member who shares their area of research and scholarly interest and agrees to function as their program advisor. This advisory relationship assumes importance as students decide upon their areas of professional specialization and develop thesis topics. Students become involved in their advisor's research through participation in research groups, and through graduate research assistantships. This involvement typically leads to the development of dissertation research. Faculty also often continue to be mentors for our students following completion of the program. They work together on collaborative research, and faculty provide support regarding career development and dealing with professional issues.

In our courses, both during lectures and in the assignments students are required to do, we typically integrate theory, research and practice. For example, students are frequently asked to apply their understanding of the scholarly literature to case studies. An emphasis is placed on interventions that are empirically supported. One of our compulsory courses is a proseminar in which students listen to colloquia featuring leading-edge research presented by department and visiting faculty. These colloquia are typically attended by department faculty who take leadership in asking questions of the presenters. In this way, we model the life-long learning process as well as the kind of critical thinking that is so important in our field. One of the key assignments in this course requires students to consider the connection between the new ideas they have been exposed to and their own research and applied interests.

Developmental-Hierarchical Curriculum

The curriculum in the MA and PhD was designed to be one coherent program. Our metaphor for the program is that of a tree. The *root* of the tree represents the background preparation our students have prior to entry. All students are required to have an undergraduate specialization in psychology. Our two year full-time MA curriculum is designed to establish a strong foundation (or *trunk*) of core knowledge and skills early in the program. This core includes fundamental professional and research courses as well as a practicum in assessment. They also do a research-based MA thesis. Doctoral students are free to specialize (or *branch* out) later on. They take advanced courses designed to enhance scientific breadth and research knowledge. They also have the opportunity to choose courses and practicum experiences that allow them to begin to establish their own professional direction and become deeply involved in scholarship and research with their doctoral thesis as the product.

Development, Diversity, and Ecology

The notions of development, diversity, and ecology permeate all of the courses in SCCP. Consistent with the recommendations of Christenson et al. (1986), we believe that students must have a solid understanding of normal development, appreciate the diverse individual learning, social, and emotional needs and behaviors of children and adolescents, and understand that these needs and behaviors must be understood within the larger context of the family, the school, and the social and cultural environment in which they live. This framework specifies a systemic approach to assessment and intervention, in which the educational and emotional needs of children and youth are seen as intertwined.

Needless to say, the core faculty in the SCCP program incorporate these principles in their work with students and in their courses. In addition, it should be noted that the SCCP program is situated in the Human Development and Applied Psychology Department at the University of Toronto. There are many advantages to this context in that the various programs in the department are inter-connected, the faculty collaborate, and some of the courses are offered to students across the various departmental programs. This collaboration is facilitated by the fact that applied developmental psychology is a unifying principle of the department and is fundamental to students' training for their respective roles as teachers, school and clinical psychologists, and researchers.

Our understanding of human development is based on four core factors. First, as children move from infancy to adulthood they undergo fundamental changes that systematically influence the ways that they perceive and respond to their world, and the ways that their families, teachers, peers and others with whom they relate respond to them. Second, the experiences of children and youth throughout their schooling, including the ways that they are prepared for it and their reactions to it, strongly influence their individual development. Third, the social experiences of children and youth, both within and outside of the family and the feelings that result from those experiences have a major impact on their individual development. Fourth, individuals have diverse learning, social and emotional needs and differ considerably from each other in the ways that they approach their world.

Both school psychology and clinical psychology have models that share similar features with those that underpin our own training model. In accordance with Bronfenbrenner (1989), we assume multiple, non-linear explanations of behavior and development. Individuals do not simply react to environmental influences; they create and change their environment and in a reciprocal manner are also affected by those environments. Consistent with the views of Garmezy and Rutter (1983), we believe that psychologists should assess both adaptive and maladaptive behaviors, and the risk and protective factors that foster them. We assume a proactive, preventive focus for professional psychologists, whether they work in schools, hospitals or mental health settings (Gutkin & Curtis, 1999).

Competencies of Graduating Students

Our training model guided us in the delineation of the competencies that we expect students in the SCCP program to have at the point that they graduate from our program. We were also guided by the requirements of the College of Psychologists and of the American Psychological Association accreditation process. These competencies specifically reflect the conviction that school and clinical child psychology should be construed as a single combined field, and by the scientist-scholar-practitioner model. Our formulation of our program involved first establishing the competencies discussed below, then articulating how the curriculum will address these competencies, and how we evaluate student attainment of these competencies. Below we discuss each of the competencies, and how they are addressed.

Broad and General Knowledge of Psychology

Practitioners who have a conceptual understanding of their work, and who base their work on scientific research must have a broad knowledge base in general psychology. This includes an understanding of the history of psychology, the cognitive-affective, biological, and social bases of behavior, and of individual differences. In order for it to be relevant to the students, it is not enough to provide this knowledge in a decontextualized way. Instead, we guide students to make the linkages between the general knowledge of psychology taught in our foundation courses with applied issues involved in research and professional work with children, youth, and families.

Research Knowledge and Skills

Practitioners who have a conceptual understanding of their work, and who base their work on scientific research, must have a solid foundation in the thinking process involved in doing research. Therefore we expect students to have an in-depth understanding of the conceptual foundations of research design in order to become critical and well-informed consumers of research as well as to do their own original research. Once this fundamental understanding has been acquired, students study advanced measurement, research design and statistics. Thus, we train practitioners who are effective in developing innovative approaches that are scientifically supported and ultimately challenge current practices, lead to better outcomes for clients, and provide feedback to researchers.

Although the basic knowledge and skills regarding research are taught directly in various courses, students learn to apply this knowledge by working together with faculty and other students in research groups led by faculty and devoted to areas of mutual interest. In these groups, students observe faculty as they are developing their research projects, and analyze and criticize each other's work. As these groups are typically comprised of faculty and students at various levels of the program, senior students frequently mentor junior students in the development of research. The major research products are masters and doctoral theses; however, students also present at professional and scholarly conferences, and publish their work in professional journals and books.

Ethical, Legal, and Professional Conduct

It is clearly important that school and clinical child psychologists perform their role in an ethical and professional manner and in a fashion that is consistent with federal and provincial legislation regarding children, youth and families. Although, in their courses, students are exposed to ethical standards for practice in psychology and the relevant legislation, we do not view simple exposure as sufficient. Instead, we emphasize the problem-solving skills necessary for decision-making regarding ethical, legal, and professional issues. We use problem-based and case-based learning techniques to teach decision-making skills. We also evaluate students' ethical and professional conduct in the context of their practicum placements. This includes ethical practice in relation to individually and culturally diverse populations. As ethical and professional standards of conduct are also required in research settings, we teach ethical issues and decision-making when students are designing research projects.

Psychological Assessment

Similar to most school psychology programs, a cornerstone of our program is the provision of training in psychological assessment of individuals who have cognitive, academic, psychosocial, and behavioral difficulties. We also do not differ from most training programs in that our students must develop a knowledge base with respect to psychometric theory, characteristics and etiology of learning and developmental disabilities, personality and socioemotional development, and classification systems in childhood psychopathology. They also develop skills in administering, scoring and interpreting psychological and educational tests, using structured and open-ended interviews, observation, communicating effectively with children, adolescents, and parents, and report-writing. In addition, consistent with our focus on development, diversity, and ecology, our students are taught to link assessment to intervention, to design, administer and interpret informal probes to assess learning in the context of a dynamic assessment, and to design, employ and interpret behavioral observation systems to assess adaptive skills and problem behavior in the context of the family, and school. They learn to consider the inter-relationship of cognitive, academic, and psychosocial problems. Furthermore, an emphasis is placed on the consideration of cultural and individual diversity.

With regard to child psychopathology, we teach students to do a differential diagnosis using traditional diagnostic classification systems such as DSM-IV. We also teach students to take a developmental psychopathology perspective in which they use a systemic approach to assess the influence of ecological factors on the development of adaptive behaviors and psychopathology, and to consider both risk and protective factors.

In order to achieve these goals, students take mandatory courses in learning disabilities, child psychopathology, and psychological assessment. The introductory psychological assessment courses focus on formal assessment. Students learn the skills under direct supervision of a faculty member in our in-house clinic before moving to a field-based practicum. In our advanced courses we focus on psychodiagnosis, and on integration of traditional approaches with dynamic assessment and systemic approaches to assessing children.

Prevention and Consultation

Although assessment is typically viewed as the major role of the school psychologist and individual psychotherapy is often seen as the traditional role of the clinical psychologist, our view of the role of professional psychologists who work with children is that a focus should be placed on prevention. This is important because multiple contextual factors such as poverty and family dysfunction place a child at-risk for mental health problems (Christenson & Buerkle, 1999; Offord, Boyle, & Racine, 1991). This entails teaching students about theories of consultation in school and mental health settings, the culture of the school and community mental health agency settings, conceptual issues related to interprofessional team functioning, assessing teacher beliefs and classroom contexts when formulating prevention programs and intervention strategies, and conceptual foundations of primary, secondary and tertiary prevention programs. We also try to teach our students to be advocates for the clients they serve.

We teach students to take this perspective in our course work with the view to them applying it in their practicum placement. In our practicum courses, for example, students are required to observe children in the classroom context, attend in-school team meetings, and interview teachers about their beliefs and practices in relation to specific children. In spite of the current literature stressing the value of this approach in school psychology (e.g., Christenson et al., 1986; Gutkin & Curtis, 1999), a major obstacle we encounter is finding supervisors who have the mandate and the skills to facilitate prevention programs in the schools. Furthermore, in mental health settings, the focus tends to be limited to short-term individual psychotherapy. Consequently, there are few role models and opportunities for our students to see systemic prevention applied in practice. Students have some opportunity, however, to observe and participate in prevention programs conducted by faculty members in the context of their research.

Psychoeducational Intervention

Typically, school psychologists assess the learning difficulties of children and make recommendations to teachers, but are not directly involved in the provision of remedial programs to children. In spite of this, we require that our students develop a knowledge base with respect to characteristics and theory about the etiology of learning and developmental disabilities, and effective instructional strategies for individuals with learning and developmental disabilities. Moreover, in practicum-based courses, we also require that they gain first-hand experience at teaching a student with learning difficulties so that they develop a better understanding of what is involved when they make recommendations to teachers. Some of the skills that they learn include analysis of curriculum materials, selecting appropriate intervention strategies on the basis of assessment data, relating psychological processing deficits and task analysis to learning and teaching, trial teaching, and monitoring and evaluating student outcome in relation to the objectives of the intervention.

Psychotherapeutic Intervention

All of our students learn basic counselling and communication skills for working with children, youth and families through course work and in their practicum placements. Through specialized courses they develop a knowledge base that includes an articulation of the theoretical principles of the major schools of therapy (i.e., behavioral, cognitive-behavioral, systemic, or psychodynamic) as well as the differences between schools. They also focus on and develop their skills in relation to a school of psychotherapy that is consistent with their aims and interests. As in our teaching of psychoeducational interventions, we focus on empirically supported approaches and on teaching our students to monitor and evaluate outcome.

Our teaching of psychotherapeutic intervention is mainly through course work and field-based practica. In our courses we use videotape, role-play and case studies to teach the application of the theoretical principles. Students receive direct supervision in psychotherapy in their doctoral practicum.

Cultural and Individual Diversity

The nature of cultural diversity varies across contexts. For example, although cultural differences are often conceptualized in terms of race and/or ethnicity, they may be based on linguistic differences rather than race (Bowman, 2000). This is particularly true in major cities in countries characterized by high proportions of immigrants or high levels of immigration. Furthermore, cultural and individual diversity varies across contexts. One of the problems we face in the Canadian and Toronto context is the question of how to assess cultural diversity. The majority of Canadians are of Anglophone or Francophone descent and have English or French as a first language, with the other official language as a second language. According to Statistics Canada Census (1996) the aboriginal population is approximately 3% of the Canadian population. Moreover, the census has shown that in urban areas like Toronto, Vancouver and Montreal, the concentration of immigrant families is much higher. For example, in Toronto more than 40% of families have a language other than English or French as a first language, and it is not uncommon for a school to have 40 or more different ethnic groups represented among its children.

Because of the complexities associated with multilingual/multicultural differences we view it as especially important that our students develop a knowledge base with respect to issues related to diversity. These include recognizing that diversity issues may impact the ways that individuals learn and interact and the ways individuals understand mental health and learning problems. Students also need to recognize that consideration of diversity issues is sometimes necessary in order to appropriately assess learning potential, as well as social and emotional difficulties. They need to understand the impact that diversity issues have on treatment planning, and become familiar with the relevant legal and ethical principles in psychology as they apply to working with diverse populations.

We believe that we are especially successful at inculcating in our students a positive attitude toward diversity and teaching them the relevant skills. We incorporate issues of diversity in all of our courses, and have some specific courses devoted to cultural and linguistic diversity. In practicum settings, students have considerable exposure to diverse populations. In addition, our students are themselves from culturally diverse backgrounds, and bring their own experience to class discussions.

Practicum

Students in the SCCP program are placed in three types of settings. The Counselling and Psychoeducational clinic is an in-house clinic whose mandate is professional training of graduate students, clinical research, and providing services to the Toronto community. Children's Services, which is mainly associated with the SCCP program, provides psychological assessments, remediation for children and adolescents with reading, writing and mathematics difficulties, and therapy for children, adolescents and families. SCCP students, who provide these assessments and interventions, are supervised directly by SCCP faculty who are registered psychologists. The Clinic has a test library that has a large collection of psychological and educational tests. The Clinical Director of the SCCP program is also the Co-Director of the Clinic and acts as principal liaison between the Clinic and the SCCP program. This person is responsible for ensuring that students working in the Clinic learn the basics of the professional role of a psychologist within a Clinic environment. The majority of children and adolescents who are referred to the Clinic receive assessments. Some children with learning difficulties receive remediation. Clients are typically self-referred. Parents hear about our services through schools, physicians, mental health agencies, OISE/UT faculty and staff, previous clients, and graduate students. The Clinic serves as a resource for clients who need to obtain low-cost services. Subsidies are provided for clients who cannot afford the standard fee.

The MA practicum is typically done in school settings. Most practicum placements are in large school districts that have psychology departments with several PhD-level registered psychologists who are committed to training our students and which serve a culturally and socioeconomically diverse population. We seek out supervisors who will provide our students with a wide range of training and educational experiences, including psychological assessment, consultation regarding learning and behavioral problems, participation in multidisciplinary teams, and in-service work shops.

The doctoral practicum is typically done in a hospital clinic or children's mental health centre. All of these centres have a very strong commitment to training students, have PhD-level registered psychologists who supervise students, have a variety of training opportunities, provide access to a culturally and individually diverse population, and have multidisciplinary teams providing services. In most of these locations, professional services are accompanied by high-level clinical research.

The minimum practicum experience required by the program in field placements is 750 hours (250 hours at the MA level, and 500 hours at the PhD level). At least 175 of those hours are direct service and 90 of those hours involve face-to-face supervision. In addition, students typically spend approximately 360 hours working in their in-house practica at the OISE/UT Counselling and Psychoeducational Clinic. In practice, our students typically get considerably more applied experience than the suggested minimum, with the average student spending approximately 1200 hours in practicum placements (including paid clinical work) prior to their internship. Prior to beginning the internship, students are required to submit to the Clinical Director five complete psychological assessment reports and documentation of at least 50 hours of intervention experience.

We employ five major strategies for integrating the academic and practicum components of our program. First, some of the practicum experiences are done in the context of in-house practicum courses in which faculty both provide the academic content and supervise students conducting assessments and intervention. Second, students in the field practicum courses meet with the Clinical Director biweekly in a seminar in which they discuss issues of relevance to the field experience. These classes provide an opportunity for students to state concerns, review strategies for dealing with ethical dilemmas, and discuss specific cases. Third, most of our field supervisors have supervised students in our program for many years. We acknowledge and formalize the relationships between the supervisors and the core program by giving 'status only' titles to the placement supervisors. Fourth, several of our clinical supervisors also teach courses, are members of thesis committees, or supervise theses of students in SCCP. The overlapping roles of field supervisors and course instructors facilitate communication between the field and the faculty and contribute to the coherence of the training experience for the students. Fifth, the Clinical Director plays a major role in providing the necessary formal communication between the field settings and program faculty. She does so by teaching the practicum seminar courses, meeting with students to assist them with decision-making regarding their placements, supporting them in the application process, telephoning practicum supervisors, visiting practicum sites, taking an active role in resolving conflicts between students and supervisors, and organizing an annual meeting during which staff at placement settings present their settings to students and faculty.

Program Organization

The faculty in the SCCP program function as an integral part of the Department of Human Development and Applied Psychology (HDAP) and participate fully in the general administration and academic life of the department. There are two leadership positions in the SCCP Program – the Program Chair and the Clinical Director. The Program Chair is a senior tenured faculty member whose role is to coordinate the program, represent the program on the HDAP Department Executive, and to chair the SCCP Program Committee in addition to the normal faculty responsibilities of research and teaching. The Clinical Director is a lecturer whose role is to coordinate the practicum and internship program, teach the two seminars accompanying the field placement practica, and advise students on career planning. The advantage of splitting the leadership of the program is that the academic leadership is provided by a faculty member who is respected for her/his scholarly work and, as a result, is a credible representative of the program in a department that values high academic and research standards. Likewise, the Clinical Director's strong clinical and administrative skills are essential for the credibility of the clinical training in the field. Working as a team, this is a very effective strategy for facilitating a strong academic and clinical program.

The core program faculty epitomize the scientist-scholar-practitioner. All are registered psychologists who engage in both basic and applied research and who have considerable experience and training as school or clinical child psychologists. The core faculty is complemented by other departmental faculty, all of whom have a background in developmental psychology, who teach courses available to SCCP students and supervise student research. In addition, several external faculty who are world-renowned clinical researchers in local hospital clinics and children's mental health centres also supervise student research and teach courses on an extra mural basis on specialized topics. Finally, our students are supervised clinically by licensed school and clinical psychologists in a variety of settings.

At any one time, the 8 to 9 core SCCP faculty teach approximately 80 students. The students are admitted on the basis of academic excellence, evidence of relevant experience working with children, and research experience. The student body is diverse in terms of age, cultural/linguistic background, and areas of interest. From the outset we ensure that students' and program goals are concordant by selecting students whose stated interests when they apply are in working with children in school or mental health settings, and whose research interests are similar to those of at least one faculty member. Although at the outset most students see themselves working in primarily clinical roles, by the time they graduate not only is there a better balance between students who want to work in schools versus clinical settings, but many want to include research as part of their responsibilities. Due to small cohorts of students who take several courses together in their first two years, and the research groups, which facilitate cross-cohort socialization, the students tend to collaborate a great deal.

The process that drives our continuous search for excellence is self-study. Core faculty, student representatives, and support staff participate in our regular program meetings where we discuss policy, curriculum, and student issues. We collect survey data from our graduates and from students in the program in order to get feedback to guide our planning. Part of our accountability process includes monitoring the clinical and academic progress of students. As a faculty, we review each student's progress annually, and revisit students for whom there are concerns.

As part of the self-study process we are continuously exploring new directions which reflect the dynamism in the model, and lead to improvement in our training. One of the new directions we are considering is to provide more intensive training in prevention and interprofessional case management. We believe that to be effective and reflective practitioners, our students need to learn techniques for initiating and implementing primary and secondary prevention programs in school and community settings. In so doing, they need to learn how to work in interprofessional teams. They also need to learn how social policy affects the situation of many children and families, and how to influence social policy themselves.

One of the problems we face is that many of our practicum placements, often in reaction to constraints imposed by government, offer traditional, brief, snap-shot style assessments that do not carefully consider the influence of context on the child, and provide short-term interventions that have limited impact. These procedures are often costly in the long-run. Therefore, we need to identify and collaborate with practicum settings where psychologists work in interprofessional teams that provide models of more flexible, long-term, innovative prevention and intervention programs.

Conclusion

One of the implications of the developmental-ecological model described at the outset of this chapter is the combining of the fields of school and clinical child psychology in training individuals to work as professional child psychologists. The SCCP program is unique in that we combine this conceptual framework with the scientist-scholar-practitioner model. Practitioners trained in this way think about children, youth, and families in a holistic or systemic way, develop flexible and innovative methods for assessing and intervening with them, and have the skills to monitor and evaluate the strategies they use and the outcomes for the client.

The SCCP program is also unique in that graduates opting to pursue research careers are trained to consider children's functioning within dynamic, complex contexts. Their training and experience in providing clinical services to children, youth, and families in school, clinic, and community settings should enhance graduates' ability to develop worthwhile hypotheses for research involving innovative prevention and intervention programs. This training should also better prepare graduates to collaborate with others and, ultimately, to undertake pivotal roles in shaping social policies that affect children's needs and children's functioning in educational and health systems.

References

Barlow, D. H., Hayes, S. C., & Nelson, R. O. (1984). *The scientist practitioner: Research and accountability in clinical and educational settings.* New York: Pergamon.

Bowman, M. L. (2000). The diversity of diversity: Canadian-American differences and their implications for clinical training and APA accreditation. *Canadian Psychology, 41,* 230-243.

Bronfenbrenner, U. (1989). Ecological systems theory. In R. Vasta (Ed.), *Annals of child development* (Vol.6, pp. 187-249) Greenwich, CT: JAI Press.

Christenson, S., Abery, B., & Weinberg, R.A. (1986). An alternative model for the delivery of psychological services in the school community. In S. Elliot & J. Witt (Eds.), *The delivery of psychological services in schools: Concepts, products and issues* (pp. 349-391). Hillsdale, NJ: Erlbaum.

Christenson, S., & Buerkle, K. (1999). Families as educational partners for children's school success: Suggestions for school psychologists. In C. R. Reynolds & T. B. Gutkin (Eds.), *The handbook of school psychology* (3rd ed., pp. 709-744). New York: Wiley.

Cole, E., & Siegel, J.A. (1990). Suicide prevention in schools: Facing the challenge. In E. Cole & J. A. Siegel (Eds.), *Effective consultation in school psychology* (pp. 247-278). Toronto: Hogrefe and Huber.

Diagnostic and Statistical Manual of Mental Disorders – Fourth Edition (1994). Washington, DC: American Psychiatric Association.

Garmezy, N., & Rutter, M. (1983). *Stress, coping, and development in children.* New York: McGraw Hill.

Geva, E., Barsky, A., & Westernoff, F. (2000). *Interprofessional practice with diverse populations.* Westport, CT: Auburn House.

Greene, R. W. (1995). Students with ADHD in school classrooms: Teacher factors related to compatibility, assessment, and intervention. *School Psychology Review, 24,* 81-93.

Gutkin, T. B., & Curtis, M. J. (1999). School-based consultation theory and practice: The art and science of indirect service delivery. In C. R. Reynolds & T. B. Gutkin (Eds.), *The handbook of school psychology* (3rd ed., pp. 598-637). New York: Wiley.

Hunsley, J., Dobson, K., Johnson, C., & Mikhail, S. F. (1999). Empirically supported treatments in psychology: Implications for Canadian professional psychology. *Canadian Psychology, 40,* 289-302.

Lewis, M. (1999). Conceptualization of developmental psychopathology. In M. Lewis & S. M. Miller (Eds.), *Handbook of developmental psychopathology* (pp. 3-27). New York: Plenum.

Meyers, J. L., & Nastasi, B. K. (1999). Primary prevention in school settings. In C. R. Reynolds & T. B. Gutkin (Eds.), *The handbook of school psychology* (3rd ed., pp. 764-799). New York: Wiley.

Nastasi, B. K. (2000). School psychologists as health-care providers in the 21st century: Conceptual framework, professional identity, and professional practice. *School Psychology Review, 29,* 540-554.

Offord, D. R., Boyle, M. H., & Racine, Y. A. (1991). The epidemiology of antisocial behavior in childhood and adolescence. In D. Pepler & K. Rubin (Eds.), *The development and treatment of childhood aggression* (pp. 31-54). Hillsdale, NJ: Erlbaum.

Prout, H. T. (1999). Counselling and psychotherapy with children and adolescents: An overview. In H. T. Prout & D. T. Brown (Eds.), *Counselling and psychotherapy with children and adolescent: Theory and practice for school and clinical settings* (pp. 1-25). New York: Wiley.

Statistics Canada Census (1996). Canadian Statistics: Immigrant Population http://www.statscan.ca

Swerdlik, M. E., & French, J. L. (2000). School psychology training for the 21st century: Challenges and opportunities. *School Psychology Review, 29,* 577-588.

Part 2

The Psychologist as a Change Agent

Chapter 7
Collaborative Consultation Training in a Multicultural Context

Solveiga Miezitis

Collaborative consultation has been recognized for its value in school psychology service delivery since the early 1970's; however, induction in this practice still presents a challenge not only for novice school psychologists, but also for highly skilled and seasoned practitioners who have focused on prescriptive diagnostic work and expert oriented models of intervention practice. Although psychologists may be well trained in data gathering and problem solving skills required for effective school consultation, there is no guarantee that they will be able to successfully apply these skills in a variety of consultation settings and cultural contexts. The aim of this chapter is to discuss my experience in collaborative consultation training in two vastly different multicultural contexts, Canada and Latvia, which has led to an examination of collaborative consultation training from a multicultural and feminist perspective and, the development of a peer supervision framework.

Historical Perspective: Learning to Practice Classroom Consultation

To begin with, I wish to acknowledge the contribution made by Seymour Sarason (Miezitis, 1991; Sarason, 1966) and David Hunt (1987, 1992) to my philosophy and practice of school consultation and my approach to consultation training.

I began the practice of classroom observation-based teacher consultation in 1973, in collaboration with a doctoral student Mary Morris, who worked with me as researcher and co-leader of a professional development workshop. We offered an inservice training program for grade 1 teachers interested in learning about ways of helping distractible children adjust to school expectations as part of a research project (Miezitis, 1973). Our twelve session weekly program consisted of theoretical presentations and the discussion of individual cases brought forward by the teachers who had volunteered for this project.

As part of the training sessions, we analyzed each case, solicited regular input and feedback from the workshop participants and suggested recommendations for ways of handling the children in various classroom situations. However, it soon became apparent that the suggestions were not always implemented or were, in fact, not yielding the expected results. After several weeks we began to sense the mounting frustration that teachers were experiencing, and began to fear that the teachers, who had volunteered for our program, would drop out and we would not be able to complete the project. We realized that we were missing some very crucial information about the teacher-pupil interactions and decided to offer to visit the teachers in their classrooms and collect some first hand observations on the referred children's behavior. We hoped to gain additional information from an "outsider's" perspective to help the teachers to understand the difficulties experienced by the "distractible" children.

When we first walked in a classroom to conduct observations and advise teachers, as the 'experts on distractibility', we felt quite overwhelmed with the complexity of classroom life. My co-leader and I began to notice that a teacher often had inconsistent or even opposite reactions to different children exhibiting similar behaviors. Our initial half day observations coupled with the information that the teachers had offered in their case presentations and the pre and post observation interviews allowed us to gain some insight into the teacher's expectations and perceptions of thriving and non thriving children in their classroom. Discussions of video taped classroom interactions with each individual teacher as well as with the workshop participants, provided further opportunities to unravel the complexities of the problems faced by the classroom teacher and clarify some of our divergent and puzzling observations. The observers' background of professional experience, philosophy of education, personality style, attitudes, expectations and understandings of the situation all contributed to the richness of the discussion and provided opportunities for bringing content into what was becoming a collaborative process rather than a structured, content driven training program. The participants became more open and enthusiastic about the meetings as time went on, an atmosphere of trust and collegial support developed. Eventually even the most reluctant participants were eager to have the "consultants" visit their classrooms and invited comments on their videos.

Working in tandem with Mary Morris, who, like myself, was a psychologist with both school and clinical experience, we learned that our perceptions and understandings of a particular situation could be quite different. While one of us might feel very comfortable and find it easy to communicate with a particular teacher, the other might falter and vice versa with another teacher or in reference to another child. As we shared our observations and held joint interviews with the teachers, we appreciated the fact that having collegial support and a sounding board to help clarify complex issues was very important, especially in the initial phase of consultation practice.

Normally we complemented each other and were able to offer the right kind of information or observation to clarify a situation or help contain or explain the teacher's reaction, but there were times when we were both puzzled. These were difficult situations when we needed to brainstorm and explore the resistances that were interfering with the problem solving process. At such times, consultants need the support and encouragement from a colleague or supervisor to overcome the impasse and move forward, or recognize when to stand back to facilitate a constructive problem solving process.

When I reflect back on our experience, I recognize that we were, in fact, engaged in what I later identified as a peer consultation relationship, as we were both learning to carry out classroom observation-based collaborative teacher consultation. We learned a lot from the teacher feedback regarding our consultation practice. Over a six month period, while working in 14 different classrooms for two half days several weeks apart, we gained considerable skill and confidence in classroom observation based assessment and the collaborative problem solving process. New perspectives emerged about the children who were initially labeled "distractible." Some were simply active children, others immature or anxious or depressed, and relatively few, were presenting with attention deficit or hyperactivity symptoms (Miezitis, 1974).

The professional development workshop experience combined with classroom observation based consultation led to the formulation of *An In-Service Training/ Classroom Consultation Model for Offering Psychological Services to Schools* (Miezitis, 1977), as well as *A Psychodynamic Teacher Consultation Model for Depressed Children* (Morris, 1978). The recognition of the prevalence of depression among "distractible" children led to further research on assessment and school based intervention and prevention approaches with depressed children (Miezitis, 1992a). Classroom consultation interventions were specifically targeted for this population in *Teacher-Mediated Intervention with Depressed Children* (Miezitis, 1992b), followed by *Parent-Mediated Intervention with Depressed Children* (Miezitis, Fiksel, & Butler, 1992), and explorations of teacher understandings of emotions and sources of resistance during the consultation process (Bergsteinson & Miezitis, 1992; Smith & Miezitis, 1992). Follow-up evaluations of collaborative classroom consultation (Butler & Miezitis, 1980; Miezitis, Butler, & Friedman, 1977; Miezitis & Scholten, 1990; Morris, 1978) showed improvement or resolution of the problem in about 80% of the referred cases.

Subsequently, prevention became a major focus of our work with my doctoral student and colleague Ester Cole. Whereas teacher and parent-mediated intervention was aimed at helping those in daily contact with depressed children to alleviate the children's distress and facilitate change, Cole's work extended *Parent Teacher Mediated Intervention as a Growth Promoting Process* (Cole, 1986). Teacher and parent consultations were supplemented with *Group Interventions Using Role Play* (Butler, Miezitis, Friedman & Cole, 1979; Cole, 1979; Miezitis, Butler, Cole, & Friedman, 1992) to improve children's social skills. A system wide prevention safety net (Heath, Humphries, & Miezitis, 1996; Miezitis et al.,1992) was proposed to ensure preventive collaboration between school, family and community resources. Finally, the idea of releasing creativity in the schools by introducing innovations and changes to anticipate and meet challenges at the system's level was proposed as a potential antidote to depression (Miezitis, 1992c). Creativity is currently widely recognized as a wellness factor and is supported by research in positive psychology (Csikszentmihalyi & Seligman, 2000).

Collaborative Consultation in a Multicultural Context

My initial experience in consultation training was with school psychology students at OISE. I was teaching a seminar and supervising the practice of classroom observation based teacher-mediated intervention using the conceptual process consultation framework proposed by Schein (1969). Research on process consultation practice in school settings indicates that this type of approach enables consultees to be active and take on a leadership role in the consultation process (Gutkin, 1999). Schein (1993) illustrates the contribution of the collaborative consultation process in teaching since it offers opportunities for flexible integration of content with process. In retrospect, I have noticed that over time my teaching and supervision practice has significantly altered and reflects the collaborative style of process consultation.

In 1997, when I began to teach consultation in the newly merged Adult Education and Counseling Psychology department at OISE, I developed courses focusing on leadership through organizational change to support educators and human resource workers in facilitating change in their workplaces. Change management models such as those proposed by Bridges (2001) and Prochaska, DiClemente, and Norcross (1992), and the emotional and social competence framework presented by Goleman, (1998a, 1998b) were introduced to help change agents to understand, plan and support personal, work, and societal transitions. Small group process and peer consultation became an integral part of these Adult education oriented courses.

Since 1991, I have also been involved in consultation training in the Faculty of Education and Psychology at the University of Latvia. Latvia is situated between the Baltic sea and the Western border of the old Soviet Union, and is one of the East European countries that regained its independence in 1991, after 50 years of Soviet occupation. Although Latvia has culturally been allied with Northern Europe and is oriented to Western ways of thinking, social relationships and communication patterns in post-Soviet countries still present challenges to educators from the West. The basic assumption that change can be facilitated through a joint problem solving process in a context of mutual trust and open dialogue is not easily embraced in a society that has lived under a coercive regime and is still cautious about openness and trust.

The challenges faced by Western consultants and trainers when working in Eastern Europe have been well documented by Horne (Horne & Mathews, in press). Based on her consultation experiences in schools, crisis centers and community projects in several vastly different Eastern and East European countries including Russia, Uzbekistan, Kosova, Romania, Macedonia, and Hungary, Horne has integrated multicultural and feminist principles of practice with collaborative consultation to develop a Multicultural Feminist Consultation model. This model extends collaborative process consultation approaches to address the values, interaction styles, and perceptions of Western ways prevalent among people who have been socialized in a collectivist authoritarian system.

In her conceptualization of multicultural school consultation, Horne introduces the basic tenets of multicultural and feminist perspectives derived from current thinking in these areas. She presents the content and process of consultation through a cultural lens focusing on "the world views, cultural backgrounds, perspectives, and group and individual differences of each member of the consultation system" (Ingraham, 2000, p. 326). Cole and Siegel (1990) have addressed multicultural issues specifically in relation to the school psychologist's response to children's needs in North America.

One of the main tenets of collaborative consultation assumes an egalitarian relationship between all participants. From a philosophical point of view, inequity issues have been addressed in feminist perspectives, which call for the consideration of context, and a dialectical approach that explores both diversities and commonalities within social contexts (Fine, 1985). Feminist theory offers an analysis of power relationships that can be applied to multiple scenarios of oppression, including ethnic and culturally different groups. Since I am working in a complex multicultural situation in my role as a Canadian-Latvian consultant/trainer in relation to my Latvian and Russian students/trainees these differences need to be addressed in the modeling of collaborative consultant/consultee/client relationships. I have recently revisited my consultation training experiences in light of Horne's Multicultural-Feminist Consultation perspectives, and would like to offer some of my observations for consideration in school consultant training.

Horne and Mathews (in press) propose a set of working principles of Multicultural Feminist Consultation (referred to as M-F) which inform consultation training practice. These include:

(1) *Setting a Context for M-F collaboration*, which involves describing the trainer's approach to consultation work and the sharing of value orientations. This process explicitly addresses the issues of power sharing among participants in collaborative consultation, cultural sensitivity and a commitment to egalitarian practices.

(2) *Consultants' self-evaluation of biases and values*. This process includes check-ins regarding cultural assumptions and language nuances and associations. I have found this component to be particularly important in multicultural contexts and in international consultation ventures. As a consultation trainer, I

have to be constantly aware of my own biases as a psychologist trained in the West, and a Canadian having lived my life in a democratic society. I also have to bring into the discussion the multicultural reality of Latvia where only 52% of the population is Latvian.

(3) *Engaging in power sharing.* This involves the creation of opportunities for alternate discourses to emerge. I engaged in the exploration of meanings and invited feedback regarding the validity and applicability of the ideas I was presenting within the Latvian, as well as the Russian cultural contexts. I was particularly aware of the Russian students in my class who, although sufficiently knowledgeable in Latvian to have passed highly competitive university entrance exams, often brought another set of associations and meanings to language.

Furthermore, the students as children were socialized in a society where the Russians were the dominant power group and Russian language the dominant language. Since independence, Latvian is the official language and Latvians are reclaiming their national status and power. This process is not without struggle and conflict. Hence open acknowledgement of these issues is essential to avoid hidden agendas and unresolved conflicts from sabotaging constructive collaboration.

(4) *Privileging consultees' needs and goals.* Acknowledgement and sharing of participants' differing personal beliefs and worldviews, as well as their goals and aspirations is a process that promotes the development of mutual understanding and trust.

(5) *Maintaining an awareness of the impact of consultation on consultants.* I have found that sharing the stories and the insights gained from the consultation experience with colleagues helps to clarify issues and integrate the transformative effect of these learning experiences in our practice. Offering recognition and celebrating successes is an important factor in promoting personal growth and self-renewal in collaborative ventures (Hunt, 1992).

In my initial in-service training work with teachers of distractible children, the program evaluation reports revealed that the positive comments offered by colleagues and seminar leaders were perceived as the most important component of the training that generalized to teachers' classroom practice. Experiencing the personal benefits of trainer and peer recognition convinced them of the value of positive reinforcement in the teaching/learning process. Hence it is important to promote the development of peer consultation networks, to provide collegial support and prevent burn-out.

(6) *Evaluating the process and following up.* I had noticed in my early work as a school psychologist that follow-up is a critical component of practice to ensure implementation and maintain the gains of assessment recommendations. The importance of follow-up was brought home by the fact that so often, as things began to improve, and the psychologist considered the task completed, teachers tended to slide back into their previous interaction patterns, and were

quick to conclude that the psychologist's recommendations were not helping to solve the referred children's problems. The "expert" diagnostic assessment model of psychological service delivery in schools leaves the psychologist open to criticism as someone who does not understand what goes on in the classroom and does not provide recommendations that can be implemented. Collaborative consultation practice helps to circumvent these perceptions because it ensures an on-going relationship between the service provider and client and helps to prevent feelings of abandonment and disappointment from arising as the "expert" leaves the scene without offering the opportunity for further contacts, if the need arises.

Follow-up is a critical component of consultant training with consultees, as well as clients to help ensure that the changes initiated through the collaborative process are maintained and that consultees have access to further consultant support as new issues arise. For example, Matthew and Horne (2002) report that consulting work participants in a women's crisis center in Hungary expressed in structured evaluation interviews that the most valuable part of the consultation was the attention to the process of the consulting interaction. Their participants had indicated that experiential participation in role-plays, exercises and games had helped them to understand the information presented, as well as the dynamics among participants on a more personally relevant level. In the evaluation of consultation training, participants both in Canada and Latvia reported that the modeling of support helped to develop a trusting collaborative training atmosphere and that role-play was one of the most powerful components of consultation training.

The Evolution of Consultation Training at the University of Latvia

When I first began to work as a visiting professor at the University of Latvia, I was teaching consultation skills to first year Master's students in the School Psychology program. Most of these students were already employed as school psychologists and their workplace served as practicum placement for their consultation training. I based the course on the three-tiered consultation framework for school psychology service delivery described by Siegel and Cole (1990) and introduced them to the Teacher-mediated intervention model (Miezitis, 1992b). Students learn about the philosophy and skills of the process consultant role in class exercises (observation, active listening, role play, and interview skills) and then go out in the schools and act as teacher consultants. Students are encouraged to elicit a referral case on the basis of a teacher interview. In my experience, withdrawn, unresponsive, low functioning, potentially depressed children respond particularly well to teacher mediated intervention.

Students were asked to observe the referred child along with a well-functioning same sex classmate in various school activities, interview the teachers about their perceptions of the two children, collaboratively identify a problem and involve the teacher in experimentation with some jointly agreed upon approaches for working with the withdrawn child using some of the strategies that the consultant had observed in the teacher's repertoire when interacting with the thriving child. The students were urged to express their appreciation of the teacher's efforts and empathy for the feelings of frustration and helplessness to help reduce anxiety and increase the teacher's awareness of the child's needs and their ability to meet these within the regular classroom structure. Consultants can help the teacher to recognize the child's unmet dependency needs (Morris, 1992), and offer support to help overcome the child's sense of inadequacy. Teachers, once relieved of their own sense of insecurity, helplessness, and frustration, can usually intuitively begin to provide the right kind of containment and encouragement to help these children succeed. Children who manifest depressive tendencies are particularly responsive to a collaborative classroom consultation process that offers some support to the teacher, who in a sense is mirroring the depressive child's feelings of helplessness and avoidant behaviors towards the child.

This type of consultation practice has proven to be quite successful in introducing beginning school psychologists to teacher consultation both in Canada and Latvia because the student can, in most cases, experience success and teacher acknowledgement and thus gain self-confidence in their practice and begin to have faith in the effectiveness of the consultative process.

Since 2000, the consultation student population at the University of Latvia has changed and class size has doubled. I am now teaching classes of 35 students of varying age, education background and experience from several universities in Latvia which offer very different programs leading to a Bachelor's degree in psychology. The consultation course students are enrolled in the first year of a two year Master's program leading to one of three specializations, clinical, school, or organizational psychology. About half of the students have no background or experience in applied psychology, and come from undergraduate programs that offer very little practical training. Those with job experience in schools, clinics, hospitals and business organizations present themselves with a variety of professional attitudes and entry skills, which are not always conducive to successful collaborative consultation practice. Furthermore, many students have limited access to a job or practicum placement, and typically there is no on site supervision due to the limited resources and paucity of trained process consultation practitioners. The situation presents challenges to the students as well as the instructor.

How to resolve the dilemma and offer a practice based course that enables a heterogeneous group of students to gain a meaningful experience in consultation practice in a wide variety of employment or practicum settings that normally do not provide role models or supervision? How to encourage students to start applying their consultative skills to real life situations so that they can expand the role model of psychological service delivery from the traditional assessment and individual psychotherapy intervention approach used in Latvia, to a more broadly based indirect systems approach which focuses on prevention rather than crisis intervention?

Collaborative Peer Supervision Model for Consultation Training

I have been experimenting with several approaches that have resulted in the development of a collaborative peer supervision model that allows the students to process their real life practicum experiences in small supervisory groups with their peers acting in a consultative role towards each other. Although this approach was dictated by circumstances, namely, working as a distance educator with only three two-week long visits to Latvia during the academic year, I discovered that the limitation of my long absences had beneficial effects on the development of professional confidence in my students, once they had overcome their initial fears and resistances. Not having direct access to an "expert," the students learned to engage wholeheartedly in a collaborative peer group process to learn and practice skills, to obtain supportive feedback needed to reduce their insecurities, and to learn to rely on each other as colleagues who are all striving to service their clients in a collaborative problem solving consultation process.

The course runs all year from October to June, and I usually meet with students during the first half of October, March, and June. I introduce students to the practicum components of the consultation training as follows:
(1) Phase I – Theory and personal change component (October-March)
    First personal evaluation report (October)
(2) Practicum case supervision (November-February)
    Practicum case report and case discussions (March)
(3) Practicum Follow-up and Evaluation (April-May)
    Follow-up report (May)
(4) Creativity Life Map assignment (March)
(5) Follow-up case discussions (June)
(6) Creativity Life Map "Show and Tell" and final celebration (June)

Phase I – Personal Change Component

I have been a long time follower of David Hunt's principle of praxis: Beginning with ourselves (Hunt, 1987). At the beginning of the course, I elicited case scenarios drawn from each participant's own repertoire of success and failure experiences in effecting change in personal or work situations. After extensive discussions about the situational factors, personal characteristics and interpersonal dynamics that contributed to their prior success and failure experiences as change agents, I asked the students to identify their personal strengths and weaknesses as potential consultants. This data served as a basis for discussing the dynamics of facilitating change.

The students were then introduced to models of emotional intelligence (Gardner, 1983; Goleman, 1995; Mayer & Solvay, 1997) and change (Bridges, 1998, 2001; Prochaska et al., 1992). They were then asked to conduct a self-analysis using Goleman's framework of Social and Emotional Competencies (Goleman, 1998b) and to identify an area of perceived weakness which they would like to work on as a personal growth project in their peer supervision group. The following week we heard about each student's self-improvement goal and helped to clarify or modify the proposed goals, if needed. After this initial discussion, the class divided up into small groups of four and held its first peer supervision meeting. During this initial meeting, each group member had an opportunity to describe their goal and break it down into observable units of change. The task of the peer consultation process was to help each group member to identify the actual steps that they could take to experiment with change in their chosen area and to receive feedback as they reported on their progress on their personal growth project. They were required to document their goals, their plan of action, and reflect on the insights gained from the personal experience and peer feedback.

Phase II – Practicum Case Supervision

Each participant was also asked to select a client in a consultation setting and identify a concrete problem to work and report on in their bi-weekly peer supervision meetings over a 3 month period, and to keep a log of the consultation sessions, as well as the supervision sessions. The peer supervision group was to provide participants the opportunity to report on their progress and seek feedback and additional suggestions from the group members. Peer consultation practice included active listening, brainstorming, joint problem solving, role play, support and other skill training, feedback on the work with clients, and collegial support. Students were asked to describe their consultation meetings with the client, as well as the peer group supervision feedback in their report. Selected cases were presented in class to illustrate and discuss a variety of issues and challenges and to provide additional theoretical and practical input. Students completed follow-up and evaluation procedures and revisited their project for a final follow-up and closure to their experience. Evaluation criteria for consultation training suggested by Brock and Donaldson (2000) were included in this process.

Phase III – Creativity Life Map

The final self-exploration assignment involves creating and presenting a personal creativity life map. These creativity maps can be based on visual representations and include reflections on creative development beginning as far back as the student can remember, identifying the people and situations that enhanced and inhibited their creative sense of self. This assignment focuses on the role of emotional intelligence and creativity in adapting to change, coping with stress, and experiencing renewal.

Theories of emotional intelligence, and their potential applications in school and organizational settings are attracting the interest of consultants in health related fields, as well as in business. Various conceptualizations of creativity and the creative process (Sternberg, 1999), with a particular focus on everyday creativity (Cropley, 1992) have rekindled the interest in the study of creativity as a protective mechanism and facilitator of change, as well as a process of self-actualization and invention. Since the role of consultant involves the facilitation of change in clients, whether they are teachers, administrators, students, or parents, understanding the creative process enables the consultant to help identify personality and systems characteristics (Csikszentmihalyi, 1999) that can act as potential facilitating or inhibiting factors in change. Thus students are invited to use the creativity map exercise to increase their self-awareness of creativity fostering and inhibiting factors, and learn to apply this knowledge in their work with their clients.

Conclusion

In conclusion, during the 30 years of consultation training using several different models of service delivery in two vastly different cultures, I have learned that what really matters in training, as well as in actual consultation work with clients, is good rapport, and an atmosphere of trust and respect that allows the participants to reach a mutual understanding of the issues involved in the problem solving process. As trainers or consultants, we are facilitators in a process that empowers people to feel confident to explore and experiment with alternative approaches to problem situations. Ability to listen, to understand, to support, to acknowledge the consultant's and consultee's efforts, and to open the space for considering other alternatives for intervention creates a climate for change. Consultants support teachers, trainers support trainees, and peers can take on the consultant or trainer role as the need arises. An understanding of the process of change and an awareness of intra and interpersonal skills or social and emotional competences contributes to successful consultation practice.

References

Bergsteinson, D., & Miezitis, S. (1992) The exploration of emotional factors in teacher-pupil relationships. In S. Miezitis (Ed.), *Creating alternatives to depression in our schools* (pp. 157-171). Toronto: Hogrefe & Huber.

Bridges, W. (1998). *Transitions*. New York: Harper Collins.

Bridges, W. (2001). *The way of transition*. New York: Harper Collins.

Brock, W. M., & Donaldson, D. L. (2000). *A developmental model for student training in consultation*. A paper presented at the Annual Conference of the International School Psychology Association.

Butler, L., & Miezitis, S. (1980). *Releasing children from depression: A handbook for elementary teachers and consultants*. Toronto: OISE Press.

Butler, L., Miezitis, S., Friedman, R. J., & Cole, E. (1979). The effect of two school-based interventions with depressive school children. *American Educational Research Journal. 17*, 111-119.

Cole, E. (1979). *Role-playing as a modality for alleviating* depressive *symptoms in 10-12-year old children*. Unpublished doctoral dissertation, University of Toronto, The Ontario Institute for Studies in Education, Toronto.

Cole, E. (1986). Parent-teacher mediated intervention: A growth promoting process. *Canadian Journal of School Psychology, 3*, 33-46.

Cole, E., & Siegel, J.A. (1990). School psychology in a multicultural community: Responding to children's needs. In E. Cole & J. A. Siegel (Eds.), *Effective consultation in school psychology* (pp. 141-169). Toronto: Hogrefe & Huber Publishing.

Cropley, A. J. (1992). *More ways than one: Fostering creativity*. Norwood. NJ: Ablex.

Csikszentmihalyi, M. (1999). Implications of a systems perspective for the study of creativity. In R. J. Sternberg (Ed.), *Handbook of creativity* (pp. 313-335). Cambridge University Press.

Csikszentmihalyi, M., & Seligman, M. E. P. (2000). (Guest Eds.). Positive Psychology. *American Psychologist*.

Fine, M. (1985). Reflections on a feminist psychology of women: Paradoxes and prospects. *Psychology of Women Quarterly, 9*, 167-183.

Gardner, H. (1983). *Frames of mind*. New York: Basic Books.

Goleman, D. (1995). *Emotional intelligence*. New York: Bantam Books.

Goleman, D. (1998a). What makes a leader? *Harvard Business Review*. Nov.-Dec.

Goleman, D. (1998b). *Working with emotional intelligence*. Toronto: Bantam Books.

Gutkin, T. B. (1999). Collaborative versus directive/prescriptive/expert school-based consultation: Reviewing and resolving a false dichotomy. *Journal of School Psychology, 37(2)*, 161-190.

Heath, N. L., Humphries, T., & Miezitis, S. (1996). Providing services for youth who are depressed. *Exceptional Children in Canada. 5*, 157-175.

Horne, S. G., & Mathews, S. S. (in press). Collaborative consultation: International applications of a multicultural feminist approach. *Journal of Multicultural Counseling and Development*.

Hunt, D. E. (1987). *Beginning with ourselves*. Cambridge, MA/Toronto: Brookline Books/OISE Press.

Hunt, D. E. (1992). *The renewal of personal energy*. Monograph Series / 25. Toronto: OISE Press: The Ontario Institute for Studies in Education.

Ingraham, C. L. (2000). Consultation through a multicultural lens: Multicultural and cross-cultural consultation in schools. *School Psychology Review, 29(3)*, 320-343.

Matthews, S. S., & Horne, S. G. (2002). *A qualitative analysis of Hungarian crisis counselors' experiences.* (Manuscript submitted for publication.)

Mayer, J., & Solovey, P. (1997). *What is emotional intelligence.* New York: Basic Books.

Miezitis, S. (1973) *Development of an in-service training program to help teachers decrease distractibility in their pupils.* Grants-in-aid project #5016, Final Report, OISE.

Miezitis, S. (1974). Distractible children in the grade 1 classroom. *Orbit, 5,* 17-22.

Miezitis, S. (1977) An in-service training/classroom consultation model for rendering psychological services to schools. In S. Miezitis & M. Orme (Eds.), *Innovation in school psychology* (pp. 59-69). OISE.

Miezitis, S. (1991). Visiting with Seymour Sarason: Reflections on the training and the professional identity of school psychologists. *Ontario Psychologist, 23(5),* 10-11.

Miezitis, S. (Ed.) (1992a). *Creating alternatives to depression in our schools: Assessment, prevention, intervention.* Toronto: Hogrefe & Huber.

Miezitis, S. (1992b) Teacher-mediated intervention with depressed children: Model and practitioner's guides. In S. Miezitis (Ed.), *Creating alternatives to depression in our schools* (pp. 287-314). Toronto: Hogrefe & Huber.

Miezitis, S., (1992c). Alternatives to depression: Releasing creativity in our schools. In S. Miezitis (Ed.), *Creating alternatives to depression in our schools* (pp. 429-437). Toronto: Hogrefe & Huber.

Miezitis, S. Butler, L., Cole, E., & Friedman, R. (1992). Group intervention with depressed preadolescents and adolescents: Research and role play manual. In S. Miezitis (Ed.), *Creating alternatives to depression in our schools* (pp. 365-414). Toronto: Hogrefe & Huber.

Miezitis, S. Butler, L., & Friedman, R. J. (1977). Teacher-mediated intervention with depressive school children. *Ontario Psychologist, 9 (4),* 45-56.

Miezitis, S., Cole, E., Heath, N., James, J., Matiss, I., & Vella, D. (1992). Towards prevention of depression in our schools. In S. Miezitis (Ed.), *Creating alternatives to depression in our schools* (pp. 417-427). Toronto: Hogrefe & Huber.

Miezitis, S., Fiksel, & Butler, L. (1992). Parent-mediated intervention with depressed children: Model and case study. In S. Miezitis (Ed.), *Creating alternatives to depression in our schools* (pp. 333-363). Toronto: Hogrefe & Huber.

Miezitis, S., & Scholten, P. T. (1990). Responding to teachers' needs: A case study in consultation. In E. Cole & J. A. Siegel (Eds.), *Effective consultation in school psychology* (pp. 81-99). Toronto: Hogrefe & Huber Publishing

Morris, M. (1978). *A study of childhood depression with special emphasis on classroom behavior.* Unpublished doctoral dissertation. University of Toronto, The Ontario Institute for Studies in Education, Toronto, ON.

Morris, M. (1992). A psychodynamic teacher consultation model for depressed children. In S. Miezitis (Ed.), *Creating alternatives to depression in our schools* (pp. 315-332). Toronto: Hogrefe & Huber.

Prochaska, J. O., DiClemente, C. C., & Norcross, J. C. (1992). In search of how people change: Applications to addictive behaviors. *American Psychologist, 47(9),* 1102-1114.

Sarason, S. B. (1966). *Psychology in community settings.* New York: Wiley.

Schein, E. H. (1969). *Process consultation: Its role in organization development.* Reading, MA: Addison-Wesley.

Schein, E. H. (1993). The role of the consultant: Content expert or process facilitator? *Personnel and Guidance Journal, 56(6),* 339-343.

Siegel, J. A., & Cole, E. (1990). Role expansion for school psychologists: Challenges and future directions. In E. Cole & J. A. Siegel (Eds.), *Effective consultation in school psychology* (pp. 3-17). Toronto: Hogrefe & Huber.

Smith, T., & Miezitis, S. (1992) Teacher's understanding of children's emotions and childhood depression. In S. Miezitis (Ed.), *Creating alternatives to depression in our schools* (pp. 127-140). Toronto: Hogrefe & Huber.

Sternberg, R. J. (Ed.) (1999). *Handbook of creativity.* Cambridge University Press.

Chapter 8
Parent-Teacher Mediated Intervention:
A Growth-Promoting Process

Ester Cole

"Nobody likes to be with me. Everything I do comes out wrong." (Tom, aged 12)

Depression in young children and adolescents represents a serious mental health problem, which may lead to feelings of hopelessness and maladjusted behaviors if not identified and treated. Research findings document that between 5% and 10% of students are depressed in their functioning (Miezitis, 1992). In the past two decades, there has been a growing interest by mental health practitioners in the study and treatment of depression in school-age children. Depression can range from mood disturbance, such as Dysthymic Disorder, to a Major Depressive Disorder, and may occur together with other affective and organic disorders. Depressive symptoms are often manifested by changes in mood, cognitive functioning, behavior, and physical condition. This complex disorder typically affects multiple areas of functioning in children including academic and social development (American Psychiatric Association, 2000; Cole, 1982, 1986, 1990, 1992; Paahaheh & Janzen, 1986; Reynolds, 1990; Rutter, Tzard, & Read, 1986).

Researchers almost universally emphasize the central importance of loss of self-esteem in depressive symptomatology (Bakwin, 1972; Connell, 1972; Gladstone & Kaslow, 1995; Glaser, 1967; Krakowski, 1970; McConville, Boag, & Purohit, 1973; Seligman & Ollendick, 1998). Self-esteem relates to self-evaluation of competence and the assessment of one's qualities in many areas including physical appearance, academic functioning, autonomy, and interpersonal relationships. Children's perception of self-worth develops gradually and is influenced by developmental factors, family dynamics, school and social supports. School-age children confront divergent problems that range from transcultural adaptation and traumatic experiences to social rejection and academic difficulties. These types of problems continually challenge professionals and parents to search for ways to enhance children's sense of security, identity, and a sense of belonging (Bracken, 1996; Crain & Bracken, 1994; Leonardson, 1986; Obiakor & Algozzine, 1994; Reasoner, 1982; Schilling, 1986; Stalikas & Gavaki, 1995).

Tom's perception of himself is typical of increasing numbers of school-age children who are referred to mental health professionals because of maladjusted, often withdrawn classroom behaviors and impaired school performance. Over the past two decades, school psychologists have become increasingly concerned that many of these children manifest pronounced depressive symptoms, such as lowered self-esteem, feelings of helplessness, and psychosomatic complaints (Cole, 1992; Cole & Brown, 1996).

As school psychologists have broadened their role and have incorporated a range of consultative services, several types of school-based intervention programs have been developed to combat depressive symptoms among children (Butler & Miezitis, 1980; Butler, Miezitis, Friedman, & Cole, 1980; Morris, 1980). Many of these programs have been influenced by increased awareness of the complex interrelationships between self-concept, psychological adjustment to school, and success in cognitive learning (Johnson, 1981; Miezitis, 1992; Winter, Cole, & Wright, 1983; Yeger & Miezitis, 1980).

The conceptualization of childhood depression adopted by the writer is derived from both Seligman's "learned helplessness" and "learned optimism" models (Seligman, 1975, 1990; Seligman & Peterson, 1986) and from the cognitive model of depression developed by Beck and his colleagues (Beck, 1976; Beck & Shaw, 1977; Beck, Rush, Shaw, & Emery, 1979; Kovacs, 1992; Kovacs & Beck, 1978).

Seligman's early theory links attributional thinking to the dynamics of feelings and behavior. He suggested that depressed people blame themselves for failure, and that this causal attribution can produce symptoms of helplessness and changes in self-esteem, cognition, and emotional responses (see also Joiner & Wagner, 1995; B. Weiner 1985; J. Weiner & Davidson, 1990).

Beck's conceptual framework of the phenomenon stems from the assumption that depressive cognitions consist of dysfunctional premises and beliefs that influence the individual's behavior, attitudes, and affective responses. Cognitive distortions are considered to develop gradually, and are probably rooted in unfavorable life experiences. These negatively self-referential and automatic thoughts cause a distorted sense of self-worth and a tendency to over-react to stimuli in a way that exaggerates the negative aspects of life.

Cognitive behavioral therapy focuses on both the behavioral manifestations and the cognitions related to depression. The behavioral techniques used in cognitive therapy aim to produce change in the patient's passivity, avoidance, and lack of gratification. The therapeutic process is designed to stimulate empirical evaluation of the patient's overgeneralized beliefs of inadequacy and incompetence (Shaw & Dobson, 1981).

A view that has gained acceptance among researchers and practitioners, as well as in the American Psychiatric Association (1980, 2000), is that childhood and adolescent depression is analogous to depression in adults (Epstein & Cullinan, 1986; Reynolds, 1984). Beck and his colleagues (Albert & Beck, 1975; Kovacs, 1981, 1992; Kovacs & Beck, 1977) have explored modifications of the cognitive theory of depression and related therapeutic strategies with school-age children. In the early 1980s, in one of the few school-based evaluations of cognitive therapy, depressive fifth and sixth grade children were taught to recognize irrational thoughts, adopt logical alternatives, and recognize the relationship between thoughts and feelings; alleviation of depressive symptoms were documented for the students in this study (Butler et al., 1980). Since then, a growing number of studies have documented the impact of similar interventions (Joiner & Wagner, 1995; Miezitis, 1992). Cognitive therapy for depressed adults was evaluated as having consistent evidence for its effectiveness, and continues to be recommended as one of the more promising intervention strategies for depressive children (Cole, 1992; Epstein & Cullinan, 1986; Teasdale, 1985).

Parent-Teacher Mediated Intervention Model: PTMI

The PTMI model was developed in an inner-city school in Metropolitan Toronto in the early 1980s. Prior to that period, the provision of psychological services in the school functioned primarily on a referral basis. Many referrals were initiated in response to crisis intervention situations, and were usually seen as a first step in seeking special education support. Beginning in the early 1980s, a new service model was implemented, focusing both on the provision of preventative services and on closer communication with students, school staff, and parents. Some of the key elements in this model included weekly multidisciplinary team conferences, intervention-oriented individual assessments, group discussions and counseling with students and parents, and short-term therapy.

As this new model of service evolved, the writer developed an intervention modality called Parent-Teacher Mediated Intervention (PTMI). This approach derives from the assumption that behavioral problems do not represent symptoms of intrapsychic disorder but, rather, are reflective of a disequilibrium in the interaction processes occurring between the individual and his or her environment (Minor, 1972). Thus, behavior can best be understood as represented outcomes of psychosocial or interpersonal processes that are current and observable. School-based psychological intervention is likely to be most effective if it is conceptualized within the context of interrelated and reciprocally influential systems in the child's life. Since home and school are two of the most important systems for the child, what occurs in one milieu is likely to affect the other substantially (Anderson, 1983; Cole, 1986; Green & Fine, 1980;

Lawrence & Heller, 2001; Petrie & Piersel, 1982; Pfeiffer & Tittler, 1983; Power & Lutz Bartholomew, 1985; Watson, Sterling, & McDade, 1997).

Both parents and teachers find it stressful to cope effectively with children who have developed a negative ideation and are less responsive to communication with others. Thus, PTMI focuses on the need to develop a voluntary and collaborative relationship among psychologist, teacher, and parent. In all phases of the process, from assessment to implementation of intervention strategies, PTMI emphasizes that the consultant and the consultees have knowledge and skills that are helpful for problem resolution (Anserello & Sweet, 1990; Cohen, 1985; Cole & Siegel, 1990; Curtis & Meyers, 1985; Graham-Clay, 1999; Gutkin, 1986).

In the PTMI model the psychologist is able to use service time more economically. By eliciting input from the student, teacher and parent(s), s/he is better able to clarify and integrate sources of information, including perceptions, attitudes and expectations for the child. However, the role of the psychologist is not to present as a provider of solutions in a hierarchical relationship, but rather to act as an animator of reciprocal communications, channeled to facilitate constructive changes in attitudes and behaviors at school and at home.

The expression of care and concern on the part of significant adults may do much to demonstrate to the child that s/he is accepted and respected. As the teacher and parent express difficulties, so too the child may learn to articulate fears and frustrations. Thus, the joint sessions provide feedback to all involved and are a source of interpersonal learning. Finally, the modeling of positive communication and coping strategies may help the child to consolidate gains made through the employment of specific therapeutic techniques, and improve his or her ability to respond effectively to stressful situations.

Assessment Phase

The goal of this phase is to identify etiological factors contributing to a child's maladjustment, and to enhance understanding of the context within which his or her difficulties are embedded. Teacher referral of children who present academic or social problems usually occurs during multidisciplinary team conferences. In order to develop a comprehensive understanding of all aspects of the child's functioning, information is derived from a variety of sources. Five sources of information are usually tapped:

   (a) discussions of the child's maladaptive characteristics as observed by teacher(s);
   (b) review of the child's educational history contained in student records;
   (c) classroom observations focusing on teacher pupil and peer interactions; the child's learning style;
   (d) psychological assessment of intellectual, perceptual, academic, learning style, and personality functioning;
   (e) parent interview data.

A detailed guide to the assessment process may be found in Appendix A.

Upon completion of the assessment phase, the data are screened against four categories of common dysfunctional indicators of depression. These categories, which have been adapted by the writer from the work of Kovacs and Beck (1977) and Forrest (1983) are presented in Table 1.

Table 1 Common Dysfunctional Indicators of Depression

Specific Affect	Sadness, anxiety, guilt, anger, fear, unhappiness, pessimism, mood variation, worthlessness, helplessness, hopelessness
Physical/ Somatic Content	Fatigue, sleep disorders, somatic complaints, eating disorders, headaches, abdominal pain
Cognitive Content	Sense of loss, negative self-concept, negative view of world, negative expectations for future, self-blame, self-criticism, loss of interest, distractibility, ambivalence, indecisiveness, suicidal ideation
Behavioral Content	Withdrawal from social contact, engaging in fewer pleasurable activities, studying alone, avoidance of groups, reduced involvement in sports and games, crying easily, procrastination

The psychologist meets separately with the student, the parent(s), and the homeroom teacher. During the course of these interviews, the structure and nature of the proposed counseling program are explained. All parties must contract to meet together at regular intervals outside class hours in order that student and teacher schedules are not disrupted. This process commits all parties to explore a variety of avenues in attempting to solve problems. The following goals are discussed:

(1) Improvement in the child's adaption to school.
(2) Enhancement of the child's self-esteem.
(3) Improvement in teacher's and parent's skills in dealing and coping with the depressive child.
(4) Facilitating effective communication and alliance between home and school.

Intervention Phase

The four participants – child, homeroom teacher, parent, and psychologist – meet for one-hour sessions twice during the first two weeks, and then (on average) for three additional biweekly sessions. Some specialized therapeutic techniques (derived from

the work of Beck, 1967, 1976) which this writer has found appropriate for use with depressive elementary school children are:
(1) *Cognitive Reappraisal* – identification and modification of maladaptive perceptions and attitudes.
(2) *Diaries/Art Work* – encouraging the child to describe both pleasurable and stressful occurrences.
(3) *Graded Task Assignments* – ensuring a series of success experiences, commencing with tasks well within the child's present capabilities.
(4) *Alternative Therapy* – considering alternative explanations for experiences; developing (through collaborative discussions) different ways of dealing with psychological and situational problems.
(5) *Homework Assignments* – learning to generalize insights gained through counseling into the child's daily experiences both at school and at home.
(6) *Cognitive Rehearsal* – guiding the child through an assigned activity, encouraging the imagination to describe the necessary steps, and working together through potential obstacles.

The first session typically begins by discussing the child's areas of strength and weakness. The child is asked to describe a maladjustive behavior or undesirable occurrence and the conditions under which it is likely to be manifested. After further discussion, one behavior is targeted. In collaboration with the other participants, the psychologist points towards more adaptive behaviors, which parent and teacher are requested to monitor during the following week by writing brief observations and impressions of the child's behavior. These "homework" assignments encourage consultees to play an active role in the consultation process as they gain increased understanding of the child's needs.

At the next session, the child's attempts at more adaptive behavior in the target area are discussed. When progress is satisfactory, additional goals may be added following further consultation. If the child continues to encounter difficulties in the target area, strategies may have to be modified to ensure success experience.

When improvement in the child's overall emotional and social functioning has been noted by all four parties, an average of two more sessions are held with the child, the teacher, and the psychologist present. These sessions concentrate primarily on the child's functioning within the school milieu.

Follow-Up Phase

During this phase, the psychologist monitors the child's progress through consultation with the teacher. Discussions following classroom observation may assist the teacher in focusing on continuing consolidation of gains made. Similarly, psychologist-teacher discussions can lead to the development of additional strategies designed to enhance the child's sense of self-worth. The psychologist should remain available as a resource person for both parent and child.

I. ASSESSMENT PHASE

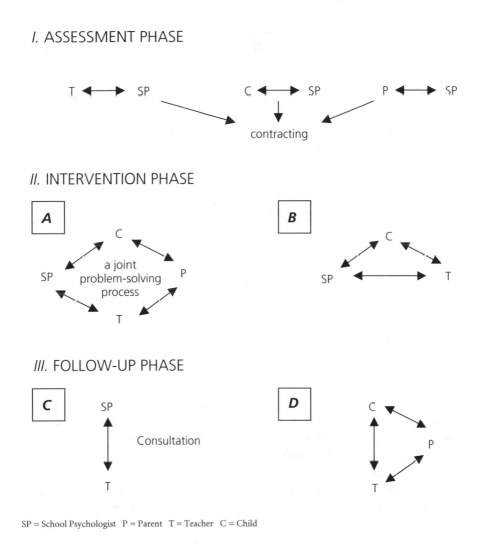

II. INTERVENTION PHASE

III. FOLLOW-UP PHASE

SP = School Psychologist   P = Parent   T = Teacher   C = Child

Figure 1 The PTMI Model

The model presented in Figure 1 has been employed over the years with children in elementary schools. An example of the use of PTMI is illustrated in the following case study.

Case Study

Assessment Phase

Dana S., a Grade 6 student, was referred for assessment because of concerns about her poor academic progress and her oppositional, uncooperative behavior in class. Her academic functioning was two years behind grade placement and a review of her school records documented a history of academic difficulties dating back to Grade 1. Dana had repeated Grade 1 and had only been promoted to Grades 5 and 6 because of her age.

Dana was described by her teacher as a moody child who at times seemed to go out of her way to seek disapproval. She was resentful when corrected, often becoming argumentative and leaving the classroom while crying. Dana's social skills were another source of concern; her teacher described her as trying to curry favor from her peers by promising to get them treats, and during game and play situations she was seen as a bad loser who had difficulty fitting in well with a team. Dana's overall school functioning was a source of stress and frustration for her teacher, who felt that she could not meet this student's needs.

During two classroom observations, Dana was restless, attending to anything but her work. She was apathetic and uninvolved in classroom discussion, was not approached by her peers, and did not initiate contact with them. She lacked confidence when facing new learning tasks, often stating, "I don't want to do that." The teacher's interaction with this child consisted of asking Dana to complete her assignments and become more involved in classroom discussions. Dana avoided eye contact with her teacher, frequently resting her head on her desk.

During psychological assessment sessions, Dana's behavior appeared to be characterized by dramatic shifts in mood over short periods of time. At times she presented as an enthusiastic, well motivated student who showed interest and curiosity about various tasks presented, but during one of her "bad" moods she became restless, disinterested, and confused, and needed considerable encouragement to perform tasks as requested. In our conversations, Dana described herself as inadequate, frequently making self-deprecating statements such as "I'm dumb." She tended to externalize blame for her social difficulties with her peers, stating "they talk behind my back." Although wishing to be socially accepted, Dana believed that her teacher disliked her and that her classmates ridiculed her. Her descriptions of her school work consisted of overgeneralizations and negative exaggerations. She felt she had trouble telling others what she meant and that she had difficulties doing what her teacher demanded.

Assessment of Dana's intellectual abilities documented cognitive functioning in the low average range. Relative weaknesses were noted in tasks tapping abstract thinking, receptive language and fund of acquired knowledge. Relative strengths were documented in visual performance tasks. Dana found nonverbal tasks rewarding and "fun."

Assessment of personality functioning suggested that Dana had developed a negative perception of herself as a student. She was inclined to become moody and agitated when facing new situations, viewed herself as inadequate, and was increasingly frustrated by her struggles with her school work. Lack of success in academic subjects resulted in feelings of helplessness, avoidance behavior, and lowered motivation at school. Dana was worried and preoccupied with some objective stresses in her home life. She wished to grow up quickly and become an independent, self-reliant adult whom "nobody tells what to do." As a developing adolescent, Dana was shy and ill at ease with her physical growth and her changing body. She perceived adults as harsh and judgmental in their communication with children. Although deeply emotionally attached to her mother, Dana felt that she was not understood by her. Her low tolerance of frustration often resulted in angry, confrontational behavior, although she craved social approval from peers and adults as a means of enhancing her sense of security and well-being.

In a parent interview, Mrs. S. indicated that she was well informed about her daughter's academic difficulties. She herself had had little formal schooling and felt unable to assist her daughter with her school work, and had decreased her involvement with the school as she had come to feel that every parent interview consisted of negative reports about her daughter's scholastic functioning. The older of two children, Dana was perceived by her mother as affectionate but "stubborn." She said that Dana shared little information with her about her school activities; that although generally healthy, she frequently complained about headaches and being "tired;" she often refused to help with house chores; and preferred solitary after-school activities, such as listening to music in her room or painting.

Mrs. S. indicated that her family had encountered recent stresses due to her job loss and her common-law husband's departure from the family. She acknowledged feeling preoccupied and somewhat ineffectual in her parenting skills. Due to these stresses, she acknowledged that she had become inconsistent in her communication patterns with her children. On occasion she shared with Dana information "as if she were an adult;" on other occasions, she presented as demanding and punitive towards the children. However, Mrs. S. seemed unaware that she was modeling depressive behaviors.

Intervention Phase

Dana, her mother and her teacher agreed to meet for joint consultation during school lunch hours. Information with regard to assessment findings was shared with both parent and teacher. Some of Dana's hobbies and special interests were identified, such as interest in music and cooking, creative expression in drawings, and helping and playing with younger students. This information was considered in the design of the intervention strategy.

The following intervention goals were formulated:
(1) Enhance Dana's self-esteem and motivation towards school work.
(2) Improve Dana's communication skills with both teacher and mother.
(3) Assist Dana in planning enjoyable after-school activities designed to enhance her social skills.
(4) Reduce Dana's uncooperative classroom behavior and improve her self-discipline.

During the first session Dana had difficulty describing any positive self-attributes. She was defensive about information shared, and pessimistic about her ability to develop more adaptive behaviors. As the sessions progressed, her behavior became more cooperative and responsive. Therapeutic techniques used included:
(1) Teacher's daily written appraisal of both positive and negative interactions in class.
(2) Discussions about Dana's chosen samples of her school and artwork.
(3) Cognitive reappraisal of Dana's perceptions of being disliked and harshly criticized by both mother and teacher.
(4) Cognitive rehearsals aimed at decreasing Dana's acting out behavior in class and suggesting alternative solutions to stress and problems.

During the intervention phase the following in-school modifications began to take place:
(1) Dana entered a daily one-hour special education program. Her withdrawal teacher concentrated on improving Dana's learning style and began to assist her with classroom assignments.
(2) Contingent upon improvement in targeted behavior (not leaving the class without permission, increased participation in classroom discussions, etc.), Dana could begin to act as a "big pal" to a kindergarten student. She visited the kindergarten class twice a week, often playing with and reading a story to a shy, inhibited child.

After-school changes were targeted as well. Mrs. S. and her daughter began baking and planning menus together. These activities were enjoyable to both and fostered increased communication with regard to school and social activities. In addition, they both acquired information about community after-school programs. Dana agreed to join the Boys and Girls Club, although her attendance at this program was inconsistent. Her mother encouraged her to invite a few classmates home, and helped plan some activities.

The intervention phase lasted over a 12-week period, and both affective and behavioral changes were noted. Dana learned to verbalize her appreciation when praise and positive attention were given to her by her teacher, volunteered to help her teacher after school, and began to share information about her activities in the withdrawal program. Although she continued to perceive her peers as ignoring her or "picking on me," she learned to talk about these incidents with her teacher and mother.

Follow-Up Phase

Dana's teacher perceived the intervention as helpful. Increased satisfaction on her part led to more consultation contacts and these ongoing meetings revealed that she was becoming increasingly pleased with Dana's overall progress. The teacher became more receptive towards Dana's academic needs and modified her program to ensure success experiences. Recommended program changes included setting short-term academic goals and charting of manageable units of work. The teacher also perceived Dana's special education program as helpful and complementary to her class program. She frequently indicated that information derived from the intervention phase sensitized her to this student's stresses and needs. She felt more tolerant when periods of regressive behavior occurred in Dana and felt more effective in planning for this student.

Both Dana and her mother found our joint meetings helpful. Mrs. S. noted an alleviation in her daughter's depressive symptoms, and reported that Dana presented as happier and closer to her. Dana learned to take pride in her scholastic achievements, but continued to verbalize her disappointment in her perceived lack of popularity amongst her peers.

Conclusion

Early intervention school-based programs have become a growing area of interest for psychoeducational consultants as they strive to meet the needs of children and their families. Studies of depression in children support the need for school psychologists to recognize the magnitude of this disorder and to assume a more active role in its assessment and treatment by initiating primary and secondary prevention modalities for home and school.

The conceptual framework for PTMI consists of an integration of consultation strategies drawing from the ecological approach to the provision of broad psychological services in school settings (Anderson, 1983; Cohen, 1985; Cole, 1986, 1996; Cole & Siegel, 1990; Gutkin, 1986; Pfeiffer & Tittler, 1983), teacher-mediated intervention and classroom consultation models developed by Miezitis (1977, 1992; Butler & Miezitis, 1980), Seligman's "learned helplessness" and "learned optimism" models (1975, 1990; Seligman & Peterson, 1986), and Beck's (1976) cognitive theory of depression (see also Kovacs, 1992). Over the past two decades, cognitive therapy has been acknowledged as one of the more recommended treatments for depressed school-aged children (Butler et al., 1980; Cole, 1992; Epstein & Cullinan, 1986).

PTMI is designed to facilitate a broad-based consultation process that encourages consultees' involvement, sharing of information, and implementation of mutual decisions. It is likely to be most effective in open climate schools characterized by a collaborative atmosphere and open communication and alliance between administration, teachers, and parents.

This multifactorial model has received positive qualitative responses from the teachers, parents, and students involved. The model can be adapted for use with nondepressive populations in the school setting. Appendix B details information for school psychologists involved in assessment and interventions with depressed children. Appendix C provides self-esteem strategies to be used by psychologists in their consultation with parents and teachers.

References

Albert, M., & Beck, A. T. (1975). Incidence of depression in early adolescence: A preliminary study. *Journal of Youth and Adolescence, 4(4)*, 301-307.

American Psychiatric Association (2000). *Diagnostic and statistical manual of mental disorders – Text revisions* (4th ed.-TR). Washington, DC; American Psychiatric Association.

Anderson, C. (1983). An ecological developmental model for a family orientation in school psychology. *Journal of School Psychology, 21*, 179-189.

Anserello, C., & Sweet, T. (1990). Integrating consultation into school psychological services. In E. Cole & J. A. Siegel (Eds.), *Effective consulation in school psychology* (pp. 173-199). Toronto: Hogrefe & Huber Publishers.

Bakwin, A. R. (1972). Depression: A mood disorder in children and adolescents. *Maryland State Medical Journal*, June, 55-61.

Beck, A. T. (1967). *Depression: Causes and treatment.* Philadelphia: University of Pennsylvania Press.

Beck, A. T. (1976). *Cognitive therapy and emotional disorders.* New York: International Universities Press, Inc.

Beck, A. T., Rush, A. J., Shaw, B. F., & Emery, G. L. (1979). *Cognitive therapy of depression.* New York: The Guilford Press.

Beck, A. T., & Shaw, B. F. (1977). Cognitive approaches to depression. In A. Ellis & R. Grieger (Eds.), *Handbook of rational emotive therapy.* New York: Springer.

Bracken, B. A. (1996). *Handbook of self-concept: Developmental, social and clinical considerations.* New York: John Wiley and Sons.

Butler, L. F., & Miezitis, S. (1980). *Releasing children from depression. A handbook for elementary teachers and consultants.* O.I.S.E. Press/The Ontario Institute for Studies in Education.

Butler, L. F., Miezitis, S., Friedman, R. J., & Cole, E. (1980). The effect of two school-based intervention programmes on depressive symptoms in pre-adolescent children. *American Educational Research Journal*, 17(1), 111-119.

Cohen, J. J. (1985). Best practices in planning interventions for elementary students. In A. Thomas & J. Grimes (Eds.), *Best practices in school psychology* (pp. 61-77). Kent, OH: The National Association of School Psychologists.

Cole, E. (1982). Childhood depression: A literature review. *Student Services Project Bulletin, 12,* Toronto: Toronto Board of Education.

Cole, E. (1986). Parent-teacher mediated intervention: A growth promoting process. *Canadian Journal of School Psychology, 3,* 33-46.

Cole, E. (1990). Parent-teacher mediated intervention: A growth-promoting process. In E. Cole & J. A. Siegel (Eds.), *Effective consulation in school psychology* (pp.101- 112). Toronto: Hogrefe & Huber Publishers.

Cole, E. (1992). Characteristics of students referred to school teams: Implications for preventive psychological services. *Canadian Journal of School Psychology, 8(1),* 23-38.

Cole, E. (1996). An integrative perspective on school psychology. *Canadian Journal of School Psychology, 12 (2)* 115-121.

Cole, E., & Brown, R, (1996). Multidisciplinary school teams: A five-year follow-up study. *Canadian Journal of School Psychology, 12 (2),* 155-168.

Cole, E., & Siegel, J. A. (1990). School psychology in a multicultural community: Responding to children's needs. In E. Cole & J. A. Siegel (Eds.), *Effective consulation in school psychology* (pp. 141-169). Toronto: Hogrefe & Huber Publishers.

Connell, H.M. (1972). Depression in childhood. *Child Psychiatry and Human Development, 4,* 71-85.

Crain, R. M., & Bracken, B. A. (1994). Age, race, and gender differences in child and adolescent self-concept. *School Psychology Review, 23(3),* 496-511.

Curtis, M. J., & Meyers, J. (1985). Best practices in school-based consultation: Guidelines for effective practice. In A. Thomas & J. Grimes (Eds.), *Best practices in school psychology* (pp. 79-94). Kent, OH: National Association of School Psychologists.

Epstein, M. H., & Cullinan, D. (1986). Depression in children. *Journal of School Health, 56(1),* 10-12.

Forrest, D. V. (1983). Depression: Information and interventions for school counselors. *The School Counselor,* March, 269-279.

Gladstone, T. R., & Kaslow, N. J. (1995). Depression and attributions in children and adolescents: A meta-analytic review. *Journal of Abnormal Child Psychology, 23,* 597-606.

Glaser, K. (1967) Masked depression in children and adolescents. *American Journal of Psychotherapy, 21,* 565-574.

Graham-Clay, S. (1999). Enhancing home-school partnerships: How school psychologists can help. *Canadian Journal of School Psychology, 14(2),* 31-44.

Green, K., & Fine, J. J. (1980). Family therapy: A case for training for school psychologists. *Psychology in the Schools, 17(2),* 241-248.

Gutkin, T. B. (1986). Consultees' perceptions of variables relating to the outcome of school-based consultation interactions. *School Psychology Review, 15(3),* 375-382.

Johnson, D. S. (1981). Naturally acquired learned helplessness: The relationship of school failure to achievement, behavior, attributions and self-concept. *Journal of Educational Psychology, 73(2),* 174-180.

Joiner, T. E., & Wagner, K. D. (1995). Attributional style and depression in children and adolescents: A meta-analytic review. *Clinical Psychology Review, 15,* 777-798.

Kovacs, M. (1981). Rating scales to assess depression in school-aged children. *Acta Paedopsychiatrica, 46,* 305-315.

Kovacs, M. (1992). *Children's depression inventory manual.* North Tohawanda, NY: Multi-Health Systems.

Kovacs, M., & Beck, A. T. (1977). An empirical-clinical approach toward a definition of child-hood depression. In J.G. Schutterbrandt & A. Raskin (Eds.), *Depression in children: Diagnosis, treatment and conceptual models*. New York: Raven.

Kovacs, M., & Beck, A. T. (1978). Maladaptive cognitive structures in depression. *American Journal of Psychiatry, 135(5)*, 525-533.

Krakowski, A. J. (1970). Depressive reactions of children and adolescence. *Psychosomatics, 11*, 429-433.

Lawrence, E. C., & Heller, M. B. (2001). Parent-school collaboration: The utility of a compentence lens. *Canadian Journal of School Psychology, 17(1)*, 5-15.

Leonardson, G. R. (1986). The relationship between self-concept and selected academic and personal factors. *Adolescence, XXI, 82*, 467-474.

McConville, B. J., Boag, L. C., & Purohit, A. P. *(1973)*. Three types of childhood depression. *Canadian Psychiatric Association Journal, 18*, 133-138.

Miezitis, S. (1977). An in-service training/classroom consultation model for rendering psychological services to schools. In S. Miezitis & M. Orme (Eds.), *Innovations in school psychology, Symposium Series/7*. Toronto: The Ontario Institute for Studies in Education.

Miezitis, S. (Ed.). (1992). *Creating alternatives to depression in our schools*. Toronto: Hogrefe & Huber Publishers.

Minor, H. W. (1972). Systems analysis and school psychology. *Journal of School Psychology, 10(3)*, 227-232.

Morris, M. (1980). Childhood depression in the primary grades: Early identification, a teacher consultation remedial model and classroom correlates of change. *Interchange, II(1)*, 61-75.

Obiakor, F. E., & Algozzine, B. (1994). Self-concept of young children with special needs: Perspectives for school and clinic. *Canadian Journal of School Psychology, 10(2)*, 123-130.

Paahanen, N., & Janzen, H. L. (1986). Incidence and characteristics of depression in elementary school children. *Canadian Journal of School Psychology, 2*, 7-19.

Petrie, P., & Piersel, W. C. *(1982)*. Family therapy. In C. R. Reynolds & T. B. Gutkin (Eds.), *The handbook of school psychology*. New York: John Wiley and Sons.

Pfeiffer, S. I., & Tittler, B. I. (1983). Utilizing the multidisciplinary team to facilitate a school-family systems orientation. *School Psychology Review, 12(2)*, 168-173.

Power, T. J., & Lutz Bartholomew, K. L. (1985). Getting uncaught in the middle: A case study in family-school system consultation. *School Psychology Review, 14(2)*, 222-229.

Reasoner, R. W. (1982). *Building self-esteem*. Palo Alto: Consulting Psychological Press, Inc.

Reynolds, W. M. (1984). Depression in children and adolescents: Phenomenology, evaluation and treatment. *School Psychology Review, 13(2)*, 171-182.

Reynolds, W. M. (1990). Depression in children and adolescents: Nature, diagnosis, assessment and treatment. *School Psychology Review, 19 (2)*, 158-173.

Rutter, M., Izard, C. E., & Read, P. B. (1986). *Depression in young people: Developmental and clinical aspects*. New York: Guildford.

Schilling, D. E. (1986). Self-esteem: Concerns, strategies, resources. *Academic Therapy, 21 (3)*, 301-307.

Seligman, L. D., & Ollendick, T. H. (1998). Comorbidity of anxiety and depression in children and adolescents: An integrative review. *Clinical Child and Family Psychology Review, 1(2)*, 125-144.

Seligman, M. E. P. (1975). *Helplessness: On depression, development and death*. San Francisco: W. H. Freeman.

Seligman, M. E. P. (1990). *Learned optimism*. New York: Pocket Books.

Seligman, M. E. P., & Peterson, C. A. (1986). A learned helplessness perspective on childhood depression: Theory and research. In M. Rutter, G. E. Izard, & P. B. Read (Eds.), *Depression in young people: Developmental and clinical aspects*. New York: Guilford.

Shaw, B. F., & Dobson, D. S. (1981). Advances in the cognitive therapy of depression. *The Ontario Psychologist, 13(1)*, 16-20.

Stalikas, A., & Gavaki, E. (1995). The importance of ethinic identify: Self-esteem and academic achievement of second-generation Greeks in secondary school. *Canadian Journal of School Psychology, 11(1)*, 1-9.

Stott, D. H. (1971). *The social adjustment of children: Manual of the Bristol social-adjustment guides* (4th Ed.). London: University of London Press.

Teasdale, J. D. (1985). Psychological treatments of depression: How do they work? *Behavior Research and Therapy, 23(2)*, 157-165.

Watson, T. S., Sterling, H. E., & McDade, A. (1997). Demythifying behavioural consultation. *School Psychology Review, 26(3)*, 467-474.

Weiner, B. (1985). An attributional theory of achievement motivation and emotion. *Psychological Review, 92(4)*, 548-573.

Weiner, J., & Davidson, I. (1990). The in-school team experience. In E. Cole & J. A. Siegel (Eds.), *Effective consulation in school psychology* (pp. 19-32). Toronto: Hogrefe & Huber Publishers.

Winter, A., Cole, E., & Wright, E.N. (1983). *Characteristics of pupils entering learning disabilities self-contained classes*. Research Service, Toronto Board of Education, 169.

Yeger, T. A., & Miezitis, S. (1980). Self-concept and classroom behavior of preadolescent pupils. *Journal of Classroom Interaction, 15(2)*, 31-37.

Appendix A: PTMI Assessment Guide

I. Student's approach to learning-interaction with teacher(s)

(a) Response to approval or attention:
  (1) appreciates praise and attention
  (2) responds negatively
  (3) distant, unconcerned about approval or disapproval
(b) Working by him/herself:
  (1) works steadily
  (2) unmotivated
  (3) only when watched or compelled
(c) Working in a group:
  (1) works steadily
  (2) unmotivated
  (3) only when watched or compelled
(d) Paying attention in class:
  (1) attends well
  (2) attends to anything but work
  (3) apathetic, cannot get his/her attention
(e) Seat work activities:
  (1) sticks to tasks
  (2) switches from task to task
  (3) difficult to stimulate
(f) Facing new tasks:
  (1) cautious but will try
  (2) lacks confidence to try anything difficult
  (3) likes challenge
  (4) impulsive approach
  (5) shows indifference

The categories in Section I were adapted from the Bristol Social Adjustment Guides – The Child in School, developed by Stott (1971). See also Cole (1986).

II. School Work

Overall academic performance:
(1) at grade level
(2) below grade level
  areas of strength   _____
  areas of difficulty   _____

III. Appraisal of Cognitive Functioning/Information

Processing skills (strength and weakness)
- Language (verbal comprehension)
- Visual Performance (perceptual organization)
- Concentration Span (distractibility)

IV. Social and Emotional Correlates

(a) Social skills:
    (1) well developed skills with peers
    (2) well developed skills with adults
    (3) difficulty with peers (e.g., excluded by peers, solitary activity, timid)
    (4) difficulty with adults (e.g., uncommunicative, withdrawn)
(b) Aggressive, acting-out behavior:
    (1) frequently
    (2) occasionally
    (3) never
(c) Frustration:
    (1) high tolerance
    (2) low tolerance
(d) Maturity:
    (1) very immature
    (2) mature for age
(e) Self-esteem:
    (1) lowered self-esteem/negative self-concept
    (2) high self-esteem/positive self concept
(f) Depressive symptoms
    (1) present
    (2) not present
(g) Anxiety:
    (1) present
    (2) not present
(h) Physique:
    (1) good health
    (2) health problems _____
       visual difficulties _____
       hearing difficulties _____
       speech problems _____
       allergies _____
       hyperactivity _____
       other _____

V. Coping behaviors

ability to verbalize feelings_____

ability to develop friendships_____

creative expressions_____

interest in extracurricular activities_____

other_____

VI. Parent interviews focusing on:

(a) parental awareness of and attitude towards the presenting problem (are parents supportive? do they use denial?)

(b) perception of the child within the family unit (is child an "identified patient?")

(c) family interaction and communication patterns (is there parental coalition in both functional and affectional terms? Is there a clear definition of generational boundaries?)

(d) parental attitudes towards education and achievement (is there a history of setting up rigid, perfectionist goals?)

(e) history of significant family stress or loss (are the adults in the family modeling depressive affect?)

Appendix B: The PTMI – Assessment and Intervention Guidelines for Health and Mental Health Professionals

General Considerations

(1) Acknowledge that depressive symptoms in children and adolescents vary as a function of developmental stage and degree of depression.

(2) Children who have experienced abuse, disappointments, severe stress, violence, or mental illness in the family are at risk for emotional and social maladjustment.

(3) Depression can be a result of a chemical imbalance in the body, and such persons may require medical treatment with antidepressants.

(4) Evaluate the presence or absence of other commonly found disorders in adolescents, including anxiety, panic and substance abuse.

(5) Note that parents and teachers find it stressful to cope effectively with children who have developed a negative ideation and are less responsive to communication with others. It is important to facilitate effective communication and alliances between home and school by identifying the child's needs and setting very short-term goals in either setting.

(6) Remember that it is relatively easy to ignore depressed children. They tend to attract little attention to themselves and their impaired academic functioning may not be linked to their emotional difficulties.

(7) Acting-out behaviors may mask a depressive condition. It is thus important not only to focus on a symptom or label. Rather, the child's behavior should be understood as reflecting difficulties between the individual and his or her environment. By adopting such an ecological approach during consultation, modifications are more likely to be made at home and at school.

Assessment

(1) Comprehensive assessment is a key to the identification of depression in children. Multiple sources of information about the child are recommended. Sources of information include classroom observations, interviews and review of past records. Assessment methods may be comprised of self-report questionnaires and projective measures.

(2) During the assessment process note the child's unmet needs which can result in low self-regard and feelings of deprivation.

(3) Identify family stressors, which are perceived by the child as threatening (e.g. potential family break up).

(4) Note school related stressors, including difficulty adjusting to a new learning environment, social isolation, poor language skills, perfectionist tendencies and poor problem-solving skills.

(5) Make sure to obtain detailed information about medical and somatic problems, which may have been overlooked or untreated.

(6) Investigate age appropriate developmental issues such as attachment, autonomy, social networks, self-awareness, the ability to express multiple emotions, and puberty factors.

(7) During the interview process, pay special attention to the child's thinking patterns. Cognitive distortions are common in depressed people. When the child describes himself/herself you will likely note:
   – arbitrary inferences (jumping to conclusion and anticipating negative outcomes).
   – overgeneralizations (a negative event is viewed as a never-ending pattern: "I didn't finish my work and the teacher will never trust me again").
   – Inflexible rules of conduct and evaluation such as "never," "always" (rigid quantifiers), "must," "have to" (categorical imperatives).
   – rejecting positive experiences by maintaining negative beliefs ("my good mark on the test doesn't count because I was just lucky").
   – personalization (overestimation of the degree to which negative events are related to the self: "It's all my fault").

(8) Identify family characteristics as depressive correlates:
   – Depressed parents may model for the child negative coping mechanisms against stress. The depressed parent may be less involved with their child due to greater feelings of incompetence, poor self-worth and impaired communication.
   – A family history of setting up rigid, perfectionistic goals for the child, which are difficult to meet.
   – Unclear roles and rules for both adults and children in the family may result in poor parental coalition and place too many responsibilities on the child.

  – Parents with substance abuse problems create a climate of stress and helplessness
     for other family members whose nurturing needs are not met.
  – Multiple losses, especially early on in life result in cumulative stress and loss of
     self-esteem.
  – Environmental stressors and precipitating events for the family including aca-
     demic problems for adolescents and social isolation.
  – Migration factors such as severance of family ties, language barriers, losses, rac-
     ism, poverty and intergenerational conflicts in a new culture.

(9) In consultation with parents and educators, emphasize the stress caregivers feel when
    attempting to support depressed children. They might feel guilty, frustrated or re-
    jected by the child. Honesty about such reactions will help put the child's problems
    in a helpful context. Indicate to all involved that when professional help is provided,
    they will note a gradual decrease in negative symptoms.

Intervention Strategies for Consultation

A. Parents

(1) Assist parents in recognizing their own feelings about their child's depression. With-
    out wanting to, they might have conveyed to the child their feelings of guilt or frus-
    tration.

(2) Discuss with parents their child's symptoms and question recent family stress. Con-
    sider family counselling for support to all involved.

(3) Indicate to parents that depression is treatable and that their child can be helped in
    overcoming unhappy feelings.

(4) Advise parents to check with the family doctor to find out if there could be a physical
    cause for some of the depressive symptoms.

(5) Parents should consult with the teacher about changes that might have contributed
    to the child's reactions and loss of self-esteem. Sharing of information is likely to sen-
    sitize all involved to the child's needs.

(6) Parents need to modify their expectations by identifying one or two goals for change.
    Multiple areas of modification are likely to increase stress for both the child and the
    parents.

(7) Stress to parents the importance of frequent contact and modelling of positive com-
    munication with the child.

(8) Parents need to identify areas of difficulties and the impact it has on communication
    at home. Help them gain insight into the value of clear statements and positive rein-
    forcement for the child ("when you smiled at me this morning, it made me happy").

(9) In consultation, identify effective management strategies, which can be employed on
    a daily basis ("after you have had your supper and done your homework, we will read
    together in your room").

(10) Help parents develop a log or simple checklist for noting positive daily changes in
     their child's behavior (e.g., decrease in negative statements, positive non-verbal com-
     munication, play with siblings, telling stories from school).

(11) Identify community services for depressed children who require long-term interven-
     tion.

B. Teachers

(1) Provide academic remediation as needed and re-evaluate expectations for the child.
(2) On a daily basis, involve student in planning short-term academic goals.
(3) Identify areas of interest (e.g., computer games), and ask the child to explain to others how the game is played.
(4) Post student work in class.
(5) Provide positive reinforcement for small steps taken by the child. This is likely to increase the child's sense of acceptance.
(6) Approach the child frequently and for short periods of time ("you seem to work very hard on your drawing...").
(7) Convey your interest and reassurance in verbal and non-verbal ways. Your smile and eye contact are likely to convey to the child that they are understood even though their behavior is withdrawn.
(8) Facilitate success experiences with tasks the child can master.
(9) Ask the child to help you in class with small jobs and express your appreciation for the assistance.
(10) Sitting arrangements in class should allow for frequent non-verbal communication with the child.
(11) Help the child learn to ask questions. Without doing so, he/she might become overwhelmed in class and view him/herself as a passive learner.
(12) Facilitate classroom discussions on coping with school stress. You might want to invite a school psychologist or social worker to discuss with the children helpful coping skills.

Appendix C: Building Children's and Adolescents' Self-Esteem

Educators and psychologists have both emphasized the impact of pupils' attitudes towards school and towards themselves as learners on academic achievement and social adjustment. The goals of curriculum and educational outcomes for students include the development of self-worth, adaptability, self-reliance and a realistic self-appraisal. These goals are particularly important for youth prone to feeling easily discouraged or less competent than others. Negative views of the self often result in a tendency to exaggerate negative aspects of daily events and may lead to dependency on others, difficulty making decisions, and low self-esteem.

General Considerations

What then are the components that family members, educators and caregivers should keep in mind?

- Self-esteem is subject to change in negative or positive ways. Overcoming a sense of failure and exclusion takes time and ongoing support from significant others.
- Listening with empathy and understanding is likely to enhance communication and constructive feedback. Judgment and perceived criticism, on the other hand, are likely to stifle communication and increase anxiety.
- High self-esteem is a result of feeling capable and able to achieve in a variety of areas. When supporting or assessing a child, ask and learn the answers to the following questions: What skills do I have? In what areas? What is easy for me to learn? Do? What can I teach someone else?
- Feeling significant enhances self-esteem and leads to increased connections with others. In order to feel significant one must receive feedback, which indicates that who we are, and what we do, or say matters to others.
- Feeling powerful refers to the sense of control over one's life. Helping youth to make decisions and exercise choices leads to more positive self-evaluation.
- Feeling worthy is central to the development and maintenance of one's positive identity. There are multiple verbal and non-verbal messages in which we indicate to others that they are valued in ways that are unconditional upon our expectations for their accomplishments. One should never underestimate the incremental feedback, which consolidates high self-esteem for individuals and for groups.

Intervention Strategies for Consultation

A. Teachers:

(1) Encourage children to set realistic goals and to test their own abilities in and out of class.
(2) Help children identify personal competencies ("I am good at....")
(3) Develop group problem-solving strategies based on co-operative learning. This is likely to enhance mutual respect.
(4) Teach children self-evaluation strategies.
(5) Define roles and responsibilities based on clear rules and expectations.
(6) Encourage inclusion of peers and provide a rational for doing so.
(7) When disciplined, make sure that the child does not feel rejected by you as an individual.
(8) Help children develop self-management techniques by discussing those in class frequently and noting efforts made by individuals and groups.
(9) Set aside time to express appreciation for group work and positive communication.
(10) When children need correction, find time to meet with them alone since they are likely to be sensitive to peer reactions.
(11) Send home positive notes which detail the child's work or behavior ("I was pleased to see how well Jim worked with his math group today...").
(12) With impulsive children, use a special signal to remind them of certain expectations without having to reprimand them in front of others.
(13) Use story writing, story telling, music and art as vehicles for self expression in a safe classroom environment.

(14) Provide regular opportunities for individual conferencing, which validate the children's experiences and work.
(15) Invite parents and community members to share their cultural customs in order to validate the link between home and school.
(16) Encourage welcoming of new students by assigning buddies and providing them with frequent contact and feedback.
(17) Practice conflict resolution skills in order to minimize bullying, blaming or name-calling.
(18) Use stories and role-playing to explain values such as trust and respect.
(19) Discuss the importance of equity and social acceptance. Ask children for examples related to their school community.
(20) Listen to children's expression of stress, note your compassion and concern when it is called for.

B. Parents:

(1) Encourage your children to become more independent by learning to make choices.
(2) Provide children with predictable routines and a sense of belonging ("we eat supper together so that our family will be able to share stories after a long day at school and work...").
(3) Model a sense of purpose and discuss how adult daily routines support all family members.
(4) Acknowledge the child's responsibilities and provide positive feedback for daily accomplishments ("I am pleased you remembered to set the table. This will save me some time which we could spend together...").
(5) Recognize the child's strengths and show him that you feel good about his achievements.
(6) Be honest about your feelings. When you withdraw privileges or punish your child, state that you are disappointed with his behavior not with him.
(7) Demonstrate your love and respect in verbal and non-verbal ways.
(8) Remember that rewards do not have to be bought. Positive activities, such as relaxing together, can be just as valuable.
(9) Make sure that your expectations are clear to your child since inconsistencies are likely to cause confusion and defensiveness.
(10) Relate to your child as an important individual and teach the child about rights and responsibilities which change with age.
(11) Develop in your children a sense of cultural and linguistic pride by modelling sharing of family stories, using humor in the first language, and planning cultural events together.
(12) When you become preoccupied, tired or busy with unexpected tasks you are likely to have less time for your child. Discuss the reasons for changing routines and indicate when you will be able to provide individual attention.
(13) Discuss with your child a range of feelings and situations. Validate their emotional reactions by listening and remembering family events.
(14) Try not to compare siblings. Each child has areas of strengths that need to be recog-

nized on a regular basis. Comparisons ("why can't you be more like your sister?") tend to stereotype behaviors and negative competition for parental approval.

(15) Help your child identify things he is proud of; worried about; hopes to achieve. Discuss ways to support the child in meeting his goals.

(16) Each day, spend some time together on a choice activity. The unit of time is less important than joint activity that allows for care and expression of affection.

(17) Accept your child's feelings, even if you do not approve of the event that resulted in his reactions. Each child is a unique individual. By supporting each member's self-worth, you will strengthen the family's self-esteem.

Chapter 9
Underachieving Adolescents: Assessment and Intervention

Janet Zarb

Academic underachievement is a frequent problem of adolescents referred to school psychologists. As used here, the term "underachievement" refers to functionally low levels of poor school performance that are not related to intellectual ability or skill. Underachievement and/or truancy are often associated with personality and emotional disorders, and may be inadequately addressed by school psychologists whose major training has been in the evaluation of cognitive and academic functioning. This is not to say that underachievement cannot exist simultaneously with learning disabilities and other deficits in intellectual, academic, or personality functioning. In fact this is often the case, and in such situations it is important to understand the multidimensional aspects of the problem, and to design interventions to address each area of difficulty.

The purpose of this chapter is to present a model for the assessment of emotional disorders that can contribute to poor school performance. The model is intended to be used in conjunction with more traditional academic and cognitive evaluations, irrespective of whether strictly academic deficits appear to be a significant component of the problem. The application of the model is illustrated by the case study of an adolescent referred to the school psychologist with presenting problems of chronic truancy and academic underachievement. The approach taken emphasizes a developmental perspective grounded in social learning theory and uses techniques from cognitive-behavioral psychology. Interventions are planned to deal with specific dysfunctional behaviors based on hypotheses about their origins and the factors responsible for their maintenance in the current situation. The application of the model for use with an adolescent population manifesting a spectrum of psychological disorders is the focus of a more comprehensive work on which this chapter is based (Zarb, 1992).

The chapter begins with a discussion of the theoretical underpinnings of the model. To illustrate the process, a series of five areas for assessment are then outlined using the specific case of one underachieving adolescent girl. In keeping with the consultation problem-solving approach of this book, the next section emphasizes the role of the school psychologist in designing interventions. The last section discusses implications for school psychologists' training.

Theoretical Influences

The essential criteria of a viable assessment/therapy model include a solid theoretical and research base, a close relationship between assessment findings and a therapy plan, a clear description of the components of the presenting problem, and provision for evaluation of behavioral change. This section provides a brief discussion of the rationale underlying the proposed cognitive/social-learning assessment model. Although the discussion will be cursory, it will be sufficient for practical application.

Similarly, a detailed description of cognitive-behavioral therapy interventions is beyond the scope of this chapter. These will be briefly discussed however, since the assessment process itself involves identification of target behaviors and cognitions for therapy intervention. Detailed descriptions of cognitive-behavioral techniques applied to adult clients are available elsewhere (Beck & Emery, 1985; Beck & Freeman, 1990; Beck, Rush, Shaw, & Emery, 1979; Bedrosian & Bozicas, 1994; Guidano, 1987; Kuehlwein & Rosen, 1993; Padesky & Greenberger, 1995). Many of the techniques have been adapted for use with an adolescent population (Zarb, 1992).

Albert Bandura (Bandura, 1969, 1985) has been one of the most influential architects of the cognitive/social-learning perspective. Bandura emphasized the importance of reinforcement contingencies stemming from parenting practices, social conditioning, and cultural norms in shaping important aspects of a child's developing personality. He was also one of the first to emphasize the role of internal cognitive processes in mediating antecedent and consequent external events. These cognitive mediators influence what a person attends to and remembers, and how he or she actually perceives events. Thus, the psychologist evaluating an adolescent must do a thorough assessment of the latter's *perception* of the presenting problem, in addition to understanding differing conceptualizations of the problem held by parents, other family members, and involved school personnel.

In keeping with the cognitive/social-learning framework, a comprehensive assessment would also need to include collection of data about the student's development in several areas. This is gathered in order to have sufficient information with which to hypothetically reconstruct current and past reinforcement contingencies responsible for shaping and maintaining present dysfunctional behaviors and thought patterns. Four basic forms of past and current learning would need to be investigated: 1) associative learning, which is under the control of immediate reinforcement contingencies, and which includes learning from parental discipline techniques and parental rules and regulations; 2) vicarious learning, which includes learning through observation and imitation of those around one, especially significant others such as parents and peers and those individuals whom the youngster admires and would like to emulate; 3) indirect learning of attitudes, beliefs, and viewpoints through the symbolic instruction of significant others; and 4) implicit learning, which takes place when the youngster draws his or her own inferences from available information from past and present experiences and memories, and uses this information to predict consequences or understand present experiences.

The pioneering work of Beck and his colleagues, cited above, and the more recent theoretical and clinical work of Jeffrey Young (Young, 1999; Young & Gluhoski, 1996) have contributed immeasurably to cognitive-social learning perspectives and techniques applied to emotional and personality disorders (Mahoney, 1993). A basic assumption of these theorists is that people's affects and behaviors are determined to a large extent by the way they perceive and structure their world. Thus, one would expect emotionally disturbed adolescents to be characterized by 1) cognitive distortions of their world and of their personal capabilities, and 2) dysfunctional behavior patterns and/or a lack of sufficient or appropriate coping skills. Assessment would therefore focus on identification of dysfunctional behavior patterns or areas of deficient coping, and concurrently, identification of the adolescent's own interpretation of events in his or her life. These interpretations, based on the youngster's self-reports about ideas, feelings, and wishes, provide the basis for understanding the maladaptive attitudes and beliefs underlying dysfunctional behaviors.

A second important assumption of this perspective is the existence of a relationship between cognitive distortions and self-defeating emotional responses such as depression and anxiety, and personality disorders, so that an individual's distorted interpretation of events leads to a specific emotional response or behavior style. A third assumption is that certain types of maladaptive cognitions characterize particular disorders (Beck & Emery, 1985; Beck & Freeman, 1990; Beck et al., 1979; Marton, Churchard, & Kutcher, 1993; Padesky, 1994; Young, 1999).

To summarize, then, a comprehensive cognitive-behavioral assessment of school problems must include identification of components of the presenting problem to be designated as target dysfunctional behaviors for therapy interventions. This necessitates a thorough assessment incorporating both a functional behavioral analysis, and a functional cognitive analysis of reinforcement contingencies shaping and maintaining these target dysfunctional behaviors and cognitions. The assessment model to be presented will include information about a youngster's direct and indirect learning from parental childrearing practices and models, and from experiences with peers, teachers, and additional significant others. This calls for a careful analysis of past and present parenting practices, and of peer and school experiences to which the youngster has been exposed. It also necessitates a careful identification of maladaptive cognitive patterns contributing to the dysfunctional target behaviors that are characteristic of the adolescent and her family, friends, and additional "significant others." Then, in order to make sense of all of this information after it has been collected, the psychologist must have an in-depth knowledge and understanding of theories of normal and abnormal child and adolescent development that are based on clinical expertise and solid research foundations.

A model of pathological sources of learning consistent with a cognitive/social-learning perspective has been outlined by Millon (1981). In his view, most of the child's behaviors and attitudes are learned from rewards and punishments spontaneously given out by parents, and from everyday activities of parents and siblings who serve as unintended models for the child to imitate and who significantly influence his or her view of how people think, talk, fear, love, and solve problems. Children are influenced by their parents' deliberate attempts at indoctrination, and later by the indoctrination of school, ethnic group, and other institutions. Daily reinforcement contingencies and observations are also influential in forming aversions, anxieties, and styles of relating and communicating. The child learns complicated attitudes, reactions, and expectancies in relation to specific events, which eventually develop into stable strategies for responding to others. Healthy adolescents have managed to develop flexibility in the use of coping strategies and the ability to match appropriate behaviors to particular situations. Healthy coping also involves some degree of employment of cognitive distortions (such as the classical defense mechanisms) to ameliorate discomfort. However, cognitive distortion becomes pathological when used indiscriminately, so that this interferes with the acquisition of more adequate coping behaviors.

In Millon's view, pathological learning arises from three sources: (1) persistent events that create intense anxieties resulting in insecurity, and consequently adaptive, self-protective reactions and long-term coping styles and anticipations that diminish anxiety initially, but are maladaptive in the long run; (2) simple conditioning or imitation of maladaptive behaviors; and (3) a lack of sufficient experiences necessary for learning adaptive coping behaviors (e.g., insufficient social experiences leading to poor social skills, insufficient self-discipline, insufficient self-control, etc.). These are three important areas that will be addressed in the assessment model presented below.

A major area of the child development literature that the school psychologist needs to be familiar with is the relationship between types of maladaptive parental child-rearing practices, and dysfunctional child and adolescent behavior patterns (Perris, 1988, 1994). For example, when a youngster is referred for truancy, the psychologist's first important task after identifying the components of the truant behavior is to make some sense of possible causes of the problem and the conditions maintaining them in terms of family, peer, and school or community factors. Since most adolescents are still living at home and thus subject to direct daily parental influences, and since parenting practices have had the longest and most consistent influence in their lives, an assessment of the relationship between parenting styles and adolescent problem behaviors is crucial. Information about the adolescent's typical reaction to parenting practices will help the psychologist to decide, for example, whether the truancy is a manifestation of a long-standing personality disorder characterized by excessive dependency related to overprotective parenting, as opposed to chronic failure to persist with unpleasant tasks related to overindulgent parenting, or characteristic disregard of rules and regulations related to oversubmissive parenting, or rebellion against extremely cruel or unfair parental practices. The psychologist must have a sufficient understanding of characteristic adolescent response patterns related to various dysfunctional parenting styles in order to generate plausible hypotheses about conditions maintaining the truancy.

Detailed discussions of rationale, assumptions, and supporting research for cognitive-behavioral therapy models have been provided by Beck (1976), Beck et al. (1979), Goldfried and Goldfried (1980), Genest and Turk (1981), Kendall and Korgeski (1979), Meichenbaum (1976) and Safran, Vallis, Segal, and Shaw (1986). Basically, cognitive-behavioral therapists agree that alteration of both maladaptive behaviors and maladaptive cognitions is crucial for a successful therapeutic outcome. Theorists such as Genest and Turk (1981) suggest that behavioral interventions are the most powerful, at least initially, since these performance-based methods not only alter dysfunctional behaviors, but also cognitive processes. This is in keeping with the notion that persuading the adolescent to actually experiment with new, more adaptive behavior patterns will be likely to result in some degree of immediate symptom relief, since these new behaviors will be likely to lead to more positive reinforcement contingencies in the youngster's environment. This demonstrates to the youngster that he can have some control over the aversive reinforcement contingencies associated with his former dysfunctional behavior pattern, and will subsequently produce greater insight into the problem and consequently, more adaptive cognitive change. Interventions growing out of the proposed cognitive/social-learning assessment model would be consistent with a cognitive-behavioral therapy approach.

The primary objective of the cognitive assessment and the application of cognitive intervention techniques is to teach youngsters to recognize and reappraise deeper dysfunctional cognitive structures that are contributing to their behavioral and emotional problems. For example, a student who is chronically truant may report the following automatic thoughts preceding a decision to skip classes: "I've always been a failure in everything, including school, so there's no point in attending classes." Specifically, the identified cognitions will be in the form of dysfunctional automatic self-statements, attitudes, beliefs, and assumptions. The rationale for cognitive therapy is that if the youngster can be taught to recognize and correct her own distortions of reality, she will then be better able to attack her problems. Just as specific maladaptive behaviors are designated as target behaviors for treatment, specific maladaptive cognitions are designated as target cognitions for therapy intervention.

Cognitive-behavioral therapists have utilized the approach in different ways, while still embracing the major underlying assumptions: (1) maladaptive cognitions do mediate dysfunctional behaviors, so a major focus of therapy is the modification of dysfunctional cognitions; (2) maladaptive cognitions are related to manifestations of unwanted emotional arousal such as depression and anxiety, so modification of distorted cognitions is a necessary prerequisite to amelioration of unwanted emotional responses; and (3) specific patterns of maladaptive cognitions are characteristic of specific psychological disorders, so identification of particular types of cognitions can facilitate identification of the particular type of disorder (e.g., depression versus anxiety).

The Assessment Model

The foregoing has been a discussion of essential components of a thorough assessment of personality and emotional disorders contributing to adolescent school underachievement, stemming from a cognitive/social-learning perspective. Although the reason for referring a youngster to the school psychologist may appear to be primarily a school-based problem such as truancy, a cognitive/social-learning assessment model would involve data collection in several critical areas in order to place the identified problem of truancy within its larger context. We have already noted several important assessment areas in addition to academic testing, including: (1) pertinent components of the presenting problems and the reinforcement contingencies maintaining each of these components (or target dysfunctional behaviors); (2) the youngster's current functioning with respect to family, peer, and school relationships; (3) current and past reinforcement contingencies stemming from parenting disciplinary practices, responsible for shaping and maintaining the youngster's maladaptive coping patterns; (4) the adolescent's distorted cognitions associated with her maladaptive coping patterns, which in turn have been responsible for further shaping and maintenance of dysfunctional response patterns; (5) an in-depth analysis of the adolescent's perception of the presenting problems, as compared to the parents', peers', and school's perceptions of the same problems; (6) parent, peer, and other models to which the youngster has been exposed over the years and which have presumably had an effect on his personality development; (7) family, peer, and school attitudes, beliefs, and other environmental and cultural influences that may have affected the youngster's acquisition of dysfunctional or distorted attitudes, beliefs, and other core cognitions; (8) behavioral or skill deficits that prevent the adolescent from normal functioning and from successful mastery of necessary developmental tasks; and (9) relevant past events involving difficult school, family, and peer relationships.

The assessment model described here was designed specifically for application to an adolescent population, and therefore focuses more closely on variables directly influencing an adolescent's world, such as parents and parenting styles, school variables, and aspects of peer relationships that are particularly relevant to crucial tasks of this developmental period. Data collection and organization are ongoing and concurrent with the design and application of therapy strategies, which may involve individual and family counseling, school-based interventions, and other community-based interventions designed to modify not only the youngster's dysfunctional behaviors and cognitions, but also the behavior of significant others as well as reinforcement contingencies maintaining the adolescent's problem behaviors.

Areas for assessment include:

(1) Initial identification of components of presenting problems.
(2) Identification of reinforcement contingencies of target dysfunctional behaviors.
(3) Influence of significant others; descriptions of the adolescent's lifestyle.
(4) Developmental analysis.
(5) Identification of dysfunctional cognitions.

Case Study: Five Areas for Assessment

Initial Identification of Components of Presenting Problem

The first step is concerned with identifying the salient components of the presenting problems, as described by the adolescent client, the parents, school personnel, and/or other referral sources. Each of these sources is encouraged to air major complaints individually, and to explain reasons for initiating the referral. The psychologist directs these initial interviews in order to secure pertinent information. He or she asks the youngster (or referring adult) to give specific examples to illustrate the problems or complaints, and information about frequency, severity, and duration of problem behaviors is elicited in order to put the problem into perspective. Information about relevant cognitions associated with each of the problems is also elicited, by asking such questions as "What thoughts were going through your head at this time?" (i.e., during the stressful situation causing the problem behaviors), and by requesting that the youngster keep a "Thoughts Diary" between sessions.

The data collected during Step One may then be organized into a list of the major complaints or problems, as defined by both referring agents and the adolescent, with accompanying cognitions noted. Each presenting problem is then broken down into components or target dysfunctional behaviors for application of subsequent intervention strategies. Possible interventions applicable to each of the identified target behaviors may also be noted at this time for future implementation. The list of target behaviors will be revised and refined throughout the assessment and intervention period. Failure of interventions to have the desired effect will provide new information and the impetus to search for reasons for the failure, which in turn provides additional assessment data. For example, failure of a father to make the necessary effort to phone the attendance counselor daily for an update report on his son's attendance after this had been carefully arranged, may suggest a pervasive tendency on the part of the parent to avoid taking action on problems and to avoid confrontation with the son.

The case of Betty, a 15-year-old girl referred to the school psychologist for chronic truancy, will be used to illustrate application of the various steps in the proposed assessment model.

Betty had grown up as the only daughter of a single mother, the father having abandoned the family several years ago and only recently returned. The mother worked long hours in order to give her daughter and an older son (who was now grown and out of the house) "the best of everything." Her tendency to cater to Betty's wishes was supported by a belief that she had to make up for her daughter's misfortune in not having had a father, for which she felt personally responsible. Betty was on her own for long periods of unstructured time after school and during the evenings while her mother worked late, and began to hang around at a neighborhood restaurant to fill in the time. Betty had never had many friends, a fact she attributed to having been a fat child. She felt that most of the students attending her current school did not like her, whereas the youngsters at the restaurant seemed to accept her. She began to adopt their lifestyle, which included long hours of talking and experimentation with drugs while skipping classes during the day. Her new group of friends praised her nonchalant attitude toward school attendance.

The mother was eventually informed by the school of Betty's truancy and involvement with drugs, and confronted her daughter and accused her of letting her down "after all I've done for you." Although Betty felt guilty, her truancy continued because she was able to deceive her mother quite easily. Although the mother disliked what was going on, she failed to inflict any consequences for it because she was afraid of jeopardizing their relationship, feeling that her daughter needed her as a friend, first and foremost.

The primary reason identified by the school for Betty's referral was truancy, the frequency and severity of which was described as daily absences from all afternoon classes and increasing absences from morning classes, so that in recent weeks she had hardly attended school at all. Lack of application to schoolwork in those morning classes she did attend was a second problem identified. In those classes she was withdrawn and appeared to daydream, and failed to complete most homework assignments so that her level of achievement was borderline.

During initial assessment interviews, Betty identified her problems as a longstanding lack of friends and lack of acceptance by peers, with the exception of fellow truants. A second problem she identified was her father's sudden return after deserting the family, and her own ambivalence about his requests for reconciliation, his continued erratic behavior when drunk, and renewal of the marital relationship, which was causing a change in the close mother-daughter relationship. Another area of concern she described was her feelings of depression. These emotional difficulties were related to perceived peer rejection, inability to discipline herself to complete assignments, and difficulty concentrating during class. She also discussed her guilt stemming from the knowledge that she was deceiving and hurting her mother by skipping classes after promising that she would attend. She said that her mother had sacrificed so much for her, and she condemned herself for her inability to say no when her new friends invited her to skip classes with them.

To summarize the information from this phase of the assessment:

School's Concerns:
- Truancy – daily absence from afternoon classes for three months, and periodic absence from morning classes.
- Lack of application to schoolwork during classes attended (e.g., daydreaming, withdrawn).

Mother's Concerns:
- Daughter's apathy, loss of interest, depression.
- Daughter's association with truant/drug-abusing peers.
- Mother's loss of control over daughter's behavior.

Betty's Concerns:
- Lack of friends and acceptance by a pro-social peer group.
- Ambivalence about new relationship with father.
- Anxiety/depression related to school; guilt for deceiving mother through her truancy.

Before going on to a discussion of other assessment areas, it is important to add that at least one in-depth interview with parents and other family members is a crucial part of the assessment and intervention process. It is preferable that the youngster be present for part of the family interview. This interview will provide a more comprehensive view of the adolescent's functioning in several settings by eliciting information about family members' personal perspectives on the adolescent's problems, sources of stress for the youngster, both past and present, parent-child interaction patterns, marital interaction patterns, pathological coping styles of parents (who serve as intentional and unintentional models for their children), and family dynamics.

Identification of Reinforcement Contingencies of Target Dysfunctional Behaviors

A second area of the assessment is concerned with further clarification of the components of the presenting problems and identification of specific dysfunctional target behaviors for application of intervention strategies. This is followed by initial attempts to identify reinforcement contingencies responsible for shaping and maintaining the target behaviors. Refining the identification of dysfunctional target behaviors, emotions, and cognitions is to be an ongoing part of the assessment process. As more and more information is obtained using more comprehensive structured interview techniques in later assessment steps, core dysfunctional patterns seminal to the youngster's psychopathology will become clearer, as well as dysfunctional patterns of significant others that may also be deemed targets for intervention strategies.

At this point in the assessment process, the youngster is only asked how family members, classmates, friends, teachers, and additional significant others typically respond to manifestations of each of the target behaviors (e.g., "How does your mother typically respond when the school informs her that you have been skipping classes? How do your friends respond when you try to refuse their offer to skip classes together?").

In addition, by asking the youngster what goes through his or her head in association with target behaviors, information is provided about cognitions related to them. For example, when Betty was asked how she usually reacted to a new school assignment and what her accompanying thoughts and feelings were, she reported that she usually expected that she wouldn't succeed in completing the assignment because she had always had great difficulty forcing herself to begin, and that she would procrastinate and become increasingly upset. Her self-statements included: "I didn't know how or where to begin," "I know I'll fail because I can never make myself finish anything," "It's hopeless," "There's no point in trying."

In addition to the adolescent, dysfunctional behaviors of significant others may also be targets for change, such as a mother's abdication of her parenting responsibility to set limits and expectations. External circumstances may be targets as well, such as a school's failure to consistently monitor the student's attendance and to promptly inform the parents about persistent truancy.

In the case of Betty, some of the target behaviors and corresponding reinforcement contingencies initially identified are listed below:

Dysfunctional Target Behaviors and Circumstances	Reinforcement Contingencies and/or Maintaining Factors
Skipping Classes	
(1) Avoidance of social anxiety in classroom setting	Relief from anxiety
(2) Avoidance of encounters with school authorities	Relief from fear of suspension
(3) Skipping with truant peers	Peer acceptance/approval
(4) Drug abuse	Temporary "high"
(5) Mother's abdication of responsibility to set limits	Mother's relief from guilt
Lack of Application to School Work	
(1) Concentration difficulties	Preoccupation with depressive concerns
(2) Lack of self-discipline skills, excessive procrastination	History of parental overindulgence; long history of poor work habits; student's belief that academic success is impossible.

Reinforcement contingencies hypothesized to be maintaining the truancy included: (1) relief following avoidance of the school and classroom setting where Betty feared negative comments from classmates and teachers about her truancy and other aspects of her personality; (2) fear of encountering the principal or other officials leading to formal suspension from school; (3) positive feelings associated with acceptance and approval for skipping classes from fellow truants; and (4) a temporary "high" from social interactions and drug abuse with truant peers. Other factors maintaining the truancy included: (5) the mother's temporary relief from guilt about her failure to provide a proper home for her children, causing her to continue to ignore the problem and to fail to impose definite expectations and consequences on Betty's behavior; and (6) Betty's (incorrect) belief that she would never be able to pass any of her courses this year so that there was no point in attending even those classes in which she had been academically successful until recently.

Important factors and contingencies maintaining Betty's lack of application to schoolwork in classes she had attended included her concentration difficulties related to depression and anxiety growing out of her preoccupation with her father; her feelings of hopelessness with respect to her chances of completing requirements for a high school diploma; and guilt feelings and self-hate related to her deception of her mother. Her lack of adequate self-discipline and study skills were shaped and maintained by a long history of parental overindulgence and the school's failure to provide extra training in study and organizational skills. A longstanding habit of extreme procrastination was partially maintained by a distorted "all-or-nothing" belief that success in any of her courses was impossible.

Systematic Survey of Influences of Significant Others and the Adolescent's Life Style

A third phase in the assessment process is a more systematic survey of the types of parent and peer models the youngster has been exposed to, a survey of her typical interaction styles with these significant others, and their evaluation of her. The next part of this phase is designed to elicit information about the youngster's daily life in the home, peer, and school environments. This phase will provide deeper insights into the shaping and maintenance of the adolescent's dysfunctional response patterns, and will further aid the psychologist in designing strategies for change.

First, the adolescent is asked to describe each of the significant others in her life (parents, siblings, classmates, best friends, teachers, etc.) and then is asked how the other person would describe her. This provides information about influential models, and also about the adolescent's self-concept in relation to parents, peers, and teachers. It also provides some important information about childrearing practices, family dynamics, and peer-group dynamics.

Next, she is asked to describe one or two stressful or upsetting situations involving each of the significant others, and her own responses and those of the other person in these situations (e.g., "Think of an upsetting situation involving your mother. Describe the situation. What was your response? Was that typical? If not, what would have been your typical response in that type of situation? What was her response? Was that typical? If not, what would have been her typical response? What thoughts were going through your head during that situation?"). For more specific information about the parents' disciplinary styles, the youngster is asked, "How does your mother (father) typically react when you do something she disapproves of? Describe an actual situation. What did she do? Then what did you do?"

The next section of the structured interview is designed to elicit information about patterns of daily living. The adolescent is asked to describe a typical weekday and a typical weekend in detail, from the time he gets up in the morning until going to bed at night. For a typical school day, he is asked to describe each of his current classes individually. This is particularly relevant for school-related problems.

In Betty's case, pertinent information from this step of the assessment included the following: (1) Betty's perception of her father's evaluation (description) of her as "not worth bothering about;" and (2) her mother's description of her as "my precious little girl who is breaking my heart." Betty perceived other family members as evaluating her as inadequate academically in comparison with her brother.

In terms of parental models, the father was described as irresponsible, moody, and violent when drunk, and the mother as self-sacrificing, nervous, and too softhearted. Current peer models, including Betty's two best friends, were school dropouts or truants who were also involved with drug abuse.

Stressful situations with the mother revolved mainly around her anger at Betty's late-night activities with friends at undisclosed locations. Betty's, and later her mother's descriptions of the response chains during these arguments indicated that the latter would almost always give in to Betty's demands. The mother's rationale for giving in was her fear of losing Betty if she tried to impose or enforce rules and regulations, as well as feeling that she had to make up for all the hardship Betty had been through with her father by indulging her and giving her the material things she wanted. The father, on the other hand, took no part in the discipline attempts on those occasions when he was staying in the home, but would periodically erupt in angry outbursts at Betty when drunk.

Betty's description of a typical weekday and weekend revealed she was alone for long periods after school and during dinner time, since her mother regularly worked late. Most of her time was spent either watching television alone, or in unstructured activities with friends which lasted late into the night, so that she would often sleep until 11:00 the next morning, missing school altogether.

Betty's description of her individual courses at school revealed several important beliefs: (1) math was perceived as her worst subject and a guaranteed failure every year; (2) she was very upset by fellow students in history class who were boisterous and who excluded her by never speaking to her; (3) she felt anxious from the start about attending two other classes in which she had no friends to talk to; (4) her geography teacher disliked her; and (5) classmates generally labeled her as a "skipper" and unattractive.

Developmental Analysis

The purpose of the developmental analysis is to collect information about persistent and/or excessively stressful events and circumstances in a youngster's life over the years that have possibly shaped maladaptive coping styles and behavior problems that are related to current problems. This includes details about parenting practices, family disruptions, and negative peer and school experiences. Data collection consists of asking both parents and adolescent to describe sources of excessive stress during preschool, elementary school, and junior high school years: older adolescents are asked about their early teenage years as well. Information is also elicited about the adolescent's interpretation of the causes of the stress and strategies for solution, as well as how he or she would have been described by significant others during those earlier periods. School records of ongoing academic and behavioral performance in the school setting (e.g., report cards, teacher anecdotal reports) will provide further data.

Betty identified the following early sources of stress: (1) lack of friends and peer acceptance due to poor image (overweight) and shyness; (2) life with an alcoholic father (inconsistency of affection, frequent violent outbursts, etc.); (3) constant negative comparison by parents and relatives with her brother who was academically superior; and (4) the father's desertion of the family, which Betty interpreted as due to his hatred for her and her mother. Betty's characteristic response to her lack of friends was a continual effort to "buy friends" by giving them presents, combined with shy withdrawal in the school setting. She reacted to her father's alcoholic outbursts with fear and anxiety, and to his desertion with anger, resentment and self-blame. For years she had reacted to negative comparisons with her brother by refusing to try and giving up.

Betty's ongoing school reports indicated that failure to complete school assignments had been a problem for years. Her insecurity, sadness, and shyness had been noted by elementary school teachers. Report cards indicated satisfactory but frequently borderline performance through Grade 8: several teachers over the years had noted poor work habits and the fact that she was working far below her intellectual potential. After Betty entered secondary school her marks had begun to slip dramatically. While up until that time she had always managed to pass on the basis of "potential," when she entered secondary school where students were expected to perform more independently, she began to fail individual subjects (two failures in Grade 9, four in Grade 10). Poor attendance and effort were noted by teachers as major contributors to failure.

Identification of Dysfunctional Cognitions

Some of the techniques to be utilized in the assessment of dysfunctional cognitions have already been alluded to, such as the use of the "Thoughts Diary" and the practice of asking the student to identify thoughts going through her head as she describes or experiences stressful situations. Relevant cognitions reported by the adolescent and significant others should be recorded verbatim from the start of the assessment process. These include automatic thoughts associated with stressful situations, past and present; perceptions of and causal theories about the problems; and distorted attitudes, beliefs, and assumptions. This information is then used in determining the subtleties and idiosyncratic nature of maladaptive target behaviors, which will vary from one individual to the next. In addition, some of the dysfunctional cognitions will be designated as targets for subsequent cognitive therapy interventions.

Data collected from the last three steps of the assessment process indicated a significant relationship between dysfunctional parenting styles and role models, and Betty's longstanding dysfunctional behavioral, emotional, and cognitive response patterns that were designated as targets for intervention. Specifically, clinical and research literature on the effects of maladaptive parenting would suggest the following conceptualization of Betty's psychopathology. The father's pattern of chronic neglect (initially associated with alcoholism and later with desertion of the family for several years), and his effect as a role model who was chronically irresponsible, were related to Betty's depressive preoccupations (e.g., angry retaliatory wishes, self-blame), which in turn interfered with concentration and self-esteem, her excessive need for approval, her tendency to drift, her poor self-discipline, and her irresponsible approach to schoolwork. The overindulgent and submissive parenting characteristics of her mother's approach were associated with Betty's tendency to act impulsively for immediate rather than delayed gratification, her inability to persist at uninviting tasks, and her lack of focus. The persistence of these maladaptive patterns over the years suggests the presence of major psychological disorders contributing to current school problems, and would indicate a need for individual psychotherapy combined with family counseling. In any case, much more will be needed to alleviate Betty's truancy than the more conventional interventions such as temporary suspension from school, or placement in a remedial class.

Planning Interventions

In planning interventions, the psychologist considers several issues:
(1) What are the characteristic maladaptive, behavioral, cognitive, and emotional responses contributing to the youngster's problem?
(2) What are the origins of and current factors maintaining these responses?

(3) What behavioral changes can bring about an alteration of the current maladaptive situation?

(4) Can the youngster's maladaptive belief systems be altered?

(5) What environmental factors can facilitate change?

(6) Are significant others in the child's life, such as peers, parents, and teachers, able to participate in the change process?

(7) What strengths or positive aspects of the situation can be capitalized on to facilitate change?

Having considered these issues, the school psychologist is in a position to select appropriate strategies for amelioration of each of the target dysfunctional behaviors or cognitions, and then take necessary steps to implement these in cooperation with the student, school personnel, parents, and other agencies and individuals who must be involved if it is to be successful. The psychologist will need to act as a coordinator of these different factions, and will also play a crucial role in sufficiently motivating the adolescent, family, and school to follow through with the recommended strategies. In addition to ongoing consultation with the various people involved, this usually necessitates personally taking responsibility for carrying out the initial steps of some of the interventions in order to bring about enough initial improvement to demonstrate their efficacy, and thereby motivate the youngster, family, and school to follow through with the recommended courses of action. This requires not only training and/or professional development in counseling skills and a thorough understanding of the theoretical and research basis of the adopted counseling model, but also a basic understanding of factors involved in the development of pathological adolescent behavior patterns in general, and of factors involved in the particular dysfunctional patterns manifested by the referred client.

In Betty's case, a variety of intervention strategies corresponding to the individual dysfunctional target behaviors may be appropriate. Individual psychotherapy may be recommended for her social anxiety, excessive need for peer approval, and lack of social skills; for self monitoring training to improve school attendance; and for her depression, which would involve cognitive therapy interventions for dysfunctional cognitions identified above. Family counseling would be another recommendation to help the mother to set appropriate expectations and limitations on unacceptable behaviors.

Recommendations for school-based interventions would include a meeting between student and principal to negotiate a partial timetable so that Betty would be able to concentrate her energy on the few courses that she was still capable of passing; meetings between Betty and teachers of those courses so that the teachers could provide her with information about missed assignments as well as providing encouragement to continue; and a meeting between student, parent, and principal in order to jointly set up a contract for attendance, a system for consistent monitoring of attendance, and a system for informing her mother of Betty's attendance patterns. Other school interventions might include attempts to involve Betty in at least one extracurricular school activity, and a study-skills program provided by the Special Education or Counseling Department.

Implications for Training Programs for School Psychologists

Repeated failure of school personnel to successfully reverse the destructive course of chronic school underachievement, especially if it has persisted for several years, is a familiar occurrence at the secondary-school level. Part of the problem often seems to stem from a poor grasp of the underlying psychopathology and failure to operationalize the pathological process in terms of specific dysfunctional behavioral, cognitive, and emotional patterns that must then become specific targets of intervention strategies. School psychologists are in a position to assume the responsibility of assessing and accurately identifying salient components responsible for underachievement, and of designing and coordinating corresponding interventions while simultaneously functioning as a consultant to school and agency personnel.

Unfortunately, psychologists working in secondary schools often lack sufficient clinical training to perform this role. They have traditionally been highly trained in the administration and interpretation of intellectual and academic tests and measures, but with much less emphasis on theories of child and adolescent psychopathology and the diagnosis of emotional and personality disorders.

The rationale for this has been that school psychologists need not pretend to be clinical psychologists since they deal with a non-clinical population. However, the reality of the situation is that the majority of adolescents with significant emotional and personality disorders are still attending school, at least sporadically. School personnel must deal with disturbed adolescents on a day-to-day basis, and consequently turn to the school psychologist for assistance. Since a high percentage of emotionally disturbed adolescents are also failing academically, an intellectual assessment is appropriate, but falls short of providing the necessary data on which to base potentially effective interventions, since recommendations would then tend to be restricted to areas of curriculum change and Special Education involvement. As a result, a high percentage of underachieving adolescents who have been receiving Special Education assistance for years still continue to fail and to skip classes, because their emotional and motivational problems have not been adequately addressed.

The tendency has been for school psychologists who lack sufficient training in clinical assessment and skills in counseling and behavior management techniques to acknowledge nonacademic components of school failure by applying global labels such as "acting-out" or "depression," combined with an equally vague recommendation for "counseling" to be provided by an outside agency. Failure to specify components of presenting problems that would be best treated by the agency, and other components that would more appropriately involve interventions by school personnel (e.g., the guidance counselor, principal, or teachers who have daily contact with the adolescent), and further failure to take responsibility for ensuring that interventions are initiated, leads to little or no amelioration of the youngster's problem.

Another difficulty frequently encountered by school psychologists is the failure on the part of students and their families to follow through with referrals to outside agencies for therapy. One method of motivating families to become engaged in therapy is for the psychologist to conduct a few preliminary family counseling sessions within the school setting, which is generally far less threatening than a clinical setting. These preliminary sessions serve to demonstrate to the family precisely how they may be helped by ongoing therapy. Again, this suggests the need for secondary-school psychologists to acquire clinical expertise in assessment of family dynamics and in family counseling.

In conclusion, it is clear that the implementation of the assessment model presented in this chapter requires school psychologists who have sufficient clinical training to precisely identify pertinent behavioral and emotional components of school underachievement. Assessment skills generally go hand in hand with a comprehensive grasp of adolescent psychopathology based on a theoretical perspective with solid research foundations, and with skills in designing, operationalizing, and implementing intervention strategies.

References

Bandura, A. (1969). *Principles of behavior modification.* New York: Holt-Rinehart & Winston.

Bandura, A. (1985). Model of causality in social learning theory. In M. Mahoney & A. Freeman (Eds.), *Cognitive and psychotherapy* (pp. 81–100). New York: Plenum.

Beck, A. T. (1976). *Cognitive therapy and emotional disorders.* New York: International Universities Press, Inc.

Beck, A. T., & Emery, G. L. (1985). *Anxiety disorders and phobias: A cognitive perspective.* New York: Basic Books.

Beck, A. T., & Freeman, A. (1990). *Cognitive therapy of personality disorders.* New York: The Guilford Press.

Beck, A. T., Rush, A. J., Shaw, B. F., & Emery, G. L. (1979). *Cognitive therapy of depression.* New York: The Guilford Press.

Bedrosian, R., & Boziacs, G. (1994). *Treating family of origin problems. A cognitive approach.* New York: The Guilford Press.

Genest, M., & Turk, D. (1981). Think aloud approaches to cognitive assessment. In T. Merluzzi, C. Glass, & M. Genest (Eds.), *Cognitive assessment.* New York: Guilford.

Goldfried, M., & Goldfried, A. (1980). Cognitive change methods. In F. Kanfer & A. Goldstein (Eds.), *Helping people change.* New York: Pergamon Press.

Guidano, V. F. (1987). *Complexity of the self; A developmental approach to psychopathology and therapy.* New York: The Guilford Press.

Kendall, P. C., & Korgeski, G.P. (1979). Assessment and cognitive-behavioral interventions. *Cognitive Therapy and Research, 3(1),* 1-21.

Kuehlwein, K., & Rosen, H. (Eds.) (1993). *Cognitive therapies in action. Evolving innovative practice.* San Francisco: Jossey-Bass Publishers.

Mahoney, M. (1993). Theoretical developments in the cognitive psychotherapies. *Journal of Consulting and Clinical Psychology, 61(2),* 187-93.

Marton, P., Churchard, M., & Kutcher, M. (1993). Cognitive distortion in depressed adolescents. *Journal of Psychiatric Neuroscience, 18(3),* 103-107.

Meichenbaum, D. (1976). A cognitive-behavior modification approach to assessment. In M. Hersen & A. Bellack (Eds.), *Behavioral assessment: A practical handbook.* New York: Pergamon Press.

Millon, T. (1981). *Disorders of personality: DSM-III – Axis II.* New York: Wiley.

Padesky, C. A. (1994). Schema change process in cognitive therapy. *Clinical Psychology and Psychotherapy, 1(5),* 267-278.

Padesky, C. A., & Greenberger, D. (1995). *Clinicians guide to mind over mood.* New York: The Guilford Press.

Perris, C. (1988). A theoretical framework for linking the experience of dysfunctional parental rearing attitudes with manifest psychopathology. *Acta Psychiatrica Scandinavica, Supplement No. 344, vol. 78,* 93-110.

Perris, C. (1994). Linking the experience of dysfunctional parent rearing with manifest psycholpathogy: A theoretical framework. In C. Perris, W. A. Arrindell, & M. Eisemann (Eds.), *Parenting and psychotherapy.* New York: John Wiley & Sons Ltd.

Safran, J., Vallis, T., Segal, Z., & Shaw, B. (1986). Assessment of core cognitive processes in cognitive therapy. *Cognitive Therapy and Research,* 10(5), 509-526.

Young, J. E. (1999). *Cognitive therapy for personality disorders: A schema-focused approach (3rd ed.).* Sarasota, Florida: Professional Resources Exchange, Inc.

Young, J. E., & Gluhoski, V. L. (1996). Schema-focused diagnosis for personality disorders. In F. Kaslow (Ed.), *Handbook of relational diagnosis and dysfunctional family patterns* (pp. 300-321). New York: John Wiley & Sons Ltd.

Zarb, J. (1992). *Cognitive-behavioral assessment and therapy with adolescents.* New York: Brunner/Mazel, Inc.

Chapter 10
Empowerment Plus®:
A "Wholistic" Approach to Cost-Effective Psychological Service Delivery in the Area of AD/HD

Teeya Scholten

The Empowerment Plus® model is a three-phase method of psychological service delivery that has been developed by the present author. It is based on a "wholistic" approach (i.e., mind, body, spirit) to personal empowerment. It incorporates aspects of primary, secondary and tertiary prevention and can be used by a psychologist practicing within or outside of a school system. It has been shown to be cost-effective in addressing concerns in the areas of attention (AD/HD – attention deficit/hyperactivity disorder), learning (LD – learning disabilities), behavior, and depression (Scholten, 1998a, 1998b, 1999a, 1999b, 1999c, 2001).

In order to be able to implement this model, a school psychologist needs to be skilled in providing in-service training, collaborative consultation, and psycho-educational assessment. They should be qualified to diagnose LD and AD/HD and have had training in Myers-Briggs personality type (MBTIT). These skills are used at the different phases of service delivery. The relationship between the Empowerment Plus® model and the framework presented by Cole and Siegel in Chapter 1 of this book has been summarized in greater detail in Table 1 below.

Application of the Empowerment Plus® model will be illustrated in this article in relation to the identification and treatment of school-age children with attention deficit/hyperactivity disorder (AD/HD). Specific aspects of the model will be described in the sections below and illustrated in detail by the two case vignettes of Aaron and Shanaz at the end of the chapter.

The purpose of this approach is to empower the classroom teacher, parents, and students and to facilitate academic success and emotional well-being. The use of Empowerment Plus® is not appropriate if one's primary goal is the formal identification

Table 1 Relationship of Empowerment Plus® Approach to Psychological Service Delivery Model proposed by Cole and Siegel (1990)

Phase of Empowerment Plus® Model	I	II	III
Level of prevention	Primary	Secondary	Tertiary
Activity	Lecture	Workshop	Consultation, assessment and treatment (only if needed)
Goal of service	Review of areas to be understood and addressed	Effect of personality and stress on academic success	Assisted interpretation and intervention re: attention, learning, personality, food sensitivities, communication, and behavior management strategies
Format	Group	Group	Individual
Time needed	1 hour	4 hours	4–6 hours
Recipients of service:	100% of school staff, parents and students 12 years and up	Only those interested in taking a wholistic approach to success	Only those parents and teachers whose students are still experiencing "challenges" after **Phases I and/or II** have been implemented
Prof.: Student ratio	1:100	1:40	1:1
The organization	School system	Classroom/family	Classroom/family
School staff	As participants in lecture and in application to all students	As participants in workshop and in application to all students	Problem-solvers with parents and psychologist in relation to single student
Teachers/parents/ students (12 years+) (indirect–lecture)	✓	✕	✕
Teachers/parents/ students (mediated– workshop)	✕	✕	✕
Teachers/parents/ students (direct)	✕	✓	✓

of a recognized "disability" for the purposes of funding. However, it can still be used as part of a formal problem-solving process that may or may not eventually culminate in a formal designation of "special needs" status. This model can also be helpful in the formulation of an appropriate Individual Educational Plan after a student has been identified and placed in an appropriate setting.

Empowerment Plus® consists of three phases of service delivery:

Phase I – 1 hour group lecture
Phase II – 4 hour group workshop
Phase III – individual consultation, assessment, and treatment

The content covered in each of these phases will be presented below.

Application of Empowerment Plus® to AD/HD

Increased awareness of ADHD, or ADD has led to an ability on the part of teachers and parents to identify attentional concerns at early ages. As the field evolves, many new ideas are emerging concerning the diagnosis and treatment of these pervasive concerns. Practitioners from a multitude of disciplines have opinions about the causes, classifications and treatment strategies for this phenomenon (Barkley, 1998, 2000; Barkley & Murphy, 1998; Berk, 2001; Brown, 2000; Haber, 2000; Nadeau, 1995; Sattler, 1998; Viveca Novak, 2001; Weintraub, 1997; Wender, 2000; Zimmerman, 1999). In the meantime, parents and school personnel continue to be faced with the question "What can we do about it?" This question has become increasingly difficult to answer where the use of psychotropic medication continues to be controversial and increasing fiscal restraint appears to be limiting the options regarding widespread implementation of comprehensive assessment and treatment programs (Park, 2001; Reichenberg-Ulman & Ulman, 1996; Richters, Arnold, & Jensen, 1995).

How, then is it possible for professionals to make recommendations to parents on newer alternative approaches when the research is still inconclusive? How can educators approach the parents in a way that fosters co-operation and builds links with other professionals? How can parents work with teachers? How can the student get the help s/he needs in the face of educational cutbacks and/or if their parents do not have the financial resources to hire private assessment and tutoring services? How does one facilitate success in the educational environment when there may be a lack of co-operation between the home and the school? How can we intervene early so as to minimize the frustrations and potential negative effects and build the maximum amount of social and emotional health of the children and families involved? How can teachers address these concerns and still have time for all of the other students and day-to-day responsibilities of managing a classroom?

It is the opinion of the present author, a long-time practitioner in the field, that there is actually a great deal that can be done for students with attentional difficulties.

Facilitating success doesn't have to take a lot of time or effort when one takes the approach advocated by the Empowerment Plus® Model.

The actual content of the material covered in **Phases I, II and III** of this model will be summarized in the following sections.

Phase I – Lecture

The purpose of this one hour lecture is to explain what is meant by a positive and "wholistic approach" to concerns in the area of attention, learning, behavior, and depression, to review areas of functioning, to share some informal assessment tools, and to identify appropriate intervention strategies. This brief overview allows the participants to make an informed choice about whether or not they wish to participate in this type of process. It also familiarizes all parties with the concepts involved. There is no limit to the size of the group. In fact, whole school staffs, parents, and any student over 12 years of age are encouraged to attend.

A More Positive View of ADD

The lecture begins by informing participants that we all have a choice as to how we view ADD. If one chooses to view the ADDers' brain as a natural resource, we can learn to channel the energies in such a way as to build success. Having a positive, yet realistic view can have a profound impact on self-esteem, as one begins to understand and learn to work WITH the special abilities of the ADDer (Scholten, 1999c). The very first step in viewing ADD in a more positive way is to use the label "*attention deluxe dimension*" instead of Attention Deficit/Hyperactivity Disorder (AD/HD). This term was formulated by the present author in 1993 and reflects the ability of the ADDers' brain to handle a great deal of information at any one time.

Attention deluxe dimension is often explained in the following way:

"The ADD brain is one that can pay attention to LOTS of different things. It's like a channel-surfing brain or picture in picture TV. For instance, a teacher might be lecturing about a topic with which the student is familiar. The student might be thinking about other things such as the goal they scored in hockey last night, the argument they had with a friend and also wondering what they will tell their teacher about the math assignment that they didn't complete. Their brain is channel-surfing. Every now and then, the student might check back with what the teacher is saying and see if there is anything new. This may usually work for them, but occasionally, they may find that the teacher has given an instruction while they were on another channel! Did they miss the directions because they couldn't pay attention, or because they were paying attention to SO MANY other things?"

Most students with ADD can relate to this explanation. Parents and teachers have indicated that it has made a significant difference in the way they view their student. Several adults with ADD have reported that once they were aware of the different channels their mind was on, and their "deluxe" amount of attention, they were able to better monitor and control the focus of their attention!

It can be helpful to students to understand that the same qualities that get them into trouble in certain situations can be an advantage at other times. It was Hartmann (1993) who first proposed that having ADD could feel *like being a hunter who is forced to live in a farmer environment*. Participants are invited to consider several cartoon examples of a hunter (Scholten, 1999a, pp. 21-22), which illustrate how the typical adjectives that are used to describe ADD – "hyperactive," "impulsive," and "distractible" could actually be considered an advantage in a "hunter" situation. Substituting the words "energetic," a "quick decision-maker" and "observant," respectively, as is shown in Table 2, can be another positive approach and empowering to those with ADD.

Table 2 Hunter Versus Farmer

Quality in a farmer environment	Quality in a hunter environment
Hyperactive	Energetic
Impulsive	Quick decision-maker
Distractible	Observant

Looking at ADD in a more positive way (i.e., through the label "attention deluxe dimension," the concept of a "channel-surfing brain" and the use of different adjectives when describing behavior) does not cost any money to implement. It simply requires a decision. It also does not excuse the student from having to complete assignments and other activities that are necessary for learning. However, it is a natural springboard for understanding the whole student and finding ways to effectively develop the natural resource of their very busy brains.

After the positive reframe on the typical qualities of ADDers, participants are given a copy of the Screening Checklist for Attentional Concerns in Adults or Children (Appendix A). This tool was based on the DSM-IV criteria for AD/HD, but it can be used by teachers, parents, and students to identify the presence of attentional concerns. The Screening Checklist tends to be a non-threatening way of describing some of the behaviors that have been observed or experienced and can also facilitate a dialogue among interested parties. As such, it is not used to make a diagnosis, but rather as a tool to initiate a problem-solving dialogue. It can also be used as an objective way to measure student functioning at baseline as well as after any intervention strategies to assess their effectiveness. If there are 4–5 checkmarks in the "pretty much" or "very much" columns of the Screening Checklist, this suggests that there are problems with attention that should be explored further. It is emphasized that the Screening Checklist indicates the presence of concerns, but does not confirm the CAUSE[1] of the attentional difficulties. See Table 3 for common causes of attentional concerns.

Table 3 Common Causes of Attentional Difficulties

Physical:	– Thyroid
	– Hypoglycemia
	– Improper nutrition
	– "Brain" allergy to substances in the environment (such as milk, wheat, corn, sugar, dust, etc.)
	– Substance abuse
Emotional:	– Depression
	– Post-traumatic stress disorder
	– Manic-depression
	– Thought disorder
	– Psychotic reactions
Environmental:	– Learned behavior through living in a chaotic environment
	– Reaction to ongoing stress at home or school
	– A reaction to past or present physical or sexual abuse
Personality:	– Personality type – some people have personality types which tend to be talkative, innovative, and flexible, but somewhat procrastinating and prone to careless errors. These "types" may "look" as though they have ADD, but may just need a little help in time-management strategies. Other personality types may actually have ADD, but NOT look like it especially if they are quiet, sensitive, and value accuracy and task completion.
Learning:	– Learning discrepancies/disabilities/difficulties may result in symptoms that look like ADD because it can be difficult to concentrate on something that is very difficult to do when LD is present along with ADD, it is important to find ways of helping the student experience success.

---

[1] It is somewhat sobering to realize that criteria similar to those outlined in the Screening Checklist (Appendix A) are used by family physicians and other professionals to diagnose AD/HD. Often, medication is immediately prescribed. The desire of the professional to provide help in a timely way is certainly understandable, but it may be this readiness to prescribe medication that has resulted in much of the present controversy over the use of drugs with AD/HD. With the Empowerment Plus® Model, medication is recommended after a formal diagnosis has been made. This occurs after ruling out all other possible causes of attentional symptoms and addressing learning and personality considerations. The Farrelly Protocol (Appendix E) is then recommended for those wishing to conduct a medication trial.

It is important that these causes be ruled out prior to a formal diagnosis of AD/HD. In more straightforward situations, potential causes may be investigated informally during *Phase I and II*. Students with more serious mental health issues may require a formal assessment by the psychologist as a part of *Phase III*.

The following five aspects of functioning are then presented to participants, irrespective of presenting concerns:

- Areas of information processing affected by attention and strategies for improving attention
- Classic patterns of learning discrepancies (LD) and interventions
- Myers-Briggs Personality Type and implications for learning, communication, organization, and time management
- Food sensitivities
- Other factors that influence the individual's functioning (e.g., areas of interest, past traumas)

What are the 4–6 Areas of Information Processing that are Affected by Attention?

Dr. Mel Levine (1992) has proposed 12 areas of information processing which can be affected by attention, irrespective of the cause of the difficulties. These are listed below and outlined in the Levine Information Processing Questionnaire (Appendix C), which is simply given out to participants. In a single individual, 4–6 areas of information processing seem to be affected by attention (not all 12):

- Maintaining consistent alertness
- Taking in information deeply enough
- Filtering out distractions
- Too passive or too active processing
- Determining the importance of information
- Preview of outcomes
- Ability to satisfy oneself
- Pacing of activities
- Self-monitoring
- Learning from experience

Participants are encouraged to complete the questionnaire at their convenience. Once these areas of difficulty are identified, Strategies for Improving Attention (Appendix D) can be implemented to address these concerns. Participants are encouraged to identify the 4–5 most challenging areas and then to select one area at a time to work on, when they are ready to do so. They are advised to choose just one strategy and to implement it for 3 weeks in order to assess its effectiveness. For instance, if the student has difficulty *filtering out distractions,* they are encouraged to wear a Walkman or ear plugs while studying. Alternatively, for problems *taking in informa-*

tion deeply enough, the strategy of repeating or paraphrasing instructions can make it possible to take in the information more deeply and remember it.

Are There Any Learning Discrepancies (LD)?

The term "learning discrepancy" is used rather than "learning disability or difficulty" because it is much more accurate and doesn't automatically carry a negative connotation.

If a specific area of "challenge" can be identified, there are strategies that can be implemented to help the learner to be successful (see the LD Chart in Scholten, 1999b, *Turning The Tides: Teaching the Student with ADD*, pp. 91-95).

Students experiencing LD may have a single area of challenge (such as spelling, reading, or math) or they may experience a cluster of difficulties, which has been termed a more "classic LD" pattern. There are two major classic kinds of LD that tend to be easily recognizable. Once identified, they can be readily addressed:

These are:

i) Visual-Spatial Learning Discrepancy (VSLD)

In the practice of the present author, approximately 80% of clients with ADD have this classic pattern of LD. In a VSLD, the student is very verbal, can understand most of what is being said to them and can express themselves well orally. They are usually good at reading. They have difficulty with written work and basic math facts. If these students are not good readers, visual co-ordination and/or the scotopic sensitivity syndrome (Irlen, 1991) should be investigated and treated. Students with a VSLD tend to be accused of being "lazy," because teachers know that they understand the concepts, but they seem to have a hard time writing them down and are very good at avoiding or putting off written work altogether.

Reduction of the written work by half and/or encouraging the use of a computer with a spell-check option is a very effective accommodation. The student feels good about the neatness of their work, the ideas they are able to express and it doesn't require 2–4 rewrites of draft copies! Because they feel good about what they are producing, gains in their self-esteem are noted and they often show increased "motivation" to complete their work. See an example of this type of VSLD in Aaron's case vignette at the end of this chapter.

ii) Language-Learning Discrepancy (LLD)

In the practice of the present author, approximately 5% of clients with ADD have this classic pattern of learning discrepancy. In a LLD, the student often has a hard time in the area of language, processing verbal information and vocabulary development. Their strengths lie in the visual areas and mathematical computations. They may understand a concept better if it can be explained through a visual diagram or concrete example.

Giving extended time in exams permits the students time to process the verbal information. It gives the time needed to read and reply to the questions. Teaching content-specific *vocabulary* for upcoming subject areas allows the students to better understand the material when it is being taught. This often facilitates their success and allows a more accurate assessment of their knowledge. Once the students start to experience success by obtaining marks that reflect their understanding, they begin to feel better about themselves and seem more motivated to learn. See an example of an LLD in Shanaz's case vignette at the end of the chapter.

The LD patterns described above are "classic ones" and fit a large percentage (85%) of clients with ADD who have been seen by the present author. It is surprising how many students fit these two "classic LD patterns" of VSLD and LLD and are able to self-identify when the characteristics are described during the lecture. Therefore, formal IQ and achievement testing are rarely needed in these cases. These students can then be helped to experience success with minimal cost and effort on the part of all concerned. The other 15% of learners may require a more in-depth investigation into causes of their difficulties before an effective intervention can be identified.

What is the Student's Myers-Briggs Personality Type?

The Myers-Briggs Type Indicator (MBTI®) is one way of looking at personality, in which there are 16 possible types (Briggs-Myers, 1987; Keirsey & Bates, 1978). MBTI® theory states that our personality influences how we prefer to interact with the world and the ways in which we learn best. *People Type and Tiger Stripes* is a handy reference in which Lawrence (1979) explains the implications of type in the classroom.

During the *Phase I* lecture, the eight basic letters (i.e., I-Introvert vs. E-Extravert, S-Sensing vs. N-iNtuiting, F-Feeling vs. T-Thinking, and J-Judging vs. P-Perceiving) are briefly reviewed with participants. Examples are given as to their relevance for energy, learning, communication, and time management and two classic MBTI® stereotypes are presented by way of example.

For instance, those who are knowledgeable about the MBTI® and ADD, know that the "classic stereotype" for the ADDer is the ENTP (Extraverted-Intuitive-Thinking-Perceiving) personality type. Whether or not they have ADD, ENTPs tend to be balls of energy. As Intuiters, they are innovative thinkers who do not particularly value detail and accuracy. As Thinkers, they may overlook how people feel and as Perceivers they are the classic procrastinators – always wanting to take in a little more information before making a decision or completing a task. An ENTP has an increased chance of being falsely diagnosed with ADD, particularly if they are living in a chaotic environment. When an ENTP actually DOES have AD/HD: hyperactive/impulsive or combined type, they often feel extremely challenged (and so do the people around them!!!). This is the most likely personality type to come to the attention of the helping professional and this has contributed to the stereotypical understanding of an ADDer as "a chaotic ball of energy." For an example of an ADDer with an ENTP personality type, see Aaron's case vignette at the end of this chapter.

The diametric opposite of the ENTP is described in the Shanaz's case vignette. She is an example of those students with an Introverted-Sensing-Feeling-Judging (ISFJ) personality type. When an ISFJ has AD/HD, it is usually the predominantly inattentive type. In the experience of the present author, there is also a high likelihood of their being misdiagnosed as having an anxiety disorder. ISFJ's tend to be very quiet, conscientious, and sensitive to the feelings of others. They value neatness and accuracy and want to finish what they start. Many teenage girls with depression may be undiagnosed ADDers without hyperactivity. They tend to stay up late trying to finish their work, can become over-tired and stressed. Their depression seems to originate from failing to achieve to their maximum potential. When someone with this personality type has ADD, they present very differently from the "classic stereotype" and need very different strategies to facilitate success.

Participants are told that the implications of their personality types will be reviewed in greater detail during the 4-hour workshop as part of *Phase II*.

Are There Any Food Sensitivities Interfering with Optimal Functioning?

Food sensitivities can cause a variety of physical as well as neurological symptoms (Randolph & Moss, 1989). The elimination of an offending food from the diet for a period of just one week can indicate whether or not it might be one cause of the attentional concerns. The Symptom and Food Diary (Appendix B) is shared with the participants for completion at their convenience. In order to choose which food group to eliminate, a number of symptoms are reviewed. See Table 4 for classic symptoms and the implicated foods. Participants are encouraged to take the suspected food out of the student's diet for 7 days and then reintroduce it for three days, while observing any changes in their student's behavior, attitude, or mood. Participants are referred to additional resources if help is needed in making up an appropriate menu (Scholten, 1998b).

The area of food sensitivities is a controversial aspect of this model, but the results to date have been very compelling. Results of the present author have shown that five percent of the students who exhibited serious attentional symptoms (according to the Screening Checklist) report the complete disappearance of their symptoms within a week of a particular food being removed from their diet! In 90% of the cases, they report feeling better, but still have attentional concerns. Of those who are ultimately diagnosed with AD/HD, one third feel that they can be successful without medication. Of the two-thirds who choose medication, 100% have responded positively to low doses of Methyphenidate (Ritalin).

Table 4 Identification of Possible Food Sensitivities	
Symptom	Type of Food to be Eliminated for 7 Days
Frequent colds, flus, runny nose, tubes in ears	All milk products, including chocolate
Moodiness – Dr. Jekyll and Mr. Hyde	All wheat products including spelt and kamut
Excessive use of corn and/or sugar products	All corn and sugar

It is important to reiterate that neither teachers nor parents can be responsible for making a diagnosis. Neither are they allergists. Although teachers cannot manipulate the student's diet, they certainly CAN provide parents with information and resources about how to choose a food to eliminate in order to see if the attentional or emotional symptoms disappear. All that is needed is a week off a particular food to suggest if it is making a difference in the student's life. If certain foods are hurting a student, removal of these (and/or eventual treatment for a particular sensitivity) can reduce the stress in an individual's life and enhance their functioning. This process doesn't have to cost a lot of money; it just takes some guidance, time, and planning.

At the end of the lecture, participants are given an explanation of how medication works for ADD. They are informed about how the effects of physical movement, time pressure, and interest can stimulate the neurotransmitters in the brain to achieve an effect similar to that created by medication. Once they understand how physical movement can help ADDers to activate their brains, they are open to learning ways to "fiddle" quietly with a small toy or to "doodle" without distracting others. Examples of some of the available nutriceutical supplements (i.e., Phytobears, Efalex Focus) are shown, but participants are encouraged to check with experts in the field of alternative health for more information. Anyone wishing to conduct a medication trial is encouraged to follow the Empowerment Plus® method, by eliminating a food from their diet, accommodating for any learning discrepancies and to enroll in *Phase II* in order to better understand the implications of their personality type. If the attentional symptoms still persist, they are advised to seek a formal diagnosis and then take the Farrelly Protocol (Appendix E) to their family physician to guide the process of evaluating the effects of medication on their functioning.

In summary, the *Phase I* lecture of the Empowerment Plus® Model involves a more positive explanation of attention deluxe dimension as well as an overview of the areas mentioned above. Checklists and questionnaires are distributed in case there is an interest in pursuing this approach (Appendices A, B, C, & D). Those who wish to try to "solve their problems" on their own are encouraged to borrow self-help resource books written by the present author. The more closely the teacher, parent, and student work together, the more effective the process can be. However, it is important to remember that the success of this method is not dependent upon the full cooperation of all parties. At each phase, the participants are encouraged to "do what they can" by implementing certain suggestions. The results are often remarkable. *Phase I* participants wishing to have some assistance in implementing this "wholistic" approach are encouraged to participate in *Phase II*.

Phase II – Workshop

The purpose of this four-hour workshop is to permit a more in-depth understanding of the implications of MBTI® personality type characteristics for learning, communication, and time-management. Examples of this are outlined in Table 5 below.

School personnel as well as all family members (12 years and up) are invited to participate.

Table 5 Implications of MBTI® Preferences for Learning

Preference	Implications for Learning
E-Extravert	Needs to talk over ideas with others; gets energy from being with people
I-Introvert	Needs time to reflect on questions and time alone every day in order to maintain energy
S-Sensing	Values neatness and accuracy; needs to proceed in a step-by-step manner; needs "concepts" identified
N-Intuiting	Innovative ideas; simultaneous rather than sequential processor; needs help with proof-reading
T-Thinking	Logical; needs to be told how others are feeling; needs to learn "active listening"
F-Feeling	Sensitive; needs to be taught how to stand up for oneself and express feelings as "I-messages"
J-Judging	Likes to finish tasks; needs to be given 5 minute warning in order to get to closure and be able to switch activities
P-Perceiving	Flexible and adaptable; needs help with time management – "work before play"

Teachers cannot be expected to know the personality type of each student in the classroom. However, they can be aware of differential needs and when alternatives are offered, students will generally select what works best for them. For instance, when given a choice after a lesson, the "Extraverts (Es)" might want to choose a partner with whom to discuss their reactions to the concepts that have been taught. The "Introverts (Is)" would benefit from some quiet time to reflect on their own. "Intuitives (Ns)" need to find ways of becoming more accurate, while "Sensing (Ss)" types often need help organizing facts into conceptual maps. "Thinking (Ts)" students often need to be taught how to communicate in a more sensitive manner and "Feeling (Fs)" ones need to learn how to identify and express their needs. Most people with "Perceiving (Ps)" preferences need time management strategies and encouragement to do their "work before play." The Judging (J's) learners value closure and need a 5-minute warning before being expected to stop an activity.

Understanding the different ways in which the students' personalities affect their learning preferences allows the teacher to provide options for enhancing learning in all of their students, not just those with ADD.

Additional time is spent reviewing the "stress bucket" (see Scholten, 1998b, p.110) and the communication tools of "I-messages" and "active listening" (Scholten, 2001, pp. 52-55).

Evaluative feedback has suggested that the information shared during *Phase II* of the Empowerment Plus® model has led to increased self-acceptance and enhanced functioning, as well as tolerance for others in all participants. The greater the number of people from a family and/or school system who are able to participate in this workshop, the greater the amount of healing that seems to takes place. Through this process, many individuals have come to accept and "celebrate" who they are, appreciating the unique characteristics they bring to their environments.

Phase III – Individual Consultation, Assessment and/or Treatment

Phase III of the Empowerment Plus® Model involves the service delivery options of individual consultation, assessment, and/or treatment by the school psychologist. The focus is usually on the student and parents. *Phase III* is reserved for those who have not been able to "solve their problems" through participation in *Phases I and II*. In the experience of the present author, the concerns can usually be resolved in three two-hour sessions. These are described below. During these sessions, the student and their family are guided through the process described thus far. The parent can then liaise with the teacher regarding the intervention strategies. If appropriate, a diagnosis of AD/HD can be made and a medication trial implemented. In more difficult cases, additional time may be needed for some formal assessment of the student's learning or behavior management training for the parents (Scholten, 1998a).

First Session – Consultation

Sometimes individual consultation with the school psychologist may be required to "put together" the information that has been previously presented. During the first of these individual sessions, some time is spent identifying relevant goals. They are stated in the positive and then the student is rated on their present level of functioning. For example, there are usually 5–15 goals that might include: "I am organized." "I do my homework independently." "We treat each other with respect." "I have 2–3 good friends." "I can focus when I want to." Most clients have scores around 3/10 at the first session. "Success" is defined by a score higher than 7/10. This is achieved in most cases by the third session after the medication trial. If not, additional assessment or intervention may be needed.

The next step is to obtain a baseline measure of attentional and physical functioning through the tools outlined in *Phase I* (i.e., Screening Checklist for Attentional Concerns, Symptom and Food Diary, Levine Processing Questionnaire). The first two are completed in the office in front of the psychologist and the Levine is sent home along with a copy of Barkley's Semi-Structured Psychiatric Interview Guide (see Scholten, 1998b, pp. 118-147). LD patterns and MBTI® type are reviewed, determined for the student and parents, and the appropriate interventions advised. If there are any reported difficulties with reading, the Scotopic Sensitivity Syndrome (Irlen, 1991) is screened using colored transparent overlays. If the student reads better with one color, a plastic overlay is loaned to the student. They are asked to read with it for 10 minutes per day for the next three weeks. Very often, improvements are reported in reading. Having their eye-coordination checked by a developmental optometrist is also recommended (Birnbaum, 1993). Lastly, one food (e.g., milk products, wheat or corn/sugar) is formally selected for removal from the diet for a week, a menu is created as a guideline and the parent is asked to ensure that a Symptom and Food Diary is completed for each day of the 10 day food trial (7 days elimination of one food and 3 day reintroduction).

Second Session – Informal Assessment and Treatment

During this second 2-hour session, information is gathered and reviewed for the purposes of ruling out any other physical or emotional causes of the attentional concerns. This session is scheduled when the student has been off the selected food for 5–7 days (and before it is reintroduced). In this way, the psychologist can observe any changes in the student's behavior or appearance. At this time, the completed Symptom and Food Diaries for each day are examined to ensure compliance with the elimination diet. The student's observations are also analyzed to detect any other possible relationship between food and behavior. The Screening Checklist of Attentional Concerns is re-administered to determine if there are any changes and to assess the impact of the food elimination on attention. The completed Barkley Semi-Structured Psychiatric Interview Guide is reviewed for the purposes of ruling out any other causes of the attentional concerns. Any other potential causes (e.g., Post-Traumatic Stress Disorder) should be treated. If attentional symptoms are still present and there are no other possible causes, a diagnosis of AD/HD is made.

Following this, a number of intervention strategies are then reviewed. These include the possibility of medication as well as nutriceutical supplements (i.e., Efalex Focus, Phytobears) and other non-invasive interventions (i.e., cognitive re-regulation). Parents and student are encouraged to carefully consider these options and investigate these in greater depth. If the parents and student are open to the use of medication, the Farrelly Protocol (Appendix E) is explained. Parents are encouraged to request that their physician use this guideline in conducting the medication trial.

Although many students report improvements with the above-mentioned steps, a very small percentage (5%–15% in the author's experience) may require additional assessment and/or treatment services. Other forms of formal (i.e., intellectual and achievement) or dynamic (i.e., Rey's Complex Figure, Word Memory Test) assessment are carried out if needed to understand the learning in greater depth. Treatment strategies such as individual social skill or time management counseling for the student and/or behavior management programs for parents such as *Riding the Wave* (Scholten, 1998a) may be needed for students who are still exhibiting difficulties. *Riding the Wave* is a behavior management technique specifically designed for parents of students with ADD for the purpose of teaching self-control. It is described in much more detail in the following section under Teaching Self-Control.

Conducting a Medication Trial

Any clients open to a medication trial are encouraged to use the Farrelly Protocol, which is outlined in Appendix E. A letter from the psychologist is given to the parents confirming the diagnosis. This is taken to the family physician along with a summary of the Farrelly Protocol. Parents and school personnel are asked to complete a Screening Checklist every day of the 3-week medication trial. This is a very prudent protocol developed by Dr. Geraldine Farrelly, a Calgary pediatrician with many years of experience in this field. It involves a careful titration of the medication dose. It begins with 1/2 tab of name brand Ritalin. The dosage is increased by only a quarter of a tab each day until side effects are experienced. Then the dose is reduced to the previous level. This type of medication trial identifies whether or not the student is a responder to a particular drug and is helpful in determining the least amount of medication that is needed for the greatest gains.

Third Session – Follow-Up

The third, and usually final session is then scheduled for three weeks from the date of the planned commencement of the medication trial. This session consists of analyzing the Screening Checklists in order to determine the minimum therapeutic dose and re-rating the student's level of functioning on the goals that were set in the first session.

Role of the Classroom Teacher

Although the classroom teacher cannot be responsible for dietary changes with their students, they can play an important role in facilitating change. Firstly, they can choose to take a more positive orientation to ADD, use the Levine Information Processing Questionnaire, and select appropriate strategies. They can understand and accommodate for LD and MBTI® personality patterns and implement *Riding the Wave* in their classroom. They can also encourage parents to access available resources in terms of reading materials, professional support, and peer support and education through International associations such as Ch.ADD (Children and Adults with ADD). This group often has local chapters and/or can be accessed on the Internet. Teachers can also encourage parents to seek a formal diagnosis of AD/HD and medication trial, if none of the strategies tried during *Phase I and II* are successful in resolving the academic, behavioral or emotional concerns being experienced by the ADDer. Teachers can also provide very useful feedback to the parents and/or psychologist as to the efficacy of various intervention strategies.

Teaching Self-Control

Some of the more successful people with ADD have learned how to overcome their many and varied challenges. These people tend to want to finish what they start and they have often developed a great deal of self-control. However, there are many others with ADD who are not being successful problem-solvers and who, for some reason, have not yet developed self-control (Barkley, 1998). Several years ago, Blakemore, Shindler and Conte (1993) developed a program specifically designed for parents of ADDers. The program was based on the assumption that these students tend to have problems with self-control. This technique has been adapted and is described in detail in both *Riding the Wave: Parenting the Child with ADD* (Scholten, 1998a) and *Turning the Tides* (Scholten, 1999b). It is a very positive and powerful approach. Results are often experienced within 10 days of applying this method.

Riding the Wave begins by establishing just one family or classroom rule. The exact rule and both positive and negative consequences are created by the adults. They should be applicable to the entire group (adults and students, alike, if possible). By beginning with one rule, everyone has an opportunity to learn how the method works. After a couple of weeks when the system has been learned, a few other rules can be introduced. No home or classroom would ever have more than about five rules. The consequences are as natural, logical, immediate, and short-term as possible. This is NOT reward and punishment; but can be easily confused with it. It is beyond the scope of this article to describe the method in greater detail, but a few examples of typical rules for the school and home settings are given below (see Tables 6 and 7).

For *Riding the Wave* to be effective, the adult needs to "notice" the student's choices that result in *positive consequences more often* than noticing the ones that have negative consequences. It is very important to ensure that the "cause–effect" relation-

---

Table 6 Riding the Wave – Examples For the School Setting

Behavior of Concern Addressed by this Rule	Rule	Consequences
Hits others, telling on others, not waiting our turns, not listening, talking when others are speaking	Treat others with kindness and respect	+ Freedom to be with others – Lose freedom to be with others for 5 minutes
Touching, pulling, poking others	Keep hands, feet and objects to ourselves	+ Freedom to stay in the group – Lose freedom to stay in the group for 5 minutes
Not being polite (e.g., not saying "please" and "thank you"), yelling, calling names, swearing	Use courteous language	+ Freedom to continue to be heard – Lose freedom to continue to be heard for 5 minutes
Running in the hallways	Walk in the hallways	+ Get to your destination faster – Get to your destination slower (since you have to go back and walk again)
Wearing outdoor shoes or boots inside classroom	Wear appropriate footwear	+ Freedom to continue your activities – Lose freedom to continue your activities (since you have to go back, take shoes off and carry them to the door)

Table 7 Riding the Wave – Examples For the Home

Behavior of Concern Addressed by this Rule	Rule	Consequences
Not getting up in the morning	We get up when our alarm goes off	+ Freedom to get up independently – Lose freedom to get up independently – I will come and "help" you get up
Not getting ready on time in the morning	We get ready on time (i.e., by 8:15 a.m.)	+ Freedom to get ready independently – Lose freedom to get ready independently – I will accompany you until you are ready
Rips up books, throws toys, misusing computer, TV, or other objects	We take care of our belongings	+ Continued access to your belongings – Lose access to your belongings for a day
Not doing chores	We complete our jobs on time	+ Freedom to get ready independently – Lose freedom to get ready independently – I will accompany you until you are ready
Not getting ready for bed on time	We get ready for bed on time (e.g., by 8:45 p.m.)	+ Freedom to get ready independently – Lose freedom to get ready independently – I will "help" you get ready for bed
Not coming home by curfew	We come home on time (i.e., by 10:30 p.m. on the kitchen clock)	+ Freedom to go out the next night – Lose freedom to go out the next night

ship is always noted. For instance, in responding to a child who has just made a choice with a:

a) Positive Consequence:

The adult would say….."Aaron, I notice that you have chosen to treat others with respect. The consequence is that you have the freedom to stay with the group."

OR

b) Negative Consequence:

The adult would say….."Aaron, I notice that you have chosen NOT to treat others with respect. The consequence is that you have lost the freedom to stay with the group for 5 minutes."

The most challenging part of *Riding the Wave* is for the adult to remember to notice the choices with positive consequences. People tend to notice when there is a problem (i.e., "the squeaky wheel that gets the oil"), so it can be a challenge to find ways to "notice" when the student chooses to follow the rule. In this case, the positive consequence needs to be brought to their attention. Within approximately 10 days of the implementation of *Riding the Wave*, changes are noted in the student and the adults consistently report a sense of relief in no longer feeling like "the bad guy." It is obvious to all parties that the student is making the choices. Soon self-control begins to develop, the student becomes more responsible, relies less on external monitoring, and self-esteem and motivation improve.

When this method is used in the classroom other students tend to pick up the language of choice. However, they should be encouraged to notice only the choices of their peers that have positive consequences. Teachers may have to put this in "rule form." One way to accomplish this might be, as follows:

The Rule: "Children make comments when others are making good choices."

+ "When you choose to make comments when others are making good choices, the consequence is that they will listen to what you have to say."

– "When you choose to comment when others are NOT making good choices, the consequence is that they may ignore what you say."

Riding the Wave is not the only behavior management tool to use in the classroom, but it is a powerful one that has been shown to result in increased self-control, responsibility, motivation, and self-esteem in students with ADD. It definitely shows the student the cause–effect relationship between their choices and immediate positive and negative consequences. As such, when used properly, it can be a very valuable adjunct to the variety of skills that most parents and teachers already possess.

In the next section, two case studies will be presented. They are fictitious examples that illustrate how the Empowerment Plus® approach can work effectively with two very different ADDers.

Case Vignettes – Aaron and Shanaz

Aaron and Shanaz, ages 8 and 15, respectively, both went to the same school (K to 12). Their parents were among those who had responded to an open invitation by the school principal in late September to attend a lecture given by the psychologist who was assigned to their school. The lecture was entitled: "A Wholistic Approach to Concerns in the Areas of Attention, Learning, and Mood."

Each set of parents had different reasons for going to the lecture. Aaron's parents knew that he was a "wild child" and they were at a loss as to how to manage him. Shanaz's parents were extremely conscientious and took every opportunity to learn whenever they could. However, they were becoming increasingly concerned that their only, beautiful, perfect, and well-rounded daughter seemed anxious and depressed for no apparent reason.

Aaron

Aaron was the youngest of 3 children and had been a "fireball" since he entered the world. His mother thought of him as "Captain Chaos"[2] and had resigned herself to the weekly calls from his teacher complaining about his incomplete homework and disruptive behavior both in class and on the playground. By the time he was in Grade 4, Aaron was spending a good deal of time each day at school in the hallway and was beginning to talk about being able to leave school as soon as he was old enough to do so.

Phase I

During the hour-long lecture, Aaron's parents were shocked to realize that he had 10/13 symptoms for attentional concerns as well as some of the classic patterns discussed in the LD and personality areas. They hadn't realized that anything was amiss, other than the behavioral challenges that the teachers reported. And yet, everything that was said during the lecture seemed to fit their little "fireball."

(1) When they filled out the Screening Checklist for Attentional Concerns (Appendix A), Aaron had 10/13 checkmarks in the "pretty much" to "very much" columns. He certainly seemed to have a problem in attention. But what was the cause? Did he have ADD, was he just a "real boy" or had his parents simply not been firm enough with him? The parents thought that it might be wise to continue with this approach to try to determine if they might be able to help Aaron improve his behavior and attitude towards school.

(2) Aaron also fit the classic LD pattern of a visual-spatial LD (VSLD) in that he was very verbal and could understand and verbally express his ideas, but he resisted doing written work. Although he enjoyed problem solving in math and seemed to be able to think in a mathematical way, Aaron just didn't seem to be able to learn his basic math facts. Parents and teachers learned that someone like Aaron would benefit greatly from being able to use a computer for all of his written work – at home and at school.

---

[2] "Captain Chaos" is a termed coined by Carol Johnston, a behavior therapist from Calgary, Alberta.

(3) Aaron had a personality consistent with the typical ADDer stereotype, in that he had an ENTP (Extraverted-Intuiting-Thinking-Perceiving) personality type. He was friendly, innovative, not always aware of the feelings of others, and flexible and adaptable. His written work (when done) was usually messy (as was his bedroom) and he didn't seem to care about being tidy. His parents and teacher learned that people with Aaron's personality type learned best under certain conditions. For instance, as an extravert, Aaron needed to work with others in groups in order to process his ideas. He liked to invent and do things in new and different ways and needed help with time management and proofreading his written work.

After the lecture, the parents called to arrange for a meeting with Aaron's teacher. They all discussed what they had learned at the lecture. Everyone was in agreement as to what he seemed to need. Although they didn't have any formal "test results," Aaron certainly fit several of the classic patterns that had been described. The parents and teacher filled out the Levine Information Processing Questionnaire and discovered that his attention affected how deeply he took in information and his ability to feel satisfied, to control his behavior, and to self-monitor. As a result of the meeting, a few changes were made at school and at home:

(1) They decided to address Aaron's VSLD by encouraging him to use the computer at home and at school for all of his written work. His parents bought a second hand lap-top computer so that Aaron could easily carry it to and from school.

(2) His teacher decided to honor his extraversion by assigning him to a group of other students. The idea was that they could help each other by sharing their different strengths. His "buddy" was a girl who loved to talk, but who was very careful with her work. She did not enjoy drawing. She could proofread Aaron's work and he could use his artistic creativity to help her illustrate her projects.

(3) In the area of food sensitivities, Aaron showed symptoms of frequent colds and flus. Therefore, his parents decided to take him off all milk products for a week and then put them back in for three days. What a difference it made! He said he could breathe much more clearly and sure enough, he became stuffed up again when milk was reintroduced. He was glad to give up milk products when he realized what they were doing to him. The family doctor advised a daily CalMag supplement (with calcium, magnesium, and vitamin D).

Once Aaron was allowed to do his work on the computer, he was proud of how neat it looked. He seemed willing to put a little more effort into it and enjoyed the creative writing parts. He still did it at the last minute, but at least he finished it and somehow his assignments began to find their way to the teacher's desk! He reported feeling better physically and he seemed to get along better with the other students at school. He loved working in a group and having an opportunity to use his artistic talent, illustrating while his "buddy" proofread his work. Within about 3 weeks his parents were delighted to hear him talking about some of the projects he was involved with at school. Gone was the focus on when he'd be old enough to leave school.

Both Aaron's parents and his teacher felt that *Riding the Wave* – a behavior management program being taught at the school – might help Aaron to develop more self-control. His teacher started to implement it right away in her classroom. Before the parents could attend this behavior-management program, they were required to participate in *Phase II* – a 4-hour workshop geared towards understanding others based on their personality type (i.e., MBTI®). They didn't really mind this, as they felt they needed all the help they could get with their "challenging child."

Phase II

Aaron was too young to come to the workshop, but Aaron's parents brought their older two children and both sets of grandparents. It was very enlightening for all to discover that both of Aaron's parents and one of his older brothers were the completely opposite personality type to Aaron. His parents and this brother liked to have a quiet house where everything was neat and tidy, where there was calm and respectful talk and reflective listening to each other. Structured routine and long-range planning were hallmarks of the Abbott family. However, the other older brother was an extravert like Aaron. He was also 8 years older than Aaron and spent most of the time with his friends. When he came home, it was usually just to sleep and so there wasn't much chance for Aaron to interact with him.

What an eye-opener it was to realize how difficult this type of environment might be for Aaron. He was a creative child whose constant chatter was his way of "thinking aloud." Rather than feeling irritated by his differences, the family resolved to try to meet some of his needs by arranging for Aaron to have friends over on a more regular basis. They also resolved to try to really enjoy his quick sense of humor and innovative ideas instead of bemoaning his lack of passion for accuracy and neatness. Soon he was regularly entertaining them with his "stand-up comic routine." They began to see some advantages to his carefree attitude and appreciated his differences as qualities that added to the richness of the family life.

Once interactions had become a little more spontaneous at home, Aaron's brother seemed to "loosen up" and started spending more time with the family. He and Aaron discovered that despite their age differences, they had some interests in common and they found some time to wrestle and "shoot some hoops" together. Aaron felt pretty special and used up a lot of his extra energy in these physically demanding workouts. Family life took on a whole different tone after this workshop. It became a celebration of differences.

Phase III

The last thing that Aaron's parents did was to learn *Riding the Wave*. Aaron's teacher was pleased with his behavior in school, but his parents were tired of chasing him to do his homework. Therefore, they chose a rule to address his lack of initiative in completing his work.

Their rule was: "Work before play." Aaron was told that if he chose to "work before play" (i.e., get his homework done before turning on the TV, using the phone or Internet) then the consequence was that he had the freedom to do his work independently, wherever he wished. However, if he chose NOT to work before play, the consequence was that he would lose the freedom to work independently. One of his parents would supervise him doing his homework in his bedroom, until it was completed. His parents were skeptical about this approach, believing that Aaron would like the one-on-one attention. Nevertheless, they were able to apply this technique properly, and within several weeks, Aaron was getting right down to his homework and then watching TV. Aaron's desire for independence had won out! His parents were very grateful to have turned in their "remote control car driver's licenses." They no longer seemed to need to tell Aaron what to do every minute. He began to take initiative in other areas, such as feeding the dog and putting his dishes in the dishwasher. Aaron even announced one day that he thought he was becoming more responsible. His parents agreed! The phone calls from the school became less frequent. On occasion, Aaron even brought home a note from his teacher saying how well he was getting along with his classmates and how much she enjoyed his creative ideas.

Shanaz

Shanaz's case was a little different. She came from a family where English was her second language.

Phase I – of using the Empowerment Plus® model consisted of the lecture which her parents had attended "just because" they were always open to learning. Shanaz went for the same reason. In reality, her parents were a little worried about Shanaz's variable emotional state, which seemed to be worsening after puberty. She was their oldest child, and they didn't really know what to expect from an adolescent girl or what exactly they could do about it if they wanted this to change. Shanaz was a nice girl, but her marks had always been lower than expected.

At first, they thought that her problems were the result of some second language confusion, after 10 years of exposure to English, they had begun to resign themselves to the fact that perhaps, she just wasn't "smart." Shanaz enjoyed drawing as well as designing and sewing clothes, and they believed that perhaps she was a "hands on" type of learner who would need to learn a trade. Shanaz had expressed some interest in being an architect, but her parents felt that this was a little unrealistic since her marks were rarely above 60%. She worked so hard for so little gain and they often wished that she could relax about school and get out a little more for some fun with her friends. The lecture was interesting but didn't seem to apply to Shanaz. However, her parents were still concerned about her increasing sadness and they planned to make an appointment to speak privately to the school psychologist later in the school year, if Shanaz didn't improve.

A few days after the lecture, Shanaz approached her parents. She had recognized herself in some of the patterns that were discussed during the lecture. Her parents were surprised to hear that it was so hard for her to concentrate (i.e., filter out the distractions of noises of people talking both at home and in class, from the TV and also from the videogames her younger brother and sister played). She even complained about the sound of the clock ticking in the classroom and said that it prevented her from thinking! That is why she couldn't get anything done in class, she said. She did her best work in the wee hours of the morning when everything was quiet. She had never complained about this before and her parents were very surprised. She had just quietly gone her own way. Shanaz also felt that she had symptoms consistent with the "5% LD" (i.e., the Language Learning Discrepancy (LLD) – but she couldn't remember what it was called). Everyone had always known that she was a slow reader, but she always got her homework done, even if she had to stay up until midnight to finish it. Her parents began to wonder if this was interfering with her sleep and had resulted in increasing levels of fatigue. Her moodiness had become more extreme in the last year – maybe this all fit together somehow. Shanaz said that it was also discouraging for her to never have time to finish her tests. She felt that she knew more than she had time to show.

Shanaz's parents were shocked with these disclosures and wondered if Shanaz was "just being suggestible." Nevertheless, they wanted to support her so they called her homeroom teacher and asked if they could all meet together to discuss some of Shanaz's observations and how it fit with the information that had been covered during the *Phase I* lecture. When they reexamined the outline from the lecture, they realized that she did indeed fit the LLD and ISFJ (Introverted- Sensing-Feeling-Judging) personality type. The teacher couldn't believe that Shanaz had as much trouble concentrating as she said she did! She was always so quiet and co-operative and her work was always so neat and complete. Nevertheless, her parents and teachers were willing to listen to her. As a result of their meeting, the following plans were formulated:

(1) The Levine Information Processing Questionnaire indicated problems in maintaining consistent alertness, taking in information deeply enough or indepth, filtering out distractions, and in the pacing of activities. Shanaz wanted to first work on the problem with noise, so she asked for permission to wear a Walkman during class and at home in the evening when trying to work.

(2) LLD – She would have extended time on all her tests and exams or when there wasn't time in the period to do this, Shanaz would be allowed to do half the questions (all of the odd or all even-numbered ones). The teachers identified

"key vocabulary words" in upcoming units and the parents promised to work with Shanaz in learning these words. Her parents had always known that Shanaz was very talented in certain areas, but now they understood more about the differences in her verbal and non-verbal functioning. They decided to encourage her to take a drawing class. They began to marvel at the intricacy of her drawings instead of focusing on their disappointment with her lack of verbal fluency.

(3) ISFJ – Her teachers and parents learned that they needed to give Shanaz thinking time to answer questions as well as time to be alone each day in order to "re-energize." They began to appreciate her perfectionism and no longer complained when she couldn't accomplish a task with the kind of speed they expected. She was a very careful person and that was a gift that she brought to the world.

(4) When she was taken off all wheat products (i.e., bread, pasta), her moodiness disappeared completely. The family learned how to use rice, rye, and other grains for bread and pasta instead of wheat.

On her very next test, Shanaz received marks of 78%. Everyone was thrilled and she stated that she finally felt as though she was getting the marks she deserved. She did not go any further at this point, because she was being so successful and because she and her parents were opposed to using medication for ADD. Instead, she took one of the nutriceutical supplements suggested at the lecture (i.e., Efalex Focus) and she found that this did indeed help her focus her attention.

Phase II was not needed for Shanaz because she, her teachers, and her parents felt that she had achieved a much higher level of success by implementing the information covered in *Phase I*. However, in order for her to receive extended time on her high school diploma exams, she needed a diagnosis of her "learning disability." For her, this was *Phase III*. She was then formally assessed and her LLD and AD/HD: Predominantly Inattentive Type was officially identified. This allowed her to have the time she needed during her final high school exams. It would also allow this accommodation during her studies at university.

A few years later, when Shanaz went to university, she arranged for accommodations similar to those she had had in high school (i.e., extended time on exams). By this time, however, she had become increasingly aware of how difficult it was to concentrate on what people were saying to her and how much energy it took for her to put her ideas together. She began to think it might be worth seeing whether or not medication for ADD might help her in these areas. Since she had already received a diagnosis of ADD, her family doctor felt comfortable putting her through a medication trial with Ritalin following the Farrelly Protocol (Appendix E). What a difference it made! Her alternating periods of alertness and fatigue disappeared and she felt that her mind was much better able to focus. She didn't need to use her Walkman anymore to screen out noises. Her marks went up even higher to around 95%. She felt that for the first time in her life, she was achieving to her potential. Her lifelong goal of becoming an architect seemed now to be within her grasp.

In summary, these vignettes illustrated how the Empowerment Plus T model was used by the school psychologist to address very different situations, using both indirect and direct methods of service delivery. Aaron had symptoms consistent with AD/HD: Combined Type and Shanaz had AD/HD: Predominantly Inattentive Type. These examples also illustrated the two classic LD patterns and how the appropriate academic accommodations were implemented. Also illustrated was how MBTI® personality type can be useful in understanding the needs of a learner and the difference some experimentation with food elimination can make.

The cost-effectiveness of these indirect methods of service delivery was seen in the lecture in *Phase I* and the workshop in *Phase II* and several years later, to conduct formal testing to document Shanaz's LD.

In Aaron's case, all three phases of the Empowerment Plus® approach were used right away to facilitate success. The indirect service delivery offered during the lecture in *Phase I* helped the parents to see some positives in Aaron's channel-surfing abilities. The workshop during *Phase II* helped Aaron's family to appreciate their differences. The direct service delivery provided in *Phase III* took the form of 3 sessions to teach behavior management to Aaron's parents. In Shanaz's case only the indirect service of the lecture in *Phase I* was needed to catalyze significant changes that were initially seen in her life.

Formal assessment was necessary for Shanaz solely for the purpose of justifying accommodations on her final high school diploma exams and at university. Eventually this would have been required for Aaron too, when he grew older in order to use the computer for "official" exams.

It may well be that someday all students will be afforded the privilege of writing exams in testing centers where they can take as long as they wish and are able to use the medium of their choice (i.e., pens and papers or computers). This type of policy would drastically reduce the often prohibitive costs to parents and/or school systems involved in the identification of "special needs" students. It would also remove the stigma from the many students who have to be tested and labeled in order to take their exams under these types of circumstances.

Conclusion

As has been illustrated above, the Empowerment Plus® model of psychological service delivery uses the principles of primary, secondary and tertiary prevention in the three phases of service delivery. Through understanding ADD in a more positive and wholistic way, school psychologists working within or outside the school system can be helpful to teachers, parents and students in cost-effective ways. They can also encourage their students to celebrate their special "channel-surfing" abilities and to use knowledge about their learning and personality patterns in order to implement practical and effective strategies for facilitating both academic and personal success.

References

Barkley, R. (1998). *ADHD and the nature of self control.* New York: Guilford Press.

Barkley, R. (2000). *Taking charge of ADHD: The complete, authoritative guide for parents.* New York: Guilford Press.

Barkley, R., & Murphy, K. (1998). *Attention-deficit hyperactivity disorder: A clinical workbook.* New York: Guilford Press.

Berk, L. (2001). *Awakening children's minds: How parents and teachers can make a difference.* New York, NY: Oxford University Press.

Blakemore, B., Shindler, S., & Conte, R. (1993). A problem-solving training program for parents of children with attention deficit/hyperactivity disorder. *Canadian Journal of School Psychology, 9(1),* 66-85.

Birnbaum, M. (1993). Vision disorders frequently interfere with reading and learning: They should be diagnosed and treated. *Journal of Behavioral Optometry, 4,* 66-71.

Briggs-Myers, I. (1987). *Introduction to type.* Palo Alto, CA: Consulting Psychologists Press.

Brown, M. (2000). Diagnosis and treatment of children and adolescents with attention-deficit/hyperactivity disorder. *Journal of Counseling and Development, Spring,* 195-203.

Cole, E., & Siegel, J. A. (1990). *Effective consultation in school psychology.* Toronto: Hogrefe & Huber Publishers.

Haber, J. (2000). *ADHD: The great misdiagnosis.* Dallas, Texas: Taylor Trade Publishing.

Hartmann, T. (1993). *Attention deficit disorder: A different perception.* Grass Valley, CA: Underwood Books.

Irlen, H. (1991). *Reading by the colours.* New York, NY: Avery, Penguin, Putnam.

Keirsey, D., & Bates, M. (1978). *Please understand me.* Del Mar, CA: Promethean Books.

Lawrence, G. (1979). *People types and tiger stripes.* Gainesville, Florida: Centre for the Application of Psychological Type.

Levine, M. (1992). *All kinds of minds.* Cambridge, MA: Educators Publishing Service.

Nadeau, K. (Ed.).(1995). *A comprehensive guide to attention deficit disorder in adults: Research, diagnosis and treatment.* New York: Brunner/Mazel.

Park, A. (2001). More drugs to treat hyperactivity. *Time, Sept.,* 63.

Randolph, T., & Moss, R. (1989). *An alternative approach to food allergies.* New York, NY: Harper and Row.

Reichenberg-Ulman, J., & Ulman, R. (1996). *Ritalin free kids* (92nd rev. ed.). Roseville, CA: Prima Health Publishing.

Richters, J., Arnold, L., & Jensen, P. (1995). NIMH collaborative multisite multimodal treatment study of children with ADHD: Background and rationale. *Journal of American Child and Adolescent Psychiatry, 34,* 987-1000.

Sattler, J. (1998). *Clinical and forensic interviewing of children and families.* San Diego, CA: Sattler.

Scholten, T. (1998a). *Riding the wave: Parenting the child with ADD.* Calgary, Alberta: Scholten Psychological Services.

Scholten, T. (1998b). *The ADD guidebook: A comprehensive, self-directed guide to addressing attentional concerns in adults and children.* Calgary, Alberta: Scholten Psychological Services.

Scholten, T. (1999a). *Attention deluxe dimension: A wholistic approach to ADD.* Calgary, Alberta: Scholten Psychological Services.

Scholten, T. (1999b). *Turning the tides: Teaching the student with ADD.* Calgary, Alberta: Scholten Psychological Services.

Scholten, T. (1999c). *Welcome to the channel-surfer's club.* Calgary, Alberta: Scholten Psychological Services.

Scholten, T. (2001). *Overcoming depression: A wholistic approach.* Calgary, Alberta: Scholten Psychological Services.

Viveca Novak (2001). New Ritalin blitz makes parents jumpy. *Time,* Sept., 62-63.

Weintraub, S. (1997). *Natural treatments for ADD and hyperactivity.* Woodland Publishing.

Wender, P. (2000). *ADHD in children, adolescents and adults: Attention-deficit hyperactivity disorder through the lifespan.* New York, NY: Oxford University Press.

Zimmerman, M. (1999). *The ADD nutrition solution.* New York, NY: Henry Holt/Owl Publishing.

Appendix A: A Screening Checklist for Attentional Concerns

Screening Checklist*
For Children And Adults With Attentional Concerns

Name:_____ Date:_____ Rater:_____

	Observation	not at all	just a little	pretty much	very much
1.	Difficulty with details – makes careless mistakes				
2.	Difficulty sustaining attention to current task				
3.	Does not **seem** to listen or sustain attention to discussions. May ask for questions/ statements to be repeated				
4.	Difficulty following through on instructions				
5.	Difficulty starting/finishing tasks				
6.	Loses things necessary for tasks or activities				
7.	Easily distracted by noises or other surrounding activities				
8.	Fidgets or doodles				
9.	Uncomfortable staying seated for periods of time or leaves seat frequently				
10.	Talks excessively or dominates conversations inappropriately				
11.	Blurts out answers before questions have been completed				
12.	Interrupts others inappropriately				
13.	Daydreams				

Comments: _____

* Adapted for use with adults and children by Dr. Teeya Scholten from checklist developed by the Calgary Learning Centre, 1996.

This form may be reproduced

Appendix B: Symptom and Food Diary

Symptom And Food Diary*

1. Write down what food you ate yesterday or on a typical day
2. Put a number in each box below which describes your symptoms or how you felt yesterday or on a typical day

Food

Breakfast_____

Lunch_____

Supper_____

Snacks: (State time of day)_____

Rate your symptoms with numbers:
0 – no symptoms, 1 – mild, 2 – moderate, 3 – severe

Symptoms					
Time of Day/ Symptom	**Before Bkfast**	**After Bkfast**	**After Lunch**	**After Supper**	**During Night**
Tired or Drowsy					
Irritable					
Overactive					
Headache					
Respiratory (Stuffy nose, cough)					
Digestive (Nausea, bellyache)					
Urinary (Frequent or wetting)					
Other (pls specify)					

Comments: (Mention anything that happened to you today that might account for your symptoms other than food.... or any observations or ideas you may have, including cravings, etc.)

*Adapted in 1996 by Dr. Teeya Scholten from a rating format used by Dr. William Langdon, a pediatric allergist from London, Ont.

This form may be reproduced

Appendix C: The Levine Information Processing Questionnaire

The Levine Information Processing Questionnaire*

Name:_____Date:_____Rater:_____

Instructions:
In the space to the left of each question place a Y or N, for what would be true in comparison to others of a similar age. Put a questions mark (?) if you are not sure of the answer or don't understand the question. Each person completing the questionnaire should do so separately.

A. Input of Information

1.0 Maintaining Consistent Alertness
1.1 Does s/he seem to be tired (i.e., yawn, stretch) during the daytime?
1.2 Does s/he fidget a lot?
1.3 Does s/he seem to "tune out" or daydream during conversations, on tests, or while working on projects?
1.4 Is there a history of unusual or difficult sleeping patterns?

2.0 Taking in Information Deeply Enough
2.1 Does s/he have a hard time remembering what is said (i.e., short-term memory)
2.2 Does s/he ask for information to be repeated right away because it has been "forgotten?"
2.3 Is there inconsistency in his/her understanding of information that has recently been given?
2.4 Is s/he absent-minded?

3.0 Passive or Active Processing
3.1 Is this someone who memorizes information rather than trying to understand it?
3.2 Does s/he seem to have a hard time relating new information or knowledge to material that has been learned previously?
3.3 Is this a person who seems to have no strong interests in any *academic* subject matter?
3.4 Does s/he complain of feeling bored much of the time?

4.0 Determining the Importance of Information
4.1 Are there indications that this person has a great difficulty deciding what's important and what's irrelevant?
4.2 Does s/he have trouble focusing on the important details?
4.3 Does s/he have a hard time summarizing or paraphrasing information?
4.4 Does s/he have trouble understanding the overall meaning of what s/he reads or hears?

* This questionnaire was developed for use with children by Dr. Mel Levine and adapted for use with adults and children by Dr. Teeya Scholten and staff of the Calgary Learning Centre.

This form may be reproduced

5.0   Filtering out Distractions
5.1   Does s/he frequently look around (i.e., stare off into space) during conversations or while working?
5.2   Are there signs of being "tuned in" to or distracted by background sights or noises?
5.3   Does this person fidget with his/her fingers or other objects at inappropriate times?
5.4   Is it especially hard for this person to "filter out" noises?

6.0   Ability to Satisfy Oneself
6.1   Is this the sort of individual who wants *things* all the time and loses interest rather quickly when s/he finally acquires what s/he wanted?
6.2   Does s/he appear to crave highly intense experiences?
6.3   Does s/he like to "stir things up" in order to produce excitement or high levels of stimulation?
6.4   Is it necessary for there to be ultra high levels of stimulation or personal interest in order to concentrate effectively?

B. Output of Information

7.0   Preview of Outcomes
7.1   Does this person fail to look ahead?
7.2   Are there signs that s/he doesn't think about the consequences before doing or trying something?
7.3   Does s/he work impulsively (i.e., without exerting sufficient planning)?
7.4   Does s/he have a hard time estimating how long tasks projects or assignments might take?

8.0   Behavioral Control
8.1   Does s/he have a hard time controlling his/her own behavior?
8.2   Does s/he seem to do many things the hard way?
8.3   Is this someone who seems to lack alternative strategies (i.e., for learning coping with stress, relating to others)?
8.4   Are there signs of poor motor control (i.e., clumsiness) when trying to start or stop an activity?

9.0   Pacing of Activities
9.1   Does s/he do many things too quickly?
9.2   Are there times when s/he operates too slowly?
9.3   Is this someone with a weak sense of time – its allocation, its sequences, its planning implications?
9.4   Does s/he make many careless mistakes because of rushing?

10.0 Consistency of Effort
10.1   Is there a lot of variability in the amount or quality of work done?
10.2   Does his/her performance deteriorate over time when he or she is trying to complete a task or assignment?

10.3 Is it often hard for this individual to *get started* with work?

10.4 Does s/he seem "lazy" or somehow poorly motivated?

11.0 Self-Monitoring

11.1 Is there a tendency to fail to notice when s/he makes errors in work?

11.2 Does s/he resist checking or proofreading their work?

11.3 In social interactions, does s/he have trouble knowing how s/he is doing (i.e., interpreting social feedback or other non-verbal cues from others)?

11.4 Does this person behave in inappropriate ways without seeming to realize early enough that s/he may be getting into trouble?

12.0 Learning from Experience

12.1 Does s/he have a hard time learning from his/her mistakes?

12.2 Does this individual seem indifferent to rewards or praise?

12.3 Are there indications that s/he fails to "learn from experience?"

12.4 Does this person seem relatively unable to make use of feedback given by others?

How to Interpret the Levine Information Processing Questionnaire:

Count the number of sections in which more questions have been answered with a "Yes" than with a "No." This will probably identify the 4-6 areas of information processing which are most strongly affected. (If you have identified more than 6 areas, you may wish to "count" only those areas where you have said "Yes" to every item.) Put an asterisk beside each area of concern and refer to Strategies for Improving Attention on the next page for ideas for appropriate interventions.

Appendix D: Strategies for Improving Attention

Strategies for Improving Attention*

Maintaining Consistent Alertness
- Sitting at the front of the class
- Getting enough sleep in order to be alert during work or class times
- Reduce the amount of work given at any one time
- Frequent breaks or opportunity to move around
- Use of hands for physical activity (i.e., "stress ball," piece of plasticene, doodling)
- Consultation with physician re: medication trial to determine if this will facilitate alertness
- Use areas of interests in school projects /workplace

Taking in Information Deeply Enough
- Use self-talk or note-taking to review information (e.g., "What it is I have just learned?")
- Self-testing techniques to see if material is being understood
- Paraphrasing
- Repetition or demonstration of instructions or explanations

Passive or Excessively Active Processing
- Reminder cards ("Am I being passive or is my mind <u>too active</u>?")
- A disciplined approach to thinking more deeply about a subject (e.g., "What are the things you already know that this new material reminds you of? How is it pretty much like it? How is it new and different? How does this new information fit into the overall scheme?")
- Put effort into developing knowledge and skills in areas of interest
- Keeping score of how often there are "channel-surfing mind trips" and/or "wake up calls"
- Recording and making use of ideas which are generated during periods of daydreaming or creative thinking

Determining the Importance of Information
- Learn how to paraphrase and summarize
- Games emphasizing vigilance and attention to fine detail
- Margin monitoring, underlining, and circling skills when reading/studying
- Practice crossing out irrelevant information (e.g., in math word problems)

Filtering Out Distractions
- Minimize distractions at home, work, and school
- Use of consistent background sounds (e.g., use of ear plugs, music on a walkman) when reading or studying
- Frequent, but timed breaks from study

* These strategies were developed by Dr. Mel Levine and are meant to be used in conjunction with the Levine Information Processing Questionnaire which identifies 12 possible areas of information processing which can by affected by problems in attention.

This form may be reproduced

Ability to Satisfy Oneself
- Use of high motivational content for learning – give choices (i.e., "What are you most interested in learning today – option a) or b)?")
- Stress on timed delays of gratification (e.g., "When it's break time in another 20 minutes, there'll be a chance to do...")
- Identification and acknowledgment of areas which are not interesting and in which there will be low motivation
- The establishment of "getting satisfied" time allocations at home

Preview of Outcomes
- Application of "what if ?" exercises to imagine future outcomes – in behavioral, social and/or cognitive-academic areas
- Practice describing *final products* (i.e., "What do I want this to look like when I finish? What is it I want to say in this report? What do I want others to think about me? How do I want to behave in a particular situation?")
- Diagramming of previewed outcomes
- Practice estimating answers

Behavioral Control
- Review of alternative (cognitive – academic, social, and/or behavioral) strategies and selection of strategy which has the best chance of working out (i.e., "best-bet"), along with "back-up" strategies in case it is needed
- Use of hypothetical (i.e., "what if...") case studies for above review
- Making plans for social survival or other challenging situations
- Using flow charts to diagram choices for behavior and possible outcomes
- Review of outcomes and exploration of other alternatives that might have worked better

Pacing of Activities
- Development of time management (in scheduling procedures at home and in school)
- Serve as a time manager at school/work
- Stress on time estimation ("How long should this take me?")
- Elimination of incentives for quick completion of tasks (i.e., no advantages to finishing or "getting it over with quickly")
- Use of time landmarks for writing/reading projects (i.e., "Where should I be three weeks before the project is due?")
- Discussions of time and time management

Consistency of Effort
- Regularly-scheduled work breaks
- Conscious attempts to monitor and document graphically "on times" and "off times"
- Self-description – verbally and/or in writing – of what it feels like to be running out of "mental energy"
  Rotation of homework or reading sites at home
- Getting assistance in getting started without being "accused" (i.e., "jump starting" efforts by saying, "It's 7 p.m., didn't you say that you wanted to begin your project at that time?" instead of "Why can't you ever get started on your own?")

Self-Monitoring
-   Stress on mid-task and terminal self assessment ("How am I doing?" or "How do I think I did?")
-   Use of self-grading and commenting before submitting tests/ work assignments, with credit for accurate monitoring
-   Proofreading exercises (e.g., COPS -Capitalization, Organization, Punctuation, Spelling)
-   Routine proofreading of own work at least 48 hours after completion
-   Use of hypothetical case studies to demonstrate the impact of poor self-monitoring on behavior and interpersonal relating
-   Inclusion of "quality control" measures in work and social plans
-   Building self-monitoring as a step in planning actions or strategies

Learning from Experience
-   Stress on very consistent consequences for actions
-   Need for changing incentives in order to maintain their novelty
-   Use of personal diaries to document outcomes of actions – possibly in diagrammatic form
-   Lists of "What I've Done Right Today" and "Where I Went Astray Today" with a stress on lessons learned for the future. These lists can be reviewed with a "mentor" (with whom one has a valued relationship and to whom one can feel accountable for attaining the personal goals which have been set)

Appendix E: The Farrelly Protocol for a Medication Trial

Farrelly* Protocol for a Medication Trial

Always begin with regular or **brand name Ritalin.** If this is desired, the physician should check "no substitutes" on the prescription or else the pharmacist may use the generic brand or SR (sustained release). Dr. Farrelly considers these to be less effective than the brand name and suggests that the generic or SR can be tried once the medication trial has been completed to see if the same results are obtained.

Begin with a dosage of S tablet of Ritalin, taken twice a day – just before breakfast and before lunch or around 8 a.m. and noon. Stay at each dosage level for three days. On the third day at each dosage level, take a third dose between 4–5 p.m. This allows one to assess the effect of this amount of medication on homework, sports, or other evening activities. Increase the dose by 1/4 of a tablet per dose *every three days*, as follows:

$$1/2 \text{ tab or } 5.0 \text{ mg}$$
$$3/4 \text{ tab or } 7.5 \text{ mg}$$
$$1 \text{ tab or } 10.0 \text{ mg}$$
$$1\,1/4 \text{ tab or } 12.5 \text{ mg}$$
$$1\,1/2 \text{ tab or } 15.0 \text{ mg}$$
$$1\,3/4 \text{ tab or } 17.5 \text{ mg}$$
$$2 \text{ tab or } 20.0 \text{ mg}$$

Complete a **Screening Checklist** every day of the trial so that responses can be monitored. Continue increasing the dosage level until signs of too much medication are noted (i.e., tiredness, irritability, light-headedness, feeling uncomfortable, or "not oneself"). Then immediately cut back to previous level. If the medication is helping, examine the Screening Checklists to see what the minimum dose was that gave the optimal results and stay on this amount. If Ritalin was not effective, other types of medication can be tried.

Some individuals may require more than 20 mg per dose, but this level should be very carefully supervised. A positive response to medication does NOT confirm a diagnosis of AD/HD. There are many reasons that a student might show attentional symptoms and respond to the items on the Screening Checklist for Attentional Concerns. If there are 4–5 checkmarks in the "pretty much" to "very much" columns, all this tells us is that there ARE attentional concerns, NOT the cause of these concerns. That is why it is so important to rule out physical and emotional causes and to understand educational and personality factors before making a diagnosis of AD/HD and engaging in a medication trial.

* This approach to a medication trial was developed by Dr. Geraldine Farrelly, a Calgary pediatrician who has worked with patients with AD/HD for years. For more information on how to use this protocol and on questions related to medication issues and ADD, see *The ADD Guidebook* (Scholten, 1998b).

Chapter 11
School Psychology in Multicultural Inclusive Communities: Responding to Children's Needs

Ester Cole and Jane A. Siegel

"...After five minutes we heard three more bombs. I was afraid. I could feel my blood freeze. It was too dangerous to wait for my parents to come back to the apartment, so we went to the basement...the next days of the bombing were terrible..."
[written by T., a 13-year-old newcomer student]

The United States and Canada are multilingual societies of increasing cultural diversity. Recent demographic trends document the transformation of North American communities and highlight the need for effective interventions in immigrant and refugee school communities. As many as half the world's refugees are children and one-quarter of all migrant children under the age of twelve enter Canada as refugees. The number of Canadian immigrants, for example, more than doubled in the late 80s, and in the early 1990s, three-quarters of immigrant children were of school age (Cole, 1998, 2000). Although Canada, like the United States, has been a country of immigrants, recently, dramatic changes have occurred in its pattern of migration with an increase in refugee applicants. Of concern, are the number of children who come from war-torn countries and those who continue to experience difficulties during the resettlement period. Surveys concerning world refugees often estimate that there are millions of displaced people throughout the world who have resettled or are in the process of applying for resettlement under safer conditions. Their needs for assistance include settlement orientation, shelter, health care, employment, legal representation, second language skills, outreach services, cultural supports, and education (Beiser, Dion, Gotowiec, & Huyman, 1995; Cole, 1996a; Cooper, 2000; United Nations High Commissioner for Refugees, 1994, 1995; Vargas, 1999).

American demographic data has called attention to the fact that immigrant and minority school-age children are the poorest in society. About 40% of children in the United States under the age of six are non-white; half of whom speak a language other than English. Many reside in racially homogeneous neighborhoods and are over-represented in lower educational streams in public schools (Barona & Garcia, 1990).

Within the education context, school psychologists, together with teachers and other mental health professionals, can help meet the needs of minority children and their families by continuing to develop a broader knowledge base, effective skills, and cultural sensitivity (Hays, 2001).

Multicultural concerns are among the recommended domains for school psychologists cited in advocacy papers by the National Association of School Psychologists (NASP) and the Canadian Association of School Psychologists (CASP), and were also the focus of national conventions (Cole, 1996b, 1998; Cole & Siegel, 1990). Although school psychologists have been providing services to multicultural students, the profession has been criticized periodically because of the role it plays as classifiers and gatekeepers of special education programs. Minority students are overrepresented in non-academic streams, and are more likely to be among the poor and to be mislabeled for their underachievement in school (Samuda, 1990). Poverty, cultural diversity, race, and language minority status are confounding factors. Assessment in all its forms has become the lightning rod for those who feel marginalized and disenfranchised.

One manifestation of inequality in education is that, in Canada and the United States, minority students tend to be overrepresented in low ability groupings and underrepresented in gifted programs, for example (Carnine, 1994). The enactment of special education regulations and laws has achieved major goals in requiring school systems to provide specialized services for the education of exceptional students. Yet, this mandate has also been criticized for labeling and placing students in special education programs following inappropriate diagnoses of children from diverse cultural and linguistic backgrounds. Moreover, the very laws enacted to maximize the protection of children's rights, became associated with inadequate assessment that provides little information for program planning. Also, measurement technologies of large-scale assessment have resulted in categorical models, which attach funding to classification. One in ten American students, for example, receive special education services (Barona & Garcia, 1990).

Criticisms of standardized tests have been fuelled, in part, not by the question of whether to test but how to test and for what purpose. Concerns on the part of professional and parent community advocates center around the fact that low achievers are removed from regular classrooms because of limited resources and fragmented curricula modifications for diverse learners. They stress that reduced expectations for learners, coupled with arbitrary interpretations of test results perpetuate a climate of mistrust in psychoeducational accountability tools. The process of misclassification has been increasingly scrutinized over the past three decades and has resulted in legal confrontations in the United States (Cole, 1992; Cole & Siegel, 1990; Reschly, 1988; Reschly, Kicklighter, & McKee, 1988).

Since the assessment of newcomer and minority students has been subjected to criticism, many boards of education fear potential bias and advise against psychological referrals of immigrant and refugee students for the first two years (Cole, 1992; Samuda, 1990; Samuda & Crawford, 1980; Samuda et al., 1989). However, such a cautious approach may delay the provision of needed services and the promotion of effective functioning.

The purpose of this chapter is to provide school psychologists with information that will help them plan assessment practices and prevention programs for children of different cultural backgrounds. It begins with a discussion of some of the complexities involved in the migration process and its impact on the family, the child, and his or her schooling. Next, we discuss assessment issues and provide a framework for an assessment-intervention model with a step-by-step elaboration of useful strategies. The chapter concludes with recommendations for role expansion, and examples of school-based primary and secondary prevention programs that psychologists can facilitate in multicultural schools.

Transcultural Children and Their Families: A Psychosocial Perspective

The demographic transformation of many North American and European cities has focused attention on issues, controversies, and concerns related to the assessment of and interventions with minority and culturally-different children. In servicing multicultural communities, school psychologists are faced with the complexities created by migration, acculturation, urbanization, language barriers, and diverse educational experiences. The interactions between cultural patterns, family dynamics, and developmental stages are crucial factors in understanding the multifaceted profile of minority children and their needs (Canino, 1988; Cole, 1996a, 1998; Fowers & Richardson, 1996).

The migration process tugs at the very roots of identity and can become one of the most stressful phases in a person's lifetime. Suberri (1987) discusses what she terms the relationship between "the separation reaction" and the degree of stress. Significant factors often include: a) developmental stage; b) self-esteem; c) generational status; d) differences between the culture of origin and the new culture; e) facility in the mainstream language; f) pressure exerted to conform to mainstream culture; and g) circumstances surrounding the relocation, such as the degree of choice and preparation for the move.

Immigrant groups come to a new society for widely diverse reasons, and these have an impact on their adjustment patterns. Presenting problems in the school milieu should be analyzed by school psychologists to consider the circumstances of the move and the potential stresses involved in adapting to a new way of life (Cole, 1998; Cole & Siegel, 1990; Wilen & van Maanen Sweeting, 1986). For example, migration by choice, although stressful, is likely to be much less traumatic than seeking political asylum. Refugee children's developmental histories often include information about disrupted lives, deprivation, significant losses, and little or no schooling (Ajdukovic & Ajdukovic, 1993).

Levy-Warren (1987) conceptualized cultural relocation as involving both an internal and an external process of separation. External separation is the actual move from one location to another, with an attendant loss of people and objects. The internal representation of cultural relocation through images of people, sights as well as values, occurs within the context of a person's identity formation. This internal process is complex, and is connected to developmental stages and to the capacity for abstraction. Thus, for a young child, relocation may only be a geographical move, as culture is associated with and transmitted through the primary caretakers. Adolescents and adults, on the other hand, are likely to have developed a stable and differentiated mental representation of their culture. For them, a new culture often represents unfamiliar norms of behavior, differences in value systems, differences in role expectations, and difficulties in communication. Thus, the move may create a situation in which fundamental aspects of identity are called into question, leading to experiences of loss, disorientation, helplessness, and personal impoverishment.

Modes of acculturation have been described as falling into four adjustment patterns: assimilation, biculturalism, rejection, and deculturation (Berry, 1985; Cole, 1996a; Cole & Siegel, 1990; Suberri, 1987). Assimilation occurs when people relinquish their cultural identity, replacing it with the new culture. Biculturalism involves a process that necessitates constant decision-making, since it includes the maintenance of cultural integrity as well as a movement to become an integral part of a larger societal framework (Esquivel, 1985). Rejection refers to self-imposed withdrawal from and limited socialization with the mainstream culture. Deculturation leads to a loss of identity and feelings of alienation as contact is severed with both cultures.

Over time, these adjustment patterns change significantly with the type of interactions and the nature of contacts with mainstream society. They are also strongly influenced by ecological factors, such as environmental receptiveness to diverse cultures and the availability of community support systems. The psychological adaptation, attitudes, and aspirations of the immigrant child must be viewed in the context of the familial mode of acculturation. The child's particular developmental state and personality structure, as well as his or her special social circumstances, are reflected in school adjustment and learning (Beiser et al., 1995; Samuda, 1990; Samuda & Crawford, 1980). In spite of migration stressors and resultant conflicts, many children seem to cope well with transitions. However, when school and home present conflicting demands and expectations, they are likely to experience academic problems and cultural discontinuity. Home-school interactions that are not viewed by the family as helpful may result in avoidant relationships (Power & Lutz Bartholomew, 1987; Yau, 1995), and when this occurs the boundary between the two systems becomes rigid. Immigrant parents may feel incompetent and threatened when they interact with the school, with the result that important information that can enhance their child's learning is not communicated (Cole & Sroka, 1997).

School psychologists and educators who have broadened their cross-cultural knowledge can do much to facilitate the adjustment of immigrant children by helping them and their families adopt a bicultural mode of functioning. Collaborative home-school relationships are more likely to develop and be sustained in schools that do not equate cultural differences with cultural deficiencies, and which have developed an environment of cultural pluralism (Cole, 1998).

Migration characteristics, however, are not always disclosed to schools. Reluctance to reveal information concerning migration status is understandable in light of the vulnerable positions in which many families find themselves. Yet, without sufficient knowledge about background circumstances, adequate care and attention may not be provided. Fragmented schooling and gaps in the children's education may also be under-reported by parents or be misunderstood by educators. Thus, the very environment which can open doors and welcome the child into a world of educational stability may inadvertently cause the students to develop negative reactions about themselves. Some students may require individualized programming in order to cope with social isolation or with confusion about academic standards. The qualitative research of Yau (1995) documents the need for clear and ongoing communication between teachers and families. Her study found that frustration experienced by refugee students was associated with obstacles such as frequent relocations, cultural disorientation, problems understanding teacher instructions, and gaps in basic skills. Resiliency on the other hand was associated with nurturing caregivers, physical security, stable personalities and a positive school climate.

Like the adults in their lives, children may have been exposed to aversive events and early losses, which can produce vulnerabilities. However, the mental health and social needs of refugee and immigrant children must be understood in context. Beiser et al. (1995) noted that research findings about children and youth are inconsistent and, at times, conflicting. Some studies report a higher risk for psychopathology while others conclude that the rate of mental health disorders among immigrant and refugee young people is not higher than for native born counterparts.

In recent years, attention has been focused on refugee children who may have suffered emotional scars related to trauma. Although post-traumatic stress disorder (PTSD) has been far more extensively studied in adults, there appears to be a growing research emphasis on children's stress reactions. It is currently estimated that up to 50% of children from war-torn countries experience PTSD symptoms (Cole, 1998). The perception of stress and the severity of events are significant correlates of the disorder (Motta, 1995; Nader, 1997; Price, 1995). Common dysfunctional PTSD indicators impact on affective symptoms (depression, guilt, grief), cognitive indicators (self-blame, intrusive recollections, suicidal ideation), psychosomatic symptoms (nightmares, sleep disturbance, fatigue) and behavioral manifestations (social isolation, startled reactions, aggression). These types of stress reactions can occur at any age. It is unclear, however, how PTSD, the age at which it occurs, the role of support systems, and the type of treatment interact in the development and resolution of the disorder (Eth & Pynoos, 1985; Motta, 1995).

Those who provide mental health services to victims of trauma have noted that children, like adults, vary in their responses and needs. Adolescents, for example, may act out, externalize, and engage in high-risk behaviors following devastating events. Young children, on the other hand, may display repetitive or obsessive play or use art as a way of expressing painful emotions related to their past. Nevertheless, traumatized individuals require specialized counseling. They need to go through a process of recovery which usually includes several stages: restoration of a stable safety net; exploration of memories related to the past events; grieving over losses; reconnection to the self in the present, and learning to trust again in order to plan for a better future (Cole, 1998; Lewis-Herman, 1992).

In spite of migration stressors and post-migration difficulties, some school-aged children successfully make the transition once their family lives have stabilized. They tend to conform to a new environment and a new way of life. A literature review by Hicks, Lalonde, and Pepler (1993) concludes that while all newcomer children experience stress associated with adjustment, expectations that this will lead to higher rates of emotional problems and maladaptive behaviors cannot be supported. The authors found that a variety of adaptive experiences are encountered, with outcomes determined by a combination of risk and protective factors related to the child, family, and community. Protective factors include competence in the mainstream language and academic skills, the development of a social network, family stability, and community services and supports.

Learning English as a Second Language

Language as a critical skill for learning and school achievement has been a theme for research studies and instructional interventions for newcomer students. Second-language students comprise heterogeneous groups whose language growth is linked to psychological, sociocultural, and educational factors. In any school, there is great variability as to how long it takes students to learn English and how much individualized help they may need in the process. These issues constitute major challenges for students, teachers, and consultants.

Learning English becomes a prime goal for immigrant children whose educational experiences and academic progress are inevitably tied to their English proficiency. Over time, slow progress in English may both reduce chances for scholastic success and also have adverse consequences for a student's self-concept, social integration, and school placement.

Failure to understand theoretical and pedagogical constructs related to language development often leads to culturally and linguistically different children with academic problems being diagnosed as learning disabled. When English as a second language (ESL) children fail to match the school performance of their peers, there is often a belief that they have deficiencies that cannot be addressed in the regular program. Underachievement has also been viewed as related to disruptions in cultural continuity and family stability, to cultural and linguistic differences between home and school, and to the family's socioeconomic status. When psychological or educational assessment issues are considered separately from pedagogical ones, they do not extend to learning plans but continue to point to the student as the locus of the problem (Benard, 1993; Cole, 1996a; Cummins, 1984, 1989, 1994; Mercer, 1983).

Misconceptions about second language learning can also lead to faulty recommendations that have a long-term impact on the educational decisions and information communicated to the parents. For example, if a child enrolled in a heritage language program has problems in the English program, the parents may be advised to withdraw him or her from the extra program because of the misconception that simultaneously learning a language other than English interferes with acquisition of the latter. In fact, the native language provides the foundation upon which to build second language competence. Parents may also become reluctant to interact with their child in the first language, thereby disrupting both the quality and the extent of the linguistic interactions their children will experience at home (Alter, 1992; Cole, 1998).

Cummins' (1979, 1980, 1981, 1984, 1989, 1994) extensive publications concerning language proficiency in bilingual children provide both a theoretical and an applied framework with implications for intervention and assessment practices. In addressing the issue of how first language (L1) proficiency is related to the development of second language (L2) proficiency, he concludes that it should not be assumed that L2 proficiency for face-to-face communication is similar to that required for performance on L2 cognitive/academic tasks. He suggests that basic interpersonal communication skills are usually achieved within two years of arrival in the host country, but that cognitive/academic language proficiency is a long-term process that takes five to seven years to develop. Thus, students who appear to learn English rapidly within the first two years may be unreasonably expected to approach grade norms in English verbal academic skills; when these advances do not occur, teachers may question the child's capabilities or intrinsic motivation to learn.

Cummins' differentiation between "basic interpersonal communication skills" (BICS) and "cognitive/academic language proficiency" (CALP) derives from earlier theories about the influence of schooling (see Bruner, 1966). He views face-to-face conversations as dependent on context for interpretation, whereas formal education calls for language usage outside the immediate context. That is, school subjects involving reading and writing call for decontextualization and explicitness in the use of language as an integrated and independent system. BICS includes basic vocabulary, grammar, phonology, and syntax, while CALP involves higher cognitive processes such as analysis, synthesis, and evaluation.

Cummins postulates that cognitive and literacy-related skills across languages are interdependent and reflect a "common underlying proficiency." This implies that transfer is more likely to occur from L1 to L2 because of greater exposure to literacy, and that first-language learning strengthens the foundation for English competence. While Cummins' contribution lies principally in his assertion that BICS and CALP dimensions of language proficiency have to be taken into account when working with children experiencing academic difficulty, he also recognizes that other social factors are correlated with academic competence. For example, the negative effects of low SES on school performance are well recognized as a complex area of child development, which must be taken into account when analyzing academic outcomes in either the first or second language (Burnaby, 1980; Corson, 1993; Wallace, 1986). Again, children's language experiences and the frequency with which they use certain verbal skills in either monolingual or bilingual homes are likely to vary extensively. These differences are often associated with educational advantage or disadvantage (Hafner & Ulanoff, 1994; Thomas, 1992; Tough, 1977, 1982). When children do not become integrated in enriching programs, what they encounter each day in school may negatively reinforce what they have learned out of school about talking, ways of thinking, and participating in their own learning.

This discussion has significant implications for teaching practices that seek to accommodate the needs of immigrant students. Teaching styles and classroom situations and interactions that result in students becoming actively engaged in the use of language for purposes they see as meaningful are more likely to lead to language development and expansion (Fillion & Wright, 1982; Fletcher & Cardona-Morales, 1990; Genesee, 1994; Hamayan, 1993; Heald-Taylor, 1986). Language encompasses many different skills whose interrelationships are multilayered. Although listening, speaking, reading, and writing are interrelated, these skills are also independent in some ways, and this can have complex implications for planning curricular activities for second-language learners. The acquisition of English is likely to be enhanced when it is both the object of instruction and a medium of communication.

In assessing individual students and in consultation with teachers, psychologists have to be cognizant of and knowledgeable about language development patterns of bilingual children. Factors related to second-language acquisition will be discussed in the next section as part of the assessment-for-intervention model.

From Static Testing to Dynamic Assessment

The role of assessment in education has been linked to accountability practices. It is thus paramount for parents to be assured that measuring what is being taught and what is being learned by their children will lead to expanded knowledge and school-based recommendations for improved learning.

The issues embedded in the assessment of learning problems of minority students have their own set of definitional problems, which are related to broader issues of social justice and equality of educational opportunities. Children's differences in abilities and learning styles may be related to social or cultural factors. However, it is not at all clear whether, or when, such differences need to be considered disabilities or impairments (Cole, 1991; Cole & Siegel, 1990; Geva, 2000; MacIntyre, 1985; Sewell, 1987).

Test bias is one of the major concerns for school psychologists performing assessments in order to determine special education placements. There has long been an acknowledgment that the assessment of cognitive functioning or academic potential of minority children poses difficult problems for practitioners and theoreticians alike, and the widespread use of standard intelligence tests as a method of establishing the amount, nature, and quality of education to be provided have come under considerable criticism (Samuda, 1975, 1990; Samuda et al., 1989; Torrance, 1982). These criticisms point to the fact that traditional psychometric techniques measure acquired knowledge only: they do not address the child's responsiveness to instruction, nor do they provide information that can be used for effective interventions (Bransford et al., 1987; Cummins, 1994; Luther, Cole, & Gamlin, 1996). Thus, they not only *predict* the failure of culturally different children, but they have also contributed operationally to the *fulfillment* of these predictions. According to Feuerstein (1979), the reason can be found in the static goal of the conventional psychometric approach, which limits itself to taking an inventory of existing information about perceptual and cognitive skills, disregarding the child's experiential, educational, and motivational background.

Repeated studies have consistently demonstrated that minority children do poorly on IQ tests, especially on verbal tasks (Samuda, 1975, 1990; Sattler, 1982, 1988, 2001). The over-representation of immigrant and minority language students in special education classes has been attributed to the use of discriminatory tests as well as to the orientation of school programs (Cummins, 1984, 1994; Mercer, 1983). Issues related to the use of standardized tests for the assessment and placement of minority group students continue to be widely debated and have impacted on legal and regulatory decisions. For example, legislation in the United States, Public Law PL 94-142 (1975), states that testing materials or procedures shall be provided and administered in the student's native language or mode of communication. Furthermore, the legislation requires educators to identify students with special needs and develop individualized programs for them.

Alternative approaches and procedures to conventional psychometric tests have been developed and are increasingly employed by psychologists as part of their assessment procedures. Attempts have been made to construct so-called unbiased "culture-free" or "culture fair" tests. However, researchers and practitioners have expressed growing skepticism about these alternatives as they maintain the assumption of intelligence as a fixed entity. Although such measures assess some aspects of cognitive functioning, many nonverbal tests have also been found to be culture-bound, as they employ materials and concepts that do not have equal exposure in all cultures and subcultures (Anastasi, 1982; M. Cole, 1975; Sattler, 1988, 2001). In addition, since they measure narrow samples of behavior, they provide limited information about the child's academic potential or remedial needs (Cummins, 1984, 1994).

Over time, the focus in assessment has shifted from test bias against minorities to include concerns over the fair use of such measures, that is to say, the use of tests that are not equally valid measures for particular groups and therefore potentially leading to unfair outcomes (Lam, 1995). In recent years, several performance-based educational assessment approaches have been documented as appropriate for all students, including linguistic minority children. Assessment modalities – such as "portfolio-based assessment," "authentic" or "performance" assessments – provide information which can be linked to instructional planning and to students' learning experiences (Estrin, 1993; Gordon & Musser, 1992).

Modifications of tests to make them more appropriate for use with culturally different children include translations, changes of instructions, substitution, elimination of time limits, special scoring systems, and renorming based on representative samples of the population (Sattler, 2001).

In contrast to psychometric procedures that have been used to provide diagnostic information to help with placement decisions, Dynamic Assessment has direct implications for intervention. The concept of Dynamic Assessment as an applied system is a novel approach, although as a philosophy it can be traced to Vygotsky's theories and the conception of the "zone of proximal development" (1978, 1986). It includes a range of approaches for integrating the assessment of abilities with the enhancement of abilities. Feuerstein (1979) developed a model of Dynamic Assessment that is considered to be one of the most comprehensive approaches, in that it links assessment practices to intervention at both theoretical and clinical levels (Luther et al., 1996; Sewell, 1987).

The construct that Dynamic Assessment has at its core is the notion that intelligence is a dynamic entity: that the human organism is an open system, accessible to structural change irrespective of etiology, condition, or stage of development. It postulates that performance failures can be attributed at least in part to deficient instruction, and that learning can change in response to environmental input.

Feuerstein's Learning Potential Assessment Device (LPAD) grew out of his longitudinal involvement in research and clinical activity dealing with acculturation, education, and therapeutic processes of disadvantaged children in Israel. It includes a battery of tests and training procedures that lead to interventions within a test-teach-retest model. Both examiner and learner are active in this process: the examiner monitors and modifies the interaction with the learner to induce successful learning, while the examinee is reinforced to assume the role of active learner. Different techniques are employed, with the common goal of modifying the functioning of the individual in an area considered critical at a particular point in the assessment. The LPAD can also be used with the Instrumental Enrichment program, an intervention strategy developed by Feuerstein (1980) with the aim of modifying cognitive functioning and the learning of new skills.

Although dealing primarily with the domain of cognitive skills, the LPAD and mediated interventions are important advances in assessment procedures. Dynamic Assessment outcomes can lead to intervention and have the potential for direct application to instruction (Cole, 1991; Cole & Siegel, 1990; Schneider Lidz, 1987).

Current Dynamic Assessment research supports the move away from traditional psychometric models of assessment. However, more research is required in order to evaluate issues related to the generalization of knowledge and its transfer to the school system. The prospect of using Dynamic Assessment both in the context of general problem-solving tasks and in the context of domain-specific activities such as reading and math is encouraging (Bransford et al., 1987; Luther et al., 1996). Dynamic Assessment seems appropriate for use with minority students when questions concerning modifiability and interventions are called for. It is not intended as a replacement for all present approaches, but as a supplement to them (Cole, 1996b).

The move away from traditional assessment and diagnostic procedures continues to have far-reaching implications for the training and practice of school psychology. Even when only used as an adjunct to traditional assessment functions, Dynamic Assessment techniques involve the unlearning of old concepts (Cole, 1998). It also requires more time commitment, and might be criticized in schools with long waiting lists for assessments.

Both practitioners and students of school psychology need to find new ways to increase training in performance-based, comprehensive psychological assessments in order to assist in appropriate educational planning for students (Shapiro, 1990). Professional development avenues that expand skills are crucial for role expansion. A wider knowledge base is likely to change the conceptualization of the practitioner's role in multicultural communities, and to lead to useful curriculum-based interventions, more comprehensive assessments, and more collaborative consultation with educators.

Psychological Assessments

Practicing school psychologists perceive their present and future roles as still requiring a strong foundation in assessment processes (Cole, 1996b; Copeland & Miller, 1985; Sattler, 1988, 2001; Wilson & Reschly, 1996), which have grown, historically, from narrow psychometric testing to encompass multiple sources of information and multidimensional functions (Cole, 1991, 1998; Pryzwansky & Hanania, 1986; Wiener, 1987). Assessment services continue to be emphasized in school systems as a legislated requirement and as a service valued by teachers and parents. Indeed, assessment can provide avenues for child advocacy as psychologists bring unique knowledge and core psychological skills to this function. Critics of assessment services within the profession may downplay the importance of this function. Nevertheless, reducing the value of assessment will not necessarily increase the profile of school psychologists. The context of assessment and its importance, however, are likely to improve when they are seen as part of a broader service model.

Much has been written to debunk cognitive assessments of immigrant students. However, relatively few publications detail developmental, broad-based assessment models that do not emphasize child deficits or diagnostic labels. Comprehensive assessments conducted in multicultural school settings call for cross-cultural awareness and consultation skills, as well as specific competencies such as knowledge of language development, knowledge of curricula, and skill in working with interpreters (Cole, 1996a; Cole & Siegel, 1990; Figueroa, Sandoval, & Merino, 1984).

Psychological assessments are conducted in order to understand "the child as a whole" and to assist in appropriate educational planning and other interventions as needed. Such an orientation is based in part on the conception that a) assessment should be linked to intervention; b) assessment must be focused on how the child learns as well as what he or she has already learned; c) the assessment should involve a process of forming and testing hypotheses; and d) understanding the interaction between the child at school and at home is necessary in order to make knowledgeable recommendations (Borghese & Cole, 1994; Christenson, Abery, & Weinberg, 1986; Cole, 1991; Meyers, 1987).

When assessment of immigrant students is considered, it should be conducted by a person who speaks the student's first language or in collaboration with an interpreter. In addition, consultation with educators and interviews with family members should become part of the assessment process. Effort should be made to obtain accurate and detailed information regarding the student's developmental, linguistic, and educational history. The student should be observed in a variety of contexts, in the classroom, the schoolyard, etc.

Assessment of the student's current functioning in various areas should reflect his or her linguistic and cultural background. In selecting standardized instruments, the psychologist must judge the appropriateness of the measures chosen on the basis of psychometric, linguistic, and cultural criteria. Consideration of norms and potential cultural bias in the interpretation of outcomes should be kept in mind throughout. If standardized tests are given, they should be used as observational tools only and the results obtained should be interpreted in light of other assessment data and factual information that is available.

The following assessment model has been developed by the writers in a school board in which psychological staff provide traditional as well as consultative services. The model provides for the evaluation of the child's cognitive skills, academic competencies, personality and social functioning, and school community interactions. It makes use of a wide variety of data sources and, unlike more traditional models, does not rely on the standardized IQ test as the sole source of information about cognitive

functioning. Rather, multiple data sources, including parent interviews, school records, personal observation, and dynamic assessment strategies are used to make inferences regarding this and other constructs. While such an approach is utilized in the
practice of many good clinicians, it becomes particularly important when working
with the multicultural child about whom standardized cognitive measures are likely
to yield biased results and misinformation.

We begin our description of this approach by outlining the various data sources in
the order in which they are usually accessed.

Consultation with Teacher and School Team

Educators refer ESL children to school psychologists because of concerns about the students' academic and/or adjustment difficulties. They often require assistance in developing appropriate programs or in making decisions about alternate placement. The
reason for referral should be discussed in consultation with the teacher and the school
team. This is considered the phase of problem clarification and the beginning of joint
problem-solving. In schools that endorse a local team model, the teacher and the psychologist together with the principal, social worker, ESL teacher, and other support staff
such as ESL consultants, discuss the child's special needs. Instead of debating the causes
for difficulty, questions are discussed in order to form hypotheses about the child in the
current learning environment. In order to obtain balanced information and reach consensus on specific concerns, the following issues should be addressed:
- What is the symptomatic reason for referral?
- What is the present level of instruction, and what does an evaluation of daily
  work suggest about the student's academic functioning?
- Does the student have the skills to complete assignments?
- Does the student understand what he/she is being taught?
- How is the student's learning style and class participation?
- What motivational manifestations are present?
- How does the student interact with teacher(s)?
- Does the student interact appropriately with peers?
- Does the student prefer the company of older or younger children?
- Is the student attending school regularly?
- Does the student exhibit strengths or interest in non-academic areas, such as
  art?
- What intervention strategies were already tried in class/school?
- Which ones were helpful?

Answering these and similar reasons for referral helps to tie assessment activities
and data collection to questions that are relevant to the student's daily classroom
functioning, and fosters joint problem-solving between teacher and psychologist.

Educational History

Factual as well as evaluative data can provide important background information about the child in school. Such an analysis is usually more complex when working with multilingual documents, and is likely to require the assistance of translators. In addition, it should be kept in mind that educational systems vary in their pedagogy and evaluation of students, and have different emphases for curriculum standards. We recommend that the following questions guide the review of student records:
- How many years has the student been in the present country?
- Did the student emigrate directly from the homeland?
- Did the student have exposure to formal educational experiences? Where? For how long? Were there gaps in formal education?
- How many schools did the student attend in each country?
- Did the student repeat any grades?
- Was the student placed in special education or other remedial programs?
- Was the student proficient in the first language?
- What were past learning strengths and weaknesses?
- Are there discrepancies between past and present evaluations of skills and/or social adjustment?
- Is there sufficient documentation to provide a profile of the student's educational experiences and social adaptation?
- Are there any previous mental health and/or educational assessments, which could be reviewed?

Understanding the student's past educational history and profile of academic skills as well as social functioning will assist in structuring the interviews with the parents and obtaining relevant background information.

Parent Interviews

Psychologists interviewing families of immigrant students often need to develop an ability to work with interpreters and to establish rapport with all participants through verbal and nonverbal communication. It is important to obtain accurate translations that are not subject to misinterpretations or evaluations by the translator. Effective interpretation involves ethical issues related to practice such as confidentiality in school settings, and can be dealt with through prior consultation or joint in-service sessions. These skills are more likely to lead to a clear understanding of the reason for referral, and help to achieve consensus on areas of concern and a plan for action. Interviewing immigrant parents also requires the psychologist to become familiar with cross-cultural mental health information in order to facilitate better communication and more comprehensive interventions. Parental attitudes towards education are likely to be influenced by their own school experience, which may bias their expectations. Expectations that are discrepant from the school's philosophy and curricular approach may lead to misunderstanding and home/school conflicts, especially for parents who are coping with discontinuity, dislocation, and readjustment. Behavioral patterns that are tolerated by families in one culture or ethnic group may be indicative of maladjustment or developmental difficulties in the host cultural setting. Social patterns, affective styles, belief patterns, and gender role differences, as well as the migration process, can have a profound impact on the child's adaptive development and school experience. All these behavioral expressions have to be conceptualized and evaluated within a cultural context. In addition, it is important to understand the parental cultural attitudes about mental illness and mental health professionals. Establishing trust is paramount in order to develop a collaborative relationship and flexible interactions between school and home. The psychologist should keep in mind the following questions, which will lead to a more comprehensive understanding of the child's developmental history, migration experience, and current needs:

A. Parents' Understanding of the School Situation

- Do the parents have school information and understand the reasons for referral?
- What are the family's perceptions about and attitudes towards the school system?
- What are their expectations of the child in school?
- Does the family understand the role of the school psychologist?
- Do they understand the process involved in the assessment?
- Do they have questions the psychologist can help answer? Should the assessment be broadened to include parental questions?

B. The Family's Migration Experience

- What were the reasons for the migration?
- Were there migration factors that led to multiple dislocations or destabilization?
- Did the family experience losses and severance of family ties?
- How does the family feel about the new way of life for the adults and the children?

C. The Student's Developmental and Medical History

- What is the student's birth date? (verification is important since birthdays might be misinterpreted or incorrect and altered on legal documents)

- Were the student's milestones (motor/language/social) reached at appropriate stages?
- Did/does the student have any major illnesses or accidents? Was drug therapy or other forms of medicine involved?
- When was the student's last physical checkup (especially visual/ hearing)?
- Was the student separated from parent(s) due to health/migration/ family reasons?
- What was the student's first language (speaking/reading/writing)? What is the student's preferred language now?
- Was the student reared and educated in a rural or an urban community?

D. The Family/Community Support System

- Does the family have community ties and support systems?
- Does the student have a social network out of school?
- What languages are spoken at home?
- What aspects of home and/or school environments are supportive or create stress for the student?
- Are there intergenerational conflicts that might impact schooling?

E. Parents' Perception of the Student

- Does the student discuss school matters at home?
- Does the student interact appropriately with siblings? With peers?
- How does the student spend time outside of school? Are the parents aware of any particular interests or talents? What television programs does the student watch?
- Does the student undertake age appropriate responsibilities in the home and perform them competently?
- What discipline strategies are used? How often? How does the student respond?

Observation of the Student at School

Observing the student at school should become an integral part of the data collection phase of the assessment. In the classroom and during recess, the psychologist has an opportunity to observe and form impressions about the interactions the child has with both teachers and peers. In addition, understanding instructional variables, classroom management, and class atmosphere, are important factors in learning about the child and the reasons for referral. Examination of classroom work is likely to enhance the frequency and style of communication between psychologist and teacher and, it is hoped, lead to ongoing consultation. If the student is attending a withdrawal (part-time) ESL program or heritage language program, observations should be made in that setting as well. During observation, attention should be paid to the following issues:

A. The Learning Environment

- Are there other immigrant students in this class?
- Does the student work alone or in a group?
- Are there frequent interactions with other children/teacher?
- How often and what kind of feedback does the teacher provide the student with?
- What kind of motivational strategies are used in the class?
- Is the classroom environment friendly?
- Do students cooperate with one another?
- Are students encouraged to participate in discussions? Does this student participate voluntarily?
- How do a) the teacher, and b) peers deal with inappropriate behaviors?

B. Learning-Related Behavior of the Child

- Does the student engage in teacher-directed academic activities?
- Does the student engage in self-directed academic activities?
- How does the student face new learning tasks?
- Does the student present him/herself as motivated?
- Does the student understand the teacher's expectations?
- Does the student pay attention in class (with/without supervision)?
- Does the child engage with interest in nonacademically oriented activities? In the classroom? At recess?
- What kind of learning strategies is the student using?

Student Interview(s)

This phase of the assessment proceeds from asking what significant others are saying about the child, to learning how the student feels about him/herself, both at school and in the community. This kind of information has general implications for the validity of formal assessment findings, inferences about hypotheses formed, and the selection of assessment devices. Obviously, the student's age and language facility will dictate the quantity of questions asked and the style of communication throughout assessment sessions:

A. The Student's Understanding of the Problem

- Is the student aware of learning/behavioral problems at school?
- How does the student feel about the school programs?
- What specific subjects in school are easy and enjoyable? Which are difficult? Why?
- Did the student have similar strengths and weaknesses in other school systems?

B. The Student's Perspective on the Migration Experience

- Does the student know or remember the reasons for migration?
- Does the student still have adjustment problems?

C. Information About the Student's Life Outside of School

- What kind of interactions with adults or peers are rewarding for the student both in and out of school?
- What is the student's daily routine?
- What out-of-school interests, hobbies, or organized activities does the student participate in? What television programs does the student watch?

D. Quality of Communication Skills

- What is the student's English language proficiency? Is his or her English understandable? Does he or she use simplified grammatical constructions? Does he or she often grope for words? Are there grammatical intrusions from the first language?
- Does the student initiate conversation?
- Does the student express feelings, opinions, concerns, wishes?
- What kind of rapport is established in the assessment situation?
- What contributes to increased motivation?

Standardized Assessment Measures

Standardized assessment approaches are fraught with the difficulties discussed earlier in this chapter. Knowledge of the limitations of assessment instruments should lead to a careful consideration of appropriate procedures by the psychologist. The student's second-language acquisition, school experiences, and degree of acculturation are likely to play a significant role in the assessment process and outcome. Information from those standardized measures that are selected should be cross-validated against other data sources, including dynamic assessment results and the observations of those who know the child both in and out of school. They may also be supplemented by informal tasks that probe significant areas in greater detail. For example, it is often instructive to observe the student actually working with reading materials from the classroom, as well as with more formal standardized measures of reading abilities. Such an approach may lead to recommendations that will be useful to the teacher in planning an instructional program.

As the child is given formal measures of cognitive, academic, and personality functioning, observation regarding the following questions will provide information that will assist in interpreting results:

- Does the student understand task instructions?
- Does the student have adequate knowledge/skills for task completion?
- Is the student's concentration span interfering with performance?
- What strategies are used in approaching tasks?
- When solving problems, is the student overly impulsive?
- Does he or she use a systematic or a trial and error approach?
- How does the student respond when probed? When receiving guided instruction? When taught? When tasks are understood and completed?
- How does the student cope with difficult tasks? – Can he or she self-correct?
- Does the student find some tasks more rewarding than others?
- Can the student transfer strategies and functions across tasks?
- Can the student monitor and evaluate completed work?
- Does the student show active involvement in the assessment process?
- What contributes to increased motivation?

Feedback and Planning Conferences

Feedback meetings should include the school psychologist, the teacher, the parents, the student, if appropriate, and a translator when necessary. (At times, the student him/herself may act as interpreter for the parents at these meetings, if a professional one is not available.) Assessment findings should be reviewed, and specific examples provided to highlight both strengths and needs. It is important for the psychologist to provide a link between assessment information and parents' and teachers' existing information about the child. The use of overly technical professional "jargon" should be avoided.

Ideally, this feedback can lead to opportunities for ongoing consultation. The discussion is likely to be productive when the focus is on the whole child and the implication of assessment findings for learning. Results should be linked to possible interventions both at school and at home. The psychologist can facilitate a problem-solving approach for the student rather than focus on the recommendation for special education services:

- What skills does the child have in core subjects? – How far are they from grade expected skills?
- What was learned from dynamic assessment tasks?
- What strategies enhanced on-task behaviors?
- What modifications need to take place? What resources are available?
- What changes at school and at home can help reduce stress for the child? What community resources can be drawn upon?

Recommendations for intervention should be specific and clear to all involved. Discussion should center around intervention plans both at school and at home. Empowering teachers and parents in the consultation process encourages home-school links and will help the implementation of agreed-upon recommendations. The psychologist must evaluate what interventions are feasible given the resources of all concerned. Agreed-upon interventions should be documented in a written report in which the psychologist specifies his or her role in providing follow-up services, such as monitoring the effectiveness of the interventions and consultation with the school team.

Areas of Functioning

Having discussed assessment methods, we turn now to the various areas of functioning that will normally be evaluated in an attempt to plan useful educational interventions. We advocate an ecological approach that takes into account the influence of the school environment, the family, and the community on learning, as well as traits indigenous to the child. In discussing each area of functioning, we identify issues that are relevant to its evaluation.

Cognitive Correlates and Information Processing Skills

Since many referrals are made for academic reasons, major effort is often directed toward evaluation of cognitive skills. Often, educators wish to have information about a student's overall cognitive ability so that they may determine if special education programming or continued support in English-language learning through ESL programming is the most appropriate course of action. The care with which this issue should be approached cannot be overemphasized. Statements about the student's overall cognitive abilities should acknowledge the limitations of standardized measures for ESL students, as discussed earlier in this chapter. Given the existence of language barriers and the lack of assessment techniques, this may be a question that cannot be fully answered. However, when converging evidence from multiple data sources point to the same conclusions, psychologists may have increased confidence in the validity of standardized assessment findings.

An approach we have found useful in the evaluation of cognitive abilities concerns itself with a student's current functioning as it may impact on his or her adjustment to the English-language environment of the classroom. The student's performance across a variety of domains can be observed and analyzed in terms of an input-elaboration-output model of mental acts (Cole & Siegel, 1990; Feuerstein, 1979; Luther et al., 1996; Schneider Lidz, 1987). This information processing approach evaluates input processes such as attending and perceiving; central processes such as comparing, transferring, retrieving and generalizing information; and output processes involving the communication or recording of a response. It is assumed that a number of such processes are involved in any cognitive task, and that performance on any task is influenced by a variety of factors. No one task should be viewed as reflecting just one process.

The evaluation of some cognitive processes may have greater implications for classroom learning than others, and may be seen as more or less relevant to the presenting concerns about the student. For example, if a student has been referred because of concerns about slow acquisition of English, it will be important to question whether deficits in auditory attentional skills may be a contributing factor. Since many tests that are thought to evaluate these abilities involve language and are confounded by second-language factors, it is important to determine that deficits in English language skills *per se* are not confused with auditory processing deficits. Such inferences can sometimes be made by comparing the student's performance on tasks of varying linguistic complexity, by making independent judgments of the youngster's English-language proficiency, and by comparing his or her skills in English and in the first language. There may be occasions when it is not possible to tease apart the importance of the two factors. Nevertheless, systematic evaluation of the student's skills in attending to, remembering, and acting upon orally presented information in English can have implications for classroom instruction. Youngsters with difficulties in this area may require significant repetition of instructions and the use of concrete demonstrations during the introduction of new concepts. Such an evaluation can provide valuable information to teachers who may have difficulty determining the extent to which the student understands what is presented on the basis of classroom observations. Many ESL students become adept at the use of nonverbal cues, and may convey the impression of having understood a concept through their successful completion of various classroom tasks when in fact they have not.

The following questions should be addressed in undertaking an evaluation of cognitive abilities. In all cases, the critical issue is not a comparison of the child's skills to those of same-aged peers, but an evaluation of how strengths and weaknesses in each skill area impact on current class functioning:

- Are the student's visual perceptual skills adequate?
- Are the student's auditory perceptual skills adequate?

- Are the student's psychomotor skills, especially as related to paper and pencil tasks, adequate?
- Are short- and long-term memory skills adequate?
- Are language skills age-appropriate? In the first language? In English?
- Are observed deficits present across both languages or only in English?
- What is the student's stage of development in conceptual reasoning and problem-solving skills? What strategies are used?

Academic Functioning

Academic growth of ESL students, especially in the language area, should be assessed through a variety of means, including observations, review of work samples, and paper and pencil tasks. Assessment methods should reflect the student's academic skills in the classroom setting and should be complementary to the curriculum plan developed by the teacher. Such an orientation is more likely to lead to effective consultation with the teacher and to bring about changes in instruction patterns for the student. Students' performance on normed referenced tests is closely related to their language development and skills. Thus, achievement tests are likely to place ESL students at a disadvantage and should be used only as part of a multiple criteria assessment. Oral language needs should be assessed in several contexts, such as social interaction, class discussions, and conversations. Attention should be paid to the student's ability to shift styles in different contexts and when possible, his or her proficiency in the native language should be assessed as part of this procedure.

Dynamic assessment techniques seem particularly appropriate for this section of the assessment, as they provide for instructional processes and mediated learning data. The test-teach-retest approach is also likely to provide the student with success experiences and reflect academic strengths and needs more accurately.

In identifying the educational implications of this aspect of the assessment, one should compare the extent of academic deficits to the student's current grade placement and chronological age. As well, the student's current English-language skills and past education need to be considered. Finally, instructional intervention will be facilitated when patterns of strength and weakness are related to curricular objectives. Thus, for example, knowing that a student does not understand the "place value" concept is more useful than knowing that his math skills are at a Grade 3 level. The following questions should guide the assessment of each academic area:

Oral Language:

- Does the student initiate conversation?
- Can the student stay on topic?

- Does the student use one-word responses? Short phrases? Simple sentences?
- What is the student's level of pronunciation and vocabulary?
- Does he/she grope for words?
- Does the student's English show intrusions from the first language?
- Can the student phrase questions? What tenses are used? Is the oral language expanded to include relationships, conclusions, expressions of thoughts and emotions?
- Does the student respond to probes, redirected questions, rephrased or repeated instructions?

Written Language:

- Does the student use basic grammatical and structural patterns?
- Do errors in written English parallel those in the spoken language?
- Does the student use capital letters, punctuation, and paragraphs?
- Is the student's spelling appropriate to age/grade placement?
- Is the student's printing or cursive writing age-appropriate?
- Does the student show ability to organize thoughts and ideas on paper?
- Does the student write about a variety of topics?
- Does the student use a restricted vocabulary?
- Does the student show a willingness to edit work?

Reading:

- Is the student's knowledge of sight vocabulary age/grade-appropriate?
- Is the student's knowledge of sound/symbol associations age/grade-appropriate?
- What does an evaluation of miscues suggest about the student's reading strategies?
- What are common error patterns (hesitations, mispronunciations, substitutions, additions, repetitions)? Do these patterns reflect the student's continuing difficulty with English?
- Is the student's reading currently limited by lack of English or by lack of basic reading skills?
- Does the student self-correct? Experiment with the pronunciation of words?
- Does the student pay attention to punctuation?
- Does the student comprehend what is read orally? Silently? Does he or she benefit from guided reading?
- Is the reading material related to the student's experiences?

Mathematics:

- Has the student mastered basic computation skills that are age/grade-appropriate?
- Are the student's mathematical problem-solving skills age/grade-appropriate?
- Which math skills are not consolidated?
- Can the student show all the steps taken in arriving at the final answer?
- Given a particular problem, can the student determine which computations are relevant to its solution?
- Can the student formulate questions?
- Can the student answer questions involving reading comprehension?
- Can the student self-correct following guided examples?

Study Skills and Learning Style:

Academic assessment findings should be integrated with information about the student's learning style and study skills:
- What is the student's preferred learning mode? Reading? Listening to others? Working alone? In a group?
- Is the student's learning style impulsive? Reflective? Independent? Dependent?
- Can the student "learn how to learn?"
- Does the student learn subject-specific as well as general study skills?
- Are any of the following areas problematic: Time scheduling? Test taking? Homework? Completing projects? Note taking techniques?

Personality Development and Functioning

Consistent with earlier assessment stages, data should be sought from multiple sources and criteria. Information sources may include classroom observations, anecdotal reports of both teachers and parents, interview and test behaviors, drawings, self-report questionnaires, and projective measures. The psychologist will have to focus attention on the process of migration and the impact it had on the child's development and school needs. In addition, standing cultural attitudes, behavioral patterns, and affective styles should play a significant role in assessment. The following questions place particular emphasis on areas that are relevant to the student's functioning in school:
- How does the child see him/herself as a student?
- What are the student's attitudes toward school, learning, and teachers?
- Is there a difference between self-concept of academic competence and other areas (e.g., athletic ability, social skills, etc.)?

- How does the student see him/herself in social interactions with peers, teachers, parents, and siblings?
- What is the student's perception of peers, teachers, parents, siblings?
- Are others seen as helpful, critical, threatening, etc.?
- What are the student's dominant behavioral characteristics?
- Are these adaptive or not? What age appropriate coping skills does the student exhibit?
- What is the student's style of interacting and communicating with others? – How does the student respond to stress, criticism, frustration?
- Are there areas of conflict that are creating tension and anxiety for the child? Does the student exhibit symptoms associated with PTSD?
- Are the student's school problems affected by the family's adjustment patterns? Does the student have unmet developmental needs?

Recommendations

Assessment findings need to be linked to a range of possible interventions in order to enhance the student's well being and overall functioning in and out of school. Through consultation and assessment, which provide a comprehensive picture about "the child as a whole," newcomer parents are likely to be reassured that second language learning gaps are not being viewed as special education needs. Moreover, they need to become confident that children at risk for educational failure will receive early programming in mainstream education and that assessment information and recommendations will be shared with parents on a regular basis.

Ideally, recommendations can encompass suggested modifications in more than one category. That is to say, strategies for home, in-class, in-school and community-based services, may become an extension of assessment data and formulation of needs and patterns of functioning. In general, practitioners need to keep in mind that helpful recommendations tend to be specific and easy to implement. On the other hand, recommendations which are perceived to be too general or time-consuming are less likely to be implemented. Consultation services by school psychologists may provide monitoring of recommendations and aid in the implementation process.

School-Based Interventions

Here we present two examples of primary and secondary prevention services with immigrant students and their families. These psychological interventions have been developed in response to the needs of children in multicultural schools who are coping with acculturation processes, academic demands, and social expectations.

Although group counseling may be appropriate for many students, relatively few school psychologists conduct counseling groups, primarily because of lack of training or experience or service time constraints (Bretzing & Caterino, 1984; Cole, 1996b; Cole & Siegel, 1990). Each of the following interventions provides the reader with an example of role expansion and avenues for counseling students and consulting with teachers and parents in mainstream education.

Example I: Role-Playing as a Modality for Alleviating Stress and Developing Social Skills

Teachers often consult with school psychologists about immigrant children whose adaptation to the new culture has been difficult, resulting in maladaptive behaviors that interfere with learning.

Although various types of intervention can be effective in approaching children who present with adjustment difficulties, role-playing techniques are considered to be particularly appropriate for use within the school milieu (Cole, 1982; Cole, 1995). In both clinically-oriented and educational research, this modality has been successfully employed to treat factors such as low self-esteem (Cole, 2000; Cole & Siegel, 1990), impaired social skills (Yalom, 1985), insensitivity to the thoughts and feelings of others, and aggressive behavior (Cole, 1995). A second reason for selecting the role-playing modality is its adaptability for use within the school context, as such short-term intervention can be easily used with groups of elementary school children, and the principles and methodology can be simply and rapidly taught to school psychologists and teachers for in-class intervention.

The selection of students for participation in the group should be done following consultation with teachers and obtaining consent from parents. Each group led by the psychologist should consist of 7-8 children of the same grade level, although not necessarily in the same class. A series of 12 weekly one-hour sessions of role-playing exercises should be developed by the psychologist with input from school staff. The objectives of the program are:

(a) to enhance self-esteem,
(b) to increase sensitivity to thoughts and feelings in oneself and others,
(c) to practice skills that facilitate social interaction,
(d) to adopt a problem-solving approach in stressful situations.

The sessions should be designed to address issues of particular interest to the students in a given school, and which reflect their adaptation needs. As can be seen from the outline of the first session presented in Appendix A, suggested time limits for each exercise are presented. However, time should be allotted for topics that the students wish to discuss. Similarly, in order to provide a measure of certainty for the children, it is recommended that the structure of each session be designed to be virtually identical.

The purpose of this group intervention is to attempt to promote psychological and behavioral changes through guided learning experiences. Role-playing is only one of the techniques used to promote these changes. Through the use of a variety of instructional techniques-role-playing, modeling, mime, and discussion – children can be encouraged to be actively involved in the learning process. Considerable emphasis should be placed on the importance of both verbal and nonverbal communication, since English proficiency is likely to vary among participants. Both during the sessions and at the conclusion of the program, discussion periods should be envisaged as a method of encouraging inexperienced children to learn more effective ways of communicating with their peers and with adults.

In our experience, teachers and parents respond positively to group counseling services. Students who are afforded an opportunity to share and discuss academic and interpersonal problems with their peers in a supportive small group setting tend to show improved self-evaluation.

Appendix A outlines, in detail, a series of sessions that use role-playing techniques to address issues of particular interest to students and teachers whose classes include refugee and immigrant children.

Example II: The Study Skills Connection

One of the more important outcomes of successful instruction is to help students become self-sufficient problem solvers. In addition to coping with problems that are specific to migration, many immigrant students lack the appropriate study skills for North American schools. In order to develop into active, independent learners, students must *learn how to learn* (Cole, 1992; Cole & Brown, 1996; Gettinger & Knopik, 1987; Weinstein & Macdonald, 1986). However, many ESL programs do not integrate learner training with language training; students are primarily taught specific cognitive strategies that relate to particular learning tasks (e.g., decoding words). Metacognitive strategies that can be used to regulate learning (e.g., planning) are taught less systematically (Cole, 1998; Wenden, 1986).

In middle and high school, adolescents face many changes and academic challenges. Regardless of their learning styles, those who have not acquired effective and efficient study skills come under a considerable amount of stress. When such students are referred for psychological assessments, they are not diagnosed as learning disabled: what they have failed to consolidate are productive learning strategies that enhance task performance. In addition, they tend to exhibit problems with transfer and generalization of learning techniques in similar contexts.

In order to address such students' needs, our former board of education formed a working committee comprised of educators, administrators, guidance counselors, and a school psychologist. The aim of the committee was to develop a study skills program that could be incorporated into ongoing curricular activities. The committee prepared drafts for general and subject-specific study skills booklets for input from teachers, students, parents, and consultants, and booklets for each age group of students were later modified to incorporate ideas and suggestions. School superintendents and principals received a proposed guide for program implementation for the new school year.

The following is a sample agenda for in-school planning. Each school team was asked to address the questions listed below:

(1) How will the booklet be distributed in your school?
- incorporated into curriculum (mainstream, ESL, special education)
- available from Guidance office
- presented at either student assembly or small groups
- gone through in class discussion

(2) What will be done to prepare teachers to be involved?
- ask staff for their help in designing and implementing a study skills program for the school
- review school policies
- list study skills strategies that are viewed by teachers as useful
- provide professional development workshops and opportunities for staff to share information and receive support when sought
- develop a resource library to be used with the booklets in each division
- discuss the program as part of the school's pedagogical objective

(3) What resources will be available to assist with planning and intervention?
- discuss collaboration with curriculum consultants, school psychologists and guidance counselors
- study skills resource materials

(4) How will study skills be incorporated into current programs?
- review curricular initiatives and government documents in relation to study skills
- in-class ongoing instruction
- teacher feedback and evaluation of homework, tests, assignments, projects, class participation

(5) How should parents be involved?
- parent information meetings and curriculum night
- share guidelines and expectations; consult with parents and stress the importance of parental involvement
- joint meetings with parents and students in middle and high schools
- use translators where appropriate

- distribution of translated booklets
- parents' association
- school newsletter translated into the necessary languages
- information letter from teacher/principal

(6) How will an ongoing program be planned?
- establish time lines
- review your school program and ask for feedback from school team, students and parents
- discuss your plan with other schools in your area

As part of the study skills initiative, the psychologist began to conduct small group interventions that focused on the following goals:
(a) provide training in metacognitive strategies helpful in planning, monitoring, and evaluating learning activities
(b) increase students' responsibility for their active learning
(c) facilitate students' learning how to learn
(d) increase student-initiated communication about learning techniques etc.

Similar to the role-playing selection process discussed earlier, students from Grades 7 and 8 were selected for group participation following consultation with the school team. With parental consent and the students' agreement, groups of eight students were formed. In each group the focus was on teachable methods of general study skills, including time management; being an effective student in class; homework; organizational skills; note making; project and research skills; studying for tests and examinations; and evaluation of schoolwork. A series of 12 weekly one-hour sessions were developed using cooperative learning methods. The sessions were based on a study skills guide, which was developed for students and parents and which complemented a teacher's guide designed with a similar format (Cole & Siegel, 1990; Cole & Warren, 1988).

Cooperative student-team learning techniques are reported to be effective for increasing cross-ethnic relationships, social interactions and academic achievement (Bohlmeyer & Burke, 1987; Cole, 1996a, 2000; Cole & Siegel, 1990; Mevarech, 1985; Slavin, 1983). In the weekly meetings, students often interacted in dyads or in groups of four, helping each other list ideas and learn new concepts related to general study strategies. In each session, there were also opportunities for constructive interactions within the group. Lists of helpful ideas and "hands on" materials were shared by all participants. The supportive social context encouraged individuals to contribute to group discussion. Peer tutoring took place on occasion when students were working on class projects.

The project and research skills topic, for example, was the focus of two successive sessions. Each group of four students was asked to list ideas about the following questions:

- How do I choose a topic?
- When should I start my project?
- What should my work look like?
- How long should my assignment be?
- Who could help me with my work?
- How do I begin my research?
- Where can I find resource material?
- Where can I work on my project?

Students were also encouraged to bring their projects to the group and explain the sequence of steps involved in their work. Following a discussion of useful ideas, the psychologist shared with the students a summary from the study skills guide, which was also brought to the teacher's attention.

Students who participated in these group interventions learned methods of acquiring and using knowledge. They reported gains in confidence and task commitment: "I learned how to study and get ready for tests;" "I learned where to get help with my work when I need it;" "I learned to share ideas and speak up in class." Teachers asked the psychologist to continue with future small group work, since they saw a transfer of knowledge and skills from the group to the classroom setting.

School psychologists who design and implement intervention programs are encouraged, together with teachers and interpreters, to facilitate parent meetings whose aim is to strengthen home-school links. Immigrant parents often feel that they lack the educational experiences or linguistic skills necessary to help their children adapt and succeed in school. Joint meetings with parents and their children are likely to clarify issues and improve communication between home and school. An example of a question and answer format relating specifically to homework issues is presented by Cole and Siegel (1990).

Implications for Service and Professional Development

This chapter has dealt with the complexities related to migration processes, and has discussed examples of avenues for meeting the needs of children in multicultural schools. For school psychologists, role expansion continues to be a challenging process involving a substantial modification in orientation and service provision during an era of declining resources and the demand for higher accountability practices in education. Yet, if psychologists wish to stop being mainly identified with assessment-for-placement problems, they must continue their involvement with prevention and mainstream-based solutions.

The education, health and mental health services needs of newcomers are too complex to be addressed by one profession or by one system at a time. Co-ordinated, multi-disciplinary approaches are likely to lead to sensitive counseling and effective consultation. Familial frames of reference are culturally based and need to become familiar to psychologists and other helping professionals. Without an inclusive cultural context, service providers may incorrectly judge behaviors as symptoms of psychopathology. Factors related to age, gender, education, and family position may impact on the assessment and counseling process. Often, cultural explanations for problems may lead to different insights and alternative modes of consultation and intervention services (Cole, 1996a, 1998).

Giordano (1994) has recommended that in order to take into account more culturally compatible services, professionals learn about expressive style and help-seeking practices of the multi-ethnic and minority populations with whom they work. He indicated that helpful mental health guidelines include: a) the assessment of behavior in the context of cultural norms and the importance of ethnicity to the family; b) the validation and strengthening of the consultee's ethnic identity and cultural background; c) the assistance of identifying and resolving family value conflicts; d) the evaluation of the pros and cons of consultant/client ethnic matches; and e) the counselor's ongoing self-assessment related to limits of ethnic knowledge.

Given the ongoing emotional, educational and social needs of newcomer children, it is important for those who service schools to develop partnerships with community agencies and ethnic organizations. Since schools are often the first system newcomers learn about, it is perceived to be a trusted environment which facilitates educational and health services. However, Hicks et al. (1993) stress the fact that there is an incongruity between some immigration policies which welcome newcomers and the reality faced by many children and their families post migration. They caution that "without primary and secondary preventive health strategies for immigrants and refugees at risk, we cannot expect those children and their families to achieve their potential" (p. 83).

Budget cuts to education and community services are increasingly dictating the new realities of social supports. Overburdened community-based services have long waiting lists and are less likely to provide ongoing supports. It is thus important for psychologists employed by school boards to develop, together with other service providers, multicultural and integrated service delivery models. By doing so, they are likely to develop frameworks which facilitate the co-ordination of prevention and intervention functions.

One of the vehicles for service delivery in many North American schools is that of multidisciplinary consultation teams. School teams are designed to support teachers in providing appropriate interventions for students in need of assistance. Some schools have expanded team mandates to include consultative services to staff, parents and community agencies. Advocates of teams highlight the following advantages to this service delivery model: teams encourage sharing of knowledge and resources; group participation often increases acceptance of recommendations made and promotes commitment outcomes; and teams provide appropriate referrals to mental health services and can monitor interventions through cost-effective consultations (Cole, 1992: Cole & Brown, 1996).

Comprehensive multicultural mental health programs in school systems must be ecological in orientation and must support a range of initiatives. The "medical model" of service delivery should be reserved only for those in crisis. Most other types of supports need to be proactive with a view that individual problems are often a reflection of poor interaction between individuals and their environment rather than symptoms of dysfunction (Cole & Siegel, 1990).

Schools are complex organizations which would benefit from mental health staff such as school psychologists assuming diversified roles. A clear commitment to equity and multicultural issues must be reflected in both pre-service and in-service models of training. The profile of communities dictate the need for better links between university trainers and supervising practitioners as well as minority faculty and student recruitment.

Ecological models of multicultural services require conceptual knowledge and skills training. A broader role for psychologists in education will likely provide an avenue for advocacy about the provision of preventative services. This, however, will require knowledge of multicultural education, cross-cultural assessment and consultation skills, anti-racist policies and programs, social skills training, crisis management, and violence prevention. The emerging issues in school communities provide opportunities for partnership between school psychologists and educators. Nevertheless, not all service providers feel competent to handle the increased demands for interventions. In line with the trend toward increased accountability in education and health, there seems to be a growing need to address outcome-based measures for training and practice in the field. Major change in service orientation will consequently require modifications in thinking, planning and professional advocacy (Cole, 1998).

For practitioners in the field of school psychology, essential elements of professional development should be based on adult learning theory. Substantive change in practice often takes several years to achieve, and requires multiple, diverse and ongoing feedback and supports. Adult learners tend to be motivated to participate when they perceive that the learning is related to their needs, rather than an attack on their competence. In addition to resources, cross-role participation is likely to stimulate shared understanding and new approaches to multicultural services.

Referring back to the model discussed in Chapter 1 (Figure 1), readers are invited to add their own examples of primary, secondary, and tertiary services for multicultural students in inclusive school communities.

References

Ajdukovic, M., & Ajdukovic, D. (1993). Psychological well-being of refugee children. *Child Abuse and Neglect, 17*, 843-854.

Alter, R. C. (1992). Parent-school communication: A selective review. *Canadian Journal of School Psychology, 8(1)*, 103-110.

Anastasi, A. (1982). *Psychological testing* (5th Ed.). New York: MacMillan.

Barona, A., & Garcia, E. (Eds.). (1990). *Children at risk: Poverty, minority status and other issues in educational equity.* Washington, DC.: National Association of School Psychologists.

Beiser, M., Dion, R., Gotowiec, A. J., & Huyman, I. (1995). Immigrant and refugee children in Canada. *Canadian Journal of Psychiatry, 40(2)*, 67-72.

Benard, B. (1993). Fostering resiliency in kids. *Educational Leadership, November*, 44-48.

Berry, J. W. (1985). Psychological adaptation of foreign students. In R. J. Samuda & A. Wolfgang (Eds.), *Intercultural counseling and assessment.* Toronto: C.J. Hogrefe Inc.

Bohlmeyer, E. M., & Burke, J. P. (1987). Selecting cooperative learning techniques: A consultative strategy guide. *School Psychology Review, 16(1)*, 36-49.

Borghese, N., & Cole, E. (1994). Psychoeducational recommendations: Perceptions of school psychologists and classroom teachers. *Canadian Journal of School Psychology, 10*, 70-87.

Bransford, J. D., Delclos, V. R., Vye, N. J., Bums, M. S., & Hasselbring, T. S. (1987). State of the art and future directions. In C. Schneider Lidz (Ed.), *Dynamic assessment.* New York: The Guilford Press.

Bretzing, B. H., & Caterino, L.C. (1984). Group counselling with elementary students. *School Psychology Review, 13(4)*, 515-518.

Bruner, J. (1966). On cognitive growth: II. In J. Bruner, R. Olver, & P. Greenfield (Eds.), *Studies in cognitive growth.* New York: Wiley.

Burnaby, B. (1980). *Languages and their roles in educating native children.* Toronto: O.I.S.E. Press, The Ontario Institute for Studies in Education.

Canino, I. A. (1988). The transcultural child. In C. J. Kestenbaum & D. T. Williams (Eds.), *Handbook of clinical assessment of children and adolescents.* New York: University Press.

Carnine, D. (1994). Introduction to the mini-series: Diverse learners and prevailing, emerging, and research-based educational approaches and their tools. *School Psychology Review, 23(3)*, 341-350.

Christenson, S., Abery, B., & Weinberg, R. A. (1986). An alternative model for the delivery of psychological services in the school community. In S. N. Elliott & J. C. Witt (Eds.), *The delivery of psychological services in schools.* New Jersey: Erlbaum.

Cole, E. (1982). Role-Playing: Theory, research, methods of implementation. *Student Services Project Bulletin*, No. 9, Toronto Board of Education.

Cole, E. (1991). Multicultural psychological assessment: New challenges, improved methods. *International Journal of Dynamic Assessment and Instruction, 2(1)*, 1-10.

Cole, E. (1992). Characteristics of students referred to school teams: Implications for preventive psychological services. *Canadian Journal of School Psychology, 8*, 23-36.

Cole, E. (1995). *Role-playing: An avenue for building inclusive classrooms for new Canadian students.* A manual for role-playing sessions for grades 4-6. Toronto Board of Education.

Cole, E. (1996a). Immigrant and refugee children and families: Supporting a new road travelled. In M. Luther, E. Cole, & P. Gamlin (Eds.), *Dynamic assessment for instruction: From theory to practice* (pp. 35-42). Toronto: Captus University Press.

Cole, E. (1996b). An integrative perspective on school psychology. *Canadian Journal of School Psychology, 12(2)*, 115-121.

Cole, E. (1998). Immigrant and refugee children: Challenges and opportunities for education and mental health services. *Canadian Journal of School Psychology, 14(1)*, 36-50.

Cole, E. (2000). Supporting refugee and immigrant children: Building bridges programme of the International Children's Institute in Canada and Overseas. *Refuge, 18(6)*, 41-45.

Cole, E., & Brown, R. (1996). Multidisciplinary school teams: A five-year follow-up study. *Canadian Journal of School Psychology, 12(2)*, 155-168.

Cole, E., & Siegel, J. A. (1990). School psychology in a multicultural community: Responding to children's needs. In E. Cole & J. A. Siegel (Eds.), *Effective consultation in school psychology* (pp. 141-169). Toronto: Hogrefe & Huber Publishers.

Cole, E., & Sroka, I. (1997). *Long term trends of the building bridges program: A thematic summary.* Montreal: The International Children's Institute.

Cole, E., & Warren, R. (1988). *The study skills connection.* Toronto: Toronto Board of Education.

Cole, M. (1975). Culture, cognition and IQ testing. *National Elementary Principal, 54*, 49-52.

Cooper, P. J. (2000). Canadian refugee services: The challenges of network operations. *Refuge, 18(6)*, 14-26.

Copeland, E. P., & Miller, L. F. (1985). Training needs of prospective school psychologists: The practitioners' viewpoint. *Journal of School Psychology, 23*, 247-254.

Corson, D. (1993). *Language, minority education and gender.* Avon, UK: Multilingual Matters Ltd.

Cummins, J. (1979). Linguistic interdependence and the educational development of bilingual children. *Review of Educational Research, 49*, 222-251.

Cummins, J. (1980). The entry and exit fallacy in bilingual education. *NABE Journal, 1*, 25-60.

Cummins, J. (1981). Age on arrival and immigrant second language learning in Canada: A reassessment. *Applied Linguistics, 2*, 132-149.

Cummins, J. (1984). *Bilingualism and special education: Issues in assessment and pedagogy.* England: Multilingual Matters Ltd.

Cummins, J. (1989). *Empowering minority students.* Sacramento: California Association for Bilingual Education.

Cummins, J. (1994). Knowledge, power, and identity in teaching English as a second language. In F. Genesee (Ed.), *Educating second language children.* Cambridge: University Press.

Esquivel, G. B. (1985). Best practices in the assessment of limited English proficient and bilingual children. In A. Thomas & J. Grimes (Eds.), *Best practices in school psychology.* Kent, Ohio: The National Association of School Psychologists.

Estrin, E. T. (1993). *Alternative assessment: Issues in language, culture, and equity. Knowledge brief. II.* San Francisco, California: Far West Lab for Education and Development. Eric, 1-8.

Eth, S., & Pynoos, R. S. (Eds.). (1985). *Post traumatic stress in children.* Washington: American Psychiatric Press Inc.

Feuerstein, R. (1979). *Dynamic assessment of retarded performers: The learning potential assessment device, theory, instruments, and techniques.* Baltimore: University Park Press.

Feuerstein, R. (1980). *Instrumental enrichment.* Baltimore: University Park Press.

Figueroa, R. A., Sandoval, J., & Merino, B. (1984). School psychology and limited English-proficient (LEP) children: New competencies. *Journal of School Psychology, 22*, 131-143.

Fillion, B., & Wright, E. N. (1982). *Recent research Re: Language learning and classroom processes.* Toronto: Research Service #162, The Board of Education for the City of Toronto.

Fletcher, T. V., & Cardona-Morales, C. (1990). Implementing effective instructional interventions for minority students. In A. Barona & E. Garcia (Eds.), *Children at risk.* September 12, 1998.

Fowers, B. J., & Richardson, F. C. (1996). Why is multiculturalism good? *American Psychologist, 51*, 609-621.

Genesee, F. (1994). *Educating second language children.* Cambridge: University Press.

Gettinger M., & Knopik, S.N. (1987). Children and study skills. In A. Thomas & J. Grimes (Eds.), *Children's needs: Psychological perspectives.* Washington, DC: The National Association of School Psychologists.

Geva, E. (2000). Issues in the assessment of reading disabilities in L2 children: Beliefs and research evidence. *Dyslexia, 6*, 13-28.

Giordano, J. (1994). Mental health and the melting pot. *American Journal of Orthopsychiatry, 64(3)*, 342-345.

Gordon, E. W., & Musser, J. H. (1992). *Implications of diversity in human characteristics for authentic assessment. CSE Technical Report 341.* Los Angeles: Centre for Research on Evaluation, Standards, and Student Testing. ERIC.

Hafner, A. L., & Ulanoff, S. H. (1994). Validity issues and concerns for assessing English learners. *Education and Urban Society, 26(4)*, 367-389.

Hamayan, E. V. (1993). Current trends in ESL curriculum. In S. Hudelson, G. Italiano, & P. Rounds (Eds.), *English as a second language.* Thousand Oaks: Corwin Press Inc.

Hays, P. (2001). *Addressing cultural complexities in practice: A framework for clinicians and counselors.* Washington, DC: American Psychological Association Press.

Heald-Taylor, G. (1986). *Whole language strategies for ESL primary students.* Toronto: O.I.S.E. Press, The Ontario Institute for Studies in Education.

Hicks, R., Lalonde, R. N., & Pepler, D. (1993). Psychosocial considerations in the mental health of immigrant and refugee children. *Canadian Journal of Community Mental Health, 12(2)*, 718-728.

Lam, T. (1995). Fairness in performance assessment. *Eric Digest. EDO-CG-95-25, 1-2.*

Levy-Warren, M. H. (1987). Moving to a new culture: Cultural identity, loss, and mourning. In J. Bloom-Feshbach, S. Bloom-Feshbach & Associates (Eds.), *The psychology of separation and loss.* San Francisco: Jossey-Bass.

Lewis-Herman, J. (1992). *Trauma and recovery.* New York: Basic Books.

Luther, M., Cole, E., & Gamlin, P. (Eds.). (1996). *Dynamic assessment for instruction: From theory to application.* Toronto: Captus University Press.

MacIntyre, R. B. (1985). Techniques for identifying learning-impaired minority students. In R. J. Samuda & A. Wolfgang (Eds.), *Intercultural counselling and assessment.* Toronto: C.J. Hogrefe Inc.

Mercer, J. R. (1983). Issues in the diagnosis of language disorders in students whose primary language is not English. *Topics in Language Disorders, 3*, 46-56.

Mevarech, Z. R. (1985). The effects of cooperative mastery learning strategies on mathematics achievement. *Journal of Educational Research, 78(6)*, 372-377.

Meyers, J. (1987). The training of dynamic assessors. In C. Schneider Lidz (Ed.), *Dynamic assessment.* New York: Guilford Press.

Motta, R. W. (1995). Childhood post-traumatic stress disorder and the schools. *Canadian Journal of School Psychology, 11(1)*, 65-78.

Nader, K. O. (1997). Assessing traumatic experiences in children. In J. P. Wilson & J. M. Keane (Eds.), *Assessing psychological trauma and PTSD* (pp. 98-135). New York: Guildford Press.

PL 94-142, Education for all Handicapped Children Act. United States Office of Education, Public Law 94-142. November 29, 1975.

Power, T. I., & Lutz Bartholomew, K. L. (1987). Family-school relationship patterns: An ecological assessment. *School Psychology Review, 16(4),* 498-512.

Price, K. (Ed.). (1995). *Community support for survivors of torture: A manual.* Toronto: Canadian Centre for Victims of Torture.

Pryzwansky, W. B., & Hanania, J. S. (1986). Applying problem-solving approaches to school psychological reports. *Journal of School Psychology, 24,* 133-141.

Reschley, D. J. (1988). Special education reform: School psychology revolution. *School Psychology Review, 17(3),* 459-475.

Reschley, D. J., Kicklighter, R., & McKee, P. (1988). Recent placement litigation: Part II, minority EMR overrepresentation-comparison of Larry P. (1979, 1984, 1986) with Marshall (1984, 1985) and S-1 (1986). *School Psychology Review, 17(1),* 22-38.

Samuda, R. J. (1975). *Psychological testing of American minorities: Issues and consequences.* New York: Dodd, Mead.

Samuda, R. J. (1990). *New approaches to assessment and placement of minority students.* Toronto: Ministry of Education.

Samuda, R. J. & Crawford, D. H. (1980). *Testing, assessment, counselling and placement of ethnic minority students.* Ontario, Canada: The Ministry of Education.

Samuda, R. J., Kong, S. L., Cummins, J., Lewis, J., & Pascual-Leone, J. (1989). *Assessment and placement of minority students.* Toronto: C.J. Hogrefe/ISSP.

Sattler, J. M. (1982). *Assessment of children's intelligence and special abilities.* Boston: Allyn and Bacon.

Sattler, J. M. (1988). *Assessment of children* (3rd ed.). San Diego, CA: Jerome M. Sattler, Pub.

Sattler, J. M. (2001). *Assessment of children: Cognitive applications* (4th ed.). San Diego, CA: Jerome M. Sattler, Pub.

Schneider Lidz, C. (1987). Historical perspectives. *Dynamic assessment.* New York: Guilford Press.

Sewell, T. E. (1987). Dynamic assessment as a nondiscriminatory procedure. In C. Schneider Lidz (Ed.), *Dynamic assessment.* New York: Guilford Press.

Shapiro, E. S. (1990). An integrated model for curriculum-based assessment. *School Psychology Review, 19,* 331-349.

Slavin, R. E. (1983). When does cooperative learning increase student achievement? *Psychological Bulletin, 94(3),* 429-445.

Suberri, K. C. (1987). Children and different cultural backgrounds. In A. Thomas & J. Grimes (Eds.), *Children's needs: Psychological perspectives.* Washington DC: The National Association of School Psychologists.

Thomas, T. N. (1992). Psychoeducational adjustment of English-speaking Caribbean and Central American immigrant children in the United States. *School Psychology Review, 21(4),* 566-576.

Torrance, E. P. (1982). Identifying and capitalizing on the strengths of culturally different children. In C. R. Reynolds & T. B. Gutkin (Eds.), *The handbook of school psychology.* New York: John Wiley and Sons.

Tough, J. (1977). *The development of meaning.* London: Unwin Educational Books.

Tough, J. (1982). Language, poverty, and disadvantage in school. In L. Feagans & D. C. Farran (Eds.), *The language of children reared in poverty.* New York: Academic Press.

United Nations High Commissioner for Refugees. (1994). *Refugee Children.* Geneva: UNHCR.

United Nations High Commissioner for Refugees. (1995). *The state of the world's refugees: In search of solutions.* New York: Oxford University Press.

Vargas, C. M. (1999). Cultural interpretation for refugee children: The multicultural liason programme, Ottawa, Canada. *Refuge, 18(2),* 32-42.

Vygotsky, L. S. (1978). *Mind in society: The development of higher psychological processes.* M. Cole, V. John-Steiner, S, Scribner, & E. Souberman (Eds. & Trans.). Cambridge, MA: Harvard University Press.

Vygotsky, L. S. (1986). *Thought and language* (3rd edition). Cambridge, MA: M.I.T. Press.

Wallace, C. (1986). *Learning to read in a multicultural society.* Oxford: Pergamon Press Ltd.

Weinstein, C. E., & Macdonald, J. D. (1986). Why does a school psychologist need to know about learning strategies? *Journal of School Psychology, 24,* 257-265.

Wenden, A. L. (1986). Incorporating learner training in the classroom. *System,* 14(3), 315-325.

Wiener, J. (1987). Factors affecting educators' comprehension of psychological reports. *Psychology in the Schools, 24,* 116-126.

Wilen, D. K., & van Maanen Sweeting, C. (1986). Assessment of limited English proficient Hispanic students. *School Psychology Review, 15(1),* 59-75.

Wilson, M. S., & Reschly, D. J. (1996). Assessment in school psychology training and practice. *School Psychology Review, 25 (1),* 9-23.

Yalom, I. D. (1985). *The theory and practice of group psychotherapy* (3rd Ed.). New York: Basic Books.

Yau, M. (1995). *Refugee students in Toronto schools: An exploratory study.* Toronto: Toronto Board of Education.

Appendix A: Role-Playing Manual: An Avenue for Building Inclusive Classrooms for New-Canadian Students (Cole, 1995)

The demographic transformation of Canadian communities has enriched schools and created new challenges for educators, students, parents and mental health professions. Schools are often faced with the complexities brought about by migration, acculturation, language barriers and diverse educational experiences. The interactions between the migration process, cultural patterns and developmental stages are important factors in understanding the needs of new Canadian students.

For refugee students and their families, the resettlement process follows traumatic circumstances related to persecution or life-threatening events. These multiple sources of stress often have a cumulative effect and may result in feelings of instability, physical and somatic problems, as well as difficulties in psychosocial adjustment. Refugee children's developmental histories often include information about disrupted lives, malnutrition, deprivation, significant losses and gaps in education. It is thus important to develop school-based programs and services which include programs for all students (Primary Prevention), programs for students at risk (Secondary Prevention), and services for students whose problems significantly interfere with their adaptation to school (Tertiary Prevention).

Although various types of intervention can be effectively implemented in multilingual, multicultural classrooms, role-playing techniques are particularly appropriate for use within the school milieu. Research findings indicate that this modality has been successfully employed to treat factors including low self-esteem, impaired social skills, insensitivity to thoughts and feelings of others and acting-out behavior. Within the school context, role playing can be easily used with small groups or whole classes and thus provide an avenue for primary or secondary interventions.

This manual was developed for grades 4 – 6 (Junior Division). It is a modified version of an earlier publication by the author (1982). The purpose of the manual is to promote psychological and behavioral changes through guided learning experiences. The sessions were designed to address issues of particular interest to students and teachers whose classes include refugee and immigrant children. The objectives of the program are:

(a) to enhance self-esteem,
(b) to increase sensitivity to thoughts and feelings in oneself and others,
(c) to practice skills that facilitate positive social interaction,
(d) to encourage tolerance and understanding,
(e) to adopt a problem-solving approach in stressful situations.

Role-playing is only one of the techniques used to meet these objectives. Each session makes use of a variety of instructional techniques – role-playing, modeling, mime, and discussion. These strategies encourage all children to become actively involved in the learning process. Since English proficiency is likely to vary among participants, considerable emphasis was placed on the importance of both verbal and nonverbal communication. Also, nonverbal behaviors are largely culture-bound and are likely to convey additional information to that communicated through language.

Both during the sessions and at the conclusion of the program, discussion periods should be viewed as a method of encouraging inexperienced children to learn more effective ways of communicating with their peers and with adults. Overall, the program is designed to emphasize immediate feedback between children's perceptions of their surroundings and the environment itself. The use of drama can provide all students with new avenues for clarification of their relations with others, their information about and expectations of society, and their evaluation of themselves.

Guidelines for Consultants and Teachers:

The series of sessions should be jointly facilitated by a consultant and the classroom teacher. Each session should be of approximately one hour's duration. Some sessions may need to be conducted in two parts to allow for maximum participation by students.

It is recommended that each meeting follow the same format in order for the children to get used to the same sequential steps: a) homework review; b) warm-up exercises; c) presentation of problem; d) preparation for drama; e) enactment; f) discussion of enactment; g) re-enactment; h) summary discussion; i) assignment of homework.

The following are important program components:
(1) Counselors and teachers should strive to create an atmosphere which is not threatening to any of the children. In order to promote positive communication, students should not be allowed to criticize their peers' performance.
(2) During role-playing, the actors should be assigned and called by their role names only. Calling children by their real names may become confusing or may create miscommunication.
(3) Facilitators should attempt to encourage the children to be tolerant toward the experimental behaviors of others during the sessions.
(4) At the outset of each exercise, the facilitators should attempt to assist the children to define the problems faced by the characters in the exercises. Questions such as: "Where does the story take place?" "Who is involved?" "How does the person feel?" should be asked.
(5) Encourage children to think about alternative ways to enact the stories. All ideas should be considered and listened to.
(6) Homework should be an option since the aim is to make it an enjoyable and supportive experience. The children should be offered the alternatives of art, writing or reporting verbally rather than writing out their answers. The students may also be given the option of working in pairs.
(7) The group discussions following each session should be developed with the following goals in mind: a) to give students a chance to verbalize any insights they have derived from the drama; b) to give players a chance to express any feelings generated by the experience; c) to help them to generalize the insights they have derived to other aspects of their lives.
(8) At the conclusion of each session, encourage each child to evaluate the session through group discussion or by filling out a card containing the following categories:
    (1) I liked it very much.
    (2) I liked it.

(3) I am not sure if I liked it or not.

(4) I did not like it at all.

The children's feedback will help the facilitators with planning future sessions and with highlighting specific issues. The children are likely to feel positive about the evaluation process and the option to contribute to the design of the sessions. At the conclusion of the program, the students should be encouraged to use visual arts as an extension of their role-playing experiences.

Session 1

Objective: To Sensitize Students to Thoughts and Feelings of Self And Others in Nonverbal Communication.

This introductory session will have a special format. Briefly explain the role-playing program. Focus on the facilitator's (and or teacher's) interest in how successfully students can make believe or pretend to be someone else. How well can children observe others make believe? How imaginative can they be?

In order to facilitate a brief discussion about role-playing ask questions such as: "Do you watch television?," "What are your favorite programs?," "Why?" "What does an actor do?," "Have you ever been an actor in a play?"

Make sure that all participants understand the concepts: imagination, make believe, mime and role-playing. Next, warm-up exercises will be initiated to increase spontaneity, emotional involvement and active participation. Pantomimic exercises are used for freeing inexperienced or shy children to perform with and/or in front of their peers.

1. Warm-up 1 (10 min.):

Choose 3 volunteers and briefly prepare them out of the class. When they return, they mime the same emotions for the group. The children guess what the actors might be thinking and feeling – happy, angry, bored, disappointed. Write the children's guesses on the board.

Warm-up 2:

The other children choose a partner and portray these emotions. The partners have to guess what feelings were conveyed in mime. The children are encouraged to watch one another's portrayals.

Warm-up 3:

Divide the children into groups of three people. Name an emotion and instruct each triad to form themselves into a sculpture conveying this emotion. Suggested emotions might include: fear, bravery, sadness, relief.

2. Presentation of Problem (4 min.):

This week is your birthday. You have just received a wrapped parcel from your family overseas. You have not seen them since you came to Canada seven months ago. Without saying a word, show how you feel when you open the parcel and find your present.

3. Preparation (5 min.):
Discuss how the parcel came to you, how it looks, what you are thinking and feeling. Students should be encouraged to express their ideas with little direction or intervention.

4. Enactment (5 min.):
Every student should take a turn. Ask for volunteers or have everyone mime simultaneously.

5. Discussion (15 min.) and Re-enactment (10 min.):
Following the role-playing, initiate discussion with questions such as: "What do you think Mary was feeling when she saw the present?" Stress the importance of watching others who communicate in nonverbal ways. Encourage positive and constructive comments from the observers. Invite the role-players to provide feedback about their own performance. Ask them what thoughts and feelings they were attempting to convey.

Many of the problems presented then allow the students to reverse roles and re-enact the drama, until all have participated.

6. Summary (10 min.):
People of all ages can often let you know how they feel or what they think without words. Ask the students to describe situations in which this has happened to them. What can happen in situations in which you misread other people's nonverbal communication? What can you do about it? Are you aware of using nonverbal communication with others?

7. Homework Assignment (5 min.):
Distribute a lined homework book to each student (print each child's name on the front of the workbook). Before the next meeting, ask each child to record a time when he/she gave 2 messages to other people without saying a word. Ask them to write about it or make a picture. Children who have language barriers may wish to draw faces to help them remember the experience. Students may also choose to cut out magazine or newspaper pictures and paste them in their workbook.

Session 2

Objective: To Examine the Effects of Social Acceptance or Rejection on Self Esteem.

1. Warm-up 1:
Ask students to choose a partner for a mirror exercise. Have them stand facing each other. One student is the reflection in the mirror, while the other student is facing the mirror. Provide specific instructions to the partners: "Look into your partner's eyes. When you move, you must move together. Try to work in a way that will make it hard to know who is the person and who is the reflection."

Warm-up 2:
Your friend went back to another country for a month to visit his grandparents. He/she just came to see you. In mime, role-play your reunion.

Warm-up 3:
Your parent is about to leave for night school and asks you to baby-sit your little brother. Your friend just arrived and wants to play with you. In groups of four, repeat the above sequences in mime. Assign roles and then reverse them.

2. Homework Review:
Ask the students to volunteer and share their homework experiences. Encourage participation of all children. Try to focus the discussion on what they have learned and how this might affect their behavior in the future.

3. Presentation of Problem:
You and your family came to Canada from a war-torn country. It was very dangerous to escape and you left some family members behind. Now, you are finally settled and going to school. One day, you go out to the yard and see a group of students fighting. They look very angry. You tell them not to fight but one student says: "Stay out of it! Why don't you just go back to where you came from!"

4. Preparation:
In groups of four, have the students discuss their thoughts and feelings and how they would express them if they were part of the group or if they were the new Canadian child.

5. Enactment:
One volunteer will portray the experience of being the rejected child. Then, ask each group to do a reversal of roles. This will help all children better understand the impact of social rejection on self-esteem.

6. Discussion:
The focus should be upon the thoughts and feelings of the students who were subjected to anger and/or social rejection. Ask what could be done in order to solve such a conflict?

7. Re-enactment:
Repeat steps 3 through 7 with a second problem:
     A television reporter came to your class for an interview. The reporter heard that you were very helpful in welcoming a group of new Canadian families and students in your community. You are describing what you did, who helped you and how your welcome was received by those involved.

8. Summary:
Ask the children to compare the two situations and the implications of each for all participants. Focus on why people experience such thoughts and feelings in these situations. Encourage realistic assessments of the situations.
     What are possible explanations for each event? Consider the feelings of disappointment, anger, and sadness, and then consider the positive feelings related to the second problem. Ask the students to discuss their experiences in similar situations. Have them describe how they felt, what they thought and how they coped.

9. Homework:
Ask the students to write or make a picture about two experiences: one in which they felt welcomed by peers and a second in which they felt excluded from social activities. Ask them to use adjectives to list their feelings and thoughts.

Session 3

Objective: To Sensitize Students to Thoughts and Feelings about Themselves and Others in Situations Involving Success and Failure.

1. Warm-up 1:
You are on a beach in a warm country. You can hear the waves while you build a sandcastle with your brother/sister. You have been working for a long time and your castle is almost finished. Suddenly, a big wave comes and sweeps your castle away. Select a partner and, in mime, pretend that you are in another country and hear the sea.

Warm-up 2:
Ask the students to change partners. Re-enact the situation using verbal communication. Stress the importance of getting ideas across by using body language as well as words.

2. Homework Review:
Have the students read or show their work. Ask for volunteers only. The children will likely describe their stories of acceptance and rejection. Briefly review what was discussed in the previous session concerning the above implications for attitude toward self. Will the children modify their behavior in similar future situations? Why? Why not?

3. Presentation of Problem:
Your teacher requested that each student prepare a short speech on the meaning of friendship. The speech is to be given in front of the class. You have only been in Canada for a year and you speak with an accent. In your home country, you were a very good speaker who was always chosen to represent your class in school plays or public speaking. Now, you are not very sure of yourself.

4. Preparation:
Discussion in groups will focus upon: What were your thoughts and feelings when the teacher presents the task? What might you say to the teacher? What might he/she tell you? Who can help you with the assignment?

5. Enactment:
Students will work in groups of three. One will be the teacher. The use of role-reversal will allow each child to play the role of the new Canadian student.

6. Discussion:
Have the children examine both what the teacher and new student might be thinking and feeling and how they felt in each role. What might they say to the child who is unsure of him/herself?

7. Re-enactment:

Steps 3 through 7 will be repeated with a second problem: You have been practicing with the school's basketball team every week. You feel ready and proud of your skills. Although you are new to the school, you have made many friends on the team. Now the game everyone has been waiting for is about to begin. When you hear the referee's whistle, you freeze. Your friends begin to play but you just stand there.

8. Summary:

The emphasis in the discussion should be on what the student wanted to say in each situation. Encourage the students to share similar experiences with one another. Hopefully, they will learn that, at times, others feel the same way they do.

Make sure to include in the discussion information about realistic and appropriate attitudes and behaviors when experiencing failure or success. Stress the importance of trying to make the best of our abilities; that everyone has weaknesses in some areas and that assistance is available in order to overcome learning or social difficulties. Ask the students to identify areas in which they feel successful. If they need assistance, who do they approach?

9. Homework Assignment:

Ask the students to briefly describe in their notebooks a time in which they experienced some failure in or out of school. Ask them to make a list of four things they would do or say to themselves if this happened to them again. Ask the students to bring to the next session pictures or items which are related to a success experience in any area of their lives.

Session 4

Objective: To Sensitize the Students to their Own Thoughts and Feelings Regarding Guilt and Self-blame.

1. Warm-up 1:

One morning, you stand with your friends in front of the school and start a snowball fight. Some students start to pitch snowballs and others duck. A car is approaching and in no time at all the entire front windshield gets covered with snowballs. The school principal stops the car and gets out!

When this exercise is finished, students return to their seats. Ask for a few comments about how they felt and what they thought as they threw snowballs at the car. When they saw the principal, were they scared? If the person were a stranger would they feel the same?

2. Homework Review:

Ask for a volunteer to summarize the problem from the previous session. Ask if the homework assignment was easy or difficult. Why? Try to get as many ideas as possible for handling difficult situations constructively. List the ideas on a flipchart or the blackboard. Then, invite the children to show what they brought from home. The items reflect success experiences that they are, no doubt, proud of.

3. Presentation of Problem:
When you fled your country, you lived for a while in a refugee camp. Your mother and father managed to bring with them very few belongings. When you settled in Canada, they showed you some pictures of your grandparents. They framed one picture and hung it in the entrance to your apartment. You have always liked this special picture. But this afternoon as you take your coat off, you accidentally knock the picture. The glass smashes when it hits the floor.

4. Preparation:
Students will discuss their reactions and plan what they might say and do. They will also consider what their parent(s) might feel and do.

5. Enactment:
Ask the students to work in pairs. Ask for one student to volunteer to portray the role of the child, from taking his/her coat off, through smashing glass, until the parent comes in later and sees the picture on the floor.

6. Discussion:
Help the children discuss typical thoughts and feelings which might be communicated in such instances. Which reactions were unsympathetic or self-defeating? Why? Help students become aware of the other person's point of view in this situation. Make sure they realize that what is said or done at the time will be influenced by stress and may not reflect true feelings.

7. Re-enactment:
Ask each pair to change roles (child and parent) and re-enact the situation. This time, each person is more aware of how the other person is feeling – "even if my parent is angry with me, maybe I could make them feel better;" "I know it is my fault that the picture frame is broken, but I did not mean to do it and feeling guilty is not going to repair it."

8. Second Problem:
Steps 3 through 7 will be repeated with the following problem:
    You and two other friends like to eat your lunch together. The new Canadian student in your class brings foods you have not seen before. She dresses differently and eats alone. You and your friends are in a silly mood. You make faces, whisper to one another, and look at the girl. She feels sad and lonely. You later learn about the hardship her family went through prior to coming to Canada. You feel ashamed of yourself.
    In groups of four role-play the situation. In the follow-up discussion focus on the relevant issues. Make sure the children understand different points of view and how to cope with feelings of guilt.

9. Summary
The students will consider the effects of self-blame and guilt on their attitudes toward themselves. Was any malice intended in cither situation? Stress the positive and constructive things that can be said and done when you feel guilty. Try to help the children understand that everyone has accidents and that dwelling on feeling negative towards yourself does not help the people involved and can become destructive.

10. Homework:
Each student will ask either a parent, sibling, or friend to describe a situation in which they did something unintentionally that caused pain or hurt feelings to someone else. The students should ask the person to tell how they felt, and what they did or said in that situation. What were the students' reactions when they heard the stories?

Session 5

Objective: To Examine the Effect of Physical Self Concept on Self-esteem.

1. Warm-up 1:
Everyone is asked to stand. In mime, ask the children to imagine that they are the tallest person in the school. Now try to imagine being the oldest person in the world.

You may try some other attributes as long as it becomes clear to the students that physical characteristics are not to be confused with who the people are, nor can we judge others by their appearance. Ask: "Can other people tell the kind of person you are by just looking at you?"

2. Homework Review:
The focus was on situations which might lead to guilt and self-blame. Did you choose to do your homework and discuss these feelings with someone else? What did you learn about the person from this discussion?

3. Problem:
Your new Canadian friend was injured when a bomb exploded during war in his country. Now he is in the hospital following reconstructive surgery. Your teacher and some students have already been to the hospital to see your friend. They told you that he feels much better but that he has got bandages "all over." You are now on your way to the hospital to visit your friend.

4. Preparation:
Students will be asked to discuss what the visiting friend might feel and think before she reaches the friend's room. Next, ask them to consider the thoughts and feelings experienced by the injured friend.

5. Enactment:
Have the students work in pairs. They are to act out the visit itself. Each pair of students will have an opportunity to present the enactment to another pair.

6. Discussion:
Ask the children to consider the most important feelings expressed by the visitor, and the patient's reaction to them. Did he believe that his friend did not care how he looked? How important was the situation to the patient?

7. Second Problem:
Steps 3 through 7 will now be repeated with the second problem:

This is your first day at school in Canada. You have never been to a class where boys and girls study together. These kids do not look like you and do not dress like you. In fact, many of them look alike. The only person who looks like adults you know is the teacher. You wonder whether these kids will befriend you or reject you because of your appearance.

8. Summary:
Have the students consider the issues presented in both problems. Focus upon the effect which a critical attitude may have upon the way they behave towards others. Are they influenced by the appearance of actors on television? Why? Do they really know what kind of people they are just by their looks?

9. Homework Assignment:
Make a list of physical features you like about yourself. Make a list of those you find unattractive. Think about the latter list, how important is it to you as a person. Next, write 3 characteristics which you have as a person that you like and consider important.

Session 6

Objective: To Encourage Tolerance Towards and Understanding of All Students.

1. Homework Review:
It may be embarrassing for students to describe and/or discuss what they wrote about their physical appearance. Consequently, it is suggested that they only be asked whether or not the assignment was helpful to them in any way. What did they learn from doing the assignment?

2. Warm-up:
In groups of three students, identify two things that are the same (alike) for people in your group. Then, list two things that are special (not alike) about each student in your group.

Have a brief discussion about the children's findings. Did they know that they had that much in common? What special things did they learn about their peers?

3. Presentation of Problem:
For the school newsletter, you would like to write a report about the new Canadian students in your school. You are not sure whether they would like to talk about their past. Who could you interview to find out more information? Would you ask the students what they miss? Why they came to Canada? What they like about this new city? What other questions are important to include?

4. Preparation:
In groups of five students, select one child to be the writer. The other students will be the newcomers. Encourage the children to be honest in the interview process and discuss their thoughts and feelings.

5. Enactment:
Ask the children to enact the situation. Then, encourage the use of role-reversal to make sure that reluctant or shy classmates have an opportunity to play the role of the interviewer.

6. Discussion:
Students should discuss how it felt to be in the role of the interviewer and in the role of a new student. Help them conclude that this was a learning experience for all involved and that newcomers who are listened to feel welcome. Writing a report about students from other countries will help them feel part of the school community.

7. Second Problem:
Steps 3 through 7 will be repeated with the second problem: Pretend that your family moved to another country, where English is not spoken. On your first morning at school, you arrive early and stand in the corridor. Several students come by, they speak to you but you do not understand a word. They repeat sentences but you can't answer in their language. You finally say: "English, I only speak English!" What do you think will happen next? How could the students communicate in nonverbal ways?

The discussion after the enactment will focus upon the behaviors, thoughts and feelings of those involved. Ask: "Do you know people who speak other languages?" "Did you ever visit a country whose people did not speak your language?" Imagine how it must feel.

8. Summary:
The discussion should allow the children to compare the two situations. Hopefully, they will conclude that understanding and tolerance build inclusive communities. Remind them about the importance of both verbal and nonverbal communication.

9. Homework Assignment:
Ask the students to interview a new Canadian student in their school. What did they learn about the person and her/his background? What did they tell the students about their background? Have them summarize the information in a question and answer format.

Session 7

Objectives: 1. To Encourage Realistic Assessment and Acceptance of One's Strengths and Needs at a Given Point in Time; 2. To Develop and Learn Strategies for Overcoming Weaknesses.

1. Homework Review:
Review the assignment. Ask for a few volunteers to either read or discuss their interview findings. What did the children learn from the process? Do they have a better understanding of their new friends or schoolmates?

2. Warm-up:
In your places, and without speaking, pretend that you are the best runner in your school. You have just won the city championship in running. Show us how happy and confident you

would look because of your success. Now pretend that you are the gym teacher. You organized the students who participated in the championship and now, it is time to drive back to school. Some of your students are happy with their participation; others are disappointed with their results.

Have a brief discussion comparing the roles of the winning student and that of the teacher. Ask about their skills and how they feel about themselves and their actions that day.

3. Presentation of Problem:

In your class, you have a big world map. The teacher asked the students: "On the map, find the country you or your family came from. Then, in groups of five, tell the children two things you know about the country. Role-play being a guide who takes a group of tourists to that country. Point out things that might be of interest to them." When you hear the teacher's instructions, you become anxious. As a new Canadian student, you know that when you speak English you often make mistakes and are at a loss for words.

4. Preparation:

Discuss the thoughts and feelings of the children in different roles. Encourage empathy and an open exchange of ideas.

5. Enactment:

Ask for a group of five students to volunteer and enact the problem in front of the class. One should play the reluctant student.

6. Discussion:

Students should attempt to understand the stress involved in such a situation. Ask questions such as: "Did the new Canadian student have self expectations which were too high?," "Was this a realistic assessment of what he/she was capable of achieving?" "How might you help others who are in a similar situation?"

7. Re-enactments:

Re-enact and discuss until all groups have portrayed their interpretation of the problem. After each re-enactment, consider new ideas that emerged, and review whether or not the conclusion was satisfactory.

Steps 3 through 7 will then be repeated with the second problem your class is planning a French quiz competition with another grade. You are told that the teachers will give oral questions to eight students from each class, and that the team, which gives the greatest number of correct answers, will be the winner. You were good in French in your home country as you went to a French school. However, since you came to Canada a year ago, you concentrated primarily on learning English. When you hear about the competition, you feel that you really want to participate and to represent your class. Two of your classmates are trying to persuade you that you should not try.

The discussion after each enactment will focus on the reactions of those involved. Specifically, how realistic was the key student's assessment of his French abilities. Were the persuading students lacking sensitivity? Ask: "Why did they behave the way they did?," "What did they learn about their classmate?," "What did he/she learn about them? Him/herself?"

8. Summary:
Have students consider differences in perceived abilities across people, and strengths and weaknesses in any one person. Hopefully, the discussion will lead to ideas about using strengths and learning ways to overcome weaknesses or lack of skills at a given point in time.

9. Homework:
The students will be asked to make two lists in their notebooks. In one they are to describe their abilities and skills, and in the other, their relative weaknesses. Give the students some examples of areas they might want to think about. They should then think about how they might best develop their strengths, and improve their areas of weakness.

Session 8

Objectives: 1. To Sensitize Students to Feelings of Loneliness, Both in Themselves and in Others; 2. To Develop Ideas for Combatting Loneliness.

1. Homework Review:
As in previous reviews, consider any effects the assignment had upon their self knowledge, without discussing actual comments made in their notebooks. Ask the students to consider what implications the two lists might have for their attitudes about themselves. Would they recommend such an assignment to students in other classes? Why?

2. Warm-up:
In mime, walk around the class to everybody else and greet them. Be aware of all these friendly people around you. Take someone's hand and imagine that you are out in a park walking with them. In mime, show us what you see.

When the children return to their places, ask them what they think about making friends. Ask: "What does friendship mean to you?" "How good a friend are you? Give an example."

Following their comments, ask the children to imagine that each one of them is alone in the classroom. "How does it make you feel?"

3. Presentation of problem:
A new neighbor, just about your age, has moved into the apartment next door. His family speaks a language you have never heard before. You are not even sure that he speaks English. One night, you hear your next-door neighbor crying. Every day for the past week you have seen this boy sitting by himself in the schoolyard. You finally decide to go and speak to him.

4. Preparation:
Consider your reactions, why it took you a week to approach the boy and how you feel now that you are about to speak to him. Then discuss how the new boy might have felt, sitting alone each day, and what he might think as he sees you coming towards him.

5. Enactment:
In dyads, students should volunteer for each role. Let the enactment proceed to a natural conclusion.

6. Discussion:
Students should share information about playing the roles of the new neighbor and the welcoming student. Ask them if they ever felt or acted like the two boys in the story.

7. Re-enactments:
Students will then be asked to reverse roles and re-enact the drama, until all children have participated. Once again, stress novel ideas or ways to draw the new neighbor away from a position of loneliness. Each time ask the students to reflect about how it feels to be a friend.

Steps 3 through 7 will then be repeated with a second problem: Since you came to Canada, you have been waiting for a letter from your best friend. Every day after school you check your mailbox, hoping to find a reply to your letter. Today, you and two other kids from your school walk home together. When you reach your building, you open the mailbox and find a letter from your friend. You read it and become sad. The children from your school ask why you look so serious. You tell them: "My friend wrote that they still have a war. He cannot go to school because it is dangerous."

8. Summary:
Have the students comment about the two situations and describe the feelings of loneliness. Help them discriminate between "being alone" and "feeling alone." Ask them to verbalize increased sensitivity to perceiving loneliness in others, and what they might do to help.

9. Homework Assignment:
Ask each student to write a list of 3 to 5 things that he/she might do when feeling lonely. Ask them to think about activities which help them overcome negative feelings.

Session 9

Objectives: 1. To Sensitize Students to Feelings of Helplessness Which They Might Experience; 2. To Develop Constructive Responses When They Become Aware of These Feelings.

1. Homework Review:
Briefly review the theme of loneliness. From the students' homework, elicit as many suggestions as possible for combating loneliness. List all ideas on the board or a flipchart. Ask if anyone experienced loneliness during the week and, if so, how they were able to cope with it.

2. Warm-up:
In mime, imagine that you and your family are in a plane on your way to Canada. This is your first flight ever! Your baby brother cries and you try not to talk about your fears. Suddenly, the captain announces that due to the bad weather, you will pass through turbulence. This will be a long flight and you feel helpless.

Discuss students' thoughts and feelings briefly and extract some suggestions about what the person might do. Ask the students to now imagine one positive activity they could do during this flight.

3. Presentation of Problem:

The fire alarm goes on in your school. The teacher asks each of you to form a line and leave the class. When you hear the alarm you are terrified. Last time you heard a similar sound, it was a warning of danger and bombing of your city in another country. These memories come back to you now. You have not thought about it for a while. You start to cry and do not know what to do.

4. Preparation:

Have students consider the child's thoughts and feelings in this situation (insecure, nervous, fearful, etc.). How do the other students and the teacher feel when they see him/her crying? Can they understand what is happening?

5. Enactment:

Have half of the students be the class and half the observers. One student should volunteer to play the teacher; another student will act in the role of the new student.

6. Discussion:

Consider themes which might emerge in the discussion, including the sensitivities of those involved. Did any of them feel this helpless in past situations? Who could be called upon to help?

7. Re-enactments:

Re-enact the drama with the remaining students who were the observers. Conclude the discussion by soliciting further suggestions for solutions in such stressful situations.

Repeat steps 3 through 7 with the second problem: Since your class is comprised of many new Canadian children, your teacher has organized a trip to downtown. A few parents join the class and you ride the subway to City Hall. You and another child talk about the fact that you saw pictures of your old country on the news last night. You look around at all these buildings and streetcars. You have never seen such high-rise buildings or such wide streets before. After a while, you and your friend realize that you are lost. You do not even know who to ask for help.

Have the students enact the roles. Try to stress the need to communicate with others in such situations in order to solve problems. Ask: "What solutions would work in this case?;" "When we feel helpless, who could help?"

8. Summary:

In comparing the two situations the students should learn to perceive that feelings of helplessness are reduced considerably by communicating and sharing with others. They should also consider the advantages of adopting a problem-solving orientation when they become aware of these feelings.

9. Homework Assignment:

Ask the students to describe a situation they have experienced which resulted in similar feelings to those discussed in the session. Ask them to describe their responses. Were they able to overcome feelings of helplessness?

Session 10

Objectives: 1. To Sensitize Students to Feelings of Exclusion and Loneliness, Both in Themselves and in Others; 2. To Develop Ideas For Combatting Exclusion and Loneliness.

1. Homework Review:
Consider any effects the assignment had upon the students' thinking and behavior. Ask for people who wish to read their work or share oral information. Did they gain new insight about themselves or their peers?

2. Warm-up:
Without talking, imagine that you are on a train by yourself. You are going to another city to visit a family member. You sit in your seat as the train pulls out of the station. Imagine that by coincidence you meet a friend you have not seen for a long time.

Now, imagine that you are on the same train by yourself. In the carriage, you see another student from school who is sitting with his family. You smile at him/her and wave. The student pretends not to know you. In mime, show us how this makes you feel.

When the students return to their places, have a short feedback discussion. What do they think about companionship? Why did the student in the second warm-up exclude someone he/she knew?

3. Presentation of Problem:
You are a new student who speaks little English. You want to be friendly but you are shy and sit by yourself. A group of students sit in the class before the bell rings. They are having fun and tell stories about a class party they had last year. Each one remembers a funny story. They all laugh and carry on. None of them even looks at you. You feel sorry for yourself because you are excluded.

4. Preparation:
Consider the behaviors, thoughts and feelings of all the students. Discuss how the new student might have felt. Sitting alone each day, and what he might think and feel as he sees the group having fun and talking about the past.

5. Enactment:
Have students volunteer for each role. In groups of six children role-play the situation. Have the children use verbal and nonverbal communication to make the story come alive.

6. Discussion:
Students should consider why the exclusion occurred. Was it intentional? Could we sometimes hurt other people without knowing that we do? Was the new student right to feel the way he/she did?

7. Re-enactment:
Following the discussion, have the students form new groups. Ask them to reverse roles and re-enact the drama, this time including the new student in the discussion. Again, stress new

ways to draw the student away from a position of loneliness. Have them reflect on how it feels to be or become a friend.

8. Second Problem:

Steps 3 through 7 will be repeated with the second problem: You sit in your home after school and feel sad. It is a cold and snowy afternoon. Your parents are out trying to find work in this new city. People at school are nice, but you cannot tell them much about yourself. Your English is not good, you do not understand their behaviors or jokes. This is your first cold winter ever and it seems very long. You find yourself thinking and dreaming about a far-away place, where everything was familiar – the weather, the people, the language and the food.

Each student will portray this role by expressing their (usually subvocal) thoughts and feelings aloud. The enactment will conclude with the children finding something to do and becoming active again. Upon concluding the re-enactments, ask students for any other ideas which they might have that would be suitable in such a situation.

9. Summary:

Have the students comment about the two situations and reflect about the impact those had on them. Help them discriminate again, between "being alone" and "feeling alone." Encourage them to describe situations in which they felt lonely, and what they might have done to overcome these feelings. They might also consider their increased sensitivity to perceiving feelings of exclusion in others, and what can be done to help those involved.

10. Homework Assignment:

Make a list of three things you might do with a new student who speaks little or no English. Consider things that might help him/her overcome feelings of loneliness or exclusion.

Session 11

Objectives: 1. To Sensitize Students to Feelings of Helplessness Which They Might Experience in the School Setting; 2. To Develop Responses Which Might Help Them Overcome These Feelings.

1. Homework Review:

Briefly review the previous session's theme. Elicit as many suggestions as possible for inclusion and/or overcoming loneliness. Ask if they thought about the session during the week and whether it changed their behavior towards themselves or others.

2. Warm-up:

Choose a partner. Imagine that you are friends and that you go to the movies together. After the show you stand near the bus stop. Your friend's bus just left and now you are standing alone. It starts to snow and it gets dark. You are cold and think that maybe you should have stayed home instead of going to the movies. Your parents must be worried about you by now, there is no bus in sight and you feel utterly helpless.

Ask the students for brief feedback and extract as many suggestions as possible about what the student might do. List some ideas on the board or a flipchart.

3. Problem:
Your teacher asks you to work in groups on your art project. You become confused and passive. In your home country, students sit in straight rows and only speak when the teacher gives them permission. You want to participate but you do not know how. The students in your group become angry and tell the teacher: "He/she does not help with the work. We need another partner!" When you hear this you feel helpless.

4. Preparation:
In groups of five choose a student who will role-play the new Canadian child. Another student will play the teacher. What art project are you working on? Consider the behaviors of all participants in the group.

5. Enactment:
Let the drama proceed until the teacher helps the group decide on how best to solve the problem. If they do not become oriented to solve the problem on their own, stop the enactment and ensure that the possibility of a constructive solution comes out in the discussion.

6. Discussion:
Some themes which should emerge in discussion are the nature of the solution, the needs and sensitivities of the new Canadian students and the role of mediation in such cases. Ask: "Does one feel less helpless when there are others who share the same feelings?"

7. Second Problem:
Repeat steps 3 through 7 with the second problem: You and your family arrive in Canada in the middle of the academic year. In order to help with your grade placement, you have to go to a reception center for an interview and some tests. The tests are in your first language. People are nice to you, but they do not know that you have been out of school for several months now. It was not easy to enter Canada and you have been waiting in another country in a camp. The tests make you feel anxious. You begin to answer questions, but you do not trust your answers and feel like giving up!

Have each student enact the role, expressing subvocal thoughts and feelings aloud. Again, try to stress problem-solving solutions or alternatives, rather than dwelling on feelings of helplessness.

8. Summary
In comparing the two situations, the students should perceive that feelings of helplessness could be reduced by sharing the burden with others. They should also consider the advantages of adopting a problem-solving orientation when they become aware of these feelings.

9. Homework Assignment:
Have students read through their notebooks and write a summary about the role-playing sessions. What did they like about them? What did they learn from them?

Session 12

This concluding session is a special one. The children should have been notified ahead of time that this will be a "party" session. Help them feel special by celebrating the cycle of role-playing meetings they have just completed. In addition to sharing some treats, conduct individual interviews with each student. In the interview, the following questions should be covered:

(1) How did you feel about the role-playing sessions?
(2) What have you learned from our sessions together?
(3) Has your behavior changed in any way as a result of the role-playing experience?
(4) Could you suggest how we might improve the sessions for other children your age?
(5) What "problem story" do you think we should add to the sessions?
(6) Would you recommend the experience to others your age? Why? (Why not)?

Thank you for sharing your information with us!

Chapter 12
Bringing Narrative Thinking into School Psychology Practice

Ilze Arielle Matiss

Words are powerful
They create meaning
They can keep us stuck or move us forward
They open windows and doors where we never thought them to be
We create our storied lives with words
Stories can make us free

The purpose of this chapter is to invite the reader into narrative ways of thinking, and to consider how they can be applied within the context of school psychology practice. I was drawn to a narrative approach because in reading about narrative beliefs, purposes, and practices I was struck by the positive, respectful, and collaborative nature of this work. Through a narrative lens there is always hope that circumstances and interactions can change, and that access to personal resources is possible.

I have been working and studying in the fields of school psychology and psychotherapy for the past 15 years. My research interests (Matiss, 1998, 2001) have been in exploring aspects of ethnic identification through life history research. This experience introduced me to the world of narrative in research and therapeutic work. Over the past three years I have been broadening the scope of my work in consultation, assessment, and therapy through the narrative lens[1].

---

1 During the past three years I have been involved in the Brief Therapy Training Centre – International Extern training program in narrative and solution-focused therapy at the Hincks-Dellcrest Centre in Toronto, Ontario. My supervisors in this setting are Jim Duvall and Eric King, and my work with them has greatly influenced my thinking and my practice. Through workshops, conferences and, the Extern training program, I have also had the good fortune of having heard first hand the ideas and thinking of internationally recognized writers, presenters, and therapists in this field. These include Judy Myers Avis, Yvonne Dolan, Jim Coyne, Don Efron, Joseph Eron, Bala Jaison , Sue Johnson, Stephen Madigan, Scott Miller, Michael White, John Walters, Michael Yapko, Karen Young, and Jeffrey Zeig.

What Is Narrative Thinking?

Narrative beliefs and practices share the theoretical underpinnings of post-modern, social-constructionist thought (see discussions in Freedman & Combs, 1996; White, 1998b, 2001; White & Epston, 1990; Zimmerman, 2001) with brief therapies and solution-focused work (see discussions in Berg & Dolan, 2001; Metcalf, 1999; Selekman, 1997). Michael White and David Epston are seen as pioneers in bringing the narrative metaphor and social constructionist thought into therapy practice (Freedman & Combs, 1996). In the narrative framework we think of people as living storied lives. The stories that people tell about themselves help to define who they are at a given time, in a given context, and in relation to whom they are telling these stories to.

In the narrative, metaphor stories are viewed as consisting of events or daily experiences, linked in a sequence, across time (with a past, present, and future), according to a plot (with meanings attributed to them), and influenced by the broader culture or context (Morgan, 2000; Young, 2002). We live many stories at once, and different stories can be told about the same events, but we develop "dominant stories" when certain events become privileged and form a dominant story (Morgan, 2000; Young, 2002). Dominant stories about gender, age, class, race, culture, sexual preference, language, education, etc. in the contexts in which we live influence our own stories. We also have alternate stories that are "more in the background," that can gain a more significant presence in our lives as we reinterpret the meaning of events in the past, present, and future. In the context of narrative thinking stories can be described as "thick" or "thin." Stories become "thicker" as more events are linked across time and have meaning attributed to them (Morgan, 2000; Young, 2002). In narrative writing these elements of stories are also organized into "dual landscapes," the "landscape of action" and the "landscape of consciousness" – the meaning or interpretation that is given to the action and its effect on one's identity, (Bruner, 1986; Freedman & Combs, 1996; Morgan, 2000; White & Epston, 1990). Alternate stories take shape when actions and the meanings attributed to them are linked to the past, present and future.

I invite you to reflect on your own stories about your life. It is likely that you can remember specific situations or periods of time where you felt positive, capable, knowledgeable, happy, lucky, courageous, caring and cared for, connected, and so on. What effect did these experiences have on: your story? your sense of yourself in the world? in relationships? in school? in your career? in your family? as a member of the community at large? What conclusions about yourself did these experiences invite you to make? Perhaps, that you are a courageous, competent person who is loved and able to connect with others. This in the narrative framework is referred to as a "positive identity conclusion." In paying attention to and gathering such positive experiences about our lives, we begin to weave a positive story about ourselves in the world. Similarly, I imagine that there are also situations and periods of time in your life that may have seemed difficult, unpleasant, painful, angry, sad, frightening, unfair, that may have challenged your sense of competence, of being loving or loveable, of being knowledgeable or capable… What "effect" did these experiences have on your sense of yourself at the time or your sense of yourself at a later time? What did these experiences "trick" you into believing about yourself? Perhaps, that you are a stupid, unlucky person who will never learn all the formulas to pass the physics exam no matter how hard you try. From a narrative perspective this is referred to as a "negative identity conclusion." In noticing and collecting mostly only negative, problem-saturated experiences, we build a "problem-saturated dominant story" about who we are. As positive energy attracts more positive energy, negative, problem-saturated energy attracts more problem-oriented energy. Problem-saturated dominant stories usually find many "allies" that help to sustain their validity. In the narrative framework "dominant stories" are explored and "unpacked" (Morgan, 2000; White, 2001) or, in postmodern terms, "deconstructed," to bring in uncertainty and tentativeness about negative identity conclusions (White, 2001), to shake up the certainty of the problem-saturated stories.

In narrative and social constructionist thinking "problems" are believed to lie in the interactions between people not within people. "Externalizing conversations" (Freedman & Combs, 1996; Morgan, 1999b, 2000; White, 1998a; White & Epston, 1990; Winslade & Monk, 2000; Young, 2002; Zimmerman & Dickerson, 1996) are used to help bring the experience of the problem outside of the person. This allows the history and the "effects" of problems to be explored. When "exceptions" and "unique outcomes" are "unpacked" and plotted in the "landscape of action" and the "landscape of identity," then opportunities are created for "alternate stories" to be brought forward, for people to come to new interpretations and meanings of their experiences. "Exceptions" and "unique outcomes" are times or situations when, for example, the person has been able "to stand up to" the problem or when the problem has not been around.

The language of narrative work at first seemed both strange and evocative, and at times, difficult to understand. It is very different from the accepted jargon of psychology. Recently I heard Karen Young (2002) speak at a workshop on "unpacking the narrative suitcase," and she addressed the issue of language. She proposed that narrative is a "way of thinking" that can be incorporated into each individual practitioner's style of working. I find the term "narrative thinking" useful. In narrative thinking and conversations people are interested in fluid concepts like ideas, beliefs, purposes, intentions, preferences, hopes, dreams, practices… In engaging in externalizing conversations, unpacking exceptions and unique outcomes, and exploring alternate stories, narrative writers and practitioners also use metaphors and language such as "standing with" (being in agreement with or embracing) narrative ideas or alternate stories vs. "standing up to" or "shrinking" problems in their narrative conversations.

I found that I embraced the ideas of narrative immediately, and that it has taken time to learn and discover ways of implementing some of those ideas in my own work. In retrospect, this happened both gradually and immediately, and continues to unfold. In being introduced to narrative thinking, it increasingly became the lens through which I view the world. "Viewing" does not always, immediately, nor consistently translate into "doing," because there are times when I do not feel or trust that my voice is strong enough, clear enough, legitimate enough to "stand with" narrative ideas in all situations. However, having embraced this way of thinking always leaves me hopeful that there is a way to bring forward yet another alternate story in my own life, the lives of the students, parents, teachers, administrators, schools, and communities within which I work and live.

Dominant Stories in the Schools

Schools have complex cultures and dominant stories. People in school communities often have diverse experiences with schools, as students, as parents, as teachers, as administrators, as members of the community, as the school board, and as the government funding schools.

In our practice as school psychologists the dominant "discourse" or story about our work is often the problem-saturated stories of children facing difficulties at school, the concerns of their teachers and parents. Janelle won't pay attention. Dylan can't read. Jessica refuses to attend school. She won't do her work. Dylan is depressed. Nicholas acts out, is disruptive, disrespectful, ADHD, ODD, maybe even CD....

Often the expectation within the dominant story is that our role as the "expert" school psychologist is to *fix* the problem, that is, "fix the *problem* child." This places the responsibility on the professionals, and creates demands that are likely impossible to meet single-handedly. Narrative practices aim to reconnect people with responsibility for their own lives. In this postmodern framework, the notion of the "expert" is challenged by a more transparent and collaborative attitude of practitioners. People, clients are seen as the true experts in their own lives, and it is believed that they already hold the knowledge that will change their stories.

One of the dominant stories in the culture of schools is that all children should be able to learn in the way that they are being taught by their teachers, and in the same way and at the same rate as most other children seem to be able to learn. When a child struggles, the dominant story is that the problem lies within the child. We as a system identify the problems within the child. Assessment is often a part of this problem-in-the-child identification process, and giving the child a label is often an outcome of this process. The child is identified with a diagnosis such as a learning disability, attention-deficit/hyperactivity disorder, oppositional defiant disorder, pervasive developmental disorder. The child is identified as "exceptional" by the school board, the child becomes eligible for a different kind of program or more support at school, and the child may also be referred for medical interventions to alleviate his/her problem.

This then becomes another dominant problem-saturated story by which that child is "invited" to live his or her life. There are many discussions in the literature addressing the impact of this dominant problem-saturated story on people's lives, and practitioners have described many examples of how they have come to challenge those dominant stories and "stand with" narrative ideas in such contexts (Gorman, 2001; Huntley, 1999; Morgan, 1998; Todd, 2000, to name a few). In my own work in the schools at present and in the process of becoming registered as a psychologist, I find myself looking for ways to "stand with" narrative ideas while at the same time working within the demands of dominant story driven professional expectations.

Issues for School Psychologists

During the process of writing this chapter I have been reflecting on the questions: What keeps me in school psychology? What excites me about working in the schools? The thoughts that immediately came to mind were about how narrative and solution-focused ideas bring energy and hope into school psychology practice at a challenging time in the profession. Experiences of people having renewed energy and passion for their work as they begin to apply narrative ideas, is cited by many authors in the literature on narrative approaches in therapy, in schools and classrooms, and other community settings (Freedman & Combs, 1996; Morgan, 1999c; O'Hanlon, 1994; Taylor, 2001). I too have experienced a sense of renewal as I have been increasingly viewing experiences, interactions, and relationships in my work in schools through a narrative lens, through a narrative story structure.

Narrative beliefs have influenced the views that I hold about children, parents, and teachers as experts on their stories and experiences, and as having the inner resources to allow changes, solutions, growth, and alternate stories to unfold. In this way of thinking, the role of the psychologist could be seen as a facilitator – a person who asks good questions that open new doors and windows of possibilities for change. In asking good questions, showing curiosity about exceptions to the dominant problem-saturated stories, and noticing and "unpacking" "sparkling moments" in a person's life during consultation, counseling and assessment interviews, school psychologists can provide their clients (children, parents, teachers) with the opportunity to deconstruct and begin to change the stories that they live by and bring forward alternate stories. The act of having conversations, of interacting with people has an effect on their stories. Conversations lead to the "co-authoring" of stories in each other's lives. These ideas bring great possibility and hope, but they also bring great responsibility. These ideas demand of us as professionals and human beings that we carefully consider the effects of our words, conversations, views, beliefs, practices, and stories on other people. Narrative thinking draws our attention to issues of power (White, 1998c).

We have a professional and ethical responsibility to consider the effects of our diagnoses and our words. Research on teacher attitudes and expectations reminds us of the impact that expectations can have on children's learning. As school psychologists, social workers, special education consultants, and educators we have put a lot of time and energy into consciousness raising about the desirability of finding the positives in all children. Narrative ideas demand of us to remain aware that our interaction with people's stories has an effect on them. Thus, even when working under the influence of dominant discourses, such as current practices of government, demands for "accountability" in education that often require the gathering of information that is not necessarily helpful in supporting alternate stories, working with narrative beliefs reminds us to, in the very least, bring balance to those views.

The Influence of Narrative Thinking on Assessment and Consultation

At first glance it may appear that the narrative and assessment/diagnostic worlds are at polar opposites which cannot be reconciled. Indeed, I have found myself in a clash of paradigms as I have been working to bring narrative ideas into my assessment work.

Assessments comprise a large proportion of my work in school boards. As I have taken on a narrative way of thinking, I have struggled with the challenge that assessments have brought to my "standing with" narrative ideas. What I have noticed is, that as my experience and experimentation with narrative ideas has evolved, this thinking has had an effect on my work within the assessment context as well. I have become more aware of the therapeutic potential of assessment encounters. These encounters offer opportunities for generating alternate stories with children and adolescents, their parents, teachers, administrators, and school support staff.

In my training in school psychology, my work has been influenced by many excellent supervisors[2] who led me to alternative ways of working with children, their parents and teachers. I was encouraged to think of the role of psychologists as a "strength detective" when working with children with difficulties. Narrative thinking has sharpened my curiosity about alternate stories and has allowed the metaphor of the "strength detective" to evolve into a richer, "thicker" idea; that of detecting alternate

---

[2] Dr. Ester Cole was my first role model for school psychology practice that extended far beyond psychometrics. This included development of school support teams, classroom interventions with students, study skills groups, and supervision in consultation and assessment that took into account the narratives of clients from inner-city and diverse multicultural communities. Dr. Anne Green cast assessment in a positive intervention frame by introducing me to the role of the psychologist as a "strength detective" when working with children who had learning difficulties. Dr. Myra Kuksis has supported the implementation of the narrative practice of giving voice to children and their families, and bringing forward alternate stories in psychological assessment reports.

stories. The narrative style of interaction in the assessment process allows us to incorporate, "punctuate," and build on the strengths that emerge in the stories.

Narrative ideas have had an effect on the kinds of questions that I ask and how I think about people and problems. In gathering children's histories from them and their parents, I try to bring forward the "stories of ability" (Morgan, 1998) as well as difficulty. I try to not assume that I know what people have experienced, thought or meant by what they say, and instead encourage "rich," "thick" descriptions of their stories. I try not to leap immediately to my dominant problem-saturated story checklists that have been deeply entrenched in my thinking, but look to children and their parents as the experts on their own lives, experiences and stories.

I have found a number of techniques used frequently by narrative and solution-focused practitioners to be helpful in the assessment process. Externalizing conversations about problems is one way of bringing narrative ideas into the assessment conversations (see Appendix A for example). Similarly exploring exceptions to the problem and "sparkling moments" are ways of bringing alternate stories forward.

Scaling questions (Berg & Dolan, 2001; Metcalf, 1999; Selekman, 1997) are a way of accessing children's, parents', and teachers' assessment of where things are at, what is most important, what needs to happen, and how to move stories in a more positive direction. They are also helpful in assessing how serious a problem is, or how safe or at-risk a young person is when they have revealed concerning information during an assessment interview. Scaling questions can also be used to "track," for example, the strength or frequency of an exception or the severity of a problem over time. This is a helpful technique that can be applied in assessment, consultation, and counseling.

Narrative Ideas in Psychological Reports and Therapeutic Documents

I have also been exploring ways of bringing narrative ways of thinking into my report writing. I have always tried to convey findings in clear straightforward language, and avoid jargon as much as possible. Now I am also consciously drawing out alternate stories about a child and his or her learning, and I try to challenge, when appropriate, the dominant problem-saturated view of the child. The aim is to bring more possibility and success into their learning, and more satisfying constructive views and experiences into their lives.

Reports can be written in ways that can help to deconstruct the dominant problem-saturated stories and amplify emerging alternate stories. Externalizing descriptions that can trace the history, "effects," "tactics," "methods of recruitment" of problems in the lives of the young people being assessed and on others (such as their peers, family, teachers, the school community etc.). Similarly, reports can draw attention to exceptions and "sparkling moments" in children's lives when they have the upper hand on the problem, as well as highlighting children's own solutions. There is an opportunity to not only bring forward alternate stories, but to ensure that the "voice" of the child and parents are also represented among the other voices within the school system (McLean, 1995; Todd, 2000).

Many practitioners (Freedman & Combs, 1996,1997; Hamilton, 2001; Huntley, 1999; Madigan & Laws, 1998; Morgan, 2000; White & Epston,1990 to name a few) whose work is influenced by narrative beliefs and practices make use of a variety of therapeutic documents such as letters, certificates, declarations, lists, drawings, handbooks, videotapes, audiotapes, and notes from the session. I have begun to use narrative documents that I call "assessment certificates" and other therapeutic documents, such as letters, lists, and pictures as an outcome of my assessment involvement with children. I have been using "assessment certificates" (see Appendix B), documents where children's strengths and areas of growth are highlighted, as a starting point for talking about assessment findings with children and their parents, often in the presence of their teachers and/or school administrators. In this way the alternate story is presented ahead of as well as in contrast to the dominant, and often problem-saturated, story. Having an audience provides "outsider-witnesses" to unfolding alternate stories (Morgan, 2000).

At present, I have found a place for my narrative thinking within the assessment framework. Narrative thinking has not changed the comprehensive approach that I take with psychological assessments, but it has primed my curiosity to also more fully explore and "unpack" the alternate stories. At the same time I wonder how my thoughts will to continue to evolve as I continue in this work.

The Story of Dylan – A Case Study from a Narrative Perspective

In the following case study I will illustrate some of the ideas that I have discussed in this chapter. This case shows a way in which a psychological assessment can support and punctuate an alternate story already in the process of unfolding in the school context. Dylan was a grade six student who had experienced long-standing difficulties in acquiring academic skills. At the age of eleven Dylan had extremely limited skills in reading and writing. He was working at a grade one level.

Dylan had been at one of my schools for just over one year when I first met him. A review of his Ontario Student Record and comments made by school personnel indicated that Dylan had carried a reputation as a trouble maker and behavior problem at his former school, and he had a history of suspensions for inappropriate behavior. In fact, he had even been placed in a behavior class at his last school – a large inner-city school. Dylan's difficulties with behavior masked his difficulties with learning. Dylan was a bright child who had learned to hide his academic difficulties. The dominant story that affected the way that Dylan, his school, and his family thought about him was one that focused on the acting out, inappropriate behaviors. To add to the dominant story was a complicated family story.

Narrative thinking can have an effect on assessment and consultation questions – how and what are we trying to answer? We are often striving for better understandings of how children learn more effectively; of what stands in the way of their learning; and of the exceptions that challenge the dominant problem-saturated stories and help bring forward preferred alternate stories. Even diagnoses may assist in bringing forward an alternate story such as LD in the story of Dylan. The following is an example of the way in which language is used in "externalizing conversations."

In the language of "externalizing conversations" a learning disability had been standing in the way of Dylan's learning in his old school. The unidentified learning disability "confused" Dylan and others, such as school personnel, and "tricked" him into drawing negative identity-conclusions about himself – such as, "since I can't read, I must not be a smart person." Frustration and confusion may have also "teamed up against" Dylan, and left him vulnerable to how his unacceptable behavior was "tricking" everyone into thinking that he was trouble. They also had people thinking that Dylan was not doing well at school because he was in with the wrong crowd and because he was not trying hard enough.

The drawing out and development of the alternate story was already well underway at Dylan's new school when I met him at the beginning of his grade-six year. His new school provided a quiet, small school setting with approximately two hundred students, and where teachers knew all the students by name. Dylan was lucky to have sensitive teachers who realized early on that they needed to modify his academic program in the regular classroom as well as through resource/withdrawal support. Dylan had been good at hiding how weak his academic skills were, and other children were not aware of his difficulties as a learner. His work and notebooks were always neatly organized in his bin at the end of the day. Sensitive teachers had provided Dylan private time and space in the resource room at the beginning of the day in which to ease into the day as well as to build his skills in reading and writing. He was also welcome to come to the resource room at the end of the day and during breaks in the school day to listen to books on CDs that were at his interest level, but well beyond his level of reading ability. This is how he was able to feel as well-versed as his grade 6 peers in the first Harry Potter story *The Philosopher's Stone* by J. K. Rowling when the movie came to the big screen and was attended by his class. In this way Dylan was able to make progress unobserved by his peers at first. Similarly, the work that was assigned to him covered the same themes as in the classroom, but at a level where he could participate. In addition to building basic literacy skills, he was also able to get support for classroom work from his resource teacher.

In the story of Dylan, the previous school's dominant problem-saturated story of Dylan as the behavior problem, had negative effects on Dylan's mother's trust of schools, how schools viewed Dylan, evaluated her as a parent, and on her view of what schools were doing for or to Dylan. She could not understand why the school had not taught him to read. Dylan's mother was worried about his frustrations and struggles as a learner. She had started to see herself as needing to be a fighter against those dominant, problem-saturated views of her child and her family. She came into the feedback meeting as a fighter. The meeting was attended by Dylan, his mother, his sisters, his school principal, and myself. We were later joined by his teachers as well. In this meeting the initial focus was on the contents of Dylan's assessment certificate (see Appendix B) in which his strengths and the beginnings of his alternate story were highlighted. The presence of these alternate views allowed the mother to become more of a collaborator with the alternate story than a fighter against the problem-saturated story. The idea of Dylan's "struggle" with a learning disability was also used in strengthening the alternate story of Dylan as a bright, capable student, who had many strengths, who was making many positive choices about his behavior, and who was learning ways to "stand up to" his learning disability and academic difficulties by taking risks and moving forward in his learning.

I have found that using the assessment certificate with children and their families has been extremely positive and helpful. In the feedback interview with Dylan and his mother, it served as an entry point into a potentially difficult conversation from a dominant story view. Beginning the feedback conversation with the contents of this document allowed the alternate story to be brought forward and made visible, and conveyed a message that we were engaging in a conversation that was much broader than the problem-saturated story. The document and conversation punctuated the ways in which the alternate story was already making gains in Dylan's life, and how Dylan and the school were working together to help this happen. The certificate put into Dylan's hand a reminder of the alternate story that he was already living in his school and of himself as a learner, which he could refer to in the future. The problem of the learning disability that had been affecting Dylan's learning in the past, and was still creating challenges at present, became something that could be worked with instead of something that was wrong with Dylan.

The alternate story of Dylan as a smart, talented person with a passion for sports, whose academic difficulties have been affected by a learning disability continues to unfold and continues to challenge the old dominant, problem-saturated story. Several months after my assessment work with Dylan had ended, his resource teacher proudly exclaimed that Dylan had "cracked the code" for reading and that he is taking enormous risks – even suggesting that he would like to read in front of his class! He was also beginning to see himself as a person who had possibilities in his future. He was becoming curious about careers. He wondered out loud about when his resource teacher had known that she was going to become a teacher. He wondered how long people went to college for. When his resource teacher explained that she had been at university for five years and then went on to do her Master's degree, Dylan responded that maybe he would go to college for ten years! The alternate story about his own career options began to take shape – he told his resource teacher that he might even decide to become a doctor! He also revealed some of the "negative identity conclusions" that the "dominant story" had been "tricking" him into believing about himself – like that he thought that his only career choice was going to be working at McDonald's. The realization that he had many options far beyond working at McDonald's allowed Dylan to begin "thickening" his alternate story. He told his resource teacher that he could even own a car. That he *was* going to own a car! The alternate story was bringing hope and positive expectations for the future.

How Do Narrative Ideas Relate to Preventive School Consultation?

In this chapter I have introduced some aspects of narrative thinking and described some ways of applying these ideas in school psychology practice. The primary focus was on using these ideas in an assessment and consultation context, since that is what I have been primarily involved with in my work in the schools and since, to my knowledge, less is written in the literature on this aspect of narrative practice. It is my belief that narrative ways of thinking can have a positive effect on the work of school psychologists regardless of the model that they work under, be it assessment, consultation, counseling, mediated-services (Cole, 1990; Cole & Siegel, 1990) or a combination of these. It is my hope that as you read the ideas presented on the previous pages you came across parts that resonated with your own experiences or your hopes for something different. One of the most powerful contributions, in my experience, of narrative ways of thinking is that they seem to re-ignite a sense of hope, excitement, energy, curiosity, and sense of purpose in those who choose to "stand with" narrative ideas. The implications of this are that in the very least this approach helps to sustain the practitioners' morale in challenging situations.

I have tried to include many references to works in the literature on various aspects of narrative and solution-focused thinking so that interested readers could continue to "thicken" their own experience and understanding of these ideas. There is a rich and growing body of literature beyond what I have been able to mention in this introduction to this way of thinking. The narrative community is making connections worldwide through publications, conferences, workshops, and websites. Although, the roots for narrative ideas were in the context of family therapy, the applications of these ideas have grown far beyond to many different types of communities and contexts, including our schools.

References

Berg, I. K., & Dolan, Y. (2001). *Tales of Solutions: A collection of hope-inspiring stories.* New York: W.W. Norton & Company.

Bruner, J. (1986). Actual minds/possible worlds. Cambridge: Harvard University Press.

Cole, A. L., & Knowles, J. G. (Eds.). (2001). *Lives in Context: The art of life history research.* New York: Altamira Press, A Division of Rowman & Littlefield Publishers, Inc.

Cole, E. (1990). Parent-teacher mediated intervention: A growth promoting process. In E. Cole & J. A. Siegel (Eds.). *Effective consultation in school psychology* (pp. 101-112). Toronto: Hogrefe & Huber Publishers.

Cole, E., & Siegel, J. A. (Eds.). (1990). *Effective consultation in school psychology.* Toronto: Hogrefe & Huber Publishers.

Freedman, J., & Combs, G. (1996). *Narrative therapy: The social construction of preferred realities.* New York: Norton.

Freedman, J., & Combs, G. (1997). Lists. In C. Smith & D. Nylund (Eds.), *Narrative therapies with children and adolescents.* New York: The Guilford Press.

Gorman, P. (2001). Teaching diagnosis from a postmodern perspective. *Journal of Systemic Therapies, 20(1),* 3-11.

Hamilton, F. (2001). Personal books as therapeutic documents. *Gecko: A Journal of Deconstruction and Narrative Ideas in Therapeutic Practice, 3,* 26-33.

Huntley, J. (1999). A narrative approach to working with students who have 'learning difficulties'. In A. Morgan (Ed.), *Once Upon a Time ... Narrative therapy with children and their families.* Adelaide, South Australia: Dulwich Centre Publications.

Madigan, S., & Law, I. (Eds.) (1998). *Praxis: Situating discourse, feminism & politics in narrative therapies.* Vancouver, British Columbia: Yaletown Family Therapy.

Matiss, I. A. (1998). *Lives in changing contexts: A life history analysis of Latvian-Canadian women's stories about being Latvian.* Ph.D. thesis, University of Toronto, Ontario, Canada.

Matiss, I. A. (2001). Moments in time. In A. L. Cole & J. G. Knowles (Eds.), *Lives in context: The art of life history research.* New York: Altamira Press, A Division of Rowman & Littlefield Publishers, Inc.

McLean, C. (1995). Schools as communities of acknowledgement – a conversation with Michael White. *Dulwich Centre Newsletter, nos. 2 & 3, pp. 51-68, Special Issue on Schooling and Education: Exploring New Possibilities.*

Metcalf, L. (1999). *Teaching toward solutions: Step-by-step strategies for handling academic, behavior and family issues in the classroom.* West Nyack, NY: The Centre for Applied Research in Education.

Morgan, A. (1998). Conversations of ability. In C. White & D. Denborough (Eds.), *Introducing narrative therapy: A collection of practice-based writings.* Adelaide, South Australia: Dulwich Centre Publications.

Morgan, A. (Ed.). (1999a). *Once Upon a Time...Narrative therapy with children and their families.* Adelaide, South Australia: Dulwich Centre Publications.

Morgan, A. (1999b). Packing your bags for school. In A. Morgan (Ed.), *Once Upon a Time ... Narrative therapy with children and their families.* Adelaide, South Australia: Dulwich Centre Publications.

Morgan, A. (1999c). Once upon a time ... In A. Morgan (Ed.), *Once Upon a Time ... Narrative therapy with children and their families.* Adelaide, South Australia: Dulwich Centre Publications.

Morgan, A. (1999d). Taking responsibility: Working with teasing and bullying in schools. In A. Morgan (Ed.), *Once Upon a Time ... Narrative therapy with children and their families.* Adelaide, South Australia: Dulwich Centre Publications.

Morgan, A. (2000). *What is narrative therapy? An easy-to-read introduction.* Adelaide, South Australia: Dulwich Centre Publications.

O'Hanlon, B. (1994). The third wave. *Family Therapy Networker, November/December,* pp. 19-29.

Selekman, M. D. (1997). *Solution-focused therapy with children: Harnessing family strengths for systemic change.* New York, NY: The Guilford Press.

Smith, C., & Nylund, D. (Eds.). (1997). *Narrative therapies with children and adolescents.* New York: The Guilford Press.

Taylor, M. (2001). Promoting respect and tolerance in schools: A teacher's perspective. *Journal of Systemic Therapies, 20(3),* 25-30.

Todd, L. (2000). "Letting the voice of the child challenge the narrative of professional practice" in *Adelaide 2000 narrative therapy and Community Work: A conference collection.* Adelaide, South Australia: Dulwich Centre Publications.

White, M. (1998a). Notes on externalizing problems. In C. White & D. Denborough (Eds.), *Introducing narrative therapy: A collection of practice-based writings.* Adelaide, South Australia: Dulwich Centre Publications.

White, M. (1998b). Notes on narrative, metaphor and narrative therapy. In C. White & D. Denborough (Eds.), *Introducing narrative therapy: A collection of practice-based writings.* Adelaide, South Australia: Dulwich Centre Publications.

White, M. (1998c). Notes on power and the culture of therapy. In C. White & D. Denborough (Eds.), *Introducing narrative therapy: A collection of practice-based writings.* Adelaide, South Australia: Dulwich Centre Publications.

White, M. (2001). Narrative practice and the unpacking of identity conclusions. *Gecko: A Journal of Deconstruction and Narrative Ideas in Therapeutic Practice, No. 1,* pp. 28-55.

White, C., & Denborough, D. (Eds.). (1998). *Introducing narrative therapy: A collection of practice-based writings.* Adelaide, South Australia: Dulwich Centre Publications.

White, M., & Epston, D. (1990). *Narrative means to therapeutic ends.* New York: W.W. Norton & Company.

Winslade, J., & Monk, G. (2000). *Narrative mediation: A new approach to conflict resolution.* San Francisco, CA: Jossey-Bass Inc., Publishers.

Young, K. (2002). Unpacking the narrative suitcase. Workshop presented at The Brief Therapy Network Annual Conference, April 23-24, Toronto, Ontario.

Zimmerman, J. L. (2001). The discourses of our lives. *Journal of Systemic Therapies, 20(3),* 1-9.

Zimmerman, J. L., & Dickerson, V. C. (1996). *If problems talked: Narrative therapy in action.* New York: The Guilford Press.

Appendix A: Sondra "Stands Up To" Distraction

Externalizing conversations are one of the foundations of narrative practices. They are generated by the belief that problems are in interactions between people, not within people. The problem is the problem. This allows the history and the effects of problems to be explored – "unpacked" and "deconstructed" – in ways that create opportunities for alternate stories to be brought forward. Resources in the literature in which the process of externalizing conversations is described in great detail include Freedman and Combs (1996), Morgan (2000), White and Epston (1990) as well as Zimmerman and Dickerson (1996). These provide an in-depth view of what externalizing conversations are and how to have them. Many sample questions and case studies are provided to illustrate both the technique and the process. The following is a case example of externalizing – "standing up to" distraction.

Sondra was a grade-5 student who had a long-standing history of academic difficulties, and who, until the middle of grade 4, had attended a French immersion program. At the beginning of her grade-4 year the program was moved to another school that was not her home school. Even though she struggled with academics, she had a group of long-time friends who she had gone to school with since kindergarten. In the middle of her grade 4 year she was transferred to the English stream program in her home school. This was a difficult transition for Sondra – she was separated from her friends and her academic struggles continued because all of her formal instruction to date had been in French. She was originally referred for a psychological assessment because she presented as withdrawn and lethargic, and appeared overwhelmed by the demands of the grade-4 curriculum.

I met Sondra when she was in grade 5, and although she continued to have difficulties, she was also beginning to take risks as a learner in areas that were her strengths. Her areas of strength (alternate story) were singing and art, and she was bringing these skills more into school life. During the assessment Sondra identified that she had difficulty paying attention in class and staying focused on her work, particularly when she was tired or did not really understand what she was supposed to do or what was being discussed in class. Her teachers had identified this as a problem, and Sondra was getting into trouble because of it. Teachers used language such as "She's so distracted. She never gets her work done. She's always bothering other students." Sondra felt discouraged because she wanted to please her teachers, she did not want to be in trouble so much, and she was not sure about how to go about it.

By the time the assessment was completed, the school was able to give Sondra extra support two periods a week with a special education resource teacher who was open to trying new approaches with her. The focus of my intervention with Sondra was on externalizing her problem with distraction. The helpful conversations were primarily with Sondra, but her mother, classroom teacher, and resource teacher were also introduced to the idea. We had conversations about how Sondra was trying to "stand up to" distraction, and wondered if they could help her by noticing times when she was able to do things differently, and not get tricked by distraction.

Sondra and I explored what effects distraction had had on her life at school. Sondra reported that in French class she had been seated by herself at the back of the room because she was always talking to her neighbors in class, she was not getting her work done, and her teacher was "mad" at her because her behavior was disruptive to the class.

We talked about ways that she could "stand up to" distraction (externalizing conversations) and what she would have to do differently, the "do something different" task (Selekman, 1997), to get to sit among her peers in French class.

Initially, I was able to touch base with Sondra weekly by visiting her in her resource classroom, where I was also observing other students that I was going to be working with in the near future. It appeared that she appreciated this contact, and it helped Sondra, her teacher, and myself keep the energy moving around "standing up to" distraction. The effects of "standing up to" distraction were that Sondra participated more confidently in class discussions, tried to get her work done during resource class time, and seemed to be happier as a learner. When my schedule did not allow me to drop in to visit as regularly, I wrote her a note as a way of maintaining the supportive contact with her. Sondra's special education resource teacher (SERT) was "recruited" (agreed) to be her contact person for the following school year to help her keep the idea of "standing up to" distraction alive and to give her support around this.

Appendix B: Examples of Certificates in Assessment and Counseling, Therapeutic Letters, and Lists

Assessment Certificate from Dylan's Story

Features of Dylan's alternate story were summarized in this assessment certificate, and it was used as the starting point for a dialogue about the assessment findings and recommendations, and his alternate story.

This is to celebrate the work of
Dylan
Dylan you have showed many strengths in your work with me:

- Dylan your answers showed that you have well-developed verbal and visual-spatial problem-solving and thinking skills
- You are a smart person who is able to understand and learn new ideas and concepts
- You have good understanding and skills in mathematics
- You are able to remember many things that you see and hear, this means that you have good memory skills that you can use to help you learn
- You are able to keep your work and notebooks neat and organized
- You show pride in your achievements
- You enjoy drawing and art activities
- You have skills in all types of sports
- You are motivated by the spirit of competition and by challenges that you can achieve
- You enjoy working against the clock to complete short paper-and-pencil tasks
- You told me that you can improve your performance on tasks and tests by studying
- Dylan your school has noticed your excellent behavior – you are cooperative, helpful, you get along with children and adults, and people can depend on you

Thank you for your cooperation and hard work!
Ilze

Therapeutic Documents in Jennifer's Story of Courage vs. Worry

Jennifer and her mother were seen in narrative family therapy at a child and family treatment center for six sessions. This therapeutic letter was sent on behalf of Jennifer and her mother to respond to school inquiries and to assist in improving communication between the home and school. It was hoped that the letter would help to "set the record straight" about Mrs. G.'s and Jennifer's intentions and points of view. The story that was unfolding during therapy sessions centered around courage vs. worry. Narrative family therapy combined with school contact through the use of therapeutic letters/documents enabled 12-year-old Jennifer to take her life back from school phobia and anxiety attacks. Jennifer's emerging alternate story is documented using her own words in the certificate that follows the letter to her school.

Dear Principal

You asked me for information during the telephone conversation on [date], regarding your stated three areas of concern with Jennifer: (1) lateness, (2) inability or unwillingness to complete school work, (3) disrespectful behavior toward teachers. The purpose of this letter is to ensure clear communication regarding my comments about our knowledge of Jennifer and Mrs. G. You reported concerns regarding the effects of conflicts between Mrs. G. and the school officials, and worries regarding Jennifer's behavior at school.

The comments that I was able to make regarding Jennifer's current emotional needs, based on our work with her in a therapeutic context, were that Jennifer: has been struggling with the effects of anxiety and worry; has experienced attending school as challenging; has expressed significant sensitivity to criticism, judgment, and perceived disrespectful behavior from others. In contrast, both Mrs. G. and Jennifer expressed positive first experiences in transferring to your school. They experienced the staff and students as welcoming. They felt the transfer was a positive step and gave them hope.

When Jennifer has experienced teacher-student relationships as supportive and nurturing, she has felt more able to take risks as a learner. Jennifer has felt better able to focus and understand what is expected of her, and more able to seek out help at those times. She very much wants to be seen as a valued and contributing member of the class, and to have her work recognized as her own. At the same time she has shown growth over the past months in her ability to stand up to worry and anxiety, as well as show courage in situations that are challenging to her in all areas of her life. She has talents and abilities in areas outside of her schoolwork, which give her strength, and they include her music – playing the alto saxophone.

I have known Mrs. G. to show great passion in defending her daughter, and in trying to support her in difficult circumstances. She also shows great concern for her daughter's wellbeing, and becomes anxious when this feels at risk. In our conversations Mrs. G. has been a strong advocate for Jennifer. She wishes to communicate openly and effectively with the school regarding Jennifer's educational needs.

We discussed that, given the work that Jennifer is doing, it may be helpful to make accommodations in the areas that are difficult for her.

You expressed an interest in my input at a school support team meeting with the G.'s and the members of your team. The Focused-Consultation Team, of which I am a member, works at the treatment center on most Tuesdays from September to June. As I was able to suggest to you fol-

lowing a consultation with my team, our next available appointment for meta-consultation with your team and the G.'s is on [date and time] at the treatment center. Please let us know as soon as possible if this consultation would be helpful in your collaboration with Mrs. G. and Jennifer in exploring how to help Jennifer feel more secure at school.

We look forward to hearing from you with regard to the focused consultation as soon as possible in order to hold that date for you.

Sincerely,

Ilze Arielle Matiss, Ph.D.
Focused-Consultation Team

This is to celebrate that
Jennifer
has discovered that:

– she has a lot of courage in her life
– friends, family, playing her music, "ignoring," and "standing up" for herself also help courage get stronger
– "every problem has a solution"
– worry is a signal that something needs her attention
– courage helps her do what needs to be done

Witnessed by:
Ilze

Liisa Shares Her Ideas About What Helps Her in Her Learning and About Friends

The following list is a summary of a narrative conversation with Liisa who was interested in helping me learn about asking kids good questions. Liisa was a grade-2 student in a French immersion program. She comes from a three-language background, which includes English, French, and Estonian. She is a talented young person who also plays the violin. At the time of this conversation Liisa was becoming easily frustrated in learning situations.

The following is the beginning of Liisa's narrative as it emerged through this helpful conversation. Liisa was given a printed copy of this document in a folder where she could continue to collect and record her good ideas:

What helps me with my learning:

– To practice and repeat new things;
– To work in a quiet environment for some things (but, not for art or free time);

- To work with a buddy to talk about ideas and brainstorm solutions to hard problems;
- To learn about more complicated and interesting ideas and topics (it gets boring when we do something more simple for too long);
- When my friends don't get into silly arguments or conflicts. A friendly environment is good for my learning.

Liisa's ideas about friends ...

- Sometimes friends get into silly arguments. Sometimes it is better to take a break from each other for a while when this happens instead of worrying about who said what and who is whose friend. When we take breaks from our friendships, then we can be friends again in a little while.

In this conversation with Liisa I invited her to talk about her learning. My goals were to be present with her and with where she wanted to lead the conversation, and to convey this to her by frequently reflecting back to her the ideas that she was formulating and sharing in her words. I found that she had a lot of ideas about her learning already, and I hoped that receiving a copy of those ideas would be validating to her.

Chapter 13
Deaf Immigrant and Refugee Children:
A Different Kind of Multiculturalism?

C. Tane Akamatsu and Ester Cole

This chapter focuses on immigrant and refugee children who are deaf. In this sense, deafness acts as a complicating factor, rather than as an explanatory factor, in how these children are to be taught. It is essential that the professionals serving these children and their families be sensitive to, and account for the cultural interpretations concerning deafness, disability, and special education services. It is necessary to acknowledge that within the realm of special education services, deafness (and more specifically deaf culture) can no longer be viewed as the central driving force informing how services are to be provided. Rather, deafness complicates an already complex situation, and constrains how intervention is to be delivered.

Introduction

Both Canada and the United States are countries of immigrants, and the rate of immigration to the country has increased over the past decade. Moreover, nearly three-quarters of immigrant children are of school age (Coelho, 1994; Cole, 1998, U.S. Census Bureau, 2000). Among these are children from war-torn countries, developing nations, and cultures where services for the disabled are minimal or non-existent. According to the U.S. Committee for Refugees, a "refugee" is defined as "a person with a well-founded fear of persecution on account of race, religion, nationality, membership in a particular social group, or political opinion, who is outside the country of his or her nationality and is unable or unwilling to return" (USCR: Evolution of the Term 'Refugee', p. 1). The increase and decline of refugees from various world regions can be traced from recent news events through to the immigration services of various countries, and finally into the resettlement patterns across the country.

Tables 1 and 2 summarize information on countries from which people frequently sought asylum and the approval rates by nationality in the year 2000 for the United States and Canada. In the U.S., asylum seekers most frequently come from Mexico and other Latin American countries (most notably Cuba, El Salvadore, and Guatemala). However, the rate of approval of refugee status for these countries is very low, under 10%. Until recently, Canada typically had not had as many asylum seekers from these countries, but had numbers of people who enter Canada from other countries via the U.S. According to the U.S. Committee on Refugees (2000), countries or ethnic groups that generate the most refugees worldwide are the Palestinians, Afghanis, Sudanese, Iraqis, and Burmese. As can be seen from Table 2, countries with high approval rates for both the U.S. and Canada have suffered from war and internal political upheaval.

Table 1 Leading Source Countries for Refugee Claims to the U.S. 1997-1999 and Canada, 1997-2000 (United States Committee on Refugees)

Source country to U.S.	1997	1998	1999
Mexico	18,684	6,677	2,542
Guatemala	9,886	5,821	2,716
El Salvadore	7,894	5,918	2,783
China	5,771	5,795	5,218
Haiti	5,230	3,375	2,977
India	4,926	2,664	Not available
Somalia	Not available	2,324	3,147

Source country to Canada	1997	1998	2000[a]
Sri Lanka	2,611	2,526	2,906
Czech Republic	1,511	Not available	Not available
India	1,340	Not available	Not available
Iran	1,226	Not available	Not available
China	Not available	2,048	Not available
Pakistan	Not available	1,757	3,111
Hungary	Not available	1,383	2,304
Chile, Argentina, Mexico, Colombia	Not available	Not available	1000 2000[b]

[a]Statistics for 1999 are not available.
[b]Figures for China, Argentina, Mexico, and Colombia were given as estimates.

Table 2 Source Countries with the Highest Aapproval Rates for U.S. and Canada (Source: U.S. Committee on Refugees, 2000)

Source Country to U.S.	Approval rate	Source country to Canada	Approval rate
Afghanistan	81.7%	Afghanistan	89%
Cuba	76–78%	Somalia	78%
Ethiopia	76–78%	Sri Lanka	77%
Sudan	71–75%	Congo	74%
Somalia	71–75%		

Issues of migration and resettlement are complicated, and deaf and hard of hearing children within the immigrant and refugee population often experience stress that can have a negative impact on their educational experience. A typical case history might include birth and early experiences in a refugee camp, living in more than one country enroute to Canada, lack of access to educational opportunities for deaf children in these countries, family separation (sometimes including the deaf child's separation from his/her own family), the family's lack of ability to cope with the child's deafness, exposure to multiple languages during the migration period, and the deaf child's lack of access to spoken language, with its cognitive and linguistic implications.

Many newly arrived deaf students lack not only English, but any form of language (spoken or signed), as well as appropriate study skills for North American schools. Their families may lack basic information about deafness, the importance of language and communication, the partnership role that families and schools can play, special education opportunities, and information about their own as well as their children's rights and responsibilities as members of a new society (Branson & Miller, 1998; Turner, 1996). Yet deaf children, like others their age, must come to feel socially and academically competent if they are to become productive members of society (Benard, 1993).

The goals of this chapter are to sensitize professionals to issues when working with "multicultural" deaf individuals and families, and to outline issues and questions to ask before considering a service delivery model. We begin by presenting information pertinent to deaf children within the refugee and immigrant population, focusing on migration, adaptation, and acculturation. Next, we examine issues of schooling, language, and cognitive development. We then conclude with implications for school psychology consultation concerning the needs of deaf and hard of hearing children.

Migration, Adaptation, and Acculturation: Implications for Deaf Children and Their Families

Immigrant children have the advantage of having had a planned migration. The new country is specifically targeted by the family as the ultimate destination for a new, and possibly improved, life. Yet, some families may come with unrealistic expectations of what the new country can offer in terms of educational and/or medical interventions for their deaf children.

In contrast, refugee migration is an unplanned move, where people are forced from their homes with little notice. There is often no target country. Families may have to travel to several different countries before one will allow them to stay on a permanent basis. It is not uncommon for education to be interrupted and languages incompletely learned.

On the other hand, both immigrant and refugee children undergo similar adaptation and acculturation stresses. Their histories may include information about disrupted lives, inadequate health care resulting in disease and malnutrition, social, emotional, and physical deprivation, significant personal losses, and educational gaps (Cole, 1998). Consequently, the children are likely to experience cognitive and emotional difficulties (Ajdukovic & Ajdukovic, 1993; Motta, 1995). In addition to the stressors mentioned above, refugee families with a deaf member face yet another stressor while waiting for the immigration decision. Concern by immigration officials that a disabled person might cause undue strain on social and medical services can be cause for denying formal entry into a country. While waiting for this decision, the family remains in limbo.

Cultural Views of Deafness

A family's perception on the needs of their deaf child is shaped by their culture's view of deafness, which can, in turn, influence decisions about enrolling the children in school, finding housing and employment, and creating a new identity and attachment to the new society (Christensen & Delgado, 1993). For example, if the child's deafness is perceived as a source of shame, then building the child's self-esteem will be a challenge. On the other hand, if deafness is believed to be the result of the parents' or the child's actions in a past life, then an attitude of helplessness may prevent proactive change from occurring. Similarly, if deafness is perceived as an unavoidable but unfortunate event, the family may react with helplessness, or conversely, may try to maximize the child's potential. Differences between a family's view and that of the medical or educational establishments can lead to challenges in service delivery. The new technology available through cochlear implants, for example, may mislead some people into believing that deafness can be "fixed" with the device, without a full understanding of the long-term educational commitment and prognoses of children with implants (Spencer & Marschark, in press).

One common misperception is that a deaf child is incapable of much learning. Many families continue to confuse the inability to speak with a lack of knowledge of a language, and to infer the inability to learn on the basis of the inability to speak. This is understandable, particularly in countries where special education services are unavailable. However, this common confusion may also lead parents to deny their deaf children the opportunity to learn to sign until after they learn to speak, thus furthering language delay and postponing understanding and acceptance of deaf children and their needs. It is well documented that specific family responses to deafness can impact on an immigrant or refugee deaf child's educational process and mental health (Akamatsu, 1993; Akamatsu & Cole, 2000; Cheng, 2000; Christensen, 2000; Cohen, 1993; Gerner de Garcia, 2000; Hammond & Meiners, 1993; Jackson-Maldonado, 1993). Counselling a family through the process of understanding the psychoeducational implications of their child's deafness is a crucial role for both teachers and school psychologists (Montanini Manfredi, 1993).

Schools are the most significant change agents at the societal and the individual level. They are becoming sites not only for academic learning and remediation, but also for mental health services to aid in acculturation and adaptation. Therefore, effective interventions with immigrant and refugee children and their families must be founded upon knowledge and awareness of the issues and challenges that face them.

Issues for Consideration by School Personnel

Issue #1: Educational Placements for Deaf Children

Once a child has been identified as having a hearing loss that impacts significantly on his or her ability to learn in the regular classroom, the question of placement arises. Typically, mildly hard of hearing children benefit greatly from the use of hearing aids, and are educated in "integrated" settings (i.e., in the regular classroom with some kind of resource support, especially for language). Moderately and severely hard of hearing children are usually educated in segregated classrooms with fewer than ten children, a trained teacher of the deaf and possibly an educational assistant. In these cases, however, the children are capable of learning through the use of their own hearing. Some profoundly deaf children may be placed in "oral" settings, where spoken language is the medium of instruction, and the expectation is that these children will learn to lip-read and speak. Other profoundly deaf children are placed in "total communication" or "bilingual" settings, where signed language is the medium of instruction. The expectation for these children is that they will learn most effectively through sign language. Lip-reading and speech are sometimes encouraged, but spoken language is not expected to play a primary role in students' communicative repertoire. In the United States, about two-thirds of the programs for deaf children use signing.

Programs for deaf students may be offered through residential schools, special day schools, or the public education system. Based on the several (U.S.) federal regulations, Marschark (1997) noted that placement decisions should be made on the basis of: "1) linguistic needs, 2) severity of hearing loss and potential for using residual hearing with or without amplification devices, 3) academic level, 4) social, emotional, and cultural needs, including opportunities for interaction and communication with peers, and 5) communication needs, including the child's and family's preferred mode of communication" (p. 113).

Since eligibility for placement into programs for deaf and hard of hearing children is initially based on audiological information, it would appear that assessing a child's degree of deafness is a rather simple matter. However, audiological needs, while appearing rather simple to address on the surface, are quite complicated. Indeed, most parents, regardless of their point of origin, have difficulty grasping the full implications of a diagnosis of deafness. On the one hand, most parents know that their child is deaf prior to entering the new country. How they react to the diagnosis and make decisions on behalf of their child will be influenced by their cultural interpretation of "deafness."

A family's immigration may have been planned around the deafness, with the (unrealistic, yet understandable) hope that the new country will have medical interventions that will "cure" the deafness. Cochlear implants in particular have this allure. Yet, the therapeutic intervention itself is expensive and requires other commitments (appointments, therapy) that the family may not be in a position to make. This is not to say that immigrant and refugee children should not receive cochlear implants. While there is not much one can do prior to the family actually arriving, schools need to work with hospital programs in counseling the parents prior to their making a decision as irrevocable as an implant.

The expectations of each kind of program interacts with the specific abilities and resources that a child brings to that program. Therefore, the kinds of interventions that school psychologists can provide or suggest will vary by program. For example, a profoundly deaf immigrant child who is unable to lip-read English may find that an oral program is extremely frustrating. In such a case, counselling parents about the child's needs and about the role that sign language can play for this child is an important service. A severely traumatized but mildly hard of hearing child may benefit from being in a segregated class to allow that child to receive more teacher attention.

One key factor in the deaf child's development is schooling and language development, which provides an avenue for further education, socialization, and the acquisition of life skills. In short, the effects of the migration experience at both the individual and familial level should not be ignored. Beiser and his colleagues conclude that the combination of supportive traditional cultural elements and new cultural norms allow for the maintenance of ethnic pride and contribute to good mental health (Beiser, Dion, Gotowiec, & Huyman, 1995; Edwards & Beiser, 1994). The immigrant or refugee deaf child's eventual acculturation to both North American society as well as to the North American Deaf culture depends on the interaction among general migration factors, as well as personal and familial factors and ethno-cultural views of deafness.

Issue #2: The Language Challenge for Deaf Immigrant and Refugee Children

Hearing students who are learning English as a second language may already possess a range of communication skills in their native language when they first arrive at school. Although some may have had little or no schooling, others may have come from communities with strong literate traditions and high educational standards. Thus, they often come equipped to build a second language on the base of their first language. Students who are already literate in their first language may bring an additional foundation on which to build their English skills.

For deaf immigrant and refugee children who arrive at school past the optimal age of language acquisition, it is paramount to expose, indeed immerse, these children in a comprehensible, language-rich environment. Because language development underlies cognitive, social, and emotional development, the lack of language logically predicts generally atypical development. Several research reviews (Marschark, 1993; Moores, 1996) have concluded that deaf children of deaf parents (who presumably are exposed to signed language from birth) typically demonstrate better academic achievement and psychosocial adjustment than deaf children from non-signing hearing families.

American Sign Language (ASL) is probably the language that is most accessible for deaf students who begin to learn their first language at a late age[1]. Because ASL uses the visual modality, it can take advantage of visual iconicity and natural gestures (Mylander & Goldin-Meadow, 1991; Newport, 1996). Skills developed even in home sign can be brought to bear on learning ASL and other natural sign systems (Fischer, 1998; Lucas & Valli, 1992; Mayer & Akamatsu, 1999).

Some researchers have concluded that ASL is the *first* and natural language of all deaf children. Building on theories from bilingual education, they argued for the use of ASL as the language of classroom instruction, with English being used for reading and writing (Israelite, Ewoldt, & Hoffmeister, 1992; Johnson, Liddell, & Erting, 1989).

However, ASL cannot be viewed as the language panacea for these children. ASL appears to have a critical period similar to that of English (Fischer, 1994, 1998;

---

[1] What holds true for English and American Sign Language (ASL) in English-speaking Canada likely holds true for French and Langue Signes des Quebecois (LSQ) in French-speaking Canada.

Mayberry & Eichen, 1991), and therefore we might expect that immigrant and refugee deaf children who arrive without a first (signed) language will be disadvantaged in ways similar to hearing children who have not acquired a solid first language. That is, although they will be able to communicate adequately in a face-to-face situation, they will have difficulty acquiring complex syntactic structures with native-like fluency.

Learning signed language, while useful for interpersonal and instructional purposes, is but one language to learn in the acculturation process. English, at least in written form, must also be mastered. Given how difficult literacy acquisition is for native-born deaf children whose parents already speak, read, and write English, it requires little to imagine the daunting task facing refugee and immigrant children. To further complicate matters, Mayer and Wells (1996) pointed out that because ASL does not have a written component, deaf children who are fluent only in ASL are doubly disadvantaged when trying to learn to read and write in English. Not only do deaf students have severely restricted access to English (and therefore to the phonological component), they also cannot transfer any literacy skills from ASL. Whereas ASL may give the children the ability to conceptualize and communicate ideas in face to face conversation, a knowledge of how English "works" (vocabulary, morphology, syntax, etc.) is also necessary to be able to read and write in English. Building on the work of Bereiter and Scardamalia (1987), Mayer (1999, p. 39) argues that "there is some minimum threshold level of [English] proficiency required" before a deaf student can productively read (Bebko, 1998) and write (Boisclair & Sirois, 1996; Moores & Sweet, 1990).

Mayer and Akamatsu (1999) questioned the exclusive use of ASL as the instructional language of choice, and suggested that natural sign systems (i.e., "the naturally evolved systems that deaf people use to communicate with hearing people," Fischer, 1998, p. 17) may provide a bridge between a native sign language and English because of their linear mapping with [English] and their use of lexical and certain grammatical constructions from ASL. They further suggested that natural sign systems can be used effectively to establish an English language base and to support engagement in literacy activities at the morphosystactic level.

It is widely accepted that it takes second language learners 5-7 years to become academically fluent in a language, a process that is facilitated through the acquisition of literacy (Cole, 1998; Cole & Siegel, 1990; Cummins, 1984). Cummins' Linguistic Interdependence theory (1991) suggests that students who can use both their newly acquired oral skills and established literacy skills from their first language are best positioned to acquire literacy in their second language. Moreover, the nature of the writing system of the child's first language may impact on how well first language literacy supports second language literacy (Cummins et al., 1984).

In the best-case scenario, refugee and immigrant deaf students may have been exposed to other languages or dialects and may not have had time to consolidate even face-to-face communication skills. Upon arrival in Canada, even students who appear to learn to sign rapidly within the first two years may be unreasonably expected to perform academically like their same-age peers who have had many years of signing. For example, Mayer and Akamatsu (2000) reported on a student who used Czech Sign Language at home and American Sign Language and English-based signing at school. Although this student was quite capable of communicating face to face with his peers, his command of written English remained rudimentary many years after his arrival in Canada.

Issue #3: Schooling and Language Learning

Approximately one-half of the world's children are refugees (United Nations High Commissioner for Refugees (UNHCR), 1994), and over half of these children come from single-parent, low-income families (Burke, 1992). Canada, which like the United States is a nation of immigrants, experienced a doubling of immigration during the late 1980s and early 1990s (Coelho, 1994), with three-quarters of immigrant children being of school age. This rise in immigration has presented schools with the tremendous challenge of meeting the educational needs of a rapidly changing population (Cole, 1996b, 1998). The implications for deaf children from disadvantaged living conditions and disruptive schooling are staggering (Hafner & Ulanoff, 1994; Thomas, 1992).

Vygotsky (1978, 1987) argued that the communicative use of language in educational contexts is essential to cognitive development. This idea, expanded further by Wertsch (1985), points to the importance of society and "more knowledgeable others" in engaging a young person in the necessary interaction to generate higher psychological processes, such as intentional attention and memory, abstract thinking, and language. By understanding the nature of interaction (particularly language-based interaction), we can come to understand how an individual learns to think, use language, and learn.

Research studies have documented that there is great variability in the length of time it takes normally hearing children to learn English as a second language and the kinds of instructional interventions necessary to promote this process (Cole, 1996a; Corson, 1993). There is little reason to expect the case for immigrant or refugee deaf children to be different or easier. Because schooling is inextricably linked to English proficiency, communicating in English is a prime goal for all immigrant and refugee children. Difficulties with language acquisition tend to hamper education, social integration and employment opportunities. For most deaf immigrant and refugee students, attendance at school provides their first accessible exposure to any language. Depending on the age of the student at the time they enter school in North America, first language acquisition may have been delayed to the point where complete acquisition in impossible, even under the best of conditions. This can have devastating consequences for subsequent cognitive and literacy development (Akamatsu, 1998; Bonkowski, Gavelek, & Akamatsu, 1991).

Many immigrant students lack the appropriate study skills for North American schooling. Their parents may not understand what these "appropriate skills" are, and therefore not be able to reinforce these skills at home. In school, regular contact with a peer helper may be of help in dealing with both social and academic issues. Co-operative learning may help to facilitate the learning process by structuring groups so that students depend on one another (and not just on the teacher). Students can become valuable resources to each other, and responsible for their own success and for the success of each group member. Co-operative learning also promotes active, hands-on learning rather than passive learning, and thus increases the motivation to learn.

Demonstration of self-initiative and assumption of responsibility in learning should be fully recognized and reinforced. Encourage the student to make decisions, such as asking how he thinks he should begin, etc. Independent decision making and problem solving should be encouraged to help the student become more actively involved in the learning process.

A teacher could help the student to set up a "binder reminder" which the student carries everyday. In it, the student is expected to put down the materials he/she needs and the different work items he/she is expected to complete for the day. Step-by-step directions or an index card for routine procedures might be taped to the student's notebook. Encourage the student to organize all materials needed for a particular task (e.g., books, pencil, eraser, etc.) before starting to work. Teaching organizational and time management strategies may be helpful, especially for developing effective work habits, study skills and test-taking strategies. An orderly work plan might be provided to help the student manage his assignments and work load (Cole & Brown, 1996; Cole & Siegel, 1990).

It is expected that the student would initially make academic progress at a slower pace. It is expected that the student would grasp abstract concepts more easily if concrete or tangible materials are used for illustrations. Demonstration learning is a good avenue for the student. A spiral approach to the curriculum, with many repetitions and gradual introduction of new concepts will be best suited to the student's learning abilities. Teaching strategies that involve frequent repetition of instructions and a language-rich environment will provide maximum exposure to each concept being taught. The vocabulary of each subject of study will need to be taught. Ensure that the student knows the terms and their meanings before further instruction with new concepts.

Issue #4: The Role of the Family

Secondary effects of deafness, such as language delay, lowered parental expectations and perceptions, experiential deficits, lack of appropriate educational experiences, and increased stress have been documented in the literature (see e.g., Calderon & Greenberg, 1993; Gregory, 1998; Lederburg, 1993 for relevant reviews). In general, this literature has suggested that deafness disrupts normal parent-child relationships by changing the nature of how deaf children experience the world and making communication difficult so that these experiences cannot be adequately mediated by the parents. As a result, the parents become psychologically unavailable and more physically controlling with their deaf children than with their hearing children. In extreme cases, interactions between deaf children and their parents can appear to be either neglectful or abusive.

School personnel must remember that immigrant and refugee parents may not view themselves as equal partners in their children's learning. Contact with a counselor who is knowledgeable about the student's cultural background and sensitive to immigration may prove beneficial. It is likely that regularly scheduled appointments (e.g., daily, weekly) would be most effective. Families will continue to require ongoing information and support in order to collaborate with the school and revalidate the value of the home language as well as sign language.

Misconceptions about sign language may inhibit parents from interacting with their children in sign, perhaps because their culture frowns upon overly expressive body language, or because they feel that signing is not a valid form of language. The parents may also recognize that their deaf child has a greater command of sign than they do, and feel powerless to interact with the child because they have no common language. Many students respond well to role-playing techniques that enhance low self-esteem, improve social skills, increase sensitivity to the thoughts and feelings of others, and decrease aggressive behavior (Cole & Siegel, 1990). These can be used in the context of the classroom, as part of an arts/drama curriculum, or in collaboration with a counsellor or school psychologist.

Although studies have concluded that parental involvement in school has a positive impact on children's academic achievement (Alter, 1992; Grace, 1993), parents may not feel empowered to work as partners with the school. As a result of linguistic barriers, cultural differences, and adjustment difficulties, immigrant parents may feel misinformed or ill-informed about the school system and yet be reluctant or unable to approach the school system for help (Cole, 1996b).

In certain cultures, the schools are charged with the responsibility for educating as well as socializing children. Parents, having provided for the basic needs of the child may feel that it is now solely the school's mandate to teach the child in order to become a functioning member of society. Because of their own limited education or inability to function in English or sign, parents may be unable to help their children with homework. They may find it difficult to participate in sign language classes because these classes are taught in English and/or because of their working conditions.

Home-school communication is often a new concept for parents. In many other countries, the school is expected to deal not only with learning, but any other behavior that the student exhibits. For students whose cultural adaptation has been difficult, maladaptive behaviors can develop and interfere with learning. Parents may respond to the school's request for cooperation as an indication that the school (or the teacher) is incompetent, and thereby lose confidence in the school. Other parents may resist involvement as a way of preserving their cultural integrity (Gerner de Garcia, 2000). This is not to suggest that home-school communication be abandoned, but rather that expectations for communication – and guidance for doing so – be set up as part of the placement and registration process.

For some parents, communicating with the school is intimidating. Particularly for refugee parents, the school represents a government institution, and a healthy distrust of any government institution may already exist. Add to this the difficulty of communicating in English and the stage is set for communication breakdowns. Teachers could reassure parents that even simple drawings and a few words go a long way in developing the kind of trust that is needed for home and school to work together. Providing examples to parents may help (see Figure 1). For parents who have some

Figure 1 Examples of Simple Techniques Useful for Facilitating Communication Between Home and School

command of English, notes could be sent between home and school when an incident is known to have set a student off, so that both are aware of what might be upsetting that student. The parents can also call the school if, for example, there is an incident at home or related to the bus that morning.

Spoken language interpreters are crucial in providing the link between the family and the school. Because finding interpreters can be difficult, particularly for languages with few local speakers, interpreters might be community social service providers, friends of the family, or family members of all ages who speak some English.

Using interpreters can be a complex process. Given the variety of English language skills to be found among users of this service, it is particularly important that the interpreter also be a cultural broker, able to interpret not only the verbal information of both parties, but also to interpret the intent of the message. Furthermore, because persons functioning in this role might be family members or close friends and therefore have a personal or vested interest in the target family, they should receive clear information about their role when functioning as interpreters.

Obviously, if there is no shared language, interpreters and their services are crucial to enhanced communication. Most schools and programs for deaf children are familiar with using signed language interpreters, but even so, difficulties tend to emerge. Relay interpreters (two or more intermediary interpreters) are needed if a teacher is deaf. That is, the deaf teacher needs an interpreter to translate from signed ASL to spoken English so that the spoken language interpreter can translate between English and the home language for the parents. Key concepts related to education systems (e.g., the difference between a special program and a specific school placement, curriculum vs. teaching strategies) might not be clear to the interpreters involved.

Implications for Assessment and Programming

The needs of immigrant and refugee deaf children are complex, and addressing these needs is equally complex. The need for a multidisciplinary team is never more pronounced than when serving these children. A systemic approach to assessment that goes beyond standardized testing is critical for understand and responding to these needs. A thorough background history is essential, including information about previous schooling in other countries, learning strengths and weaknesses, behavioral difficulties at home and school. Any documentation of the student's educational, medical, and mental health histories should be obtained. This information should be discussed with the team to further refine any referral questions. Figures 2 and 3 contain sample interview protocols for gathering background information.

The role of assessment is an integral part of instruction, guided learning, and accountability. Assessment should be a process of gathering information about a student in order to identify learning strengths and needs, and to develop appropriate

Country of birth:

Years in present country:

Number of countries prior to present:

Is there sufficient documentation to provide a profile of the student's educational experiences and social adaptation?
❑   Yes
❑   No   If not, what is still needed?

Previous formal educational experience:

Country	Number of schools	Grade	Language	Special Ed?

Home language(s):
(who speaks what?)

Student's preferred language/ modality:

Past learning strengths and weaknesses:

Discrepancies between past and present evaluations of skills and/or social adjustment?

Previous mental health and/or educational assessments?

Date	Facility	Type of Assessment	Results

Figure 2 Sample Interview Protocol for Gathering Background Information (Adapted from Cole & Siegel, 1990)

What is the symptomatic reason for referral?
- ❑ Academic:
- ❑ Behavioral:
- ❑ Socio-emotional:
- ❑ Health/Physical:

Present level of instruction: Language   Math

What does an evaluation of daily work suggest about the student's academic functioning?

Does the student have the skills to complete assignments?
- ❑ Yes, independently
- ❑ Some, needs support
- ❑ No, needs exensive support

Student's learning style (circle all that apply)

Auditory   Visual   Tactile Kinesthetic Motoric
Good rote memory Good thematic memory
Understands the large ideas but gets lost in detail Surface/shallow understanding only
Easily distracted Maintains good attention Good eye-hand coordination
Impulsive Reflective
Overly active Overly passive

Class participation

What motivates this student?
Interaction with teachers: ❑ good   ❑ satisfactory   ❑ poor
Interaction with peers: ❑ good   ❑ satisfactory   ❑ poor
Prefers company of children who are   ❑ older   ❑ younger   ❑ same age
School attendance: ❑ regular   ❑ irregular
Non-academic strengths:

Intervention strategies already tried:

Strategy   Outcome _____

_____

_____

_____

_____

Figure 3 Sample Pre-interview Protocol for Consultation with Resource People. For Teachers' Use (Adapted from Cole & Siegel, 1990)

educational services (Cole, 1991, 1996b). Concern about assessment practices for deaf children has centred largely on two major issues: 1) validity and reliability of the measures, and 2) subsequent educational practices that encourage maximal achievement. Many writers, educators, and researchers have cautioned against the use of verbal tests to measure intelligence in deaf and hard of hearing populations (Maller, 1996, 1997, 1999; Maller & Ferron, 1997). These cautions were raised earlier with equal fervor in the multilingual and multicultural literature (Cummins, 1994; Genesee & Hamayan, 1994). Nevertheless, ongoing measures of language-related abilities (whether in signed or printed language) are necessary for formulating a comprehensive view of a deaf immigrant or refugee student (Akamatsu, 1998; Marschark, 1993), although finding appropriate methods for doing this is extremely difficult.

To add to the complexity of assessment, the practice of restricting assessment to nonverbal measures in the early years of an immigrant or refugee child's experience can be problematic. For example, a child's performance on standardized nonverbal measures may be tainted by a lack of experience with the materials used in the assessment. It may be unreasonable to expect decontextualized problem solving (e.g., social problem solving based on hypothetical situations) based on experiences that are very different from the population on whom the measure was standardized. Given the degree of early deprivation, cultural background, and migration experience, the picture is understandably more complicated with deaf immigrant and refugee students. What holds true for assessing immigrant/refugee or language minority students may hold doubly true for immigrant/refugee deaf students.

Because ASL will always be a part of deaf children's lives, instruction in ASL as well as opportunities to interact in ASL should be provided. Assessment tools for ASL are being developed, but there are no widely available standards or norms against which to measure the development of ASL (Supalla, Singleton, Wix, & Maller, 1998). Similarly, formal curricula for teaching ASL are only now being developed for use in schools (Singleton, Supalla, Litchfield, & Schley, 1998). The assessment of deaf students' English skills has a large literature (see Marschark, 1993 and Moores, 1996 for relevant reviews), but even here, debate continues to focus on fairness in testing, and on the advisability of using assessments to continuously demonstrate that even the most advantaged deaf students have enormous difficulty with English (Luetke-Stahlman & Luckner, 1991; Paul, 1993; Vernon & Andrews, 1990).

The literature on deafness is fairly consistent about the disadvantage at which deaf students find themselves when faced with measures of ability which do not adequately differentiate between language-related difficulties and the actual level of knowledge or skill the students possess (Marschark, 1993). Furthermore, differences in linguistic, social, and educational experiences affect native-born deaf students' performance on the various tasks that usually comprise tests of intelligence. It is therefore important not to misperceive linguistic deficits as deficits in ability since decontextualized language may present difficulties for children from culturally different homes. Moreover, Marschark (1993) notes that even when deaf and hearing children have equivalent non-verbal IQs, the academic achievement of the deaf students is several grade levels below that of their hearing peers. Vernon and Andrews (1990) also note that neurological damage associated with the deafness (e.g., certain medical syndromes, prematurity, maternal rubella, high fever during infancy) can also contribute to both greater variability and lower scores on tests of non-verbal intelligence within the deaf population. Therefore, one must exercise caution when interpreting the results even of non-verbal intelligence tests.

Educators and parents must be aware of lowered expectations of immigrant or refugee deaf students, either because of their migration experience or their hearing status. While actual levels of achievement, particularly in the early years, may not accurately reflect their abilities, ongoing dynamic assessment can aid in setting realistic goals for these students.

Currently, assessment (particularly in the form of standardized testing) acts as a lightening-rod for those who feel marginalized and disenfranchised (Cole, 1996a), including deaf and hard of hearing children. Assessment may be viewed as the very process that causes marginalization and disenfranchisement. In the interest of preventing further discrimination and limitations in opportunities based on their performance on various assessments, delay or exemption from participation in assessment is tabled as a viable alternative. However, indefinitely delaying or exempting these individuals from any kind of assessment puts them outside the system of accountability, and can have serious implications for the provision of appropriate programs and services and the preparation of students who are self-sufficient and able to exercise the rights and responsibilities of citizenship (Samuda, 1990). Therefore, a systemic approach to assessment that goes beyond standardized testing to include informal curriculum and instruction-based techniques should be adopted (Dunst, Trivette, & Deal, 1988; Palinscar, Brown, & Campione, 1991; Rueda & Garcia, 1997).

Normative data for deaf students is difficult enough to acquire due to the low incidence of deafness. This type of data on immigrant/refugee deaf students will be even more difficult to collect. Therefore, when assessing the academic achievement and social adjustment of deaf immigrant and refugee students, it is important to measure progress in four ways. First, how well has the individual student done academically and socially since arrival? Second, how does the student compare to others with similar immigrant or refugee backgrounds? Third, how does he or she compare with the general deaf population? Fourth, how does the student compare with normally hearing peers?

Alternative assessment procedures, such as portfolio-based assessment and the use of authentic or performance-based assessments, alone or in combination with culturally sensitive tests, have been advocated because they provide information that can be applied directly to instructional planning, and incorporated into students' individual education plans (Cole, 1996b; Estrin, 1993; Gordon & Musser, 1992). One practical and immediately applicable procedure is to perform dynamic assessments over a period of time, creating and analyzing portfolios of the student's work. For example, samples of the student's schoolwork can be collected. Changes in individual education plans can be documented. Standardized ability and achievement tests can be administered and compared across, say, a one-year time span. Diagnostic teaching and close observation of the student performing various tasks can be made and different kinds of intervention offered. Where appropriate, the "test-teach-test" method will yield information to allow educators and parents to understand what the student can do without help. It can also help determine what kinds of intervention/teaching create the most learning for the student. Documentation of the kinds of interventions that seem to be most helpful can be made and discussed with the classroom teacher and parents.

Concerns have been raised, however, that such evaluations are not equally valid for all groups, and may lead to unfair outcomes (Cole, 1996a). Assessment continues to be emphasized in school systems as a legislated requirement and as a valued service by teachers and parents (Green, 1998). Psychologists trained in both deafness and multicultural issues bring many skills and areas of knowledge to the assessment and consultation process (Cole, 1991; Cole & Siegel, 1990; Martin, 1991; Vernon & Andrews, 1990). Such skills include observation and interview skills, selection and evaluation of appropriate measures, and interpretation of the effects of language, culture and personality on adjustment and performance. Knowledge domains include developmental, learning and personality theories, individual differences, and multilingual education. This evolution toward comprehensive and equitable psychological assessment is timely in light of the diverse student population, the reform movement in education and the re-evaluation of special education services. Through consultation and assessment, which provide a comprehensive picture about children, parents are likely to be reassured that in spite of their child's early history, significant and relevant gains in language and learning can be made by their child, and that favorable outcomes are possible.

Summary

The education, health and mental health service needs of deaf immigrant and refugee children are too complex to be addressed by one profession or by one system at a time. Instead, co-ordination must occur among the many systems with which the family comes into contact if effective, efficient, and culturally sensitive services are to be provided (Cole, 1998).

Service providers need to become familiar with the frames of reference of the families with whom they work (Turner, 1996). Cultural values, in general and those specifically related to deafness must be explored and understood. Without a cultural context and knowledge of deafness, factors related to age, gender, education and family position may be misinterpreted, and professionals may incorrectly judge the behaviors of deaf children as symptoms of psychopathology (Pollard, 1998). Giordano

(1994) has indicated helpful clinical guidelines for mental health professionals working in a multicultural milieu. His guidelines may be modified to include: a) the assessment of behavior and learning in the context of cultural norms, the importance of ethnicity to the family, and the cultural implications of deafness to the family; b) validating and strengthening the student's and family's ethnic identity and cultural background; c) identifying and resolving family value conflicts, particularly around deafness and the use of sign language; d) an evaluation of the teacher's own hearing status and ethnicity and its impact on the student's willingness to learn, and finally, e) the teacher's ongoing self assessment related to limits of knowledge about the impact of deafness in the context of the student's ethnic background. As we pointed out earlier, families from different cultures may view deafness not only as an inability to hear, but also as an inability to learn. Furthermore, a teacher who is also deaf may be viewed as less competent than a normally hearing teacher. On the other hand, the teacher may serve as a concrete role model for positive educational outcomes for a deaf child. Gender differences may also influence a family's perception of the teacher's competence. Families who do not have confidence in a teacher, for whatever reason, may undermine that teacher's attempts at teaching their deaf child. It is important for the school personnel to be aware of the impact of the particular hearing status, ethnic, and sometimes gender match between the teacher, student, and family.

Schools are often the first system recent immigrants learn about, but special education services, under whose auspices deaf and hard of hearing children receive education, may be uncharted territory. Parents may not realize that special education services are available in North America, or not understand their rights and responsibilities with regard to receiving appropriate educational services for their children. Due to language, educational, and/or cultural barriers, they may be unable to advocate effectively for their children.

Because schools are perceived to be a trusted environment which facilitates education and eventual access to North American society, parent outreach is vital at point of contact with the education system. Given the ongoing emotional and social needs of immigrant and refugee children, it is important for schools to develop partnerships with external agencies and ethnic organizations. It is thus important for psychologists and social workers employed by school boards to develop multicultural and integrated service delivery models, which can facilitate the co-ordination of prevention and intervention functions (Cole, 1996b).

One such vehicle for service delivery in many North American school boards is that of in-school multidisciplinary consultation teams, comprised of educators, school psychologists and social workers (Cole, 1992). Generally, these teams are designed to support teachers in providing appropriate interventions for students in need of assistance. Expanded team mandates can include consultative services to staff, parents and community agencies. In their five-year follow up study on school teams, Cole and Brown (1996) found that teams continue to be utilized for consultation about immigrant and refugee students, particularly around the common difficulties in coping with adjustment to a new language and culture. About a quarter of those surveyed saw refugee needs as an attribute that was most often related to student referral for team consultation.

Consultation services in Canadian schools have been documented as providing valued services to educators (Sladeczek & Heath, 1997). Siegel and Cole (1990) developed a consultation framework for organizing programs which link primary, secondary and tertiary prevention initiatives. This model provides both for direct intervention by mental health professionals as well as for preventative programs delivered by teachers and other in-school staff. For example, primary prevention programs such as anti-racist education, self-esteem or social skills training can be provided by mental health staff in partnership with teachers. Given the severity of the problem, primary prevention programs could also include consultations with hospitals and ethnic-community organizations who make referrals for deaf children. It is hoped that a broader role for mental health professionals in education will provide an avenue for advocacy about the provision of preventatively-oriented services. Secondary prevention programs, formulated in consultation with schools, are directed toward students who are at-risk emotionally or socially. Tertiary prevention programs should be directed to students and families in crisis. Primary and secondary prevention programs might best be provided in a collaborative model, with one expert on refugee issues, and one expert on deafness. Tertiary prevention (or active intervention) might best be accomplished by someone who has primary expertise in deafness, in consultation with informed others. A schematic of this model, with examples for deaf children is presented in Table 3.

Substantive change in practice often takes several years to achieve. Cross-disciplinary participation among psychologists, social workers, teachers, public health nurses, and language/cultural interpreters is likely to stimulate shared understanding and new approaches to multicultural services. Educational options for newly arrived immigrants and refugees must be explored with individuals knowledgeable about both deafness and multicultural services. It would seem vital that when immigrant or refugee deaf students are identified, a multidisciplinary team should meet to evaluate the student's and family's history and expectations so that the parents are able to make an informed decision about special education services and placement. In line with the trend toward increased accountability in education and mental health, there is a growing need to address outcome-based measures for training and practice in the field. Ecological models for multicultural services require conceptual knowledge and skills training. This, however, will require knowledge of multicultural education, anti-racist policies and programs, social skills training, crisis management and violence prevention. As Vygotsky (1997) once stated, "Education is a process of mutual and continuous adaptation of both camps, where sometimes it is guide or leader which represents the most active and the most original effective side, and sometimes those who are being led" (p. 349). Effective change and exemplary practice will be developed best through the collaborative efforts of multidisciplinary teams.

Table 3 Preventatively-Oriented Interventions for Immigrant and Refugee Deaf Students

Recipient and level of service	Primary prevention: Identify resources, provide and analyse information; program for all deaf students	Secondary prevention: Program for deaf students "at risk"	Tertiary prevention: Programs for deaf students whose problems significantly interfere with their adaptation to school
School System	Present in-service workshop on deaf refugee/immigrant issues	Develop plan for identifying deaf students at risk for adjustment difficulties	Develop plan for responding to needs of deaf refugee students and their families
School Staff	Invite community-based workers to consult on issues relevant to specific ethno-cultural groups (e.g., cultural implications of deafness)	Discuss relevance of migration background of specific ethno-cultural groups with teachers of deaf students	Liaise between school and community service providers to provide services for those in need
Students or Parents, mediated service	Co-lead, with a teacher, a series of social-skills workshops for an entire class	Consult with teachers on learning and emotional needs of newly arrived students	Consult with teacher prior to formal referral
Students or Parents, direct service	Inform parents about local resources for deaf children and their families	Facilitate group for new immigrant and refugee students; liaise with ethnic community agency to co-lead a group	Conduct individual assessment and/or counselling

References

Ajdukovic, M., & Ajdukovic, D. (1993). Psychological well-being of refugee children. *Child Abuse and Neglect, 17,* 843-854.

Akamatsu, C. T. (1993). Teaching deaf Asian and Pacific Island American children. In K. Christensen & G. Delgado (Eds.), *Multicultural issues in deafness* (pp. 127-142). White Plains, NY: Longman.

Akamatsu, C. T. (1998). Thinking with and without language: What is necessary and sufficient for school-based learning? In A. Weisel (Ed.), *Deaf education in the 1990's: International perspectives* (pp. 27-40). Washington, DC: Gallaudet University Press.

Akamatsu, C. T., & Cole, E. (2000). Immigrant and refugee children who are deaf: Crisis equals danger plus opportunity. In K. Christensen (Ed.), *Deaf plus: A multicultural perspective* (pp. 93-120). San Diego, CA: DawnSignPress.

Alter, R . C. (1992). Parent-school communication: A selective review. *Canadian Journal of School Psychology, 8,* 103-110.

Bebko, J. (1998). Learning, language, memory and reading: The role of language automatization and its impact on complex cognitive activities. *Journal of Deaf Studies and Deaf Education, 3,* 4-14.

Beiser, M., Dion, R., Gotowiec, A. J., & Huyman, I. (1995). Immigrant and refugee children in Canada. *Canadian Journal of Psychiatry, 40,* 67-72.

Benard, B. (1993). Fostering resiliency in kids. *Educational Leadership, November,* 44-48.

Bereiter, C., & Scardamalia, M. (1987) *The psychology of written composition.* Hillsdale, NJ: Erlbaum.

Boisclair, A., & Sirois, P. (1998). Text comprehension in hearing impaired children in grade 3 and grade 6. *CAEDHH Journal, 22,* 71-92.

Bonkowski, N., Gavelek, J., & Akamatsu, C. T. (1991). Education and the social construction of mind. In D. Martin (Ed.), *Advances in cognition, education and the deaf* (pp. 185-194). Washington, DC: Gallaudet University Press.

Branson, J., & Miller, D. (1998). Achieving human rights: Educating deaf immigrant students from non-English-speaking families in Australia. In A. Weisel (Ed.), *Issues unresolved: New perspectives on language and deaf education* (pp. 88-100). Washington, DC: Gallaudet University Press.

Burke, M. A. (1992). Canada's immigrant children. *Canadian Social Trends,* Spring: 15-20.

Calderon, R., & Greenberg, M. (1993). Considerations in the adaptation of families with school-aged deaf children. In M. Marschark & M. D. Clark (Eds.), *Psychological perspectives on deafness* (pp. 27-47). Hillsdale, NJ: Lawrence Erlbaum Assoc.

Cheng, L. (2000). Deafness: An Asian/Pacific perspective. In K. Christensen (Ed.), *Deaf plus: A multicultural perspective* (pp. 59-92). San Diego, CA: DawnSignPress.

Christensen, K. (Ed.). (2000). *Deaf plus: A multicultural perspective.* San Diego, CA: DawnSignPress.

Christensen, K., & Delgado, G. (1993). *Multicultural issues in deafness.* White Plains, NY: Longman.

Coelho, E. (1994). Social integration of immigrant and refugee children. In F. Genesee (Ed.), *Educating second language children.* Cambridge: Cambridge University Press.

Cohen, O. (1993). Educational needs of African American and Hispanic deaf children and youth. In K. Christensen & G. Delgado (Eds.), *Multicultural issues in deafness* (pp. 45-68). White Plains, NY: Longman.

Cole, E. (1991). Multicultural psychological assessment: New challenges, improved methods. *International Journal of Dynamic Assessment and Instruction, 2,* 1-10.

Cole, E. (1992). Characteristics of students referred to school teams: Implications for preventive psychological services. *Canadian Journal of School Psychology, 8,* 23-38.

Cole, E. (1996a). Immigrant and refugee children and families: Supporting a new road travelled. In M. Luther, E. Cole, & P. Gamlin (Eds.), *Dynamic assessment for instruction: From theory to application* (pp. 35-42). Toronto: Captus University Publications.

Cole, E. (1996b). An integrative perspective on school psychology. *Canadian Journal of School Psychology, 12,* 115-121.

Cole, E. (1998). Immigrant and refugee children: Challenges and opportunities for education and mental health services. *Canadian Journal of School Psychology, 14,* 36-50.

Cole, E., & Brown, R. (1996). Multidisciplinary school teams: A five-year follow-up study. *Canadian Journal of School Psychology, 12,* 155-168.

Cole, E., & Siegel, J. (1990). School psychology in a multicultural community: Responding to children's needs. In E. Cole & J. Siegel (Eds.), *Effective consultation in school psychology* (pp. 141-169). Toronto: Hogrefe & Huber Publishers.

Corson, D. (1993). *Language, minority education and gender.* Clevedon: Multilingual Matters LTD.

Cummins, J. (1984). *Bilingualism and special education: Issues in assessment and pedagogy.* England: Multilingual Matters Ltd.

Cummins, J. (1991). Language development and academic learning. In L. Malave & G. Duquette (Eds.), *Language, culture and cognition.* Philadelphia: Multilingual Matters.

Cummins, J. (1994). Knowledge, power, and identity in teaching English as a second language. In F. Genesee (Ed.), *Educating second language children* (pp. 33-58.). Cambridge: University Press.

Cummins, J., Swain, M., Nakajima, K., Handscombe, D., Green, D., & Tran, C. (1984). Linguistic interdependence among Japanese and Vietnamese immigrant students. In C. Rivera (Ed.), *Communicative competence approaches to language proficiency assessment: Research and application.* Clevedon: Multilingual Matters.

Dunst, C., Trivette, C., & Deal, A. (1988). *Enabling and empowering families: Principles and guidelines for practice.* Cambridge, MA: Brookline Books.

Edwards, G. J., & Beiser, M. (1994). Southeast Asian refugee youth in Canada: The determinants of competence and successful coping. *Canada's Mental Health, Spring,* 1-5.

Estrin, E. T. (1993). Alternative assessment: Issues in language, culture and equity. Knowledge Brief, II. *Far West Lab for Education and Development.* San Francisco, California. ERIC, 1-8.

Fischer, S. (1994). Critical periods: Critical issues. In B. Schick & M. P. Moeller (Eds.), *Proceedings of the 7th annual conference in issues in language and deafness: The use of sign language in educational settings: Current concepts and controversies* (pp. 1-11). Omaha: Boys Town National Research Hospital.

Fischer, S. (1998). Critical periods for language acquisition: Consequences for deaf education. In A. Weisel (Ed.), *Deaf education in the 1990's: International perspectives* (pp. 9-26). Washington, DC: Gallaudet University Press.

Genesee, F., & Hamayan, E. V. (1994). Classroom – based assessment. In F. Genesee (Ed.), *Educating second language children.* Cambridge: University Press.

Gerner de Garcia, B. (2000). Meeting the needs of Hispanic/Latino deaf students. In K. Christensen (Ed.), *Deaf plus: A multicultural perspective* (pp. 149-198). San Diego, CA: DawnSignPress.

Giordano, J. (1994). Mental health and the melting pot. *American Journal of Orthopsychiatry, 64*, 342-345.

Gordon, E. W., & Musser, J. H. (1992). Implications of diversity in human characteristics for authentic assessment. CSE Technical Report 341. Los Angeles: Centre for Research on Evaluation, Standards, and Student Testing. ERIC.

Grace, C. (1993). A model program for home-school communication and staff development. In K. Christensen & G. Delgado (Eds.), *Multicultural issues in deafness* (pp. 29-42). White Plains, NY: Longman.

Green, J. (1998). Constructing the way forward for all students. *Education Canada, 38*, 8-12.

Gregory, S. (1998). Deaf young people: Aspects of family and social life. In M. Marschark & M. D. Clark (Eds.), *Psychological perspectives on deafness* (pp. 153-170). Hillsdale, NJ: Lawrence Erlbaum Associates.

Hafner, A. L., & Ulanoff, S. H. (1994). Validity issues and concerns for assessing English learners. *Education and Urban Society, 26*, 367-389.

Hammond, S. A., & Meiners, L. (1993). American Indian deaf children and youth. In K. Christensen & G. Delgado (Eds.), *Multicultural issues in deafness* (pp. 143-166). White Plains, NY: Longman.

Israelite, N., Ewoldt, C., & Hoffmeister, R. (1992). *Bilingual-bicultural education for deaf and hard-of-hearing students.* Toronto, Ontario: MGS Publication Services.

Jackson-Maldonado, D. (1993). Mexico and the United States: A cross-cultural perspective on the education of deaf children. In K. Christensen & G. Delgado (Eds.), *Multicultural issues in deafness* (pp. 91-112). White Plains, NY: Longman.

Johnson, R., Liddell, S., & Erting, C. (1989). *Unlocking the curriculum: Principles for achieving access in deaf education.* Gallaudet Research Institute Working Paper 89-3. Washington, DC: Gallaudet University.

Lederburg, A. (1993). The impact of deafness on mother-child and peer relationships. In M. Marschark & M. D. Clark (Eds.), *Psychological perspectives on deafness* (pp. 93-119). Hillsdale, NJ: Lawrence Erlbaum Assoc.

Lucas, C., & Valli, C. (1992). *Language contact in the American Deaf community.* Washington, DC: Gallaudet University Press.

Luetke-Stahlman, B., & Luckner, J. (1991). *Effectively teaching students with hearing impairment.* New York: Longman.

Maller, S. J. (1996). WISC-III verbal item invariance across samples of deaf and hearing children of similar measured ability. *Journal of Psychoeducational Assessment, 14*, 152-165.

Maller, S. J. (1997). Deafness and WISC-III item difficulty: Invariance and fit. *Journal of School Psychology, 35*, 299-314.

Maller, S. J. (1999). The validity of WISC-III subtest analysis for deaf children. Paper presented at the American Educational Research Association, Montreal, Canada, April 19-23.

Maller, S. J., & Ferron, J. (1997). WISC-III factor invariance across deaf and standardisation sampled. *Educational and Psychological Measurement, 7*, 987-994.

Marschark, M. (1993). *Psychological development of deaf children.* New York: Oxford University Press.

Marschark, M. (1997). *Raising and educating a deaf child: A comprehensive guide to the choices, controversies, and decisions faced by parents and educators.* New York: Oxford University Press.

Martin, D. (Ed.). (1991). *Advances in cognition, education, and deafness.* Washington, DC: Gallaudet University Press.

Mayberry, R., & Eichen, E. (1991). The long-lasting advantage of learning sign language in child-hood: Another look at the critical period for language acquisition. *Journal of Memory and Language, 30*, 486-512.

Mayer, C. (1999). Shaping at the point of utterance: An investigation of the composing processes of the deaf student writer. *Journal of Deaf Studies and Deaf Education, 4*, 37-49.

Mayer, C., & Akamatsu, C. T. (1999). Bilingual-bicultural models of literacy education for deaf students: Considering the claims. *Journal of Deaf Studies and Deaf Education, 4*, 1-8.

Mayer, C., & Akamatsu, C. T. (2000). Deaf children creating written texts: Contributions of American Sign Language and signed forms of English. *American Annals of the Deaf, 145(5)*, 394-403.

Mayer, C., & Wells, G. (1996). Can the linguistic interdependence theory support a bilingual-bi-cultural model of literacy education for deaf students? *Journal of Deaf Studies and Deaf Education, 1*, 93-107.

Montanini Manfredi, M. (1993). The emotional development of deaf children. In M. Marschark & M. D. Clark (Eds.), *Psychological perspectives on deafness* (pp. 49-63). Hillsdale, NJ: Lawrence Erlbaum Associates.

Moores, D. (1996). *Educating the deaf: Psychological principles and practices.* 4th ed. Boston: Houghton Mifflin.

Moores, D., & Sweet, C. (1990). Factors predictive of school achievement, In D. Moores & K. Meadow-Orlans (Eds.), *Educational and developmental aspects of deafness.* Washington, DC: Gallaudet University Press.

Motta, R. W. (1995). Childhood post-traumatic stress disorder and the schools. *Canadian Journal of School Psychology, 11*, 65-78.

Mylander, C., & Goldin-Meadow, S. (1991). Home sign systems in deaf children: The development of morphology without a conventional language model. In P. Siple & S. Fischer (Eds.), *Theoretical issues in sign language research: Psychology.* Chicago: University of Chicago Press.

Newport, E. (1996). Sign language research in the Third Millennium. Paper presented at the Theoretical Issues in Sign Language Conference, Montreal, Canada, September 19-22.

Palinscar, A. S., Brown, A., & Campione, J. (1991). Dynamic assessment. In H. L. Swanson (Ed), *Handbook on the assessment of learning disabilities* (pp. 75-94). Austin, TX: Pre-Ed.

Paul, P. (1993). Deafness and text-based literacy. *American Annals of the Deaf, 138*, 72-75.

Pollard, R. (1998). Psychopathology. In M. Marschark & M. D. Clark (Eds.), *Psychological perspectives on deafness*, Vol. 2, (pp. 171-198). Mahwah, NJ: Erlbaum.

Rueda, R., & Garcia, E. (1997). Do portfolios make a difference for diverse students? The influence of type of data on making instructional decisions. *Learning Disabilities Research and Practice, 12*, 114-122.

Samuda, R. J. (1990). *New approaches to assessment and placement of minority students.* Toronto: Ministry of Education.

Siegel, J., & Cole, E. (1990). Role expansion for school psychologists: Challenges and future directions. In E. Cole & J. Siegel (Eds.), *Effective consultation in school psychology* (pp. 3-17). Toronto: Hogrefe & Huber Publishers.

Singleton, J., Supalla, S., Litchfield, S., & Schley, S. (1998). From sign to word: Considering modality constraints in ASL/English bilingual education. *Topics in Language Disorders, 18*, 16-29.

Sladeczek, I. E., & Heath, N. L. (1997). Consultation in Canada. *Canadian Journal of School Psychology, 13*, 1-14.

Spencer, P., & Marschark, M. (in press). Cochlear implants: A review of linguistic, social and educational implications. In M. Marschark & P. Spencer (Eds.), *The handbook of deaf studies, language, and education.* New York: Oxford University Press.

Supalla, S., Singleton, J., Wix, T., & Maller, S. (1998). The development and psychometric properties of the American Sign Language Proficiency Assessment (ASL-PA). *Journal of Deaf Studies and Deaf Education, 4,* 249-269.

Thomas, T. N. (1992). Psychoeducational adjustment of English-speaking Caribbean and Central American immigrant children in the United States. *School Psychology Review, 21,* 566-576.

Turner, S. (1996). Meeting the needs of children under five with sensori-neural hearing loss from ethnic minority families. *Journal of the British Association of Teachers of the Deaf, 20,* 91-100.

United Nations High Commissioner for Refugees. (1994). *Refugee Children.* Geneva: UNHCR.

United States Census Bureau (2000). Current Population Reports, P25-917 and P25-1095; and "Resident Population Estimates of the United States by Age and Sex: April 1, 1990 to July 1, 1999; with short-term projections to April 1, 2000;" published 24 May 2000; <http://www.census.gov/population/estimates/nation/intfile2-1.txt>.

United States Committee on Refugees.
(http://www.refugees.org/worldcountryrpt/amer_carib/1998/canada.htm),
(http://www.refugees.org/worldcountryrpt/amer_carib/1999/canada.htm),
(http://www.refugees.org/worldcountryrpt/amer_carib/canada.htm),
(http://www.refugees.org/worldcountryrpt/amer_carib/1998/us.htm)
(http://www.refugees.org/worldcountryrpt/amer_carib/1999/us.htm)
(http://www.refugees.org/worldcountryrpt/amer_carib/us.htm)
(http://www.refugees.org/news/fact_sheets/refugee definition.htm)

Vernon, M., & Andrews, J. (1990). *The psychology of deafness.* New York: Longman.

Vygotsky, L. S. (1978). *Mind in society: The development of higher psychological processes.* Cambridge, MA: Harvard University Press.

Vygotsky, L. S. (1987). *Thought and word.* (trans. N. Minnick). In R.W. Rieber & A.S. Carlton (Eds.), *The collected works of L.S. Vygotsky: Volume 1.* New York: Plenum.

Vygotsky, L. S. (1997). *Educational psychology.* (trans. R. Silverman). Boca Raton, Florida: St. Lucie Press.

Wertsch, J. (1985). *Vygotsky and the social formation of mind.* Cambridge, MA: Harvard University Press.

Chapter 14
Collaborative Consultation in French Immersion: Observing Communication and Interaction Patterns

Laurie Carlson Berg

The study discussed in this chapter provides information for French immersion teachers, school psychologists, and others in the school staff and the educational organization. It provides an example of a primary prevention model of psychological services at the school level. An observation grid and a consultative process were used to gather and analyze information to aid individual French immersion teachers in program planning for students (Carlson & Cole, 1993).

This research is situated within a context which assumes that the school psychologist is a change agent and engaged in a collaborative problem-solving process with teachers. "Teaching is thus perceived as a cooperative task, governed by a culture of inquiry. The workplace then becomes the locus of ongoing professional learning, guided by principles of school-based development, adult learning, cooperative planning, ongoing evaluation, and active knowledge transfer within the school" (Vandenberghe & Huberman, 1999, p.10). It also views the teacher as decision-maker. Finally, consultation is seen as a collaborative process involving mutual respect from all participants (Cole & Siegel, 1990).

The traditional way of providing consultation or implementing change was for the school psychologist to act as expert and make plans for change and give these plans to teachers for them to put into practice (Cole & Siegel, 1990). For decades, the professional literature has urged school psychologists to assume a broader role. It has also been demonstrated that school psychologists rank consultation as the preferred, or one of their most preferred, job functions (Shpuniarsky, 1988). Nonetheless, the results of a recent study indicate that only 17% of their time is spent in problem-solving consultation (Reschly, 2000). Perhaps what is needed is a model of how to engage in a problem-solving consultation process. This chapter is intended to illustrate one such method.

Teachers, as informed professionals, have also been urged to become partners in the change process (Brophy, 1989; Fullan, 1991; Wells, 1990). Wells (1990) provides three compelling reasons for teachers to partner with change agents, such as school psychologists. First, each class is a unique grouping of individual students and a teacher, each of whom have their own style, strengths, limitations, and set of past experiences. To plan for change in a particular classroom, then, one must know its dynamics well. The instrument used in this research is one such way for a teacher and school psychologist to study the dynamics. Secondly, in order to make effective change, one needs to have the control which comes from setting one's own goals, planning how to achieve them, and revising when necessary. Thirdly, one learns best when one is the agent of one's own learning; when one identifies problems and issues and is responsible for seeking out information and then experimenting with and evaluating a variety of possible solutions. Through the process described in this chapter, the teacher and school psychologist work collaboratively to identify issues, seeking out information about them, and then planning possible solutions. By so doing, the teacher and school psychologist are providing an example of action research for their students. Furthermore, the school, as a centre of inquiry, can share in advancing professional knowledge in education through joint investigations with university personnel.

The example of consultation that will be outlined in this chapter is an observational study that was carried out in six French immersion classrooms at one school over an eight-week period. An observation grid was developed for use in order to determine the predominant language and the type of communication strategies used by teachers and students.

Step 1: Identifying the Area of Concern

This research was carried out at a school where the writer was doing a student practicum placement with a school psychologist. The area of focus, namely communicative output of French immersion students, came out of discussions with both the supervising psychologist and teachers at the school. It is suggested that the most appropriate use of this methodology would be to begin by identifying the area of concern through a dialogue between consultants, in this case the school psychologist and practicum student, and the consultees, in this case the French immersion teachers.

In this research, the area of concern was how to increase the amount of French spoken in class by French immersion students. The starting point was an interview with each of the six teachers. The teachers were asked about their goals and the methods they used to attain them.

Step 2: Development of the Data Gathering Tool

Once the need, or area of concern, was identified, the student school psychology consultant reviewed the relevant literature to design a data-gathering tool. An observation grid was chosen in order to make a careful and systematic analysis of the instructional environment and its influence on the amount of French spoken. This decision was influenced by the classic work of Ysseldyke and Christensen (1987) who maintain, as do others (Bandura, 1978), that learning and behavior are not independent of their surroundings. The use of observations for collaborative problem solving is also encouraged by scholars who maintain that these collective school development projects can help prevent teacher burnout (Vandenberghe & Huberman, 1999).

The area of concern, as identified by the teachers, was communicative output. The French immersion teaching guidelines at the school board in which this research was carried out maintained a philosophy that second language teaching is most effective when the communicative approach is used (Clarke, 1988; Laplante, 2000; Lyster, 1995). The communicative approach emphasizes the importance of creating situations in which meaningful communication can occur on a one-to-one basis, in small groups, and in whole-class groupings. The observation grid (see Appendix A) was designed to determine which classroom situations and activities maximize communication in French as a second language and the context and purposes for which French and English are spoken in the classroom.

A review of the relevant literature revealed that: 1) there had been relatively few studies of the communicative approach as it manifests itself in daily classroom processes in immersion classrooms (Cleghorn, 1981; Lentz, Lyster, Netten, & Tardif, 1994; Wode, 2000), 2) the importance of the teacher as language model (Bayliss & Vignola, 2000; Bruck & Schultz, 1977; Center for Advanced Research on Language Acquisition, 2000), 3) the importance of talk to learning (Wells, 1990, 2001), and 4) the types of talk that have been identified (Goodwin & Coates, 1977; Tough, 1979; Wode, 2000). Guidelines for French immersion programs reflect a broadening of focus from the traditional emphasis on the development of proficiency in French to include a consideration of teaching practices and classroom atmosphere (Clarke, 1988; Lentz, 2001; Netten, 2001).

Cleghorn (1981) conducted research on patterns of language use and interactions, both formal and informal, among French immersion teachers and found that children's performance in French is influenced by the teacher's pattern of language use in the classroom. This information contributed to the decision to have an observational category on teacher-to-student (T-S) interactions and student-to-teacher (S-T) interactions. The final speaker category on the observation grid is student-to-student (S-S).

At each of the six observational sessions, five students were selected by a random selection without replacement method. An effort was made to select boys and girls for each observational period and, in the case of classes with combined grades, at least one student from each grade level was selected per period. Teacher-to-student interactions included all communications initiated by the teacher and directed to any of the five students selected for observation during that particular period. Teacher-to-student interactions also included communications initiated by the teacher and directed to the whole class. Student-to-student interactions included all communications initiated by one of the five selected students and directed at any of their classmates or to the whole class. Marks on the observation grid were made in one color of ink for French communications and in another color of ink for English communications.

The types of talk included in the grid (see Appendix A) were informed by the work of Goodwin and Coates (1977), Tough (1979), and Wells (1990a, 1990b). The individual talking behaviors were grouped into five categories: telling, asking, discussing, socializing, and disciplining/acting out. The types of communication were also subgrouped according to the number of people involved in the interaction, the three categories being one-to-one, small group, or whole class.

Step 3: Collecting the Data

Classroom observations were carried out to determine the relationship between the academic subject being taught, as well as instructional groupings and activities, and the amount and kind of student communication in French and English in the French immersion classroom. The data were analyzed in order to answer the following questions: *What classroom situations and activities maximize communication in French as a second language?* and *In what context and for what purposes are French and English spoken in the classroom?*

The six teachers who participated in this study were women teaching Grades 1–5 French immersion in a large metropolitan school board. The amount of French instruction within the grade levels was uniform. The teachers had been teaching for between three and fifteen years overall, with between one and eight and one half years experience. The six groups of children who participated were two Grade 1 classrooms, two Grade 2/3 classrooms, one Grade 3/4/5 classroom and one Grade 4/5 classroom. Six observation periods were spent in each classroom, as follows: two periods of mathematics; two periods of French Language Arts; and two periods of social studies. The three subjects were chosen so as to include sessions in which the second language is taught (French Language Arts), sessions in which the learning is primarily language-based (social studies), and sessions in a subject area that is less dependent on second language proficiency (mathematics). For each academic subject, observations were made both of lessons in which primarily new material was being presented and of review lessons. Each observational period was approximately 45 minutes in length. It should be noted that, in a non-research consultation, a detailed grid like the one described above would not necessarily be used. The important consideration when designing the grid is how much detail is necessary to answer the question. Another consideration is whether all the data needs to be, or indeed can be, gathered at the same time. For example, the teacher may want information about one specific behavior, such as whether s/he is initiating communication with a variety of students. In this case, a more global concern was raised that required a review of the relevant literature, to explore what was known regarding the concern, and a detailed grid to provide the necessary information.

Step 4: Joint Review of Data

Once the observations have been carried out by the school psychologist, or indeed another teacher, a review of the data can be done by the consultant and consultee to address the questions of the consultee. The review is aimed at highlighting the behaviors that promote the teacher's goal, in this case increased French output by students, and addressing behaviors or situations which do not appear to be promoting the goals and objectives of the teacher consultee.

In this case, which was a formal research study, statistical analysis of the data was performed. Since the sample was made up of a small number of teachers and classrooms, non-parametric statistics were used, including frequency counts and percentages. An initial overview of the data revealed similarities in the communication and interaction patterns according to grade grouping. Therefore, a decision was made to combine the data from the three groups, which consisted of the two Grade 1 classes as the first group, the two Grade 2/3 classrooms made up the second group, and the third group was made up of the Grade3/4/5 classroom and the Grade 4/5 classroom.

Communication Types by Interaction Types

The overall findings for communication types by interaction type, for all grades combined, can be seen in Table 1. Overall, teacher-to-student interactions were the most numerous, making up 55.7% of all interactions in this study. The remaining interactions were evenly divided between student-to-student and student-to-teacher interactions.

As Table 1 shows, the total number of interactions for each communication category (telling, discussing, asking, social, and disciplining/acting out) was also tabulated. Asking communications were the most numerous, accounting for 45.6% of all interactions in this study. Asking communications occupied nearly half of all teacher-to-student interactions and nearly three-quarters of student-to-teacher interactions.

Telling communications made up over 30% of all interactions observed. Almost all of the telling took place in teacher-to-student interactions. The students engaged in few telling communications, with only 5% of student-to-teacher interactions and only 12.5% of student-to-student interactions being telling communications.

Table 1 Communication Type by Interaction Type

Communication Type	Total n	Total %	T-S n	T-S %	S-S n	S-S %	S-T n	S-T %
Telling	1345	36.5	1110	82.5	168	12.5	67	5.0
Discussing	267	7.3	28	10.5	185	69.3	54	20.2
Asking	1681	45.6	877	52.2	215	12.8	589	35.0
Social	344	9.3	26	7.6	238	69.2	80	23.3
Discipline/Act Out	47	1.3	10	21.3	14	29.8	23	48.9
Overall	3684	100	2051	55.7	820	22.3	813	22.1

Discussing and social communications each made up less than 10% of the total interactions observed. Most discussing and social talk occurred between students, accounting for nearly 70% of all discussing behaviors and social behaviors observed. The least discussing occurred in teacher-to-student interactions.

Another important finding is that the students exhibited the most balanced distribution among the five types of communications. The teachers, in contrast, appeared to be telling and asking for the most part with only 1.3% of teacher-student communications involving each discussing or social communications. It is also interesting to note that teacher-to-student communications relating to disciplining/acting out accounted for less than one half of 1%.

Interaction Types by Classroom Grouping

The total number of communicative interactions by classroom grouping (whole class, small group, one-to-one) was tabulated for all grades combined, as shown in Table 2. Nearly half of the interactions occurred in the whole class grouping and 40% oc-

Table 2 Interaction Types by Classroom Grouping

Interaction Type	Total n	Total %	Whole Class n	Whole Class %	Small Group n	Small Group n	One-to One n	One-to-One n
Teacher to Student	2051	100	1170	57.0	655	31.9	226	11.0
Student to Student	820	100	181	22.1	532	64.9	107	13.0
Student to Teacher	813	100	396	48.7	291	35.8	126	15.5
Total	3684	100	1747	47.4	1478	40.1	459	12.5

curred in small groups. Only 12.5% occurred on a one-to-one basis. Nearly half of all interactions observed in this study occurred between teachers and students in the whole class grouping. The lowest number of interactions occurred from student-to-student on a one-to-one basis. The greatest number of student-to-student interactions took place in small groups.

Classroom Grouping by Grade

The number of interactions that occurred in each of the classroom groupings, as calculated for each grade, can be seen in Table 3. While the greatest number of interactions took place in the whole class setting, for the students observed in this study, there was an increase in the number of one-to-one interactions as the students got older so that by Grade 4/5, one-to-one communications accounted for 30% of the interactions. In the same way, the whole group interactions decreased as the students got older, going from over 61% in Grade 1 to 36.5% in Grade 4/5.

Table 3 Classroom Groupings by Grade

Grade	Total *n*	Total %	Whole Class *n*	Whole Class %	Small Group *n*	Small Group %	One-to One *n*	One-to-One %
One	1240	100	760	61.3	405	32.7	75	6.0
Two/Three	1399	100	606	43.3	723	51.7	70	5.0
Four/Five	1045	100	381	36.5	350	33.5	314	30.0
Total	3684	100	1747	47.4	1478	40.1	459	12.5

Step 5: Collaborative Problem-Solving and Planning

Once the data has been analyzed either formally, as in this study, or informally, the collaborative problem-solving between school psychologist and teacher can begin. In this study, we proceeded by bringing together the relevant data to respond to two questions. A summary of the response to each question and a discussion of both questions follows.

What classroom situations and activities maximize communication in French as a second language?

Overall, the highest percentage of French interactions for all grades combined occurred in the whole-class grouping. The greatest number of communications in English took place when the students were in small groups. The greatest number of student-to-student interactions took place in small groups. When students were working in small groups on activities, assignments, or projects, communications to model correct speech were more likely to occur. Discussing and reading activities both seemed to encourage more social communication but, with that, there were also more disciplining and acting out communications. However, the older students in this study did not have any disciplining/acting out communications during student-to-student communications. This may be an indication that, as the students mature, they are able to remain on task more independently. The greatest variety of communication in both French and English occurred in student-to-student interactions. The percentage of interactions is most evenly distributed across the five categories of communication (telling, discussing, asking, social, disciplining/acting out) for student-to-student interactions. Teacher-to-student and student-to-teacher interactions were mainly telling and asking communications. Student-initiated communications accounted for close to half of all communications in this study. There were more student-initiated communications to other students than to teachers. In this study, students initiated more discussion than did teachers.

In what context and for what purposes are French and English spoken in the classroom?

In terms of the purposes for which each language was used, French was used in the majority of asking, telling, and disciplining/acting out communications. English was used for the majority of social communications and French and English were used with equal frequency for discussions. French was the predominant language used in all three subject areas (French Language Arts, math, and social studies). French was the language which was predominant in the whole class setting while English predominated when students were in small groups. For teachers who claim that group work is counterproductive because of the amount of English spoken, Allen, Swain, Harley, and Cummins (1990) propose use of certain pedagogical strategies. One strategy is to give the students a task that requires the outcome to be a spoken or written text in French. Another strategy is for the teacher to contrive an activity that will naturally elicit certain forms of language, particularly those which may be problematic for the students. Allen et al. (1990) contend that student opportunities for output be carefully planned so that students have the opportunity to produce the full range of target language forms.

Discussion and Recommendations

When asked, the teachers indicated that an area of concern for them was how to increase the amount of French spoken in class by French immersion students. The observation grid helped to identify the components of oral output and put these components into the talk categories of telling, asking, discussing, social, and disciplining/acting out. By identifying the categories of talk, their sub-components, as well as classroom groupings, the recommendations for how to modify the teaching of French in immersion classrooms could be more specific. The following are an example of some recommendations which came out of the analysis of data in this study.

Increase Student Discussion Opportunities

Teacher talk accounted for more than half of all the interactions in this study. It consisted mainly of asking and telling communications. Teacher talk is important in French immersion classrooms because the teacher is a linguistic role model, perhaps the only one, in many Canadian school communities where English is the predominant language. Receiving comprehensible input from the French teachers is an important factor in oral language development of French immersion students (Allen et al., 1990; Cummins & Swain, 1986). However, it is important that this input occur in a situation where meaning is negotiated through a process of learning and interacting that leads to comprehension (Snow, 1989). It is possible that such meaning was negotiated through the asking and answering communications in this study. Nonetheless, future planning could include facilitating more discussing communications. This could lead to situations in which meaning is defined and this would be of benefit to the students' future oral output. This is consistent with the work of Harley and Swain (1984) who concluded that comprehensible input, while necessary, is not sufficient to promote proficiency in a second language. They recommend that teachers provide opportunities for students to be involved in activities which require the productive use of various language constructs in meaningful situations.

Continue to Provide Feedback on Errors in Student Speech

According to Cummins and Swain (1986) *negative input* is also needed to push the student to produce precise, coherent, and appropriate speech. This *negative input* was observed in this study when the teachers and students used the telling communications *corrects student speech* and *models correct speech*. It is recommended that the teachers continue to engage in these behaviors and to encourage the students to engage in them as well. Allen et al. (1990) acknowledge the dilemma of providing feedback on errors: if teachers correct errors, they may interrupt the flow of communication; if they do not correct errors, the opportunities for students to make links between form and function are reduced.

Broaden Variety of Talk Experiences

As important as it is for students to have good linguistic role models and hear correct French speech, it is also important for them to have opportunities to talk. Wells (1990) maintains that one of the principal ways a child learns to talk is by talking. According to research into verbal communication (Tough, 1979; Wells, 1990) and French immersion methodology (Snow, 1987), students need a variety of talk experiences, both one-on-one and in small and large groups. In this study, most student talk occurred in small groups. A greater variety of talk experiences, including large group and one-to-one, could give students the opportunity to further develop their communicative skills. Presentations of current events, reciting of poetry, debate are examples of large group forums for communication. These activities could also facilitate discussion, a communicative activity to which the students in this study could use more exposure. One-to-one activities could be proofing each other's written work and providing verbal feedback or any activity done in pairs requiring verbalizing. Providing whole class and one-to-one activities would broaden the talk experiences of the students in this study.

Implications

The observation grid used in this study could also be used in other second language classrooms, both nationally and internationally. For example, in the United States, there are various forms of bilingual education (Faltis & Hudelson, 1998). In some forms, Spanish/English education is provided to a mixed group of students, some who speak English as their mother tongue and others for whom Spanish is their first language. In this context, examination of which language is used for which purposes could be helpful in two important ways. First, it could serve to ensure that a variety of types of communication are modeled to and practiced by the students. Second, an observer could monitor the messages given regarding the relative importance of each language. For example, if important school announcements are given in English, the students may interpret this to mean that English is a higher status language.

In Germany, there are programs in which students begin one immersion program when they enter school at age 3 and then begin a second immersion program at around age 10 (Wode, 2000). Wode has studied how the children learn the second languages and the types of errors they make in terms of semantics, phonology and lexicon. Further study could be done to examine whether the students are learning to use their non-native languages in a variety of communicative interactions. If, as in this study, most of their communication consists of telling and asking, they could succeed well in their schooling but perhaps not have full communicative competency when engaging with native speakers.

In any setting, the observation grid could also be used to gather data to inform making individual education plans for students having particular difficulty. Although the six classrooms observed in this study are not necessarily representative of all French immersion programs, the findings can provide insights to school psychologists who may be unfamiliar with French immersion classroom practices. The observation grid could be used by school psychologists, even if they do not speak French, to observe the pattern of teacher-to-student, student-to-student, and student-to-teacher interactions and to note the instructional grouping arrangements, instructional content, and the activities and behaviors in which the students are engaging. Observation of the learning environment and the interactions of the student with his or her teacher, peers, and environment is a key part of consultation. Observation can be a powerful learning tool for teachers (Wajnryb, 1992) and psychologists. The knowledge gained using observation methods is likely to enhance psychoeducational assessments as well. By including observations of the learning environment of the student being assessed, a clearer profile of the student's educational needs will likely emerge. Furthermore, the collaborative consultations based on the observations are likely to lead to sound classroom-based interventions since the observer has first-hand knowledge of the classroom environment and dynamics. It is not likely that each child observed in this study will be individually assessed by a school psychologist. Nonetheless, each can benefit from the recommendations made through this collaborative consultation process.

The results of this study can also inform the training of French immersion teachers. Teacher educators could make their students aware of the observation grid and the categories of communication. Knowledge of the types of communications and situations which can facilitate their development will aid the future teachers to focus their teaching not only on grammar and vocabulary acquisition but also on facilitating the full range of communicative competencies in their students.

The methodology used in this study could serve as a model of consultation that could be taught at the graduate level to students preparing to be school psychologists. It provides a way for them to access concerns of teachers and explore the concerns and questions in a collaborative manner. The recommendations that can be generated from such a process are likely to be more readily used and accepted by teachers since they have been informed by the teacher's current practices and classroom environment and the teacher has been an active participant in the process from start to finish.

Conclusion

This chapter has outlined a method of collaborative consultation. This process was engaged in by a school psychology student researcher and a group of six teachers. This process could be used not only by school psychologists and teachers but also teams of teachers working collectively and collaboratively. The process began with a question from the teachers. This question identified the area of concern. Next, a data-gathering tool was developed. The observation method and grid were informed by research. The necessary data to inform the collaborative problem solving and planning were collected through interviews with teachers and classroom observations using the grid. In terms of the review of the data, in this research project a statistical analysis was undertaken and then recommendations came out of both the quantitative and qualitative analysis of the data and relevant previous research. Since the statistical analysis consisted mainly of frequency counts and percentages, this could also be done in a school-based consultation or the data could be reviewed more informally by both the school psychologist and the teacher. Once the data has been jointly reviewed, the next step is the collaborative problem-solving and planning. The cycle comes full circle when new observation is done to provide feedback as to whether there are improvements in the area of concern and whether further planning and intervention may be necessary.

References

Allen, P., Swain, M., Harley, B., & Cummins, J. (1990). Aspects of classroom treatment: Toward a more comprehensive view of second language education. In B. Harley, P. Allen, J. Cummins, & M. Swain (Eds.), *The Development of Second Language Proficiency* (pp. 57-81). Cambridge: Cambridge University Press.

Bandura, A. (1978). The self system in reciprocal determinism. *American Psychologist, 33,* 344-351.

Bayliss, D., & Vignola, M.-J. (2001). FSL teachers in French immersion: How good should they be and how do they get there? In *The state of French second language education in Canada 2001* (p. 20). Ottawa: Canadian Parents for French.

Brophy, J. (1989). *Advances in research on teaching.* Greenwich: JAI Press.

Bruck, M., & Schultz, J. (1977). *An ethnographic analysis of the language use patterns of bilingually schooled children. Working papers on bilingualism, 13.* Toronto: Ontario Institute for Studies in Education, Bilingual Education Project.

Carlson, L., & Cole, E. (1993). Communication and interaction patterns in French immersion classrooms: Implications for consultation. *Canadian Journal of School Psychology, 9(2),* 133-149.

Center for Advanced Research on Language Acquisition (2000). Immersion Teaching Strategies Observation Checklist [On-line]. Access: http://carla.acad.umn.edu/checklist.html, last updated on October 30, 2000.

Clarke, J. (1988). *French immersion language arts guidelines.* Toronto: Metropolitan Toronto School Board.

Cleghorn, A. (1981). *Patterns of teacher interaction in an immersion school in Montréal.* Unpublished doctoral dissertation, McGill University.

Cole, E., & Siegel, J. A. (Eds.). (1990). *Effective consultation in school psychology.* Toronto: Hogrefe & Huber Publishers.

Cummins, J., & Swain, M. (1986). *Bilingualism in education.* New York: Longman.

Faltis, C., & Hudelson, S. (1998). *Bilingual education in elementary and secondary school communities.* Boston: Allyn & Bacon.

Fullan, M.G. (1991). *The new meaning of educational change.* Toronto: OISE Press.

Goodwin, D. L., & Coates, T. J. (1977). The teacher-pupil interaction scale: An empirical method for analyzing the interactive effects of teacher and pupil behavior. *Journal of School Psychology, 15(1)*, 51-59.

Harley, B., & Swain, M. (1984). The interlanguage of immersion students and its implications for second language teaching. In A. Davies, D. Criper, & A. Howatt (Eds.), *Interlanguage,* (pp. 292-311). Edinburgh: Edinburgh University Press.

Laplante, B. (2000). Apprendre en sciences, c'est apprendre à "parler sciences": Des élèves de l'immersion nous parlent des réactions chimiques. *Canadian Modern Language Review/La Révue Canadienne des Langues Vivantes, 57(2)*, 245-271.

Lentz, F. (2001). Reflections on immersion pedagogy: Food for thought. In *The state of French second language education in Canada 2001* (p. 22, 24). Ottawa: Canadian Parents for French.

Lentz, F., Lyster, R., Netten, J., & Tardif, C. (1994). Table ronde vers une pédagogie propre à l'immersion. *Le Journal de l'Immersion, 18(1)*, 15-27.

Lyster, R. (1995). *Instructional strategies in French immersion: An annotated bibliography.* Ottawa : Canadian Association of Immersion Teachers.

Netten, J. (2001). Are French classrooms sufficiently male-friendly? In *The state of French second language education in Canada 2001* (pp. 8-9). Ottawa: Canadian Parents for French.

Reschly, D. (2000). The present and future status of school psychology in the United States. *School Psychology Review, 29(4)*, 507-522.

Shpuniarsky, M. (1988). *Psychological consultation in schools.* Unpublished Master's thesis, University of Toronto.

Snow, M. (1987). *Immersion teacher handbook.* Los Angeles: University of California, Los Angeles.

Snow, M. (1989). Negotiation of meaning in the immersion classroom. In *Negotiation of meaning: Teacher's activity manual.* Rockland, MD: Board of Education of Montgomery County.

Tough, J. (1979). *Talk for teaching and learning.* London: Ward Lock International.

Vandenberghe, R., & Huberman, A. M. (1999). *Understanding and preventing teacher burnout.* Cambridge: Cambridge University Press.

Wajnryb, R. (1992). *Classroom observation tasks: A resource book for language teachers and trainers.* Cambridge: Cambridge University Press.

Wells, G. (1990). Talk: A medium for learning and change: An inquiry orientation. In *Readings on assessing language arts* (pp. 77-81). Toronto: Ontario Ministry of Education.

Wells, G. (Ed.) (2001). *Action, talk, and text: Learning and teaching through inquiry.* New York: Teachers College Press.

Wode, H. (2000). *Multilingual education in Europe: What can preschools contribute?* Paper presented at the 5th European Conference on Immersion Programs, Vaasa, Finland.

Ysseldyke, J. E., & Christenson, S. L. (1987). *The instructional environment scale.* Austin: Pro-Ed.

Appendix A: Types of Communication

One-to-One/Small Group/Whole Class

Telling	T-S	S-S	S-T
Instructs/explains/describes			
Corrects S speech (S-S: O = Own; P = Peers)			
Models correct speech			
Gives instructions/reinforces rules			
Provides S with P/N feedback on her performance			
Indicates needs/wants			
Justifies behavior			
Repeats instructions			
Discussing			
Discusses task at hand			
Makes comparisons			
Analyzes			
Reflects on meaning of experiences			
Justifies judgments			
Predicts possible problems, solutions, and consequences			
Asking			
Asks questions			
Answers questions			
Social			
Shares past, present, and future experiences			
Communications not oriented to class activity but which are non-disruptive, e.g. greetings, sharing of non-academic information (S/G)			
Disciplining/Acting Out			
Constructive or negative response to undesirable behavior of S (C/N)			
Constructive or negative response to teacher communication (C/N)			

Total observation time: _____ **minutes**
Type of Lesson: Primarily New Material/Application & Consolidation
Subject: Math, French Language Arts, Social Studies

Chapter 15
Consulting About Young Children: An Ecosystemic Developmental Perspective

Sharone Maital and Anat Scher

Introduction

Practitioners have become increasingly concerned with adapting psychological consultation to meet the needs of specific groups of consultees and clients (Harris & Zetlin, 1993; Ingraham, 2000; Maital, 2000; Westby & Ford, 1993). At the same time, child development experts have been calling for careful consideration of how the results of developmental research are being translated into specific practices and policies (Damon, 1995; Horowitz, 2000; Lerner, Fisher, & Weinberg, 2000; Shonkoff, 2000; Sigel, 1990). In particular, studies have focused on when to intervene, how to best address current and future needs of the child, which partners to collaborate with, and how to consult effectively in light of cultural diversity (Meisels & Shonkoff, 2000). In working with young children, professionals are challenged to adopt a sensitive and effective approach that can account for the needs of the child, the parents, and the educators. This chapter presents a model for consultation that focuses on the needs of those working with young children. However, the model is also relevant for school psychologists and consultants seeking a systemic approach to working in other settings.

As more mothers of young children across the world join the work force, millions of children are in need of good daycare and preschool arrangements. Hence, we may expect to see an increase in the demand for psychological services for this age group. In some areas daycare centers and preschool programs have been a part of the community school system, and school psychologists have been involved in providing early childhood services from the outset (Barnett, 1986; Ershler, 1992). In other settings, school psychologists may be involved only at the point of transition from kindergarten to school. In both cases, a solid background in early development is essential for consultation with individual caregivers as well as at the system level. As we gain more empirical data regarding the importance of specific features of early intervention programs to later school adjustment (Blair, 2002; Ershler, 1992) psycho-educational services will need to translate this information into practice. Moreover, given the influence of sensitive parenting during the early years on the subsequent well-being of children (e.g., Blair, 2002; Rutter & Rutter, 1993) consultation aimed at establishing primary prevention programs as well as secondary interventions are both effective and economical (Cole,1996).

In consulting about young children, school psychologists have an important role to play in formulating, organizing, and delivering these types of services. School psychologists are in a unique position, at the intersection between developmental research and its application to practice and policy. There is a considerable body of scholarly work on early intervention efforts that are grounded in developmental research (e.g., Blasco, 2001; Shonkoff & Meisels, 2000). However, few have elaborated on an approach to *consulting* about young children.

Psychological consultation is widely advocated as an effective means of helping children with difficulties, in part by helping those who are responsible for them. Beginning with the early work of Gerald Caplan (1970), consultation has been defined as an indirect process of providing psychological services aimed at both resolving existing problems and preventing future difficulties. Since then, it has been adopted as an effective and widely used tool in school psychology (Cole & Siegel, 1990). Many textbooks and chapters have been written to present a variety of approaches to school consultation (e.g., Brown, Przwansky, & Shulte, 1995; Cole & Siegel, 1990; Conoley & Conoley, 1992; Erchul & Martens, 1997; Parsons & Meyers, 1984). The triadic nature of consultation in educational settings (involving consultant-consultee-child) and the collegial nature of relations between a professional consultant and consultee are widely assumed as the basis for consultation. The target of change may be seen as ranging from a more direct focus on the *child* who is experiencing difficulty, the *consultee's* difficulties in coping with the child, to a broader focus on creating *organizational* or *system-wide* change as a means of resolving and preventing future difficulties (Meyers, 1995; Meyers, Parsons, & Martin, 1979).

Three widely advocated approaches to consultation are behavioral, mental health, and organizational. *Behavioral consultation* focuses on helping consultees develop strategies for coping with children's difficulties based on principles of social learning theory. This approach has been most widely applied in educational settings (e.g., Brown et al., 1995; Conoley & Conoley, 1992). *Mental health consultation* focuses on promoting the psychological growth of consultees and helping them resolve internal processes that preclude effective problem resolution. *Organizational consultation* is concerned with understanding the structure and social interaction processes that occur in systems that may be affecting the individual (e.g., Schein, 1999). In addition, ecological or systemic approaches to consultation (e.g., Siegel & Cole, 1990; Conoley & Conoley, 1992; Plas, 1989) represent attempts to arrive at a more eclectic and integrative model that encompasses problem-solving approaches of several consultation models.

Approaches to consultation also vary with respect to their views concerning the role of the consultant and the influence processes used. Some have suggested that the consultant's role can be placed on a continuum from a more directive, expert role to a more collaborative stance in which consultants and consultees share responsibility for helping the client (e.g., Noell & Witt, 1996). Caplan and Caplan (1993) suggested that collaboration among mental health professionals and direct service providers is predominant when consultants work within an organization, whereas a more expert counseling role with respect to the consultee may be better suited to consultants external to the organization. Behavioral consultation is often seen as focused on the client's difficulties thus relying on a more directive, expert stance; a mental health focus on consultee difficulties places greater emphasis on the importance of collaboration. However, recent evidence suggests that consultants can be both directive and collaborative in their relations, regardless of the focus of change (e.g., Caplan & Caplan, 1993; Erchul, Raven, & Whichard, 2001; Gutkin, 1999).

How can we adapt these consultation models to the unique needs of parents and teachers who seek help in coping with young children? The ecological nature of early risk is well documented (e.g., Garbarino & Ganzel, 2000; Lerner et al., 2000; Meisels & Shonkoff, 2000) and an ecological stance has been advocated for choosing targets of intervention (Vincent, Salisbury, Strain, McCormick, & Tessier, 1990). The importance of an ecological approach to providing psychological services for children has been noted since the early involvement of school psychologists in preschool settings for children at risk (Barnett, 1986; Ershler, 1992). Less has been written specifically about adapting consultation processes to providing services focused on young children. Donahue, Falk, and Provet (2000) recently presented a clinically oriented, collaborative mental health approach to consultation in early childhood educational settings. Their work emphasized the integration of the goals of early childhood education and mental health practices through establishment of collaborative partnerships among caregivers, parents and professional service providers. Blasco (2001) also emphasized the importance of collaboration and the integration of direct and indirect services for young children. In this chapter we propose an ecosystemic developmental approach to consulting about young children. Our model aims to provide consultants with an organized framework for examining the systemic nature of developmental processes, the context of early development, and the difficulties frequently experienced by young children and their caregivers. School psychologists concerned with young children need to be versed in developmental theory and research. They also should be familiar with methods for bridging science and practice with respect to childrearing issues faced by parents and educators. Moreover, they need to be able to work collaboratively, taking into account the different perspectives of the various participants in the ecological system that forms the young child's "developmental niche."

In the following sections, we first discuss some of the unique features of early child development and early childrearing contexts that are particularly salient for consultation about children from birth to five or six years of age. Following this, we present an ecosystemic perspective for consultation about young children. We then examine how such a systemic approach can be used in conjunction with knowledge of child development to guide the various stages in the consultation process.

Developmental Considerations in Consulting About Young Children

There are a number of developmental phenomena that have direct implications for consulting about young children. These include the interdependence and bi-directional influences of children and their caregivers during early childhood, and the wide variability and rapid change among normally developing young children.

Interdependence Among Young Children and Their Caregivers

The interdependence of children and the adults responsible for them is a hallmark of early childhood. Young children are not yet capable of seeking professional help independently (and developmental disabilities may even prolong the chronological period of dependency). Seen from this perspective, most intervention programs for young children recommended consultation with the adults responsible for them. Although school age children continue to rely upon adults to gain access to psychological services, as they get older they become more autonomous and more capable of independently seeking help from mental health professionals such as the school psychologist or counselor. However, with younger children, even direct services require the cooperation of parents and/or other adults responsible for the child.

Because young children are so dependent upon others, it is often difficult to differentiate a single locus of developmental difficulty or to isolate a single target for change. Rather, difficulties experienced by young children are generally interactive in nature and may be associated with the parent-child or teacher-child relationship itself (Garbarino & Ganzel, 2000; Stern, 1995). Attachment research suggests that there is variability in the quality of relations that young children experience with different family members and non-parental caregivers, especially in child care and early education settings (Pianta, 1999; Van Ijzendoorn, Sagi, & Lambermon, 1992; Weinraub & Lewis, 1977). This may account for some of the variability in the behavior of young children across interpersonal settings. Even in cases where a disability is clearly associated with the child (for example, children with genetic abnormalities, organic defects such as deafness, or perinatal complications), the expression of the disability and readiness to seek help can vary quite widely. The *goodness of fit* between a child's needs and temperament, the needs and style of the parents and of other responsible adults, along with environmental supports may be more important than the severity of a disability in determining whether the child's behavior becomes a problem and which intervention may be most effective (e.g. Horowitz, 1987; Rutter & Rutter, 1992; Simeonsson, Bailey Jr., Huntington, & Comfort, 1986). Thus, eco-systemic factors – responses of family members to the child, supports that family members provide for one another, as well as resources, social policies, and cultural beliefs and attitudes – all may be relevant to the consultation process.

Difficulties presented in each context may also reflect the quality of relations among settings; there may be tensions within and among the different settings in which the child participates, rather than a problem associated with the child or the setting alone (Honig, 1995; Howes & Matheson, 1992; Pugh, 1989). For example, mothers and caregivers may hold different expectations for self-control or independent exploration by the young child. Several studies have found significant differences in developmental expectations of parents and preschool teachers (e.g., Edwards, Gandini, & Giovaninni, 1996; Hess, Price, Dickson, & Conroy, 1984; Holloway, Gorman, & Fuller, 1988), and in the teaching strategies that they use. In general, differences in parents' expectations across contexts were more extreme and reflected their specific culture, whereas a cross-cultural comparison of teachers' views suggests that they share more universal developmental timetables in keeping with their professional training (Edwards et al., 1996). Thus, a child's difficulty may be expressed in one setting and not in another, or the problem may reflect confusion and frustration associated with discrepant expectations and conflicting messages from different caregivers. Such cases call for consultation focused on interpersonal relations among the different settings and consideration of the need for system-wide change.

Variability and Rapid Change in Early Childhood

The rapid rate of change and wide variability normally associated with early development is another set of issues that require careful consideration when school psychologists consult about young children. Awareness of normally occurring rapid change and variability in rates of growth among young children has implications for beliefs of both consultants and consultees about the need for early intervention. The case of early language acquisition is illustrative. Among toddlers, wide variability appears quite normative (e.g., Dromi, 1999; Bates et al., 1994; Fenson et al., 1994). For example, a recent U.S. study reported a mean vocabulary size of 302 words for 24-month-olds with a standard deviation of 179 words (Feldman et al., 2000). Similar variability has been reported for Spanish (Jackson-Maldonado, Thal, Marchman, Bates, & Gutierrez-Clellen, 1993) and Hebrew speaking toddlers (Maital, Dromi, Sagi, & Bornstein, 2000). Developmental studies such as these challenge school psychologists to help consultees differentiate between true developmental delays and perceived problems that arise due to unrealistic adult expectations.

The task of differentiating problems that reflect unrealistic expectations from real developmental difficulties is further complicated by assumptions of universal developmental trajectories typically based on classical (Western) theories of psychosocial development (Chait, Barnett, & Hyde, 2001; Rothbaum, Weisz, Pott, Miyake, & Morelli, 2000). This presents several challenges to school psychologists working in early childhood settings. The first challenge is the need to consider the cultural validity of widely held ideas about development and family behavior (Chait, Barnett, & Hyde, 2001; Rothbaum et al., 2000). Harkness and Keefer (2000) reviewed evidence for cultural variability in parents' goals and expectations that clearly have implications for behavior in different settings and for planning interventions. For example, a teacher's emphasis on individual cognitive development may be resisted by parents who hold collectivist views and are concerned about the child's social functioning in the group. American and Dutch parents held different educational concerns and different concepts of independence and dependence. The American parents were more concerned with cognitive aspects of development, whereas the Dutch parents were more focused on their children's social qualities and were more tolerant of young children's dependent behaviors as well as their assertions of independence. Other research has shown how the "difficult" temperament of young Ethiopian children was valued as it elicited greater adult attention and feeding (deVries & Sameroff, 1984).

A second challenge is to differentiate confirmed developmental findings from more speculative assertions that serve policy makers and practitioners (McCartney & Rosenthal, 2000; Shonkoff & Meisels, 2000). This requires careful consideration of the research methods used and critical consideration of the generalizability of results from different studies. It also requires critical consideration of pressures on school psychologists to rely on norm-referenced testing and early classification of children in need of services (Ershler, 1992).

Variability in children's behavior occurs normally over the course of development. Shaffer (2000) recently reviewed evidence concerning continuities from early to later development and concluded that "direct connections between early experiences and later personality functioning have proved difficult to demonstrate" (p. 12). For example, evidence for wider variability than expected in relations between early attachment and later outcomes, has led some to question the long term developmental implications of early attachment security and other early social-emotional experiences (Lewis, 1997; Thompson, 2000). Rather, there appear to be multiple pathways and chains of events expressed in the interactive influences of the child's temperament, contextual opportunities, and the timing of influences; all of which may lead to different outcomes. An over-emphasis on the primacy of early events for children's subsequent well-being, and failure to appreciate the potential for resilience of young children as they develop across the life span, may result in undue pressure for early interventions (Lewis, 1997). At the same time, there is increasing evidence that protective conditions both within the child and in the context of childrearing, such as sufficient nurturing to establish interpersonal trust, maternal competence, and community support for families, may serve as potential buffers that moderate young children's responses to adversity and increase their resilience (Werner, 2000). Particularly from a preventive perspective, this challenges school psychologists to help those involved with young children to chart a suitable developmental trajectory – one that is sufficiently flexible to accommodate opportunities that present themselves along the way and that considers the optimal timing for intervention.

Providing parents, caregivers and early educators with accurate, up-to-date information about development, and formulating a set of common developmental goals should be an important goal for school psychologists in consulting about young children. Above all, this task requires that early childhood consultants gain expertise in the translation of research findings to practice and policy. In particular, consultants need to be aware of the pitfalls and ethical implications of applying research to practice. Sigel (1990) proposed that the ethical application of developmental research requires careful attention to the limitations of findings and caution in making undue claims that all children will profit from interventions under all circumstances. Practitioners may view intervention goals and strategies that are consistent with developmental theory and research as more objective than interventions that are congruent with the culture of the consultees. However, there is an increasing recognition of the rights of parents to take part in establishing interventions that fit with their family and cultural values (Meisels & Shonkoff, 2000). Experts in cross-cultural early intervention also point to the need to fit interventions to the cultural perceptions and developmental goals of the consultees in order to insure effectiveness (Eldering & Leseman, 1999). Similarly, the values and organizational culture of each early educational system need to be taken into account. Thus, in addition to interpreting research findings, consultants need to be sensitive and skilled in culturally suitable means of applying them.

The Needs of Parents and Teachers of Young Children

Ecological influences emanating from common pressures of modern life, such as the need for both parents to work while raising young children or the relative isolation of the different adults responsible for a young child, also need to be considered in evaluating the difficulties of young children and consulting about them. From an ecosystemic perspective, parenting (and caregiving in general) may be conceptualized as multi-determined by factors that are both proximal and distal (Belsky, 1984). Many caregivers are challenged to balance the demands of attending to young children, while also meeting their own personal needs. With the growing prevalence of nuclear and even single parent families, Western childrearing has become an increasingly lonely and child-centered task with little consideration of adults' needs (Bronfenbrenner, 1992; Kagitcibasi,

1996). Even in group care settings, teachers may have little time for interactions with parents or other caregivers (Long, Peters, & Garduque, 1985; Pugh, 1989). Yet such naturally occurring social supports for parenting have been associated with reduced risk for developmental problems (Werner, 2000). Moreover, cross-cultural developmental research suggests that in Western society, adults are expected to adapt their behaviors and the surroundings to meet the needs of the young child (Rogoff, Mistry, Goncu, & Mosier, 1993). Paradoxically, in Western society, adults also are encouraged to focus on their own self-fulfillment (Damon, 1995), often leading to premature pressures for mature behavior (Elkind, 1987).

Another source of stress among parents that should be considered in consultation about young children is parental satisfaction with combining work and childrearing, or with full-time homemaker roles. Mothers' satisfaction has been associated with maternal well-being and the quality of mother-child relationships (e.g., Hock, 1980; Hoffman & Youngblade, 1999). For example, there is some evidence that employed mothers are more likely to place early demands on the child for independence in order to facilitate their functioning in dual roles, whereas full-time homemakers may foster dependency in their children. The changing role of fathers is also an important influence on child development that needs to be taken into account (Cabrera, Tamis-LeMonda, Bradley, Hofferth, & Lamb, 2000). A recent study found that fathers in dual-wage families were more involved in household tasks and child care and held fewer gender specific expectations (Hoffman & Youngblade, 1999). This study also found that both the work status of mothers and their sense of psychological well-being related to patterns of parenting – working mothers tended to be less permissive or authoritarian and more authoritative. Yet, child outcomes such as acting out were multi-determined, and not clearly related to one or another variable. Although this study considered families of children in early elementary grades, the findings are equally relevant to preschool children. The results highlight the need to consider the complex interactive influences of parents' work status, their attitudes toward work, the networks of support available – including the social climate that may or may not support parents' work decisions together with child-related variables such as gender and age, when consulting about young children and developing interventions.

An important goal in the early stages of consultation with those responsible for young children is to help families and educators identify difficulties and to help them come to terms with the recognition of their child's limitations (Blasco, 2001; Fine, 1991; Garguilo, 1985). The developmental status of young children often makes direct assessment more difficult than the evaluation of older children. In addition to the caution required in using normed-based measures (due to the dynamic nature and wide variability among young children), consultants also need to take into account that young children are relatively limited in their awareness of their difficulties as well as in their verbal ability to report their situation. Also, most normally developing young children are quite guarded in relating to an unfamiliar adult in an unfamiliar setting (Bronfenbrenner, 1979). Consequently, the initial evaluation of whether there is a need for intervention may be based on the knowledge, perceptions and needs of the adults who care for the young child as much as an objective, developmental assessment of the child's behavior. For example, Scheeringa, Peebles, Cook, and Zeanah (2001) found that a majority of the symptoms used in diagnosing PTSD in young children were observed and reported by parents, but could not be confirmed by independent observations of the child by professionals. Paradoxically, these same adults who are close to the child may have conflicting interests with respect to acknowledging the child's difficulty. Responses of parents to confirmation of their child's difficulty has been likened to patterns of mourning (Bradley, Rock, Whiteside, & Caldwell, 1991; Fortier & Winlass, 1984; Gowen, Johnson, Goldman, & Appelbaum, 1989). Often, parents respond with avoidance, shock, denial and anger, and they may blame the messenger. Consultation with teachers or non-familial caregivers of young children may be especially important for helping parents with the needed support so they can accept alternative, but more realistic views of the child's development. Ershler (1992) has noted that parental factors predict children's coping with disabilities more than the child's skills. In turn, early childhood educators also may need support in their efforts to contain frustrations that arise in trying to help children with challenging difficulties.

At times, the developmental and cultural variability noted above, as well as normally occurring changes over time, may be cited by parents who wish to deny that there is a problem and maintain their idealized hopes for their child. In other cases, parents or educators may be overly demanding or may expect developmental tasks to be accomplished with little direction, when in reality adult involvement is critical to the child's developmental level. They may even base their expectations on their understanding of theories and findings proposed by developmental psychology (e.g., Damon, 1995; Horowitz, 2000). For example, some parents and teachers may expect children to develop self-control and appropriate social behavior based on "natural" maturational processes, with little need for adult guidance. When this does not happen, and more direct instruction is required, some may become unduly alarmed and others may resist suggestions for change in their parenting strategies.

An over reliance on organismic models of development that emphasize a deterministic view of individual growth may exacerbate conflicts between the needs of adults and their children. An eco-systemic perspective in consultation can help provide a more balanced view of the interacting individual developmental and contextual influences on the child's behavior. It is conducive to helping all the parties involved to maintain a healthy sense of balance between internal organismic aspects of development, direct responsibilities for coping with children's difficulties, and recognition of more distal social influences that may impact on change. While changes in the approach of the individual parent or caregiver to a child with signs of attention deficits may lead to significant gains, the problem might be alleviated even more effectively by advocating changes in the organization of the preschool setting or in educational policies that dictate the early childhood curriculum.

Contexts of Early Childcare

In considering contextual issues, we use Bronfenbrenner's (1979) levels of the ecology of development. The difficulties of young children are rarely experienced in isolation from interactions in the immediate family and the larger social context. Difficulties experienced by young children often reflect problems with parent-child relations (as well as teacher-child relations), and also may be related to risk conditions such as maternal depression or family discord, the quality of the educational setting, or poor community resources, over which the child has no control (Leventhal, Brooks-Gunn, McCormick, & McCarton, 2000; Meisels & Shonkoff, 2000; Werner, 2000). Other risks may result from distal aspects of the child's ecosystem such as regulations concerning quality of childcare facilities and preparation of caregivers. The behavior of young children may be especially sensitive to variables associated with quality of care, like group size, adult-child ratios, and caregiver education as well as early education curricula (e.g., Burchinal et al., 2000; National Institute of Child Health and Human Development (NICHD) Early Child Care Research Network, 2000; Rosenthal, 1990). However, determination of these factors can be seen as a matter of policy decisions based on cultural norms as much as any direct consideration of children's needs (Broberg & Hwang, 1992; Hyun, 1998; Lubeck, 1995; Tobin, Wu, & Davidson, 1989) or universal developmental considerations.

Increasingly, young children throughout the world participate in early education and childcare programs. In some cultures, especially those with national social welfare policies, early education facilities are publicly supported and regulated by national policies (e.g., Cochran, 1993; Lamb, Sternberg, Hwang, & Broberg, 1992; Melhuish, 2001; Penn, 1997; Woodwill, Bernhard, & Prochner, 1992) and almost all young children attend. In other cultures, such as the U.S. and Canada, early care for normally developing children is provided mainly through the private market and associated decisions are a matter of parental choice (Goelman, Rosenthal, & Pence, 1990; Honig, 1995). Concern for children from disadvantaged families or those with disabilities has led to legislation and a variety of public early educational intervention programs such as Head Start (Blasco, 2001; Lubeck, 1995; Mallory, 1994; Shonkoff & Meisels, 2000). Goelman and colleagues (1990), for example, noted that the differences between child care in Canada and Israel reflects macro-system and exosystem variables such as the degree to which provision of public support for early childcare is considered a remedial, welfare service (Canada) compared with an emphasis on policies to enable mothers to gain access to employment. Even when there are laws that mandate public psychological and educational services for disabled and disadvantaged toddlers and young children (as in the U.S.), attaining services for the child may be a source of further difficulty for parents. Consultants may be called upon to help families navigate among multiple agencies (Blasco, 2001; Telzrow, 1999).

Some division of labor between the immediate family and others, as well as a degree of discontinuity between settings is inherent in early childcare arrangements.

Bronfenbrenner (1979) proposed that the negotiation of discontinuities and the ability to adapt to different settings is an important developmental task. Assumptions about the critical importance of early attachments to a single nurturant caregiver, and the inherent discontinuity of settings experienced by young children in daycare, has generated considerable research and debate (see, for example, Clarke-Stewart, Allhusen, & Clements, 1995; Fox & Fein, 1990; McGurk, Caplan, Hennessy, & Moss, 1993; Phillips, 1987; Sagi & Koren-Karie, 1993; Scarr & Eisenberg, 1993). Some have argued that young children are not yet ready for the discontinuities inherent in non-familial care and urge utmost caution due to risks associated with development of insecure attachments (e.g., Belsky, 1990). For example, results from studies of kibbutz (communal settlements) child care in Israel have found a relatively high proportion of insecure-ambivalent attachments among these infants, particularly among those who experienced communal rather than family sleeping arrangements (e.g., Sagi et al., 1985; Sagi, van IJzendoorn, Aviezer, Donnell, & Mayseles, 1994). These Israeli studies suggest that risks for insecure attachments relate to the extent of the discontinuities involved – for example, if the children slept with their young peers in separate homes, apart from their parents (Aviezer, van Ijzendoorn, Sagi, & Schuengel, 1994) or if mothers were away from home for many hours (Scher & Mayseless, 2000). Others have noted the mixed evidence concerning risks associated with divided responsibility for childcare. For example, in the large U.S., NICHD day care study, type of non-maternal group care had no effect on quality of attachment (NICHD Early Child Care Research Network, 1997), but other studies have found that quality of child care (in both the U.S. and Canada) is associated with later cognitive and language development, especially among children from lower income families (e.g., Burchinal, Campbell, Bryant, Wasik, & Ramey, 1997; Goelman & Pence, 1987; NICHD Early Child Care Research Network, 2000).

Rather than focus only on risks for children, a balanced consideration of the issues of shared childcare arrangements calls for thoughtful appraisal of the needs of parents and caregivers as well (e.g., Clarke-Stewart et al., 1995; Honig, 1995; Scarr & Eisenberg, 1993). Thompson (2000) suggests that shared narratives about children's responses to separations involved in early education and care rather than direct experiences may contribute to different outcomes. Thus, another important role for consultants working with parents and early childhood caregivers from an ecosystemic developmental perspective is to help them establish co-constructed narratives and scripts for intervention that promote healthy adjustment.

Differing views concerning the cultural validity of one or another approach to understanding child development is another factor that impacts the relations among the contexts in which young children participate. Approaches to socialization in early child education settings vary within and across cultures – ranging from those with a humanistic developmental caregiving focus to more didactic educational emphases (Boocock, 1995; Penn, 1997; Tobin et al., 1989; Woodwill et al., 1992). Some would argue that the humanistic emphasis in Western early education, adopted as "developmentally appropriate practice" by organizations such as the National Association for the Education for Young Children (NAEYC), are insufficiently sensitive to cultural dictates (Hyun, 1998; Lubeck, 1995; Tobin et al., 1989). In keeping with Western cultural assumptions, most Western childcare settings are age-segregated and arranged specifically for young children. There are small tables and chairs, and adults adjust their speech and practices to meet children's needs. In other cultures, children are expected to learn incidentally as they accompany and observe more experienced older children or adults (Rogoff, Mistry, Goncu, & Mosier, 1993; Whiting & Edwards, 1988; Tobin et al., 1989). In the latter groups (which are likely to include minority cultural groups within Western countries), there is less deliberate adult instruction; adults are likely to guide children in adult activities in which the children can participate.

Several other aspects of social and education policies may be expected to influence young children's well-being as well as early detection of developmental difficulties. In some countries, like Canada, the UK, and Israel, early screening and health care facilities are widely available through the public health system. In other countries, as in many parts of the U.S., access to health care and to early education facilities is largely dependent upon the ability to pay. Low-income parents may place children in large groups or with less qualified caregivers, as a result of financial considerations. In other settings, there may be insufficient attention to the need for parent-caregiver communications, or such sharing might be viewed as undermining the professional status of early educators (e.g., Long et al., 1985; Pugh, 1989).

In sum, in helping consultees identify problems and find solutions to problems of young children, consultants need to consider a complex set of conditions, including the characteristics of the individual child, as well as multiple perspectives associated with each level of the developmental context. It is more important for consultants to consider the impact of different approaches to child development and caregiving than to take sides with one or another view. The ways in which parents and other caregivers relate to one another may be the product of power struggles engendered by debate. Moreover, it is important for consultants to be culturally sensitive in advocating specific practices that meet the needs of young children and of those responsible for them.

An Ecosystemic Model for Consulting About Young Children

Entry to the System and Problem Assessment

An eco systemic approach to consultation suggests that school psychologists working with young children should consider the problems from the perspective of different points in a dynamic, multi-dimensional space (see Figure 1). As increasing numbers

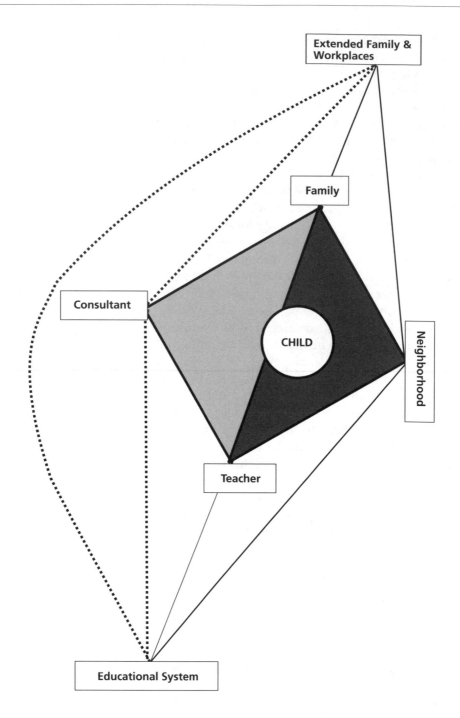

Figure 1 An Eco-Systemic "Map" of the Developmental Niche

of parents work, the experiences of even very young children can be viewed as occurring in settings defined by social networks of parents and early childhood educators. In turn, these mesosystem relations are nested within a larger neighborhood and community context. Both parents and teachers may be pressed by multiple influences from more distal levels of the system, including the work environment, educational policies, and professional demands placed on early educators. These relations are further influenced by broader social forces that affect families and early childhood settings. The model depicted in Figure 1 presents a general map of the three most direct forces involved in forming the "developmental niche" of the child. Other elements of the system are represented as more distal influences. In practice, a unique map should be developed specifically for each consultation case.

Since young children are so interdependent with those responsible for them, it is particularly important to consider the multiple systemic influences both at the initial stages of problem identification and while presenting a collaborative problem-solving process. At the entry stage of consultation, school consultants use the eco-systemic model as a structural "road map" to chart the interactions among the different elements of the context as they relate to the difficulties of young children and the adults responsible for them. Use of the ecological map at the initial stages of consultation points up multiple entry points at which the consultant may choose to "join" the system. An eco-systemic perspective may be especially useful as a tool for uncovering both immediate and more distal influences (for example, the views of grandparents about a mother's work) that often act as hidden forces in maintaining a problem situation and engendering resistance to change (White & Loos, 1996).

The eco-systemic nature of early childhood contexts calls for consultants to examine difficulties with respect to the interactive processes among the parts of the system in an effort to promote collaborations among key participants in the child's developmental niche. Individual development and the associated expression of difficulties also may be seen as an interactive, systemic process. A multimodal approach to problem assessment suggests that a problem may be expressed through different interacting modalities (Lazarus, 1997). We suggest that six facets of the problem should be considered in eco-systemic developmental consultation. A primary consideration in early childhood is the *developmental status* of the child and those caring for them. Against the backdrop of the individual developmental factors, a problem assessment should account for the *behaviors* of each of the different participants in the system, their *affect* or feelings about the difficulty, the physical properties of the *setting, interactions* among participants in the system, and the *cognitions* of participants expressed through their ideas, images and beliefs about childrearing. The components to be assessed can be recalled with the shorthand acronym: D-BASIC (*development, behavior, affect, setting, interactions, cognitions*). By assessing the D-BASIC facets of the problem systemically, consultants may be alerted early on in the consultation process to differences in perceptions, and potential conflicts between different key players that may contribute to the maintenance of the problem or preclude effective intervention. The

Table 1 Assessment of Six Facets of a Problem in Developmental Consultation

The following are examples of questions concerning each facet of a problem in a developmental niche.*

D- *Developmental Status*	B *Behavior*	A *Affect*	S *Setting*	I *Interpersonal Interactions*	C *Cognitions (Beliefs and ideas)*
What is the developmental stage of the child? Are there delays in development relative to norms? Are there discrepancies in different areas of development? What is the developmental status of parents or caregivers (e.g. very young parents, older caregivers,)? Are caregivers trained and experienced? Is the preschool organization new or well established?	*What* are the manifestations of the problem in functional behavioral terms? *What* are the child's behaviors and the behavior responses of the different caregivers or policy makers? *When* does the problem present? *When* have consultees come to seek help? *Where* (in what contexts is the problem expressed)? *How* are the difficulties expressed (frequency, duration)?	*What feelings are* associated with the difficulty for each of the participants in the developmental niche? (e.g. Feelings of frustration, helplessness, anger, depression) *What is the Affective Climate* of the more distal parts of the eco-system? (e.g. relaxed, laid-back atmosphere vs. feelings of tension and stress within the family or preschool)	*How is the setting organized?* What is the quality of the preschool or setting? What are *the daily routines and practices* associated with the problem? *Who and what considerations determine the organization of the* setting? Is the setting *flexible or does it have a fixed structure and practices?* Who are the *gatekeepers?*	*How do different members of the system interact with* one another – especially with respect to the child's difficulty or developmental issues? *What is the quality of relations among* members of the developmental niche? *Who is in contact with whom –* within the system? With whom are there *contacts outside* the immediate niche? *Who are the leaders and followers in the system?*	*What are the beliefs and ideas* about parenting and childcare that guide the behavior of the different participants in the developmental niche? *How do parents/ teachers/ policymakers each* explain the difficulty brought to the consultant? Do participants in the niche exhibit *irrational, stereotypical thinking or inaccurate knowledge* of developmental issues associated with the problem?

*From an eco-systemic perspective it is important to consider the responses of the different participants concerning each of the facets of the difficulty and the functioning of the system.

D-BASIC approach can also point up specific strengths in the system as to be addressed in generating solutions. Table 1 presents some examples of questions that can be used for problem identification across each of these multimodal components in ecosystemic consultation.

The Problem Solving Process – Generating Solutions

A primary goal of eco systemically oriented consultation is to promote a more comfortable fit among the elements that make up the developmental niche. As with other ecological approaches, this perspective supports the flexible use of different existing models of intervention, particularly approaches that emphasize conjoint work with parents and educational settings (O'Callaghan, 1993; Sheridan, Kratochwill, & Bergan, 1996). In early childhood, the consistency of relations with parents and the changing nature of relations with other caregivers is especially important. An integrative, systemic approach to consultation emphasizes the benefits of linking changes in one part of the system to changes in other elements (Maital, 1996; Omer, 1993; Plas, 1986), rather than a simple eclectic matching of alternative consultation techniques for different problems. For example, changes in consultee responses to a child's disruptive behavior may be more or less difficult to attain depending on interactions between the child's Developmental Status and Behavior, the consultee's own Behavior repertoire, Affective responses to the situation, the organization of the physical and social Setting, Interpersonal relations, and Cognitive beliefs about the child.

A multimodal approach to assessing problems with respect to interactions among different elements of the context can be integrated with Caplan's (1970) ideas concerning alternative sources of difficulty faced by consultees and the levels of intervention proposed by Meyers and his colleagues (1979). Caplan proposed that consultees may experience difficulties in coping with a client due to lack of knowledge, lack of skills, lack of confidence, or lack of objectivity. When difficulties experienced by different members of the immediate setting reflect the lack of knowledge or skills needed to handle the child's problematic behavior, consultants may try to help consultees gain those skills. From an eco-systemic perspective, it is important to increase consultee awareness of resources available within the system and to gain skills in accessing those resources. For example, information about community medical and educational resources may be particularly important for parents or teachers who are first confronted with a handicapped child. However, an eco-systemic approach also points up potential difficulties that may arise due to factors such as an imbalance in access to information. For example, some professionals may perceive that their status as child development experts would be undermined if parents were equally knowledgeable, creating problems associated with issues of control rather than with the child's difficulty itself. A multimodal approach to understanding different facets of consultee difficulties also leads to questions about factors such as how the structure of the health care system may support parents' beliefs that these settings cannot be easily approached. Such a multifaceted understanding of the problem could lead to greater consultant involvement in helping consultees with advocacy activities (West & Idol, 1987), or it could lead to more careful examination of difficulties associated with the beliefs of the consultee or conflicting beliefs that arise in conjoint consultation situations.

Providing consultees with information and helping them gain skills in problem resolution is often accomplished through behavioral consultation techniques. In developing behavioral interventions for young children from an ecological perspective, it is particularly important to account for their developmental status and to consider ways in which the expectations and related organization of the setting fits young children's needs as well as the needs of those responsible for them. For example, in establishing preschool social skills interventions, consultants may be expected to draw on their expert knowledge of developmental psychology to help analyze social skills tasks into their developmental components, establish a reasonable timetable for acquiring various skills, and to help maximize the use of normally occurring growth processes (for a good example, see Stevahn, Johnson, Johnson, Oberle, & Wahl, 2000). As noted earlier, it is also important to examine developmental expectations for behavior within their cultural context and to decide conjointly on goals for change.

When consultees' difficulties stem from lack of confidence, an eco-systemic approach points to the importance of helping consultees find or create resources for support and reinforcement in coping within the natural context, as well as providing direct support from the consultant. Consideration of the different facets of the ecology may also point up structural or interactive aspects of the system that may undermine confidence, as well as promote lack of objectivity in dealing with children's problems. For example, in some cases, multi generational neighborhoods may provide younger parents with role models and supports that reinforce confident parenting. In other cases, over-reliance on social comparisons and media presentations of ideal parenting may lead to unduly self-critical parental behavior, and even unrealistic beliefs and expectations about young children.

From the perspective of mental health consultation, lack of objectivity or irrational beliefs about child development may in themselves be the source of a consultee's difficulties. An ecosystemic developmental approach points up the need to consider the multiple forces that may lead to lack of objectivity in consultees' beliefs about children and caregiving that may produce ineffective practices. It is especially important for consultants who are expert in child development to consider the accuracy of parents' and teachers' understanding of developmental research (Horowitz, 2000). For example, those responsible for young children may lack information more about normal variability in development among children at young ages, which they need in order to maintain reasonable expectations and engage in suitable practices. However, lack of objectivity may also be associated with interpersonal influences from within a consultee's past, as well as current needs of caregivers that result from broader systemic influences such as work pressures noted above. Thus, expectations that children develop empathy and moral reasoning over the course of maturation without explicit education may lead to a laissez faire approach to misbehavior that also fits the needs of parents or early educators who are overburdened with other pressures (e.g., Damon, 1995). It may do little good to help a parent adopt a more assertive and authoritative approach to their child if there are also powerful influences in the ecosystem that suggest that parent-child relations should *always* be fun for both parent and child. In such cases, it may be important for consultants to help consultees examine their beliefs and find alternative reference groups that can support more rational thinking.

As noted throughout, many interventions proposed on the basis of an eco-systemic, developmental view may involve changes in the organization of the developmental niche. For example, helping to increase or improve communications between parents and early childhood educators may require changes in the roles that parents and teachers each play with respect to one another. Encouragement of significant adults to provide children with more individual attention may require advocacy of changes at distal levels of the system – influencing policy makers, for example, to require a higher ratio of adults to children or to hire well trained caregivers. Many early intervention projects require that the consultant consider systemic changes that can promote the well-being of whole groups of disadvantaged children who are at risk (Shonkoff & Meisels, 2000). However, most organizational systems value routine patterns of relating and may resist change. An eco-systemic, developmental perspective should be useful for helping consultants discern systemic patterns and the effect of interacting forces with respect to the problem child's developmental functioning. It also suggests the need to accommodate changes in relationships among participants in the developmental niche that may result from (at times rapid) shifts in the needs of the child over the course of normal development. From an organizational perspective, consultants may be called upon to help members of a professional team or parents and educators formulate agreed upon goals and a common core culture that can guide effective functioning of the developmental context as a whole (Harris & Zetlin, 1993). In this respect, consulting about young children requires consideration of several distinctive cultures associated with early childhood, particularly with respect to developmental science, early childcare and education, and the specific culture of the family.

Summary

In this chapter we contend that consulting about young children requires a unique set of considerations. These include not only a solid base in developmental theory, but also an awareness of the pitfalls and risks of its translation into practice. In line with recent theory and research about early development, an eco-systemic perspective has been adopted. In translating this perspective to consulting about young children, we highlighted four broad sets of developmental issues.

The first developmental principle is the total dependence of young children on their parents and other caregivers. Emphasizing this characteristic of early childhood is significant to consultants both for uncovering the child's difficulties and for planning intervention and change. The relations among the different others in the life of the child are also a significant factor, thus it is important for consultants to consider the interactions among the elements of the developmental niche.

The second issue refers to continuity and change in development. Specifically, child development is dynamic, has multiple pathways and is characterized by variability in outcomes and in rate of change. These principles of individual growth along with the appreciation of their interdependence on the contribution of child, parent/teacher and context variables provide an essential guideline for intervention with young children. However, decisions about the timing, the recipients and the setting of intervention require ecological and cultural sensitivity. Thus in consulting about young children, a collaborative stance is essential.

The third premise highlights the relevance of the needs of the significant adults in the child's world. In line with eco-systemic principles, stressors and discord in the family system, in the pre-school environment, and/or conflicts between the two settings risk the development and adjustment of young children. As factors like well being, role satisfaction, frustration and support experienced by parents and educators impact both the proximal and the distal processes in the eco-system surrounding the young child – these variables should be tapped upon when consulting. Furthermore, since the emotional state of the adult can sometimes mask developmental difficulties, or, alternatively, exaggerate the reported problem – the systemic approach is particularly suited for meeting the challenges posed by working with young children.

The fourth issue within the framework of developmental, eco-systemic consultation refers specifically to the educational and child-care contexts. In considering the interplay between the context and the child's functioning, the quality of education, the specific needs of the individual child and the continuity between home and school are to be considered. Moreover, the above characteristics should also be examined in terms of their match with cultural norms and expectations.

In order to encompass the expression of the various developmental issues, we adopted a multi-modal approach to assessing the difficulty and planning interventions across the different levels of the system. Consideration of the interactions of six facets (*development, behavior, affect, setting, interpersonal interactions, and cognitions, *D-BASIC) through which problems may be expressed, across the different participants in the developmental niche points up the complexity of an eco-systemic, developmental approach to consultation. At the same time, it highlights the multiple opportunities for joining the system and emphasizes the flexibility gained through consideration of a wide range of possibilities for intervention.

Although this chapter has focused on toddlers and preschoolers, most of the developmental principles examined and discussed here are relevant to school-aged children as well. The advantages of using a developmental perspective when consulting about children are not age specific. Thus, we propose that the developmental considerations and the use of a multi-faceted D-BASIC model to assess children's difficulties that we presented in this chapter can be adapted to eco-systemic consultation with children across development.

Taken together, the present eco-systemic approach represents a comprehensive, indirect service delivery model for both primary and secondary interventions that is particularly suitable for the educational challenges and constraints as we enter the 21st-century. The practice of school psychology is situated at the intersection of the child-parent-teacher. Thus, a developmental approach to consultation like the one outlined above is particularly suited to their needs. An important role of school psychologists is to initiate change proactively in order to enhance children's psychological well-being (e.g., Cole & Siegel, 1990). Developmental consultation with teachers of young children and their families at the preschool stage is a valuable avenue for enhancing positive developmental trajectories. As many parents naturally seek professional input when their child is young, involvement in early consultation may not only be more comfortable for parents but it also may have long term impact on children's adjustment, parenting, and school-family interactions. Finally, we recommend that the study of consulting about young children should become part of the academic and professional training of all school psychologists.

References

Aviezer, O., Van IJzendoorn, M. H., Sagi, A., & Schuengel, C. (1994). "Children of the dream" revisited: Collective child-rearing in Israeli kibbutzim. *Psychological Bulletin, 116*, 99-116.

Barnett, D. W. (1986). School psychology in preschool settings: A review of training and practice issues. *Professional Psychology: Research and Practice, 17*, 58-64.

Bates, E., Marchman, V., Thal, D., Fenson, L., Dale, P., Reznick, J. S., Reilly, J., & Hartung, J. (1994). Development and stylistic variation in the composition of early vocabulary. *Journal of Child Language, 21*, 85-123.

Belsky, J. (1984). The determinants of parenting: A process model. *Child Development, 50*, 83-96.

Belsky, J. (1990). The effects of infant day care reconsidered. In N. Fox & G. G. Fein (Eds.) (1990), *Infant day care: The current debate* (pp. 3-40). Norwood, NJ: Ablex Publishing Corporation.

Blair, C. (2002). School readiness: Integrating cognition and emotion in a neurobiological conceptualization of children's functioning at school entry. *American Psychologist, 57*, 111-127.

Blasco, P. M. (2001). *Early intervention services for infants, toddlers, and their families*. Boston: Allyn & Bacon.

Boocock, S. S. (1995). Early childhood programs in other nations: Goals and outcomes. *The Fu-*

ture of Children (Special issue – Long term outcomes of early childhood programs), 5(3), 94-114. www.future of children.org/information2826/

Bradley, R. H., Rock, S. L., Whiteside, L., & Caldwell, B. M. (1991). Dimensions of parenting in families having children with disabilities. *Exceptionality, 2,* 41-61.

Broberg, A. G., & Hwang, C. P. (1992). The shaping of child-care policies. In M. Lamb, K. Sternberg, C. Hwang, & B. Broberg (Eds.), *Day care in context: Historical and cross cultural perspectives* (pp. 509- 521). Hillsdale, New Jersey: Earlbaum.

Bronfenbrenner, U. (1979). *The ecology of human development.* Cambridge, MA: Harvard University Press.

Bronfenbrenner, U. (1992). Child care in the Anglo-Saxon mode. In M. Lamb, R. Sternberg, C. Hwang, & A. Broberg (Eds.), *Nonparental child care: Cultural and historical perspectives* (pp. 281-291). Hillsdale, NJ: Lawrence Erlbaum Associates.

Brown, D., Pryzwansky, W. B., & Schulte, A. C. (1995). *Psychological consultation: Introduction to theory and practice.* Boston: Allyn & Bacon.

Burchinal, M. R., Campbell, F. A., Bryant, D. M., Wasik, B. A., & Ramey, C. T. (1997). Early intervention and mediating processes in cognitive performance of children of low-income African-American families. *Child Development, 68,* 935-954.

Burchinal, M. R., Roberts, J. E., Riggins Jr., R., Zeisel, S. A., Neebe, E., & Bryant, D. (2000). Relating quality of center-based care to early cognitive and language development longitudinally. *Child Development, 71,* 339-357.

Cabrera, N. J., Tamis-LeMonda, C. S., Bradley, R. H., Hofferth, S., & Lamb, M. E. (2000). Fatherhood in the twenty-first century. *Child Development, 71,* 127-136.

Caplan, G. (1970). *The theory and practice of mental health consultation.* NY: Basic Books.

Caplan, G., & Caplan, R. B. (1993). *Mental health consultation and collaboration.* San Francisco: Jossey-Bass.

Chait Barnett, R., & Hyde, J. S. (2001). Women, men, work, and family: An expansionist theory. *American Psychologist, 56,* 781-796.

Clarke-Stewart, K. A., Allhusen, V. D., & Clements, D. C. (1995). Nonparental caregiving. In M. H. Bornstein (Ed.), *Handbook of Parenting, Volume 3* (pp. 151-176). Hillsdale, NJ: Lawrence Erlbaum.

Cochran, M. (Ed.). (1993). *International handbook of day-care policies and programs.* Westport, CT: Greenwood.

Cole, E. (1996). An integrative perspective on school psychology. *Canadian Journal of School Psychology, 12,* 115-121.

Cole, E., & Siegel, J. (Eds.). (1990). *Effective consultation in school psychology.* Toronto, Ontario: Hogrefe & Huber Publishers.

Conoley, J. C., & Conoley, C. W. (1992). *School consultation: Practice and training (Second Edition).* Boston: Allyn & Bacon.

Damon, W. (1995). *Greater expectations: Overcoming the culture of indulgence in our homes and schools.* NY: Free Press.

deVries, M. W., & Sameroff, A. J. (1984). Culture and temperament: Influences on infant temperament in three East African societies. *American Journal of Orthopsychiatry, 54,* 83-96.

Donahue, P. J., Falk, B., & Provet, A. G. (2000). *Mental health consultation in early childhood.* Baltimore, MD: Paul H. Brookes Publishing Co.

Dromi, E. (1999). Early lexical development. In M. Barrett (Ed.), *The development of language.* London: UCL Press.

Edwards, C. P., Gandini, L., & Giovaninni, D. (1996). The contrasting developmental timetables of parents and preschool teachers in two cultural communities. In S. Harkness & C. Super (Eds.), *Parents' cultural belief systems* (pp. 270-288). NY: Guilford Press.

Eldering, L., & Leseman, P. P. M. (1999). Enhancing educational opportunities for young children. In L. Eldering & P. P. M. Leseman (Eds.), *Effective early education: Cross-cultural perspectives* (pp. 3-16). NY: Falmer Press.

Elkind, D. (1987). *Miseducation: Preschoolers at risk.* NY: Knopf.

Erchul, W. P., & Martens, B. K. (1997). *School consultation: Conceptual and empirical bases of practice.* NY: Plenum Press.

Erchul, W. P., Raven, B. H., & Whichard, S. M. (2001). School psychologist and teacher perceptions of social power in consultation. *Journal of School Psychology, 39,* 483-498.

Ershler, J. L. (1992). Model programs and service delivery approaches in early childhood education. In M. Gettinger, S. N. Elliott, & T. R. Kratochwill (Eds.), *Preschool and early childhood treatment directions* (pp. 7-54). Hillsdale, NJ: Lawrence Erlbaum Associates.

Feldman, H. M., Dollaghan, C. A., Campbell, T. F., Kurs-Lasky, M., Janosky, J. E., & Paradise, J. L. (2000). Measurement properties of the MacArthur Communicative Development Inventories at ages one and two years. *Child Development, 71,* 310-322.

Fenson, L., Dale, P. S., Reznick, J. S., Bates, E., Thal, D. J., & Pethick, S. J. (1994). Variability in early communicative development. *Monographs of the Society for Research in Child Development (Serial No. 42), 59* (4).

Fine, M. J. (1991). The handicapped child and the family: Implications for professionals. In M. J. Fine (Ed.), *Collaboration with parents of exceptional children* (pp. 3-20). Brandon, VT: Clinical Psychology Publishing Company.

Fortier, L. M., & Winlass, R. L., (1984). Family crisis following the diagnosis of a handicapped child. *Family Relations, 33,* 13-24.

Fox, N., & Fein, G. G. (Eds.). (1990). *Infant day care: The current debate.* Norwood, NJ: Ablex Publishing Corporation.

Garguilo, R. (1985). *Working with parents of exceptional children: A guide for professionals.* Boston. Houghton Mifflin.

Gowen, J. W., Johnson, M. N., Goldman, B. D., & Appelbaum, M. (1989). Feelings of depression and parenting competence of mothers of handicapped and nonhandicapped infants: A longitudinal study. *American Journal of Mental Retardation, 94,* 259-271.

Garbarino, J., & Ganzel, B. (2000). The human ecology of early risk. In J. P. Shonkoff & S. J. Meisels (Eds.), *Handbook of early childhood intervention (Second Edition)* (pp. 76-93). NY: Cambridge University Press.

Goelman, H., & Pence, A. R. (1987). Some aspects of the relationships between family structure and child language development in three types of day care. In D. Peters & S. Kontos (Eds.), *Annual advances in applied developmental psychology, Vol. 2: Continuity and discontinuity of experience in child care* (pp. 129-146). Norwood, NJ: Ablex.

Goelman, H., Rosenthal, M. K., & Pence, A. R. (1990). Family day care in two countries: Parents, caregivers, and children in Canada and Israel. *Child and Youth Care Quarterly, 19,* 251-270.

Gutkin, T. B. (1999). Collaborative versus directive/prescriptive/expert school-based consultation: Reviewing and resolving a false dichotomy. *Journal of School Psychology, 37,* 161-190.

Harkness, S., & Keefer, C. H. (2000). Contributions of cross-cultural psychology to research and interventions in education and health. *Journal of Cross-Cultural Psychology, 31,* 92-109.

Harris, K. C., & Zetlin (1993). Exploring the collaborative ethic in an urban school: A case study. *Journal of Educational & Psychological Consultation, 4,* 305-317.

Hess, R. D., Price, G. G., Dickson, W. P., & Conroy, M. (1984). Different roles for mothers and teachers: Contrasting styles of child care. In S. Kilmer (Ed.), *Advances in early education and day care, Vol. 2.* Greenwich, CT: Johnson Associates, Inc.

Hock, E. (1980). Working and nonworking mothers and their infants: A comparative study of maternal caregiving characteristics and infant social behavior. *Merrill-Palmer Quarterly, 26,* 79-101.

Hoffman, L. W., & Youngblade, L. M. (1999). *Mothers at work: Effects on children's well-being.* NY: Cambridge University Press.

Honig, A. S. (1995). Choosing childcare for young children. In M. H. Bornstein (Ed.), *Handbook of Parenting, Vol. 4* (pp. 411-435). Hillsdale, NJ: Erlbaum.

Horowitz, F. D. (1987). *Exploring developmental theories: Toward structural/behavioral model of development.* Hillsdale, NJ: Lawrence Erlbaum.

Horowitz, F. D. (2000). Child development and the PITS: Simple questions, complex answers, and developmental theory. *Child Development, 71,* 1-10.

Howes, C., & Matheson, C. C. (1992). Contextual constraints on the concordance of mother-child and teacher-child relationships. In R. C. Pianta (Ed.), *Beyond the parent: The role of other adults in children's lives. New Directions in Child Development, 57,* (pp. 25-40). San Francisco: Jossey Bass.

Hyun, E. (1998). *Making sense of developmentally and culturally appropriate practice in early education.* NY: Peter Lang.

Ingraham, C. L. (2000). Consultation through a multicultural lens: Multicultural and cross-cultural consultation in schools. *School Psychology Review, 29,* 320-343.

Jackson-Maldonado, D., Thal, D., Marchman, V., Bates, E., & Gutierrez-Clellen, V. (1993). Early lexical development in Spanish-speaking infants and toddlers. *Journal of Child Language, 20,* 523-549.

Kagitcibasi, C. (1996). *Family and human development across cultures: A view from the other side.* Hillsdale, NJ: Lawrence Erlbaum Associates.

Lamb, M., Sternberg, K., Hwang, C., & Broberg, B. (Eds.). (1992). *Day care in context: Historical and cross cultural perspectives.* Hillsdale, NJ: Erlbaum.

Lazarus, A. A. (1997). *Brief but comprehensive psychotherapy: The multimodal way.* NY: Springer Publishing Company.

Lerner, R. M., Fisher, C. B., & Weinberg, R. A. (2000). Toward a science for and of the people: Promoting civil society through the application of developmental science. *Child Development, 71,* 11-20.

Leventhal, T., Brooks-Gunn, J., McCormick, M. C., & McCarton, C. M. (2000). Patterns of service use in preschool children: Correlates, consequences, and the role of early intervention. *Child Development, 71,* 802-819.

Lewis, M. (1997). *Altering fate: Why the past does not predict the future.* NY: Guilford Press.

Long, F., Peters, D. L., & Garduque, L. (1985). Continuity between home and day care: A model for defining relevant dimensions of child care. *Advances in Applied Developmental Psychology, 1,* 131-170.

Lubeck, S. (1995). Nation as context: Comparing child-care systems across nations. *Teachers College Record, 96,* 467-491.

Maital, S. L. (1996). Integration of behavioral and mental health consultation as a means of overcoming resistance. *Journal of Educational and Psychological Consultation, 7,* 291-303.

Maital, S. L. (2000). Reciprocal distancing: A systems model of interpersonal processes in cross-cultural consultation. *School Psychology Review, 29,* 389-400.

Maital, S. L., Dromi, E., Sagi, A., & Bornstein, M. H., (2000). The Hebrew CDI: Language specific properties and cross-linguistic generalizations. *Journal of Child Language, 27,* 43-76.

Mallory, B. L. (1994). Inclusive policy, practice, and theory for young children with developmental differences. In B. L. Mallory & R. S. New (Eds.), *Diversity and developmentally appropriate practices: Challenges for early childhood education* (pp. 44-61). NY: Teachers College Press.

McCartney, K., & Rosenthal, R. (2000). Effect size, practical importance, and social policy for children. *Child Development, 71,* 173-180.

McGurk, H., Caplan, M., Hennessy, E., & Moss, P. (1993). Controversy, theory and social context in contemporary day care research. *Journal of Child Psychology & Psychiatry, 34,* 3-23.

Melhuish, E. C. (2001). The quest for quality in early day care and preschool experience continues. *International Journal of Behavioral Development, 25,* 1-6.

Meisels, S. J., & Shonkoff, J. P. (2000). Early childhood intervention: A continuing evolution. In *Handbook of early childhood intervention (2nd edition)* (pp. 3-31). New York: Cambridge University Press.

Meyers, J. (1995) A consultation model for school psychological services. *Journal of Educational & Psychological Consultation, 6(1),* 59-71.

Meyers, J., Parsons, R., & Martin, R. (1979). *Mental health consultation in the schools.* San Francisco: Jossey-Bass.

National Institute of Child Health and Human Development (NICHD) Early Child Care Research Network. (2000). The relation of child care to cognitive and language development. *Child Development, 71,* 960-980.

National Institute of Child Health and Human Development Early Child Care Research Network, (1997). The effects of infant child care on infant-mother attachment security: Results of the NICHD study of early child care. *Child Development, 68,* 860-879.

Noell, G. H., & Witt, J. C. (1996). A critical re-evaluation of five fundamental assumptions underlying behavioral consultation. *Journal of School Psychology, 11,* 189-203.

O'Callaghan, J. B. (1993). *School-based collaboration with families: Constructing family-school-agency partnerships that work.* San Francisco: Jossey Bass.

Omer, H. (1993). The integrative focus: Coordinating symptom-and-person-oriented perspectives in therapy. *American Journal of Psychotherapy, 47(2),* 283-295.

Parsons, R., & Meyers, J. (1984). *Developing consultation skills: A guide to training, development, and assessment for human services professionals.* San Francisco: Jossey-Bass.

Penn, H. (1997). *Comparing nurseries: Staff and children in Italy, Spain, and the UK.* London: Paul Chapman Publishing.

Phillips, D. (Ed.). (1987). *Quality in child care: What does the research tell us?* Washington, DC: National Association for the Education of Young Children.

Pianta, R. C. (1999). *Enhancing relationships between children and teachers.* Washington, DC: American Psychological Association.

Plas, J. M. (1986). *Systems psychology in the schools.* New York: Pergamon Press.

Pugh, G. (1989). Parents and professionals in pre-school services: Is partnership possible? In S. Wolfendale (Ed.), *Parental involvement: Developing networks between school, home and community* (pp. 1-19). London: Cassell Educational Ltd.

Rogoff, B., Mistry, J., Goncu, A., & Mosier, C. (1993). Guided participation in cultural activity by toddlers and caregivers. *Mongraphs of the Society for Research in Child Development, 58* (8, Serial No. 236).

Rosenthal, M. K. (1990). Behaviors and beliefs of caregivers in family day care: The effects of background and work environment. *Early Childhood Research Quarterly, 6,* 263-283.

Rothbaum, F., Weisz, J., Pott, M., Miyake, K., & Morelli, G. (2000). Attachment and culture: Security in the United States and Japan. *American Psychologist, 55,* 1093-1104.

Rutter, M., & Rutter, M. (1993). *Developing minds: Challenges and continuity across the life span.* N.Y.: Basic Books.

Sagi, A., & Koren-Karie, N. (1993). Day care centers in Israel: An overview. In M. Cochran (Ed.), *International handbook of day-care policies and programs* (pp. 269-290). Westport, CT: Greenwood.

Sagi, A., Lamb, M. E., Lewkowicz, K. S., Shoham, R., Dvir, R., & Estes, D. (1985). Security of infant-mother, -father, and metapelet attachments among kibbutz reared Israeli children. *Monographs of the Society for Research in Child Development, 50,* 257-275.

Sagi, A., van IJzendoorn, M. H., Aviezer, O., Donnell, F., & Mayseles. (1994). Sleeping out of home in a kibbutz communal arrangement: It makes a difference for infant-mother attachment. *Child Development, 65(4),* 992-1004.

Scarr, S., & Eisenberg, M. (1993). Child care research: Issues, perspectives and results. *Annual Review of Psychology, 44,* 613-644.

Schaffer, H. R. (2000). The early experience assumption: Past, present, and future. *International Journal of Behavioral Development, 24,* 5-14.

Scheeringa, M. S., Peebles, C. D., Cook, C. A., & Zeanah, C. H. (2001). Towards establishing procedural, criterion, and discriminant validity for PTSD in early childhood. *Journal of the American Academy of Child and Adolescent Psychiatry, 40,* 52-60.

Schein, E. H. (1999). *Process consultation revisited: Building the helping relationship.* NY: Addison-Wesley.

Scher, A., & Mayseless, O. (2000). Mothers of anxious/ambivalent infants: Maternal characteristics and child-care context. *Child Development, 71,* 1629-1639.

Sheridan, S. M., Kratochwill, R. R., & Bergan, J. R. (1996). *Conjoint behavioral consultation: A procedural manual.* NY: Plenum Press.

Shonkoff, J. P. (2000). Science, policy, and practice: Three cultures in search of a shared mission. *Child Development, 71,* 181-187.

Shonkoff, J. P., & Meisels, S. J. (Eds.) (2000). *Handbook of early childhood intervention (Second Edition).* NY: Cambridge University Press.

Siegel, J. A., & Cole, E. (1990). Role expansion for school psychologists: Challenges and future directions. In E. Cole & J. A. Siegel (Eds.), *Effective consultation in school psychology* (p. 18). Lewiston, NY: Hogrefe & Huber Publishers.

Sigel, I. (1990). Ethical concerns for the use of research findings in applied settings. In C. B. Fisher & W. W. Tryon (Eds.), *Ethics in applied developmental psychology. Advances in applied developmental psychology, 4,* 133-142.

Simeonsson, R. J., Bailey Jr., D. B. Huntington, G. S., & Comfort, M. (1986). Testing the concept of goodness of fit in early intervention. *Infant Mental Health Journal, 7,* 81-94.

Stern, D. N. (1995). *The motherhood constellation: A unified view of parent-infant psychotherapy.* NY: Basic Books.

Stevahn, L., Johnson, D. W., Johnson, R. T., Oberle, K., & Wahl, L. (2000). Effects of conflict resolution training integrated into a kindergarten curriculum. *Child Development, 71,* 772-784.

Telzrow, C. F. (1999). IDEA Ammendments of 1997: Promise or pitfall for special education reform? *Journal of School Psychology, 37,* 7-28.

Thompson, R. A. (2000). The legacy of early attachments. *Child Development, 21,* 145-152.

Tobin, J. J., Wu, D. Y. H., & Davidson, D. H. (1989). *Preschool in three cultures: Japan, China, and the United States.* New Haven: Yale University Press.

Van Ijzendoorn, M. H., Sagi, A., & Lambermon, M. W. E. (1992). The multiple caretaker paradox: Data from Holland and Israel. In R. C. Pianta (Ed.), *Beyond the parent: The role of other adults in children's lives. New directions in child development, 57,* (pp. 5-24). San Francisco: Jossey Bass.

Vincent, L. J., Salisbury, C. L., Strain, P., McCormick, C., & Tessier, A. (1990). A behavioral-ecological approach to early intervention: Focus on cultural diversity. In S. J. Meisels & J. P. Shonkoff (Eds.), *Handbook of early childhood intervention* (pp. 173-195). NY: Cambridge University Press.

Weinraub, M., Brooks, J., & Lewis, M. (1977). The social network: A reconsideration of the concept of attachment. *Human Development, 20,* 31-47.

Werner, E. E. (2000). Protective factors and individual resilience. In J. P. Shonkoff, & S. J. Meisels (Eds.), *Handbook of early childhood intervention (Second Edition)* (pp. 115-132). New York: Cambridge University Press.

West, J. F., & Idol, L. (1987). School consultation (Part I): An interdisciplinary perspective on theory, models, and research. *Journal of Learning Disabilities, 7,* 388-408.

Westby, C. E., & Ford, V. (1993). The role of team culture in assessment and intervention. *Journal of Educational and Psychological Consultation, 4,* 319-342.

White, L. J., & Loos, V. E. (1996). The hidden client in school consultation: Working from a narrative perspective. *Journal of Educational and Psychological Consultation, 7,* 161-178.

Woodwill, G. A., Bernhard, J., & Prochner, L. (Eds.). (1992). *International handbook of early childhood education.* NY: Garland Publishing.

Part 3

Consultation in School-Based Programs

Chapter 16
Appraisal for Better Curriculum

Jane A. Siegel and Ester Cole

"As part of the A.B.C. program in my Grade 4 classroom, the school psychologist, in observing my particular teaching style and how it suited some students, was able to help me identify students who could best learn through alternative teaching approaches. With her suggestions, I was able to offer a variety of teaching techniques and to be more adaptive to the learning needs of my pupils."
(Dinny, Grade 4 teacher)

Appraisal for Better Curriculum (A.B.C.) was a broad-based formative evaluation program involving psychological staff, classroom teachers, school administrators, and curriculum consultants working as a team. The program was initially implemented in the 80s with the goal of assisting teachers in developing classroom curricula that would better meet students' learning needs. This chapter describes the role of the school psychologist in such a program, with a particular emphasis on developing our understanding of practices that result in effective implementation. As the program evolved over time, there was a shift in the role of psychological staff toward one in which consultation rather than assessment became the primary function. This shift in emphasis required the learning of new skills and attitudes that have ultimately had a positive impact on the psychological service as a whole, as well as resulting in more effective implementation of the A.B.C. program itself.

The program, which was implemented for a decade, shaped other class-based appraisal. It has had a significant impact on the role of school psychologists as consultants in the past two decades, especially with regards to primary and secondary prevention service (Cole, 1992, 1996; Cole & Brown, 1996). This chapter documents the development of a system wide program and is included for its historical value and its far reaching implications for ongoing consultation services.

In terms of the model presented in Chapter 1, the A.B.C. had a primary prevention focus, i.e., it involved psychological staff in services that were targeted toward classroom teachers or school administrators and only indirectly toward individual students. The program evolved from an early identification program that had been ongoing at the school board since the early 1970s (Brown, Landrus, & Long, 1974). That program also had a primary prevention emphasis; however, the form of intervention taken was often the provision of special education services, rather than intervention in the regular classroom. The role of the school psychologist was assessment-oriented, and involved the administration of multiple "screening" tasks for identifying children who might be at risk. Such students frequently received more in-depth individual assessments, followed by special education programming. Thus, while having a preventative focus, the early identification program followed the traditional test-and-place model for school psychology (see Bardon, 1982; Sheridan & Gutkin, 2000)

While the intent of the program was obviously positive, both educators and psychologists developed concerns about a) the proliferation of special education programs, b) the wisdom of targeting children for such programs at an early age, and c) the opting out by regular classroom teachers of the responsibility for educating children at risk. As well, teachers legitimately resented the involvement of psychological staff who would administer a series of tests to their class and then be cast in the role of "experts" on the needs of students.

Because of these concerns, the early identification program was replaced by the A.B.C. in 1980 with a different purpose and function. While continuing to have a primary prevention orientation, this new program focused on the regular rather than the special education classroom as the point of intervention. This shift in emphasis required new strategies for successful program implementation and the learning of new skills and attitudes by all involved.

This chapter is divided into several sections. First, we provide an overview of the A.B.C. program. We then discuss ten key factors that, in our experience, contributed to its success. Although these practices did not typify the operation of the program in every school, they were, in our judgment, correlated with the achievement of its objectives.

In the next section, we provide specific examples of how appraisal information was related to students' needs and led to practical curriculum change. We then briefly discuss ethical issues that arise for school psychologists who function as consultants in the implementation of a primary prevention program such as the A.B.C. The final portion of the chapter documents the impact of this program on the functioning of a psychological services department, its delivery of services, and the professional development of its staff.

Overview of the Program

The A.B.C. evolved over time and changes were documented at the school and the system level. Figure 1 provides an overview of the program in its early stages. The goals were oriented toward mainstream education with a primary prevention focus.

Students' learning needs were identified on a classroom, rather than on an individual basis. The implication of these needs for the curriculum were discussed and areas for possible change were targeted. It should be acknowledged that many teachers already undertake an evaluation at the beginning of each school year to determine their students' academic skill levels. The purpose of the A.B.C. was to broaden and enhance these efforts by expanding the focus of the evaluation, and by bringing resources to the resolution of problems that individual teachers would not normally be able to access.

As shown in Figure 1, the A.B.C. program functioned at five points that are considered to be critical transitions during a student's school career: entry to school in Kindergarten (Phase I) and at Grades 1 (Phase II), 4 (Phase III), 7 (Phase IV), and 9 (Phase V). The first three phases of the program were mandated throughout the school system, while Phases IV and V operated on a pilot basis, with schools and teachers volunteering to participate.

GOALS
− Understand the educational needs of students
− Adapt the classroom program to meet identified needs

TIMING
− Phase I	− School Entry
− Phase II	− Grade 1
− Phase III	− Grade 4
− Phase IV*	− Grade 7
− Phase V*	− Grade 9

THE SCHOOL TEAM
− School Principal
− Classroom Teacher(s)
− School Psychologist
− Other(s)

*pilot phases

Figure 1 Appraisal for Better Curriculum (A.B.C.)

The focus of the evaluation had a somewhat different emphasis at each level, in keeping with the developmental and educational needs of children at different ages. The school entry level was primarily concerned with the child's physical health and initial adjustment. In Phase II (Grade 1), the focus of the evaluation became broader in that the development of the child's skills in areas considered to be vital to early school learning was assessed, including confidence and attitudes toward school, language and motor skills development, attention span, and preferred learning style. These areas of functioning continued to be examined in subsequent levels of the program, with increasing emphasis on the evaluation of academic achievement levels.

The final key component of the program shown in Figure 1 is the school team. Members of the team included the principal, classroom teacher or teachers, and the school psychologist. At the request of the principal, other members of the school staff, such as the vice-principal, special education teacher or curriculum specialist, became members.

Although some aspects of the A.B.C. at each level were mandated throughout the school system, local school team members had a fair amount of decision-making authority regarding the program in their school. Table 1 identifies some of the issues that were discussed. Ideally they were resolved in a collaborative manner during the course of meetings throughout the academic year.

The actual implementation of the program, as well as the roles played by school team members, varied markedly from school to school. As with any program of this kind, the approach could be a relatively superficial one in which each participant goes through the motions but little or no meaningful educational goals are achieved. Alter-

---

Table 1 Questions for the A.B.C. School Team

Questions related to planning:
- What are our chief concerns for this group of students?
- What information do we need in order to understand our concerns more fully and plan interventions to address them?
- How should we go about obtaining this information?
- Who will take responsibility for gathering the information and organizing it?
- When will we meet to evaluate the information we have, and plan what needs to be done next?

Questions related to curriculum implementation:
- Do the students have needs that are not being met by the present programs?
- What program changes are feasible?
- How do these changes fit in with overall curriculum planning for the school? For the school system?
- What resources, both personal and material, are required to implement them?

Questions related to evaluation:
- Has the program been successful?
- How do we know?
- What could we do better next time?

natively, the program was used as a vehicle for the solution of significant educational problems.

Our experience was that with a superficial approach, school teams tended to focus on the "what" and "when" of the program, but not the "why." Much time was spent in information gathering, but relatively little attention was given to understanding the purpose of collecting that information or analyzing its implications. Even though the participants may have worked very hard, the lack of significant outcomes often left them with a feeling of frustration.

A number of variables that influenced the degree to which the A.B.C. operated successfully and accomplished its stated purpose are discussed more fully in the next section. Unhelpful practices are contrasted with helpful ones, with a particular focus on the role of the psychologist.

What Contributed to a Successful A.B.C. Program?

1. Principal's Support

The A.B.C. program was a system-wide "top-down" initiative, which both implied that changes were desirable and that intended outcomes were clear to its participants. The program further assumed the cooperation of the administrative leadership in each school, and placed the principal in a change agent role. Thus, administrative support was a crucial factor in the implementation of this program.

It was our impression that some principals had difficulty functioning in such a role. In those schools, appraisal meetings tended to be delayed, clarification of goals was not encouraged, and implementation procedures were weak. In addition, shared responsibility around decision-making was not promoted in either the planning or the follow-up phases.

In other schools, principals seemed more receptive to the concept of change. They fostered the development of an open, collaborative atmosphere and saw the program as a means of achieving important educational goals. Such principals focused team discussions on goals of the A.B.C. (i.e., the appraisal of students' skills, competencies, and preferences; developing a broader understanding of students' learning needs; planning appropriate curriculum). They also facilitated implementation by releasing teachers from the classroom for planning and evaluation meetings, participation in related professional development meetings, and joint teacher-psychologist activities. This kind of support resulted in a large number of consulting relationships evolving naturally and voluntarily among the school staff, which had positive implications for many joint programs in the school.

2. A Team Approach

From the outset, the program employed a multidisciplinary team approach. Members included the homeroom teacher, the principal or designate, and the school psychologist. The team's major responsibilities included data collection and interpretation, followed by planning for curriculum adaptation. Although teamwork conceptually implied positive and productive efforts and outcomes, it was also challenging. Our experiences in this regard echoed Sarason's (1988) perceptions of the complexities involved in working towards change in a school system.

When school psychologists adopt more traditional roles, relationships and responsibilities tend to be clear and predictable (Cole, 1996; Maher, Illback, & Zins, 1984; Siegel & Cole, 1990). Discussions between psychologists and educators usually then center around individual children whose learning or social needs are not being met in the regular classroom, and solutions tend to emphasize modifications outside of the regular program, such as the provision of special education and/or the involvement of community services. In such a model, it is easy to assume that psychologists provide assessments for placement only; that teachers are responsible for classroom instruction; and that principals deal with administrative services and decision-making *per se* (Fullan, 1982, 1988, 1991, 2001; Fullan & Miles, 1992).

The A.B.C. team departed from such a traditional approach. Team meetings required an expanded role and the development of new skills for all involved. These changes and new initiatives were sometimes stressful for team members who were influenced and at times overwhelmed by new interpersonal processes that required them to re-evaluate their own role and that of other members in the group. Especially at the beginning of the program, many principals were uncooperative and many teachers resistant. Figure 2 illustrates some of the tensions faced by the psychologist in such meetings.

Role ambiguity, and at times loss of confidence, could also be felt by psychologists, especially by those who were committed to direct services of assessment and counseling. The A.B.C.'s new avenues tended to produce feelings of being out of control, fears of a backlog of referrals, and a general sense of having "too much to do." An additional problem was that many psychologists felt obliged to "carry" the program by themselves, either because they believed in its goals, or conversely, were eager to complete it in order to return to more direct service delivery. Such self-chosen leadership tended to associate the program with being the "psychological services program" and sometimes induced passivity in other members of the team.

Ideally, the principal assumed the position of team leader. Other team members felt supported when this occurred, as such a role was consistent with the principal's status as the school's administrative and curriculum head. Frustration could also be reduced when the team had a scheduled time for discussion and follow-up meetings. Program objectives and ventilation of negative feelings could be discussed, but shared responsibility became the goal in such cases. Team members did not "take over"

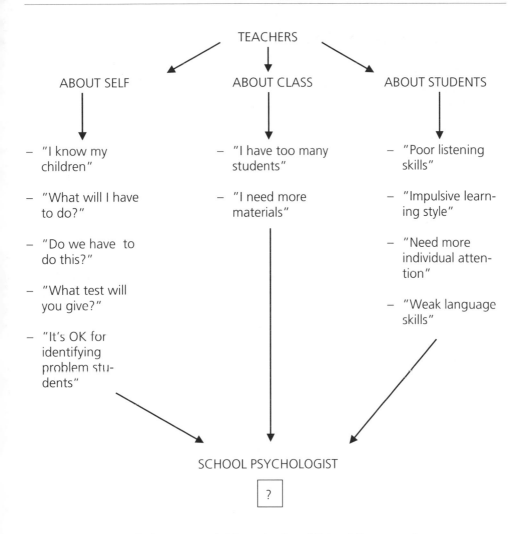

Figure 2 Pre-Appraisal "Automatic Thoughts" and Other Misconceptions

functions, but were stimulated to collaborate around common goals. They viewed one another as possessing different and complementary skills and perspectives. Over the years, professional development sessions involving principals, teachers, and psychologists stressed the need for such multidisciplinary cooperation.

The psychologist's effective consultation skills can facilitate the kinds of interpersonal, listening, and communication skills necessary for positive group dynamics and interprofessional collaboration. In teams where psychologists felt secure as consultants and were supported by the principal, territoriality concerns on the part of team members were avoided (Cole, 1992; Cole & Brown, 1996; Cole, Siegel, & Yau, 1990, 1992; Pfeiffer & Heffernan, 1984).

3. Asking Questions About Students

An A.B.C. program was more likely to achieve its goals if the first team meeting was devoted to identifying questions and emerging issues. Such questions may have been derived from the teacher's initial observation in the early days of the school year or previous experiences with similar groups of students, or from some broader concern within the school. These tentative hypotheses could be later used to focus data collection and analysis.

This essential first step proved to be difficult for many team members. Both teachers and psychologists are "busy doers" who face a hectic work pace on a daily basis. Many teams were tempted to start new programs with planning *what* to do rather then *why* to do it. However, such faulty planning usually led to elaborate appraisal projects that did not necessarily correspond to the teacher's needs in a given classroom.

It was our impression that difficulties were more likely to occur in less democratic school teams in which the members exhibited poor motivation for change and where the psychologist acted or was placed in the "expert" role. In contrast, teams in which members were open to change usually began their planning meetings by addressing teachers' concerns and needs. Psychologists who felt secure in their role as consultants could facilitate discussion around a teacher's plans for the first term of the academic year and the relevance of the program for the class. Discussion was more likely to be productive when it began with questions about the aims and expectations of the program. Agreement in principle about the following issues was key:

(1) What does the teacher want to learn about the students?
(2) What are the teacher's goals for the class?
(3) What are class needs?
(4) How are appraisal questions going to be answered?
(5) What is the purpose and format of future meetings?
(6) How is the teacher prepared to act on appraisal results?

Once these issues were discussed, specific plans could be made and responsibilities assigned. Tasks involving various aspects of data collection and organization were clarified. The agenda was concluded by scheduling several meetings throughout the year in order to monitor progress. Decisions were often recorded by an appointed team member, and a summary was shared with all involved.

4. Multiple Interactions with Teachers and Students

In its planning-to-practice sequence, the A.B.C. program was facilitated by frequent in-class interactions between the teacher and the psychologist. Such multiple contacts allowed for ongoing communication, verification, and re-evaluation of hypotheses, as well as the implementation of practical interventions. When teachers and psychologists spent time observing children together, they developed shared impressions about students' approaches to learning based on joint knowledge of classroom dynamics and interpersonal behavior. Issues related to learning strategies during individual, small-group, and large-group activities could be addressed. Among the questions that could be discussed were: How do children process new information? How do they solve problems? What class activities do they select? Who are the active learners? Who depends on the teacher's help? What behaviors interfere with learning?

In schools where the psychologist and/or the teacher felt reluctant to employ such an approach, there were fewer opportunities for ongoing consultation contacts. This often occurred when the purpose and focus of classroom observation was not clear and agreed upon by both parties. For many teachers, the presence of the psychologist in the classroom represented an unacceptable departure from seeing the latter's primary responsibilities as related to testing individual problem students. In addition, these teachers may have felt that their knowledge and effective teaching skills were being evaluated. Thus, classroom observations were perceived as an imposition and as interfering with daily routines.

Sensing the teachers' concerns, psychologists who lacked confidence in their own consultation skills tended to distance themselves from the classroom. In contrast, those who were sensitive to the teachers' feelings tried not to come across as judgmental, and used their classroom visits as opportunities to strengthen their relationship with the teacher. They attempted to increase their credibility as helpful professionals, and to establish an informal classroom presence with both teachers and students (Abel & Burke, 1985; Fagan & Wise, 1994; Hawryluk & Smallwood, 1986; Shinn & McConnell, 1994).

5. Moving Toward Classroom-Based Assessment

Linking appraisal methods to curriculum and to concerns expressed by the teacher were central to the program's success. However, in some schools, the selected evaluation strategies did not answer many of the teachers' questions about student needs and competencies: rather, the appraisal phase was viewed as the responsibility of the psychologist, and this "handing over" of appraisal responsibilities to one team member tended to induce passivity and lowered interest. The psychologist skilled in the administration of normed referenced batteries became less concerned with identifying teacher needs, and instead tended to grapple with research data in order to select the best format for measuring a particular skill or ability. Many embarked on ambitious programs involving the "testing and scoring" of multiple forms in the quest to obtain important information about the "whole child" and the "whole class." Such psychologists often presented their teams with too much "wrong data" (Deno, 1986). Tests used were the same measures appropriate for a differential diagnostic model, and tended to focus on broad aptitudes rather than skills, behaviors, and attitudes more relevant to classroom decision-making. With such an emphasis, the appraisal phase tended to become an end in itself rather than a means to curriculum adaptation.

Overworked and staying close to their traditional role definition, these psychologists had few opportunities for informal interactions with teachers and students. In addition, long periods of time usually elapsed without providing feedback to teachers. Follow-up meetings took place up to six months after the data had been collected, by which time class dynamics had usually changed and findings ceased to be relevant to teacher concerns. Since the appraisal was not time-efficient, teams met for full days to hear assessment findings on 25 to 30 children. Little time or energy was left for considering better curriculum ideas and suggestions.

With experience, those school teams able to adopt an open collaborative style of problem-solving gradually modified their appraisal practices. More time was spent clarifying the goals of the appraisal, with the result that the data-gathering phase became shorter and more focused. Both the content of the appraisal and the methods used were altered. Rather than evaluating broad aptitudes (i.e., language ability), the appraisal focused more on student behaviors and attitudes (L. Carlson & Cole, 1993; Kratochwill, 1982) that were important for success in the existing class program (i.e., participation in group discussion). As well, appraisal methods became more direct in that they reflected more clearly the setting, methods, and materials actually used by teachers; thus, results could be more appropriately generalized to curriculum decision-making (Shapiro, 1990; Shinn & McConnell, 1994; Ysseldyke & Mirkin, 1982).

From this it may be seen that the appraisal no longer focused exclusively on the administration of standardized paper and pencil tests to groups of students outside of the classroom. Instead, the teacher and psychologist worked together within the classroom, often making use of actual curriculum materials (see Estrin, 1993; Gordon & Musser, 1992; Tucker, 1981) as the basis of the evaluation. Other methods included informal inventories of student attitudes, examination of work samples, interviews, discussions, in-class observations, and teacher-completed checklists. The use of commercially available paper and pencil tests came to form only a part of, rather than the entire, appraisal battery.

Gradually, school teams learned to center their planning discussions around alternate appraisal techniques. Those psychologists who were sensitive to teacher preferences for ongoing and more informal methods of evaluation (Fullan, 1982, 1991), appreciative of teachers' skills as observers of children (Boice, 1983; L. Carlson & Cole, 1993), and knowledgeable about the pros and cons of alternate measurement strategies, were able to assist school teams to devise evaluation methods that achieved their goals by using an appropriate mix of formal and informal procedures. A more detailed description of some of these strategies and their impact on curriculum planning is presented later in this chapter.

6. Study of Student Record Information

Student records contain valuable information about children's educational histories, but are often underutilized by teachers. Over the years, new report cards are added, but the records are usually reviewed by teachers and psychologists only when problem students are discussed. In many instances, the fact that records are housed in the school office rather than in the classroom tends to create a barrier to teachers' access. In other cases, teachers have an active mistrust of the information they contain: "I don't read the school records because I want to form my own impressions about my students."

Because of their expertise in the evaluation and assessment of students, most school psychologists were aware of the wealth of factual, as well as interpretive, information that school records contain. Thus, they were in a position to suggest that school teams access them as part of the appraisal, particularly at the Grade 4 level and beyond. Class information (such as the number of students involved in special education programs, the number who had recently transferred into the school, and attendance patterns) were helpful as school teams developed a deeper understanding of student needs. Often the process was begun by recording basic data regarding entry to school and the number of school changes. More extensive investigation of the records could proceed as a means of providing additional information about questions that arose during the course of the appraisal. A guide for summarizing school record information is shown in Appendix A.

7. Understanding Class Needs

Once the appraisal was complete, what was done with the data gathered? How was it recorded? How was it presented for team discussions so that student needs became apparent? When large amounts of information were gathered in the absence of clearly defined appraisal goals, both teachers and psychologists seemed to gravitate towards using the data to identify students at risk. Hours were spent in endless anecdotal discussions about "interesting students" in each class. While useful in clarifying the learning needs of individuals, such discussions were inordinately time-consuming. Exhausted at the end of such sessions, team members often had little time or energy to make generalizations or identify classroom trends. Teachers tended to feel overwhelmed by the large amount of information presented, and had difficulty understanding the relevance of the findings to curriculum planning.

These obstacles were often overcome by moving the focus of discussion from individual to class needs. Using teacher concerns as a starting point, team discussions could be more class-centered, and groups of children with similar needs could be identified. Appraisal areas explored were usually related to both the content and the process of learning.

Appraisal data could be summarized for an entire class, often using a one-page grid (see Table 2). Students' names were listed on the left-hand side, and areas of investigation were stated across the top. Student results were recorded numerically, but were frequently encoded using a symbol system that allowed patterns and trends to be discerned through visual inspection.

Such visual aids were one strategy designed to simplify data and led to more time-efficient analysis of child-class-program interactions. Information about individual children was evaluated in relation to peers, and was a first step in forming a composite picture of groups with similar characteristics and of the entire class. Team discussions became more objective and analytical. They were more likely to address appraisal findings in relation to curriculum objectives, and to focus on the implications for teaching and working arrangements in the classroom.

8. An Ongoing Process Within the School

Positioning the program as an integral part of the school's culture was another key to its success. Successful programs generally arose in schools in which the principal's leadership, participation, and attention to early planning was the norm. This kind of assertiveness and modeling allowed for more indirect consultation services by the psychologist, and increased teachers' commitment to the program.

It was especially useful to devote time early in the school year to planning agendas for and scheduling team meetings. Table 3 provides an example of the meetings planned by one school. Such a scheme emphasized continuity and the cyclical nature of the curriculum planning process. It also allowed the psychologist increased opportunities to discuss children's developmental changes and needs, and to link such factors with the consideration of curriculum adaptations.

Careful planning also allowed for better information dissemination amongst the teaching staff. When appropriate, implications of results derived from the appraisal for the entire school program were discussed. For example, identified learning gaps at the Grade 4 level could lead to the introduction of new teaching strategies in Grades 1 through 3. Alternatively, if the school staff decided to focus professional development in a given year on a particular topic (for example, the use of computer programs), the A.B.C. process provided information that facilitated the tailoring of programs to teacher and student needs.

9. Post-Appraisal Team Conferences and Curriculum Adaptation

Curriculum adaptation was the core of the A.B.C. Following the delineation of areas of strength and weakness, program alternatives were usually outlined. Psychologists

Table 2 An A.B.C. Class Profile

ABC PHASE IV

Grade 7

School:

Room:

NAME	Student Record Info. Age	Years in Canada	School Changes					Academics Math Measurement	Math Geometry	Math/Arithmetic	Math/Graphs	Reading Level	Writing Score	Coping Skills Writing Speed	Writing Form	Listening	Self Concept Class Positive (No.)	Negative (No.)	Other	Better Class Physical Changes	Academic Changes	Social Changes	Other	Comments re: Learning Style Information – Teacher's Concerns
1.																								
2.																								
3.																								
4.																								
5.																								
6.																								
7.																								
8.																								
9.																								
10.																								
11.																								
12.																								
13.																								
14.																								
15.																								
16.																								
17.																								
18.																								
19.																								
20.																								
21.																								
22.																								

Table 3 A.B.C. Implementation Plan

Phase	1. Planning	2. Feedback/Follow-up	3. Follow-up/Evaluation	4. Evaluation
When	Early September	Mid-October	Mid-November	Mid-May
Who	Principal (or designate), classroom teacher(s) psychologist, rotary teacher(s)			
Agenda For Team Meetings	1. What do teachers want to learn about their students from the appraisal? 2. What appraisal format and package will address class needs? 3. How are teachers prepared to act on appraisal results? 4. What questions are identified for the class? 5. Assign responsibilities for various aspects of data collection and organization. (Who? When?) 6. Schedule all future team meetings. Plan several meetings throughout the year.	1. Identify general issues and concerns emerging from classroom observations. 2. Examine general class profile. 3. Identify additional appraisal information to be analyzed prior to the next meeting. Assign responsibility for this task. 4. Consider appropriate follow-up strategies by teacher, psychologist, curriculum consultants. 5. Consider feedback to students. 6. What additional information is required?	1. Teacher and psychologist give evaluation of interventions tried to date. 2. Examine appraisal results in depth as agreed upon in previous meetings. 3. Consider implications of additional academic data and follow-up. 4. Identify areas where consultant help is required. 5. Assign responsibility for tasks and ordering supplies provided for in the A.B.C. budget.	1. Consider appraisal strategies and materials. What was effective? What needs improvement? 2. Evaluate the process. What could have been done to make the program more effective? 3. Consider follow-up interventions. What was successful? What was not? 4. What are some issues that need to be addressed in the coming year? 5. Suggestions including appraisal materials; data organization; follow-up strategies; use of consultant(s) help; administrative support.

experienced in consultation and group interaction processes could help to move the program from appraisal into intervention. They could assist the problem-solving process by steering discussions away from global statements, excluding strategies that could not or would not be implemented by teachers (Gutkin, 1986; Gutkin & Curtis, 1982; Shapiro, 1990), and by helping team members to focus instead on clear, practical solutions (Fullan, 1991; Fullan & Miles, 1992; Schmuck, Runkel, Arends, & Arends, 1977; Sheridan & Gutkin, 2000).

Among the issues that could be discussed were the following:

- Should the physical environment be rearranged to allow for more spontaneous interactions and activities?
- Should timetables be altered?
- How might students respond to changes made in techniques of instruction?
- What steps should be taken to provide remedial help for problem students?
- What social or academic challenges can be provided for problem students?
- What supplies and equipment are required for planned interventions?
- Who are the best resource staff?
- Who is responsible for the implementation of suggestions made?

Attempts to change the classroom instructional behavior of teachers have been shown to be most successful in situations where teachers perceive the changes to benefit the learning of students (Fullan, 1982). Teachers are more likely to evaluate proposed changes positively when they flow from a process in which they have been involved and comfortable from the beginning. As stressed throughout this section, ongoing group interactions among team members, principal support, and clean agenda plans tended to strengthen the program.

We have also found that the likelihood of curriculum change was enhanced when some of the discussion took place with teachers as an intact group, rather than only appealing to them as individuals (Fullan, 1991; Sharan & Hertz-Lazarowitz, 1982; Speck, 1996). Such group discussions usually tapped a multitude of topics, ranging from general issues across the curriculum to more specific grade- and class-based needs. Teachers often shared programming strategies with their peers and demonstrated new initiatives and materials they had developed. Such supportive exchanges often led to plans that had an ongoing and widespread impact upon the life of the school.

10. Follow-Up Interventions Involving the School Psychologist

The involvement of the school psychologist in ongoing curriculum initiatives educated school teams to view the supportive role of psychological staff as multidimensional, as opposed to seeing them exclusively affiliated with the appraisal stage.

Psychologists involved at all phases of the program began to include in their role a continuum of direct as well as indirect service delivery options (see Chapter 1). Follow-up initiatives that included psychologists became an important support system for teachers undergoing change. More psychologists became involved in such activities as leading groups, being involved in class discussions, and similar classroom activities as a follow-up to needs identified through the appraisal. Frequent consultant-consultee meetings led to reinforcement of positive class practices and open one-to-one discussions as teachers led the way towards program modifications. These contacts also allowed for joint reflection and occasional reformulation of answers to questions previously discussed at team meetings. What problems did teachers identify in the process or the outcomes of the program? What aspects did they find useful? How could they improve the program to make it more useful in adjusting curricula to meet their class needs?

Moving from Appraisal to Intervention

This section provides some illustrative examples of how appraisal information contributed to curriculum planning. Over the years school teams developed many creative appraisal strategies and interventions to address concerns identified in their local schools. The examples presented employ several different appraisal methods, and focus on aspects of student abilities, behaviors, and attitudes. These were selected because they illustrate some of the major themes of this chapter and emphasize the changing role of the school psychologist. However, they represent only a very small subset of the procedures actually used in schools during the program.

Example 1: Observing and Planning at the Grade 1 Level

Our first example describes the development and use of an observational checklist for Grade 1 teachers. The reasons for developing this alternate appraisal method are outlined in Table 4. These reasons were articulated in a multidisciplinary meeting involving the writers, school superintendents, and a curriculum consultant. This group met two or three times a year for the purpose of monitoring the implementation of the program and solving any problems arising at the systems level.

Acknowledging teachers as experienced observers of young children (Elkind, 1976, 1978; Fullan, 1991), as well as reflecting the policy of the school system to make more use of teacher observations in student evaluation, a working committee including three Grade 1 teachers was established. These teachers were selected because of their understanding of the goals of the A.B.C. The questions with which they were presented included: What have you learned about observing children that could be

Table 4 Goals of the Grade 1 Observational Checklist

- Access teacher observational data
- Improve link between appraisal and curriculum planning
- Enhance teacher ownership of process
- Reduce formal testing
- Speed up understanding of classroom needs

shared in a useful way with other teachers? How do you record your observations and communicate them to other members of the A.B.C. team? Thus, the teachers were seen as key to the achievement of the committee's objectives. Other committee members (including psychological staff and a curriculum consultant) were assigned supportive roles. Their involvement with this committee provides an example of systems level consultation as discussed in the model described in Chapter 1.

During several meetings over the course of one academic year, the working committee developed an observational checklist for use by teachers. The items selected were adapted from a much larger pool on the basis of their relevance to curriculum decision-making early in the Grade 1 program, and their content reflects the "child-centered" educational philosophy of this particular group of teachers. Items were positively worded, covered most areas of classroom functioning, and were intended to identify both learning strengths and weaknesses. Most described specific student behaviors and skills that could be assessed through ongoing day-to-day observation, rather than through a contrived "testing" situation.

The focus was not on absolute or enduring characteristics of a child, but rather on the child's interaction with the particular classroom of which he or she was a part. The checklist was designed to help teachers be more analytical and less subjective in making their observations. In addition, it enabled them to present information to the school team in a format that could readily be understood and acted upon.

As may be seen in Figure 3, the checklist consisted of the items themselves, a "cookbook" for the teacher on the meaning of the items, and a class summary grid. As the teacher evaluated a child on each item, he or she could record the result directly on the grid. What emerged at the end of the process was a class summary of needs and abilities. As the record was color-coded, patterns and trends could be rapidly discerned through visual inspection of the summary sheet. Table 5 describes the general areas of functioning covered by the checklist, and provides examples of items in the areas of reading and adaptability.

Role of the School Psychologist. If classroom teachers used the observational checklist or some similar systematic method of evaluation, the main burden of information-gathering in the appraisal shifted from the psychologist to them. While this change had many benefits (see Table 4), both the teacher and psychologist had to adjust to this shift in roles. Under the old model, the psychologist's area of responsibility was clearly defined as the gathering and ownership of test data while that of the teacher was defined in terms of the class program. Under the new model, the psychologist gave up control of the data and exercised power only through his or her ability to influence the thinking and decision-making processes of the teacher. For some psychologists this change in role was anxiety provoking. Many distrusted observational methods (Boice, 1983) and questioned teacher objectivity. Others, who saw their main expertise as "testing," lacked confidence in their ability to contribute to the program when testing per se was no longer a part of it.

Those psychologists who were comfortable embracing the role of consultant and skillful at developing the kind of rapport with teachers that was essential to a collaborative relationship, valued the freedom and opportunity to develop new skills. Such individuals moved easily into the role of assisting teachers in a variety of ways, including collaboration on adapting the checklist to address local concerns, clarifying the meaning of individual items, assisting in the interpretation of results, and supporting the process of curriculum change.

Evaluation and Curriculum Follow-up. In the year following its development, the Observational Checklist was piloted by a larger number of teacher volunteers work-

---

FORMAT
- List of Items
- "Cookbook"
- Class summary grid

Names						Comment
Mary						
Susan						
John						
Trevor						

- 3 Category, Color-Coded Response System
  Red .... Yellow .... Green

TIMING
- Early to mid-October

Figure 3 Grade 1 Observational Checklist

Table 5 Grade 1 Observational Checklist: Areas Covered and Sample Items

Areas covered

1. Learning style	2. Adaptability	3. Organization
4. Talking	5. Listening	6. Reading
7. Written Language	8. Mathematics	9. Creative Expression
10. Motor Skills		

Sample items from the adaptability area
1. Enjoys school
2. Approaches new people, situations, and routines with confidence
3. Shows appropriate independence
4. Accepts guidance and suggestions from others when appropriate
5. Shows a wide range of emotions appropriate to the situation
6. Plays/works cooperatively with other children
7. Sets realistic expectations for self

---

ing in a broad-based sample of schools. During an evaluation meeting in January of that academic year, the teachers and their respective school psychologists met to share their experiences in small group discussions. As well, suggestions for revision were actively solicited.

Most of the teachers responded positively to the use of the checklist. They reported that completion required approximately 20 minutes per child over a one- to two-week period. While the actual decision-making and recording was done in quiet moments away from the hurly-burly of the classroom, the teachers said that they often confirmed their impressions through direct observation. They described the usefulness of the checklist in the following ways:

- It helped them to evaluate their ideas concerning the class more objectively.
- It helped them to organize their thinking and present their concerns to others.
- It ensured that the "quiet" children in the class were not overlooked.
- It highlighted strengths, both for the class and for individuals. This was considered especially valuable as such strengths often provided a departure point for corrective programming.
- It was useful as an aid in preparing written reports for parents.

Most importantly, teachers reported that the checklist met the goal of suggesting areas for possible curriculum adaptation. For example, it provided the catalyst for one teacher to introduce a different set of reading materials, for another to reorganize her classroom groups, for a third to alter the pace of instruction, and for a fourth to place the emphasis in the math program on sorting and classifying, rather than computation.

Example 2: Effective Use of Commercially Available Group Measures

Throughout this chapter, we have suggested that psychological staff could contribute most effectively to the A.B.C. when they functioned as consultants rather than testers. Nevertheless, there were occasions when group-administered tests could make a useful contribution to the program. The key to success was to begin by asking these fundamental questions: What were the teacher's concerns for this group of students? What information was needed in order for the team to better understand these concerns and suggest methods for addressing them?

Educators tend to have strong opinions about commercially available group-administered tests: there is a tendency either to accept results uncritically, or to reject them categorically as biased, unfair, or irrelevant. While acknowledging the preference that many teachers have for more informal appraisal methods (Fullan, 1982, 1991), school psychologists had an important role to play in pointing out some of the advantages of commercially developed instruments, especially the existence of reliability data, rigorous item screening procedures, easily quantifiable results, and the availability of appropriate norms (Ebel, 1982; Shinn & McConnell, 1994). We suggested that information about appropriate tests be made available to all members of the appraisal team and that, if a test was to be given, teachers and psychological staff collaborate in the process. Joint observation of students as they took the test could provide useful opportunities for consultation.

In the A.B.C., group-administered measures were often given to provide information about the students whom teachers were not able to evaluate easily. They were more likely to be given only in phases III, IV, and V, as children at these age levels seemed to cope more effectively with paper and pencil tasks than younger children.

One area of student competency about which teachers often had questions was cognitive abilities. Group testing has been the subject of much public debate. It is rightly regarded as poor psychological practice when results are used to sort youngsters into special education programs or stream them into homogeneous classes. Nevertheless, standardized cognitive ability measures can be useful as part of an assessment directed toward curriculum planning (Kratochwill, 1982). In our experience, teachers often asked questions such as:

- Were there students in the class who were underachieving in relation to their abilities?
- Was the curriculum too challenging for some students, but not challenging enough for others?
- Was the material presented to students beyond their ability levels?

When such questions arose, the first task was to select an appropriate cognitive ability measure. Within our school board, the Raven's Standard Progressive Matrices (Raven, Court, & Raven, 1977) was often the measure that was given. It had many features to recommend it as a group-administered test of cognitive abilities in a multilingual, multicultural school board. The test consists of 60 problems in the form of a two-dimensional matrix or geometric design from which some part has been omitted. The child selects the missing section from a set of choices given below the design, and records his or her choice on an answer sheet. The test does not involve reading or language and therefore is not biased against children who are poor readers or for whom English is not a first language. Experience suggests that children enjoy taking the test. They tend to be unaware of incorrect answers and, although some of the items are quite difficult, most youngsters do not finish the test with an impression that they have performed inadequately. Since the Raven's is a self-paced measure, the speed of performance can provide additional information about learning styles.

In addition, the test has been extensively researched. Correlations with academic achievement are moderate though respectable (Raven et al., 1977; Sattler, 2001); thus, results could supplement the kinds of observations teachers were able to make as they evaluated students' academic achievement. The test has been researched from a number of theoretical perspectives and spans a wide range of cognitive abilities. It has been described as a measure of "Simultaneous Processing" (Jarman & Das, 1977); as tapping both "Gestalt" and "analytic" thinking skills (Hunt, 1974); and as a method of evaluating complex cognitive processing (Snow, 1980). As well, it has been discussed from a developmental perspective using a neo-Piagetian framework (Bereiter & Scardamalia, 1979) which is well-known to educators (see for example Elkind, 1976, 1978). Finally, because the test is self-paced, the speed of performance can provide an indication of a student's impulsivity in approaching tasks (J. Carlson & Wiedel, 1979). Each of these perspectives could offer a point of view for discussing the implications of results for curriculum planning.

In order to provide some examples of curriculum issues that could be addressed with this kind of measure, actual results from four classes of Grade 4 students in two different schools are presented in Figure 4.

School A was a typical inner city school with a low income, multiracial population, while School B had culturally more homogeneous students from middle class families. Raw scores are shown for each student in the class, and the arrows designate class means. Raw scores rather than age-normed scores are given since comparison of abilities among individual students was not the goal.

Examination of the four classes revealed both similarities and differences that could provide provocative information to teachers. For example, the average score of one of the inner city classes was almost as high as that of those from the middle class school-a fact that in and of itself might have been surprising to some teachers. Again, in three of the four classes, there were a number of students who were able to solve some of the more difficult problems. To have achieved such success, these students must have been adept at identifying patterns and relationships, at reasoning about several unrelated pieces of information, and at generalizing from one context to another. A question for the teacher was whether these skills were reflected in the stu-

SCHOOL A

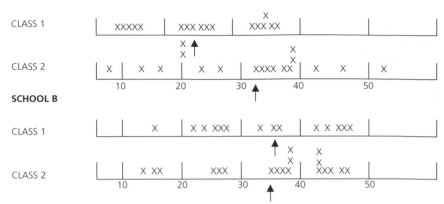

Figure 4 Distribution of Raven's Raw Scores in Four Classes

dents' achievement. If they were not, then the challenge was to provide such students with educational experiences that would stimulate them to make more use of these skills in the classroom.

A third issue was the degree to which disparate results were obtained. In this case, results in three of the four classes were quite heterogeneous. Were students with low scores also impulsive in their approach? If their impulsivity also characterized their approach to everyday classroom tasks, then their achievement levels might have been improved by teaching them a more reflective response style. In any event, the challenge for the teacher was to provide a program that met the needs of students with a variety of abilities and learning styles. Attempts to meet this challenge could lead to a discussion of student activities to allow individuals with a wide range of ability levels to work together without excessive competition.

All of these ideas were discussed with teachers as hypotheses to be tested in light of their own observations, rather than accepted uncritically as truths engraved in stone. Regardless of whether the insights suggested by the results ultimately turned out to be useful, the fact that the test was given allowed teachers to think about their students from a somewhat different perspective and to ask questions that might not otherwise have occurred to them.

Example 3: Building Self-Esteem – Appraisal to Intervention

Both educators and psychologists have emphasized the impact of pupils' attitudes towards school and towards themselves as learners on academic achievement and social adjustment (Blumenfeld, Pintrich, & Hamilton, 1986; Chiu, 1988; Hightower et al., 1987; Marsh, 1986; Stalikas & Gavasi, 1995; Tierno, 1983; Walker & Greene, 1986). Thus, the study and development of a positive self-concept was an important part of the A.B.C. Initially, psychologists were viewed as the team members who were "responsible" for any aspect of the appraisal associated with the affective area. Taking their responsibilities seriously, and aware of the fundamental problems associated with the definition and measurement of this domain (Keyer & Sweetland, 1984; Korchin, 1976; Kramer & Conoley, 1992; Marx & Winne, 1978; Robinson & Shaver, 1974; Wylie, 1974), psychologists undertook extensive reviews of research data in order to select appropriate self-report scales. Such factors as the suitability of the scale for administration to students, its length, its reliability and validity, and the avoidance of scales with a focus on problem behavior or on issues of a sensitive or clinical nature, were among those considered.

Having selected a self-concept scale and verified its acceptability to other members of the school team, psychologists were usually faced with the task of administering and scoring it. However, as teachers often left the class when the psychologists entered it, they were frequently unable to take advantage of the opportunity to observe the students at work. Furthermore once the results were scored, information presented at team meetings tended to be expressed in terms of students with "high" or "low" self-concepts. All too often neither the meaning of such global labels nor their implication for classroom programming was clearly understood by teachers.

Therefore, alternate avenues for the study of self-concept that would actively involve classroom teachers were sought. Various measures were developed by psychologists. The self-concept booklet described here (entitled "About Me") was developed by one of the authors (Cole, 1983) with two main purposes in mind. First, it aimed to provide school teams with information that would enhance their understanding of the interactions between students' motivational states, social-emotional characteristics, and learning styles. Second, the measure was designed to complement other appraisal approaches and to provide information that would lead to programming decisions in connection with appraisal objectives (Hambleton, 1982; Ysseldyke et al., 1997)

"About Me" is based on work by Canfield and Wells (1976). It uses many of the strategies suggested by those writers for enhancing the development of self-concept in the classroom. These strategies are familiar to teachers and are similar to activities they frequently use. Thus, the booklet not only appraises issues related to self-concept, but the act of administering it to students is seen in and of itself as a self-concept enhancing activity.

The booklet has two versions, for Grades 4 and 7. The items tap content areas such as friendship, perception of self in and out of school, and attitudes towards learning. In developing the booklet, the author sought the advice of psychologists, teachers, and school administrators. Periodically, questions were modified and items were adapted or excluded following interviews with the users of the measure. Particular attention was paid to students' developmental needs through the use of age-appropriate words and phrases and content reflecting their interests, reasoning abilities, and organizational skills.

"About Me" lacks the psychometric rigor of many of the self-concept scales described in the research literature which have been developed for the identification of children with special needs. Moreover, like other self-report scales it may be both susceptible to response biases and limited by students' willingness to write candidly about themselves. Nevertheless, it was often preferred by school teams over more formal measures because it offered an easy and simple avenue towards understanding school adjustment (Cole & Brown, 1996; Hightower et al., 1987).

The "About Me" booklet (at the Grade 7 level) is reproduced in Appendix B. The appendix also contains instructions for administering the booklet to students, as well as a general scoring guide. This scoring guide categorizes the responses using a classification scheme based on data obtained from students over a six-year period. A suggested "grid" for developing a class profile is also presented.

Follow-up Strategies for Grade 7

"About Me" afforded both teachers and psychologists a joint opportunity to address students' self-concept through teamwork. It also allowed for the study of students' perspectives and integration of social and affective education into ongoing curriculum and instruction (Elias & Clabby, 1984; Merrell, Cedeno, & Johnson, 1993).

The information derived from student responses to the booklet could be used in several ways to assist in creating a classroom environment conducive to learning and social growth. Psychologists were able to discuss appraisal findings from a cognitive-developmental perspective and within the context of understanding emerging student needs (Byrne & Shavelson, 1986; Crain & Bracken, 1994; Damon & Hart, 1982; Dusek & Flaherty, 1981; Leonardson, 1986; Noppe, 1983; Tierno, 1983).

Table 6 illustrates a suggested movement from assessment to curriculum adaptation. The reader will notice the interrelationship among the four cells, which aim to relate appropriate curriculum goals and teaching approaches to early adolescents' needs. For example, cell A emphasizes the child's cognitive development and the move from concrete to more abstract thought patterns. Cell B ties this development with specific learning needs, such as students' need for more intellectual freedom to question and challenge information taught, side by side with their emerging need for greater autonomy and a desire to exercise choices and new capacities. Cell C lists the areas investigated in "About Me" that match the adolescents' developmental changes and learning needs, and lead to the specific teaching techniques and alterative modes of instruction listed in cell D. Small group discussions or debates will allow for peer interactions while the students learn to hypothesize, judge, and develop values. Taken together, the four cells show that curriculum planning can foster social interac-

Table 6 The Self-Concept Domain – Early Adolescence

A. Rapid Changes/New Capacities
1. Physical Growth
2. Social-Emotional Development:
   - range of powerful emotions and reactions
   - self-awareness
   - influence of peer group/social identity $\longleftrightarrow$
   - self-absorption
   - conflicting feelings about self, authority, and independence
   - subjective descriptions of self
3. Cognitive Development: "Formal operations" – emerging abilities to:
   - develop abstract thought
   - make more objective judgments
   - hypothesize; understand the past
   - plan realistically for near future
   - increase interest in social issues

B. Social Learning Needs
1. Freedom intellectually to:
   - explore/question/challenge
2. Positive communication
3. Supportive attitudes
4. Greater autonomy
5. Acceptance by peers and adults
6. Value system
7. Psychological security and sense of competence
8. Opportunities to test beliefs/ exercise choices and new capacities

C. Areas of Investigation in "About Me"
1. Personal attributes
2. Friendship, social skills
3. Perception of adults
4. Acceptance of responsibility
5. Out of school activities
6. Sports and hobbies
7. Perception of academic abilities
8. Feelings about class, school

D. General Approaches/Teaching Techniques
1. Small group discussions
2. Class problem-solving sessions
3. Skill practice exercises
4. Role-playing
5. Experience sharing discussions
6. Interviews
7. Debates
8. Dialogue

tions among students as they acquire new academic skills and more insight into themselves as learners. Once these relationships were understood, specific teaching strategies such as those listed in Table 7 could be considered in consultation with the classroom teacher. Often, it was advisable for the psychologist to participate with the teacher in a joint intervention. It was important to select follow-up strategies that were seen by the teacher as complementing his or her curriculum goals, and which could be viewed as valuable and enjoyable by all involved.

Case Study

The use of a "questions and suggestions box" (strategy 4 in Table 7) was discussed by the author with a Grade 7 teacher following the analysis of A.B.C. findings. Mr. A. viewed his students as being "reserved, not talking, not sharing," and wished "to do something about it." Data from the "About Me" class profile revealed that, in comparison to the two other classes, students in 7A tended to view adults as possessing many annoying qualities ("angry" -30%; "bossy, unfair" -46%). In addition, they

---

Table 7 Some Specific Teaching Strategies

1. A series of classroom sessions can be held, during the course of which concerns raised by the students are discussed with both teacher(s) and school psychologist(s):
   - Social acceptance and rejection and its effects on self-esteem (how do we cope with feelings of disappointment, anger?)
   - Situations involving success and failure at school
   - The effects of physical self-concept on self-esteem (views, feelings, values)
   - Motivation, study skills, and academic success (explore ideas, assumptions)
   - Communication with peers and adults (role-playing, enactment of teacher-student discussion)
   - How to combat feelings of loneliness? (have students discriminate between "being alone" and "feeling alone")
   - Students' rights and responsibilities (school/family/community)
   - Planning for the future – why? how?
   - Students should be encouraged to evaluate these discussion sessions by filling out a card containing the following categories:
     (a) I liked our class discussion
     (b) I am not sure whether I liked it or not
     (c) I didn't like it at all
     (d) Suggest how we might improve our next discussion

2. "About Me" classroom profiles can be discussed with students. Themes of information should be analyzed together.

3. Each student meets with the teacher and/or psychologist to review and discuss his/her answers to questions posed in the booklet. This dialogue also provides an opportunity to address pupils' questions and concerns.

4. Collect anonymous questions from students in a class "questions and suggestions" box. The psychologist and/or teacher reads the questions to the class for a guided problem-solving discussion.

were not happy with the atmosphere in their class ("teacher getting angry" -40%; "others' misbehavior" -35%; "too much school work" -25%). The students wrote, however, that they wished to improve their class environment and that they would like grown-ups to "understand us" (31%), "respect us" (50%), and "be nice to us" (29%).

Mr. A. supported the idea of devoting one hour each week to class discussions as an avenue to opening dialog between himself and his students. In joining this and other class discussions, the author's role was to serve as an "organization-development consultant" to class groups (Anscrello & Sweet, 1990; Schmuck, 1982).

The "questions and suggestions box" remained empty for the first two weeks. However, each week the teacher and the author encouraged the students to share their questions, and reinforced their promise to set aside an hour a week to address their requests for information and to listen to their opinions. Weekly feedback and nonjudgmental openness to suggestions were offered.

The third visit to the class proved to be pivotal as the following sessions produced 10-30 questions a week. Once a week we all would help in the physical rearrangement of the classroom and create a circle of chairs. The meetings became part of the weekly timetable, agreed upon by the class and the teacher. Once a month the students were asked whether they wished to continue the meetings. As the process proved enjoyable and supportive, the meetings continued for most of the academic year.

The questions from the box usually could be classified in the following categories:

(1) **Knowledge**
   - "What is stress?"
   - "What happens when you die?"

(2) **Relationships**
   - "Why do people make fun of kids who wear glasses?"
   - "I get along with my parents, and I think I get enough respect and responsibility. Is something wrong with me?"

(3) **School**
   - "Why do people think the smarter you are the more work you can do?"
   - "Why do we have so many tests?"

(4) **Sexuality**
   - "Why is sex referred to as 'the Birds and the Bees?'"
   - "If you have special feelings for someone, should you or should you not express them?"

Pupils and adults jointly sought to answer these questions, which in turn increased students' comfort in sharing their feelings, thoughts, and opinions about the many topics they chose to address. The meetings became more constructive as class cohesiveness increased. In addition, the teacher reported enhanced interpersonal communication and more frequent group problem-solving experiences in other areas of the class program.

In the early spring, students gravitated towards discussing adolescence. Following consultation with the teacher and the class, the author presented two short movies, following which all were asked to share their impressions. When the students were requested to write anonymously about their own adolescence, they welcomed the opportunity and wrote extensively about physical, social, cognitive and emotional changes. The following quotations were typical:

Socially
– "I am more picky about my friends."
– "I want to go to a lot more social events."

Physically
– "My voice is deeper."
– "Your body changes, hair grows. I listen to Dr. Ruth."

Thinking
– "I find myself constantly thinking about the opposite sex."
– "It's hard for me to concentrate in class because songs keep running through my mind."

Emotionally
– "My emotions confuse me. I find myself crying a lot more lately."

At the end of the academic year, the students were asked for feedback about the effectiveness of the program. The majority of the class expressed strong and positive opinions of support. Typical answers to the three questions asked were:

(1) What did you think and how did you feel about the meetings?
"I think it was a very smart thing to do. I felt it was really interesting listening to other students' opinions."
"I felt it helped answer a lot of questions I had about the world."

(2) What did you learn from it?
"I learned that a lot of people in my class worry about the same subjects I do."
"I am not the only one with problems."

(3) Would you recommend such meetings for other students your age? Why?
"Yes, talking with other students the same age makes you feel better."
"Yes! It is a good learning experience and with each question you question yourself."

For the author as the school psychologist, the experience brought her closer to day-to-day realities of the classroom and the teacher. Having employed this intervention strategy for several years, she saw it as time-efficient and often effective. The underlying conception was based on the widely used, social cognitive approach (Elias & Clabby, 1984), and the strategy led to class discussions that broadened understanding of relationships, increased coping and decision-making skills, and enhanced self-esteem. The modality worked best when it was implemented following teacher (consultee) initiated discussions. This allowed for the development of a collaborative relationship between the teacher and the psychologist as professional peers (Conoley & Conoley, 1982; Fagan, 1990; Fagan & Wise, 1994; Sheridan, 2001; Speck, 1996). In terms of the model presented in Chapter 1, this intervention should be seen as a primary prevention program.

Example 4: Integrating Multiple Sources of Information

In the samples presented so far, we have addressed the question of how various sources of information could be used as data in curriculum planning and follow-up interventions. In this section, we demonstrate how different information sources could be integrated for instructional planning purposes.

Tables 8, 9, and 10 present appraisal measures, findings, and suggested curriculum strategies that were typical of the A.B.C. program at Grades 1, 4, and 7, respectively. In accordance with the practices laid out in a previous section (ten strategies for a successful program), a blend of formal and curriculum-based measures is illustrated at each level. Teacher consultation is listed first, for it is through this process that initial teacher concerns could be identified. Then, other sources of information such as student records (especially in Grades 4 and 7), the "About Me" self-concept booklet, the teacher observational checklist (for Grade 1), and test data could be evaluated with these concerns in mind. While the follow-up suggestions for curriculum intervention derived logically from the data presented, such proposals were or were not seen by a teacher as something that he or she would want to implement. Thus, these suggestions were viewed as an exploration of what was possible, rather than as a description of what would be implemented in a real classroom. Ideally, intervention strategies resulted from joint problem-solving by team members reacting to the information generated by the appraisal. Follow-up suggestions for curriculum modification and program development also included making use of resources from outside the school, such as curriculum consultants.

Ethical Issues in the A.B.C.

In their role as consultants and as members of the A.B.C. team, psychologists had a responsibility to evaluate the degree to which their activities conform to the ethical standards required of the profession. In most jurisdictions, they must adhere to clearly stated standards of practice and conduct as a condition of license. As well, such professional organizations as the National Association of School Psychologists have adopted ethical principles to guide the behavior of their members. As has been pointed out by Hughes (1986), however, these ethical guidelines address many aspects of psychologists' work in schools only indirectly. In particular, although consultation is

Table 8 From Appraisal for Better Curriculum – Examples

Grade 1	Appraisal Strategies	Appraisal Results	Possible Follow-up Interventions
	– Teacher consultation – "Observational Checklist" – Classroom observations – Evaluation of work samples	*Teacher consultation* Identified teacher concerns are that many students: – fail to follow routines – do not complete seat work or participate in discussions – disrupt by seeking attention from teacher Identified strengths are that most students: – enjoy school, especially being read to – have good large muscle coordination *Observational Checklist* Confirms above, and identifies the following additional strengths for most students: – are curious – enjoy opportunities for artistic expression *Classroom Observations* – confirm teacher's concerns – a group of quiet shy students sits at the back of the class – a core of students (about 1/4) does participate – teacher sits at desk during seat work time – structured seat work activities dominate the curriculum *Evaluation of Work Samples* – little work completion – art work is colorful, detailed	– Physical rearrangement of the classroom (more activity and work centers), seat shy students closer to teacher – Limit large group instruction to activities children really enjoy such as reading stories, physical activities – Use small groups for teaching specific academic skills – Decrease number of structured seat work activities; increase creative activities (artwork, role-playing, crafts, outdoor games). – Monitor activities in order to make necessary adjustments to meet the changing needs of class – Involve curriculum consultants in implementation.

Table 9 From Appraisal for Better Curriculum – Examples

Grade	Appraisal Strategies	Appraisal Results	Possible Follow-up Interventions
4	– teacher consultation – classroom observation – review of student record information – "About Me" – Raven's Progressive Matrices – written language samples	*Teacher consultation* The identified concern is students' relatively low reading levels (mainly beginning Grade 3). Otherwise, these students are described by the teacher as a cooperative well-motivated group. *Classroom Observation* – well-behaved class – existing class program allows little opportunity for verbal interaction among students *Review of Student Records* – 7 of 25 students attend special education withdrawal classes – 4 students come from non-English-speaking backgrounds *"About Me" Self Concept* Students report that: – they feel positively about their class and teacher – they are worried about their reading *Raven's Progressive Matrices* – average scores predominate *Written Language Samples* – creative writing samples are short; phrases are simple	– For language enrichment increase group/class opportunities for oral expression. – Increase group project work to provide opportunities for successful experiences. – Use alternative modes of instruction, including audiovisual aids – Review textbooks to assess reading levels – Discuss with students how they learn best – Consider out-of-class visits in the community followed by discussion, artwork, reading, and creative writing – Consider the use of drama, role-playing, poetry, reading etc. – Involve ESL and special ed. consultants for reading etc.

Table 10 From Appraisal for Better Curriculum – Examples

Grade	Appraisal Strategies	Appraisal Results	Possible Follow-up Interventions
7	– teacher consultation – classroom observation – review of student record information – "About Me" – Raven's Progressive Matrices – written language and math samples	*Teacher consultation* The teacher expresses general concerns about the achievement levels, work habits, and behavior of those students. Of particular concern are three students who regularly disrupt the class. *Classroom Observation* – Too much wandering of students in and out of class – Disruptive students engage in power struggle with teacher and peers who sit near them – Students rush through their class work *Review of Student Records* Four students repeated a grade and attend a special education program. *"About Me"- Self Concept* Students: – are worried about their scholastic abilities – have a negative perception of adults – have a strong interest in sports *Raven's Progressive Matrices* – Heterogeneous results: those with low scores worked too quickly *Written Language and Math Samples* – show evidence of impulsive style, i.e., sloppy handwriting, spelling errors – average scores in math	– Class discussions should address study skills, expectations, goals. Consistent application of rules – Discuss students' concerns about academic needs and social problems with peers. – Encourage students to write about topics of interest – Set short-term goals – Find ways of promoting positive relationships between teacher and class, i.e., frequent use of verbal approval and encouragement – Identify students in need of individualized programming, and vary instructional approaches – Involve students in formulating class rules and behavioral expectations in order to promote the development of social skills – Language materials used should include areas of interest to students, e.g., sports, teen stories

often mentioned explicitly as a legitimate psychological service, many of the ethical dilemmas that can arise in the course of consultation are not explicitly discussed.

Psychologists' role in the A.B.C. involved the provision of service primarily to teachers and principals, and only secondarily to children and parents (Stewart, 1986). Nevertheless, both as psychologists and as members of the larger school community, there was an obligation to safeguard the rights of anyone who may be influenced by the program-children and parents as well as school personnel. Our experience was that ethical issues were most salient with respect to teachers' and parents' rights, each of which is discussed below (Ysseldyke et al., 1997).

Teachers' Rights

As the primary recipients of the services provided by psychological staff in the A.B.C., school personnel had a right to be aware of the nature of the services to be provided, and to be ensured of the confidentiality of any information about them which may have been acquired as the program was implemented. As well, their ongoing responsibility for the class program and their right to accept or reject any advice or recommendations needed to be explicitly recognized.

Although the A.B.C. was a mandated program, the role of psychological staff was a matter to be negotiated with other members of the school team. When psychologists primarily fulfilled the "testing" role, teachers had little concern about their own rights, as the focus was clearly on the evaluation of students' needs and characteristics. However, when the role expanded to include both consultation and extensive classroom observations, teachers needed to be reassured regarding the nature and purpose of the psychologist's activities. They had to feel confident that their privacy would be respected, and that concerns discussed in collaborative consultation with the psychologist were shared with others only with their consent. They expected that information discussed in team meetings was focused on student and program variables, rather than their personal qualities and teaching skills. Finally, they needed to be assured that the psychologist would avoid being forced into the role of conveying evaluative information about them to well intentioned, but possibly overly zealous, school administrators.

Parents' Rights

It is generally acknowledged that parents have the right to review educational records pertaining to their child and to participate in educational decision-making that affects them. Such rights are legally sanctioned in most jurisdictions. Regardless of the legal obligation, however, educators make the assumption that parents are concerned about their children, have their best interests at heart, and are their most forceful advocates. As well, practical experience suggests that parents are more supportive of the decisions made by educators when they have been involved in the process (Cole, 1992; Cole & Brown, 1996; Hughes, 1986).

Each time their child participated, parents were informed about the A.B.C. by means of a brochure, which described the goals of the program, listed the school personnel involved, and identified the steps to be followed. Parents were invited to contact the principal if they had any questions or concerns. In addition to this, many schools provided parents with information about the program through special meetings of the parent association. School personnel involved in the program, including psychological staff and classroom teachers, were often invited to attend. Frequently, a film describing the program and its goals was shown.

In a few instances, parents asked that their child not participate in the program, and when such a request was made it was honored. Other parents wished to receive specific feedback regarding the results of their child's appraisal. Typically, information was provided in a joint meeting involving psychological staff and school personnel; however, such requests were relatively rare. Apparently, most parents accepted the notion that the A.B.C. was mainly designed to facilitate program planning by teachers, and were confident that they would be informed of any important educational decisions affecting their child.

Because the A.B.C. was seen as classroom-based with outcomes that related to within-class programming rather than special education placement, parental consent for a child's participation was not obtained. Psychological staff involvement was in the role of providing assistance to the classroom teacher and school principal who retained decision-making responsibility for all aspects of the program and any recommendations arising from it. They did not, themselves, provide direct service to children and did not maintain records about individual students participating in the A.B.C.

Occasionally, recommendations for individual children involved program alterations that went beyond customary classroom procedures. Whenever a child was singled out, identified as different, or involved in programming support outside of his or her regular classroom, parental consent was obtained (Bersoff, 1982). It was also obtained whenever a child was referred to psychological staff, whether for assessment, small group interventions, or individual counseling.

The Process of Role Expansion for the School Psychologist

While no comprehensive evaluation of the A.B.C. was undertaken by the school board, it was our impression that the effects of the program were far-reaching. For psychological services staff, the program acted as a catalyst for role expansion and skill development. It was our impression that staff improved their consultation skills, and that those added skills had a pervasive influence on their work. Gradually, the focus of the service was changing from an assessment-for-placement model to one in which both psychological staff themselves and the educators with whom they worked had the expectation that the psychologist's main goal was problem-solving in the educational interests of the child.

In the remainder of this chapter, we will attempt to document these impressions by presenting data describing both the attitudes and behaviors of the psychological staff. To anticipate the discussion, we will argue that consultation played a somewhat greater role in this particular service than was often the case, and that the A.B.C. program had an influence on this development. Of course, in the absence of well-controlled studies, such assertions are difficult to support conclusively. However, the information that we had was consistent with this line of reasoning.

Since our concern in this volume is with the role of school psychologists, we will focus here on the changes that occurred in the role, behavior, and attitudes of psychological staff since the program's inception. Again, in the absence of well-designed evaluation studies, it is by no means certain that all of the points raised here were clearly attributable to the program. As well, during the time that the program was in place, the high-level administration of both the school board and the psychological services department attempted to foster a consultation role for psychological staff. The A.B.C. was, therefore, but one of several initiatives that were taken in this direction.

Earlier in this chapter, we documented ten factors that in our experience contributed to the effectiveness of A.B.C. teams in meeting their goals. The question we address first is whether the psychological staff themselves valued the strategies that we have identified. In the fifth year of the program, the psychological services department surveyed its staff concerning its A.B.C. practices. The questions asked paralleled the issues raised in Part II. Staff were asked to rate on a three-point scale each activity in terms of its importance for their role as an A.B.C. team member. One can see from Table 11 that the results supported the description of effective practices outlined earlier.

Fostering an ongoing process of multiple class-based interactions was rated as most important. Least important to effective practices was the use of standardized, norm-referenced tests; indeed, this last item was the only one listed with a predominance of "not important" ratings. This finding appeared to reflect the growing emphasis on the use of curriculum-based measures and classroom observation, increased participation in post-appraisal adaptations, and reliance on consultation as a means of achieving program goals.

Our next question is whether the values articulated within the context of the A.B.C. extended to other activities within the psychological service. As part of the questionnaire mentioned earlier, the psychological staff were also asked to rank-order 16 "domains of school psychology" in terms of the "personal importance you attribute to each." The "domains" were those identified by the National Association of School Psychologists (NASP) document "School Psychology Blueprint for Training and Practice" (NASP, 1984). Results are shown in Table 12 (see also the updated Blueprint in Ysseldyke et al., 1997).

Interpersonal communication and consultation was the top ranked area of concern, followed closely by assessment. Research and school-community relations were the lowest ranked, possibly because the school board employed specialist personnel to whom these responsibilities were specifically assigned. These results contrast with those of McKee et al. (1987), who asked their respondents to rank-order a similar list of "professional competencies." Their data identified assessment-related activities, such as cognitive assessment and report writing, as the top ranked competencies in terms of importance to practice, with skills related to consultation and intervention ranked somewhat lower. While direct comparisons are hazardous, it may well be that the psychological staff at this particular school board were able to achieve a somewhat better balance between assessment and consultation than was typical of many of their colleagues in other jurisdictions. A common finding for both groups, however, was that questions pertaining to professional development needs indicated a clear interest for more in-depth knowledge in areas related to interventions, both in and out of the classroom, and consultation.

Table 11 Importance of A. B.C. Practices as Seen by the Psychological Staff

Importance of A. B. C. Practices	Average Rating*
1. Help in identifying questions to be addressed in the appraisal	2.6
2. Facilitate the team approach, encouraging participation by each team member	2.7
3. Foster an ongoing process (including multiple interactions)	
– with teachers	2.8
– with students (individual; small group)	2.5
4. Use norm-referenced tests	.7
5. Use criterion-referenced measures	2.1
6. Use classroom observation	2.6
7. Prepare student/individual profiles	2.2
8. Prepare class profiles	2.4
9. Help in planning post-appraisal program changes/curriculum implementations	2.6
10. Participate in follow-up interventions	2.4
11. Encourage the team to evaluate its efforts	2.4

*Ratings are on a three-point scale, 1=not important, 3=very important
*N = 40

Table 12 Importance of School Psychology "Domains"

		x̄	Rank Order
1.	Class Management Procedures	6.1	6
2.	Interpersonal Communication and Consultation	4.1	1
3.	Basic Academic Skills (consultation on major theories of learning, research on teaching basic skills, study skills ...)	5.4	5
4.	Basic Life Skills (offer assistance in designing curricula to develop adaptive behavior, functional life skills ...)	8.3	10/11
5.	Affective/social skills	4.5	3
6.	Parental Involvement (help design and operate programs involving school-family contacts. . .)	7.7	9
7.	Classroom Organization and Social Structures	6.7	8
8.	Systems Development and Planning (help in developing systems for integrating assessment and instructional activities; assistance in evaluation instructional systems ...)	6.4	7
9.	Personal Development	10.4	13
10.	Individual Differences in Development and Learning	4.7	4
11.	School-Community Relations	11.6	16
12.	Instruction (consult on matters relating to the general improvement of instruction ...)	8.3	10/11
13.	Legal/ethical and professional issues	11.3	14
14.	Assessment	4.4	2
15.	Multicultural Concerns	9.9	12
16.	Research	11.4	15

*N=32 ; In addition, eight psychologists responded that all domains remained equally important.

How did the attitudes and priorities identified above translate into actual behavior? From Table 13, which presents staff estimates of the amount of time spent on various activities, it may be seen that approximately 25% of their time during a typical school year was spent on A.B.C., a figure that compares favorably with the amount of time devoted to individual assessment work (34%). As well, staff reported spending an additional 25% of their time on consultation over and above their A.B.C. involvements. This figure is approximately double that reported by McKee et al. (1987) in a survey of school psychologists in the United States. The results are consistent with the idea that this group of school psychologists did spend more time than was typical in consultation-oriented work.

Table 13 Percentage of Time Spent on Functions

Functions	Mean (%)
1. A.B.C.	25.6
2. Consultation	25.3
3. Assessments	33.9
4. Counseling with children	7.7
5. Counseling with parents/families	6.4

Additional information regarding changes in the activities of the school psychologist during the A.B.C. program is presented in Table 14, in which the number of individual psychological assessments in 1982-1986 is documented. Assessments during that period declined dramatically (by over 40%), while both the elementary school enrollment and the number of psychological services staff remained relatively steady. Part of this decline may reflect the beneficial effects of the A.B.C. program on instruction, as it provided a vehicle for intervening while problems could still be resolved through the regular class program. It may also, however, reflect an increasing reliance on consultation rather than assessment as a method of responding to problems. It was also our impression that during that same period, assessments changed qualitatively. They were more likely to include information reflecting the child's actual functioning

Table 14 Individual Assessments in 1982 and 1986

	1982	1986	% Change
Number of Assessments	3,660	2,110	42
Elementary Enrollment	41,625	33,902	19
Number of Psychological Staff	52	52	0

in the classroom as obtained from classroom observations and teacher interviews, and to include instructional recommendations rather than diagnostic formulations. Thus, rather than inhibiting consultation, assessment work came to be a vehicle for fostering it.

The discussion so far has focused on the attitudes and activities of the psychological staff. During the period in question, the Board of Education also made several administrative and structural changes that demonstrated its recognition of the expanded role of the psychological staff. These changes included: a) the incorporation of the student services department (of which psychological services was a part) into the Curriculum Division, as opposed to the Special Service Division of the school board; b) the establishment of local school teams focusing on educational and primary prevention goals, and including the school psychologist as a member; c) the establishment of families of schools served by consultative teams, including both curriculum experts and psychological staff; and d) an increase in joint professional development activities for psychological staff, school administrators, and teachers.

Conclusions

This chapter has described the implementation of a comprehensive program involving school psychologists in the curriculum planning process. Although the role of the psychologist in this program initially focused on group assessment activities, experience with the program has underscored the need for much broader involvement. As demonstrated in the examples in this chapter, psychologists' involvement in the program could encompass many aspects of the model presented in Chapter 1.

Figure 5 presents a version of that model with examples drawn from the A.B.C. program. The reader will note that most of the examples given relate to primary and secondary prevention activities, and that many of them have been discussed in earlier sections of this chapter.

In many cases, the psychologist undertook a supportive, professional development, or consultative role with respect to school administrators and teachers. Direct services to students followed a prevention model. Also shown are services to students who were "at risk" (tertiary prevention). These students did not respond to interventions in the regular classroom and were referred to the school team of which the psychologist was a part (see Chapter 2 by Cole & Brown). This aspect of the model is shown here because, as a result of evaluating a class as a whole, students with special needs emerged as a matter of course. Ultimately, the involvement of the psychologist in curriculum planning for regular class students enhanced his or her planning for those students with special needs.

Of course the extensive involvements shown in Figure 5 did not characterize the role of the psychologist in every school's A.B.C. program. Factors such as the receptiveness of school administration to consultation and the interest and skills of the psy-

RECIPIENTS OF THE SERVICE	PRIMARY PREVENTION	SECONDARY PREVENTION	TERTIARY PREVENTION
	– A.B.C. Team – Identify resources	– A.B.C. Team – Programs for students with special curriculum needs	– School Team – Programs for students whose problems interfere significantly with their adaptation to school
Services to the organization (school system or school) as advisors, consultants	Facilitate functioning of A.B.C. Team. Assist Team to define program goals, plan solutions to common problems identified through the appraisal	Assist in planning strategies for addressing the problems of special needs groups as identified in the appraisal	Develop school-wide strategies for assisting students with serious academic difficulties in the regular class
Services to teachers and administrators as providers of information, advisors, consultants	Assist in data collection, in developing class profiles, making plans for program modifications	Workshops for teachers on strategies for addressing problems identified through the appraisal	Assist in planning classroom modifications for students with serious academic difficulties
Indirect services to students/parents using teachers as mediators. Providers of consultation, information	Support teacher as program modifications to meet identified class needs are implemented	Support teacher as special strategies for groups of children are implemented	Consult with teacher as strategies for children with serious academic difficulties are implemented
Direct Services to students/parents	Discuss issues (e.g. learning style, self- concept) arising from program with the class	Work with special needs group as follow-up to the appraisal, e.g. study skills group, self-concept group, social skills group	Direct services (assessment, counseling) for students with serious academic difficulties

Figure 5 The Role of the School Psychologist In the Appraisal for Better Curriculum

chological staff interacted to produce a wide variety of implementation strategies.

In conclusion, it appears that the A.B.C. program had an impact beyond its intended goals. The attitude of the school system toward psychological staff moved increasingly toward acceptance of their involvement in consultation and preventative activities. As well, psychologists themselves appeared to have developed a broader view of their mission, going well beyond the assessment-for-placement model of service. Involvement in the A.B.C. exposed them to curriculum issues and made them more sensitive to teachers' needs in their consultation in other domains. Their broadened perspective on educational planning, classroom dynamics, and the teaching-learning process had a positive impact even on assessment services, which became more oriented toward problem-solving than to special education placement. Teachers seemed more open to engaging in consultation, as they learned about the continuum of relevant services psychologists could provide. Finally, parents and the larger school community learned that psychologists were not only involved with "problem" children, but could serve as a useful educational resource.

References

Abel, P. R., & Burke, J. P. (1985). Perceptions of school psychology from a staff perspective. *Journal of School Psychology, 33*, 121-131.

Anserello, C., & Sweet, T. (1990). Integrating consultation into school psychological services. In E. Cole & J. A. Siegel (Eds.), *Effective consultation in school psychology* (pp. 173-199). Toronto: Hogrefe & Huber Publishers.

Bardon, J. I. (1982). The role and function of the school psychologist: The psychology of school psychology. In C. R. Reynolds & T. B. Gutkin (Eds.), *The handbook of school psychology.* New York: Wiley.

Bereiter, C., & Scardamelia, M. (1979). Pasqualeone's M-Construct as a link between cognitive-developmental and psychometric concepts of intelligence. *Intelligence, 3*, 41-63.

Bersoff, D. N. (1982). The legal regulation of school psychology. In C. R. Reynolds & T. B. Gutkin, (Eds.), *The handbook of school psychology.* New York: Wiley.

Blumenfeld, P. C., Pintrich, P.R., & Hamilton, L. (1986). Children's concepts of ability, effort and conduct. *American Educational Research Journal, 23(1)*, 95-104.

Boice, R. (1983). Observational skills. *Psychological Bulletin, 93(1)*, 3-29.

Brown, A. E., Landrus, G. D., & Long, E. R. (1974). *The Toronto Early Identification and Developmental Program.* Toronto Board of Education.

Byrne, B. M., & Shavelson, R. J. (1986). On the structure of adolescent self-concept. *Journal of Educational Psychology, 78(6)*, 474-481.

Canfield, J., & Wells, H. C. (1976). 100 *ways to enhance self-concept in the classroom: A handbook for parents and teachers.* New York: Prentice Hall.

Carlson, J. S., & Wiedel, H. (1979). Toward a differential testing approach: Testing the limits employing the Raven matrices. *Intelligence, 19*, 323-344.

Carlson, L. D., & Cole, E. (1993). Communication and interaction patterns in French immersion classrooms: Implications for consultation. *Canadian Journal of School Psychology, 9(2)*, 133-149.

Chiu, L.-H. (1988). Measures of self-esteem for school-age children. *Journal of Counselling and Development, 66,* 298-301.

Cole, E. (1983). *About me.* Psychological Services: Toronto Board of Education.

Cole, E. (1992). Characteristics of students referred to school teams: Implications for preventive psychological services. *Canadian Journal of School Psychology, 8,* 23-36.

Cole, E. (1996). An integrative perspective on school psychology. *Canadian Journal of School Psychology, 12(2),* 115-121.

Cole, E., & Brown, R. (1996). Multidisciplinary school teams: A five-year follow-up study. *Canadian Journal of School Psychology, 12(2),* 155-168.

Cole, E., Siegel, J. A., & Yau, M. (1990). The local school team: Goals, roles, and functions. *Research Services, 194.* Toronto: Board of Education.

Cole, E., Siegel, J. A., & Yau, M. (1992). Multidisciplinary school teams: Perceptions of goals, roles, and functions. *Canadian Journal of School Psychology, 8,* 37-51.

Conoley, J. C., & Conoley, C. W (1982). *School consultation: A guide to practice and training.* New York: Pergamon Press.

Crain, R. M., & Bracken, B. A. (1994). Age, race, and gender differences in child and adolescent self-concept. *School Psychology Review, 23(3),* 496-511.

Damon, N., & Hart, D. (1982). The development of self-understanding from infancy through adolescence. *Child Development, 53,* 841-864.

Deno, S. L. (1986). Formative evaluation of individual student programs: A new role for school psychologists. *School Psychology Review, 15(3),* 358-374.

Dusek, J. B., & Flaherty, J. F. (1981), The development of self-concept during the adolescent years. *Monographs of the Society for Research in Child Development, 46(4),* Serial No. 191.

Ebel, R. Q. (1982). Evaluation and selection of group measures. In C. R. Reynolds & T. B. Gutkin (Eds.), *The handbook of school psychology.* New York: John Wiley.

Elias, M. J., & Clabby, J. F. (1984). Integrating social and affective education into public school curriculum and instruction. In C. A. Maher, R. J. Illback, & J. E. Zins (Eds.), *Organizational psychology in the schools.* Springfield, Illinois: Charles E. Thomas.

Elkind, D. (1976). *Child development and education: A Piagetian perspective.* New York: Oxford University Press.

Elkind, D. (1978). *The child's reality: Three developmental themes.* New York: John Wiley & Sons.

Estrin, E. T. (1993). *Alternative assessment: Issues in language, culture and equity. Knowledge brief, II.* San Francisco: Far West Lab for Education and Development (ERIC 1-8).

Fagan, T. K. (1990). A brief history of school psychology in the United States. In A. Thomas & J. Grimes (Eds.), *Best practices in school psychology – II.* Washington, DC: National Association of School Psychologists.

Fagan, T. K., & Wise, P. S. (1994). *School psychology: Past, present, and future.* White Plains, NY: Longman.

Fullan, M. G. (1982). *The meaning of educational change.* New York: Teachers College Press.

Fullan, M. G. (1988). *What's worth fighting for in the principalship?* Toronto: The Ontario Public School Teachers' Federation.

Fullan, M. G. (1991). *The new meaning of educational change.* Toronto, ON: OISE Press.

Fullan, M. G. (2001). *Leading in a culture of change.* San Francisco: Jossey-Bass.

Fullan, M. G., & Miles, H. B. (1992). Getting reform right: What works and what doesn't. *Phi Delta Kappa, 6,* 745-752.

Gordon, E. W., & Musser, J. H. (1992). *Implications of diversity in human characteristics for au-*

thentic assessment. CSE Technical Report 341. Los Angeles: Centre for Research on Evaluation, Standards, and Student Testing. ERIC.

Gutkin, T. B. (1986). Consultees' perceptions of variables relating to the outcome of school-based consultation interactions. *School Psychology Review, 15(3),* 375-382.

Gutkin, T. B., & Curtis, M. J. (1982). School based consultation: Theory and techniques. In C. R. Reynolds & T. B. Gutkin (Eds.), *The handbook of school psychology* (pp. 796-828). New York: Wiley.

Hambleton, R. K. (1982). Advances in criteria-referenced testing technology. In C. R. Reynolds & T. B. Gutkin (Eds.), *The handbook of school psychology.* New York: John Wiley.

Hawryluk, M. K., & Smallwood, D. L. (1986). Assessing and addressing consultee variables in school-based consultation. *School Psychology Review, 15(4),* 519-528.

Hightower, A. D., Cowen, E. L., Spinnel, A. P., Lotyczewski, B.S., Guare, J. C., Rohrbeck, C. A., & Brown, L. P. (1987). The child rating scale: The development of a socio-emotional self-rating scale for elementary school children. *School Psychology Review, 16(2),* 239-255.

Hughes, J. N. (1986). Ethical issues in school consultation. *School Psychology Review,* 15(4), 489-499.

Hunt, E. (1974). Quoth the raven? Nevermore! In L. Gregg (Ed.), *Knowledge and cognition.* Hillsdale, NJ: Erlbaum.

Jarman, R. F., & Das, J. P (1977). Simultaneous and successive synthesis and intelligence. *Intelligence, 1,* 151-169.

Keyer, D. J., & Sweetland, R. C. (Eds.) (1984). *Test critiques.* Kansas City: Test Corporation of America.

Korchin, S. J. (1976). *Modern clinical psychology.* New York: Basic Books.

Kramer, J., & Conoley, J. (Eds.). (1992). *The eleventh mental measurement yearbook.* Lincoln, NB: Buros Institute of Mental Measurements.

Kratochwill, T. R. (1982). Advances in behavioral assessment. In C. R. Reynolds & T. B. Gutkin (Eds.), *The handbook of school psychology.* New York: Wiley.

Leonardson, G. R. (1986). The relationship between self-concept and selected academic and personal factors. *Adolescence, XXI, 82,* 467-474.

Maher, C. A., Illback, R. J., & Zins, J. E. (Eds.). (1984). *Organizational psychology in the schools.* Springfield, Illinois: Charles C. Thomas.

Marsh, H. W. (1986). Self-serving effect in academic attributions: Its relation to academic achievement and self-concept. *Journal of Educational Psychology, 78(3),* 190-200.

Marx, R. W., & Winne, P. H. (1978). Construct interpretations of three self-concept inventories. *American Education Research Journal, 15(1),* 99-109.

Mckee, W. T., Witt, J. C., Elliott, S. N., Pardue, M., & Judycki, A. (1987). Practice informing research: A survey of research dissemination and knowledge utilization. *School Psychology Review, 16(3),* 338-347.

Merrell, K. W., Cedeno, C. J., & Johnson, E. R. (1993). The relationship between school behavior and self-concept in school settings. *Psychology in the Schools, 30,* 293-298.

NASP (1984). *School psychology: A blueprint for training and practice.* Minneapolis: National School Psychology In-Service Training Network.

Noppe, I. C. (1983). A cognitive developmental perspective on the adolescent self-concept. *Journal of Early Adolescence, 3(3),* 245-286.

Pfeiffer, S. I., & Heffernam, L. (1984). Improving multidisciplinary team functions. In C. A. Maher, R. J. Illback, & J. E. Zins (Eds.), *Organizational psychology in the schools.* Springfield, Illinois: Charles C. Thomas.

Raven, J. C., Court, J. H., & Raven, J. (1977). *Manual for Raven's Progressive Matrices and Vocabulary Scales.* London: H. K. Lewis.

Robinson, J. P., & Shaver, P. L (1973/4). *Measures of psychological attitudes.* Ann Arbor, Michigan: Survey Research Center, Institute for Social Research.

Sarason, S. B. (1988). *The making of an American psychologist.* San Francisco: Jossey-Bass Publishers.

Sattler, J. M. (2001). *Assessment of children: Cognitive applications* (4th ed.). San Diego: Jerome M. Sattler, Publisher, Inc.

Schmuck, R. A. (1982). Organization development in the schools. In C. R. Reynolds & T. B. Gutkin (Eds.), *The handbook of school psychology.* New York: John Wiley.

Schmuck, R. A., Runkel, P. J., Arends, J. H., & Arends, R. I. (1977). *The second handbook of organization development in schools.* Palo Alto: Mayfield.

Shapiro, E. S. (1990). An integrated model for curriculum-based assessment. *School Psychology Review, 19,* 331-349.

Sharan, S., & Hertz-Lazarowitz, R. (1982). Effects of an instructional change program on teachers' behavior, attitudes and perception. *The Journal of Applied Behavioral Science, 18(2),* 185-201.

Sheridan, S. M. (2001). Approach to the task of editor of School Psychology Review: Conceptual and practical frameworks. *School Psychology Review, 30(1),* 3-10.

Sheridan, S. M., & Gutkin, T. B. (2000). The ecology of school psychology: Examining and changing our paradigm for the 21st century. *School Psychology Review, 29,* 485-502.

Shinn, M. R., & McConnell, S. (1994). Improving general education instruction: Relevance to school psychology. *School Psychology Review, 23,* 351-371.

Siegel, J. A., & Cole, E. (1990). Appraisal for better curriculum. In E. Cole & J. A. Siegel (Eds.), *Effective consultation in school psychology* (pp. 201-245). Toronto: Hogrefe & Huber Publishers.

Snow, R. E. (1980). Attitude processes. In R. E. Snow, P. Federico, & W. E. Montague (Eds.), *Aptitude, learning and instruction, Vol. 1: Cognitive process analysis of aptitude.* Hillsdale, NJ: Erlbaum.

Speck, M. (1996). Best practice in professional development for sustained-educational change. *Spectrum – Journal of School Research and Information, 14(2),* 33-41.

Stalikas, A., & Gavaki, E. (1995). The importance of ethnic identity: Self-esteem and academic achievement of second-generation Greeks in secondary school. *Canadian Journal of School Psychology, 11(1),* 1-9.

Stewart, K. J. (1986). Disentangling the complexities of clientage. In S. N. Elliott & J. C. Witt (Eds.), *The delivery of psychological services in schools.* Hillsdale, NJ: Erlbaum.

Tierno, M. J. (1983). Responding to self-concept disturbance among early adolescents: A psychological view for educators. *Adolescence, 18,* 577-584.

Tucker, J. A. (Ed.). (1981). *Sequential stages of the assessment process: A training module.* Minneapolis: National School Psychology In-Service Training Network.

Walker, L. S., & Greene, J. W. (1986). The social context of adolescent self-esteem. *Journal of Youth and Adolescence, 15(4),* 315-322.

Wylie, R. C. (1974). *The self-concept (Vol. 1).* Lincoln, NB: University of Nebraska Press.

Ysseldyke, J. E., Dawson, P., Lehr, C., Reschly, D., Reynolds, M., & Telzrow, C. (1997). *School psychology: A blue-print for training and practice II.* Bethesda, MD: National Association of School Psychologists.

Ysseldyke, J. E., & Mirkin, P. K. (1982). The use of assessment information to plan instructional interventions: A review of the research. In C. R. Reynolds & T. B. Gutkin (Eds.), *Handbook of school psychology.* New York: John Wiley.

Appendix A: A Guide For School Record Information
A.B.C. Phase IV Grade 7

Name: _____
Room: _____
School: _____

1. Date of Birth:_____   Age:_____

2. How long has the student been in Canada? (Record number of years.)

3. How long has the student been enrolled at this school? (Record number of years.)

4. How many school changes has the student had? (Record number of years.)

5. How many times has the student changed schools in mid-year? (Record number of changes in mid-year.)

6/7. How many grades has the student-repeated? (Record the number of grades.)– transferred? (Record the number of grades.)

8/9. Do reports record absenteeism as a problem?
    ( ) No   ( ) Yes, family reasons/truancy
    ( ) Yes, health reasons   ( ) Other
    Record (P) for Primary Division, (J) for Junior Division and (S) for Senior Division

10. What Special Education program did/is the student attend/ing? Record LC for Learning Center LD for Self-Contained Learning Disability B for Self-Contained Behavioral Rc for Reading Clinic etc. ( ) past ( ) present

11. Did the student attend ESL/ESD classes? ( ) Primary Division ( ) Junior Division ( ) Senior Division

12. Does the student have any health problem(s)? ( ) No ( ) Yes, specify

13. Areas of academic performance at grade level or above in grades 6-7:

Grade 6	Grade 7		Grade 6	Grade 7	
( )	( )	Language Arts	( )	( )	French
( )	( )	Maths	( )	( )	Arts
( )	( )	Environmental Studies	( )	( )	Physical Education
( )	( )	Study Skills	( )	( )	Effort
( )	( )	Overall adjustment			

14. Other

Appendix B: Assessment of Self-Concept Administration and Data Analysis

Time Requirements

30 to 45 minutes are usually required to administer the booklet "About Me," but there are no time limits.

Instructions

The booklet should be completed by students with both the Psycho-educational Consultant and the home room teacher present. Before distributing the booklets, inform the students that other Grade 7 youngsters are asked to complete similar questions as we would like to learn more about their opinions, thoughts, and feelings about themselves. It should be stressed that this is not a test, that there are no right or wrong answers, and that upon reviewing results, the booklet will be given back to each student. One or two words in the instrument may be difficult for some students and should be defined. Students' questions are usually necessary and should not be discouraged. It should be explained that it is recognized that everyone feels differently at different times in different situations, but that they should respond the way they *generally* feel.

A General Guide for Self-Concept ("About Me") Information A.B.C. – Grade 7

10 words that best tell about me:

- cognitive   (P) smart, bright, intelligent . . .
                    (N) stupid, not good at school . . .
- physical   (P) pretty, athletic . . .
                    (N) ugly . . .
- social   (P) generous, helpful . . .
                    (N) sneaky, greedy . . .
- neutral/other . . .

N.B. A "Grid" for a suggested class profile is attached.

Complete The Following Sentences

a. Cooperation is important because . . .
   - helps build a good relationship
   - helps accomplish a goal
   - answer not specific
b. I am worried about . . .

- parents, other relatives
- future (work, school)
- passing to grade 8
- other

c. My best friend can be counted on to...
- be loyal, trustworthy
- help me when in need
- reliable
- other

d. When somebody is nice to me, I . . .
- am nice to them
- other (feel good . . .)

e. A person I learn a lot from is . . .
- parent(s)
- teacher(s)
- friend(s)
- other

f. One thing I could teach someone else is . . .
- to be friendly, polite
- school/sports activities
- skills
- other

g. I like being with people when . . .
- I am in a good mood
- they are friendly
- I am lonely, upset, mixed up
- other

h. At school I am . . .
- smart, happy, a good student
- well behaved, diligent
- other

i. I wish grown ups would . . .
- understand us
- listen to us
- respect us
- other

j. I am proud that I . . .
- am myself
- do well at school
- gender
- relationships
- attributes
- other

Getting to know you

a. What are you doing to prove you can accept more responsibility?
    - completing work
    - out of school duties/jobs
    - being more mature
    - other
b. What do you see yourself doing 2 years from now?
    - high school
    - school and working
    - non-academic activities
    - don't know
c. How do you spend your time after school and on weekends?
    - sports
    - homework
    - T.V.
    - see friends
    - help at home
    - reading
    - other
d. Of all the things you do in your free time, which do you like the most?
    - seeing friends
    - sports
    - T.V. and videos
    - other
e. What are some things you have to do out of school that you do not like doing?
    - chores, housework
    - homework
    - doing nothing
    - other
f. What are your favourite sports and hobbies?
    - any sports mentioned
    - collecting things
    - arts, crafts
    - other
g. What are some of the things about adults you respect and admire the most?
    - kind, helpful
    - understanding
    - caring
    - hard-working
    - other
h. What thing don't you like about adults?
    - angry
    - unfair, authoritarian
    - disrespectful
    - other

About school and friendship

a. What do your friends have in common?
  - like same activities
  - attitudes
  - qualities
  - other
b. What does friendship mean to you?
  - talk to, share with
  - trust, loyalty
  - mutual liking, help
  - other
c. How good a friend are you? Give an example.
  - I help when asked
  - I comfort, give advice
  - I am trustworthy
  - other
d. What do you think about school?
  - like it
  - like it sometimes/necessary
  - negative
  - other
e. What is your favourite book? What in it has personal meaning for you?
  - themes: animals, music, future, love, friendship, sci-fi
  - diary
  - other
f. What do you like about this class
  most?
  - teacher
  - students
  - atmosphere
  - other
  least?
  - others' misbehavior
  - work
  - teacher getting angry
  - other
g. How would you change this class to make it better?
  - more cooperation
  - physical changes
  - academic changes
  - no changes

Table 15 "Self Concept" Class Profile Grid

ABC PHASE IV

Grade 7

School:

Room:

Student Names	"10 words"-attributes					Worried About					Proud Of						Friends			Class		Better Class					More Responsibility			Adults – Qualities					
	Cognitive (No.)	Physical (No.)	Social (No.)	Neutral	Other	Relatives	Future	Self	School	Other	Self	School Work	Relationships	Skills	Sports	Other	Many	Few	Other	Positive (No.)	Negative (No.)	Other	Physical Changes	Academic Changes	Social Changes	Other	Schoolwork	Jobs/Duties	Other	Kind/Helpful	Understanding	Other	Disrespectful	Authoritarian	Other
																														Positive			Negative		
1.																																			
2.																																			
3.																																			
4.																																			
5.																																			
6.																																			
7.																																			
8.																																			
9.																																			
10.																																			
11.																																			
12.																																			
13.																																			
14.																																			
15.																																			
16.																																			
17.																																			
18.																																			
19.																																			
20.																																			
21.																																			
22.																																			

Chapter 17
Suicide Prevention in Schools: Facing the Challenge

Ester Cole and Jane A. Siegel

"A little girl looked up to heaven when she felt the *loneliness* wouldn't *subside* and asked God, "Will you put your arms around me and take me to the sky? For I have this *urge I* want to *die ...*

To keep from telling a *lie*
I just *smile* saying *nothing*

The *gate of life* was closed to you one day. I have a lot *of anger* and deep regret."

(written by Mary, age 16)

Mary's suicidal poem, dedicated to her teacher, was a clear and loud cry for help. She survived a suicidal crisis and lived to get the help she needed. Unfortunately, such signals of distress are not always recognized or acted upon by educators.

Suicide occurs more often than many of us realize. It is the second most frequent cause of death among young people in Canada, and the third leading cause of death for American adolescents and young adults. Moreover, reported suicides reflect only a fraction of those committed: many actual suicides are not identified as such or are disguised as accidents by family, friends, and even official authorities. Suicide threats and attempts by adolescents may not be seen by the adults around them as serious efforts to end their own lives.

Traditionally, school psychologists have been uninvolved with this problem. In some cases they may not even be made aware of suicide attempts in the school system and at best they may be asked by educators to assist with crisis intervention. Given our current understanding of suicide and its causes, however, school psychologists are in a position to adopt a more proactive role. They can help, not only forestalling the completion of actual suicide attempts, but also by sensitizing educators to recognize, understand and react to signs of distress among young people (Cole, 1992; Cole & Siegel, 1987, 1990; Davis, Sandoval, & Wilson, 1988; Mazza, 1997; Pagliaro, 1995; Sandoval & Brock, 1996; Silverman & Felner, 1995; Smith, 1990).

The purpose of this chapter is to document the introduction of a suicide prevention program in a large metropolitan school system, to describe how the program was implemented, and to discuss the many roles of school psychologists during the course of its introduction and evolution. In addition, resource materials providing background information on adolescent suicide and suggestions for crisis management are presented to assist those practitioners who wish to become involved in this area.

Suicide Prevention: The Role of School Psychologists

To provide a framework for this discussion of the role of school psychologists in suicide prevention, the model in Figure 1 is presented as a reference. This model for psychological services, initially introduced in Chapter 1, is an extension of similar models proposed by Caplan (1970) and Parsons and Meyers (1984). It conceptualizes the role that school psychologists perform as varying along two dimensions. The horizontal dimension specifies who benefits from the service: a) an organization itself (school board or local school), b) teachers and administrators within the organization, or c) students and parents. The psychologist's services to students and parents may be indirect, as indicated in the third row – that is, as a back-up consultant to educators who provide the main service. Of course, the psychologist may also work with students and parents directly (row 4).

The vertical dimension specifies the *goals* of the service. Primary prevention services are intended to forestall problems before they arise by providing information and identifying resources, secondary services are intended to provide help to students "at risk," and tertiary services are directed toward students whose problems significantly interfere with their school progress.

For the purposes of this chapter, the cells of the model provide examples of services related to suicide prevention. The reader will want to refer to these examples repeatedly as specific steps in the implementation of the suicide prevention program are discussed. Prior to its introduction, psychological services related to suicide were crisis-oriented and concentrated at the lower right-hand comer of the table (cells 3c, 4b, 4c). As the program evolved, services came to include examples from all cells.

In this particular school board, the psychological service was part of a student services department, which also included psychiatrists and social workers. The suicide prevention program was a multidisciplinary project including professionals from all

Recipients of Service	Primary Prevention Identify resources, provide and analyze information; program for all students	Secondary Prevention Program for students "at risk"	Tertiary Prevention Programs for students whose problems significantly interfere with their adaptation to school
Services to the organization (school system) as advisors, consultants	1a – Planning a suicide prevention program at the systems level – Information pamphlet for students "A Cry for Help"	1b – Develop a plan for identifying students "at risk"	1c – Prepare resource materials on crisis management – Develop a school crisis response plan
Services to teachers and administrators as providers of information, advisors, consultants	2a – Professional development sessions on adolescent stress and youth suicide for teachers and administrators	2b – Provide information on the "signs of distress" among troubled youth to teachers	2c – Liase between school and community agencies to provide services for those in crisis
Indirect services to students/parents using teacher's as mediators; providers of consultation, information	3a – Student assembly/ discussion on the signals of depression and suicide – Parent meetings on suicide	3b – Provide consultation to teachers working with depressed students	3c – Provide consultation to school staff in crisis
Direct services to students/parents	4a – Class discussion of emotional development led by school psychologists – Parent meetings on suicide	4b – Provide counseling to depressed youngsters	4c – Crisis intervention

Figure 1 The Role of the School Psychologist in Suicide Prevention

three fields who collaborated in its development. In the discussion that follows, the program is referred to as a "Student Services" effort, in order to acknowledge explicitly the contributions of all the professionals involved.

Step 1: Identifying the Need

The impetus for the suicide prevention program came from the trustees of the school board. Aware of the increasing incidence of adolescent suicide as reported in the media, they requested information about the prevalence of suicide in the city and the availability of services to troubled youth in the school system. In the course of their discussions, the trustees identified suicide as an area of concern to educators, and recommended that steps be taken to develop a greater sensitivity among teachers, administrative staff, and students on this issue. To facilitate the achievement of this goal, the trustees directed student services staff to prepare an information booklet on suicide suitable for distribution to young people in Grades 7 through 13. Finally, they recommended that all schools be required to develop a plan for dealing with adolescents at risk.

At this phase in the development of the program, consultation occurred at the system level (see cell 1a of Figure 1). Senior staff from the student services department were invited to have input into documents prepared by the Board's administrators for consideration by the trustees, and were involved in their discussions of the issue.

Step 2: An Information Booklet for Adolescents

As requested by the trustees, the booklet "A Cry for Help"[1] was developed by a psychologist and a psychiatrist from the student services staff in consultation with others. In terms of the model, preparation of the booklet can be thought of as a primary prevention service at the level of the system (cell 1a of Figure 1).

Based on underlying theory and indicators of adolescents at risk, the booklet was designed to give all students a better understanding of the problem. The following key messages were stressed:

(a) suicide prevention is possible,

(b) professional help is available,

(c) signals of distress can be recognized.

As well, basic facts about suicide and information about counseling and crisis intervention services in the school board and the community were provided. After reviewing the content of the booklet, the trustees approved its distribution to students

---

1 The booklet is reproduced for your information in Appendix A

and recommended that it be made available in all secondary and senior elementary schools.

Step 3: Planning for Implementation

The trustees had sanctioned the distribution of the booklet, but had not provided the school system with any specific plan as to how to accomplish this. As mental health professionals, student service staff were concerned about the negative consequences of distributing the booklet without appropriate preparation of teachers, guidance staff, and administrators. The department therefore decided to accompany the distribution of the booklet with an offer of consultation to school personnel. In terms of the model, this consultation would initially involve the first row of Figure 1, as planning could involve primary, secondary, or tertiary prevention. Thus, assisting school administrators to develop a crisis response plan would be an example of systems consultation regarding the provision of tertiary services (cell lc). At later stages, it was expected that student services personnel would become involved in activities covering most other aspects of the model as well.

Given the size of the school board and the complexity of the project, the student services department decided to establish a Central Resource Team (CRT) on suicide prevention to plan and coordinate the program. This team consisted of student services staff whose interests and skills extended to both clinical and administrative aspects of the project. The CRT determined that before proceeding with large-scale distribution of the booklet a modest experiment with a small number of pilot schools would be helpful. The CRT also developed a number of short-term goals, including (1) training of consultants whose schools would participate in the pilot project, (2) acting as facilitators of information about the booklet, and (3) preparing resource materials for student services. Long-term goals included (1) implementation of the program in all target schools, and (2) facilitating of primary and secondary prevention programs.

The pilot phase involved six schools whose staff demonstrated particular concern with students' depressive symptoms. Some of them had recently encountered one or more suicidal crisis. In others, student services staff assigned to the schools were already members of the CRT. Initial consultation between the CRT and the schools was designed to foster a collaborative relationship. The CRT discouraged requests for a "packaged," one-shot training approach in favor of discussions aimed at tailoring the program to each school's needs. Among the projects planned were in-service programs for teachers, workshops for students and parents, and the establishment of a local suicide prevention team. Not surprisingly, principals were the key decision-makers in determining the length and elaborateness of the program. A committed student services staff at the local level was also felt to be a key ingredient for success.

Step 4: Professional Development for Student Services Staff

In anticipation of suicide prevention programs being implemented in all schools, an introductory in-service day was held for student services staff. The agenda included material on suicides in adolescents, a review of the booklet "A Cry for Help," and an opportunity for staff to react to the topic in small group discussions. Staff were also asked to comment on the following questions:

(1) How should schools be prepared to handle suicidal students?
(2) How can professional development on the subject of suicide prevention be provided to all Board personnel?
(3) What are effective ways of presenting the booklet to students?
(4) What further components should be added when introducing the program to students?

Staff overwhelmingly endorsed the concept of incorporating the distribution of the booklet into an overall suicide prevention program in each school. They also expressed a desire for support from the CRT in implementing the project, and requested further professional development on the topic of suicide.

Additional professional development sessions were held just prior to the system-wide implementation of the program, involving both student services administration and those providing direct service to schools. The goals of the sessions were to (a) sensitize staff to the topic, (b) broaden their knowledge base, (c) enhance confidence, and (d) prepare them to offer consultation to schools at all levels (See Figure 1). Thus staff were not only presented with background information on suicide and materials on crisis management techniques, but were also given information on program planning that would be helpful in their consultation with school administrators. Throughout the in-service, small-group discussions enabled staff to express their concerns and come to terms with their emotional responses to the topic. As well, staff were presented with materials that they themselves would find useful as consultants to the schools.

Thus, on Day 1 of the in-service, staff were presented with an abbreviated version of the resource materials on suicide and assessment technique found at the end of this chapter. Days 2 and 3 reinforced the theoretical background through the use of videos on the subject that had been successfully presented to students and staff in the pilot schools. Days 2 and 3 also offered practical information regarding the more successful programs in the pilot schools and case presentations on crisis management.

Following the in-service sessions, an interest/support group was established for staff, which met on a regular basis to share information during implementation of the program. Agenda included discussion of mutual problems, invited speakers from the community, and the sharing of information resources and materials.

Step 5: Implementing the Program

To initiate system-wide implementation of the program, student services administrative staff met with secondary and senior school principals in each area of the city. Copies of the "Cry for Help" booklet were distributed, and principals were informed of their obligation to make it available to students. The purpose of these meetings was to make principals aware both of adolescent suicide and of the role that student services staff can play in the implementation of a school-based prevention program (see cell 2a of Figure 1). Following these meetings, student services staff approached school principals on an individual basis.

Implementation of the program at the local school level frequently began with the establishment of a school-based suicide prevention team consisting of locally assigned student services staff and interested members of the school's guidance department, teaching staff, and administration. Members of the CRT consulted with these local teams on request. The Agenda for In-School Planning reproduced in Table 1 summarizes issues that were often addressed during the team's initial meetings.

The evolution of the program varied from school to school. As the following examples illustrate, primary prevention was a major focus.

(1) Full staff meetings were held to familiarize teachers with the topic (see cell 2a of Figure 1). Presentation techniques consisted of small group guided discussions, lectures, and audiovisual presentations. Such meetings almost always occurred near the beginning of a project. Teachers responses were wide-ranging, from support – "thank God the subject is not taboo any longer"– to feelings of anxiety and resistance – "I'm only a math teacher and I teach ten classes a week!" These reactions pointed yet again to the need for frequent ongoing discussions with teachers, so that they may develop a degree of comfort with the subject of suicide prevention that would allow them to address it with their students. It was clearly stated that teachers were not expected to be therapists; professional development was designed to assist them simply to recognize a student at risk through verbal, behavioral, and situational indicators, and to deal appropriately with the issue of suicide through the curriculum.

(2) Group discussions with students (cells 3a and 4a). In group discussions led by either teachers, guidance, or student services staff, Grade 12 and 13 students were encouraged to discuss stress and common myths about suicide including the following:

"People who talk about suicide don't attempt it."

"Suicide threats are a bid for attention and should be ignored."

"A person who makes an unsuccessful suicide attempt is less likely to try it again."

"Only mentally ill people attempt suicide."

Table 1 Agenda for In-School Planning

(1) How should the information booklet on suicide "A Cry for Help" be distributed to students?
  - Display in school library or guidance office
  - Student assembly on suicide
  - After-school discussions with students
  - Class discussions with students during "homeroom"

(2) How should the school staff be prepared?
  - Discuss the general problem of suicide and suicide prevention
  - Discuss the booklet "A Cry for Help"
  - Provide opportunities for staff to ask questions and receive support
  - Include staff suggestions in implementing a program
  - Examine school plans for responding to a crisis situation

(3) What resources are available to assist with school planning?
  - School staff
  - Community services/agencies
  - Mental health professionals at the school board (psychologist, social worker, psychiatrist)
  - Student Council
  - Parents' Association

(4) What resources are useful for responding to a crisis?
  - Who will be the contact person(s)?
  - How will the school psychologist, social worker or psychiatrist be involved?
  - How should community agencies and hospitals be involved?
  - How should school staff be informed of the crisis plan?

(5) Can the topic of suicide prevention be included in existing curriculum dealing with students' emotional development and needs?
  - Health
  - Physical education
  - Guidance
  - Family studies
  - Homeroom
  - Extracurricular activities

(6) How should parents be involved?
  - Parents' Association (PTA)
  - School newsletter
  - Information letter from the principal
  - Special information meeting

(7) How can an ongoing program for future years be planned?
  - Incorporate suicide prevention into the curriculum
  - Plan an annual program for students

Sessions emphasized that adolescents were most likely to turn to their friends when distressed, and that it was crucial to recognize and respond to friends at risk.

(3) A special evening presentation for parents, students and staff on "teenage stress" took place (cells 3a and 4a). Discussion centered around the creation of a more positive environment for students at school.

(4) A full day's conference was held at school staff's request (cells 2a, 2b, 2c). Small group sessions were led by invited Board and community speakers. These included the following topics:

   (a) signals of distress
   (b) emergency resources and legal responsibilities
   (c) a case study involving a suicidal student
   (d) role-playing a classroom vignette emphasizing differing perceptions of student and teacher
   (e) discussion of youth stress at school/home/peer group
   (f) understanding adolescence as a period of rapid developmental changes.

Ongoing evaluation was a feature of the suicide prevention project in those schools that implemented multifaceted programs. The local suicide prevention team met frequently to discuss staff feedback and plan future events. A questionnaire that was used to solicit reactions from teaching staff is reproduced in Table 2. As a result, those staff who were not actually on the planning team had input into the evolution of the project. Such a strategy helped to foster an image of the program as a collaborative effort, rather than as something foisted on the teaching staff by the administration.

Table 2 Questionnaire for Teaching Staff

(1) What was the most/least valuable part of the program for you?

(2) How do you think the program could be improved?

(3) In what ways was the workshop useful to your classroom situation?

(4) What suggestions can you make as to how the staff should proceed with the project?

(5) Would this format and content be suitable for students?

Conclusions

Prior to the implementation of the suicide prevention program, psychological services in this area were oriented toward tertiary prevention (see Figure 1). If school psychologists were involved with suicide at all, it was on a crisis management basis. In a typical high school, psychological staff would become aware of suicidal behavior in perhaps two or three students during the course of an academic year. Their role was to assist educational personnel in the evaluation of risk and to arrange for referral to appropriate community agencies. Such services had little influence on the students' educational experience, and most probably reached only a fraction of those who in one way or another contemplated suicide.

In implementing the suicide prevention program, psychological staff had the opportunity to offer a much broader range of services. Both administrative and front line staff played a role in systems-wide planning of the program. Other opportunities for system-wide consultation included preparation of "A Cry for Help" and the resource materials on suicide and risk assessment presented in the second section of this chapter.

At the local school level, psychological staff were involved in program planning, multiple in-service sessions for teaching staff on suicide and adolescent emotional development, consultation regarding the identification of students at risk, liaison with community services, and presentations to students and parents. As they became identified with the program, they were more frequently asked by school personnel to provide consultation on the mental health needs of students. The staff grew more confident in its mastery of the topic and its crisis management skills due to the professional development components of the program.

In addition to providing opportunities for expanding services, the program enhanced the profile of psychological staff both at the local school and on a system-wide basis. Interest groups, including guidance counselors and special education teachers, requested and received workshops on such topics as adolescent stress and emotional development.

While not all schools opted for the program, approximately 50% of those to whom consultative services were offered implemented some aspect of it. Many of the schools that chose not to participate cited such issues as competing priorities for teachers' times or administrative changes that made the program inappropriate to introduce to staff. Such schools were anticipated to opt in the program at some point in the future.

In those schools that did participate, organizational factors seemed to have played a significant role in developing effective programs. It was our impression that "open-climate" schools characterized by a collaborative atmosphere were more receptive to a consultative relationship. Such schools were able to understand the educational orientation of the program and endeavored to incorporate it as an ongoing facet of school life.

We will conclude this section by reminding readers that involvement of psychological services in a wide-ranging thrust on suicide prevention had not been mandated by the trustees of the school board. The student services department, including psychological staff, had only been requested to prepare an information brochure for students. It was the decision of the department itself to offer consultation to schools and to embark on intensive professional development for its own staff. The fact that such initiatives occurred within the context of suicide prevention rather than some other mental health issue simply reflects the fact that this was a priority for the trustees of this particular school board. As in any consultation process, it was important to respond to the needs of the school system as perceived by educators. School psychologists seeking to expand their roles need to be assertive in their response to such needs and take advantage of opportunities presented.

Resource Materials for School Psychologists

In presenting background information on suicide, we are well aware that a little knowledge can be a dangerous thing. Our goal is not to make teachers, administrators, and school psychologists experts on this topic: rather, we wish to provide sufficient information to heighten their awareness of the emotional needs of students; to sharpen their ability to identify students at risk; and to facilitate an appropriate response, including referral to professionals experienced in coping with adolescents in severe distress. The provision of therapy to severely suicidal students is clearly *not* the domain of a school system. However, since educators see students nearly every day, they are in a unique position to identify those in need and to make arrangements for appropriate help.

It has been our experience that both educators and school psychologists who are unfamiliar with suicide require multiple exposures to become comfortable with the topic. We recommend several sessions with an emphasis on small group discussions that allow participants to share experiences and emotions. Community services and agencies should be involved in staff development wherever possible and made aware of the school board's suicide prevention program.

The resource materials included here begin with a brief discussion of incidence of suicide among adolescents. Such data are important, since educators frequently think that suicidal behavior among students is so infrequent that the matter need not concern them. Next, theoretical perspectives on suicide, including the psychodynamic, psychobiological, social, and developmental points of view, are presented. The relationship between depression and suicide is also discussed. Each perspective alerts school psychologists to complementary and overlapping aspects of the topic. With this background as a framework, specific strategies for crisis intervention are presented, including the evaluation of signals of distress, assessment techniques, and referral procedures. The chapter concludes with a discussion of a suicide in a school.

Why Should We Concern Ourselves with Suicide?

Because suicide rates among school age-children and adolescents are low, actual suicides among students in any particular school occur infrequently. Teachers and administrators, therefore, often question the relevance of suicide prevention to them.

In fact, however, suicide is a leading cause of death among young people across North America. In Canada, it is the second leading cause of death for those under 30 years of age (Joffe, Offord, & Boyle, 1988; Statistics Canada, 1994); in the United States, it is the third leading cause of death in the 15-24 year old age group after accidents and homicides (Vital Statistics of the United States, 1980). Among 15- to 19-year-olds, the age range roughly encompassing the high school population, suicide rates have been increasing with the rate more than doubling from 1961-1975 (Holinger, 1978). Data to 1982 continued to show steady increases (Shaffer, 1986). More recent statistics put the suicide rate for this age group at 12.9 per 100,000 in Canada (Statistics Canada, 1997) and at 14.9 per 100,000 in the United States (American Association of Suicidology, 1996).

The above statistics are based on suicides as determined from coroners' reports. However, it has been found that many suicides are disguised or not reported as such (Shaffer, 1974), possibly as many as 50% (McKenry, Tishler, & Christman, 1980). Many factors contribute to this underreporting. It is often difficult to distinguish suicide from death by "accidental means," as in motor vehicle accidents or drug overdoses. Coroners' criteria for the definition of suicide vary between jurisdictions, and often confirmed or indisputable evidence is required (Garfinkel & Golombek, 1984; Schuyler, 1973). Both the family of a suicide victim and professionals may be inhibited from providing information to authorities that would clearly confirm a case of suicide. Among professionals, there has been an assumption that since children, and even some adolescents, lack an appreciation of death's finality, suicide is an impossibility (Pfeffer, Plutchik, & Mizruchi, 1983; Shaffer, 1974). Families may wish to avoid the perceived social stigma and may fear that an admission that suicide has occurred will lead to attempts by other family members (McKenry et al., 1980; Metha, Chen, Mulvenon, & Dode, 1998; Schuyler, 1973).

Suicide attempts occur far more often than actual suicides-as much as 20 to 100 times as often (E. Smith, 1981). While suicide attempts are frequently misperceived as manipulation, follow-up death patterns in those who have attempted suicide reveals that they are more likely to die by their own hand than from any other cause (Tefft, Peterson, & Babigian, 1979). Thus, a suicide attempt should be construed as a "cry for help" by the young person concerned and should not be dismissed or ignored.

More recent U.S. surveys of normal high school students (Ross cited by Davis, 1985; Smith, 1985) reveal that 10% to 12% had made at last one "suicide attempt." Even though such attempts only infrequently resulted in a medical contact for assistance (Smith, 1985), these data highlight the fact that suicide is a matter of concern for many young people. In a high school with 2,000 students, as many as 200 may have made a suicidal gesture at some point in their lives. Suicidal behavior occurs more frequently among teenagers than most adults realize and it needs to be recognized and dealt with openly by the schools (Metha et al., 1998; O'Donnell, 1995).

Some Basic Facts About Suicide

Educators may dismiss suicide as an aberration of normal development, assuming that only a person who suffers from a significant mental disorder would do it and that it is a problem that they can do little about. In fact, this is a myth: while a small minority of suicidal young people do have psychotic symptoms, for many suicide is a final solution for coping with life stresses. Such individuals frequently exhibit multiple adjustment difficulties that can be easily noticed by educators-for example, acting out, truancy, academic underachievement, and social withdrawal (see Barrett Hicks, 1990; Husain & Vandiver, 1984; Kurtz & Derevensky, 1993). Such signs of distress signify that they are in trouble and need help.

Looking only at overall suicide rates can give misleading impressions of group risks. For example, completed suicides in males are four to five times more common than in females[2], while suicide attempts are three times more common in females (Garfinkel & Golombek, 1974; Hawton, O'Grady, Osborn, & Cole, 1982; McKenry et al., 1980). Suicide is extremely rare among elementary school children, but after puberty the rate shoots up. The increase is particularly dramatic among white males, rising from approximately 6 per 100,000 to over 20 per 100,000 between the ages of 15 and 19 (Shaffer, 1986).

There is evidence that sociocultural factors influence suicide rates, which vary markedly among young people from country to country. In North America, rates among adolescent blacks are substantially lower than for whites, while those for native young people are consistently much higher, more than 40 per 100,000 (Cole & Siegel, 1990; Husain & Vandiver, 1984; Mazza, 1997; National Center for Health Statistics, USA, 1998). Such variations suggest that suicide rates may be influenced by factors peculiar to a particular school system or even to a particular school. Educators and school psychologists should familiarize themselves with local conditions by obtaining coroners' reports and hospital emergency ward data for their areas.

Theoretical Perspectives on Suicide

Because its victims are so young, adolescent suicides are especially tragic events. Families, teachers, and friends ask themselves why a young person could come to see the

---

[2]   Males tend to use more lethal methods than females, including firearms, hanging and poisoning (National Center for Health Statistics, USA, 1998).

taking of his or her own life as the only solution. Also, they feel guilty – wondering if they are somehow at fault and what they might have done to prevent the occurrence.

There are no easy answers to these questions. All young people and their particular circumstances are unique, and there is no simple way of knowing if someone will become a suicide victim. Nevertheless, studies of the phenomenon have identified some common factors. Often, the suicidal adolescent has been the victim of a long-standing series of problems beginning in early childhood. Multiple signs of poor adjustment are often present in his or her history. These problems are exacerbated by cognitive, emotional, social and physical changes accompanying the onset of adolescence. Finally, in the period immediately preceding the event, there is a series of stressful occurrences – often seemingly unimportant but devastating to the adolescent who has few resources for coping with difficulties (Brent, 1995; Cole, 1992; Husain & Vandiver, 1984; Pfeffer, 1986).

Keeping this general framework in mind, one can view adolescent suicide from a number of different perspectives, including the psychodynamic, the psychobiological, the sociological, and the developmental. Suicidal behavior can also be thought of as a symptom of depression. These various points of view contribute somewhat different, though overlapping and frequently complementary ideas that will be useful to school psychologists in working with educators and troubled adolescents. These perspectives are highlighted in the following brief discussions.

A. The Psychodynamic Perspective

The psychodynamic theory represents one of the first attempts to organize a heterogeneous and confusing symptom picture into a system tied to theoretical constraints. For the school psychologist working with depressed or suicidal adolescents, it emphasizes the following key aspects:
  (1) a link between depression and suicide,
  (2) actual or perceived losses in the person's background,
  (3) feelings of guilt and anger turned towards the self,
  (4) loss of self-esteem.

In his discussion of depression in the classic paper "Mourning and Melancholia", Freud (1917) conceptualized suicide as an act of "unconscious hostility toward a lost love object." The lost love object could be anything that precipitated sharp disappointment, including the death, absence, or rejection by a loved one, or even some more abstract loss, such as an ideal or liberty. Briefly, the mechanism by which such disappointments depart from feelings of simple grief or mourning and can lead to depression and at times to suicide is as follows.

Disappointment produces feelings of loss, frustration, and anger directed toward the lost love object. In the normal person, these feelings can be overcome as one can rely on other, healthy aspects of one's personality coming into play. However, individuals whose life experiences have led to arrested personality development lack such resources. For them, the sense of loss and the feelings of guilt, emptiness, and self-reproach that result from their anger cannot be tolerated in their conscious thinking (Klerman, 1978). The reasons for the angry feelings are repressed into the subconscious. The person becomes confused, turns the anger inward instead, and suffers from lowered self-esteem, thus failing to discriminate between the self and the lost love object as the proper source of the difficulties (Reis, Peterson, & Evon, 1977). Instead of overcoming the loss, the person becomes depressed and at risk for suicidal behavior.

While some modern writers in the psychoanalytic tradition have questioned whether the conflicts postulated by Freud are possible in the only partially developed personalities of young people (Beres, 1966), others have argued that elements of the theory often manifest themselves in suicidal adolescents. For example, losses are common in their backgrounds (Husain & Vandiver, 1984). As well, Toolan (1975) postulated that the adolescent who experiences rejection or loss develops feelings of anger toward the depriving person for the denial of love and nurturing. These negative feelings lead to guilt and a sense of "badness," which in turn may result in suicidal thoughts and self-destructive behavior (DeHouter, 1981; McKenry et al., 1980).

B. The Psychobiological Perspective

Biological factors and their relationship to suicidal characteristics in adolescents is a challenging area of research. In interviewing and working with maladjusted youth and their families, the school psychologist should pay close attention to information concerning:
(1) a history of chronic health problems,
(2) information or clues of substance abuse,
(3) a history of psychiatric illness, especially depression.

In these instances, it is advisable for the psychologist to seek medical consultation.

The biological perspective on suicide focuses on the importance of organic stressors as correlates. Physical ill health is one such factor (Hawton et al., 1982; Husain & Vandiver, 1984), and may be especially problematic when it occurs in conjunction with psychological and social difficulties. Drug abuse also has been identified as a possible stressor in suicidal adolescents (Clark, 1993; Fowler, Rich, & Young, 1985; Vajda & Steinbeck, 2000)). Its actual significance is difficult to confirm statistically, however, since there is a large incidence of drug abuse and a small incidence of suicide.

Psychiatric illness is another factor that must be considered. In adults, there is an accumulating body of evidence to suggest that psychiatric illnesses are related to genetically transmitted abnormalities in brain function (Ahearn et al., 2001; N. Anderson, 1984; Lopez et al., 2001). There is also a growing body of literature documenting the prevalence of mood and psychiatric disorders in children and adolescents who commit, attempt or consider suicide (De Hert, McKenzie, & Peuskens, 2001; Flisher, 1999).

Depression is often associated with suicide in both adults (Carlson, 1983) and children (Birmaher, Ryan, Williamson, & Brent, 1996; Esposito & Clum, 1999; Pagliaro, 1995). In adults, a biological origin for depression is supported by genetic studies, the existence of neurophysiological markers for depressive states, and the positive effects of medication on depressive symptoms. Increasingly, studies with child and adolescent populations are reporting similar findings (Birmaher & Heydl, 2001; Dahl & Ryan, 1996). To some extent the research in this area has been hindered by the lack of methodological rigor that is found in work with adults (Angold & Costello, 2001; Cantwell, 1983; Puig-Antic, 1986; Rice, Harold, & Thaper, 2002) as well as by the lack of well-defined diagnostic criteria for major depressive illness in children. In addressing these issues, researchers are increasingly exploring the possibility that there are etiological differences between depressive symptoms in childhood and adolescence such that the neurological mechanism involved may change developmentally (Duggal, Carlson, Sroufe, & Egeland, 2001; Puig-Antic, 1986). Recent revisions to the DSM-IV as well as to existing assessment scales are also serving to increase the utility of standardized evaluation and diagnostic measures in clinical and research settings (Chorpita, Yim, Moffitt, Umemoto, & Francis, 2000). The psychobiology of affective illness in children is a rapidly changing research area in which school psychologists will want to update their knowledge on a regular basis.

C. The Sociological Perspective

School personnel are frequently privy to information about psychosocial stressors in troubled students' lives, but often become overwhelmed and discouraged by such knowledge, and may tend to confuse possible correlates as causes of suicidal behaviors. The school psychologist is in a position to explain and share information that will lead to a deeper understanding of the needs of students with inadequate coping skills. The summary that follows should assist in such efforts.

The sociological perspective on suicide considers rising suicide rates to reflect changes in the values and norms of society. While suicide continues as one of the last remaining taboos to which considerable social stigma is attached, violence as a whole is increasingly condoned (Anderson, 1982; Cole, 1995). Over time, rates of suicide and violence correlate with one another, and adolescents who are suicidal also sometimes express a desire to kill other people (Finch & Poznanski, 1971). Steinmetz's (1977) study of the relationship between family violence and suicide concluded that young people who kill themselves have frequently witnessed violence between their parents or were themselves targets of physical abuse. Similar findings concerning violence have been documented since then (see for example Kurtz & Deverensky, 1993). Thus adolescent suicide needs to be viewed in the context of a growing cultural acceptance of violence, both in the society at large and within the family.

The breakdown of traditional family support systems is thought to be another social factor in increasing suicide rates (Durkheim, 1951). Individuals who are poorly integrated into a supporting network of social relationships are less able to cope with life stresses and more prone to suicide. In adolescence, isolation and loss of social contact have been related to suicide. Easily quantifiable indicators that may signal a lack of family cohesiveness include the loss of one or more parents through divorce, separation or death; single parent families; working parents; parents who are alcoholic or mentally ill; and family and school disruptions caused by frequent moves. All of these factors have been found more frequently in the families of suicidal young people (DeHouter, 1981; Dorpat, Jackson, & Ripley, 1965; Garfinkel & Golombek, 1974; E. Smith, 1981; Teicher, 1970). Although it would be a mistake to conclude that such factors cause suicide, they can contribute to conditions within the family that provide a young person with less support and fewer resources for coping with stress (O'Donnell, 1995).

Poverty is another factor sometimes associated with family breakdown and frequently found in the backgrounds of suicidal adolescents (Teicher, 1970). It would be wrong, however, to assume that adolescent suicide is restricted to or typical of low socioeconomic classes. In societies that promote and glamorize the goals of wealth, the stresses placed on young people from high economic status families to achieve financial success can be as devastating as those associated with poverty (Brent, 1995; McAnarney, 1979).

Many writers stress negative family variables as correlates of suicide (Anderson, 1982; Barrett Hicks, 1990; Cole & Siegel, 1987; McKenry et al., 1980; Pfeffer, 1986). Common denominators related to family characteristics include a) parent-child conflict, b) maladaptive patterns of interrelationships, including ambivalence, high rigidity, setting up perfectionistic goals, and overprotection, c) lack of appropriate generational boundaries, d) poor parental coalition, both in functional and affectionate terms, e) multiple losses, especially early on in the child's life, and f) depression in parent(s), which can lead the child to mirror and identify with parental behavior as a coping mechanism against stress. Such parents are usually less involved with their children due to greater feelings of guilt, impaired communication, and poor self-worth. Jacobs (1971) noted that families of suicidal young people were more likely to deal with discipline problems by criticizing, nagging, yelling, withholding approval, or using physical force. It is easy to imagine how such tactics if used frequently and repeatedly could lead the young person to feel both angry and unwanted, emotions that are common among suicidal adolescents (see Cole & Siegel, 1990; Husain & Vandiver, 1984; Kurtz & Deverensky, 1993). Such tactics may be more likely to be employed by parents who are themselves under stress, thus explaining the association between suicide and sociocultural variables. However, their use is by no means restricted to the disadvantaged, and they may be employed unthinkingly by parents with the best of intentions.

D. The Developmental Perspective

Suicide is a rarity in young children and increases with age after puberty. The developmental perspective focuses on cognitive, physical, emotional, and social changes in adolescence that might be associated with this phenomenon. Issues related to adolescent development that should be considered by school psychologists working with troubled youths, their teachers, and parents include the following:

    (1) in the cognitive domain, the adolescent's improved ability to consider alternatives, and his or her understanding of the consequences of death,

    (2) in the physical domain, the adolescent's rapid growth and the onset of puberty,

    (3) in the emotional domain, the ability to experience guilt and shame,

    (4) in the social domain, the need for acceptance by others, and conflicting feelings regarding authority and independence.

While the developmental changes associated with adolescence are well documented, hypotheses concerning the nature of their relationship to suicide are frankly speculative and, for the most part, unsubstantiated. Shaffer (1986) has suggested that the adolescents' growing social independence may be the most important factor that makes them vulnerable to suicide in comparison to younger children. Social support systems provide an opportunity to correct inaccurate perceptions through discussions with family and teachers. For young children, the opportunities for such corrective feedback are multiple. However, adolescents' striving for independence and autonomy may lead them to reject these sources of support (Metha et al., 1998; Reynolds & Mazza, 1994).

A more widely discussed hypothesis concerns the impact of cognitive development on adolescent thinking related to suicide (Carlson, 1983; Davis, 1985; Shaffer, 1986). For example, one consequence of adolescents' growing cognitive capacities may be the ability to experience the emotion of guilt (Izard & Schwartz, 1986). As well, having just entered the period of formal operational thinking, adolescents are able to consider possibilities that are not a part of their personal experience. They may be more prone to suffer the despair that is a hallmark of suicidal thinking (Beck, Kovacs, & Weissmann, 1975) when they are able to contemplate multiple life alternatives and conclude that all of them offer negative prospects. Thus, they may be led to choose death as a solution to their problems.

Using a Piagetian perspective, Koocher (1974) investigated developmental changes in children's understanding of death. In the earliest stage, death is thought of as temporary and reversible, akin to sleep. In the middle stage, it is understood to be permanent (irreversible), but is seen as something that happens only to old people, not young children. Adolescents understand the permanence of death, and also that it can happen to them. However, only the more cognitively mature are able to fully understand their own deaths as final and irreversible. Thus, for very young children, deliberate suicide is a logical impossibility since death is not seen as permanent. Somewhat older children are protected because death is not seen as relevant to them. However, adolescents are vulnerable, because although they can conceive of their own death, they do not fully understand its disastrous personal consequences.

Studies of the concept of death in suicidal young people support this view. They are more likely to feel that life processes continue after death, and that their own death might be reversible as compared with peers who have not contemplated suicide (McIntire & Angle, 1980; Orbach & Glaubman, 1979a, b). As well, this explanation makes some of the suicidal "types" (Davis, 1985) that occur in adolescents more understandable. It is conceivable that a young person who did not fully anticipate the permanence of his or her own death could contemplate suicide as a retaliation (Elkind, 1978), a method of manipulation, or as a means of rejoining a lost loved one (McKenry et al., 1980; Rosenkrantz, 1978). Without such a perspective, these explanations seem irrational to adults.

E. Understanding Depression in Adolescents

Although suicidal behavior has long been associated with depression in adults, depression in children and adolescents was not even thought to exist until recently. Today, however, this is a rapidly expanding research area (see Rutter, Izard, & Read, 1986), and a growing body of literature establishes its connection to suicide (Anderson, 1982; Birmaher et al., 1996; Dahl & Ryan, 1996; Esposito & Clum, 1999; Goldberg, 1981; Hawton, 1982; Konopka, 1983; Pfeffer et al., 1983; Robbins & Conroy, 1983). While the relationship between suicide and depression is by no means perfect, the link is sufficiently strong that school psychologists concerned with suicide prevention should also have a broad understanding of childhood and adolescent depression. Such knowledge will sensitize them to the following characteristics amongst distressed and potentially suicidal young people:

(1) Feelings of sadness, unhappiness, emptiness, pessimism, helplessness, and hopelessness, as well as feelings of anger, guilt, and fear. Irritability and loss of pleasure in usual activities.

(2) Physical complaints such as fatigue, sleeping disorders, eating disorders, headaches, or stomach-aches.

(3) Negative thinking, including negative view of self, self-blame and criticism, negative view of the world, pessimism about the future, suicidal thoughts, distractibility, ambivalence, and indecisiveness.

(4) Behaviors such as withdrawal from social contact, engaging in fewer pleasurable activities, studying alone, reduced involvement in sports or games, crying easily.

Depression involves a complex of dysfunctional symptoms, including changes in affect, cognition, behavior, and physical condition. School psychologists should acknowledge that although childhood depression has become an accepted clinical diagnosis, legitimized by its inclusion in the DSM-IV as a psychiatric disorder, depressive symptoms are also quite common in the general population. To date, research has not clarified whether those who meet the DSM-IV criteria for major depression have a qualitatively different illness or simply a more severe form of a problem that is quite common.

Although depression among children and adolescents was ignored until recently, the field is currently an exciting research area (see Rutter et al., 1986). Some of the questions being researched include the following: (a) the similarities between depression in adults, adolescents, and young children, (b) etiology and long-term prognosis for depression in children and adolescents, (c) the relationship between depression and mourning, and (d) appropriate criteria for identifying depression in young people.

What are the origins of depression? Freud attributed it to the inability of an unhealthy personality to cope effectively with loss, while psychobiologists point out that genetic links (at least in adults) suggest the inheritance of an organic predisposition. Noting that the symptom structure of depression incorporates cognitive and behavioral as well as physical and emotional features, contemporary theorists propose a complex etiology in which emotional, cognitive, behavioral and biological systems interact with one another in ways that are maladaptive and inefficient in coping with life stresses (Izard & Schwartz, 1986). Separate, but related ideas include (a) the role of cognitive processes in depression, (b) the concept of learned helplessness and, (c) the importance of lowered self-esteem (Cole, 1982; Petersen et al., 1993).

1. Cognitive Mechanisms in Depression

Beck and his colleagues (Beck, 1976; Beck, Rush, Shaw, & Emery, 1979; Beck & Shaw, 1977; Kovacs & Beck, 1977) have developed a cognitive model of depression that stresses the role that negative thinking can have on the individual's behavior, attitudes, and affective responses. Such negative thinking often involves three components (the "cognitive triad"): negative views of the self, negative views of life experiences, and a negative view of the future. Life experiences are assessed in terms of these dysfunctional beliefs, resulting in a tendency to exaggerate their negative aspects in spite of objective evidence to the contrary. The depressed person sees him or herself as a deprived and defective person to whom only negative things can happen and whose prospects for the future are therefore hopeless. Beck has found that hopelessness is the symptom of depression most closely related to suicide.

Such distorted thinking is felt to develop gradually and to be rooted in the individual's life experiences. Beck suggested that the best therapeutic approach to relieve depression is to help the person break his or her circular, negative thinking, and has developed strategies that have been shown to alleviate depressive states. Although most of Beck's work has been conducted with adults, he and his colleagues (Albert & Beck, 1975; Kovacs & Beck, 1977) have explored modifications of the cognitive theory and related therapeutic strategies with school-age children. Others have also explored the cognitive mechanisms of depression including looking at various psychological determinates such as hopelessness, locus of control, anger, and perfectionism (Boergers, Spirito, & Donaldson, 1998; Hammond & Romney, 1995).

2. Learned Helplessness

Lack of control over reinforcement or trauma is central to the development of what Seligman (1975) termed "learned helplessness." Seligman and his colleagues (Abela & Seligman, 2000; Abramson, Seligman, & Teasdale, 1978; Dweck & Bush, 1976; Miller & Seligman, 1975) have conducted considerable research into the phenomenon of helplessness with animals and humans. The concept was initially developed to describe the behavior of animals who were shocked repeatedly with no means of escape. Such animals showed multiple signs of distress, including some behaviors that resembled those of depressed humans. They became apathetic, and took no steps to help themselves even when means of escape were later provided.

Seligman hypothesized that learned helplessness provides a model for depression in human beings. Thus, depressed states are thought to develop when repeated life experiences over which the person has no control result in negative consequences (Seligman, 1978). Extensions of the theory (Abramson, Garber, & Seligman, 1980; Gladstone & Kaslow, 1995; Joiner & Wagner, 1995; Schwartz, Kaslow, Seeley, & Lewinsohn, 2000) highlight the importance of a person's attributions regarding life events. Those who are depressed have been found to be more likely to attribute life's outcome to forces that are internal, rather than external, global rather than specific, and stable rather than unstable. Recently, these findings have been extended to children as young as 9 years of age (Abela & Seligman, 2000; Seligman & Peterson, 1986).

3. Negative Self-Esteem

Numerous writers consider that loss of self-esteem or the development of a negative self-concept is a central aspect of depression, either as a precipitating factor, as an outcome of depression, or both. As well, lowered self-esteem is a central feature of both the psychoanalytic (Bibring, 1953; Jacobson, 1954) and the cognitive (Beck,

1976) theories of depression. Adolescents may be particularly vulnerable to lowered feelings of self-esteem, as this is a phase of development that is marked by progress towards emotional independence and a heightened sense of self. At the same time, adolescents tend to experience an increase in their reactions and in the intensity of their feelings towards self and others. During this developmental stage their self-confidence becomes vulnerable and their self-perceptions fluctuate as they undergo changes associated with their physical, cognitive, and social growth (Bracken, 1996; Kostanski & Gullone, 1998; Lewinsohn, Seeley, & Gotlib, 1997).

Responding to Signals of Distress

Each of the theoretical perspectives on suicide just discussed suggests clues for identifying potentially suicidal youth. These clues, as well as others, are summarized as Signals of Distress in Table 3.

Although these signs are noticed by many parents and teachers, they are frequently ignored and are not seen as indicators that a young person is in serious trouble and requires professional help. These distress signals should be discussed with educators, and plans should be made for an appropriate response. It is especially important to emphasize that young people who talk about suicide are not "just talking." It is a myth that if they talk about suicide they won't attempt it (Anderson, 1982; Hennig, Crabtree, & Baum, 1998).

A psychologist who learns that a student is experiencing multiple symptoms of distress should directly ask questions such as, "Are you thinking of killing yourself?" or "It sounds as if you're having a rough time of it – do you ever think of killing yourself?" Raising the topic of suicide assures the adolescent that one is willing and able to understand his or her feelings (Fichette, 1982; Schuyler, 1973; E. Smith, 1981). There is no formula or infallible checklist of suicidal risk (Husain & Vandiver, 1984). However, the questions in Table 4 appear to canvass some of the predictors of imminent suicide attempts (Beck et al., 1979; Fichette, 1982; Schuyler, 1973; Smith, 1981; Toolan, 1975).

A. Assessment Techniques

When facing a suicidal adolescent, one is likely dealing with an individual whose capacity to see adult authority figures as positive resources has diminished. The assessment of suicidal risk in teenagers is complex and difficult, as multiple correlates, expressions, symptoms, and signs can be associated with suicidal behavior. The overall aim of the assessment, then, is to create an atmosphere of care, concern, and willingness to help the student immediately. The following principles and specific techniques will assist you during the assessment phase.

Table 3 Signals of Distress

1) **Preoccupation with Themes of Death**
   - Repeated threats of suicide
   - Previous suicide attempts
   - Statement(s) of wishing to be dead, being a burden on others
   - Communication of themes of death through art, writings
   - Description of plans for death
   - Making out a will

2) **Behavioral Indicators**
   - General withdrawal and noticeable change in motivation
   - Decreased school activity, isolation, aloofness
   - Altered school performance
   - Unexpected and unexplained absence from school
   - Unexplained procrastination or persistent lateness
   - Apparent loss of involvement in previous interests and hobbies
   - Tendency to become uncommunicative and apathetic
   - Sudden "improvement" from a depressed state
   - Disposing of valued possessions
   - Outbursts of frustration
   - Frequent accidents

3) **Profound Sense of Personal Failure and Social Inadequacy**
   - Self-dislike, low self-regard
   - Feelings of loss, deprivation
   - Sense of gloom, "feeling down about life"
   - Feeling misunderstood and not appreciated
   - Life too painful or too difficult
   - Feeling overwhelmed by responsibilities

4) **Physical/Somatic Indicators**
   - Loss of appetite, loss of weight
   - Tiredness, exhaustion
   - Chronic sleeplessness
   - Somatic complaints
   - Restlessness
   - Excessive use of alcohol or drugs as an escape
   - History of ill health or psychiatric disorder

5) **Affective Indicators**
   - Unhappiness, pessimism
   - Anger, guilt, fear
   - Mood variation
   - Anxiousness, extreme tension, agitation
   - Feelings of helplessness and hopelessness

6) **Cognitive Indicators**
   - Self-depreciation, self-blame
   - Distractibility
   - Problems in judgment and memory
   - Extreme and rigid thinking patterns
   - Escapist and suicidal wishes

7) **Common Environmental Stressors**
   - Recent suicide of friend or loved one
   - History of losses
   - Rejection by friends, loved ones or family
   - School difficulties
   - Family problems such as illness, divorce, etc.

Table 4 Student Questions – Psychologist's Focus

Questions for Students	Focus for the School Psychologist
1) Have you thought of killing yourself? How will you do it?	Ask questions that will help you decide whether the attempt is impulsive or well planned. Note existence of specific plan, method, availability and accessibility of means, and timing.
2) How serious are you?	Ask if there were previous communications of intent. Determine the frequency and intensity of thoughts about self-harm, sense of losing control, and feelings of helplessness.
3) Have you tried before?	Note the history of previous attempts (how many, when, method, reasons for remaining alive, responses of significant others). Ask if the student has recently withdrawn from therapeutic help.
4) What has happened to make life worthless?	Examine the circumstances that preceded the attempt. Explore information about recent separations and losses (especially if public), recent geographical moves, breaks in usual support network, physical ill health.
5) How do you think your family and friends would feel?	Does the student feel disconnected from family or friends? Was there any thought given to other people's reactions?
6) Are you able to make this decision alone?	Explore the strength and flexibility of the student's internal resources. Has she/he considered alternatives? Is the student overly influenced by troubled peers? What resources are available to support continued living? Has the student revealed suicidal thoughts/feelings to anyone else?
7) What do you know about death or dying?	Inquire whether the student comprehends death as final and irreversible. This information will assist in your assessment of risk as well as directions for therapy.
8) Do you know that your feelings can be understood?	Examine the student's ability to communicate his/her need for help. Is the student comfortable in asking for or receiving it? Does she/he believe that potential helpers care and are available? Explore the belief that change cannot, or will not, occur.
9) Is there something else we need to discuss?	Make careful note of any answers not previously canvassed.

Recognize your own uneasiness in discussing suicide and your fear that a student might carry through on a threat

Accept the fact that the adolescent's own ambivalence must be addressed and he or she must be protected from self-destruction. Acknowledge that immediate intervention is called for. Commit yourself to be available, and show your willingness to discuss any problem without being judgmental. Do not act shocked or panic at what you are told, as it will jeopardize your own ability to act. Remember that the stress you are experiencing is often felt by other caregivers.

Establish a positive and trusting rapport with the student in order to facilitate gathering of information and to help determine the seriousness of intent and level of suicidal risk

Ask specific questions about the adolescent's state, and actively listen to what is said. Convey empathetic understanding and reflect the feelings expressed by acknowledging any anger, pain, or panic. Note how the adolescent perceives and copes with a sense of loss. Watch for information that implies a lack of value for life. Pay special attention to noting indirect and subtle themes of helplessness, hopelessness and death.

Be affirmative. Do not be fearful or apologize for being intrusive

You cannot assume that the adolescent is in control, nor treat him or her as if this is the case. Keep track of your reactions during the interview, and trust your intuition and judgment if you become suspicious that the student may attempt self-harm.

Focus on a problem solving-approach, and stress that help is available

It is wrong to support blaming, as well as to make light of the situation. Do not dismiss distress as a normal adolescent experience (e.g., the intense reaction to the loss of a first love), and do not minimize it as mere attention-seeking or manipulation. The student may feel inadequately understood or believe that you do not care to listen, respect, or appreciate his or her needs and feelings. Emphasize that there are professionals who are especially trained to help children and adolescents who feel depressed and isolated.

Understand that suicidal gestures may be a response to intolerable stress

Do not reassure too liberally by saying such things as "things are not as bad as they seem," "things will improve," or "you have a number of reasons to go on living."

While these may be true, they deny the adolescent's feelings of hopelessness. Bear in mind that suicidal children succumb to intense pressures and are overwhelmed by painful emotions. They need to hear from you that you care about them and that you don't want them to die!

The student may wish to have "someone to lean on." Express your genuine concern about his or her welfare and indicate the reasons why

A reticent attitude on your part may be seen as rejection and a justification for pessimism and despair. Offer compassion and permit yourself to be as emotionally close as possible; however, do not act as the student's only "lifeline": help identify other resources needed to improve the situation. If the student has revealed nothing to anyone else, take the responsibility to explore whether parents or other significant adults at school or in the community can be enlisted for help.

B. Responding to Your Assessment of Risk

1) When you decide that the suicide risk is high

The student who has expressed a lethal intent, either by having developed a clear plan for death or by attempting self-harm, should receive professional care as soon as possible.

Inform the principal or designate (vice-principal, guidance teacher, student services personnel, school nurse) of your concern and your recognition of the immediate need to refer the student to a treatment facility

Act specifically to make arrangements for prompt assessment by qualified experts. If possible, consult with other professionals in order to share the burden of making decisions.

Discuss how the parent/guardian will be informed of the school's observations and worries and how aid will be enlisted

The person who is assigned to contact the parent/guardian should be aware that some parents may deny information that points to the fact that their child is at risk. Anger, fear, and guilt are other common feelings and responses for families of troubled youth.

Help the student realize that a crisis situation has occurred

Emphasize that he or she can be helped, but that confidentiality will have to be breached. Until an adequate assessment confirms that the adolescent has sufficient self-control, do not accept a promise not to commit suicide. Do not permit the student to leave a safe, supervised, or secure environment while you make arrangements: stay with the adolescent until you have transferred the responsibility for his or her safety to someone trustworthy, e.g., a parent.

2) Suicide Crisis Management Procedures

Principals and school personnel are usually guided by a standard procedure that outlines the actions of a school to ensure communication with the parent/guardian, and adequate supervision and protection of the student. However, in extremely life-threatening situations in which the student is out of control, do not hesitate to bypass this if necessary and call the police. The following are suggested guidelines for responding to suicidal crises and emergencies.

(1) Prompt accompaniment of the adolescent to the nearest hospital emergency department, crisis intervention unit, or mental health treatment facility with an emergency service should be undertaken when the family physician cannot be reached or if the situation appears too urgent for delay.

(2) Advance warning to the treatment setting may facilitate more immediate intervention. Where possible, call for consultation and/or advance warning.

(3) The principal or designate should be available to the emergency staff of the treatment center, who may wish to alert the school to specific concerns or provide directions on further management.

(4) Arrange for appropriate follow-up in cooperation with the treatment facility. Do not hesitate to initiate contact if major concerns continue at the school.

(5) Following the emergency, review the school's crisis response procedures and programs for suicide prevention. Improve these procedures as necessary, using resources from both inside and outside the school board that can provide assistance.

3) When you decide that the risk is low

Following your assessment, confirm the soundness of your judgment by reviewing the evidence quickly. If possible, consult with other professionals. Inform the parent(s) of your concerns and stress that their child might benefit from professional help.

Arrange follow-up meetings with the student, even months later. Do not hesitate to ask how he or she is feeling and coping with everyday demands. Be alert to the signs of cumulative stress, isolation, or failure. Maintain contact with those significant adults who know the student, to confirm that the risk remains low. For some adolescents, emotional and social development can lag behind intellectual and academic aptitudes. Although this lag in development is recognized, it is often ignored; parents and educators may make the mistake of assuming that such youngsters are happy and risk-free.

Discuss the situation with school personnel and identify how the school can be supportive, for example by providing counseling, putting academic stress in proper perspective, changing class routines, teaching study skills, encouraging development of new interests, arranging for academic support, and assisting the student to communicate better with family members. Goal-setting can focus on coping with learning and the daily routine of school. Short-term goals are recommended. Daily planning permits the student to succeed with tasks and goals such as establishing schedules of activities, time budgeting, planning for the weekend, and concentrating on studying-all easily supported by teachers.

Dispel misconceptions by offering basic information about suicide in children and youth. Determine if there is a need to discuss suicide prevention with school staff and students. If the school decides to embark on the implementation of such a program, use the questions in Table 1 as a guide for planning.

Management after a Suicide

"A man's dying is more the survivor's affair than his own." (Thomas Mann)

When a suicide occurs, it arouses many overwhelming feelings in those who knew the deceased. This is especially true when a young person takes his or her life. One of the first reactions is denial, which is a universal response to death. Grief causes many emotions to surface: shock, disbelief, anxiety, confusion, sorrow, guilt, and anger. Following a suicidal trauma, the school psychologist may become involved with the survivors who manifest one or more of these responses. During this period, the following information will assist you in your work with bereaved families, teachers, and peers (Hazell & Lewin, 1993; Silverman & Felner, 1995).

Once parents overcome the stage of denying the reality of their child's death, in their confusion and panic they frequently tend to direct anger not only at themselves but at others who were in contact with their child, particularly the school. Yet, because of the stigma and imposed shame, they are often unable to express their feelings openly or deal with them.

Parents consumed by a sense of failure and abandonment can become a high-risk group for suicide themselves. A sudden and chosen death of a loved one raises feelings that are extremely difficult to cope with. Parents often wonder if the suicide might have been their fault or if they could have prevented it: self-doubt and desperation activate memories of the last encounters with the dead. Repetitive questions are voiced: "Why did it happen to us?" "If he really cared for us would he have done this?"

Buried or unacknowledged grief can be harmful and destructive in any family, and can be particularly dangerous in the case of death by suicide as the mourning process is disturbed by exaggerated feelings of guilt and depression. Grief can put unbearable stress on relationships. Denial or silence will further exacerbate the sense of isolation from society at large and from other family members.

A separate tragedy is the sibling of a suicide victim. Feelings of rage and worthlessness were typical of a teenager who stated in a counseling session: "I was angry at my sister for checking out, and afraid my parents secretly wished I'd been the one to die." A sibling may feel like a precipitant to the event. He or she may have been given the responsibility to "watch" and feels responsible for having failed, or may have been aware of the preparations for the suicidal act and told no one. Some have discovered the body, or have unwittingly assisted in the suicidal act itself. The reactions of these youths vary from guilt – "I should have stopped her"– to identification – "the future is gone, suicide is the way out." They must deal with the remaining family members' grief and with the separation and loss of the deceased, and to learn to cope with the new alignment in the family that follows the loss. Commonly observed after-effects include depression or suicidal behavior on anniversaries.

Family members may have trouble reaching out for help. In your role as school psychologist, you should offer basic information about youth suicide and strongly urge them to seek professional counseling, as open communication with the aid of a qualified professional will reduce misplaced feelings of guilt and inappropriate acceptance of blame. Joining a local survivor support program is a recommended mode of therapy. In such groups, participants are keenly aware of each others' feelings and reactions as they go through the same mourning stages.

How should the school respond to and cope with the loss of one of its students? Consult with the principal about the urgency of immediate planning and action. At first, it is important to ascertain the facts. It is necessary to work quickly, for students often sense that something is wrong and rumors begin to circulate. All teachers should be informed about the death and must tell the truth and establish a support system that will meet the needs of the students.

Expert resource services in the community and mental health professionals at the school board should join to assist in responding to the needs of students, educators, and parents. It is necessary to talk about death in order to help adolescents work through their grief without relying solely on behavioral responses. Teachers must share their own feelings in open discussion and encourage students to do so too, in order to acknowledge that we are entitled to our feelings and that sharing makes it easier.

In the search for meaning, other feelings are encountered: unfairness, loneliness, fear. Normal class schedules should be set aside by teachers and students and time allowed for personal reflection and discussion of the tragedy of the suicide and stigma. "Mourning assemblies" and small group sessions can provide an opportunity to express mutual and communal feelings of loss by staff and students. However, giving too much prominence to the tragedy may tend to sensationalize the act of suicide.

Students should be encouraged to find personal expressions for their sorrow. Participation in the funeral and mourning process will confirm what is difficult to believe – that a classmate is dead. It also helps students to reflect on their friend's absence and their own loneliness and sadness. It is necessary to remind students that their own thoughts and actions did not cause the suicide, thus helping to relieve them of feelings of guilt. The need to address this grief is important if contagion is to be minimized. Looking ahead to coping, without forgetting the sadness, should be underlined.

Appendix B provides school psychologists with a summary guide for coping with tragic events. It includes information concerning crisis teams, coping with bereavement and constructive consultation strategies.

If your school is not involved with suicide prevention, as the school psychologist you can encourage the administration to develop and introduce such a program to students and staff. Table 1 will be of help to you at this phase. We cannot afford not to educate ourselves in suicide prevention as even one senseless death is one too many!

References

Abela, J. R. Z., & Seligman, M. E. P. (2000). The hopelessness theory of depression: A test of the diathesis-stress component in the interpersonal and achievement domains. *Cognitive Therapy and Research, 24(4),* 361-378.

Abramson, L. Y., Garber, J., & Seligman, M. E. P. (1980). Learned helplessness in humans: An attributional analysis. In J. Garber & M. E. P. Seligman (Eds.), *Human helplessness: Theory and applications.* New York: Academic Press.

Abramson, L. Y., Seligman, M. E. P., & Teasdale, J. D. (1978). Learned helplessness in humans: Critique and reformulation. *Journal of Abnormal Psychology, 87,* 49-74.

Ahearn, E. P., Jamison, K. R., Steffens, D. C., Cassidy, F., Provenzale, J. M., Lehman, A., Weisler, R. H., Carroll, B. J., & Krishnan, K. R. R. (2001). MRI correlates of suicide attempt history in unipolar depression. *Biological Psychiatry: Special Issue, 50(4),* 266-270.

Albert, M., & Beck, A. T. (1975). Incidence of depression in early adolescence: A preliminary study. *Journal of Youth and Adolescence, 4(4),* 301-307.

American Association of Suicidology (1996). Washington, DC.

American Psychiatric Association. *Diagnostic and Statistical Manual of Mental Disorders* (4th ed.). Washington, DC: American Psychiatric Association.

Anderson, L. S. (1982). Understanding and working with the depressed suicidal adolescent. *Counseling and Human Development, 15,* 1-12.

Anderson, N. C. (1984). *The broken brain: The biological revolution in psychiatry.* New York: Harper & Row.

Angold, A., & Costello, E. J. (2001). The epidemiology of depression in children and adolescents.

In I. M. Goodyer (Ed.), *The depressed child and adolescent (2nd ed.). Cambridge child and adolescent psychiatry* (pp. 143-178). New York, NY: Cambridge University Press.

Barrett Hicks, B. (1990). *Youth suicide.* Bloomington: National Educational Services.

Beck, A. T. (1976). *Cognitive therapy and emotional disorders.* New York: International Universities Press, Inc.

Beck, A. T., Kovacs, M. V., & Weissmann, A. (1975). Hopelessness and suicidal behavior. *Journal of the American Medical Association, 234,* 1146-1149.

Beck, A. T., & Shaw, B. F. (1977). Cognitive approaches to depression. In A. Ellis & R. Grieger (Eds.), *Handbook of rational emotive therapy.* New York: Springer.

Beck, A. T., Rush, A. J., Shaw, B. F., & Emery, G. L. (1979). *Cognitive therapy of depression.* New York: The Guilford Press.

Beres, D. (1966). Superego and depression. In R. M. Loewenstein, L. M. Newman, M. Schur, & A. J. Solnit (Eds.), *Psychoanalysis: A general psychology.* New York: International Universities Press.

Bibring, E. (1953). The mechanism of depression. In P. Greenacre (Ed.), *Affective disorders: Psychoanalytic contributions to their study.* New York: International Universities Press.

Birmaher, B., & Heydl, P. (2001). Biological studies in depressed children and adolescents. *International Journal of Neuropsychopharmacology. Special Issue, 4(2),* 149-157.

Birmaher, B., Ryan, N., Williamson, D. E., & Brent, D. (1996). Childhood and adolescent depression: A review of the past 10 years, Part 1. *Journal of the American Academy of Child & Adolescent Psychiatry, 35(11),* 1427-1439.

Boergers, J., Spirito, A., & Donaldson, D. (1998). Reasons for adolescent suicide attempts: Associations with psychological functioning. *Journal of the American Academy of Child and Adolescent Psychiatry, 37(12),* 1287-1293.

Bracken, B. A. (1996). *Handbook of self-concept: Developmental, social, and clinical considerations.* New York: John Wiley and Sons.

Brent, D. A. (1995). Risk factors for adolescent suicide and suicidal behavior: Mental and substance abuse disorders, family environmental factors, and life stress. *Suicide and Life-Threatening Behavior, 25,* 52-63.

Cantwell, D. P (1983). Family genetic factors. In D. P Cantwell & G.A. Carlson (Eds.), *Effective disorders in childhood and adolescence.* New York: Spectrum.

Caplan, G. (1970). *The theory and practice of mental health consultation.* New York: Basic Books.

Carlson, G. A. (1983). Depression and suicidal behavior in children and adolescents. In D. P Cantwell & G. A. Carlson (Eds.), *Effective disorders in childhood and adolescence.* New York: Spectrum.

Chorpita, B. F., Yim, L., Moffitt, C., Umemoto, L., & Francis, S. E. (2000). Assessment of symptoms of DSM-IV anxiety and depression in children: A revised child anxiety and depression scale. *Behavior Research & Therapy, 38(8),* 835-855.

Clark, D. C. (1993). Suicidal behavior in childhood and adolescence: Recent studies and clinical implications. *Psychiatric Annals, 23(5),* 271-283.

Cole, E. (1982). Childhood depression: A literature review. *Student Services Project Bulletin,* No. 8, Toronto Board of Education.

Cole, E. (1992). Characteristics of students referred to school teams: Implications for preventive psychological services. *Canadian Journal of School Psychology, 8,* 23-36.

Cole, E. (1995). Responding to school violence. *Canadian Journal of School Psychology, 11(2),* 103-116.

Cole, E., & Siegel, J. A. (1987). Alleviating hopelessness: Suicide prevention in the schools. *Public Health Reviews, 15,* 241-255.

Cole, E., & Siegel, J. A. (1990). Suicide Prevention in Schools: Facing the challenge. In E. Cole & J. A. Siegel (Eds.), *Effective consultation in school psychology* (pp. 247-278). Toronto: Hogrefe & Huber Publishers.

Dahl, R. E., & Ryan, N. D. (1996). The psychobiology of adolescent depression. In D. Cicchetti & S. L. Toth (Eds.), *Adolescence: Opportunities and challenges. Rochester symposium on developmental psychopathology, Vol. 7* (pp. 197-232). Rochester, NY: University of Rochester Press.

Davis, J. M. (1985). Suicidal crises in schools. *School Psychology Review, 14,* 313-324.

Davis, J. M., Sandoval, J., & Wilson, M. P. (1988). Strategies for the primary prevention of suicide. *School Psychology Review, 17(4),* 559-569.

De Hert, M., McKenzie, K., & Peuskena, J. (2001). Risk factors for suicide in young people suffering from schizophrenia: A long-term follow-up study. *Schizophrenia Research: Special Issue, 47 (2-3),* 127-134.

DeHouter, K. V. (1981). To silence oneself: A brief analysis of the literature on adolescent suicide. *Child Welfare, 60,* 3-10.

Dorpat, T. L., Jackson, J. K., & Ripley, H. S. (1965). Broken homes and attempted suicide. *Archives of General Psychiatry, 12,* 213-216.

Duggal, S., Carlson, E. A., Sroufe, L. A., & Egeland, B. (2001). Depressive symptomatology in childhood and adolescence. *Development & Psychopathology, 13(1),* 143-164.

Durkheim, E. (1951). *Suicide: A study in sociology.* J. A. Spaulding & G. Simpson (Trans.). New York: Free Press.

Dweck, C. S., & Bush, E. S. (1976). Sex differences in learned helplessness: 1. Differential debilitation with peer and adult evaluations. *Developmental Psychology, 12,* 147-156.

Elkind, D. (1978). *The child's reality: Three developmental themes.* New York: John Wiley & Sons.

Esposito, C. L., & Clum, G. A. (1999). Specificity of depression symptoms and suicidality in a juvenile delinquent population. *Journal of Psychopathology & Behavioral Assessment, 21(2),* 171-182.

Fichette, B. (1982). Suicide in youth: What counselors can do about it. *School Guidance Worker, 38,* 23-26.

Finch, S. M., & Poznanski, E. O. (1971). *Adolescent suicide.* Springfield, IL: Charles C. Thomas.

Flisher, A. J. (1999). Mood disorders in suicidal children and adolescents: Recent developments. *Journal of Child Psychology & Psychiatry & Allied Disciplines, 40(3),* 315-324.

Fowler, R. C., Rich, C., & Young, D. (1985). *San Diego suicide study.* American Association of Suicidology, 18th Annual Meeting, Toronto, 1985.

Freud, S. (1917). Mourning and melancholia. In *Sigmund Freud Collected Papers Vol. IV.* London: Hogarth Press, 1950.

Garfinkel, B. D., & Golombek, H. (1974). Suicide and depression in childhood and adolescence. *Canadian Medical Association Journal, 110,* 1278-1281.

Gladstone, T. R., & Kaslow, N. J. (1995). Depression and attributions in children and adolescents: A meta-analytic review. *Journal of Abnormal Child Psychology, 23,* 597-606.

Goldberg, E. L. (1981). Depression and suicide ideation in the young adult. *American Journal of Psychiatry, 138,* 35-40.

Hammond, W. A., & Romney, D. M. (1995). Cognitive factors contributing to adolescent depression. *Journal of Youth & Adolescence, 24(6),* 667-683.

Hawton, D., O'Grady, J., Osbom, M., & Cole, D. (1982). Adolescents who take overdoses: Their characteristics, problems, and contacts with helping agencies. *British Journal of Psychiatry,* 140, 118-123.

Hazell, P., & Lewin, T. (1993). An evaluation of postvention following adolescent suicide. *Suicide and Life-Threatening Behavior, 23,* 101-109.

Heath, C. P. (1990). Children and reactions to death-Handouts, *Communique.* Washington, DC: The National Association of School Psychologists.

Hennig, C. W., Crabtree, C. R., & Baum, D. (1998). Mental health CPR: Peer contracting as a response to potential suicide in adolescents. *Archives of Suicide Research, 4,* 169-187.

Holinger, P. C. (1978). Adolescent suicide: An epidemiological study of recent trends. *American Journal of Psychiatry, 135,* 754-756.

Husain, S. A., & Vandiver, T. (1984). *Suicide in children and adolescents.* New York: Spectrum.

Izard, C. E., & Schwartz, G. M. (1986). Patterns of emotion in depression. In M. Rutter, C. E. Izard, & P. B. Read (Eds.), *Depression in young people: Developmental and clinical aspects.* New York: Guilford Press.

Jacobs, J. (1971). *Adolescent suicide.* New York: Wiley & Sons.

Jacobson, E. (1954). Transference problems in the psychoanalytic treatment of severely depressive patients. *Journal of the American Psychoanalytic Association, 2,* 595-606.

Joffe, R. T., Offord, D. R., & Boyle, M. H. (1988). Ontario child health study: Suicidal behavior in youth 12-16 years. *American Journal of Psychiatry, 145(11),* 1420-1423.

Joiner, T. E., & Wagner, K. D. (1995). Attributional style and depression in children and adolescents: A meta-analytic review. *Clinical Psychology Review, 15,* 777-798.

Klerman, G. (1978). Affective disorders. In A. M. Nicholi (Ed.), *The Harvard guide to modern psychiatry.* Cambridge: Harvard University Press.

Konopka, G. (1983). Adolescent suicide. *Exceptional Children, 49,* 390-394.

Koocher, G. P. (1974). Talking with children about death. *American Journal of Orthopsychiatry, 44,* 404-411.

Kostanski, M., & Gullone, E. (1998). Adolescent body image dissatisfaction: Relationships with self-esteem, anxiety, and depression controlling for body mass. *Journal of Child Psychology & Psychiatry & Allied Disciplines, 39(2),* 255-262.

Kovacs, M., & Beck, A. T. (1977). An empirical-clinical approach toward a definition of childhood depression. In J. G. Schutterbrandt & A. Raskin (Eds.), *Depression in children: Diagnosis, treatment and conceptual models.* New York: Raven.

Kurtz, L., & Derevensky, J. L. (1993). Stress and coping in adolescents: The effects of family configuration and environment on suicidality. *Canadian Journal of School Psychology, 9(2),* 204-216.

Lafond, R. (1990). *Personal services: Psychosocial planning for disasters.* Health Canada: Minister of Supply and Services Canada.

Lewinsohn, P. M., Seeley, J. R., & Gotlib, I. H. (1997). Depression-related psychosocial variables: Are they specific to depression in adolescents? *Journal of Abnormal Psychology, 106(3),* 365-375.

Lopez, P., Mosquera, F., de Leon, J., Gutierrez, M., Ezcurra, J., Ramirez, F., & Gonzalez-Pinto, A. (2001). Suicide attempts in bipolar patients. *Journal of Clinical Psychiatry, 62(12),* 963-966.

Mazza, J. J. (1997). School-based suicide prevention programs: Are they effective? *School Psychology Review, 26(3),* 382-396.

McAnarney, E. R. (1979). Adolescent and young adult suicide in the United States: A reflection of societal unrest? *Adolescence, 56,* 765-774.

McHutchion, M. E. (1991). Student bereavement: A guide for school personnel. *Journal of School Health, 61(8),* 363-365.

McIntire, R. I. S., & Angle, C. R. (1980). *Suicide attempts in children and youth.* Hogerstow, MD: Harper & Row.

McKenry, P. C., Tishler, C. L., & Christman, K. L. (1980). Adolescent suicide and the classroom teacher. *Journal of School Health,* 130-132.

Metha, A., Chen, E., Mulvernon, S., & Dode, I. (1998). A theoretical model of adolescent suicide risk. *Archives of Suicide Research, 4,* 115-133.

Miller, W. R., & Seligman, M. E. P. (1975). Depression and learned helplessness in man. *Journal of Abnormal Psychology, 84,* 228-238.

O'Donnell, C. R. (1995). Firearm deaths among children and youth. *American Psychologist, 50(9),* 771-776.

Orbach, I., & Glaubman, H. (1979a). Children's perception of death as a defensive process. *Journal of Abnormal Psychology,* 671-674.

Orbach, I., & Glaubman, H. (1979b). The concept of death and suicidal behavior in young children. *Journal of the American Academy of Children Psychiatry, 18,* 668-678.

O'Toole, D. (1989). *Growing through grief: A K-12 curriculum to help young people through all kinds of loss.* Burnsville, NC: Rainbow Connection.

Pagliaro, L. A. (1995). Adolescent depression and suicide: A review and analysis of the current literature. *Canadian Journal of School Psychology, 11(2),* 191-201.

Parsons, R. D., & Meyers, J. (1984). *Developing consultation skills: A guide to training, development and assessment for human services professionals.* San Francisco: Jossey-Bass.

Perry, P. E. (1990). *Beyond content – Uncommon interventions with people in crisis.* Calgary: Synergy Library.

Petersen, A. C., Compas, B. E., Brooks-Gunn, J., Stemmler, M., Ey, S., & Grant, K. E. (1993). Depression in adolescence. *American Psychologist, 48(2),* 155-168.

Pfeffer, C. R. (1986). *The suicidal child.* New York: Guilford.

Pfeffer, C. R., Plutchik, R., & Mizruchi, M. S. (1983). Suicidal and assaultive behavior in children: Classification measurement and interrelations. *American Journal of Psychiatry, 140,* 154-156.

Pitcher, G., & Poland, S. (1992). *Crisis intervention in the schools.* New York: Guilford.

Poland, S. (1994). The role of school crisis intervention teams to prevent and reduce school violence and trauma. *School Psychology Review, 23(2),* 175-189.

Poland, S., & Pitcher, G. (1990). Best practices in crisis intervention. In E. Thomas & J. Grimes (Eds.). *Best practices in school psychology – II.* Washington, DC: The National Association of School Psychologists.

Puig-Antic, J. (1986). Psychobiological markers: Effects of age and puberty. In M. Rutter, C. Izard, & P. B. Read (Eds.), *Depression in young people: Developmental and clinical perspectives.* New York: Guilford.

Purvis, J. R., Porter, R. L., Authement, C. C., & Born, L.C. (1991). Crisis intervention teams in the schools. *Psychology in the Schools, 28,* 331-339.

Reis, S., Peterson, R. A., & Evon, L. (1977). *Abnormality: Experimental and clinical approaches.* New York: Macmillan.

Reynolds, W. M., & Mazza, J. J. (1994). Suicide and suicidal behavior in children and adolescents. In W. M. Reynolds & H. F. Johnston (Eds.), *Handbook of depression in children and adolescents* (pp. 525-580). New York: Plenum Press.

Rice, F., Harold, G., & Thaper, A. (2002). The genetic etiology of childhood depression: A review. *Journal of Child Psychology & Psychiatry & Allied Disciplines, 43(1),* 65-79.

Robbins. D., & Conroy, R.C. (1983). A cluster of adolescent suicide attempts: Is suicide contagious? *Journal of Adolescent Health Care, 3,* 253-255.

Rosenkrantz, A.L. (1978). A note on adolescent suicide: Incidence, dynamics and some suggestions for treatment. *Adolescence, 13,* 209-214.

Rutter, M., Izard, C. E., & Read, P. B. (Eds.). (1986). *Depression in young people: Developmental and clinical aspects.* New York: Guilford.

Sandoval, J., & Brock, S. E. (1996). The school psychologist's role in suicide prevention. *School Psychology Quarterly, 11(2),* 169-185.

Schuyler, D. (1973). When was the last time you took a suicidal child to lunch? *Journal of School Health, 43,* 504-506.

Schwartz, J. A., Kaslow, N. J., Seeley, J., & Lewinsohn, P. (2000). Psychological, cognitive, and interpersonal correlates of attributional change in adolescents. *Journal of Clinical Child Psychology, 29(2),* 188-198.

Seligman, M. E. P. (1975). *Helplessness: On depression, development and death.* San Francisco: W. H. Freeman.

Seligman, M. E. P. (1978). Comment and integration. *Journal of Abnormal Psychology, 87,* 165-179.

Seligman, M. E. P., & Peterson, C. A. (1986). A learned helplessness perspective on childhood depression: Theory and research. In M. Rutter, G. E. Izard, & P. B. Read (Eds.), *Depression in young people: Developmental and clinical aspects.* New York: Guilford.

Shaffer, D. (1974). Suicide in childhood and early adolescence. *Journal of Child Psychology and Psychiatry, 15,* 275-291.

Shaffer, D. (1986). Developmental factors in child and adolescent suicide. In M. Rutter, G. E. Izard, & P. B. Read (Eds.), *Depression in young people: Developmental and clinical aspects.* New York: Guilford.

Silverman, M. M., & Felner, R. D. (1995). Suicide prevention programs: Issues of design, implementation, feasibility and developmental appropriateness. *Suicide and Life-Threatening Behaviors, 25,* 92-104.

Smith, E. J. (1981). Adolescent suicide: A growing problem for school and family. *Urban Education, 16,* 279-296.

Smith, K. (1985). *Psychoanalytic theories of suicide: A half-century of change.* American Association of Suicidology, 18th Annual Meeting, Toronto, 1985.

Smith, K. (1990). Suicidal behavior in school aged youth. *School Psychology Review, 19(2),* 186-195.

Statistics Canada (1994). Ottawa: Vital Statistics and Health Status Sector.

Statistics Canada (1997). Ottawa: Vital Statistics and Health Status Sector.

Steinmetz, S. K. (1977). *The cycle of violence: Assertive, aggressive, and abusive family interaction.* New York: Praeger.

Tefft, B. M., Peterson, A. M., & Babigian, H. (1979). Patterns of death among suicide attempts: A psychiatric population and a general population. *Archives of General Psychiatry, 34,* 1155-1161.

Teicher, J. D. (1970). Children and adolescents who attempt suicide. *Pediatric Clinics of North America, 17,* 687-696.

Toolan, J. M. (1975). Suicide in childhood and adolescence. *American Journal of Psychotherapy, 29,* 339-344.

Vajda, J., & Steinbeck, K. (2000). Factors associated with repeat suicide attempts among adolescents. *Australian & New Zealand Journal of Psychiatry, 34(3),* 437-445.

Vital Statistics of the United States: Vol. II – Mortality (1980). Washington, DC: National Centre for Health Statistics.

Waddell, D., & Thomas, A. (1989). Children and response to disaster – Handouts, *Communique*. Washington, DC: The National Association of School Psychologists.

Appendix A: "A Cry for Help"

Preface

There are times when people's thoughts and feelings about themselves and their problems can lead them to consider suicide as the only way of ending their pain, unhappiness, and difficulties.

You or your friends may have known someone who felt unhappy, unwanted and discouraged, someone who felt that problems couldn't be solved, or that nothing was going right and that nothing would change for the better in the future. You may have felt that way yourself at times. Such feelings are not uncommon.

Suicidal persons often tell others about their thoughts. It's their way of communicating how unhappy they feel and of asking for help.

How should you react if one of your friends makes a suicide threat or attempt? What if you yourself feel unhappy, troubled, or have thoughts of suicide?

This booklet tells you how to seek help. It has been prepared by the Student Services Department of the Board of Education for the City of Toronto to encourage students and staff to develop a better understanding of suicide in the hope of preventing it.

Introduction

Suicide occurs more often than most of us realize. It is the second most frequent cause of death among young people in Canada.

Suicide has occurred throughout history among people of all age levels, cultures, social, and economic backgrounds. Today, suicide and its causes are better understood. As a result, we are more able to deal with stresses that can lead to suicide.

Persons who have thoughts and feelings of suicide are not alone, even though in their troubled state they may believe otherwise. Many people think that no one else feels as they do or understands their problems. Many people think of suicide at one time or another.

Prevention of suicide is possible. There are people who understand the problems, the sense of shame, fear, loneliness, helplessness, and hopelessness related to thoughts of death by suicide. Professional help is available; anyone who feels suicidal should seek that help.

Basic Facts about Suicide

Threats of suicide must be taken seriously. More than 75% of young people who have ended their lives by suicide have talked to others about their intentions.

Although suicidal people are extremely unhappy, they are not necessarily mentally ill. Often, their unhappiness follows emotional disturbances, long painful illness, loss of someone important to them, or feelings and thoughts of helplessness and hopelessness.

People's thinking patterns change when they become very unhappy. They tend to think more than they usually would on how sad and hurt they feel and about the emptiness of their lives.

Suicide is common to all groups in society. It does not distinguish between genders, or among social and economic backgrounds, cultures, or age levels. It is an individual matter related to personal problems and it is possible to prevent it.

Suicidal people often cry for help by letting others know how they feel. Most of them are unsure of themselves and struggle with the difficulty of choosing to live or die. They tend to leave it to others to save them.

Observed improvement following a suicidal crisis does NOT mean that a suicide risk is over. Many suicides occur within about three months after the beginning of "improvement" – when the person has regained the energy to act in a self-destructive manner.

If saved from self-destruction and given professional help, suicidal people can go on to lead meaningful and productive lives. Suicidal crises last only a limited time, but the problems that created them may be ongoing.

A Cry for Help

People who are seriously thinking of suicide are undergoing a crisis in which they are not their normal selves. Suicide attempts reflect deeply-felt unhappiness and a desperate need for understanding and caring. Every effort should be made to get at the cause of unhappiness.

Evidence shows that if a person is prevented from committing suicide, he or she is very thankful afterwards. Suicide only leaves a trail of tragedy. It places an unusually heavy burden on those left behind. Family members and friends may identify with the victim and become preoccupied with the fear that they too may resort to suicide if life becomes very difficult.

Family and friends are in the best position to give emergency assistance. The first step is the frank recognition that the person is at present very unhappy and thus potentially suicidal.

There is no substitute for professional assistance in the treatment of a suicidal crisis. Don't hesitate to ask for this assistance if there is any doubt about whether or not a person is at risk of death by suicide.

Signals of Distress

Some of the following are conditions and concerns for us to recognize. (One or more might be observed when a person is suicidal.)
  - Direct threats of suicide and repeated references to death
  - Description of plans for death
  - Unexpected and unexplained absences from school or work
  - General withdrawal and noticeable change in motivation; such as decreased social activity, altered school performance and attitude, apparent loss of involvement in interests and hobbies, and disposing of possessions
  - Self-dislike and a profound sense of personal and social inadequacy and failure, "feeling down about life"
  - Anxiousness, restlessness, extreme tension, agitation, loss of appetite, loss of weight, tiredness, exhaustion, chronic sleeplessness, lack of concentration

– Attempts at escaping painful thoughts and feelings, perceived losses, or troubled relationships by over-indulging in alcohol or drugs

Understanding Suicidal Situations

Crises occur when life's pressures become too great and intolerable. Professional help and reassurance are needed as these periods are painful and dangerous.

Impulsive Suicidal Behavior

In moments of anger, hurt, disappointment, or frustration, a person can react with unplanned suicidal behavior. In reality, sudden impulsive reactions to stress arise from unsuccessful struggles with the tensions and confusions of living.

Serious or Chronic Illness

As long as a person is alive, there is hope for improvement in his or her condition. Constant pain or fear of incurable illness may lead to thoughts of suicide as an escape from suffering.

Suicide Attempts as Ways of Communicating

Suicide attempts may communicate a "message" to another person. They may be a way of striking back at others, or of persuading them not to take an unwanted action, or of expressing feelings without using words. A suicide attempt cannot correct basic difficulties between people.

Thoughts and Feelings That Life Is No Longer Worth Living

Feeling troubled, isolated, inadequate, or alienated from school, parents, and friends, may result over time in "depression." The loss of a loved one, through death or separation or rejection, or the loss of good feelings about oneself through failure in achievement or in important relationships may deeply intensify unhappiness.

You Can Be Helped

Talk to a responsible friend, teacher or adult whom you can trust.
Ask them to assist you in finding help:

Family Doctor
Crisis Centers and Distress Lines
Hospitals and Psychiatric Centers and Children's Treatment Centers

Religious Counselors
Family and Friends

Board of Education

Teacher	Guidance Counselor
Vice-Principal	Principal
School Nurse	Social Worker
Psychoeducational Consultant	Psychiatrist

Community Agencies

Suicide Prevention Resources In Your Community

Distress Centers
Provide a 24-hour telephone response to the emotionally distressed, anxious, lonely and suicidal; they offer a listening ear and/or help in life-threatening situations.

Hospitals
Emergency Department in your local General Hospital: numbers listed in your local yellow pages under Hospitals.

Youth Services
Offer counseling advice and support.

Student Services
See your school psychiatrist, psychologist, psychoeducational consultant or social worker; contact can be arranged through your school office or through the Student Services Office.

Guidance Services
See your Guidance Counselor at school or phone Guidance and Counseling Services.

Other Services
For counselling and assistance:
Family Service Association
Public Health Nurses

Conclusion

Suicide is an act of despair which grows out of an individual's sense that his or her life has moved completely beyond personal control. Our understanding of the human condition has refined our ability to recognize and prevent this occurrence. The problems and personal turmoil which lead one to consider suicide are real and seem overwhelming. They are to be taken seriously.

Very often confusion and uncertainty interfere with decision making. While in a suicidal crisis, thinking processes, inferences and evaluation of information are distorted. With professional help these thinking patterns can change. Negative self-perceptions and feelings of alienation, unhappiness and despair can be alleviated.

There is a tendency to leave the ultimate decision to others. Signs are communicated to those who are watchful. These signs are cries for help. The problem the person is wrestling with is not that he or she actually wants to die. The real question is whether or not there is a way to continue living.

Many people might feel uncertain of how to respond to a suicidal threat. When confronted with suicide one's first reactions are ones of great concern and an overwhelming desire to do the "right thing." As has already been indicated in this booklet, acting appropriately and quickly is important. Any threat or attempted suicide should be treated as an emergency. Every effort should be made to obtain professional help.

People who feel suicidal should not hesitate to seek professional help. Assistance is available from many sources.

The Board of Education for the City of Toronto gratefully acknowledges the Canadian Mental Health Association for the opportunity to adapt the information contained in its own pamphlet, which served as a basis for this booklet.

This pamphlet was prepared by:
Michael Brotman, Ester Cole and Mel LaFountaine
Others who contributed were:
Ted Brown, Marlinda Freire, Greg McClare and Jane Siegel

This pamphlet is also available in: French, Chinese, Greek, Italian, Polish, Portuguese, Spanish, and Vietnamese.

"Remember that a 'cry for help' should always be taken seriously. The best response is fast, professional help." [Canadian Mental Health Association]

Appendix B: Coping with Tragic Events

As in a personal crisis, when a tragedy takes place in a school community, students, staff and parents experience feelings of grief, shock, denial, confusion, sorrow and helplessness. If a crisis is not resolved, overwhelming feelings of depression or burnout may occur. School-age children who have faced traumatic events in their past, are particularly vulnerable in such situations. For them, a school crisis is likely to activate past fears and memories and may result in cumulative stress reactions. Such children will likely require individualized or small group support facilitated by a mental health professional (Cole, 1992; Lafond, 1990; Poland & Pitcher, 1990).

Disasters and tragedies can take many forms. In some cases, pre-planning can be done (i.e., an anticipated death). Others may be sudden and allow little or no time for pre-planning. Specific situations call for specific responses. However, given the challenges faced by schools, education systems, have established crisis intervention teams which can be called to provide assistance with management procedures and mental health supports (Purvis, Porter, Authement, & Born, 1991; Toronto Board of Education, 1991; Waddell & Thomas, 1989).

Crisis Teams

(1) Team membership is usually comprised of mental health professionals, administrators and educators. The role of the team is to support staff in decision making following a tragedy; to assist in identifying at-risk students; to support effective coping behaviors during extreme emotional states; to provide information about resources and community supports.

(2) When teams are formed, it is recommended that training include: warning signs of at-risk students; active listening skills; reporting procedures; crisis interviews; grief reactions; explaining death to children; postvention; legal considerations in emergency situations; changes in confidentiality dealing with the media; documentation of action plans and activity checklists, and sharing of information. The training may include case studies, which are included at the end of this appendix; role play intervention techniques; dealing with caregivers' reactions; communication techniques; team debriefing and multicultural and religious considerations.

(3) During a crisis, the role of the team cannot be viewed as static. Needs may change very quickly and members may be called upon to act as consultants, spokes people, crisis counsellors, providers of information and organizers of activities. Mental health professionals should indicate to the team leader and the school principal their areas of competence and preference in working with staff, students or parents. This is likely to assist in administrative planning and maximize appropriate services.

(4) Crisis teams need to maintain active lists of resources, emergency telephone numbers, referral procedures, lists of trained translators/interpreters and appropriate community agencies.

(5) When called upon, a crisis team should conduct a brief needs assessment and plan intervention steps, which should be reviewed as the needs change during the school day. At the end of the day, the team should have a debriefing, record administrative procedures and plan follow-up activities.

Crisis Intervention Steps

(1) Determine how staff, students and parents will be informed about the tragedy. If a death occurred outside the school, the principal or designate should confirm the information by contacting the affected family to discuss their wishes. Immediate action is called for. The administration needs to be prepared to deal with staff and students as soon as possible.

(2) All teachers should be informed if possible, in a short staff meeting. The circumstances will determine whether it is desirable or possible first to convene a teachers' meeting. Mental health professionals should take part in such a meeting since vulnerable reactions are to be expected.

(3) Staff members must talk to students about the event in order to help control the spread of rumors. Immediate attention will show students care and respect for their reactions.

(4) Decide about scheduling changes. This decision will likely depend on the nature and extent of the crisis and might vary from grade to grade. In general, the sooner the needs of individuals or groups are met, the less complex it will become to return to a normal routine.

(5) Regular classes will need to be suspended while discussions take place. Teachers have to know who will provide immediate out of class assistance to needy children and where to send them.

(6) An effective method for informing parents may be to prepare a letter by the principal, with input from a mental health professional, to be sent home with the students.

(7) Parents whose children's reactions are assessed as extreme should be contacted by phone and counselling services offered.

(8) In case of a death, funeral and memorial services will require decisions about staff and/or student attendance. If possible, parents should accompany their children.

(9) Following a suicide, it is important to support students without giving too much prominence to the tragedy in order not to sensationalize the death. Students may feel anxiety, confusion and guilt. It is thus important to stress that the death was not their fault. They should be encouraged to re-establish routines so they can begin to feel more control. Staff should stress that they cannot fully answer the question "why did it happen?" However, large group and small group sessions can provide opportunities to express mutual and communal feelings of loss by staff and students.

(10) Mental health professionals should consult with the school about on-going opportunities to deal with the crisis. This may include long-term counselling in and out of the school.

(11) Teachers who deal with students' reactions on a daily basis may require support and information about additional resources. It is important for the helpers to take time to deal with their own reactions in order to prevent burnout and maximize functional working relationships at school.

(12) Counsellors should inform staff and parents about delayed reactions in children. A similar crisis in another location may trigger intense renewed feelings of stress. Also, anniversary dates may reactivate depressive feelings. Planning remembrance events or acknowledging the date may divert renewed stress reactions.

Coping with Bereavement

The acceptance of a tragic event concerning death varies from person to person, and reactions may continue to occur for a long period. It may be months before the significance of a death is fully realized. In some people the grief process may cause depression; in others it may result in numbness or anger. Children's reactions must be understood in the context of developmental stages. Children's cognitive development plays a significant role in the extent to which a child will understand the meaning of death (Heath, 1990; McHutchion, 1991; Perry, 1990; Pitcher & Poland, 1992; Poland, 1994).

(1) Caregivers need to consult with educators and parents about developmental phases in understanding death and children's process of grieving:

Ages	Interventions
Ages 3-5 Death is seen as reversible. Magical thinking makes children feel that good behavior will reverse events.	Children need to ask the same questions over and over. Reassure them by trying to answer questions and by being available to engage in activities. Regression and angry outbursts should be recognized as stress reactions.
Ages 6-9 Children begin to understand the finality of death and the fact that it is irreversible; they do not understand death as a universal concept.	Note that children may express fears and worry about death of loved ones. Reassure them by helping them to name and describe their feelings. Death is likely to be viewed in a concrete and personified way.
Ages 10-12 Many children have the emotional security to express an understanding of death as final and inevitable. They begin to associate death with cessation of bodily functions.	Reassure them that it is normal to feel sad or angry. Encourage questions and give permission to grieve. Guilt may increase when children are unable to understand why the loss occurred. Explain the death in a clear and direct manner.
Adolescence As teens begin to gain more independence and start to plan for the future, they also begin to realize the finality of all life.	Teenagers need to be provided with opportunities to grieve. They require adult support and close communication with peers. They may exhibit intense and/or unpredictable reactions and need reassurance that some aspects of their lives have not changed.

(2) Cultural differences must be considered when working with students during a tragic event. Some backgrounds encourage overt expression of grief while others condone suppression of such feelings. It is thus important for caregivers to familiarize themselves with cross-cultural expressions of grief in order to understand children's reactions and to identify accurately those in need of more individualized support.

(3) Mental health professionals should consult with educators and parents about the developmental phases of grief resolution. The *first phase* is often characterized by shock and numbing of feelings. Denial and disbelief may also be expressed at this stage. The *second phase* of acute grief follows reactions of alarm. It may be characterized by disorganization, sadness, internal conflict and guilt. It may take over three months for these intense feelings to subside. In children who have experienced early losses, it may take two years before the grief process is completed. The *third phase* involves the understanding and acceptance of the loss and a decrease in symptoms such as frequent crying. Most children are able to verbalize their awareness of the loss and increase their self-reliance.

(4) Mental health professionals should share with educators relevant literature on tragic events. Many school systems have developed central resource materials and curricula, which are likely to help school-age children deal with their feelings and stressful experiences (see for example, O'Toole, 1989). Through age-appropriate readings, children are likely to learn that their thoughts and feelings are seen as a normal part of the bereavement process. Books for teachers, parents and counsellors should also be included in the central resource materials. It is important to select multicultural and multilingual readings which represent an inclusive school community.

(5) Help identify for staff and parents normal grief reactions in school-aged children. Symptoms may include: sadness, distraction, withdrawal from activities, anxiety, fears and bad dreams. Indicate that delayed grief may result in suppression of feelings, preoccupation with morbid thoughts, increased isolation or aggression.

(6) When mental health professionals become involved during a tragic event they are likely to provide an example of appropriate caring, openness and immediate availability. Parents should be encouraged to inform educators about changes they have noticed in their child's functioning. This is likely to facilitate an appropriate assessment of the situation and a referral for counseling if the reactions are prolonged or disturbing in their intensity (for example frequent nightmares; bedwetting or regressive behaviors).

(7) Counselors who provide secondary prevention activities in classrooms may consult with teachers about the following activities:

   - *Discussion* – this constructive group activity may support the healing process following a debriefing about the tragedy. The students are likely to have questions and associations. They might choose to share memories or brainstorm about coping strategies. Based on the students' developmental stages, different issues will likely be addressed. Encourage communication since it is a powerful avenue for alleviating negative pressures.
   - *Drama* – this type of flexible activity allows children to project their feelings in safe ways. For younger children, use puppets as a way to encourage communication and validation of emotions. Older children may like to use mime or act out a short skit, which they have created about the event.
   - *Creative expression* – writing, art, music or sharing of poems from home may be presented to the group ("I brought a tape of a song I like to listen to when I am sad..."). Some older students may not wish to share their writings or artwork with others. Their privacy should be respected in order to minimize stress and pressure.

- *Physical play* – during a crisis period students' time is often structured. However, physical play and choice activities in and out of class can release tension and is viewed as an important way to channel feelings and stress reactions. Although children may exhibit different levels of activity, the inclusion of play will provide a balance during a difficult day or period.
- *Readings* – children may choose to be read to since this is a familiar activity associated with attention and care. The reader may choose a story or poem with a theme related to the tragic event. This can be followed by a discussion in a caring atmosphere.
- *Group projects* – this type of activity is likely to enhance children's sense of belonging and control. By planning and working together, children are likely to feel less isolated with their thoughts. Activities such as writings, memory projects, murals or planning an assembly will allow for projection of emotions and decrease of anxiety.

(8) Some students may benefit from participating in peer counseling or a bereavement support group. This will likely help them integrate their crisis experiences and losses. This type of group counseling is usually facilitated by a mental health professional. The objectives of this secondary or tertiary intervention are a) to provide opportunities to express feelings related to the event, b) to provide sharing opportunities and learn effective copying skills, c) to assist students in problem identification and sharing of problem-solving strategies, and d) to enhance self-esteem and social skills.

(9) Specific efforts should be made by educators and mental health professionals to identify students whose personal adjustment is fragile. In individual counselling, review the circumstances surrounding the event. Listen with empathy and reflect back the reactions expressed. Indicate that the feelings and reactive behaviors are understandable. Establish a relationship, which will facilitate future meetings for support and the restoration of coping skills.

(10) When consulting with parents about helpful interventions share some of the following strategies:
- Children under stress benefit from hearing that they are not alone and that a parent will stay with them to comfort and reassure them.
- Establish continuity in the daily routines for the child.
- Let the children stay close to you in order to feel secure, and answer questions with simple and accurate information.
- Provide extra attention and allow children to express their feelings. Your comfort will reassure them.
- Acknowledge that regressive behaviors may reflect children's fears rather than misbehavior. Encourage age appropriate conduct by focusing on joint activities and verbalizing your approval and acceptance.
- Model for the children how to cope with a crisis situation. Try to have activities, which involve all family members. Allow children to help others in the family.
- If the children continue to experience signs of stress or grief, counselling may be necessary. Contact the school for a referral to an appropriate mental health professional at school or to a counselling service in the community.

Tragic Events Support Team (T.E.S.T.)

Vignettes for small group discussion

(1) Mary Smith is a grade 3 student. On Friday after school, she had a birthday party at her home. Many of her classmates came to the party and were picked up by their parents at 6:00 p.m. Her father and his business partner were killed in a car accident on Friday evening. On Monday morning, the school staff and some students learned about Mary's tragedy.

   (a) What is the role of the school in such a case?
   (b) What should Mary's teacher do in order to get support for herself and the class?
   (c) Should the class have a discussion about the tragedy? What should be the focus of activities?
   (d) Should the parents of the class be contacted?
   (e) Should the T.E.S.T. be contacted? Why? When?
   (f) How do you see your role in supporting the school?

(2) On Sunday evening at 9:00 p.m. a teacher in a senior school calls the Principal at her home to tell her that he learned about the sudden death of a teacher who had been depressed for a long time. The teacher heard from a friend that it might have been a suicide. They are both shocked and overwhelmed. The Principal ends the conversation by saying: "Leave it with me, I will deal with it." On Monday morning a student comes to his teacher and asks if it is true that Mr. X died. The student heard about it from his mother. The student wants to know how Mr. X died. Other students come into the class and stand around.

   (a) When should the school staff be told about the death?
   (b) When and how should the students be told?
   (c) What process should be used to help staff deal with students' reactions and concerns?
   (d) What should be the procedure for identifying "high risk" students during this week?
   (e) Who should contact the family?
   (f) What resources would the school benefit from?
   (g) How do you see your role in supporting the school?

Chapter 18
Violence Prevention in Schools: Knowledge, Skills, and Interventions

Ester Cole

Violence is a barometer of social stress. It is a major problem in many homes and communities. Youth aggression and violent behaviors are among the most challenging issues facing educators and mental health professionals. Schools, which are a mirror of society, have become intervention sites for numerous learning and social problems affecting children and adolescents. The range of educational goals, which have expanded far beyond the traditional academic curriculum, and the transfer of family and social problems to the school have reinforced the need for coordinated school and community-based services (Cole, 1995, 1998; Welsh, 2001).

Violence directed toward the self has steadily increased over the past three decades. Suicide has become the second or third cause of death for young people in North America (Cole, 1992). In the United States, rates of violence and victimization have increased significantly. Homicide and suicide are leading causes of death among children and youth under the age of 21. Sixteen to nineteen–year–olds have the highest rate of handgun victimization among all age groups. It is estimated that 1 of 16 adolescents are victims of violent crimes (Hughes & Hasbrouck, 1996; C. O'Donnell, 1995; Soriano, Soriano, & Jimenez, 1994).

Data concerning school violence has been well documented in several countries. Although caution should govern the analysis of crime statistics (Hyman & Perone, 1998b), recent studies point out troubling facts and figures. Canadian studies have documented that nearly half of the 15-year-old boys and one-quarter of the girls took part in bullying activities at school (Canadian Council on Social Development, 1997). An Ontario study by Craig and Pepler (1997) concluded that the majority of bullying episodes (68%) took place close to school buildings.

In a five-year follow-up study in Ontario, Cole and Brown (1996) found that 46% of secondary and 59% of elementary school consultees described students as often or sometimes exhibiting violent behaviors. Overall, the characteristics of students referred for consultation continued to emphasize academic and social-emotional needs, which tended to be more prevalent in the higher age groups. The impact of youth aggression was recently documented in a UK study which surveyed school-age children about their reactions to violent incidents. One-third of those surveyed expressed real concerns about being victimized in school, and the ratio was similar for both boys and girls. More generally, the study concluded that for a substantial number of pupils, school was therefore associated with feelings of insecurity and vulnerability (Noaks & Noaks, 2000).

The phenomenon of violence must be understood in the context of change in society at large and the psychosocial risk factors associated with higher rates of mental health problems in children (Cole, 1998, 1999). These risk factors include poverty, parental psychopathology, and maltreatment. Mental health problems have also been linked to alienation, poor socialization, deficits in interpersonal communication, and poor school performance (Offord, Boyle, & Racine, 1990; Offord & Lipman, 1996; Osofsky, 1995; Paavola et al., 1995; Wolfe, Scott, Wekerle, & Pittman, 2001).

Many Canadian and American schools have undergone demographic changes consistent with migration patterns. Refugee children may have been victimized by wars and trauma; cultural barriers for newcomers may result in feelings of exclusion and marginalization from mainstream culture; prejudice and discrimination result in alienation and are believed to be related to behavioral maladjustment (Cole, 1996). In addition, the structure of families has undergone changes. More school-aged children witness family break-ups and experience significant stress associated with abuse and maltreatment. This implies losses of support systems, nurturing adults, and stable living conditions (Conway, 1990; Emery & Lauman-Billings, 1998; Juby & Farrington, 2001; Thompson & Wilcox, 1995). Also, economic restructuring has resulted in new trends for some and in increasing poverty for others. Poverty and economic gaps are contributing factors to poor living conditions in urban neighborhoods and to higher unemployment rates. This in turn increases frustration, family stress, and instability (Advisory Committee on Children's Services, 1990; Children and Youth Project Steering Committee, 1994; Herrenkohl, Egolf, & Herrenkohl, 1997; Human Resources Development Canada, 1996; Thompson & Wilcox, 1995).

Access to firearms, involvement in antisocial groups, and drug abuse have increased people's awareness and fears of violence (Hughes & Hasbrouck, 1996; Hyman & Perone, 1998b). However, the phenomenon of violence has also led to demands for public education about violence prevention in and out of the home. Child abuse and domestic violence policies and reporting procedures, for example, have become the norm in many communities (Hyman & Perone, 1998a; Osofsky, 1995; Paavola et al., 1995; Thompson & Wilcox, 1995).

Within the framework of advocacy and demands for coordinated prevention efforts, media violence has been subject to growing criticism. American studies document that children and youth watch on average between 23 to 28 hours of television per week and are exposed to distorted versions of glamorized violence towards women, minorities, and youth. Media violence tends to desensitize viewers and can contribute to children's levels of aggressiveness (Hughes & Hasbrouck, 1996). Although children can be taught critical viewing skills, in reality many children are unsupervised when they watch television or play video games and continue to be exposed to violent behaviors. The American Psychological Association Commission on Violence and Youth (1993), concluded that higher levels of viewing violence on film and television are correlated with increased acceptance of aggressive attitudes and increased acting-out behaviors.

In recent years, the need for coordinated prevention efforts resulted in educational policies and programs (see for example Ontario Ministry of Education, 1994, 2000; Paavola et al., 1995). In addition to the documentation of procedures for reporting violent incidents, schools were directed to include educational and violence-prevention initiatives. Common directions often lead to staff development; codes of behavior; procedures for dealing with violent incidents; strategies for coping with the aftermath of violence; early identification of high risk students, and mental health prevention and intervention services.

Such frameworks are consistent with psychological knowledge that brought the study of violence and aggression into the realm of science. We have come to learn that children who are exposed to violence and who exhibit early aggression are at a risk for antisocial behavior later in life if effective intervention is not provided (Latimer, 2001; Moffitt, Caspi, Dickson, Silva, & Stanton 1996; Towberman, 1994; Wolfe et al., 2001).

The focus on the prevention continuum of programs highlights the partnership between psychology and education. School psychology areas of knowledge and skills are needed as schools grapple with societal pains of economic inequality, prejudice, and desensitization towards violence and adverse social circumstances. Effective prevention and intervention programs draw on understanding developmental and sociocultural risk factors for antisocial behavior and link this knowledge to the development and evaluation of programs (APA, 1993; Stage & Quiroz, 1997; Sterling-Turner, Robinson, & Wilcznski, 2001).

Risk Factors for Anti-Social Behaviors

Children and Youth Characteristics

Children at risk for conduct problems often exhibit low tolerance for frustration in early childhood. They tend to be more impulsive and angry when their wishes are not met in social situations. They often resent perceived authority figures and may associate with delinquent subgroups. They frequently have attributional biases: over-perceiving hostility in others and habitually blaming others for wrongdoing. During conflict, they underestimate their own aggressiveness and rely excessively on nonverbal action. In a study about the effects of hostile attribution on adolescents' aggressive responses, it was found that perceived hostile intent influenced the level of aggressive responses used by adolescents in social situations. Study findings point to the relevance of an information-processing model to the prediction of aggressive behavior in adolescents (Van Oostrum & Horvath, 1997).

Without proper interventions, these characteristics and behaviors may increase in frequency and continue to include attention-deficit problems, academic frustration, poor problem-solving strategies, and low expectations for non-aggressive means to resolve problems (Herrenkohl et al., 1997; Kazdin, 1997; Phillips, Schwean, & Saklofske, 1997). School bullies, for example, may intimidate and victimize peers. They may feel powerful and draw others into aggressive behavior. However, without corrective interventions, bullies are at risk for antisocial behaviors in adult life and unstable relationships (Charach, Pepler, & Ziegler, 1995; Craig & Pepler, 1996; Larson, 1994; Lewin, 1999; Ziegler & Pepler, 1993).

Studies of youth violence have expanded to include characteristics of both aggressors and victims. Pope and Bierman (1999), for example, found that children who are characterized by irritable-inattentive behavior in late childhood experience ostracism and peer victimization in early adolescence. The authors suggested that victims of bullying may be characterized by deficits in emotional regulation, which leads to pervasive difficulties responding to social situations. Another study by Schwartz (2000), investigated the behavioral profile and psychosocial adjustment of subgroups of victims and aggressors in elementary school peer groups. Findings indicated that impairments in behavioral and emotional regulation were most evident for aggressive victims. They were also characterized by academic problems, peer rejection, and emotional distress. Study findings stress the need to consider subgroups of victimized children.

Family Characteristics

Early onset of antisocial child behavior is associated with several family dynamic characteristics. These include poor parental management, unclear family boundaries, poor parental communications, adults modeling poor self-control, inconsistent roles and rules of discipline, contradictory behavioral standards, erratic exercise of control, lack of family cohesiveness, negative interactions including physical threats and assaults, drug and alcohol abuse, history of losses, and mistrust in school-home communication (Emery & Laumann-Billings, 1998; Paavola, et al., 1995; Sprott, Doob, & Jenkins, 2001; The Task Force on the Health Effects of Woman Abuse, 2000).

Studies indicate that abused or neglected children are at increased risk for developing antisocial disorders in later years regardless of gender, race, age, or socioeconomic status (American Psychiatric Association, 1994; Dauvergne & Johnson, 2001;

Finkelhor & Dziuba-Leatherman, 1994; Luntz & Widom, 1994; Patterson, 1986). For example, preschool antecedents of adolescent assaultive behavior were researched in a longitudinal study by Herrenkohl et al. (1997). The results concluded that the harsher the physical discipline during the preschool years, the greater the likelihood of the child developing assaultive behavior in late adolescence. A more recent study by Wolfe et al. (2001) examined the relationship between child maltreatment, adjustment problems, and dating violence. Results were consistent with earlier findings by concluding that maltreatment is a significant risk factor for adolescent difficulties. Youths with maltreatment histories reported significant adjustment problems in adolescence that differed by gender. Females reported considerable emotional distress, including anger, depression, and anxiety. Males reported fewer symptoms of emotional turmoil but were significantly more likely to be abusive toward their dating partners.

These types of correlations between family violence and later maladjustment have called for early interventions. Unlike chronic family situations, with mild to moderate abuse, multilevel programs, which include stress management and relationship skills, may reduce the likelihood of continued aggression in children and adults (Emery & Laumann-Billings, 1998; Lumsden, 2000; Sprague & Walker, 2000).

Safe Schools

School effectiveness research emphasizes the quality of children's school experience and its relationship to socialization, self-esteem, and achievement outcomes. This literature also indicates that strong leadership and staff, parents, and students participating in decision making enhance safe school effectiveness. Also, clear expectations for student behavior and learning and frequent monitoring of performance contribute to a cooperative climate and a sense of ownership of the school (Cesarone, 1999; Cole, 1995; Morrison & Morrison, 1994; Stephens, 1994; Sugar & Horner, 1999).

There is encouraging evidence that programs employed on a school-wide basis can be effective in reducing levels of antisocial behavior and improving the school climate (Cesarone, 1999; Johnson, 1998; Offord & Boyle, 1993). Several countries have adapted anti-bullying programs modeled after the Norwegian national intervention developed by Olweus (1987, 1991, 1994, 1997, 1999). Longitudinal studies documented a significant reduction of bullying incidents when a comprehensive intervention plan was developed and employed consistently. Olweus' model operates at the level of community, whole school, classroom, and individual students. Given the complex problems related to bullying and victimization, the pervasive nature of the phenomenon and the under-reporting of the prevalence of aggression, an ecological approach to restructuring is called for. When this is achieved through collaborative planning, the social environment of the school tends to change, thereby indicating to all involved that aggression is regarded as inappropriate and unacceptable behavior.

Program goals include staff's, parents' and students' information about the problem; communication of clear rules against aggressive and violent behavior (i.e., "zero tolerance" school policies); and provision of individual and group counseling to victims of aggression. Through educational leadership, community meetings, and staff in-service, appropriate decisions are made to strengthen school-home ties and enforce behavior standards (Cesarone, 1999; Craig & Pepler, 1997; Nettles, Mucherah, & Jones, 2000; O'Connell, Pepler, & Craig, 1999; Ziegler & Pepler, 1993).

The transformation of safe school communities includes additional characteristics. First, through curriculum planning and coordination with social support systems, schools provide programs which acknowledge the ethnic and cultural diversity of the learners and staff. Second, school grounds are well-maintained and supervised by staff, students, and parent volunteers. Third, the physical setting of the school is used by the community both during the school day and in off-hours. Fourth, school needs are clarified with input from all stakeholders and multidisciplinary approaches are developed in order to address the needs. Last, school and community support programs are monitored and outcomes are assessed. When the culture of safe schools changes, there is a reduction in over-attachment and over-reliance on very few individuals in leadership positions and a demystification of the uniqueness of community systems. Rather, complementary programs are developed by emphasizing a team approach, staff development, peer coaching, and mentoring (Cole, 1995; Farrell, Meyer, Kung, & Sullivan, 2001; McLaughlin, Leohe, & Henderson, 1997; Ziegler, Stevenson-Finn, & Stem, 1997).

Prevention and Intervention Programs

Comprehensive violence prevention programs are ecological in orientation by supporting complementary initiatives. Rather then viewing students' problems of under-achievement and social misconduct as symptoms of dysfunction, they are seen as a reflection of poor interaction between individuals and their environment (Cole, 1995). A conceptual framework for organizing prevention approaches links three types of interrelated programs and services familiar to school psychologists. Primary prevention initiatives are programs intended to maximize the educational progress and personal development of all students. These types of programs are usually implemented when the school system or high-level administrators identify needs and document policies which guide the organization towards change. Secondary prevention programs are directed toward students who are at risk. Although their difficulties have not yet led to a crisis, they require some specialized social or academic intervention if their progress is to continue. Tertiary prevention programs are oriented towards students who are in crisis. For them, the problems experienced are of a magnitude that significantly interferes with their academic gains and social adjustment (Cole, 1996; Cole & Siegel, 1990).

Collaborative consultation is a key component in planning and facilitating the implementation of prevention and intervention initiatives. Primary prevention programs are supported by evidence which indicates that interventions in early childhood can reduce aggression and can also affect risk factors associated with antisocial behaviors, including poor school achievement and inconsistent parenting (APA, 1993). Educational programs geared at health issues and preschool readiness skills are examples of interventions that include multiple components in children's social context in and out of the family (Hyman & Perone, 1998a; Jaffe & Baker, 1999; Offord & Boyle, 1993).

Early prevention programs can also prepare children for dealing with developmental challenges and transitions (Steinberg, 1999). Because antisocial behaviors tend to increase during adolescence, it is likely that early violence prevention efforts will lead to a reduction in maladjustment. Also, there is evidence that indicates that success in treating aggressive and antisocial youth after the disturbances are underway is limited (APA, 1993; Lewin, 1999; Lumsden, 2000; Resnick & Burt, 1996).

Primary prevention of school violence can encompass a range of efforts through the curriculum and school-based activities. These types of initiatives create a climate that makes disclosures of aggression safe and promotes the development of alternatives to antisocial behaviors. Prosocial skills include examples such as peer programs (buddy systems, peer tutoring); staff mentoring (e.g., students are assigned to staff members for support); conflict resolution programs (peer mediation and students trained as peacemakers aim to reduce schoolyard conflicts by focusing on verbal mediation and anger management); school-wide curriculum that teaches equity concepts and critical thinking skills (through projects, cooperative learning activities, and media literacy education) staff in-service; parental support through committees and information meetings; and student training in social skills and mediation techniques (Bear, 1990; Committee for Children, 1997; Community Board Program, 1995; Gibbs, 1995; Girard & Koch, 1996; Larson, 1994; Lions Quest, 1997).

Secondary prevention programs aim to improve the behavior, cognitive, and affective skills of children at risk for later adolescent antisocial conduct. Both proactive and reactive services can be operationalized through multidisciplinary consultations that focus on problem solving. This type of consultation utilizes a series of stages that structure activities including problem analysis, plan implementation, and plan evaluation. Through this process, examples regarding the severity of the problem are identified (threats, tantrums, assaults). Those are followed by an analysis of events preceding the child's behavior or factors that exacerbate the frequency of problem behavior (grieving over losses, abuse, academic frustration, problems with peers). Areas of strength related to the child, family, and school are identified, as are skills and attitudes related to interventions (Bruskewitz, 1998; Ceballo, 2000; Kratochwill, Elliott, & Rotto, 1990).

Direct counselling with child, family or groups of children can be monitored through multidisciplinary consultation teams. Indirect services can include consultations with family, school, teacher(s) or agencies. Examples of indirect consultation are
– planning behavior modification reinforcement techniques, behavior goal setting

and contracting, parent management training, and monitoring of alternative behavioral techniques.

Anger-coping interventions with aggressive children have been described in several studies which utilize cognitive-behavioral techniques. The interventions train groups of children to recognize the interrelationship between cognition, emotional responses, and behavior. Using role-playing, self-instruction, physiological cues to anger, goal setting, and problem solving in social situations, children learn to gain more insight into their own behavior and better cope with anger-arousing situations (Phillips et al., 1997; Smith, Siegel, O'Conner, & Thomas, 1994). Stage and Quiroz (1997), for example, studied interventions to decrease disruptive classroom behaviors. They conducted a meta-analysis of 99 studies and concluded that group contingencies, self-management, differential reinforcement, functional assessment, and cognitive-behavioral interventions are likely to result in a substantial reduction of disruptive behavior for students treated.

Social skills training programs are likely to be more effective when combined with other initiatives, such as parent management training. Because aggressive behavior in children has many correlates, parent training programs tend to complement and strengthen direct interventions with aggressive youngsters. Typical aspects of parent programs include the reinforcement and modeling of pro-social communication and behavior, learning and using non-physical discipline procedures, self-management anger techniques, and monitoring of behaviors (Larson, 1994). Overall, secondary prevention programs that involve multi-modal approaches in treatment and curriculum are viewed as cost-effective (Johnson, 1998; Nettles et al., 2000).

Tertiary prevention programs are directed toward those who have had a history of repeated aggression. Those children and adolescents were either not identified earlier for intervention or failed to respond to short-term programs. At school, the frequency of their conduct problems can lead to victimization of others and at times requires crisis interventions. Although tertiary interventions are reactive to severe problems, they nevertheless aim to reduce the frequency of aggressive patterns of behavior.

Adolescent anger-control programs and stress inoculation training approaches aim to reduce the intensity, frequency, and duration of acting-out behaviors. More adaptive anger control skills are the main goal of training. Programs use strategies such as self-statements, relaxation, coping with emotional arousal, self-assessment, and skill application behaviors (Meichenbaum, 1985). These types of strategies can be used with small groups or modified for individual or family therapy.

Clearly, multi-modal treatment approaches tend to be more effective for youth with serious aggressive and violent behavior. These types of programs require the coordinated efforts of school and treatment settings. As well, family treatment and ongoing consultation with the school system or job training programs are likely to assist aggressive youth (APA, 1993; Centre for Educational Research and Innovation, 1998; Eber & Nelson, 1997; Kazdin, 1997; Myaard, Crowford, Jackson, & Alessi, 2000; Paavola et al., 1995; Resnick & Burt, 1996).

Table 1 provides an organizational framework for building safe schools and prevention services.

Table 1 An Organizational Framework for Safe Schools and Prevention Programs

Risk Indicators	Effective-functional Indicators
Community Characteristics	
– Poverty and unemployment	– Stable neighborhoods
– Desensitization to violence	– Steady employment
– Prejudice and racial discrimination	– Inclusive community leadership
– Access to firearms and drugs	– Community support systems
– Antisocial groups, gangs	– Outreach services
– Frequent mobility	– Crime prevention in partnership
– Poor health service	with police and schools
– Lack of social supports	
School Characteristics	
– Ineffective response to community diversity	– Programs promote equity and diversity
– Behavioral and academic expectations are unclear	– High expectations for learning
– Bullying and intimidation are common	– Schools coordinate prevention programs with community services
– No emergency response plans and procedures	– Staff inservice and team work are the norm
– Little parental involvement	– School grounds are clean and secure
– Limited inservice for staff	– Parents are partners in decision making and program planning
– Limited collaboration with community systems	– Students feel safe and respected
– Grounds are not well-maintained	– Discipline and expectations are clear and consistent
– School discipline is inconsistent	
Family Characteristics	
– Poor family cohesiveness	– Family cohesiveness
– Inconsistent rules of discipline	– Clear roles and rules
– Erratic exercise of power and control	– Shared power
– Threats and physical assaults	– Open communication
– Drug and alcohol abuse	– Appropriate family and individual boundaries
– History of losses and mental problems	– Positive coping skills
– Poor communication and defensive responses	– High academic expectations
– Poor relationship with school	– Bi-cultural supports
	– Modeling of positive social skills
	– Home-school partnership

Table 1 continued

Student Characteristics
- Poor impulse control
- Substance abuse
- Truancy and/or delinquency
- School failure
- Resentment of authority
- Repetitive pattern of anger and aggressive conduct
- Attributional biases – overperceiving hostile intentions
- Underestimation of own aggressiveness
- Habitual blame onto others
- Attention deficit problems
- Poor problem-solving strategies
- Unstable relationships

- High self-esteem
- Good verbal problem-solving strategies
- Positive social skills
- Ability to cope with stress and frustration in constructive ways
- Feeling supported in family and school
- Has academic success and positive perception of self as student and friend
- Sensitive to feelings of others
- Stable relationships
- Able to work cooperatively with others

Intervention Program Characteristics
- Fragmented services
- Lack of consultation
- Reactive short-term programs for high risk students and families
- Lack of evaluation of services
- Little knowledge of multicultural service needs
- Unimodal treatment services "top-down" communication style

- Interlinked prevention services
- Consultation which facilitates program planning
- Early interventions with children and families
- School-wide conflict resolution and peer mediation programs
- Proactive and reactive services
- Life skills programs
- Social skills training (role-playing, reinforcement feedback, peer support)
- Stress-inoculation training
- Anger control programs
- Parenting and family treatment programs
- Multimodal treatment
- Evaluation of programs

Implications for School Psychologists

Ecological models for violence prevention provide school psychologists with an opportunity to play a key role in program development. Safe school models require psychological knowledge and skills in order to sustain effective initiatives over time. In this regard, APA (1999) has provided leadership with its public education campaign in schools and community outreach events. The video "Warning Signs" and special involvement kits contain information and sample materials for carrying out educational and primary prevention programs in school communities. Since its publication, this program has had a positive impact on bottom-up and top-down initiatives in many school systems. However, although several national associations have been proactive in developing position papers and conferences on violence prevention, it is the day-to-day participation in school systems that will clarify the role and broaden the services of school psychologists. Social skills training, early childhood interventions directed towards parents, conflict resolution, communication and consultation skills, self-esteem programs, anger management, and tragic-events support teams are all examples of psychological services consistent with violence-free school movements (Horner & Sugar, 2000; Hyman & Perone, 1998a; Osofsky, 1995; Stage & Quiroz, 1997).

A diversified role for school psychologists will continue to provide an avenue for advocacy about the provision of preventively oriented services. However, this will require in-depth knowledge about educational systems, prevention activities, and involve parent management training, anti-racist curriculum, small group social skills training, multicultural needs and services, and program evaluation skills (Cole, 1996). Psychologists who work in education must recognize school violence as a systems problem and be prepared to deal with emerging issues that grow and change. Conceptual knowledge and skills training in the area of violence prevention should also become priority domains for training future school psychologists.

References

Advisory Committee on Children's Services. (1990). *Children first*. Toronto, ON: Queen's Printer.

American Psychiatric Association. (1994). *Diagnostic and statistical manual of mental disorders* (4th edition). Washington: Author.

American Psychological Association. (1993). *Commission on violence and youth* (Report, Vol.1). Washington DC.

American Psychological Association. (1999). *Warning signs – A youth anti-violence initiative*. Washington DC: Author.

Bear, G. C. (1990). Best practices in school discipline. In A. Thomas & J. Crimes (Eds.), *Best practices in school psychology II*. Washington, DC: National Association of School Psychologists.

Bruskewitz, R. (1998). Collaborative invention: A system of support for teachers attempting to meet the needs of students with challenging behaviors. *Preventing School Failure, 42(3)*, 129 – 134.

Canadian Council on Social Development. (1997). *The progress of Canada's children 1997*, Ottawa: CCSD.

Ceballo, R. (2000). The neighborhood club: A supportive intervention group for children exposed to urban violence. *American Journal of Orthopsychiatry, 70(3)*, 410-427.

Centre for Educational Research and Innovation (1998). *Coordinating services for children and youth at risk : A world view.* Paris: Organization for Economic Co-operation and Development.

Cesarone, B. (1999). Fostering resilience of children. *Childhood Education, 75(3),* 182-184.

Charach, A., Pepler, D., & Ziegler, S. (1995). Bullying at school: A Canadian perspective. *Education Canada, 35,* 12-18.

Children and Youth Project Steering Committee (1994). *Yours, mine and ours: Ontario's children and youth.* Toronto, ON: Queen's Printer.

Cole, E. (1992). Characteristics of students referred to school teams: Implications for preventative psychological services. *Canadian Journal of School Psychology, 8(1),* 23-36.

Cole, E. (1995). Responding to school violence: Understanding today for tomorrow. *Canadian Journal of School Psychology, 11(2),* 108-116.

Cole, E. (1996). An integrative perspective on school psychology. *Canadian Journal of School Psychology, 12 (2),* 115 – 121.

Cole, E. (1998). Special feature: Violence prevention in schools. *Youth Update, 16 (2),* 4-5.

Cole, E. (1999). Whole school approach to overcoming violence. *Orbit, 29 (4),* 38-39.

Cole, E., & Brown, R. (1996). Multidisciplinary school teams: A five-year follow-up study. *Canadian Journal of School Psychology, 12(2),* 155-168.

Cole, E., & Siegel, J. A. (Eds.). (1990). *Effective consultation in school psychology.* Toronto: Hogrefe & Huber Publishers.

Committee for Children (1997). *Second stop – A violence prevention curriculum* (Grades K – 9). Seattle, Washington: Committee for Children Publishers.

Community Board Program (1995). *Conflict resolution: A secondary school curriculum.* San Francisco, CA : Community Board Program Publishers.

Conway, J. F. (1990). *The Canadian family in crisis.* James Lorimer & Company, Publishers.

Craig, W. M., & Pepler, D. (1996). Bullying and victimization at school: What can we do about it? In S. Miller, J. Brodine, & T. Miller (Eds.), *Safe by design: Planning for peaceful school communities.* Seattle, Washington: Committee for Children.

Craig, W. M., & Pepler, D. (1997). Observations of bullying and victimization in the school yard. *Canadian Journal of School Psychology, 13(2),* 41-60.

Dauvergne, M., & Johnson, H. (2001). Children witnessing family violence. *Juristat.* Canadian Centre for Justice Statistics. Ottawa: Statistics Canada.

Eber L., & Nelson C. M. (1997). School-based wraparound planning: Integrating services for students with emotional and behavioral needs. *American Journal of Orthopsychiatry, 67(3),* 385-395.

Emery, R. E., & Laumann-Billings, L. (1998). An overview of the nature, causes, and consequences of abusive family relationships. *American Psychologist, 53(2),* 121-135.

Farrell, A. D., Meyer, A. L., Kung, E. M., & Sullivan, T. N. (2001). Development and evaluation of school-based violence prevention programs. *Journal of Clinical Child Psychology, 30(1),* 207-220.

Finkelhor, D. & Dziuba-Leatherman, J. (1994). Victimization of children. *American Psychologist, 49 (3),* 173-183.

Gibbs, J. (1995). *Tribes: A new way of learning and being together.* Sausalito, CA: Center Source Systems.

Girard, K., & Koch, S. J. (1996). *Conflict resolution in the schools: A manual for educators.* California: Jossey-Bass Inc.

Herrenkohl, R. C., Egolf, B. P., & Herrenkohl, E. C. (1997). Preschool antecedents of adolescent assaultive behavior: A longitudinal study. *American Journal of Psychiatry, 67*, 422-432.

Horner, R., & Sugar, G. (2000). School-wide behavior support: An emerging initiative (Special Issue). *Journal of Positive Behavioral Interventions, 2*, 231-233.

Hughes, J. N., & Hasbrouck, J. E. (1996). Television violence: Implications for violence prevention. *School Psychological Review, 25 (2)*, 134-151.

Human Resources Development Canada (1996). *Growing up in Canada*. Ottawa: Author.

Hyman, I. A., & Perone, D. (1998a). Introduction to the special theme section on school violence. *Journal of School Psychology, 36 (1)*, 3-5.

Hyman, I. A., & Perone, D. (1998b). The other side of school violence: Educator policies and practices that may contribute to student misbehavior. *Journal of School Psychology, 36(1)*, 7-27.

Jaffe, P. G., & Baker, L. L. (1999). Why changing the YOA does not impact youth crime: Developing effective prevention programs for children and adolescents. *Canadian Psychology, 40 (1)*, 22-29.

Johnson, G. M. (1998). Effectiveness of interventions for at-risk students: Inner-city school teacher evaluation. *Special Services in the Schools, 14(1-2)*, 77-103.

Juby, H., & Farrington, D. P. (2001). Disentangling the link between disrupted families and delinquency. *British Journal of Criminology, 41*, 22-40.

Kazdin, A. E. (1997). Practitioner review : Psychosocial treatments for conduct disorder in children. *Journal of Child Psychology and Psychiatry, 38(2)*, 161-178.

Kratochwill, T. R., Elliott, S. N., & Rotto, P. C. (1990). Best practices in behavioral consultation. In A. Thomas & J. C. Crimes (Eds.), *Best practices in psychology II*. Washington, DC: National Association of School Psychologists.

Larson, J. (1994). Violence prevention in the schools: A review of selected programs and procedures. *School Psychology Review, 23(2)*, 151-164.

Latimer, J. (2001). A meta-analytic examination of youth delinquency, family treatment and recidivism. *Canadian Journal of Criminology, 43 (2)*, 237-253.

Lewin, L. M. (1999). Childhood social predictors of adolescent antisocial behavior. *Journal of Abnormal Child Psychology, 27(4)*, 277-292.

Lions Quest (1997). *Skills for action* (secondary). Granville, OH: Quest International.

Lumsden, L. (2000). Early intervention to prevent violence. *Research Roundup, 17-1*.

Luntz, B. K., & Widom, C. S. (1994). Antisocial personality disorder in abused and neglected children grown up. *American Journal of Psychiatry, 151*, 670-674.

McLaughlin, M. J., Leohe, P. E., & Henderson, K. (1997). Strengthen school and community capacity. *Journal of Educational and Behavioral Disorders, 5(1)*, 15-23.

Meichenbaum, D. H. (1985). *Stress inoculation training*. New York : Pergamon Press.

Moffitt, T. E., Caspi, A., Dickson, N., Silva, P., & Stanton, W. (1996). Childhood-onset vs. adolescent-onset conduct disorder in males. *Development and Psychopathology, 8*, 399-424.

Morrison, G. M., & Morrison, R. L. (1994). School violence to school safety: Reframing the issue for school psychologists. *School Psychology Review, 23*, 236-256.

Myaard, M. J., Crowford C., Jackson, M., & Alessi, G. (2000). Applying behavior analysis within the wraparound process: A multiple baseline study. *Journal of Emotional Behavioral Disorders, 8(4)*, 216–229.

Nettles, S. M., Mucherah, W., & Jones, D. S. (2000). Understanding resilience: The role of social resources. *Journal of Education for Students Placed at Risk, 5(1-2)*, 47-60.

Noaks, J., & Noaks, L. (2000). Violence in schools: Risk, safety and fear of crime. *Educational Psychology in Practice, 16(1)*, 69-73.

O'Connell, P., Pepler, D. J., & Craig, W. M. (1999). Peer involvement in bullying: Insights and challenges for intervention. *Journal of Adolescence, 22(4)*, 437-452.

O'Donnell, C. R. (1995). Firearm deaths among children and youth, *American Psychologist, 50(9)*, 771-776.

Offord, D., & Boyle, M. (1993). Helping children adjust: A tri-ministry project, *ORBIT, 24*.

Offord, D., Boyle, M., & Racine, Y. (1990). *Ontario child health study: Children at risk*. Toronto, ON: Queen's Promise.

Offord, D. R., & Lipman, E. L. (1996). Emotional and behavioural problems. *Growing up in Canada*. Ottawa: Human Resources Development Canada, Statistics Canada.

Olweus, D. (1987). Schoolyard bullying – Grounds for intervention. *School Safety, 6*, 4-11.

Olweus, D. (1991). Bully/victim problems among school children: Some basic facts and effects of a school based intervention program. In D. Pepler & K. Rubin (Eds.), *The development & treatment of childhood aggression* (pp. 411-438). Hillsdale, NJ: Erlbaum.

Olweus, D. (1994). Annotation: Bullying at school: Basic facts and effects of a school-based intervention program. *Journal of Child Psychology and Psychiatry, 35*, 1171-1190.

Olweus, D. (1997). Bully/victim problems in school: Facts and intervention. *European Journal of Psychology of Education, 12*, 495-510.

Olweus, D. (1999). Norway. In P. K. Smith, Y. Morita, J. Junger-Tas, D. Olweus, R. Catalano, & P. Slee (Eds.), *The nature of school bullying*. New York: Routledge.

Ontario Ministry of Education. (1994). *Violence-free school policies*. Toronto: Author.

Ontario Ministry of Education. (2000). *Violence-free school policies*. Toronto: Author.

Osofsky, J. D. (1995). The effects of exposure to violence on young children. *American Psychologist, 50(9)*, 782-788.

Paavola, J. C., Cobb, C., Illback, R. J., Joseph, H. M. Jr., Torreulla, A., & Talley, R. C. (1995). *Comprehensive and coordinated psychological services for children: A call for service integration*. Washington, DC: American Psychological Association.

Patterson, G. R. (1986). Performance models for antisocial boys. *American Psychologist, 41*, 432-444.

Phillips, D., Schwean, V., & Saklofske, D. (1997). Treatment effects of a school based cognitive-behavioural program for aggressive children. *Canadian Journal of School Psychology, 13(1)*, 60-67.

Pope, A. W., & Bierman, K. L. (1999). Predicting adolescent peer problems and antisocial activities: The relative roles of aggression and dysregulation. *Developmental Psychology, 35*, 335-346.

Resnick G., & Burt, M. (1996). Youth at risk: Definitions and implications for service delivery. *American Journal of Orthopsychiatry, 66(2)*, 172-187.

Schwartz, D. (2000). Subtypes of victims and aggressors in children's peer groups. *Journal of Abnormal Child Psychology, 28 (2)*, 181-192.

Smith, S. W., Siegel, E. H., O'Conner, A., & Thomas, S. B. (1994). Effects of cognitive-behavioral training on angry behavior and aggression of three elementary-aged students, *Behavioral Disorders, 19*, 126-135.

Soriano, M., Soriano, F. I., & Jimenez, E. (1994). School violence among culturally diverse populations: Sociocultural and institutional considerations, *School Psychology Review*, 204-215.

Sprague, J., & Walker, H. (2000). Early identification and intervention for youth with antisocial and violent behavior. *Exceptional Children, 66(3)*, 367-379.

Sprott, J. B., Doob, A. N., & Jenkins, J. M. (2001). Problem behavior and delinquency in children and youth. *Juristat.* Canadian Centre for Justice Statistics. Ottawa: Statistics Canada.

Stage, S. A. & Quiroz, D. R. (1997). A meta-analysis of interventions to decrease disruptive classroom behavior in public education, *School Psychology Review, 26(3),* 333-368.

Steinberg, L. (1999). *Adolescence* (Fifth Edition). Boston: McGraw-Hill.

Stephens, R. D. (1994). Planning for safer and better schools: School violence prevention and intervention strategies. *School Psychology Review, 23(2),* 204-215.

Sterling-Turner, H. E., Robinson, S. L., & Wilcznski, S. M. (2001). Functional assessment of distracting and disruptive behaviors in the school setting. *School Psychology Review, 30(2),* 211-226.

Sugar, G., & Horner, R. (1999). Discipline and behavioral support: Preferred processes and practices. *Effective School Practices, 17(4),* 10-22.

Chapter 19
Violence Prevention in Secondary Schools:
A Project for Raising Awareness and Facilitating Action

Glenn DiPasquale

Introduction

"Violence in America is a public health problem of the highest magnitude. Today 1 in every 10,000 people will become the victim of homicide, a rate that has doubled since World War II. America's youth are especially vulnerable. Nearly 3 in every 10,000 young males will be murdered. Among minority males between the ages of 16 and 25 who live in impoverished areas of large cities, the rate is more than 10 times higher – one in every 333. These young men are more likely to die by homicide than from any other cause."
Reducing Violence: A Research Agenda
American Psychological Association, 1996

"Preliminary results from a current CDC study indicate that between July 1, 1994, and June 30, 1998, there were 188 violent deaths on or near school grounds or at school-associated events. The majority of these incidents were homicides involving firearms. These violent deaths occurred in communities of all sizes, racial and ethnic make-up, and locales."
Best Practices of Youth Violence Prevention
Thornton, Craft, Dahlberg, Lynch, & Baer (2000, Centers for Disease Control)

Psychologists, especially those working in schools, have been concerned about youth aggression and violence for some time. Constant media coverage of high profile school shootings, particularly at the turn of the 20th century, exacerbated this already serious concern, and convinced the general public that youth violence is on the increase and that our schools are no longer safe. Although the majority of such acts of violence occurred in the United States where firearms are relatively easy to obtain, a widespread determination to address the problem has found resonance throughout North America. There is debate in the research literature regarding the urgency of the issue since youth violence has decreased in the last decade (e.g., Holhut, 1996; Mulvey & Cauffman, 2001). However, schools and communities have responded to the perception that youth violence is worsening, and a wide array of preventative initiatives have resulted (Thornton et al., 2000; Tolan & Guerra, 1994). This chapter describes one such initiative based on a program produced by a partnership of the American Psychological Association (APA) and Music Television (MTV), and details the implementation of the program in a suburban school system near Toronto, Canada.

The Program

In early 1999, APA and MTV were preparing to release a large anti-violence public education campaign centered on a video documentary entitled *Fight for Your Rights: Warning Signs.* The video, over 20 minutes in length, features a popular MTV personality interviewing high school students who had been involved in serious violent incidents. For example, one segment focuses on a young man currently serving a life sentence for killing two people in a school shooting, another features friends and family of a teenage couple who carried out a suicide pact, and others feature young people who managed to avoid a tragedy because someone recognized the potential problem and took action.

Interspersed among the interviews are clips from actual television news coverage of the incidents, as well as spots featuring psychologists who provide analysis of the incidents. Generally, the analysis is driven by research findings showing that virtually all such violent outbursts are preceded by warning signs that clearly indicate the perpetrator is in significant psychological difficulty, often involving suicidal intent (Dwyer et al., 1998). The premise underlying the project holds that these warning signs are evident to people close to these individuals, especially their peers. By getting help immediately peers might prevent these individuals from carrying out their violent plans, and assist them on the road to regaining a reasonable level of mental health. The video is preventative in the sense that it educates youth, parents and educators about the warning signs, and the main goal of the program is to encourage the viewer to seek assistance immediately when such signs are recognized.

As one press release put it:

"APA and MTV hope that by educating youth about the common precursors to violent behavior and how to seek help when problems arise, the disturbing trends that exist in today's schools can be reversed.

When you recognize the warning signs of violence in someone else, it is important to do something about it by getting help...

Hoping that someone else will handle it is not a solution – the risk for violent behavior won't go away by itself."

The video, which features a contemporary, rock music sound track, is very well produced, fast-paced, powerful, and often moving. The intended audience according to APA is students in middle school and high school, as well as adults in the wider community. The video and supporting printed materials were available free of charge to psychologists across North America, and recommended use was as the centerpiece of a series of community-based Youth Forums organized by psychologists. The showing of the video would be followed by a panel discussion "... to engage teenage participants in a dialogue about violence" (Alvarez, 1999). Suggested members of the panel included various experts such as psychologists, school district officials, police personnel, and community leaders. As will be seen below, the project profiled here took a somewhat different direction that attempted to utilize the more supportive, intimate climate available within school classrooms to afford students the opportunity to discuss the video with peers and a trained teacher.

On April 20, 1999 the extremely tragic school shootings in Littleton, Colorado made headlines around the world and lent an unexpected relevance and urgency to the release of the program.

The School District

York Region is a suburban municipality on the northern border of the city of Toronto, Ontario, Canada. The region is densely populated and affluent in the south, but maintains a mix of rural land and bustling small towns in the north. Since the 1980s, it has been one of the fastest growing jurisdictions in North America, with a high and growing level of ethnic and religious diversity. The local public school authority has more than doubled its enrollment in the last two decades, nearing 95,000 pupils at the time of this project. Of these, over 35,000 attended the region's 23 high schools, and therefore were the intended participants for the project.

As required in the province of Ontario, governance of the school authority is shared by a political arm, (elected trustees), and a professional management arm consisting of educator and non-educator managers (superintendents). The management group meets regularly in the Director's Council, consisting of all supervisory officers and several other key administrators. School board projects with region-wide scope are typically introduced first at the Director's Council for approval and support, and implemented collaboratively with appropriate school and board staff, and often with community-based partners. The corporate culture within the school system places a high value on collaboration with a wide array of "system partners" from both within the system and outside it to ensure a rich mix of diverse opinion and input.

The school board employs approximately 25 psychologists and psychological associates. The latter are registered professionals who practice autonomously under licensure by the College of Psychologists of Ontario, but hold Masters degrees, as opposed to psychologists who hold PhD degrees. The board also employs about a dozen attendance counselors who are certified social workers, but there is no social work department.

Relative to similar jurisdictions in the United States, student violence has always been at a low level in this school district. Compared to similar Canadian jurisdictions, however, the prevalence of violence is quite typical. Firearms are rare and the only instance of a school shooting was a non-lethal incident in the early 1970s. Fighting, weapon use (other than firearms), and gang-related activities are as frequent as in other Canadian school districts with similar demographics. There is a perception, and some data to support it, that the level of violence in the schools is on the increase here as elsewhere in North America, and the board has initiated a number of policies, procedures, and programs to deal with it.

Proposing the Program

Shortly after the release of the Warning Signs video, with the shootings in Colorado still dominating the news, the Ontario Psychological Association arranged a screening at a meeting of the Association of Chief Psychologists of Ontario School Boards. The present author, the Chief Psychologist with the York Region District School Board, was among the attendees.

Impressed with the video, the author made arrangements to present it at a meeting of the Director's Council along with a proposal to integrate it as a resource into the board's ongoing Safe Schools initiatives. The proposal was well received and the discussion that followed was lively and productive. The superintendents were highly supportive, particularly the chair of the Safe Schools Committee. Several decisions were made including that:

   (a) every secondary school student in the board would have the opportunity to view the video;
   (b) immediately after viewing the video, every student will attend a "debriefing" class led by a teacher trained to conduct such sessions;
   (c) school guidance departments, assisted by other board staff, will be available to assist students requesting support after viewing the video and attending a debriefing class;

(d) key board staff, including psychology staff and attendance counselors, will be available to assist with planning and implementation;

(e) trustees, student councils, and parent councils should be given the opportunity to view the video prior to its presentation to the student body;

(f) community agencies who deal with youth, such as religious organizations, the police, community-based mental health centers, hospital counseling centers, etc. should be offered a viewing of the video, provided with the details of the project, and kept informed of progress;

(g) responsibility for all aspects of the project will rest with an implementation team consisting of the Superintendent responsible for the Safe Schools Committee, the board's Guidance Consultant, and the board's Chief Psychologist, all assisted by the board's Information Officer.

Planning and Implementation

The Plan

Early in the planning process the implementation team recognized that with a project so logistically large, collaboration with various system partners would be essential. The approach that seemed to make the most sense was a "train-the-trainer" model that would put expertise and support into each school. The success of the project would hinge on the commitment and support of school staff, both administrators and teachers, who would bear the ultimate responsibility for delivering the program to the students.

After a great deal of discussion and consultation, a plan emerged which was laid out in the following steps:

(1) The video would be screened at meetings of all secondary school principals and vice principals, followed by a discussion of the implementation model, and solicitation of input.

(2) Administrators in each school would select a team of three or four staff to attend a half-day workshop where they would be trained to present the video to the entire school staff and select and train volunteer teachers to conduct the student debriefing sessions. These school teams could include any school staff, but were required to have at least one administrator (i.e., the principal or a vice-principal), and at least one guidance teacher (preferably the head of the guidance department) on board.

(3) All psychology staff and attendance counselors would attend the workshop and would be available to the school teams as planning and implementation resource people.

(4) Enough copies of the video would be acquired so that in any given school staff

could complete the project within a few days. Since the schools ranged in size from about 1000 to over 2000, this appeared to be a reasonable expectation.

(5) Students would view the video in groups of "reasonable size." It was hoped that this would be no more than 35, but if necessary larger groups could be workable with sufficient supervision.

(6) Immediately after viewing the video students would move into a debriefing session. In these sessions the groups could not exceed 35 students.

(7) At the end of each session any students who indicate a desire to discuss the video further, who have personal questions, or who are disturbed by what they've seen, would be encouraged to visit the Guidance Office where various staff would be available to meet with them. Again, psychology and attendance staff would be available to support each school's guidance department during this time, and community-based counseling agencies could also be approached about providing assistance.

Resource Materials

As mentioned earlier, APA provided a variety of print materials to accompany the video. The most important of these was a booklet for students that summarizes the key messages in the video. Topics covered include *Reasons for violence, Recognizing violence warning signs in others, What you can do if someone you know shows violence warning signs, Dealing with anger, Are you at risk for violent behavior?, Controlling your own risk for violent behavior, and Violence against self.* With permission from APA, the author modified the booklet, gave it a somewhat more Canadian focus, and added a list of local agencies that students could contact in an emergency. This modified document is reproduced as Appendix A. This student guide was translated into Chinese to accommodate the school district's largest immigrant population, and plans are ongoing for translation into other languages such as Urdu, Gujarati, and Vietnamese.

The author also produced a two-page guide for those teachers selected to conduct the debriefing sessions. This guide describes the purpose of the debriefing session as "…two-fold: first, to ensure that the messages the students got from viewing the video are the messages that were intended; and second, to allow students to discuss the video and ask questions in a positive, supportive environment supervised by a teacher." The guide then goes on to suggest a simple, five-step structure for the session that should ensure both goals are met and students leave feeling supported. This guide, reproduced as Appendix B, was also used by the school teams to help prepare selected teachers to lead debriefing sessions.

Using samples provided by APA as guides, the board's Information Officer produced an article for schools to include in their parent newsletters (shown as Appendix C), as well as a series of press releases and newspaper articles describing the project and promoting community awareness. As the project unfolded, local television news broadcasts also featured items pertaining to the program.

Planned Involvement of School Psychology Staff

The project was designed to be highly collaborative. That is, school psychology staff would function very much as part of a team, serving multiple roles. The preventative service model that is a theme of this book (Siegel & Cole, 1990) serves as a useful heuristic for understanding the planned involvement of psychology staff, as summarized in Figure 1. Being system wide and involving service to all students and all staff, the psychology staff activities are mainly clustered in the left-hand cells of the table, under Primary Prevention. (A limitation here is that only secondary schools were fully involved, but eventually elementary schools did receive some "spin-off" benefit from the project. Details are provided in a later section below.) Certain resources were identified, and in fact the Chief Psychologist actually initiated the project and obtained or created most of the resource materials. Clearly these activities would be fit nicely into cell 1a.

Most of the psychology staff were expected to be involved in the workshop where the school teams were prepared. As well, they would be available to the schools to assist with training teachers and other staff. These activities slot into cell 2a.

Psychology staff would also attend some of the parent sessions where the video was screened, and participate in discussions afterward. Similarly, the Chief Psychologist screened and discussed the video at meetings of the Board of Trustees, the Safe Schools Committee, and the School Board/Police Services Liaison Committee. At every high school, when the video was being screened, psychology staff were to be available to assist teachers and talk with students. As well, psychology staff have long been available to discuss violence or suicide prevention with classes of students as part of the curriculum, so this activity happened routinely prior to the project. All of these activities would fall into cells 3a and 4a. The other activity generally found in cell 4a, primary prevention services directed to individual students or parents, was expected to be less frequent, happening whenever students visited the guidance office to discuss the impact of the video.

In the Secondary Prevention column, several cells are also relevant to this project. Cell 1b is particularly relevant since the actual goals of the project include identification of students at risk for violent or suicidal behavior. In cell 2b, we have the workshop for school teams and later in-school workshops for the rest of the staff where the warning signs would be thoroughly discussed. Assisting teachers and guidance staff in dealing with students who expressed discomfort after seeing the video is the kind of activity referenced in cell 3b, and some staff would deal with those students directly, which is referenced in cell 4b.

The column titled "Tertiary Prevention" might not be as applicable to the present

Recipients of Service	a. Primary Prevention Identify resources, provide and analyze information; Program for all students	b. Secondary Prevention Program for students "at risk"	c. Tertiary Prevention Programs for students whose problems significantly interfere with their adaptation to school
1. The Organization – School system or school – Provide information, consult, advise	– Planning a violence/suicide prevention program at the systems level – Producing student and teacher guides	– Prepare guidance staff for dealing with students "at risk" – Program educates students re: peers "at risk"	– Consult with administration re: students at risk for violence or suicide
2. School Staff – Teachers or administrators – Provide information, consult, advise	– Planning & jointly presenting workshop for school teams – Supporting teams in presenting to school staff & training teachers	– All school staff learn warning signs for violence/suicide	– Consult with school staff re: at risk students
3. Students/Parents (Mediated) – Provide information, consult, advise	– Present to classes re: violence and suicide prevention (with and without video) – Present to parent meetings re: violence and suicide prevention (with and without video)	– Provide brief group counseling for students who seek help after viewing video – Provide referral for students/ families & liaison with outside agencies	– Consult with at risk students and their parents; liaise with community agencies
4. Students/Parents (Direct) – Group and individual counseling – Assessment – Consultation	– Discussion with groups and individuals who were alarmed by the video & sought out assistance – Parent meetings re: video & violence/suicide prevention	– Provide brief counseling for students who seek help after viewing video – Provide referral for students/ families & liaison with outside agencies	– Crisis intervention

Figure 1 The Role of Psychological Services in Violence Prevention

project. Certainly cell 3c is relevant, since community agencies were alerted and there was some liaison with them concerning referring students. As well, in a few cases, staff were expected to get involved in crisis intervention as a result of the reaction of one or more students (cell 4c).

Figure 1 illustrates, then, that the present project can be nicely analyzed using this model, and there are aspects that fit the descriptors for the various cells in the diagram. This kind of system-wide project is a time-limited departure from the typical perception of psychology staff as the administrators and interpreters of test instruments. It raises the profile of the psychology staff, and broadens the perception of school system partners regarding our expertise and skills. What's more, there were spin-offs for other staff such as attendance counselors who also had the opportunity to function outside their normal working mode and use their social work skills in a different context.

Implementation: The Workshop to Train the School Teams

As was mentioned above, each secondary school was mandated to send a school team to a half-day workshop. The team was to consist of an administrator, a guidance teacher (preferably the head of the guidance department), and one or two other teachers. All schools participated and compliance with regard to team make-up was excellent. Participants were seated at large tables that could accommodate two or three teams. Most attendance counselors and psychology staff were also in attendance, and for the planning portion of the workshop they were seated with a team from a school they served in their regular work. The workshop was presented in mid October, with the expectation that the entire project would be completed before the winter break in mid March.

The day began at 8:30 a.m. with coffee, juice, and a variety of baked goods. The program began at 9:00 a.m. with a welcome from the Superintendent with responsibility for the Safe Schools Committee. The Superintendent next led a discussion to: a) emphasize the importance of the project with regard to system goals, b) review management expectations regarding the project, and c) provide a general overview of the implementation plan.

The Chief Psychologist spoke next and after briefly discussing the origin and background of the video, presented it to the group. With the exception of the school administrators, few of the attendees had seen the video prior to the workshop, so after it was shown the teams were given 10 minutes to share their reactions at their tables, and another few minutes to share with the entire group.

Reactions were consistent with those seen in previous screenings of the video. Participants were impressed with the quality and the "hard-hitting" content. Some concerns were expressed regarding reactions from younger students, and probably from some parents. Fortunately by this time the video and support materials from APA had a track record, in that large numbers of community forums had already been conducted in the United States. As well, an estimated four million young people had already seen the video on MTV, particularly in one week in the summer when it had aired every evening in prime time (Alvarez, 1999). These factors reassured participants that there was a low risk of students having seriously negative reactions to the program. Overall, the teams were quite positive and enthusiastic that the program was worthwhile and of some importance.

The next phase of the workshop focused on the resource materials. Each school team was given a copy of the video. They were informed that almost 120 additional copies were available at the board's library and schools could sign out as many as 20 at a time for up to one week. The student guide and the teacher's debriefing guide were distributed and studied in some detail. Several messages in the guides were emphasized, particularly the following:

- York region schools are extremely safe, but with accurate information and a caring attitude, violence and suicide can be reduced even further.
- Students who consider violent acts against themselves or others are usually in emotional pain and psychological difficulty, and we all sometimes make things worse through bullying, teasing, or insensitivity to their need for support.
- There are almost always warning signs when someone is preparing for a violent act, and those most likely to notice are friends and other peers.
- Students are not encouraged or expected to take action directly to prevent violence, but it is vital that they seek help from caring adults such as parents, teachers, religious leaders, or police.

The teams were also provided with a checklist to assist them with logistical and organizational planning, and a series of surveys or "feedback forms" to be distributed to students, teachers, and parents. These surveys asked open-ended questions soliciting input on what schools and authorities could do to make schools safer.

After some discussion of the materials, the agenda turned to planning. The implementation team had concluded that the project could not be successful if the procedural steps were too strictly defined. These high schools are sufficiently unique that the school teams needed considerable latitude in planning exactly how the project would proceed. Therefore the next phase of the workshop focused on defining the tasks the teams needed to accomplish, and then giving them time at their tables to begin planning how best to accomplish those tasks.

The Guidance Consultant led the group through the following list of required steps or tasks that the school team needed to consider in their planning:

- The entire school staff, both teaching and non-teaching, had to be shown the video and provided with the student and teacher guides, following which they would need time for reflection and discussion.
- A subset of willing teachers had to be selected to do the debriefing sessions with class-sized groups of students (no teacher should be coerced into being involved).

- The teacher "debriefers" had to go through a brief training session based on the teacher guide, and here the psychology staff could help if desired.
- Guidance staff needed to prepare to receive any students who might want to talk further about personal issues after the debriefing session, and both attendance and psychology staff would be available to assist.
- The student council needed to be consulted and perhaps shown the video prior to the school-wide screening.
- The parent council needed to be consulted, and it was highly recommended that there be a meeting to screen the video for any interested parents prior to the school-wide screening – psychology and/or attendance staff would attend to help answer questions if desired.
- Local community agencies involved in counseling young people, as well as the police "street beat" officers, had already been alerted about the project, but the school teams were encouraged to make contact again simply to confirm screening dates, and perhaps to invite them to be in the school on those dates, if desired.
- A person or group on staff should be given responsibility for reproducing the printed materials in sufficient quantities, for booking the videos and for arranging for the required audio-visual equipment.

Clearly the school teams had a great deal to plan, and in the workshop they merely had time to make a beginning. It was clear that the real planning would occur at the school in consultation with the entire staff, and support was available to assist them if desired.

In a large group discussion following the small group planning sessions, certain areas of uncertainty emerged and were discussed. For example, some participants were concerned about the nature of the debriefing sessions. Specifically, the concern centered on the ability of "an ordinary teacher" to handle what could be a delicate or disturbing group discussion. This was an excellent question that took us into a more detailed discussion of the purpose of the debriefing sessions. Most importantly it gave us an opportunity to emphasize that the debriefing sessions were definitely not counseling or therapy milieus.

In these sessions teachers would be expected to do what they typically do – teach. As with any sensitive issue teachers might tackle in classroom discussions, guidelines were provided. As well, teachers would be aware that if any student appeared to need extensive support, trained people would be available in the school. In many ways these debriefing sessions were not expected to be that different from classroom discussions on other difficult topics such as homosexuality, abortion or terrorism. Secondary school teachers handle these situations frequently and they have excellent instincts regarding student needs. We invited the workshop participants to share our confidence in the excellence of our teaching staff, and to pass that confidence on to the teachers themselves.

Implementation: Executing the Plan

The first surprise for the implementation team was the swiftness with which the school teams responded. Within days of the workshop, schools were already reserving copies of the video and approaching psychology and guidance staff to schedule their participation. Not surprisingly, unforeseen difficulties also appeared relatively swiftly. The first was a shortage of audio-visual equipment. Although schools could obtain 20 copies of the video, none in fact had 20 VCRs on hand. This problem was just as easily solved in typical fashion, with teachers bringing their own personal equipment from home to keep the project on track.

A more serious complication arose when one of the high schools had a student commit suicide while staff there were still in the planning stage. The incident was impactful and destabilizing, requiring the assistance of the board's Tragic Event Response Team. Since the video does touch on suicide, school staff made the decision to put off the antiviolence project indefinitely to allow for healing. As it turned out, the school did complete the project the following spring, missing the original deadline by less than eight weeks.

Other problems that arose were comparatively minor and were solved in most cases without involvement of resources outside the schools. By and large, the schools completed the project efficiently, and with a high degree of caring and professionalism.

The Role of Psychology Staff

In the workshop several areas were highlighted where psychology staff could be of assistance. For example, all schools had psychology staff involved in the initial planning that took place at the workshop. They were then offered assistance from one or more psychology staff in:
- completing the planning process,
- presenting the video to the school staff and conducting follow-up discussion,
- preparing teachers to lead debriefing sessions,
- presenting the video to members of the Student Council, Parent Council, or community,
- counseling students after the debriefing sessions,
- arranging referrals to outside agencies for students or families feeling a need for longer term follow-up, and
- virtually any other part of the project where it appeared psychology staff could be helpful.

The school teams varied widely in terms of how much use they made of the psychologists and psychological associates who work for the board. While each of the services listed above was requested at least once, no schools involved psychology staff in each and every one of those processes. The most common services requested were counseling students after the debriefing sessions (every school had at least one psychology staff on hand during the video screenings), and helping to arrange referrals to outside agencies. Most of the psychology staff felt pleased with their involvement, though some felt somewhat underutilized. None felt overtaxed or outside their comfort zone for the demands made of them.

It should be noted that the student reaction to the video was very positive. They reportedly thought it was very well done and quite "cool," but not terribly intense. The mass exodus to the guidance office for counseling that some feared and expected, did not materialize except in one school. In that one school about 30 students arrived in the guidance office after the debriefing sessions, most fairly upset. All were girls and all but one were there to disclose their own suicidal ideation. While other schools did have similar experiences, none dealt with as high a number of needy students.

In a nonscientific, random sample of brief interviews with a number of teachers who had conducted debriefing sessions, the author was given the impression that students were responsive and very interested in the topic. They asked good questions and the discussions were focused and thoughtful. The teachers showed considerable enthusiasm for the project and generally felt it was very worthwhile.

Follow Up

Surveys

As mentioned above, brief surveys were distributed to students, parents and staff after the program was completed. Filling out a survey was optional, but it was hoped that a representative sample could be obtained from across the grade levels in each school. The surveys were unstructured and open-ended, hopefully to glean a wide array of input. Each survey asked three questions:
  - "What can (students/teachers/parents) do to make this school safer?"
  - "What can the school board do to make schools safer?"
  - "What can the police do to make schools safer?"

Responses were clustered and tabulated by frequency. Data analysis was qualitative with no attempt made to apply any statistical tests of significance.

Student Survey Results

Nine of the board's 23 secondary schools (39.1%) returned student surveys, with a total of 1,956 being available for analysis. One school returned only 28, while the others returned anywhere from 175 to 284 with a mean of 241, which is about 17% of the average enrolment per high school. Each of the board's distinct geographical communities was represented in the data, and there was a fairly even distribution across grade levels. The size of the sample is adequate for data of this type, but how representative it might be is difficult to know. Interpretation of the data, then, should be viewed with some caution.

For each question the responses were categorized conceptually and tabulated in terms of the percentage of surveys that included each concept. The percentages do not add to 100 since students were encouraged to list as many ideas as they wished in response to each question. As might be expected there were large numbers of suggestions that ranged far and wide with respect to the issues. Below is a summary of only the most common responses that might suggest broad areas of agreement among the respondents.

Question 1: What can students do to make this school safer?

It is gratifying that the most frequent response to this question involved the concept that students should make an effort to prevent problems of school violence by respecting others, being friendly and inclusive, and/or refraining from teasing or isolating others. This type of response was found in 69.5% of the surveys. Typical comments included:
- don't make fun of others
- respect others
- be supportive
- listen to each other's problems
- look out for each other
- stick together

The fact that this response was the most frequent is important because one criticism of the video and similar types of violence prevention approaches, is that they can lead to stigmatizing individuals who are eccentric but may not be at risk for violence at all (Dwyer et al., 1998; Mulvey & Cauffman, 2001). The student and teacher guides used in this program were designed to emphasize that the way we treat individuals could be an important causal factor in their being at risk for violence. More to the point, the guides emphasize that identifying those who exhibit warning signs is important specifically so that they can receive support, not so that they can be punished in some way. The survey results suggest that this message was effectively communicated.

The second most frequent response to this first question involved some reference to watching for and/or reporting suspicious behavior that corresponded to that described in the video. In all, a total of 58.4% of the surveys mentioned "violence," "warning signs" and/or "suspicious behavior" as things to watch for and either report to authorities, or use as a cue for vigilance, flight or warning others. There was clear evidence in these responses that the video had had an impact, and often comments from the video were echoed in the responses, indicating good attention to and retention of the material.

The third most frequent response, found in 32.7% of the surveys, focused on a need for students to control their own tendencies toward being violent or promoting violence. Typical comments here included:

- don't fight or bully others
- don't pick on other kids
- don't bring weapons to school
- don't encourage fights
- break up fights
- stop people who are bullying or teasing others

Suggestions that anti-violence counseling or education be provided for all students constituted the fourth most frequent response, appearing in 13.7% of the surveys. Specific suggestions included:
- anger management programs
- school-wide discussion groups or clubs
- regular guidance appointments
- peer groups
- more videos similar to the Warning Signs video

Interestingly, calls for stricter policing and security measures were fifth on the list of student suggestions, being mentioned in only 6.9% of the surveys. The solutions proposed here were fairly predictable including:
- metal detectors
- stricter rules with more serious consequences
- increased staff and police presence
  security cameras
- security guards
- student selection procedures to ban persistently violent students

The rather low frequency of this type of response should not be taken as an indication that students don't see a need for more security. As will be seen, this issue resurfaces in the next two questions. In terms of the students then, the four most frequent types of responses, namely improving the way students treat each other, increasing student vigilance regarding warning signs, reducing student violence and increasing the availability of counseling and education, all tend to be proactive, preventative and positive strategies.

Question 2: What can the school board do to make schools safer?

The most frequent type of response to this question focused on helping students re-duce violence by providing counseling, support and education. A remarkable 83.2% of the surveys contained some mention of programs, services or activities of this na-ture. Examples of this positive, proactive response include:
- more educational videos like this one
- professional counselors/therapists
- promote awareness of safety and causes of violence with slogans, posters, etc.
- more guidance teachers, regular guidance appointments
- anger, stress management courses
- school assemblies with speakers discussing violence
- help each other with problems

The second most frequent response to the second question suggests the school board increase security or policing. In 54.0% of the surveys, there is some mention of tighter security measures of various kinds. The list of responses was very similar to that reported for question one, with the most frequently mentioned being metal de-tectors, stricter rules with harsher consequences, security cameras, security guards and increased police presence in schools. Comparing the two questions, one can con-clude that students see these security measures as important, and clearly the respon-sibility of the school board.

The only other response to question 2 that appeared in more than ten percent of the surveys focused on paying attention to and reporting the warning signs discussed in the video. In 11.4% of the surveys, students mention that the school board some-how should take responsibility for detecting and reporting suspicious behavior that might denote a propensity for violence.

Question 3: What can the police do to make schools safer?

The responses to this question were the most scattered and tended not to be easily clustered. Many of the responses were repeats of previous suggestions and didn't seem to really involve the police at all. Those responses that were directly related to police action fell into only two categories. The most frequent type of response, ap-pearing in 42.3% of the surveys, merely suggested a greater police presence in and around the school. Examples of comments include:
- more police presence
- police patrolling around the school grounds
- constant police presence all day
- undercover police in schools

- prompt response by police
- random checks/patrols

The second most common response involved the police not simply being present, but being engaged in specific activities. This type of response was found in 39.5% of the surveys, and examples include:
- police can talk to students about violence/life experiences
- enforce punishments/suspensions/the law
- teachers, admin., police should be nicer, more caring, respectful
- quit hassling the students
- random searches

In general then, the student surveys were suggestive of a successful program in which the messages of compassion, hope and proactive action were conveyed effectively. We turn now to the teacher surveys to look at the same questions from the perspective of the adults responsible for the safety of the school environment.

Teacher Survey Results

Eight schools submitted teacher surveys for analysis, and for the most part they were the same schools that submitted the student surveys. The number submitted was 150. The number from each school ranged from 2 to 44, with a mean of 18.5. This constitutes a small sample, on the order of 10 to 15% of the teaching staff in most high schools, so the following description of results should be considered only as an indicator of teacher opinion.

Specific comments recorded by teachers tended to be extremely similar to those found in the student surveys, so only those that were unique will be reported verbatim.

Question 1: What can we do to make this school safer?

The number one class of response to this question in the teacher surveys involved the concept of watching for and acting on the warning signs highlighted in the video. In the teacher surveys, this was mentioned 88.0% of the time, compared to 58.4% for the students where this response was the second most frequent. Specific comments mirrored those reported in the student surveys, which in turn were reminiscent of points made in the video and the student guide. This would suggest that the program had a considerable impact on the teaching staff, perhaps more so than on the students.

The second most frequent type of response to this question in the teacher surveys was focused on security and policing, with 58.6% of the surveys including such comments. Recall that in the student surveys this class of response was fifth in frequency in question one, with only a 6.9% inclusion rate. However, the teacher-student comparison on this issue makes more sense in the context of question two. What can clearly be taken here is that teachers see it as the school's role to implement such security measures, the students do not.

Moving on to the third most frequent response from teachers to this question, we find the concept that was number one for the students, namely preventing violence by respecting others, being friendly and inclusive, and helping those who need support. In the teacher surveys this concept appeared 55.3% of the time as opposed to almost 70% for the students. This is once again a gratifying finding since it does suggest that we avoided the trap of stigmatizing or vilifying students who may have mental health or adjustment problems. There is a clear suggestion in this data however, that compassion toward students experiencing the pain of suicidal or violent feelings is somewhat greater among the students than among the teachers, at least in this small sample of respondents.

The fourth most frequent response to this question in the teacher surveys (and in the student surveys) was the suggestion of providing counseling or education to students as a violence prevention measure. One third of the teacher surveys mentioned this idea, as opposed to 13.7% for the students. Most of the responses were very similar but with a higher proportion of teachers than students mentioning each. The largest disparity involved the idea of safety promotion presentations to educate students in emergency measures which was mentioned by 10.7% of teachers but only 0.4% of students. The one idea mentioned by students only was to increase guidance department strength, involvement and accessibility. No teacher surveys mentioned this idea while it appeared in 1.8% of student surveys.

Finally, the fifth most frequent response in the teacher surveys involved the concept of students taking responsibility for reducing their own violent or immature behavior. Only 6.1% of the teacher surveys made reference to students themselves simply putting a stop to fighting, bullying and teasing, while almost one third of the student surveys proposed this solution.

Question 2: What can the school board do to make schools safer?

As was the case with the students, the number one response to this question on the teacher surveys was that students should be provided with help, counseling and/or education to prevent violence by supporting those who are at risk. In fact, 100% of the teacher surveys contained at least one such suggestion, and the majority contained two or more. Specific comments were very similar to the examples listed above in the student survey descriptions.

Again echoing the student survey results, the second most frequent response from the teachers to this question involved increased security and policing measures. This response was found in 84.7% of teacher surveys, as compared to 54% of student surveys. For the most part, the same kinds of suggestions were made, but a higher proportion of the teachers than the students mentioned each. Similar to the results reported above, exceptions included about five times as many students as teachers suggesting metal detectors and security guards in the schools.

It is noteworthy here that the nature of the comments around security and policing were quite different in question 1 versus question 2. That is, although they agreed on many of the specific needs, students and teachers did not necessarily see the school and the board responsibilities in the same way. The table below demonstrates some of these complex interactions.

Table 1 Percentage of Students and Teachers Comments Relating to Security and Policing Issues

Comment	Students	Teachers
More rules, stricter consequences and policies		
Question #1 ("student/teachers")	0.3%	16.0%
Question #2 ("the board")	7.3%	14.0%
Zero tolerance for violence		
Question #1	0.5%	12.7%
Question #2	1.8%	6.0%
Staff/administration presence/visibility as a deterrent		
Question#1	0.0%	11.3%
Question#2	0.0%	4.0%
Enforce punishment/suspensions for violence		
Question#1	0.1%	6.0%
Question#2	5.3%	21.3%
Security Cameras		
Question#1	0.5%	0%
Question#2	7.8%	6.7%
Metal Detectors		
Question#1	1.8%	0%
Question#2	13.1%	2.7%

These differences are not necessarily unexpected, except perhaps for the student support for metal detectors. In general, it makes sense that teachers are more inclined to think of security and policing solutions given their legal responsibility for the safety of their students, and that such solutions vary in terms of who should implement them. The students, on the other hand, are at a stage of development where their sense of vulnerability to dangers in the environment is low, and they might be less inclined to trust authority figures such as the police. As a result they seem to see less need for security measures, except for those of a technological (unbiased?) nature such as metal detectors and cameras. They also have surprisingly strong opinions about who should bear the responsibility for having such measures implemented – the school board.

The only other concept that appeared in a significant number of the teacher surveys for question 2 involved watching for and acting on the warning signs highlighted in the video and print materials. This concept was mentioned in 11.3% of the teacher surveys, which is almost identical to the student surveys.

Question 3: What can the police do to make schools safer?

Once again the teacher responses were surprisingly similar to those of the students. The most frequent response alluded simply to a greater police presence in and around the school, with 98.1% of the surveys mentioning this type of suggestion. The second most common teacher response suggested police do something specific such as speak at assemblies or randomly search lockers, etc., with 42.0% of surveys containing suggestions of that nature.

Parent Survey Results

Only 11 parent feedback forms were returned for analysis. School staff made the forms available at School Council meetings and other parent activities, and parents did show a great deal of interest in the video project, but very few ever returned a completed feedback form to the school. The reason for this is not readily apparent, but clearly the data reported below are gleaned from a very small sample of parents and therefore could not be generalized with any confidence.

Question 1: What can parents do to make schools safer?

The majority of responses to this question involved improving communication with the school and/or with the students. These responses were in 72.7% and 45.5% of the surveys respectively. Other responses that appeared in one or two of the surveys included knowing your child and his/her friends, lobbying school board and Ministry officials to increase funding for safety initiatives, encouraging other parents to see the video, and helping the school to arrange for speakers to address safety.

Question 2: What can the school board do to make schools safer?

There were a wide variety of responses to this question. The most common response, found in 45.5% of the surveys, was for the board to increase resources for counseling or educating students around violence. The number two response, found in 18.2% of the surveys, was for the board to implement stiffer penalties for violent behavior.

Question 3: What can the police do to make schools safer?

The pattern of responses to this question was similar to that noted in the teacher and student surveys. The most common suggestion, found in 54.5% of the surveys, was for an increase in police presence in and around schools. The second most common response, found in 45.5% of surveys, was for the police to participate in school programs as a speaker or even as a curriculum resource. In 36.4% of the surveys, parents suggested that police improve their relations with the students by being less intimidating, "hassling" the students less and being more understanding.

Summary of Survey Results

While the emphasis sometimes varied, the survey results for students and teachers were very similar. Both place a high priority on taking the warning signs of violent or suicidal behavior seriously and acting upon them by alerting authorities. Both seem to have integrated the concept that individuals at risk for violence are not monsters to be vilified and punished, but are in psychological pain and need support from peers and teachers. And related to that, both understand that all of us may exacerbate the problem by treating each other in ways that attack self-esteem and increase isolation.

Not only do students and teachers seem to have grasped the same important messages from the video and print materials, but they also prioritize them the same way in terms of school board and police responsibilities. With regard to what the students and staff can do however, their priorities diverge in predictable ways. Compared to students, teachers place a much higher value on in-school security and policing measures, and a somewhat lower value on prevention approaches characterized by students helping and supporting peers at risk, or on students simply abandoning their aggressive behavior.

As mentioned above, teachers and students agree to a marked degree on appropriate actions for school boards and police officers. The board is encouraged to increase counseling and education for all students (especially those at risk), to increase security and policing measures, and to take warning signs seriously. The police are seen as needing to increase their visibility in and around the school, and to play a greater role in preventing violence.

Parent survey results are clearly compromised by the very small sample size. The few parents who did respond focused most on communication, particularly among themselves, their children, the school and the police. Increasing the availability of counseling and educational resources was also a high priority with these parents.

Follow-up: Secondary Schools

A follow-up meeting was called for the school teams to discuss their experiences. They reported that the students appeared to enjoy the program, especially the video. In all schools the teachers who conducted the debriefing sessions reported increased student willingness to discuss their concerns about their friends, and even themselves. Students also expressed a desire for more programs of this type in the future. The student guides were judged to be excellent since "almost none were found left on the floor, in desks or in the garbage."

Other teaching staff appeared to give the program a positive rating as well, but expressed some concerns. They were unsure about follow-up for students who asked for referrals to outside agencies for counseling, and expressed a desire for more activities to follow-up in class after the program. The teacher guide was judged to be very useful, providing a good framework.

Overall, the program was deemed to be a success. As a result it was recommended that all secondary schools use the video each year as part of the provincially mandated grade nine orientation process known as the Teacher Advisor Program or TAP. In this way the video would be shown to and discussed with all students as they begin their high school years. As well, individual teachers were encouraged to use the video in the years following grade nine if it was deemed to be appropriate for meeting curriculum goals.

Follow-up: Elementary Schools

Copies of the video were distributed to all of the board's elementary schools, but strictly for the use of the staff. All staff were encouraged to watch the video and discuss it, and psychology staff could participate if desired. Elementary schools could also arrange screening sessions for parent groups if they wished, again with assistance from the psychology staff.

Although they might have seen it on television, the video was considered to be less appropriate and perhaps too intense for use with students below the grade nine level. Even if teachers felt that some grade seven or eight classes would be able to benefit from seeing the video, it was decided to restrict its use to the high schools.

The Broader Context

Clearly in the broader context of violence prevention the program described here is but a single, small piece of a very large puzzle. Many recent publications have summarized findings from years of research, and have concluded that effective violence prevention is far more complex than anything that might be addressed in a single project of the scope described here. For example, recent reports from the Surgeon General of the United States (Shalala, 2001), The Centers for Disease Control (Thornton et al., 2000), The Center for the Study and Prevention of Violence (Tolan & Guerra, 1994) and others, have delineated the multi-faceted nature of best practices in this area, involving school, family and community initiatives.

The "Warning Signs Project" described here, though logistically large, was quite small in scope, and it was successful as far as it went. Follow-up evidence suggested that awareness was raised, and that students, parents and teachers engaged in dialogue about an important issue. In the end a greater understanding ensued. Most importantly, as a direct result of the program, some students did reach out for help because they recognized themselves or their friends in the warning signs described in the video, and clarified in the teacher-led discussion groups. As a result, many students were referred to outside agencies for counseling.

Of course, as with any prevention initiative, proving a suicide or a violent incident was actually prevented is almost impossible without expensive, long-term research. Even student self-reports are anecdotal and subject to exaggeration or distortion. Nonetheless, the goals set for the program, namely educating the community, staff and students, providing direction for seeking help, and empowering students to play an active role in making their schools safe, were accomplished. When viewed as a part of the school board's overall strategy for creating safe schools, the investment of time and resources would appear to be well justified.

Finally, the project succeeded in raising the profile of the psychology department and highlighting the breadth of expertise available to schools through their psychologists and psychological associates. This is important for a number of reasons, but at the top of the list is the welfare of the students. If school boards can "exploit" all of the skills, abilities, expertise and experience of the psychology staff they employ, it has to benefit the students in the long run. Using such staff only as testers or special education gate-keepers deprives students of a range of services that might well provide far more benefit than would one more assessment. Projects such as that described here can be one step in altering perceptions and illuminating the large prevention "toolkit" that can be accessed through school psychology staff.

References

Alvarez, T. (1999). APA and MTV launch youth anti-violence initiative. *Practitioner, 12 (1)*, 1-7.

American Psychological Association (1996). *Reducing violence: A research agenda*. Washington, DC: The Human Capital Initiative.

Dwyer, K., Osher, D., Warger, C., Bear, G., Haynes, N., Knoff, H., Kingery, P., Sheras, P., Skiba, R., Skinner, L. & Stockton, B. (1998). *Early warning, timely response: A guide to safe schools: The referenced edition*. Washington, DC: American Institutes for Research.

Holhut, R. T. (1996). Teen violence: The myths and the realities. Internet Document, URL: http://www.mdle.com/WrittenWord/rholhut/holhut25.htm, *3pp.*

Mulvey, E. P. & Cauffman, E. (2001). The inherent limits of predicting school violence. *American Psychologist, 56(10),* 797-802.

Shalala, D.E. (2001). *Youth Violence: A Report of the Surgeon General.* Rockville, MD: U.S. Department of Health and Human Services, Centers for Disease Control and Prevention, National Center for Injury Prevention and Control; Substance Abuse and Mental Health Services Administration, Center for Mental Health Services; and National Institutes of Mental Health.

Siegel, J. & Cole, E. (1990). Role expansion for school psychologists: Challenges and future directions. In E. Cole & J. Siegel (Eds.), *Effective consultation in school psychology* (pp. 3-17). Toronto: Hogrefe & Huber Publishers.

Thornton, T. N., Craft, C. A., Dahlberg, L. L., Lynch, B.S. & Baer, K. (2000). *Best practices of youth violence prevention: A sourcebook for community action.* Atlanta: Centers for Disease Control and Prevention, National Center for Injury Prevention and Control.

Tolan, P. & Guerra, N. (1994). *What works in reducing adolescent violence: An empirical review of the field.* Boulder, CO: Institute of Behavioral Science, Regents of the University of Colorado.

Appendix A: Warning Signs: Take a Stand Against Violence – A Guide for Students

Introduction

"Being on either end of a violent situation, whether you seem to have come out with the upper hand or whether you don't seem to, it doesn't resolve anything. It escalates the problem. Hatred leads to more hatred. Violence leads to more violence."

Adam Yauch of the Beastie Boys

After watching the video "Warning Signs", you might be worried about the safety of your school. You can be sure that York Region schools are among the safest anywhere. And it's important to know that terrible events like those shown in the video are very rare, even though they are more common now than in the past.

So why is this video being shown to all high school students in York Region public schools? Because it would be great to prevent even one of these tragic events from happening. There are almost always warning signs when someone is about to commit an act of violence, and since students are far more likely than adults to see these signs, it makes sense to present this video to our students.

Before listing the warning signs mentioned in the video, it's important to mention that violent acts are usually committed by people in pain, and there are factors that make that pain worse. Sometimes we are all a part of the problem. These factors include:
- Constant bullying, mean teasing, isolation or public humiliation
- Peer pressure
- Early childhood abuse or neglect
- Witnessing violence in the home, community, or even in the media
- Easy access to weapons

The Warning Signs

When the above factors are present, warning signs are even more likely to indicate a serious problem. The warning signs that suggest violence is an immediate possibility include:
- Loss of temper on a daily basis
  Frequent physical fighting
- Frequent vandalism or property damage
- Increased use of drugs or alcohol
- Threatening to commit an act of violence, or describing plans for such an act
- Enjoying hurting animals
- Carrying a weapon

Other behaviors can signal the possibility of violence if they build up or repeat over a period of time. These include:

- A history of violent or aggressive behavior
- Being a victim of bullying
- Serious drug or alcohol use
- Gang membership or a strong desire to be in a gang
- Access to or fascination with weapons, especially guns
- Threatening others regularly
- Trouble controlling feelings, especially anger or sadness
- Withdrawing from friends and usual favorite activities
- Feeling neglected or alone
- Poor school performance
- Discipline problems at home or at school, or frequent trouble with authority
- Feeling constantly disrespected
- Ignoring the rights and feelings of others

What You Can Do to Help Prevent Violence

If you see some of the signs listed above in someone you know, you can and should do something. Here are some important things to think about:

- Be safe! Don't spend time alone with people who show warning signs. Try to get them help.
- Tell an adult! Go to an adult you trust and ask for help. It could be a family member, a teacher or guidance counselor, the principal or vice-principal of your school – any adult you can talk to comfortably and in confidence.
- If you're worried about being a victim of violence, ask someone in authority to protect you. It's not wise or safe to try to protect yourself by using violence or by carrying a weapon.
- Be safe! Don't try to go it alone.

What You Can Do to Help Prevent the Pain That Can Lead to Violence

As mentioned above, sometimes all of us add to other people's problems without realizing it. We all have a responsibility to help each other and make our schools and communities safe for everyone. If we don't make things better, or if we make things worse, we increase the possibility that someone might become a danger to him/herself or others. Here are some suggestions:

- Don't be part of the problem by hurting other people, especially by bullying, intimidating, teasing, rejecting, or isolating someone. These behaviours cause a great deal of pain, frustration, and anger, which can eventually lead to violent outbursts.
- Do be part of the solution by being civil and respectful to everyone you meet and by including others when you can. And although it may sound old fashioned it's still tough to beat "The Golden Rule" – treat other people the way you would like to be treated.
- Do have the courage to report it if you witness bullying or intimidation, and to seek help if you see the warning signs of violence.

Violence Against Self – Suicide

Another type of violent behavior is when someone tries to hurt or kill themselves – suicide. Like all violent behaviors, there are almost always warning signs that a person is planning to attempt suicide. Some of the signs are similar to those that might signal a violent act, and in fact many of the life experiences are the same. Some factors that are more often related to suicide, however, are these:
- A recent death or suicide of a friend or relative
- A recent break-up with a boyfriend or girlfriend
- Trouble with parents and other authority figures
- Recent news reports of suicides of other young people

While the events listed above are factors that increase the risk of a person committing suicide, the more serious warning signs are these:
- Previous suicide attempts
- Heavy alcohol or drug use
- Threatening to commit suicide
- Constantly talking about suicide, death, dying or the afterlife
- Sudden increase in moodiness, or time spent alone
- Sudden change in eating or sleeping habits
- Talking a lot about feeling lonely, hopeless, guilty, or worthless
- Losing control, being impulsive or aggressive
- A sudden drop in school performance
- A sudden loss of interest in friends or favorite activities
- Giving away important belongings, e.g., CDs, jewelry, posters, clothing
- Hinting about not being around for upcoming events
- Making final arrangements, e.g., saying good bye to friends, making a will, etc.

What You Can Do to Help Prevent a Suicide

It's important to remember that most young people who are thinking about committing suicide don't really want to die. They just want the pain to stop, and they want their lives to be better. When they get the appropriate help, they are seldom ever suicidal again. Suicide is usually an act of desperation – a permanent solution to a temporary problem – and it is never the right answer to life's problems. If you see the signs listed above in a friend, here are some things you can do:
- If a friend mentions suicide, take it seriously.
- Listen carefully, then seek help immediately.
- Never keep someone's talk of suicide a secret, even if they ask you to. Remember, you risk losing that person forever.
- When you recognize the warning signs for suicidal behavior, in yourself or someone else, *do something about it*. Tell a trusted adult who can get the person professional help. Together we could save a life.

Some Agencies That Can Help

If you can't approach an adult in the school or the community for help, no matter what the reason might be, you can still get help by telephone, often without giving your name. Here are some phone numbers you can try:

Community Crisis Response Service (12 noon to 4:00 a.m.) 310 2673
(310-cope)
Crime Stoppers 1-800-222-8477
Kids Help Phone 1-800-668-6868
Markham Stouffville Hospital Emergency 472-7111
York Central Hospital, Crisis Team 883-2290
York County Hospital, Child & Adolescent Crisis Unit 853-2227
Youthdale Treatment Centre, Crisis Support Team 416-363-9990

Appendix B: Warning Signs: Take a Stand Against Violence – A Debriefing Guide for Secondary School Teachers

This guide has been produced as a support document for the video "Warning Signs: Take a Stand Against Violence." The video, a joint effort by the American Psychological Association (APA) and Music Television (MTV), represents one response to the large number of incidents of extreme violence in high schools in the United States. The video strongly promotes the prevention of violence and suicide through educating young people about the warning signs, which are almost always present before such incidents occur. Viewers are urged to get help from a trusted adult if they see these warning signs in other students or even themselves.

Despite the differences between the U.S. and York Region, the message of this video is important enough to justify showing it to all of our high school students. Due to the powerful nature of the video, it has been mandated that as soon as possible after seeing it, students attend a small group "debriefing" session. The purpose of these debriefing sessions is twofold:

(1) To ensure that the messages the students got from viewing the video are the messages that were intended; and

(2) To allow the students to discuss the video and ask questions in a positive, supportive environment supervised by a teacher.

The debriefing session will be short, perhaps only 20 to 30 minutes in some schools, so it will likely need to be fairly structured. The suggestions below should help to make the session as effective as possible. Resource staff such as Attendance Counsellors and Psychological Services staff will be available to support school staff and students.

Step 1: To introduce the video, share the background information above. To guide their viewing, ask students to pay particular attention to the warning signs mentioned by the experts featured in the video. (Students will be getting a handout, so they don't need to take notes.) After the video, begin the debriefing with some brief comments to assure students that *York Region schools are safe*, particularly compared with some regions in the United States. Then reiterate the following main messages in the video:

(1) Young people who commit acts of violence or suicide are in emotional pain, sometimes intensified by the way we treat them, and we need to identify and help them *before* they do something reckless.

(2) With help, most if not all of these tragic, violent events *can* be prevented.

(3) Before a violent act or suicide attempt, there are almost always *warning signs*. It is important for young people to be aware of these warning signs because students are more likely than adults to notice them. This is the key to preventing such incidents.

(4) If a young person sees these warning signs, in a fellow student or even in themselves, he/she should get help from an adult in the school or community. Students should not try to handle it themselves, and should *never* put themselves in danger.

Step 2: Distribute the handout, which lists the warning signs mentioned in the video, in addition to other information. Emphasize that the warning signs or characteristics are usually the result of painful life experiences such as being *openly disrespected, rejected* or *bullied* by peers, being *abused* or *exposed to violence* in their lives, having repeated experiences of *failure or frustration*, or having difficulty dealing with *intense feelings of anger or depression*.

Step 3: Open the floor for questions. Try to facilitate any ensuing discussion by keeping it focused on the topics at hand. Model both a realistic attitude to caution and safety, and a sense of compassion for young people in pain. Keep in mind that we are hoping to foster a sense of responsibility for the safety of the community, and the welfare of *all* students.

Step 4: Each debriefing session should produce some written record of the students' feelings about three questions:
    (1) What can *students* do to make their school safer?
    (2) What should *the school board* do to make schools safer?
    (3) What should *the police* do to make schools safer?

Feedback sheets will be provided to record students' thoughts. The recorder can be the teacher or a student, perhaps coordinated in partnership with the student council. These feedback sheets should be handed in to a school administrator at the end of the day so that they can be easily collected and analyzed later.

Step 5: End the session with a strong assurance that any student, who has concerns about a friend or acquaintance, or even him/herself, will be supported if they come for help. Encourage them to speak with a favorite teacher, a guidance counselor or an administrator in the school, or to seek help from an adult in their home or community. If all else fails, the student handout contains telephone numbers of several crisis response hot lines.

Point out that the greatest risk of all would be to do nothing.

Appendix C: Newsletter Insert – Making Our Schools Safer: A Focus on Prevention

The focus for our Safe Schools initiative in York Region is prevention. We are very fortunate that our schools are among the safest anywhere.

The Colorado and Alberta incidents in the early spring highlighted for every school board and every community the need to continually assess and focus on meeting the social and emotional needs of our students. Many school boards, in partnership with the local police, have embarked on innovative initiatives.

By the end of February 2000, every secondary school student will view the video titled, "Warning Signs: Take a Stand Against Violence." The viewing will be followed by a debriefing with a teacher which will highlight and reinforce the messages in the video, ask questions and explore the role and responsibility of every member of a school community. Each student will receive a guide, which we encourage you to read and discuss with him or her.

This video was developed by the American Psychological Association and produced by MTV as part of a youth anti-violence initiative before the incident in Colorado. It has been aired extensively on MTV and has been seen by over four million adolescents in U.S. high schools with very positive and encouraging responses. It gives viewers an opportunity to hear young people speak in their own words about violent behavior and ways to prevent it.

Our school will be showing the video to our School Council on <date> and to students on <date>. We invite you to join us to view the video at any of the times which may be convenient for you. We are asking students, parents, staff and community members to give us feedback on how we can make our schools safer.

Violence is not a school issue, but rather a community issue. We will be working with the police and media to raise awareness in our communities. In order to continue to support and reinforce the non-violence message in our schools we need communication, co-operation, and the coordination of energy and resources among staff, students, parents and the community.

"Safe Communities: Safe Schools": that is our goal.